Women and Work

Garland Reference Library of Social Science (Vol. 679)

# Women and Work
## *A Handbook*

Edited by
Paula J. Dubeck
Kathryn Borman

Assistant Editors
Sonia Carreon
Amy Cassedy

GARLAND PUBLISHING, INC.
*New York & London*
*1996*

**Library of Congress Cataloging-in-Publication Data**

Women and work : a handbook / edited by Paula J. Dubeck, Kathryn Borman.
     p.    cm. — (Garland reference library of social science ; vol. 679)
    Includes bibliographical references and index.
    ISBN 0-8240-7647-8 (case : alk. paper)
    1. Women—Employment—United States.    I. Dubeck, Paula, 1944–
II. Borman, Kathryn M.
HD6095.W678   1996
331.4'0973—dc20                                    95-49853
                                                       CIP

Cover by Lawrence Wolfson Design, New York.
Cover photograph ©Tony Stone Images.

Printed on acid-free, 250-year-life paper
Manufactured in the United States of America

# Contents

## Section III. Women in Diverse Occupations

## Section V. Legal Factors Affecting Women's Work and Opportunity

## Section VI. Work Experiences and the Organizational Context of Work

WOMEN'S WORK EXPERIENCES

# Section VIII. Cross-Cultural Issues and International Studies

# Introduction

## Origins of the Handbook

Twenty-five years ago, this volume could not have been written. At that time, both of us were in graduate programs, preparing to launch professional careers in a discipline (sociology) in which women held fewer than 15 percent of the Ph.D.s, with an even smaller percentage on university faculties. Studies in sociology at the time rarely focused on women, except to examine their roles as members of the family unit. Groundbreaking stratification studies analyzed sons' inheritance of fathers' occupations. Similarly, the discussion of women's labor-force participation presented women's employment as "part-time" and "secondary"—not so much a necessity as simply an expendable means to provide a better lifestyle for the family. Few universities had given support to women's studies programs, suggesting the relative unimportance of this area.

Relatedly, in the United States in 1970, women represented 5 percent of the practicing lawyers and 8 percent of the practicing physicians; they were 13 percent of the Ph.D. recipients overall. Their presence in the labor force and in high-profile, high-status occupations was characterized by invisibility and by a lack of social, political, and economic "muscle."

During the last two and a half decades, a combination of factors have brought about significant changes with regard to both the status of women and research on the status of women. Among these changes are the passage of federal legislation, including the 1964 Civil Rights Act, defining sex as a basis upon which employers and others may not discriminate; Title IX, tying nondiscrimination policies to educational institutions receiving federal funds; and Executive Order 11375, implementing Equal Employment Opportunity Commission and affirmative-action directives for business and government with regard to the recruitment, hiring, and promotion of women.

Further, women were taking advantage of expanded opportunities in higher education. In 1970, approximately one-third of bachelor's degrees were awarded to women; by 1990, more than half (52 percent) of the B.A. and B.S.s awarded were earned by women. Relatedly, more women sought and attained high-status professional degrees—in law, medicine, engineering, management, and the sciences. By 1990, 35 percent of M.D. degrees, 40 percent of law degrees, and

37 percent of Ph.D.s were received by women. Indeed, the importance of opening access to the study and practice of law cannot be understated. It gave women the means and leverage to make corporations and government agencies accountable to legislation barring discrimination against women.

At the same time, the public increasingly supported women's right to equal pay for equal work, to hold public office, and to hold (or choose among) multiple roles as housewives, mothers, and members of the labor force. Indeed, the discrepancy between women's and men's support for women's rights with regard to work and pay had been virtually eliminated by the mid-1980s.

Coupled with these various legal, educational, and attitudinal changes were basic demographic and economic changes in American society. An increase in divorce rates and changing laws with regard to financial support after divorce meant that more women were becoming heads of households and sole providers for children. The restructuring of the U.S. economy in the 1980s reduced the number of high-paying manufacturing jobs and increased the number of low-paying service jobs. These changes propelled growing numbers of women into the ranks of workers out of necessity, to meet the basic needs of a two-parent family unit, or as single parents responsible for the economic well-being of children.

Indeed, economic restructuring has had far-reaching effects for women both here and abroad. In recent years, international attention has focused on formal equality for women and a conviction that women as individuals contribute something distinctive to the public order. This emphasis was part of the 1985 United Nations-sponsored world conference held in Nairobi, Kenya, to review and appraise achievements of the United Nations's Decade for Women. The conference celebrated women's contributions while also examining the status of efforts to gain full legal equality for women in all nations.

Although a variety of changes have worked to redefine the role and status of women in American society, the nature of issues that confront women and work also have evolved. At first, particularly following the passage of Title IX, the most immediate concerns focused on monitoring changes in the representation of women as they entered a growing number of occupations, especially traditionally male-dominated occupations. Soon thereafter, issues of mobility and success were framed, as women sought to achieve the same level of success in their work as men. Barriers to success embedded in organizational practices also emerged as fertile areas for investigation. As such, research on mentoring, opportunity structure, and sex-typing within occupational specialties came to be the dominant issues for assessing women's status and their progress with respect to work. More recently, research has focused on how organizational culture and the competing realms of work and family present women with sometimes inhospitable work environments, or at least as settings with conflicting pressures. Issues such as sexual harassment, comparable worth, and women's push to define "family-friendly" firms emerged as key concerns of those investigating the status of women.

It is within the context of these transformations over the past twenty-five years that the present volume was developed. Our primary focus is the status of women and work in the United States. At the same time, changes in the status of women in the U.S. are part of worldwide changes that have taken place with regard to the status of women. Accordingly, we pay attention to cross-national research that places American women in a broader social context and to studies on the status of women in a variety of countries.

## Contents of the Volume

This volume's 150 entries are organized into eight major categories: I.) Women's Labor-Force Participation in the U.S.: Patterns and Issues; II.) Approaches to Analyzing Women and Work; III.) Women in Diverse Occupations; IV.) Factors Influencing Career and Occupational Choice; V.) Legal Factors Affecting Women's Work and Opportunity; VI.) Work Experiences and the Organizational Context of Work; VII.) Issues Emerging from the Intersection of Work and Family; and VIII.) Cross-Cultural Issues and International Studies. Within each of the eight major categories, the contents are arranged topically to provide an understanding of the trends and patterns influencing current research and scholarship in the social and behavioral sciences.

The first section, Women's Labor-Force Participation in the U.S., is arranged to present an overview of women's labor-force activity, both in general and as is characteristic of various segments of the population. The latter includes young, working-class, and immigrant women, as well as the employment patterns of women in various ethnic and cultural groups. Significant dimensions of labor-force activity, including women's union affiliations, unemployment, and retirement, are discussed as factors that have different consequences for women and men. In this section, we also include entries that address two related forces that structure employment opportunities for women: occupational sex-typing and the gender-based segregation of work. The effect of these factors on women's earning capacity and the economic well-being of their families is presented in the final set of essays in this section. Attention is given, as well, to comparable worth as a strategy to diminish the effects of such gender-based practices.

While the first section of the handbook provides an overview of participation, the second section, Approaches to Analyzing Women and Work, presents a variety of perspectives that are used to examine women's work experience at individual, organizational, and societal levels. In addition, we include essays that present efforts to reconceptualize women's role and status in society, in order to provide a more dynamic model for research on women and work.

In the third section, Women in Diverse Occupations, entries focus on how women fare in a variety of occupations. The initial essays provide an overview of women in high-status occupations and professions, the service sector, and blue-collar occupations. The remainder of the section is devoted to summarizing women's representation in a series of occupations, the problems they face, and key issues to be addressed in future research.

In Factors Influencing Career and Occupational Choice (Section IV) the influences of religious and educational institutions are examined. The gender-role expectations reflected in the education of women at the turn of the century set the stage for examining the career plans of contemporary college women. Shifting the focus to interpersonal relations, essays explore how role models and gender stereotypes operate to legitimate career choices for women. In Section V, Legal Factors Affecting Women's Work and Opportunity, the history of protective legislation is reviewed. These essays—concerning sexual harassment, affirmative action, and family leave—set the stage for those chronicling the emergence and implementation of legislation currently in force and intended to bring gender equality to the workplace.

The volume then focuses on the experiences of working women and how organizational context influences those experiences. Essays in Section VI, Work Experiences and the Organizational Context of Work, detail current research on women's work interest, commitment, and satisfaction before exploring the implications of the pervasive influence of gender on the culture and practices in organizations. Discrimination, gender bias in job evaluations and personnel decisions, sexual harassment, and sexual coercion are explored. We pay special attention to women in management, where the issues of opportunity and success are most visible. At the end of this section, essays explore various strategies for reducing or eliminating sex discrimination, sexual harassment, and wage discrimination.

Following this, the volume focuses on an increasingly prominent concern with which working women—and men—deal: the work/family intersection. Over time, we have become ever more aware that the scope of concerns associated with the work/family intersection are present for most of the years of employment for women. The most visible issues today emerge as children are brought into the family. Thus, in Section VII, Issues Emerging from the Intersection of Work and Family, issues of when to have children, the difficulties that arise from the competing demands of work and child care, and the consequences for women's careers are addressed. So is the research examining the effects of mothers' employment on children's development and behavior. Yet pressures also come from the other end of the age spectrum. Today, there is an increasing likelihood that middle-aged workers—particularly women—also will be responsible for caring for their own parents. As such, we include an essay that addresses "eldercare" and the value of employer programs that address this issue.

The final section in this volume (Section VIII), Cross-Cultural Issues and International Studies, examines the status of women in an international framework. An overview is presented through a series of essays based on cross-national comparisons. These are followed by segments that examine women and work in selected countries, arranged to reflect the varying levels of development that influence the nature of employment opportunities for women.

## Final Thoughts

Our intent throughout this volume has been to present the reader with a broadly based understanding of women's work experiences. An additional goal has been to make available, for each entry, a set of references to guide the reader toward the most useful set of sources for further, in-depth research on the topic. To do this, we have sought contributions from researchers in a range of social and behavioral sciences. We reviewed recently published journal articles and books to determine who was involved in what kinds of research and scholarship on the topics related to women and work. We also asked several well-known researchers in the field to consult with us as members of an editorial board for the project. In turn, they proposed topics to be addressed and nominated individual authors to develop entries on a number of the topics included in the volume. Finally, we actively solicited contributors to write on a number of specific topics.

We were heartened by the response to our call for contributors, a response that demonstrated the wealth of research accomplished to date on the status of women and work. We believe that this volume represents both the strength and diversity of such research. Those who consult this volume will, we hope, find it a useful source of timely information on the topic of women and work across a wide variety of domains. It should serve as a useful reference for both the student and the researcher wishing to move into women and work as an area of study and research.

As with any volume of this kind, we are sure that our aim has, in particular instances, out-stretched our grasp. For example, we have not addressed all of the international studies and cross-cultural issues that might have been dealt with. As editors, we take full responsibility for both the content and omissions in coverage. At the same time, our responsibilities were eased by the ongoing commitment of our editorial review board members: Arlene Kaplan Daniels, George Farkas, Margaret Marini, David J. Maume, Joanne Meyerowitz, Brian Powell, Rachael Rosenfeld, Susan Searing, and Doris Wilkinson. They helped define the scope of coverage, reviewed manuscripts, and suggested contributors. We are extremely appreciative of their commitment to this volume of work and to seeing it through its various stages.

Finally, we wish to acknowledge the help and support of others along the way who made the preparation of this volume possible. A number of scholars served as special reviewers, including Marcia Bellas, Wallace Borman, Romy Borooah, Silvia Cancio, Janice Dyehouse, Elizabeth Fernea, Mark Ginsberg, Norris Johnson, Barbara Ramusack, and Suzanne (Tolliver) Shipley. In addition, we had excellent help and support from staff at the University of Cincinnati, including Cheryl B. Fuhrmann, Dale Wilburn, and Pamela Hoffman. Likewise, our assistants, Sonia Carreon and Amy Cassedy, provided the commitment, energy, and support that kept a focus to our efforts and brought the volume to completion.

As might be expected, the development of this volume highlighted the changing roles and status of women that we, too, faced through our own careers. Issues of access, opportunity, and success on the "work" side of our lives were paralleled by issues framed by having to choose when to give priority to "work" and when to give priority to "family," and by our attempts to accommodate both roles. We have been fortunate to have supportive families during our careers and as we undertook this volume. Frank, Jordan, Wally, Greg, and Geoff have our thanks and enduring appreciation for moving through many of those changes with us.

*Paula J. Dubeck*
*Kathryn Borman*

# I

# Women's Labor-Force Participation in the U.S.
*Patterns and Issues*

# General Patterns of Employment/Unemployment

## Women's Changing Labor-Force Participation in the U.S.

The proportion of working-age women who are in the labor force (either working or actively seeking work for pay outside the home) has increased dramatically during the twentieth century. In particular, married women (at first older and then younger married women in the prime child-bearing and -rearing years) have entered the labor force in greater and greater numbers. These changes have been associated with women's increasing educational attainment, increasing demand for services provided by traditionally female occupations, changes in family and life patterns, and changing social norms. Understanding how and why women's labor-force participation has changed in the last hundred years requires an examination of economic, institutional, and sociological factors, and is essential for explaining the nature of and prospects for women's economic progress.

The overall changes in women's labor-force participation since 1890 have been frequently observed, although the explanations for these changes have been subject to changing and controversial interpretations (see Goldin 1990; Wright 1991). Women, who made up less than 20 percent of the civilian labor force before 1900, constituted more than 45 percent of that force by 1990. The overall changes in women's labor-force participation rates from 1890 to 1991 were characterized by moderate increases in the early part of the twentieth century succeeded by accelerated rates of increase that began with the decade of the 1940s. The most recent data show an interruption in the twenty-five-year pattern of significant year-to-year increases (see Table 1).

Determining what underlies these changes should begin with an examination of the life-cycle changes in women's labor-force participation. In 1890, fewer than 5 percent of married women (2.5 percent of white, 22.5 percent of nonwhite, and 3 percent of foreign-born married women) were in the labor force, while more than 40 percent of single women (38.4 percent of white, 59.5 percent of nonwhite, and 70.8 percent of foreign-born single women) were in the labor force. By 1988, almost 60 percent of married white women and 65 percent of married nonwhite women were in the labor force, as were 69 percent of single white women and 56 percent of single nonwhite women (Goldin 1990).

TABLE 1. Female Civilian Labor-Force Participation Rates, 1890 to 1992

| Year | Percentage of Female Working-Age Population in Labor Force (working or looking for work) |
|------|------|
| 1890 | 18.9 |
| 1900 | 20.6 |
| 1920 | 23.7 |
| 1930 | 24.8 |
| 1940 | 25.8 |
| 1950 | 29.5 |
| 1960 | 37.7 |
| 1970 | 43.3 |
| 1980 | 51.5 |
| 1990 | 57.5 |
| 1991 | 57.3 |
| 1992 | 57.8 |

Sources: 1890 to 1950: Goldin, Claudia D. (1990) *Understanding the Gender Gap: An Economic History of American Women.* New York: Oxford University Press, p. 17.

1960 to 1990: U.S. Bureau of the Census, *Statistical Abstract of the United States, 1991,* Table 631.

1991: U.S. Department of Labor, Bureau of Labor Statistics, "Women's Labor Force Growth Appears Stalled," January 1992.

1992: U.S. Department of Labor, Bureau of Labor Statistics, *Employment and Earnings,* January 1993.

The most striking changes in the labor force during this century have come from the increasing participation of married women, especially after World War II. At first, the significant increases were from older married women (over age thirty-five). Since the 1960s, however, the labor force participation of younger married women has increased dramatically. Goldin (1990) has recently demonstrated that, for most of the history of the United States, marriage itself has been the factor that determined women's labor-force status. That is, most women dropped out of the labor force upon marriage. Those that remained in the labor force tended to stay there. Married women's work experience (in years) has been high since the beginning of the century, although it has not increased significantly in the last fifty years. Married women's labor-force participation rates increase with their age, and, when women are grouped in cohorts by date of birth, each cohort from 1866–1875 to 1956–1965 has had increasingly higher participation rates (with most reentering the labor force for the first time since marriage).

Since 1960, married women with young children have more than tripled their labor-force participation to almost 60 percent (see Table 2). Married women with children between the ages of six and seventeen had a labor-force participation rate of over 73.5 percent by 1990.

The determinants of these important changes have been and are still being studied by economists, sociologists, and historians. It is often unclear whether a factor is a cause or an effect of women's increasing labor-force participation. There are, however, a number of components that may be included in the explanation. First, higher educational attainment has been clearly associated with women's par-

TABLE 2. Labor-Force Participation of Married Women by Presence and Age of Children, 1960 to 1990

*Percent of Married Women in the Labor Force*

| Year | with no children under 18 | with children 6–17 only | with children under 6 |
|------|------|------|------|
| 1960 | 34.7 | 39.0 | 18.6 |
| 1970 | 42.2 | 49.2 | 30.3 |
| 1980 | 46.0 | 61.7 | 45.1 |
| 1990 | 51.1 | 73.6 | 58.9 |

Source: U.S. Bureau of the Census, *Statistical Abstract of the United States, 1992,* Tables 620 and 621.

TABLE 3. Female Labor-Force Participation Rates by Educational Attainment, 1970 to 1990

*Percent of Women in the Labor Force*

| Year | who did not graduate from high school | who graduated from high school | who completed 1–3 years of college | with 4 or more years of college |
|------|------|------|------|------|
| 1970 | 43.0 | 51.3 | 50.9 | 60.9 |
| 1975 | 44.1 | 53.9 | 57.3 | 62.7 |
| 1980 | 43.7 | 61.2 | 66.4 | 73.4 |
| 1985 | 44.3 | 65.0 | 72.5 | 78.6 |
| 1990 | 46.5 | 68.8 | 75.7 | 81.3 |

Source: U.S. Bureau of the Census, *Statistical Abstract of the United States, 1992,* Table 611.

ticipation in the labor force. The more education a woman has, the more likely she is to be in the labor force (see Table 3). In 1990, more than 80 percent of women who had completed four or more years of college were in the labor force, compared with about 69 percent of female high-school graduates and 46 percent of those with less than a high school education. Because women's potential earnings increase with education, it now costs more to remain *out* of the labor force (in terms of forgone income). During this century, women's educational attainment has increased dramatically and has become closer to that of men's at the higher levels. In 1991, 19 percent of women and 24 percent of men had completed four or more years of college. With increasing life spans, women can realize higher returns on their educational investment. Therefore, increasing education attracts more women to the labor force, and women in the labor force may in turn seek more education.

Another factor in the explanation of women's increasing labor-force participation during this century has been the increasing demand for workers in the service, clerical, and other white-collar areas, which tend to be predominantly female. Not only did this raise women's wages above what they otherwise would have been, but employers also began to realize that they could not satisfy the demand exclusively with young, single women (Oppenheimer 1970).

Demographic changes have also been associated with rising labor-force participation (although cause and effect are not clear). The median age at first marriage has increased for both men and women. There has been a long-run decline in the birth rate and the number of children per family. More women are having children at an older age. The divorce rate has increased. Studies have shown that women now expect to be in the labor force for a longer period of time, although women still plan to work fewer years than men (Blau and Ferber 1991, for example).

Finally, there have been institutional and social changes that must be included in the explanation. For most of the century, women in the labor force were viewed as temporary, marginal workers: Single women would quit when they married or became pregnant, and married women were supplemental in terms of family income. Therefore employers were not likely to invest in training for female workers, and they were paid less than men. Protective legislation also limited women's occupational opportunities. Women were viewed as too delicate and small for many jobs. In fact, many employers actually implemented written rules that prohibited married women from being hired (particularly in teaching and clerical occupations). These "marriage bars" began in the 1800s and did not disappear until the 1950s. In 1942, for example, 87 percent of American school districts forbade hiring married women, and 70 percent fired single women who married. Goldin (1990), who brought this information to light, suggests that at their height, marriage bars affected about 50 percent of all office workers.

Employers' perceptions and social norms regarding appropriate labor-force behavior for single and married women (especially those with children) have been slower to change than women's actual labor-force participation. The women's movement and public policies such as the Equal Pay Act of 1963, the Civil Rights Act of 1964, affirmative action (1965), and Title IX (Education Amendments of 1972) have helped to reduce discrimination against women in education and the labor force.

The rate of further growth in women's labor-force participation will probably be slower for the rest of this century than it has been for the last twenty-five years (U.S. Bureau of Labor Statistics 1992). However, factors such as future birth patterns, the strength of the economy, and demographic changes among different groups of women may affect this trend.

*Dayle A. Mandelson*

## Bibliography

Bergmann, Barbara. 1986. *The Economic Emergence of Women*. New York: Basic Books.

Blau, Francine D., and Marianne A. Ferber. 1991. "Career Plans and Expectations of Young Women and Men: The Earnings Gap and Labor Force Participation." *Journal of Human Resources* 26:581–607.

Blau, Francine D., and Marianne A. Ferber. 1992. *The Economics of Women, Men, and Work*. Englewood Cliffs, N.J.: Prentice-Hall.

Blau, Francine D., and Anne E. Winkler. 1989. "Women in the Labor Force: An Overview." In *Women: A Feminist Perspective*, edited by Jo Freeman. Mountain View, Calif.: Mayfield.

Fuchs, Victor. 1988. *Women's Quest for Economic Equality*. Cambridge, Mass.: Harvard University Press.

Goldin, Claudia D. 1990. *Understanding the Gender Gap: An Economic History of American Women*. New York: Oxford University Press.

Oppenheimer, Valerie Kincade. 1970. *The Female Labor Force in the United States*. Berkeley: University of California, Institute of International Studies.

Rix, Sara E., ed. 1990. *The American Women 1990–91: A Status Report.* New York: W.W. Norton.

U.S. Bureau of Labor Statistics, Department of Labor. *Employment in Perspective: Women in the Labor Force.* (Quarterly.)

———. 1992. "Women's Labor Force Growth Appears Stalled." *Labor Statistics.* Summary 92:2.

U.S. Bureau of the Census. 1991, 1992. Abstract of the United States. Washington, D.C.: U.S. Department of Commerce.

Wright, Gavin. 1991. *"Understanding the Gender Gap:* A Review Article." *Journal of Economic Literature* 29:1153–63.

## Women and Part-Time Work

Growing numbers of American women continue to make the occupational decision to engage in part-time work. Apparent since the 1950s, this trend perpetuates the existence of a female-dominated part-time labor force. Several factors contribute to this growth. Of primary interest are the social factors that influence the occupational choices available to women in the U.S. Examined here are the social factors that serve, at least in part, to constrain the occupational choices available to women. This is done by considering the interplay of labor-market demand, cultural ideology, and national policy issues that affect women's labor-force decisions.

### Trends in Part-Time Labor

It is no secret that many American women work outside the home. Women constitute a substantial share of the U.S. labor market and their employment numbers are growing. In 1988 approximately 54 percent of white women, 51 percent of African-American women, and 49 percent of Hispanic women over the age of sixteen were employed either full- or part-time (U.S. Department of Labor 1989, pp. 70–75). This represents an increase in women's employment from 1980, when 48 percent of whites, 46 percent of African Americans, and 42 percent of Hispanics were counted among the ranks of the employed (U.S. Department of Labor 1989, pp. 70–75).

Generally speaking, the federal government defines part-time employees as those individuals working fewer than thirty-five hours a week (U.S. Department of Labor 1989). Full-time employees are those who work thirty-five hours or more a week.

Between 1954 and 1985, the proportion of the federal labor force filled by part-time workers rose from 8 to 12 percent (Chamallas 1986). Between 1968 and 1988, full-time employment in the United States rose 46 percent while part-time employment displayed an 86 percent increase (U.S. Department of Labor 1989, pp. 54–55). This expansion appears to be continuing (Feldman 1989). From 1980 to 1989 the number of workers employed part-time increased by more than 23 percent, twice the growth experienced in the full-time labor force (Belous 1989). The data indicate the importance of work status when considering women's labor-force participation.

Women are most likely to occupy part-time employment positions (Rotchford and Roberts 1982; Smith 1983; Chamallas 1986). In 1982, approximately 33 percent of all married women worked part-time (Smith 1983, p. 2). As of 1988, female employees accounted for 67 percent of the part-time labor force but only 40 percent of all full-time workers (U.S. Department of Labor 1989, pp. 54–55; U.S. Bureau of the Census 1990, p. 387). The contemporary part-time employee is typically female, married with school-age children, and works outside the home approximately twenty hours per week (Chamallas 1986; Wakefield et al. 1987).

As interest in women's part-time employment expands, it is increasingly clear that distinct properties separate part-time from full-time work. The differences raise pertinent questions about the occupational choices made by many part-time workers.

### Differences According to Work Status

Employers and society as a whole often evaluate part-time work as second-class employment (Chamallas 1986). Part-time positions are often concentrated in the lowest levels of the occupational structure and in areas implying female-specific demand (Smith 1983). The concentration of part-time work in the lower levels of the occupational structure affects employees in two ways. First, it influences the rewards part-time workers receive for their labor-force participation. Second, it directly affects the way society assesses both the work and the worker.

The reward structures for full-time and part-time work are distinctly different. As opposed to full-time employees, part-time workers tend to receive little or no training when entering a given position. Part-time workers enjoy few promotional opportunities and are vulnerable to periods of unemployment. Perhaps the greatest distinction appears when considering the monetary rewards associated with employment. Part-time employees in the United States tend to receive lower wages than do their full-time counterparts and seldom qualify to receive employer-provided fringe benefits (Smith 1983; Chamallas 1986). If employers do provide fringe benefits to part-time workers, benefits are prorated according to the hours worked. These structural differences help to perpetuate the societal notion that part-time work is second-class employment.

It is clear that compensatory and prestige differences exist between full-time and part-time employment. Given these differences, it is not readily apparent why women workers so often choose part-time employment. One finds at least a partial explanation by examining the supply and demand factors associated with part-time work.

### Part-Time Work as an Occupational Choice

The increased demand for part-time female labor evolves from two primary sources. First, changes in the market structure of the U.S. economy during the 1970s and 1980s brought about the growth of certain jobs that are both part-time and gender-specific (Smith 1983). Second, employers are increasingly recognizing the organizational benefits of using part-time employees. Modern organizations thus rely on part-time workers both in response to changing market structures and as a cost-effective method of maximizing profits.

The rise of particular industries in the U.S. economy is largely accountable for the proliferation of part-time employment (Smith 1983). This is especially true in the service and retail sectors of the economy, where part-time work tends to be most heavily concentrated. The service and sales industries must respond to daily or seasonal fluctuations in output demand. At the same time, employers strive to maximize profits by minimizing operating costs. Part-time labor serves this purpose by providing low-cost workers who can be scheduled around the output demands of the organization.

Cultural ideology and national policy issues represent key supply-side factors affecting the gender-specific nature of part-time work. Of particular interest here are the overlapping issues of expected role fulfillment and child-care needs. American women fulfill many roles, but society considers them first and foremost family caregivers (Smith 1983). The multiple role demands women experience appear to make part-time employment an attractive occupational choice, especially among women with children. Employers often use this rationale to both legitimate and explain the gender-specific nature of part-time work. At the same time, they reinforce the culturally dominant view of women as primary caregivers and secondary wage earners.

The presence of children in the home represents perhaps the single greatest constraint to women's labor-force participation. Two factors associated with the parental role constrain women occupationally. The first is an ideological constraint, the second a pragmatic one. First, society expects women to maintain primary responsibility for the care and rearing of children (Smith 1983; Chamallas 1986). Second, affordable child care is often inaccessible to working women in the United States, as is the availability of paid parental leave following the birth or adoption of a child (Allen 1988).

For women working out of desire or necessity, the issue becomes one of constrained choice. As secondary wage earners, women are limited in their ability to purchase adequate child care. The cost of paid child care merely minimizes the contributions made by the earned wages. Therefore, many women arrange their work schedules around the availability of nonpaid child care provided by husband or relatives (Smith 1983). It is easy to comprehend the attraction that part-time work holds for many married women with children. Society first dictates women to place primacy on their roles as family caregivers. Women then face occupational constraints that appear in the form of national policies that are slow to respond to the needs of working mothers. This intersection of ideological and national policy considerations accounts, in large part, for the gender-specific supply of part-time employees.

## Consequences and Conclusions

Since the 1950s, female workers in the United States have dominated a growing part-time labor force. A combination of demand and supply factors is largely accountable for this phenomenon. Broad changes in the market structure of the U.S. economy have necessitated the construction and growth of certain part-time positions. This is especially true in the retail and service sectors, where poorly paid, low-skill jobs are concentrated. At the same time, employers continue to promote part-time work as an attractive option for working women. Part-time employment appears to provide a desired fit between women's home and work responsibilities. The logic of this argument ignores the manner in which part-time work reinforces women's status as secondary wage earners.

Social factors have historically constrained the occupational choices of working women. These constraints emanate from two sources. First, cultural ideology dictates that women place priority on their family roles. Second, national policy makers have been slow to respond to the needs of working women. The lack of comprehensive child care and parental-leave policies prohibits many women from seeking full-time employment. The intersection of three main factors—market demand, cultural ideology, and national policy—actively channels many women into part-time employment. In so doing, it reinforces the image of women as marginal workers. It also influences both the future occupational opportunities and the self-concepts of female part-time workers.

In summary, the issue surrounding women and part-time work is one of constrained occupational choice. For many women, the decision to enter into part-time employment represents something other than freedom of choice in the labor market. Rather, for many it represents a decision made in light of constrained occupational opportunities. One must look beyond the obvious to understand the employment decisions of women. Part-time work provides an obvious fit between women's home and work responsibilities. The social factors that precipitate the need for this fit are not always as obvious.

*Martha L. Shockey*

## Bibliography

Allen, Joseph P. 1988. "European Infant Care Leaves: Foreign Perspectives on the Integration of Work and Family Roles." In *The Parental Leave Crisis: Toward a National Policy*, edited by Edward F. Zigler and Meryl Frank. New Haven: Yale University Press.

Belous, R.S. 1989. *The Contingent Economy*. Report No. 15. Washington, D.C.: National Planning Association.

Bianchi, Suzanne M., and Daphne Spain. 1986. *American Women in Transition*. New York: Russell Sage Foundation.

Chamallas, Martha. 1986. "Women and Part-Time Work: The Case for Pay Equity and Equal Access." *North Carolina Law Review* 64(4):709–75.

England, Paula, and George Farkas. 1986. *Households, Employment, and Gender: A Social, Economic, and Demographic View*. New York: Aldine.

Feldman, D.C. 1989. "Reconceptualizing the Nature and Consequence of Part-Time Work." *Academy of Management Review* 15(1):103–12.

Hom, Peter W. 1979. "Effects of Job Peripherality and Personal Characteristics on the Job Satisfaction of Part-Time Workers." *Academy of Management Journal* 22(3):551–65.

Huber, Joan, and Glenna Spitze. 1983. *Sex Stratification: Children, Housework, and Jobs*. New York: Academic.

Rotchford, Nancy L., and Karlene H. Roberts. 1982. "Part-Time Workers as Missing Persons in Organizational Research." *Academy of Management Review* 7(2):228–34.

Smith, Vicki. 1983. "The Circular Trap: Women and Part-Time Work." *Berkeley Journal of Sociology* 28:1–17.

U.S. Bureau of the Census. 1990. *Statistical Abstract of the United States: 1990*, 110th edition. Washington, D.C.: U.S. Government Printing Office.

U.S. Department of Labor, Bureau of Labor Statistics. August 1989. *Handbook of Labor Statistics: Bulletin 2340*. Washington, D.C.: U.S. Government Printing Office.

Wakefield, Douglas S., James P. Curry, Charles W. Mueller, and James L. Price. 1987. "Differences in the Importance of Work Outcomes between Full-Time and Part-Time Hospital Employees." *Journal of Occupational Behaviour* 8:25–35.

## Self-Employed Women in the United States

The rate at which women have entered self-employment has increased dramatically in recent decades. The self-employment rate increased 45 percent from 1970 to 1983 (Becker 1984). While the number of self-employed women is far below that of men, their percentage in the work force has increased five times faster than that of self-employed men and more than three times faster than that of female wage and salary workers. Self-employed women tend to be older, married, slightly better educated, white or Asian, and more concentrated in female-dominated personal-service and retail-sales industries. Although all self-employed workers on average work longer hours, women are more likely to work part-time and to earn less than their wage and salary counterparts (U.S. Small Business Administration 1986). Despite these economic disadvantages, self-employment may be attractive for women who have few employment options or require more flexibility in their work lives. This is especially true for mothers of young children.

Despite some movement into occupations and industries dominated by men, the large and growing numbers of women in the labor force still tend to be segregated in a small number of "female" occupations. Women's share of the increase in self-employment has also been confined to gender-typical occupations (Wharton 1989). While the news media have focused attention on successful female entrepreneurs, most self-employed women hold sales or nonhousehold personal- and business-service jobs. Although professionals, such as doctors and lawyers, have a history of self-employment (for example, setting up a private practice), women are self-employed in those occupations on average one-third as often as men (Aronson 1991). In fact, women's exclusion from these male-dominated professional jobs is a form of "hidden segregation" (Wharton 1989). Other barriers to self-employment for women include less access to financial capital with which to finance a business (particularly in nontraditional industries and occupations) and customer discrimination against women-owned businesses in nontraditional industries. It is likely that self-employed women are most commonly found in personal-service jobs because those occupations require less start-up capital. Self-employed women, however, have increased their numbers in construction and precision-skill occupations dominated by men (Aronson 1991).

Self-employed women earn significantly less than self-employed men and wage and salaried workers of both sexes. Women who were full-time, sole business owners earned only 31 percent of the amount comparable men did in 1983, whereas female wage and salaried workers earned about 60 percent of what their male counterparts did (Haber, Lamas, and Lichtenstein 1987). Female proprietors earned only about 30 percent of the wages of comparable female wage and salaried workers. (Self-employed earnings are often difficult to assess because it is common to underreport earnings to avoid taxes.)

Most studies that have predicted self-employment have focused exclusively on men. One theory suggests that the "entrepreneur" believes that he or she has special abilities that will lead to success. A second theory proposes that the self-employed are motivated to work for themselves because they are dissatisfied with, or have lost, their jobs. Motives for becoming self-employed do not seem to differ substantially for men and women. Both sexes indicate the ability to be independent and the expectation of more money as the top reasons for being self-employed (Hakim 1989).

The greater numbers of women going to work and their tendency to stay at their jobs for a long time have created new opportunities. Longer work histories provide women with the assets, contacts, and knowledge to start businesses. Small studies of female business owners have found that women are self-employed for a variety of reasons, only one of which is economic need (Cromie and Hayes 1988). Self-employment can be an option for women wanting or requiring a more flexible means of balancing family and work responsibilities. It is also a means for some women to overcome occupational subordination in the labor market, and a means of personal growth and identity for women who otherwise might not be in the labor force. It may also be the only means that unemployed or under-employed women have to earn sufficient income.

### Self-Employment and Family Responsibilities

To truly understand self-employment among women, one has to consider the family context. Sexual segregation at work may persist because women's competing role obligations influence their choice of occupations. Women are drawn to certain occupations where low training requirements make it easy and relatively cost free to withdraw from the labor force when their children are young (Polachek 1979), or that provide nonmonetary benefits that make it easier to combine family and work responsibilities (Ross 1987).

Self-employment, like certain occupations, can provide time flexibility that can make it easier to combine family and work. Self-employment represents a work option between market work and family responsibilities. With more women in the labor force, many need substitutes to do household work and child care. As a result, there are increased opportunities to work at home, substituting lower wages for more time to devote to homemaking and child rearing, and with fewer work-related expenses.

Despite its lower earnings, self-employment can provide more flexibility and allow a woman more control over her schedule. That may be particularly attractive for women with small children. Boyd-Davis (1991) found that exclusively self-employed wives and wives who had a wage job plus a second business had more children living in the household. In particular, self-employment with or without a second job is a more attractive work option for wives with two or more children of five and under (although nonparticipation is still more common). Connelly (1992) found the same relationship for women regardless of marital status. She found that the number of young children increased the probability of a woman's being self-employed or a child-care provider. There is a financial price to pay, however. The average hourly wage of self-employed child-care providers was $1.20 in 1985, compared with $4.26 for other self-employed women and $2.27 for child-care providers who were not self-employed.

### Conclusion

Self-employment is an increasingly popular work alternative for a growing number of women. It is popular with mothers of small children because of the potential for greater time flexibility and the ability to control the work schedule. There is a price to pay for this flexibility, however. Despite some progress in male-dominated occupations, gender segregation has increased in the self-employed sector of the economy. Most self-employed women (particularly child-care workers) earn substantially less than self-employed men and wage and salaried workers of both sexes. So, while self-employment can provide the means to overcome discrimination or balance home responsibilities while earning income, it is not a choice for everyone. Further research is needed on the "choice" of self-employment.

*Sandra Boyd-Davis*

## Bibliography

Aronson, R. 1991. *Self-Employment: A Labor Market Perspective*. Ithaca, N.Y.: ILR.

Becker, E. 1984. "Self-Employed Workers: An Update to 1983." *Monthly Labor Review* 197:14–18.

Boyd-Davis, S. 1991. "Self-Employed Wives in the Labor Force." Paper presented at the Population Association of America, Washington, D.C.

Connelly, R. 1992. "Self-Employment and Providing Child Care." *Demography* 29 (1):17–29.

Cromie, S., and J. Hayes. 1988. "Toward a Typology of Female Entrepreneurs." *Sociological Review* 36 (1):87–113.

Haber, S., E. Lamas, and J. Lichtenstein. 1987. "On Their Own: Self-Employed and Others in Private Business." *Monthly Labor Review* 110 (5):17–23.

Hakim, C. 1989. "New Recruits to Self-Employment in the 1980s." *Employment Gazette* 97 (6):286–97.

Kent, C., D. Sexton, and K. Vesper, eds. 1982. *Encyclopedia of Entrepreneurship*. Englewood Cliffs, N.J.: Prentice Hall.

Polachek, S. 1979. "Occupational Segregation among Women: Theory, Evidence and a Prognosis." In *Women in the Labor Market*, edited by C. Lloyd, E. Andrews, and C. Gilroy, pp. 137–57. New York: Columbia University Press.

Ross, C. 1987. "The Division of Labor at Home." *Social Forces* 65:816–33.

U.S. Small Business Administration, Office of the Advocacy. 1986. "Self-Employment as Small Business." Chapter 4 of *The State of Small Business: A Report of the President*, pp. 105–35. Washington, D.C.: Government Printing Office.

U.S. Department of Commerce. 1986. *Women and Business Ownership: An Annotated Bibliography*. Washington, D.C.: U.S. Government Printing Office.

Wharton, A. 1989. "Gender Segregation in Private-Sector, Public-Sector and Self-Employed Occupations, 1950–1981." *Social Science Quarterly* 70 (4):923–39.

## Working-Class Women and Work

Besides facing issues such as occupational segregation, the wage gap, and the lack of mobility, which affect all working women, working-class women confront problems that differ dramatically from those of women in middle-class and professional occupations. Typically, working-class women work in jobs considered unskilled, usually with little job security, with low pay and few or no benefits (health and retirement insurance or paid vacations). The work is often repetitive, tedious, physically demanding and, most of all, boring (Rosen 1987; Cavendish 1982).

These women work because they need the money, but respect rather than sympathy is due them. They are not simply tied to wretched work conditions by economic need; most find a level of satisfaction in their work (Hess and Ferree 1987; Rosen 1987; Sacks 1988). Satisfaction may arise, in part, from their recognition of the contribution they make to their families' economic well-being, but it is also often related to pride in doing a difficult job well, to meeting the challenges of quantity and quality of work, and to their awareness of their value as workers and women. Pride in their hard work and awareness of their exploitation in the workplace contribute to their active resistance to oppression at work. Uncertainty over changing trends in work structure and the decline in the U.S. economy create ambivalence and undermine women's ability to demand better work conditions (Rosen 1987; Cavendish 1982).

Recent changes in work structure have had a profound effect on the character of working-class women's work. Factory jobs that provided some women with relatively high wages, compared with other types of women's work, have begun to disappear as employers move operations to other regions or countries in search of a lower-paid labor force. Concurrently, service-sector occupations have grown rapidly, creating new jobs so disproportionately filled by women that they are sometimes called "pink-collar" (Smith 1984; Bose et al. 1987; Amott and Matthaei 1991). The expansion of service-sector employment has created fundamental changes in the character of work, especially for working-class women (Smith 1984). Service occupations are increasingly part time or less than full-year jobs that pay low wages. Both market factors and personal preferences have stimulated the increase in part-time employment. Contrary to the common belief, however, statistics suggest that availability of jobs rather than worker preference is the key factor in the trend toward higher levels of part-time employment (Smith 1984; Beneria and Stimpson 1987).

Another change in the character of work is the disappearance of the so-called family wage earned by a male breadwinner to support his family (Smith 1984). Most service work, the fastest-growing sector of the economy, does not pay enough to support workers and their families. Therefore, families often must have two paid workers to remain above the poverty line, and many women who head households are poor despite their full-time employment.

Changes in technology and work structures also affect women's work experiences, through changing job skills and levels of managerial control. Some researchers suggest that technological advances ultimately create higher-skilled jobs (Bell 1973; Piore and Sabel 1984; Zuboff 1988), while others conclude that skill levels are reduced and managerial control over workers is increased by current uses of technology and shifts in work structures (Beneria and Stimpson 1987). Several authors in the edited collections by Sacks and Remy (1984) and Bose, Feldberg, and Sokoloff (1987) discuss "de-skilling" of low-level service work in such occupations as clerical work, word processing, and retail sales, occupations that employ large numbers of women. Computer technology is also being used to increase managers' ability to control and monitor work. Computers can record the number of documents produced, sales made, or telephone calls answered, even allowing managers to listen in on telephone conversations without workers' knowledge (Bose, Feldberg, and Sokoloff 1987; Sacks and Remy 1984). While technological and organizational changes can often be used to simplify the work process and increase managerial control over workers, researchers however increasingly recognize that the impact of these changes is contingent on a variety of organizational and societal factors (Spenner 1988; Form et al. 1988). Clearly, increased technology will continue to affect the work structures and experiences of all workers, and will provide interesting research material in the future.

Women recognize the skills necessary to do their jobs well, although these skills may be less apparent to others. Changes in work organization toward more flexible production patterns that encourage workers to develop new skills—as in the recent experiments in the auto industry (Piore and Sabel 1984)—are slow to reach most female working-class workers. Typically, factory production jobs are tiny parts of the whole process, with each worker repeating one part over and over throughout the day. Largely confined to these "unskilled" production jobs, women often experience the speed of the work as the hardest part of the job (Cavendish 1982; Rosen 1987). Speed itself, however, is a learned skill. Only with experience and skill can women workers assemble 170 electric cords per hour (Rosen 1987), attach pickets to 3,168 garments per day (Sacks and Remy 1984), or pack precise amounts of spinach into two thousand cans each day (Zavella 1988). Women know that their work requires strength, energy, coordination, and skill unrecognized by management or outsiders (Rosen 1987). Pressure to increase speed through computerized machines and simplified work processes is a key factor in shaping the experiences of women factory workers.

Finally, the changing character of women's work increasingly includes periods of involuntary unemployment. Computerization may reduce clerical employment by 27 to 46 percent by the year 2000 (Bose et al. 1987:24), although clerical work will continue to be the largest occupation for women. The need for easy expansion and contraction of the labor market, a key factor in low-level service work and female-typed factory jobs (Smith 1984), requires that women change jobs to maintain their earnings—often with periods of unemployment in between. Ambivalence is a common feeling about their unemployment when viewed within the context of women's various work and family commitments (Rosen 1987). Households then have less money, but women can spend more time with their families and gain temporary relief from the need to balance paid work with caring for their families. They know, however, that they must return to paid work. This is the "bitter choice" (Rosen 1987) that women must make.

Diverse family responsibilities highlight the connections between work and family experienced by all workers, but especially women. Recently, scholars have begun to recognize what working women have always known: Women experience neither paid work nor home life as isolated parts of their lives. Furthermore, the shapes and structures of both work and home are dependent upon each other (Bose et al. 1987; Bookman and Morgen 1988; Beneria and Stimpson 1987; Ward 1990; Zavella 1988). This understanding reveals the contradictions that working-class women manage daily and illuminates the complexities of both families and work as factors legitimating the inequality of men, women, and children. Both paid employment and unpaid work at home offer advantages and disadvantages for women that affect their work patterns, employment choices, child-care decisions, purchasing patterns, and even decisions about when and if to marry or to divorce, and whether to have children.

Connections between work and family also help explain working women's resistance strategies and patterns. Although changes in work structures and available employment undermine female workers' ability to become independent and remain out of poverty, women continue to resist the structures and ideologies that define them as marginal, exploitable labor (Sacks and Remy 1984; Rosen 1987; Amott and Matthaei 1991; Bookman and Morgen 1988; Bose et al. 1987; Beneria and Stimpson 1987; Ward 1990; Zavella 1988). Family structures and responsibilities, as well as work structure and culture, combine to either support or oppose working women's resistance (Zavella 1988; Bookman and Morgen 1988) and help to determine the type of resistance women engage in (Zavella 1988; Sacks 1988; Amott and Matthaei 1991; Ward 1990).

Several researchers have explored individual and collective informal resistance strategies. For example, Kessler-Harris (1982) and Amott and Matthaei (1991) place women's resistance in historical perspective, while Zavella (1988) and Hossfeld (1990) look at contemporary female workers. Most studies of resistance, however, have focused on participation in labor unions. Working-class women's participation in unions has historically been low, in part because of their responsibilities outside the workplace, but also because of the orientation and structures of the unions (Bose et al. 1987). Larger, male-dominated unions often absorb smaller women's unions and tend to ignore issues of concern to women (Bookman and Morgen 1988; Bose et al. 1987). As overall union membership has declined with job losses in heavily unionized, male-dominated industries, large national unions have moved toward organizing female clerical and health-care workers (Sacks 1988; Bookman and Morgen 1988). As this occurs, women increasingly demand recognition of issues unique to their experiences.

Recently, scholars have begun to consider the importance of connections between race, ethnicity, class, and gender to understanding women's experiences of work and family, and their resistance to oppression and exploitation (Amott and Matthaei 1991; Zavella 1988; Sacks 1988; Bookman and Morgen 1988; Ward 1990; Bose et al. 1987). Research that focuses on paid domestic work and the women who do it specifically explores these issues. Understanding resistance within the context of women's race, ethnicity, class, and gender exposes even more subtle forms of resistance. Supervisors often use gender and racial and ethnic stereotypes to manage workers' behavior and gain control over the workplace.

> *The bosses here have this type of reasoning like a seesaw. One day it's "You're paid less because women are different than men," or "Immigrants need less to get by." The next day it's "You're all just workers here—no special treatment just because you're female or foreigners."*
>
> *Well, they think they're pretty clever with their doubletalk, and that we're just a bunch of dumb aliens. But it takes two to use a seesaw. What we're gradually figuring out here is* how to use their own logic against them. *(Hossfeld 1990:149).*

Recognizing how management uses gender and racial and ethnic stereotypes against them, women often turn the stereotypes around and use them as a form of resistance (Hossfeld 1990; Bookman and Morgen 1988). Much more work needs to be done to understand how the interconnections among race, ethnicity, class, and gender affect working women's lives.

When looking at working-class women and work, several key issues emerge. The changing character of work is creating extensive changes in women's work experiences through the growth in the service sector, decreasing wages, changing skill levels, control of workers through technology, and increases in involuntary unemployment. Women often experience work as both good and bad because of the multiple responsibilities they manage at home and at paid work. The connections between paid work and families are especially important for female workers. Women work to meet family as well as personal needs, and family affects all aspects of women's employment decisions. Although women need to work, they also resist exploitation in the workplace. It is working-class women's strength, courage, and determination we must remember when studying the demeaning, devalued paid work they do.

*Nanette Page*

## Bibliography

Amott, T., and J. Matthaei. 1991. *Race, Gender, and Work*. Boston: South End.

Bell, D. 1973. *The Coming of Post-Industrial Society*. New York: Basic Books.

Beneria, L., and C. Stimpson. 1987. *Women, Households, and the Economy*. New Brunswick, N.J.: Rutgers University Press.

Bookman, A., and S. Morgen. 1988. *Women and the Politics of Empowerment*. Philadelphia: Temple University Press.

Bose, C., R. Feldberg, and N. Sokoloff, eds. 1987. *Hidden Aspects of Women's Work*. New York: Praeger.

Cavendish, R. 1982. *Women on the Line*. London: Routledge and Kegan Paul.

Form, W., R.L. Kaufman, T.L. Parcel, and M. Wallace. 1988. "The Impact of Technology on Work Organization and Work Outcomes: A Conceptual Framework and Research Agenda." In *Industries, Firms and Jobs: Sociological and Economic Approaches*, edited by G. Farkas and P. England, pp. 303–28. New York: Plenum.

Hess, B., and M. Marx Ferree. 1987. *Analyzing Gender*. Newbury Park, Calif.: Sage.

Hossfeld, K. 1990. "Their Logic against Them: Contradictions. In Sex, Race, and Class in Silicon Valley." In *Women Workers and Global Restructuring*, edited by K. Ward, pp. 149–78. Ithaca, N.Y.: ILR.

Kessler-Harris, A. 1982. *Out to Work*. New York: Oxford University Press.

Piore, M., and Sabel, C. 1984. *The Second Industrial Divide: Possibilities for Prosperity*. New York: Basic Books.

Rosen, E. 1987. *Bitter Choices: Blue-Collar Women in and out of Work*. Chicago: University of Chicago Press.

Sacks, K. 1988. *Caring by the Hour*. Urbana: University of Illinois Press.

Sacks, K., and D. Remy, eds. 1984. *My Troubles Are Going to Have Trouble with Me*. New Brunswick, N.J.: Rutgers University Press.

Smith, J. 1984. "The Paradox of Women's Poverty: Wage-Earning Women and Economic Transformation." *Signs* 10:291–310.

Spenner, K. 1988. "Technological Change, Skill Requirements and Education: The Case for Uncertainty." In *The Impact of Technological Change on Employment and Economic Growth*, edited by R. Cyert and D. Mowery, pp. 131–83. Cambridge, Mass.: Ballinger.

Ward, K. 1990. *Women Workers and Global Restructuring*. Ithaca, N.Y.: ILR.

Zavella, P. 1988. *Women's Work and Chicano Families*. Ithaca, N.Y.: Cornell University Press.

Zuboff, S. 1988. *In the Age of the Smart Machine: The Future of Work and Power*. New York: Basic Books.

## Young Women at Work

Work is perhaps the single most common out-of-school activity among America's teenagers. Data from "High School and Beyond" (HS&B), a national representative study of high-school students, indicate that 90 percent of American high-school teenagers will be employed at some time during the course of their secondary-school experience (Sebring et al. 1986). The number of teenagers currently working in the United States is considerable: Census statistics reveal that slightly more than half of America's teenagers (51.3 percent) ages sixteen to nineteen who are enrolled in secondary school are also paid workers (U.S. Department of Labor 1993).

While the proportion of young men's participation in the labor force has remained relatively constant over the past twenty years, young women's participation has increased significantly (U.S. Department of Commerce, Economics and Statistics Administration 1993). Analyses of the Department of Labor's National Longitudinal Survey (DOL-NLS) and HS&B data showed that roughly 45 percent of men and 40 percent of women ages sixteen to seventeen were employed during the 1980s (Lewin-Epstein 1981; Lewis et al. 1983; D'Amico 1984). More recent estimates indicate that the percentage of young women who work may, in fact, have surpassed that of young men. Reports from the third follow-up of the National Education Longitudinal Study of 1988 (NELS:88), a nationally representative survey of high-school seniors, reveal that, in 1992, 47.5 percent of young men and 51.6 percent of young women were employed while in school (Green et al. 1994).

Although the labor-force participation rates of young women and men have reached parity, gender differences persist with respect to wages, the number of hours worked, and the type of jobs held. Most teenagers who work part time earn wages at or slightly above the minimum wage; several studies, however, show that young men are paid at a significantly higher hourly rate than young women (Lewin-Epstein 1981; Lewis et al. 1983; Stevenson 1978; U.S. Department of Commerce, Economics and Statistics Administration 1993). Similar wage differentials are found among fifteen to twenty-four-year-olds who work full time; young men earn an average of one thousand dollars more per year than young women (U.S. Department of Commerce, Economics and Statistics Administration 1993).

The majority of students work about twenty hours or less a week, but young women appear to work fewer hours than young men (Green et al. 1994; see also Charner and Fraser 1988). Data from the third follow-up of NELS:88, conducted in 1992 among high-school seniors, show that 37.5 percent of women were working twenty hours a week or less during the school year, while 14.1 percent were working more than twenty hours a week. The profile for men is significantly different: 28.7 percent of them worked twenty hours a week or less during the school year, but almost 19 percent of them were working more than twenty hours a week (Green et al. 1994).

Gender differences in hours worked can be linked to differences in the type of work undertaken by young women and men. Even at this young age, women and men tend to be employed in sex-stereotypic fields. Charner and Fraser (1988), in their review of data from HS&B, conclude that women tend to have jobs in the fields of child care and clerical work, whereas most men tend to earn money doing odd jobs and manual labor. In tenth grade, 50 percent of young women held child-care-type jobs, whereas the most frequently held jobs for young men were "other" (30 percent), followed by odd jobs (14 percent), manual labor (13 percent), farming (11 percent), and food service (10 percent). By twelfth grade these employment categories had shifted, and many more women worked as store clerks (25 percent), in food service (22 percent), clerical (18 percent), and other jobs (15 percent). For men the category "other" decreased (26 percent), whereas employment as sales clerks (18 percent), manual laborers (14 percent), in food service (12 percent), and skilled trades (11 percent) all increased.

The process that adolescents use to locate employment has yet to be systematically investigated. There is some evidence from a purposive sample of young workers who were entering their first jobs following high-school graduation that men are more effective than women in finding and keeping jobs (Borman 1988). When searching for work, men tend to use contacts with friends or relatives, whereas women tend to use want ads or apply directly to employers. Even though women use a wider variety of job-search strategies which expend more resources than men, they often achieved less favorable results. Borman (1991) partially attributes these gender differences in job searching strategies and longevity of employment to the inexperience of women in obtaining work outside traditional roles and to sexual discriminatory practices in hiring and retaining workers at some places of employment.

The relationship between adolescent work experiences and academic outcomes is somewhat mixed. Lewis et al. (1983) found significant gender relationships between hours worked and class rank. Using NLS data, his analyses showed that work experience had no effect on grades or class rank for young men. However, for young women, work experience had a small negative relationship on grades but a small positive relationship with class rank.

No differences in gender effects are reported by D'Amico (1984), who, in his analysis of data from the National Longitudinal Surveys of the Labor Market Experience of Youth, found no relationship between working and grades or class rank for either sex. Similarly, Schill et al. (1985), in a study involving 4,587 students from public and private high schools in Washington State, found that students who work fewer than twenty hours a week have higher grades than those students not working or working more than twenty hours, regardless of sex.

Scholars studying the working patterns of teenagers tend to disagree about the value of these influences on socializing values of work or career choices. Mortimer and Borman (1988) contend that work experiences in adolescence begin to shape values and attitudes toward a work career. Work is seen as a socializing experience in which an individual can acquire work habits, learn how to manage social situations, and have the opportunity to participate in socially useful activities.

Taking a more negative position, Greenberger and Steinberg (1986) suggest that the type of jobs in which most teenagers are employed have serious limitations with respect to their developmental potential. They maintain that the low level of cognitive complexity associated with most such jobs offers limited access to roles requiring responsibility and authority. Consequently, adolescent work roles typically do little to pave a solid path to adulthood. Since many adolescents have little contact with adults at work, working does more to tie a young worker to the adolescent community than to the adult world. Claiming that the money teenagers earn is often used to buy luxuries that enhance their status among their peers rather than to fulfill a genuine need, Greenberger and Steinberg (1986) assert that such experiences undermine "work values" and do not strengthen ties to the adult world or foster attachment to norms and values of mainstream society.

Few empirical studies have examined whether teenage attitudes and values toward work vary systematically by gender. One exception is a new national longitudinal study of youth development, which is examining how adolescents come to think about work and career choices over time (Bidwell et al. 1992). Using data from this ongoing project in an analysis of self-esteem and work, Schneider et al. (1994) found that adolescent women exhibit higher levels of self-esteem, control, and satisfaction when working at paid jobs than do men. Upon closer investigation of the job experience, Schneider et al. show that for women it is actually the perception of doing worklike activities, rather than simply being at a paid job, that leads to these positive feelings. For example, young women who have jobs but do not feel that what they are doing is "like work" tend not to experience the heightened self-esteem and satisfaction evidenced in young women who feel that what they are doing on the job is "like work." This finding provides further evidence to the Greenberger and Steinberg argument (1986) that many of the less cognitively engaging types of jobs available to teenagers may not provide the benefits that are presumed to emerge from the job experience.

The experiences women and men have on the job and the consequences these experiences have for future career choices remain unexplored. Using data from the National Longitudinal Study of Youth to study the dynamics that underlie young women's traditional job choices, Berryman (1988) suggests that the choices they make might indirectly revolve around the basic issue of choosing between family and work. According to Berryman, educational investments and occupational choices for young women are essentially derived from their commitment to family formation. Berryman contends that this commitment to family may not be a conscious decision process but nevertheless serves as a driving force in the determination of their choices—unlike young men, who place other issues before family. Contrasted with this position, Weis (1990) found in her qualitative study of a working-class high school in an economically depressed city that young women tend to reject future roles as homemakers, whereas young men expect that they and their spouses will assume traditional family roles after high-school graduation.

Evidential data that support gender career determination are inconclusive. The extent to which perceptions of the occupational structure affect psychological and social development remains unclear. Different jobs undoubtedly offer different opportunities for learning, autonomy, and social interaction. Which type of jobs young women are likely to pursue and why they make those choices is largely unexplained. How work contributes to human development for both men and women continues to be unresolved, particularly in today's society, where gender roles and responsibilities are being questioned and redefined (Fuchs-Epstein 1987).

Teenage work experiences provide adolescents with opportunities to observe the actions, motivations, and reward structures associated with certain types of employment. These experiences are likely to influence the judgments young women and men have about themselves and others, which we suspect have long-term consequences on their orientations toward their adult lives. Thus, continued intensive study of the variation in teenage work experiences will provide significant insights into the formation of attitudes and values.

*Barbara Schneider*
*Jennifer A. Schmidt*

## Bibliography

Berryman, S.E. 1988. "A Commentary on I. Charner and B.S. Fraser's *Youth and Work: What We Know; What We Don't Know; What We Need to Know.*" In I. Charner and B.S. Fraser *Youth and Work: What We Know; What We Don't Know; What We Need to Know.* Washington, D.C.: W.T. Grant Foundation Commission on Work, Family and Citizenship.

Bidwell, C., M. Csikszentmihalyi, L. Hedges, and B. Schneider. 1992. "Study of Career Choice: Overview and Analysis." Unpublished pilot study report.

Borman, K.M. 1991. *The First "Real" Job: A Study of Young Workers.* Albany: State University of New York Press.

———. 1988. "The Process of Becoming a Worker." In *Work Experience and Psychological Development through the Lifespan,* edited by J.T. Mortimer and K.M. Borman. AAAS Selected Symposium. Boulder, Colo.: Westview.

Charner, I., and B.S. Fraser. 1988. *Youth and Work: What We Know; What We Don't Know; What We Need to Know.* Washington, D.C.: W.T. Grant Foundation Commission on Work, Family and Citizenship.

D'Amico, R. 1984. "Does Working in High School Impair Academic Progress?" *Sociology of Education* 57:152–64.

Fuchs-Epstein, C. 1987. *Deceptive Distinctions: Sex, Gender, and the Social Order.* New York: Sage.

Green, P.J., B. Dugoni, S. Ingels, and E. Camburn. 1994. *A Profile of the American High School Senior in 1992*. In press.

Greenberger, E. 1988. "Working in Teenage America." In *Work Experience and Psychological Development through the Lifespan*, edited by J.T. Mortimer and K.M. Borman. AAAS Selected Symposium. Boulder, Colo.: Westview.

Greenberger, E., and L.D. Steinberg. 1986. *When Teenagers Work: The Psychological and Social Costs of Adolescent Employment*. New York: Basic Books.

Lewin-Epstein, N. 1981. *Youth Employment during High School*. Washington, D.C.: National Center for Education Statistics.

Lewis, M.V., J.A. Gardner, and P. Seitz. 1983. *High School Work Experience and Its Effects*. Columbus, Ohio: National Center for Research and Vocational Education.

Mortimer, J.T., and K.M. Borman. 1988. *Work Experience and Psychological Development through the Lifespan*. AAAS Selected Symposium. Boulder, Colo.: Westview.

Schill, W.J., R. McCartin, and K. Meyer. 1985. "Youth Employment: Its Relationship to Academic and Family Variables." *Journal of Vocational Behavior* 26:155–63.

Schneider, B., J. Schmidt, and L. Song. 1994. "Adolescent Self-Esteem and Salience: Influence of Gender and Perceptions of Work." Paper presented at the annual meeting of the American Educational Research Association. New Orleans, La.

Sebring, P., B. Campbell, M. Glusberg, M. Spencer, M. Singleton, and M. Turner. 1986. *High School and Beyond: 1980 Senior Cohort Third Follow-up*. U.S. Department of Education, Washington, D.C.

Stevenson, W. 1978. "The Relationship between Early Work Experience and Future Employability." In *The Lingering Crisis of Youth Unemployment*, edited by A.V. Adams and G.L. Mangum, with W. Stevenson, S.F. Dogiger, and S. Mangum. Kalamazoo, Mich.: W. Upjohn Institute for Employment Research.

U.S. Department of Commerce, Economics and Statistics Administration; Bureau of the Census. 1993. *Statistical Abstracts of the United States*. Washington, D.C.

U.S. Department of Labor, Bureau of Labor Statistics. 1993. *Geographic Profile of Employment and Unemployment 1992*. Bulletin 2428. Washington, D.C.

Weis, L. 1990. *Working Class without Work: High School Students in a De-Industrializing Economy*. New York: Routledge.

## Women and Unemployment in the U.S.

A woman is officially defined as unemployed if she is seeking paid work but is unable to find a job. As a demographic group, women generally experience a higher unemployment rate than men. Women suffer adverse consequences of unemployment as wives, daughters, and as unemployed persons themselves. There are often economic and psychological impacts. Public policies are needed to strengthen the situation of unemployed women as well as men. In addition, specific policies are required to address the particular situation of women.

Women's unemployment is computed officially by dividing the number of those unemployed (that is, unsuccessfully looking for paid work) by the total number of employed and unemployed women during a survey week. The unemployment rate for men is calculated in a parallel fashion. Unemployment rates are also calculated for other demographic groups in society, including those based on age and race, thus enabling numerous subgroup comparisons. Generally, women who are young (especially age twenty-four or younger) or minorities have higher unemployment than those who are older or white. Historically, women's unemployment rate has been higher than men's. The exception to this pattern occurred early in the 1980s (1982 and 1983), when men's unemployment increased more rapidly than, and surpassed, that of women. From 1984 to 1989, women's unemployment rates again exceeded men's, but the gender gap was quite small.

Changes in women's and men's unemployment rates reflect the size of and changes in several labor-market transitions. For the past twenty years, the unemployment rate of adult men (twenty years or older) has risen, largely because of the increased probability of losing a job, and because, once unemployed, men have faced increasing difficulty in finding a job. A major reason for this was men's employment concentration in industries, especially within manufacturing, in which plants increasingly have closed down entirely or permanently laid off large portions of their workforces as part of the restructuring of the American economy known as deindustrialization. During this same period, some offsetting trends for adult women contributed to the current narrowing of the female-male unemployment gap. Between 1968 and 1979, the rise in women's unemployment was caused primarily by the increased probability of women outside the labor force (such as, housewives or volunteers in the community) seeking, but failing, to enter paid work, and by employed women losing their jobs. At the same time, there was a decline in the proportion of employed women who dropped out of the labor force. This was probably due to a longer delay in marriage and less likelihood of women exiting the labor force when becoming wives and mothers. During the period 1979–1988, there was a continued decline in the number of employed women exiting the labor force and a decline in the probability of employed women losing their jobs, which were concentrated in high-growth service areas (rather than manufacturing). These declines resulted in a decline in women's unemployment rate during this decade and in the smaller male-female unemployment rate differential (Deitch et al. 1991; Howe 1990).

Unemployment results in economic hardship for women. They are likely to be out of work longer than their male counterparts. However, it is unclear whether or not a woman's marital status affects the length of her unemployment. There is some evidence that single-parent women are more likely than male heads of households to experience protracted periods of unemployment. Women, in comparison to men, are more likely to be reemployed in low-paying sales and service jobs, rather than production jobs. In addition, women are more likely to be reemployed in part-time rather than full-time jobs (Perrucci et al. 1987).

Not all women, or their families, are equally vulnerable to economic strain and other adverse ramifications of unemployment, because of their varying resources and coping reactions. The degree and duration of economic strain experienced by women varies by the number and type of alternative sources of income they have, such as a spouse's income or unemployment compensation or severance pay. Similarly, when it is the husband/father who is unemployed, wives/daughters may enter or stay in the labor force and bolster the family income. Other coping strategies that can ameliorate the economic impact of unemployment include forgoing or postponing expenditures in a number of areas, including medical care; increasing home production of goods and services; and generally striving to get the most for whatever financial resources one has. Eventual reemployment is often not a panacea because new jobs may be lower paying and lacking in fringe benefits, and because the financial difficulties produced by long periods of unemployment persist (Perrucci et al. 1988).

Obviously, economic hardship caused by women's unemployment is important in its own right. It is also significant because the stress of job and income loss may impinge on women's mental health. Research documents various negative psychological effects of men's unemployment on the women who are their wives or daughters. For the wives of workers, the unemployment of their spouse produces a variety of mental-health problems—increased levels of subclinical symptoms, depression, anxiety, and stress. These psychological effects for wives are affected by financial difficulties and conflict over money as well as by the husband's level of disturbance. Problems are sometimes long term and do not necessarily improve with the worker's reemployment (Targ and Perrucci 1990).

At the individual level, wives' prior mental-health status is an important predictor of symptomatology after husbands' unemployment. Negative personal coping such as emotional withdrawal, denial, and increased eating, drinking, and smoking have been shown to adversely affect wives' well-being after husbands become unemployed. Beyond themselves, potential resources for wives include social support from spouses, relatives, and friends. However, findings are mixed as to the significance of social support. Recent research indicates that it is the maintenance of support that exists before job loss that is most important (Targ and Perrucci 1990).

In addition, there is some evidence that an adolescent daughter in an intact nuclear family may experience impairment in psychological well-being (anxiety over finances, self-esteem, and general mental health) because of the father's unemployment, particularly the income loss entailed. This occurs primarily if the father becomes rejecting and the mother nonsupportive. Other impacts of parental unemployment on children can include financial deprivation; changes (downscaling) of parental vocational aspirations and socialization practices regarding children; increased anger, hostility, and even abuse of children; and impaired physical health of the children (Elder and Liker 1982).

As women have increasingly obtained or tried to obtain paid jobs, they have experienced unemployment directly, rather than indirectly through their husbands or fathers. Recent studies indicate that the severity of the negative mental-health impact of unemployment on women workers is similar to the impact on men workers. Financial difficulties are a major factor in precipitating psychological symptoms among unemployed women. Married and single women as a whole are equally affected by losing their jobs. However, there is some evidence that single mothers who are heads of households are especially disadvantaged as a result of job loss. Reemployment does not necessarily have a positive effect on women's mental health status (Nowak and Snyder 1983; Rosen 1987; Schlozman 1979).

Women workers utilize personal or individual resources such as a sense of mastery, or a feeling of control over life, to ameliorate the effects of unemployment. In addition, they may have various sources of support available to them. However, the evidence regarding social support for women workers is not consistent. Research indicating that women are more likely than men to ask for help from family and friends and less likely to receive support from spouses contrasts with research findings showing no difference between women and men in the percentage that receive "lots of love and support" from spouses, family, and friends. Among women displaced by plant closings, social support is negatively related to depression (Perrucci et al. 1988).

Despite evidence of major human costs of high unemployment for women, there is controversy as to whether or not women's unemployment is important to themselves, their families, and their communities (Targ 1983). Existing policy and recommendations to prevent or ameliorate the effects of unemployment seldom focus on women specifically. Although strategies are needed that apply to all unemployed workers and their families, policies are also needed to address the situations of women affected by joblessness, whether as wives, daughters, or workers. First, the unemployment itself could be prevented; this is especially relevant in the case of plant closings. Other Western, industrialized countries are more stringent in requiring companies to show cause why they should be allowed to close plants, devastating the individuals and communities involved (Perrucci and Targ 1988).

Second, the economic impacts of unemployment could be softened. One way is through lengthening the period of unemployment benefits beyond the current twenty-six-week period. Although current law allows for a twenty-week extension, it is only under emergency situations as defined by the president. To benefit women workers especially, the definition of workers covered by unemployment insurance could be broadened. In addition, as regards closings, legislation requires a sixty-day warning from corporations that intend to close. However, the legislation does not provide for funds to monitor whether employees are receiving that notification. For wives, Aid to Families with Dependent Children-Unemployed Parent (AFDC-UP) could be instituted in every state. In contrast to the usual AFDC situation, AFDC-UP pays support even if there is an unemployed man in the home. Private initiatives, often required only under union contract, including severance pay, continued insurance benefits, and assistance with job search, could be more widespread. In order to search for jobs, unemployed women with small children as well as wives with small children who want to reenter the labor force as a result of a husband's job loss require short-term child care. Therefore, both money to pay for child care as well as the availability of this type of child care are needed (Targ and Perrucci 1990).

Third, because the prior situation of husbands, wives, and female workers is an important predictor of how well they will cope with unemployment, educational and social services that assist with financial management and psychological well-being are relevant. Undoubtedly, the most important policy to lessen and possibly prevent the negative effects of unemployment would be a comprehensive full-employment policy including full-time jobs that offer the potential to support the basic needs of families. Short of that, public policy that ensures the basic nutrition, housing, and health care of U.S. families is needed (Targ and Perrucci 1990).

*Carolyn C. Perrucci*
*Dena B. Targ*

## Bibliography

Deitch, C., T. Nowak, and K. Snyder. 1991. "Manufacturing Job Loss among Blue Collar Women: An Assessment of Data and Policy." In *Gender Differences: Their Impact on Public Policy*, edited by M.L. Kendrigan, pp. 33–65. Westport, Conn.: Greenwood.

Elder, G.H., Jr., and J.K. Liker. 1982. "Hard Times in Women's Lives: Historical Influences across Forty Years." *American Journal of Sociology* 88:241–69.

Howe, W.J. 1990. "Labor Market Dynamics and Trends in Male and Female Unemployment." *Monthly Labor Review* 13:3–11.

Nowak, T.C., and K.A. Snyder. 1983. "Women's Struggle to Survive a Plant Shutdown." *Journal of Intergroup Relations* 9:22–44.

Perrucci, C.C., R. Perrucci, D.B. Targ, and H.R. Targ. 1987. "Plant Closing: Comparison of Effects on Women and Men Workers." In *Redundancy, Layoffs and Plant Closures: Their Character, Causes and Consequences*, edited by R.M. Lee, pp. 181–99. London: Croom Helm.

Perrucci, C.C., R. Perrucci, D.B. Targ, and H.R. Targ. 1988. *Plant Closings: International Context and Social Costs*. New York: Aldine De Gruyter.

Perrucci, C.C., and D.B. Targ. 1988. "Effects of a Plant Closing on Marriage and Family Life." In *Coping Strategies and Social Policy*, edited by P. Voydanoff and L.C. Majka, pp. 55–71. Newbury Park, Calif.: Sage.

Rosen, E.I. 1987. *Bitter Choices: Blue-Collar Women in and out of Work*. Chicago: University of Chicago Press.

Schlozman, K.L. 1979. "Women and Unemployment: Assessing the Biggest Myths." In *Women: A Feminist Perspective*, edited by J. Freeman, pp. 290–312. Palo Alto, Calif.: Mayfield.

Targ, D.B. 1983. "Women and the New Unemployment." *Humboldt Journal of Social Relations*, 10:47–60.

Targ, D.B., and C.C. Perrucci. 1990. "Plant Closings, Unemployment and Families." *Marriage and Family Review* 15:131–45.

Voydanoff, P. 1990. "Economic Distress and Family Relations: A Review of the Eighties." *Journal of Marriage and the Family* 52:1099–115.

## Women and Retirement in the U.S.

The retirement transition has demarcated the last phase of the life course in advanced Western economies. The onset of this transition is marked by one or more of three status changes in individual lives: full exit from the labor force, partial exit from the labor force (usually measured as reduced hours of work), and pension (including Social Security and other private and governmental pensions). These changes can occur simultaneously or in sequence over a protracted period, spanning more than ten years. As such, the retirement transition is not always a crisp, instantaneous, and absorbing change from work to nonwork or from income based on earnings to income based on pensions, entitlements, or personal assets.

A trend toward "early retirement"—that is, toward retirement at ages younger than those associated with public pension eligibility (prior to age sixty-five in the U.S.)—has been observed across advanced industrial societies (Kohli et al. 1991). This trend has been attributed to a number of factors. Chief among them are industrial shifts away from older manufacturing systems and toward newer manufacturing and service sectors, and governmental programs benefiting older populations (such as Supplemental Security Income and Medicare in the U.S.). These changes have pushed and pulled older workers out of the labor force at earlier ages. Related to these changes has been the fact that older men retiring since the early 1970s have benefited by employee pension systems that emerged strongly in the post–World War II era as a result of corporate prosperity and unionization. This set of historical circumstances is no longer applicable to the employment sectors of most Western, advanced economies, including the U.S.

Women's labor-force participation patterns over the past three decades reveal two countervailing trends with respect to retirement (O'Rand et al. 1992). On the one hand, women's labor-force attachments have been increasing steadily, with older women (those aged fifty-five to sixty-four) displaying among the steepest upward trends of labor-force participation. Older women are working later and later in their lives. One reason is that, on average, they enter their career jobs (that is, their longest-lasting jobs) later in their worklives (an average of ten years later than men) and work fewer years over their lifetimes (Ruhm 1990). As a result, their earnings trajectories and pension savings (if these are available at their jobs) are low and require job attachment until later ages. Another is that even after controlling for the timing of their entry into and the duration of their work careers, their average earnings and retirement savings are low as a result of occupational segregation and the highly variable patterns of employer pension coverage across industries. Women work in industries that have significantly lower rates of pension coverage or else smaller pension plans with modest benefit packages (especially service and retail sales) (O'Rand 1986, 1988). Finally, recent trends reveal that older women are returning to work after initially retiring at higher rates of pay (Hayward et al. 1988). These returns are associated with a number of factors including the loss of a spouse through widowhood or divorce, catastrophic illness and related financial need, and other economic strains.

On the other hand, women have historically retired at earlier ages than men because of their gender roles and restricted employment opportunities. Women have retired at earlier ages (before age sixty-two) for two reasons. The first is marital status, which allocates Social Security benefits to a woman based on her husband's history of earnings, which is typically larger than her own. This leads women to retire with their husbands, who are usually older. The second reason women retire at earlier ages than men is their lower relative earnings, making the replacement rates of Social Security (that is, the ratio of retirement benefit level to preretirement wages) higher and leading them to exit the labor force. Women's retirement benefits are directly associated with their years out of the labor force in caregiving activities. Every year of child-rearing and elder care translates into benefit loss, with the latter proving to be more costly to older women (Kingson and O'Grady-LeShane 1993).

Notably, the U.S. Social Security System systematically favors "traditional" married couples (husband-worker, wife-nonworker) over single individuals and dual-career couples in the calculation and distribution of retirement benefits. This bias encourages women to retire as spouses rather than as workers. As such, pension receipt as widows (possible at age sixty) and as spouses (possible at age sixty-two with reduced benefits) propels many women into retirement (Gilbert 1994).

However, the social security systems of most Western countries—even those identified as social-welfare states as well as the U.S.—provide very poorly in the long run for survivors and widows. Recent cross-national studies have documented that survivor benefit policies contribute significantly to persistent poverty among widows and other older women. In the U.S. surviving worker wives and widows receive 50 percent and 67 percent, respectively, of their family benefits before the deaths of their husbands. This loss of already low and relatively fixed incomes among older women makes them vulnerable to poverty. Recent estimates are that survivors live an average of seventeen years after the deaths of their spouses. The allocation of small incomes over this extended and increasingly costly period of life leaves older women in retirement alone and with fewer and fewer resources. Although the trends of recent decades have included increasingly more affluent elderly populations in many countries, there has nevertheless been a persistent component of these populations that has remained poor—older women (Duncan and Smith 1989; Burkhauser et al. 1994).

Future trends suggest that women's labor-force attachments will continue to rise and achieve relative parity with men's over most of their adult lives

(Goldscheider 1990). Yet pension systems are not changing in ways to make retirement easier or fairer for women. Pensions, in particular, are changing in the direction of higher risk and lower certainty. The fastest-growing pension instruments in the industries where most women work, referred to as defined contribution plans, have features that increase the risks for economic insecurity in retirement. These plans do not "promise" a specific benefit upon retirement in the manner that traditional (defined benefit) pensions have; rather they are individualized market investments whose pay-offs are unclear. Also, these plans have short-term benefits that incur long-term risks: They are portable tax shelters that can nevertheless be cashed out (liquidated with minimal penalties) to handle such financial demands as hospitalization charges, bankruptcy, college costs, and divorce. Accordingly, intervening financial needs (which are highly likely circumstances in women's lives) can preclude effective retirement saving for future cohorts of older women (O'Rand 1995).

*Angela M. O'Rand*

### Bibliography

Burkhauser, R.V., G.F. Duncan, and Richard Hauser. 1994. "Sharing Prosperity across the Age Distribution: A Comparison of the United States and Germany in the 1980s." *Gerontologist* 34:150–60.

Duncan, G.R., and K. Smith. 1989. "The Rising Affluence of the Elderly: How Far, How Fair, How Frail? " *Annual Review of Sociology* 15:261–89.

Gilbert, N. 1994. "Gender Equality and Social Security." *Society* (May/June):26–33.

Goldscheider, F. 1990. "The Aging of the Gender Revolution: What Do We Know and What Do We Need to Know?" *Research on Aging* 12:531–45.

Hayward, M.D., W.R. Grady, and S.D. McLaughlin. 1988. "The Retirement Process among Older Women: Changes in the 1970's." *Research on Aging* 10:358–82.

Kingson, E.R., and R. O'Grady-LeShane. 1993. "The Effects of Caregiving on Women's Social Security Benefits." *Gerontologist* 33:230–39.

Kohli, M., M. Rein, A.-M. Guillemard, and H. van Gunsteren, eds. 1991. *Time for Retirement: Comparative Studies of Early Exit from the Labor Force*. New York: Cambridge.

O'Rand, A.M. 1988. "Convergence, Institutionalization and Bifurcation: Gender and the Pension Acquisition Process." *Annual Review of Gerontology and Geriatrics* 8:132–55.

———. 1986. "The Hidden Payroll: Employee Benefits and the Structure of Workplace Inequality." *Sociological Forum* 1:657–83.

———. 1995. "Stratification and the Life Course." In *Handbook of Aging and the Social Sciences*, edited by R.H. Binstock and L.K. George. 4th ed. New York: Academic (forthcoming).

———, J.C. Henretta, and M.L. Krecker. 1992. "Family Pathways to Retirement." In *Families and Retirement*, edited by M. Szinovacz, D.J. Ekerdt, and B.H. Vinick, pp. 81–98. Newbury Park, Calif.: Sage.

Ruhm, C. 1990. "Career Jobs, Bridge Employment, and Retirement." In *Bridges to Retirement: Older Workers in a Changing Labor Market*, edited by P.B. Doeringer, pp. 92–107. Ithaca, N.Y.: ILR.

## Women in the U.S. Labor Movement

Despite their long-standing involvement in the U.S. labor movement, women have been less represented and less active than men in the labor movement (Foner 1987; Milkman 1990; Needleman and Tanner 1987; Roby and Uttal 1988; Strom 1983). This gender difference in labor movement involvement has been attributed to sexist, exclusionary, and discriminatory actions of male trade unionists; the allegedly, greater psychological passivity of female workers; patterns of occupational and industrial sexual segregation in employment; inattention of unions to recruiting female members and to working women's employment issues; and the constraints of household and family gender roles. The labor movement, however, has become increasingly attuned to working women's issues, such as child care, pay equity, and occupational safety and health, as it has "feminized"—that is, as women have come to be a larger proportion of U.S. labor union membership and leadership during the post–World War II era (Cornfield 1987, 1989, 1990). Nonetheless, unions may approach women's issues haltingly when these issues jeopardize collective bargaining and seniority-based personnel systems, as in some instances of implementing comparable-worth reforms (Acker 1989).

Female workers have been less likely than male workers to belong to unions. Roughly 11 to 15 percent of all female workers in the U.S. have belonged to unions since the 1950s. In contrast, the percentage of all male workers who were union members has exceeded that of women but has decreased from 31 percent to 19 percent between 1956 and 1991, with the decline of blue-collar and manufacturing employment. The labor movement, consequently, has feminized in that the percentage of all union members who were women increased from 19 percent to 37 percent between 1956 and 1991 (LeGrande 1978; Needleman and Tanner 1987; U.S. Bureau of Labor Statistics 1992, p. 228).

The underrepresentation of women in unions has traditionally been attributed to women's alleged psychological passivity and to male craft-union hostility toward, and exclusion of, female workers (Cornfield 1987; Milkman 1990; Strom 1983). Opinion surveys of nonunion workers, however, indicate that nonunion women are at least as pro-union as nonunion men (Cornfield 1987; Fiorito and Greer 1986; Milkman 1990). Also, craft-union hostility is at best a partial explanation in light of the feminization of the labor movement (Cobble 1990).

Rather, recent explanations of women's representation in the labor movement have focused on variations in women's union membership and in factors that motivate, facilitate, and hinder the unionization of female workers (Cobble 1990). Milkman (1990), for example, suggests that the feminization of the labor movement results from the more inclusionary organizing strategies of the new unions in the growing, predominantly female white-collar services and government employment sectors, as well as from the more ideologically liberal national political conditions that prevailed in the late twentieth century when these unions emerged, compared with those of the surviving building-trades craft unions that had emerged in the late nineteenth century. Others have argued that women's unionization has been motivated by increased women's labor-force participation and deteriorating employment conditions, such as declining real earnings and the depersonalization of work associated with bureaucratization and office automation. Other factors have been the enactment of anti–sexual discrimination law, the advent of women's movement organizations such as the Coalition of Labor Union Women, which actively encouraged women's unionization during the 1970s and 1980s, and increased organizing efforts among female white-collar and service workers by declining unions attempting to recoup their blue-collar, male membership losses. It has been hindered by increased employer resistance to the unionization of women and men workers (Cornfield 1987; Milkman 1990; Needleman and Tanner 1987).

Little is known about the impact of labor-movement feminization on female union members' level of activism—that is, volunteering to participate in union governance and operations—in part because of the paucity of longitudinal studies of activism. Labor-movement feminization has been accompanied by an increase in the proportion of female labor leaders, although women continue to be underrepresented in union offices (Cornfield 1989; Milkman 1990; Roby and Uttal 1988). Cornfield's (1989) status-conflict theory holds that women, as well as other union member minority groups who are low in socioeconomic status, may emerge as union leaders, especially in ideologically universalistic unions, when they are deemed by the existing leadership to be of strategic importance to the revival of union growth in the face of antiunion employer hostility. Studies of low-level union officers and rank-and-file union members indicate that women are comparably active or less active than men and that their activism is more constrained than men's by household and family responsibilities (Cornfield et al. 1990; Roby and Uttal 1988).

The feminization of the labor movement may be one of the chief factors that influences the directions taken by unions at the bargaining table and in national politics (Cornfield 1990). More research on the conditions that promote and hinder feminization and on the determinants and outcomes of gender differences in union membership activism will illuminate how the labor movement addresses the problem of gender inequality in the U.S.

*Daniel B. Cornfield*

## Bibliography

Acker, Joan. 1989. *Doing Comparable Worth*. Philadelphia: Temple University Press. Burton, Joan. 1987. "Dilemmas of Organizing Women Office Workers." *Gender and Society* 1:432–46.

Cobble, Dorothy. 1990. "Rethinking Troubled Relations between Women and Unions: Craft Unionism and Female Activism." *Feminist Studies* 16:519–48.

Cornfield, Daniel. 1989. *Becoming a Mighty Voice: Conflict and Change in the United Furniture Workers of America*. New York: Russell Sage.

——. 1990. "Labor Unions, Corporations and Families: Institutional Competition in the Provision of Social Welfare." *Marriage and Family Review* 15:37–57.

——. 1987. "Women in the Automated Office: Computers, Work, and Prospects for Unionization." In *Advances in Industrial and Labor Relations*. Vol. 4, edited by David Lewin, David Lipsky, and Donna Sockell, pp. 177–98. Greenwich, Conn.: JAI.

Cornfield, Daniel, Hilquias Cavalcanti, and Bang Jee Chun. 1990. "Household, Work, and Labor Activism: Gender Differences in the Determinants of Union Membership Participation." *Work and Occupations* 17:131–51.

Fiorito, Jack, and Charles Greer. 1986. "Gender Differences in Union Membership, Preferences, and Beliefs." *Journal of Labor Research* 7:145–64.

Foner, Philip. 1987. "Women and the American Labor Movement: A Historical Perspective." In *Working Women: Past, Present, Future*, edited by Karen Koziara, Michael Moskow, and Lucretia Tanner, pp. 154–86. Washington, D.C.: Bureau of National Affairs.

LeGrande, Linda. 1978. "Women in Labor Organizations: Their Ranks Are Increasing." *Monthly Labor Review* 101:8–14.

Milkman, Ruth. 1990. "Gender and Trade Unionism in Historical Perspective." In *Women, Politics, and Change*, edited by Louise Tilly and Patricia Gurin, pp. 87–107. New York: Russell Sage.

Needleman, Ruth, and Lucretia Tanner. 1987. "Women in Unions: Current Issues." In *Working Women: Past, Present, Future*, edited by Karen Koziara, Michael Moskow, and Lucretia Tanner, pp. 187–224. Washington, D.C.: Bureau of National Affairs.

Roby, Pamela, and Lynet Uttal. 1988. "Trade Union Stewards: Handling Union, Family, and Employment Responsibilities." In *Women and Work: An Annual Review* 3, edited by Barbara Gutek, Ann Stromberg, and Laurie Larwood, pp. 215–47. Newbury Park, Calif.: Sage.

Strom, Sharon. 1983. "Challenging 'Woman's Place': Feminism, the Left, and Industrial Unionism in the 1930s." *Feminist Studies* 9:359–86.

U.S. Bureau of Labor Statistics. *Employment and Earnings* 39. Washington, D.C. 1992.

## Women's Status in American Labor Unions

Women have historically been underrepresented in American labor unions. Although the various labor organizations have had divergent attitudes toward women workers and their potential for organization, none have welcomed women with the same enthusiasm reserved for men. This is especially true when considering women's representation in union leadership. Certainly, some unions have done better than others: The Congress of Industrial Organizations (CIO) unions made dramatic progress in organizing and integrating women into their unions. Unfortunately, its expulsion of eleven left-wing unions in 1949 and 1950 and its subsequent merger with the American Federation of Labor (AFL) in 1955 slowed the process of women's inclusion. Despite the fact that unions underrepresent women, most have policies that affect female workers. They have supported protective legislation for female workers and, more recently, equality legislation, although they pursue these policies with unequal vigor.

### The History of Women's Membership and Representation in Unions

A union's organizing strategy determines, in large part, its willingness to incorporate women (as well as minorities) into its ranks. In its heyday, the Knights of Labor, which sought to unite all wage earners, succeeded in organizing an impressive number of women. In its peak year of 1886, women constituted 17 percent of the labor force and 8 to 9 percent of its membership (although women were segregated in separate locals and some were not in the labor force). While the percentage of females in the labor force continued to increase yearly, their proportion of the union population dropped precipitously after the collapse of the Knights, and then grew very slowly thereafter. This can be explained by the fact that the AFL (the dominant labor organization at the time) practiced exclusionary policies. The AFL was organized around skilled crafts and, as most women were unskilled, it had no vision of their place within the organization. Although the AFL usually paid lip service to the needs of women workers, it didn't encourage their organization in practice, and after the collapse of the Knights it became even less interested in women workers. In light of the AFL's inactivity on women's issues, the Women's Trade Union League was formed in 1903 to assist (mainly AFL unions) in organizing women and to promote protective legislation and women's suffrage.

The Industrial Workers of the World (IWW), formed in 1905, echoed the AFL's vocal concerns, but fortified them with concrete actions. It sought to organize the skilled as well as the unskilled and, in doing so, became conscious of the special problems faced by women workers. Women were more visible in the IWW's leadership and their rights more strongly supported. Yet in times of male unemployment, even the IWW encouraged women to release their jobs to men (Foner 1979, pp. 392–412). The IWW was considerably weakened as a result of its antiwar activities during World War I and its internal dissension.

It wasn't until the birth of the CIO in 1935 that women workers once again had a union organization that was genuinely interested in their welfare. In contrast to the AFL's exclusionary policy, the CIO had a strategy of inclusion: It proposed to organize workers, regardless of race, creed, or sex, along industrial lines. Given this strategy, the CIO had important decisions to make concerning its priorities. Which industries should be organized first? Where should the CIO put its organizational capacity? Since industries then (as now) were characterized by different compositions of men and women, the CIO's organizing decisions affected the composition of its potential membership. Although some argue that the industries that employed large numbers of women were, for the most part, ignored and the traditionally male industries favored (Milkman 1980), patterns of CIO financial assistance to organizing efforts suggest otherwise. In fact, a substantial proportion of large CIO grants (those over $80,000) during the CIO's founding period (1935 to 1941) were given to unions organizing in industries with large percentages of women workers. One of the CIO's first major organizing drives was in textiles, with approximately 40 percent women workers.

Women were active in the early CIO organizing drives. A few women, such as Gladys Dickason of the Amalgamated Clothing Workers (ACWU), ended up in leadership roles: Dickason was appointed assistant director of the CIO's postwar organizing drive in the South. More often, rank-and-file women assisted men in building (mainly) male local unions through women's auxiliaries (made up of workers' wives and sometimes working women). Women's auxiliaries were especially important in the early days of the United Automobile Workers (UAW), during the sit-down strikes. Here and elsewhere, women provided food to the striking workers, enabling them to continue occupying the factories. With such activities, women basically accepted the traditional division of labor based on gender. Unfortunately, when it was their turn, women strikers didn't receive comparable aid from the men (Milkman 1980).

So although the CIO did better overall, women still were not recruited into labor unions in equal numbers to their representation in the labor force. While they constituted 35 percent of the labor force in 1944, they made up only 22 percent of union membership. Although the percentage of women in unions increased substantially, so has the percentage of women in the labor force. The percentage of women in the labor force who are in unions probably increased slightly from 1960 to 1980 (Goldfield 1987, pp. 126–27). The persistent gap in women's union membership can be attributed, in large part, to the types of work they perform. Women are more likely to work in sectors that have been traditionally hard for unions to organize (such as nonmanufacturing industries, white-collar, and service sectors) (Dickason 1949). Differences in women's economic interests may also account for some of the discrepancy (Freeman and Medoff 1984). And another contributing factor is the failure of the Southern union organizing drive in the post–World War II period, which left the predominantly female Southern industrial labor force unorganized (Kenneally 1981). Finally, union policies and lack of interest in recruiting women have contributed to their underrepresentation. Witness, for example, the lack of union support for women in the postwar period that resulted in the displacement of women by returning servicemen and a return to more rigid sex segregation in the workplace.

Some CIO and a few AFL unions succeeded in organizing numerous women. The United Electrical, Radio and Machine Workers (UE) and the UAW had the most women members (about 280,000 each in 1946, constituting 40 and 28 percent of their memberships respectively), while the International Ladies Garment Workers Union (ILGWU) and ACWU each had fewer numerically (about

200,000 each) but more proportionally (75 and 66 percent respectively). The textile (both CIO and AFL), steel, retail and wholesale, railway clerks and bakery and confectionery unions also had substantial numbers of women members. More recently, the public-sector unions have organized impressive numbers of women workers.

The Coalition of Labor Union Women (CLUW) was founded in 1974 to challenge the slow progress of women's integration. It helped to establish a position within the AFL-CIO to boost the organization of women, promote affirmative action on the job and within unions, press for legislation, and increase women's participation within unions (Cook 1991). While the CLUW's efforts have resulted in important advances for women, overall, progress remains limited.

Women's representation in union leadership has also lagged behind their numbers in the unions. Most unions have only a token number of women leaders. In 1958, for example, less than 5 percent of all union officials were female. As could be expected, former CIO unions had better records than former AFL unions. And within the CIO, certain unions proved to be exemplary. Most impressive is the record of the UE, with 40 percent female membership. A full third of the UE's organizing staff was female, and in the 1940s it had one woman on its general executive board and two by 1953. The United Federal Workers (UFW) was the first national union to elect a woman to its presidency. UFW's president, Eleanor Nelson, was also the first woman to serve on the CIO's executive board. More recently (1970–1984), the United Furniture Workers accomplished gender integration in its leadership (see Cornfield 1989a).

Women's representation in AFL-CIO union leadership is still problematic, though efforts beginning in the 1970s that were aimed at training women for leadership positions may eventually produce results.

## Union Policies: Support for Legislation and Collective Bargaining
Unions address women's issues through two channels: supporting legislation and collective bargaining. Most AFL-CIO unions supported protective legislation in the past, although most haven't spent much time promoting it, and some haven't always used it in the best interest of women workers. At times, it was used to limit women's open access to better jobs (Raphael 1974). The UAW has opposed protective legislation, probably because of its particular experiences with that form of legislation and the ways it affected its female members (Cook 1968). In the World War II period, the UE and the UAW both wrestled with the issue of women's rights and equal pay. While the UAW demanded equal pay for equal work, the UE went further in demanding equal pay for comparable worth (which put into question the overall basis of job segregation by sex). Both unions fought against the displacement of women after the war, but, as it turned out, it was rehiring, not seniority, that made the difference for women's positions, and the unions had little control over the rehiring process (Milkman 1987). Although the UE's progress was cut short by its expulsion from the CIO, its pioneering activities continue to inspire current debates on women's job rights. The UAW's Women's Bureau vigorously defended women's rights and continued to make gains. By the mid 1960s, UAW women leaders were able to play important roles in the rebirth of the women's movement (Gabin 1990).

In 1973, the AFL-CIO officially endorsed the Equal Rights Amendment. Still, the commitment of individual unions to equality legislation varies greatly. Cornfield (1989b) found that unions in the service, white-collar, and, to a lesser degree, manufacturing sector are more likely to support redistributive legislation. Women workers themselves have had various responses to legislation: When they thought protective legislation and equal pay would result in losing their jobs to men, they opposed them; when there was no such threat, they supported them, since better pay and working conditions would result (Cobble 1988).

Unions' attention to women's issues in collective bargaining also varies. Cook's research suggests that a union's success in achieving family-support programs (including child and elder care), flextime and job sharing is more likely when women are highly represented in the union. When women are less represented, unions sometimes approve policies supporting the needs of women (like equal pay and seniority rights) by emphasizing how these policies enhance male wages and seniority (Kenneally 1981, pp. 184–85).

In conclusion, women have yet to attain full representation and equal treatment in labor unions. They are underrepresented in numbers and in leadership positions. In addition, women actively continue to prod unions to seek an end to the pay inequity between male and female workers.

*Judith Stepan-Norris*

## Bibliography

Cobble, Dorothy Sue. 1988. "'Practical Women': Waitress Unionists and the Controversies over Gender Roles in the Food Service Industry, 1900–1980" *Labor History* 29:5–31.

Cook, Alice H. 1968. "Women and American Trade Unions." *Annals of the American Academy of Political and Social Science* 375:124–32.

———. 1991. "Women and Minorities." In *The State of the Unions*, edited by George Strauss, Daniel Gallagher, and Jack Fiorito. Madison, Wis.: Industrial Relations Research Association.

Cornfield, Daniel. 1989a. *Becoming a Mighty Voice*. New York: Russell Sage.

———. 1989b. "Union Decline and the Political Demands of Organized Labor." *Work and Occupations* 16:292–322.

Dewey, Lucretia. 1971. "Women in Labor Unions." *Monthly Labor Review* 94:42–48.

Dickason, Gladys. 1949. "Women in Labor Unions." *Annals of the American Academy of Political and Social Science* 251:70–78.

Foner, Philip. 1979. *Women and the American Labor Movement: From Colonial Times to the Eve of World War I*. New York: Free Press.

———. 1980. *Women and the American Labor Movement: From World War I to the Present*. New York: Free Press.

Freeman, Richard, and James Medoff. 1984. *What Do Unions Do?* New York: Basic Books.

Gabin, Nancy. 1990. *Feminism in the Labor Movement: Women and the United Auto Workers, 1935–1975*. Ithaca, N.Y., and London: Cornell University Press.

Goldfield, Michael. 1987. *The Decline of Organized Labor in the United States*. Chicago and London: University of Chicago Press.

Kenneally, James. 1981. *Women and American Trade Unions*. Montreal: Eden.

Milkman, Ruth. 1987. *Gender at Work: The Dynamics of Job Segregation by Sex during World War II*. Urbana and Chicago: University of Illinois Press.

———. 1980. "Organizing the Sexual Division of Labor: Historical Perspectives on 'Women's Work' and the American Labor Movement." *Socialist Review* 49:95–150.

Raphael, Edna. 1974. "Working Women and Their Membership in Labor Unions." *Monthly Labor Review* 97:27–33.

Strom, Sharon Hartman. 1983. "Challenging 'Woman's Place': Feminism, the Left, and Industrial Unionism in the 1930s." *Feminist Studies* 9 (Summer 1983):359–86.

# Intersection of Gender, Race/Ethnicity, and Work

## African-American Women and Work

From 1940 to 1990, the African-American female labor force grew from 1.8 million to about 11.6 million. The growth of the labor force has been associated with a number of factors, such as population increases, changing demographic characteristics of the population (such as fertility, marital status, education, and age), the overall status of the economy, and structural transformations of particular industries and occupations, as the economy shifted from an emphasis on agriculture to the service sector.

### Labor-Force Participation of African-American Women

Historically, African-American women have been more likely to participate in the labor force than white women. Yet a racial convergence in women's labor-force participation occurred between 1940 and 1993. In 1940, 37.3 percent of African-American women over fourteen years of age were engaged in gainful employment, while only 24.1 percent of white women were. Over the intervening fifty-year period, however, African-American women had slower growth in labor-force participation rates than did white women. As a result, by 1993, African-American women were almost as likely to participate in the labor force as white women (58.3 percent for African-American women, 58.4 percent for white women) (U.S. Bureau of the Census 1940; U.S. Bureau of Labor Statistics 1994).

In the past, African-American women tended to work more continuously than white women. Maintaining economic independence was often more crucial for African-American women than for white women because they were more likely to be the main breadwinners of their families: They were more likely to be single mothers and less likely to be able to rely on a spouse's income for economic survival because of the relatively higher rates of unemployment among African-American men (Wallace 1980).

The age pattern of labor-force participation of African-American women between 1940 and 1993 shows that labor-force participation has increased among all ages under sixty-five. This pattern looks like an inverted U, similar to the pattern of their male counterparts. As African-American women finish school, their labor-force participation rates increase. As of 1993, over three-quarters of African-

American women are in the labor force by their thirties, and they remain in the labor force more or less continuously until they retire, around their fifties or sixties. This age profile appeared quite distinct from that of their white counterparts. White women used to have U-shaped rates: Their participation rates were highest in their early twenties before they started having children, then fell as they withdrew from the labor force during their child-bearing years, and climbed as they returned to work after their youngest child reached school age (Bianchi and Spain 1986). By the early 1990s, however, the age profile of white women became very similar to that of their African-American counterparts, as increasing numbers of mothers returned to work less than a year after giving birth (U.S. Bureau of the Census 1991). A more recent study indicates that white women's and African-American women's labor-force participation rates following childbirth may not be so different, that white women return to work after birth as fast as African-American women do (Yoon and Waite 1994).

Comparison of the labor-force participation rates among African-American and white women by marital status between 1940 and 1988 shows that married African-American women are more likely to participate in the labor force than are married white women, while the pattern is just the opposite among single women (Goldin 1990, p. 17). The presence of children is more likely to depress the labor-force participation of married white women than of married African-American women (Bell 1974). More recent data also indicate that, among married women who have children younger than six years of age, African-American women are significantly more likely to be in the labor force than white women. However, the racial difference is not significant among women ever married with children.

## Occupational Changes

At the turn of the century, most (88 percent) African-American women worked either in domestic and personal-service occupations or in the agriculture, forestry, and fishing industries. By 1930, a substantial decline had occurred in the proportion of African-American women working in farming and other related occupations, as a result of the accelerated movement of African-Americans out of the South to job opportunities in the industrial areas of the North. In both the North and the South, African-American workers were hit especially hard by the Great Depression of the 1930s. In 1940, private-household service occupations alone accounted for 57.4 percent of the employment of African-American women, who also sustained moderate increases in unskilled factory jobs. In the fifty years following 1940, however, tremendous changes were made in the occupational distribution of employed African-American women.

During that time, African-American women moved out of low-paying, unskilled jobs, such as private-household service occupations, to more skilled and better paying white-collar occupations, partially because of the enforcement of affirmative-action requirements in the late 1960s and early 1970s and the rapid job growth in these occupations in the government sector. For example, in 1940, about 57.4 percent of all employed African-American women were working in private-household services. In 1960, the proportion dropped sharply to 39.3 percent, and by 1990, only 0.3 percent were employed in those occupations. Clerical occupations accounted for only 1.5 percent of all African-American female employees in 1940; by 1960, the proportion had increased over fivefold. The proportion of African-American women in clerical occupations continued to increase over the next three decades and reached 25.8 percent in 1990. African-American women also made progress in professional and managerial occupations. Between 1940 and 1990, the proportion of women in those occupations increased dramatically, rising from 4.9 percent in 1940 to 25.1 percent in 1990. Relatedly, African-American women are far more likely to be employed in the government sector than in the private sector (King 1993; Sokoloff 1992). According to the March 1990 Current Population Survey, 35.5 percent of African-American female managers are employed in the public sector, compared with only 14.5 percent of white female managers.

With wider opportunities for African-American women in the job market, occupational differentiation between white women and African-American women has dramatically decreased. Using micro-data samples from the U.S. Census and the Current Population Survey, King (1992) found that the dissimilarity index of occupational differentiation fell by half for African-American and white women between 1940 and 1988. With the decrease in racial segregation on the job, earning differentials narrowed between white and African-American women over time. Cunningham and Zalokar (1992) found that African-American women's real hourly wages were about 44 percent of those of white women in 1940; by 1980, African-American women's wages had increased to 99 percent of white women's. Among all female workers with college degrees between the ages of twenty-five and sixty-four, the median earnings for African-American women in 1989 were considerably higher than for white women: $23,928 for African-American women versus $19,966 for white women (Meisenheimer, 1990). Because African-American women tend to work longer hours, their median earnings were higher than those of white women. Among year-round, full-time workers, the gap in annual earnings between African-American and white women grew smaller. White college graduates earned $708 more per year than their African-American counterparts: $26,765 for African-American women versus $27,473 for white women.

Despite the overall decrease in occupational segregation by race, the narrowing racial gap in earnings, and the upward mobility that African-American women have attained, the occupational tipping model suggests that many African-American women gain access to clerical and professional positions only when the jobs become de-skilled and routinized, so that white women shift to better opportunities, leaving space for African-American women at the bottom. Based on wage data, King (1993) suggests that with the rapid expansion of clerical occupations, white women shifted to higher-paying clerical positions. That allowed African-American women to gain access to less well paid clerical positions, such jobs as file clerk, typist, keypunch operator, machine operator, and social-welfare clerical assistant. In professional occupations, Sokoloff (1992) found that African-American women made inroads into female professions and technical fields between 1960 and 1980, such as elementary school teaching, nursing, social work, and clinical-laboratory technology; white women were not pursuing these occupations at the same rate in 1980 as they had in the past. As a result, Sokoloff (1992) argues that racial segregation between African-American women and white women increased in certain professional fields, contrary to what King (1992) has observed in the overall decline in occupational segregation by race.

To conclude, the labor-market experience of white women became more continuous and more like that of their African-American counterparts. The economic status of African-American women has improved as these women moved away from menial jobs, such as domestic, to white-collar service occupations. However, the occupational tipping model has suggested that progress has been capped before African-American women have reached professional and financial parity with men or with white women.

*Young-Hee Yoon*

## Bibliography

Amott, T.L., and J. Matthaei. 1991. *Race, Gender and Work: A Multicultural Economic History of Women in the United States.* Boston: South End.

Bell, D. 1974. "Why Participation Rates of Black and White Wives Differ." *Journal of Human Resources* 9 (4):465–79.

Bianchi, S.M., and D. Spain. 1986. *American Women in Transition.* New York: Russell Sage.

Cunningham, J.S., and N. Zalokar. 1992. "The Economic Progress of Black Women, 1940–1980: Occupational Distribution and Relative Wages." *Industrial and Labor Relations Review* 45 (3):540–55.

Goldin, C. 1990. *Understanding the Gender Gap: An Economic History of American Women.* New York: Oxford University Press.

King, M.C. 1993. "Black Women's Breakthrough into Clerical Work: An Occupational Tipping Model." *Journal of Economic Issues* 27 (4):1097–125.

———. 1992. "Occupational Segregation by Race and Sex, 1940–88." *Monthly Labor Review* 115 (4):30–7.

Meisenheimer, J., II. 1990. "Black College Graduates in the Labor Market, 1979 and 1989." *Monthly Labor Review* 113 (11):13–21.

Sokoloff, N.J. 1992. *Black Women and White Women in the Professions: Occupational Segregation by Race and Gender, 1960–1980.* New York: Routledge.

U.S. Bureau of the Census. 1940. *Census of Population. Employment and Personal Characteristics.* Washington, D.C.: Government Printing Office.

———. 1990. *Census of Population. Social and Economic Characteristics, United States.* Washington, D.C.: Government Printing Office.

———. 1991. *Fertility of American Women: June 1990.* Current Population Reports, Series P-20, No. 454, Washington, D.C.: U.S. Government Printing Office.

U.S. Bureau of Labor Statistics. 1994. *Employment and Earnings.* Washington, D.C.: Government Printing Office.

Wallace, P.A. 1980. *Black Women in the Labor Force.* Cambridge, Mass.: MIT.

Yoon, Y., and L.J. Waite. 1994. "Converging Employment Patterns of Black, White, and Hispanic Women: Return to Work after First Birth." *Journal of Marriage and the Family* 56:209–17.

## Latinas in the U.S. Labor Force

As the Latino population in the United States grows to become the largest minority group, their labor-force participation will have dramatic effects on the economy. (The term Latino is used in place of Hispanic except when referencing the works of another author. Because Hispanic is a term imposed by the U.S. government to categorize all Latinos, there is controversy among Latinos about which term is preferred.) There is a misconception that Latinas, Latino women, have only recently become members of the labor force. But the reality is that Latinas have always been active members. The Latino population is composed of many different groups, with the largest four groups being Mexican Americans, Puerto Ricans, Cuban Americans, and Central/South Americans. Latinas are generally overrepresented in the lower-skilled jobs with the lowest wages, although it is important to note that there are differences among these groups in their labor-force participation. Literature on Latinas' labor-force participation has focused on either their culturally based gender roles or their lack of human capital. Closely related to human capital is the impact of immigrant status on access to resources with which to build Latinas' market capital.

In 1993, the 4.07 million Latinas in the labor force constituted only 3.2 percent of the total labor force (U.S. Bureau of the Census 1994). In comparison, Non-Latina women constituted 42 percent of the total labor force. Among Latina subgroups, Central and South Americans had the highest labor-force participation in 1993 (57.2 percent), followed by Mexican Americans (51.6 percent), Cuban Americans (48.4 percent), and Puerto Rican women (46.2 percent). The U.S. Census Bureau's *Current Population Reports* (1973, 1993) show that the percentage of Latinas participating in the labor force increased from 39.7 percent in 1973 to 51.9 percent in 1993. For the same periods, labor-force participation of Mexican-American women increased from 38.7 percent to 51.6 percent; Puerto Rican women's participation increased from 31.8 percent to 46.2 percent. Other subgroups were not reported separately in 1973.

Historically, it has been assumed that Latinas' participation in the labor force has been constrained by their subordinate role in a "machismo" culture. Because of a view that women in the Latino culture must stay home and take care of the family while their husbands provide for them, Latinas, when forced to work out of financial necessity, are assumed to choose jobs that allow the family to be first priority. These jobs, of course, are either low paying or part time. Ortiz and Cooney (1984) examined sex-role attitudes and labor-force participation of Hispanic and non-Hispanic white females and found that women with traditional sex-role attitudes were less likely to participate in the labor force. Hispanics may have more traditional sex-role beliefs, but those beliefs were not the overriding factor in their decisions to participate in the labor force. Cooney (1975) determined that college-educated Mexican-American wives with middle to high incomes have higher rates of labor-force participation than college-educated Anglo wives, even when preschool children are in the home.

In another study, Fernandez Kelly (1990) looked at Mexican-American and Cuban women's labor-force participation. Because of their economic successes, Cuban men have been better able to provide for their families. Their wives, as a result, initially worked to help the family economically, but once their husbands succeeded they either stopped working or worked to supplement their husbands' income. Mexican-American men, however, for a number of reasons have not succeeded financially at the same levels as Cuban men. Consequently, they are not able to provide for their families, and their wives often work out of financial necessity.

Some researchers have claimed that because of their cultural responsibility of staying home to care for the family, Latinas have not developed the human capital required to be active, competitive members of the labor force. The argument is that the discrepancies in the wages and jobs of women and minorities is not based on discrimination practices but rather is due to their lack of the education, skills, and training required for higher-skilled and higher-paying jobs. The reality is that Latinas do have the lowest levels of education, with Mexican-American and Puerto Rican women at the bottom level of education. Of all Latina groups, Cuban women are the best educated, have the smallest families and do well in the labor market (Tienda and Guhleman 1985; Smith and Tienda 1988). However, Tienda and Guhleman (1985) argue that equalizing Latinas' characteristics with those of non-Hispanic white women would not eliminate the disparities between the two groups. In their study, they found that education was the most salient determinant of Latinas' occupational position. They attributed Latinas' stratification to differential access and control over resources such as education and market skills.

At the same time, Escutia and Prieto (1988) found that even if Mexican-American and Puerto Rican women had the same educational attainment and language competence as non-Hispanic white women, they would still have lower occupational status. In addition, Latinas' lower educational attainment levels influence their occupational distribution, earning levels, and unemployment levels more negatively than the same attainment by non-Hispanic white women. Notably, Firestone and Harris (1994) found that Latinas' family income in Texas had declined between 1980 and 1990, compared with the total Texas population, despite increases in labor-force participation, increases in paid labor hours per week, and increases in education.

Smith and Tienda (1988) surveyed women of color and found that differences in labor-force participation exist among all women even when educational attainment is controlled for. Mexican-American women had the lowest educational attainment of all women and were least likely to be employed in professional occupations. Cuban women were the most likely of all Latinas to graduate from high school and to be employed in managerial positions. Among women of color who did not complete college, Cuban women had the highest percentage of earnings in comparison to those with college degrees, while Puerto Ricans earned the lowest incomes. Relatedly, as U.S. populations continue to upgrade their schooling, women of color will have restricted labor-market opportunities as a result of their below-average educations.

Immigration status is also relevant when considering Latinas' access to resources for improving labor-market skills and human capital. Immigrants for the most part have less access to resources that will benefit their labor-market skills (such as knowledge of the U.S. educational system and language competence). Because the Latino population has a greater number of immigrants than any other minority group, their access to the necessary resources will determine their success in the U.S. labor market. According to Stier and Tienda (1992), characteristics that determine female labor supply for immigrant women include years of residence in the U.S., English proficiency, and national origin, as well as education and work experience. They looked at whether an immigrant factor existed in women's decision to enter the labor force and found that "pure" immigration effects on labor supply quickly give way to other factors. Earning potential and children are wives' main considerations in the decision about labor-market activity, irrespective of nativity.

Where Stier and Tienda (1992) looked at immigrant wives' decision to enter the work force, Torres (1992) studied the effects of nativity on earnings, specifically for Puerto Ricans already participating in the labor force. When Puerto Ricans are born on the island and educated in Spanish, they have characteristics similar to those of other Latino immigrants, even though they are technically

American citizens. His findings indicate that mainland-born Puerto Rican women earn higher wages and have higher educational levels than island-born women. He also found that second-generation Puerto Ricans in the U.S. have increased labor-force experience and English language proficiency, compared with first-generation arrivals. These findings suggest that immigrant status per se is a source of earning inequalities.

Overall, the literature on Latinas in the labor force includes three major components. First, in terms of culture, Latinas, like all women, must balance family and work, but in addition they must come to terms with their role as women within a Latino culture. It is unclear how this role actually affects Latinas' labor-force participation. Second, in terms of human capital, Latinas have lower levels of education and labor-force experience, which restricts opportunity for upward mobility. Furthermore, immigrant status may have no effect on the decision to enter the labor force, but it does influence the earning potential of those in the labor force. Once culture, education, and labor-force experience are taken into account, discrimination against Latinas still exists, restricting access to education and job opportunities.

> Susan E. Moreno
>
> Chandra Muller

## Bibliography

Cooney, R.S. 1975. "Changing Labor Force Participation of Mexican American Wives: A Comparison with Anglos and Blacks." *Social Science Quarterly* (56):252–61.

Escutia, M., and M. Prieto. 1988. *Hispanics in the Workforce Part II: Hispanic Women*. Washington D.C.: National Council of La Raza.

Fernandez Kelly, M.P. 1990. "Delicate Transactions: Gender, Home, and Employment among Hispanic Women." In *Uncertain Terms: Negotiating Gender in American Culture*, edited by F. Ginsburg and A.L. Tsing, pp. 183–95. Boston: Beacon.

Firestone, J., and R. Harris. 1994. "Hispanic Women in Texas: An Increasing Portion of the Underclass." *Hispanic Journal of Behavioral Sciences* (16):176–85.

Ortiz, V., and R.S. Cooney. 1984. "Sex-Role Attitudes and Labor Force Participation among Young Hispanic Females and Non-Hispanic White Females." *Social Science Quarterly* (65):392–400.

Smith, S., and M. Tienda. 1988. "The Doubly Disadvantaged: Women of Color in the U.S. Labor Force." In *Women Working: Theories and Facts in Perspective*, edited by A. Stromberg and S. Harkess, pp. 61–80. Mountain View, Calif.: Mayfield.

Stier, H., and M. Tienda. 1992. "Family, Work, and Women: The Labor Supply of Hispanic Immigrant Wives." *International Migration Review* (26):1291–313.

Tienda, M., and P. Guhleman. 1985. "The Occupational Position of Employed Hispanic Women." In *Hispanics in the U.S. Economy*, edited by G. Borjas and M. Tienda. Orlando, Fla.: Academic.

Torres, A. 1992. "Nativity, Gender, and Earnings Discrimination." *Hispanic Journal of Behavioral Sciences* (14):134–43.

U.S. Bureau of the Census. May 1974. *Persons of Spanish Origin in the United States: March 1973*. Current Population Reports Series P20-264. Washington, D.C.: U.S. Department of Commerce, Social and Economic Statistics Administration.

———. May 1994. *The Hispanic Population in the United States: March 1993*. Current Population Reports Series P20-475. Washington, D.C.: U.S. Department of Commerce, Social and Economic Statistics Administration.

## Immigrant Women in the U.S. and Work

The work of immigrant women in the United States has always played a vital role in many areas of the economy, despite the often extreme hardships that confronted these workers. Generalizing about patterns of work among female immigrants is difficult because their circumstances have varied greatly by ethnicity, marital status, and other factors. Those that chose to work outside the home, however, shared a common experience of employment discrimination on the basis of racism, sexism, and xenophobia. Such discrimination often forced these women to work long hours in unsafe workplaces for very low wages. Immigrant women also often worked in repetitive manufacturing jobs, especially in the textile and garment industries, or in other unskilled and low-paying types of labor such as domestic service, laundering, prostitution, and childcare (Katzman 1981). These workers experienced significantly more exploitation, hazards, and abuses in the workplace than either native-born women or immigrant men. Other immigrant women chose not to work outside their own homes because of the cultural traditions of their ethnic groups or their personal preferences. These women, however, often did produce income by doing home-based manufacturing, helping in a family business, or taking in boarders (Daniels 1988).

Many immigrants came to America throughout the nineteenth and twentieth centuries, with the highest concentration arriving between 1880 and 1921. They often came fleeing poverty or political and religious oppression in their native lands. The Irish were one of the earliest non-Anglo ethnic groups, arriving in the mid 1800s, followed by successive waves of Germans, Italians, Eastern Europeans, Jews, and other groups before 1920. Many Chinese and Japanese immigrants arrived in the 1800s seeking employment on the burgeoning West Coast, as did large numbers of French Canadians and Mexicans. Immigration was severely restricted after 1920, with only certain groups thereafter selectively allowed entry to the United States. Selective exceptions were made for those facing political or humanitarian crises in their homelands. Refugees fleeing both the Cuban revolution in the early 1960s and war in Southeast Asia in the mid 1970s were legally allowed to enter in large numbers (Dinnerstein 1988).

Immigration in 1990, however, retained strong parallels to immigration in the nineteenth century. At the same time, illegal immigration continued at a steady rate, with many Mexicans and Central Americans entering the United States along its southern border and an increasing number of Chinese being smuggled in aboard ships. Regardless of the era in which immigrants came, their ethnicity, or their country of origin, most shared the common experiences of discrimination, poverty, and relegation to the most difficult and undesirable jobs.

The ethnicity of immigrant women often played a major role in the type of employment that was available to them. Employers used ethnic stereotypes in selecting workers, and recruited and hired women from certain ethnic groups for particular types of work. Such stereotypes were frequently rooted in types of work common to the immigrants' countries of origin, the perceived suitability of some groups to certain tasks, or simply to racist misinformation. For example, stereotyping made millwork the province of young Italians, the Welsh, and the Irish, while cigar-making was deemed to be the work of Bohemians, Russians, and Germans. Jobs in sewing and other "needle trades" were consistently filled by Jewish women. Asian women were most often relegated to even lesser employment, such as laundry work and prostitution (Daniels 1988).

In addition to being ethnically typecast by employers, women from different backgrounds often showed distinct preferences for particular types of employment. For example, Hasia Diner, in *Erin's Daughters in America* (1983), indicates that domestic service, rather than work in manufacturing, was the preferred and often stereotypic employment for Irish women. Such domestic service was similarly the choice of other ethnic groups, especially those with large numbers of unmarried females. Gary Ross Mormino, in *Immigrants on the Hill* (1986), tells how Italian immigrant women preferred to work in the tobacco industry until marriage and then chose home-based employment. Showing ethnic preference for certain types of work or industries was one of the few small ways that immigrant women could help to determine their own economic destinies.

Most immigrant women faced common problems and obstacles in employment. Immigrant women were often restricted to low-level employment by the combined factors of sexism in the paternalistic American and immigrant cultures and by pervasive feelings of extreme nativism, racism, and ethnocentricity among native-born Americans. At the turn of the century, this was not unlike some of the problems facing native-born women, who were denied the most basic political or legal rights or economic equality. This prevalent sexism denied American women voting rights in elections and usually forced them to work in sex-typed support roles, manufacturing, or home-based employment. For immigrant women, these limitations were often exacerbated in immigrant communities by the male-dominant Old World traditions of many ethnic groups.

Periods of intense xenophobia throughout the nineteenth and twentieth centuries led to further discrimination against many immigrants. Groups opposed to non-Anglo immigration, called Nativists, viewed immigrants as a threat to the status quo of American life. They claimed that immigrants, especially those from Catholic Ireland and Southern and Eastern Europe, subverted American patriotism, undermined Protestantism, and led to racial "mongrelization." Nativists incited anti-immigrant riots, passed restrictive immigration and naturalization legislation, and prohibited newcomers from many areas of employment. Denied lucrative employment, immigrants were often forced to work in low-paying and dangerous jobs.

A tragic example of such brutality and exploitation against immigrant women was at the Triangle Waist Company. At Triangle, young Jewish immigrant women were overcrowded into the top three floors of a ten-story building, sewing shirtwaists, a popular women's garment in the early 1900s. In addition to forcing these women to work long hours for very low wages, the Triangle Waist Company's supervisors locked the fire exits to deter thefts and early departures, a common practice in the garment industry. On March 25, 1911, fire broke out at Triangle, quickly engulfing the upper floors and killing 146 workers. This tragedy, known to history as the Triangle Shirtwaist Fire, dramatized the plight of these immigrant women, stimulating some Progressive Era reform movements led by middle-class women. The fire also became a rallying point for organizing immigrant women laborers, who were often slow and erratic in unionizing (Milkman 1985).

Immigrant women faced the same obstacles in labor organization that they faced in securing decent employment. Early labor organizations such as the American Federation of Labor were often elitist, allowing only skilled and native-born workers into their membership. Unskilled workers, immigrants, and African Americans were usually perceived as outsiders, or even worse, as potential competitors for jobs. Unions viewed women and children, and especially immigrant women, as a pool of cheap labor that could undermine the power of organized labor. Rather than including women in the mainstream of the labor movement, many unions worked to exclude them from workplaces or marginalize them in undesirable jobs. Nevertheless, in 1900 women constituted 19 percent of the paid labor force in the United States.

The International Workers of the World, commonly known as the "Wobblies," were a noted exception to this exclusionary trend against women. The IWW organized immigrant women in many female-dominated industries throughout the United States and led several labor strikes. Notable among these IWW-led strikes were a successful strike against the American Woolen Company in Lawrence, Massachusetts, in 1912, and the failed Paterson Silk Strike of 1913, involving over twenty-five thousand female workers. Despite encouragement and organizing assistance by a few groups such as the IWW, the labor movement largely ignored the plight of immigrant women, or actively worked to undermine their efforts (Golin 1988).

Throughout American history, immigrant women often worked at unrewarding and difficult jobs, facing constant hazards, discrimination, exploitation, and even death. In spite of the long hours they spent toiling in factories or domestic service, many immigrant women successfully established new lives in America, raising families and contributing to the strength of the economy and the diversity of the culture. They endured the extreme hardships of the workplace, while also shouldering most of the domestic tasks in their own homes. Carrying insurmountable burdens, with only scant rewards or gratitude, was seemingly the common thread among immigrant women in America.

*David G. Hogan*

**Bibliography**

Daniels, Roger. 1988. *Asian America: Chinese and Japanese in the United States since 1950*. Seattle: University of Washington Press.
Diner, Hasia. 1983. *Erin's Daughters in America*. Baltimore: Johns Hopkins University Press.
Dinnerstein, Leonard. 1988. *Ethnic Americans: A History of Immigration*. New York: Harper and Row.
Golin, Steve. 1988. *The Fragile Bridge: Paterson Silk Strike 1913*. Philadelphia: Temple University Press.
Katzman, David M. 1981. *Seven Days a Week: Women and Domestic Service in Industrializing America*. Urbana: University of Illinois Press.
Kerber, Linda K. 1991. *Women's America: Refocusing the Past*. New York: Oxford University Press.
Manning, Caroline. 1970. *The Immigrant Woman and Her Job*. New York: Arno.
Matthaei, Julie A. 1982. *An Economic History of Women in America*. New York: Schocken.
Milkman, Ruther, ed. 1985. *Women, Work & Protest*. London: Routledge and Kegan Paul.
Mormino, Gary Ross. 1986. *Immigrants on the Hill: Italian-Americans in St. Louis, 1882–1982*. Urbana: University of Illinois Press.
Strasser, Susan. 1982. *Never Done: A History of American Housework*. New York: Pantheon.

## Domestic Workers and Their Employers

Domestic work encompasses a series of household and child-care tasks. It is typically characterized by relatively low pay, hard physical labor, the absence of opportunities for advancement or promotion, low status and prestige, and the lack of guaranteed benefits such as paid vacation, sick leave, Social Security, and dental or medical insurance plans. Traditionally, a defining feature of the job has been the psychological exploitation that occurs in the close relationship established between employer and employee, both of whom are usually women. While both employer and employee share subordinate gender status in the United States, they are frequently differentiated by class, race, and legal status. Women of color and immigrant women have traditionally predominated in domestic work and they continue to do so today. Occupational arrangements, however, have undergone important historical shifts. By the 1920s in the United States, live-out domestic work arrangements became more prevalent than live-in work. Live-in arrangements, however, did not disappear, and today these jobs are filled by new immigrant women, many of whom lack legal status. Unlike the nineteenth century or the early twentieth century, when upper- and middle-class households employed multiple servants, today many employers can afford only one employee, so domestic work often occurs in an isolated and privatized environment. Remuneration varies widely by employer and by region of the country. Live-in domestics generally receive part of their salary in kind, in the form of room and board.

In the United States, the growth of the domestic service occupation arose with urbanization and industrialization, processes accompanied by rural–urban migration and growth of the urban-based middle class. Between 1870 and 1910, the number of female domestic workers in the U.S. nearly doubled as the expanding urban middle classes' needs for domestic service were met by European immigrants and African-American rural–urban migrants (Katzman 1981). From 1850 until 1930, domestic work was the single largest category of employment for women in the United States (see citations in Glenn 1986, p. 99).

Historically, African-American women predominated in the South, Irish women and then later African-American and Caribbean women in the Northeast, and Asian and Latina women in the West and Southwest (Glenn 1986; Rollins 1985; Romero 1988). Although domestic work is defined as "women's work," class, race, and, increasingly, legal status define which women work as, and which women employ, domestics. The people who perform domestic duties for pay are still primarily poor women of color, and in particular areas of the U.S. with large immigrant populations, such as California, New York, and south Texas, domestic work is today nearly institutionalized as a job performed by immigrant women from Latin America and the Caribbean (Ruiz 1987; Solorzano-Torres 1987; Wrigley 1991).

Lewis Coser (1973) predicted the obsolescence of domestic servants, whose work would be replaced by the fragmented services offered by various persons and agencies, such as part-time housecleaners, dry cleaners, and caterers. To a limited extent this shift has occurred, and Mary Romero (1987, 1988) characterizes the shift from live-in servants to live-out cleaning women as occupational modernization. When they work for several different employers on a contractual basis, domestic workers are afforded greater job flexibility and are less likely to become dependent on deeply personalized employer-employee relations. Personalized employer-employee relations are most intense for domestic workers who live with their employer and for those who care for small children and work for the same employer on a daily, "live-out" basis (Wrigley 1991).

Intensely personalized employer-employee relations may no longer be as critical as they once were, and the psychic needs of employers to expect their domestic employees to act subserviently may have peaked in the 1930s and 1940s (Palmer 1989), but employee deference and employer maternalism still prevail

(Rollins 1985). Many employers, for example, routinely give their domestic workers unwanted advice, used furniture, old clothing, and rotting food and then expect their employees to reciprocate with gratitude and deference. Domestic workers are keenly aware that part of the job requires conforming to these expectations (Glenn 1986; Rollins 1985). These exchanges between nonequals confirm for the female employers their own sense of racial superiority and justify their view of the employee as their inferior (Palmer 1989; Rollins 1985).

Major modifications in domestic work have occurred, but it is not an occupation in decline. While some commentators dismissed the occupation as an archaic holdover from premodern, precapitalist eras, domestic work appears instead to be enjoying a period of expansion and resurgence. Although it is virtually impossible to document occupational growth because of the informal, under-the-table aspect of the work, many observers agree that the growing demand for domestic work derives from the mass entrance of women into the labor force. During the 1960s and 1970s, female U.S. citizens entered the labor force in unprecedented numbers, and by the late 1980s a majority of women with children under the age of three were either employed or seeking work. Men have not responded to women's employment by taking equal responsibility for household work and child care, so many dual-income families have solved their household needs by hiring domestic workers.

There are two competing views on the role of domestic work in the lives of intra- and international female migrants. One view emphasizes domestic work as an occupation that promotes acculturation and social mobility. Accordingly, domestic employment serves as an occupational stepping stone or bridge linking less advanced, agricultural areas of the economy to more modern sectors, such as manufacturing or retail. An alternative perspective sees domestic work as a dead-end job, as an occupational ghetto. The extent of individual and intergenerational mobility provided by domestic work in the United States has generally varied by race and ethnicity, with European immigrants experiencing upward mobility and African-Americans and Mexican women finding themselves confined to domestic work for their entire lives, especially in the years prior to World War II. Glenn (1986, pp. 102–5) suggests that Japanese-American domestic workers assumed an intermediate position, as many second-generation domestics left the occupation when they married. The extent of occupational mobility that occurs among the many Latina and Caribbean immigrants who are currently employed as domestics constitutes an important inquiry for future research.

In Latin America, domestic workers have formed organizations and trade unions in response to low pay and working conditions that sometimes resemble servitude (Chaney and Castro 1989). These domestic workers' unions are engaged in political education, in dispensing legal advice, in job placement, as well as in recreation and other expressive activities. In California, Latina immigrant women have begun to form housecleaning cooperatives that provide job placement and job training and promote workplace rights. These efforts mitigate the privatized and personalized nature of domestic work. An innovative information and outreach campaign for domestic workers in Los Angeles attempts to reach Latina, undocumented, immigrant women as they ride public buses to and from work. This project attempts to overcome the inherent isolation of the job by providing legal referrals, basic employment and legal rights, and advice in the form of novelas (leaflets with captioned illustrations) (Hondagneu-Sotelo 1993).

Unlike au pairs, young women from Europe and the Midwest taking temporary child-care jobs and enjoying the protection of legal status, many Latina child-care workers and housecleaners lack legal work authorization. Some employers promise to help their domestic workers obtain legal status, and the domestic workers who are undocumented immigrants may tolerate substandard working conditions and pay in hopes that this promise will be fulfilled. Employers may rationalize poor treatment of their domestic employees on the basis that they do not speak English or lack legal status; some employers have successfully imposed conditions much like servitude by threatening to have their domestic workers deported. An undocumented immigrant woman's position within the occupation is not static; it may improve if she makes a transition from live-in to live-out work. This transition is facilitated if she gains experience, learns to utilize informational resources made available through friends and relatives who also do domestic work, and establishes routine employment (Hondagneu-Sotelo, 1994). Undocumented women and women who are not U.S. citizens constitute the major supply of paid domestic workers in the United States today. It is no longer just race and class, but also language proficiency and, most saliently, legal status, that divide domestic employers and employees.

*Pierrette Hondagneu-Sotelo*

## Bibliography

Chaney, Elasa M., and Mary Garcia Castro. 1989. *Muchachas No More: Household Workers in Latin America and the Caribbean*. Philadelphia: Temple University Press.

Coser, Lewis. 1973. "Servants: The Obsolescence of an Occupational Role." *Social Forces* 52:31–40.

Glenn, Evelyn Nakano. 1986. *Issei, Nisei, Warbride: Three Generations of Japanese American Women in Domestic Service*. Philadelphia: Temple University Press.

Hondagneu-Sotelo, Pierrette. 1994. "Regulating the Unregulated?: Domestic Workers' Social Networks." *Social Problems* 41:50–64.

———. 1993. "Why Advocacy Research?: Reflections on Research and Activism with Immigrant Women." *American Sociologist*.

Katzman, David M. 1981. *Seven Days a Week: Women and Domestic Service in Industrializing America*. Urbana: University of Illinois Press.

Palmer, Phyllis. 1989. *Domesticity and Dirt: Housewives and Domestic Servants in the United States, 1920–1989*. Philadelphia: Temple University Press.

Rollins, Judith. 1985. *Between Women: Domestics and Their Employers*. Philadelphia: Temple University Press.

Romero, Mary. 1988. "Chicanas Modernize Domestic Service." *Qualitative Sociology* 11:319–34.

———. 1987. "Domestic Service in the Transition from Rural to Urban Life: The Case of La Chicana." *Women's Studies*. 13:199–222.

Ruiz, Vicki L. 1987. "By the Day or the Week: Mexicana Domestic Workers in El Paso." In *Women on the U.S.–Mexico Border*, edited by Vicki L. Ruiz and Susan Tiano, pp. 61–76. Boston: Allen and Unwin.

Solorzano-Torres, Rosalia. 1987. "Female Mexican Immigrants in San Diego County." In *Women on the U.S.–Mexico Border*, edited by Vicki L. Ruiz and Susan Tiano, pp. 41–60. Boston: Allen and Unwin.

Wrigley, Julia. 1991. "Review Essay: Feminists and Domestic Workers." *Feminist Studies*. 17:317–29.

## Appalachian Women and Work

Appalachian women are women who were born, or whose parents were born, in the Appalachian Region (a federally defined area including West Virginia and portions of thirteen other states situated along the Appalachian Mountain range). They include the original Indian women of the region (Cherokee, Appalachee, Shawnee, Choctaw); Anglo-Saxon and Celtic women settlers and refugees; black women settlers who were free and runaway or freed slaves; and European and other immigrant women who came later to the coalfields or farms, or to work in stores. Appalachian women's work has been influenced by their harsh physical environment in isolated, mountain "hollers"; by values shaped for survival in this environment, such as familism, attachment to the land, individualism, and self-reliance; and by a patriarchal family structure. Subsistence and small cash-crop farming, coal mining, railroads, and lumbering were the traditional industries. "Boom and bust" economies forced many to leave their rural homes during the Great Migration of the 1940s, 1950s, and 1960s to seek work opportunities in defense factories in the cities of the North and East.

Traditionally, Appalachian women's work was in and around the home, taking care of children, other family members, a garden, and management of the household. Although the patriarchal culture in Appalachia placed women in a secondary status, elderly women had a special status. They carried on the health-care traditions of the family; many were "granny women" who knew of herbs and teas to cure almost any ailment. They received respect for their wisdom and knowledge. With increasing age, women attained positions of authority and recognition; their advice was freely given and accepted, even by their husbands.

Appalachian women were also applauded for their resourcefulness and domestic industry. They churned their own butter; dried shuck beans, pumpkin, and other fruits; smoked meats; pounded corn to make bread; canned and pickled much from the garden; made their own lye soap; made the family's clothing; made their own cleaning utensils; made their own medicines; and sometimes made their own cloth and recycled old pieces of clothing into quilts. Women also helped in the fields to bring in the crops, worked in the garden, and performed all other domestic chores (Campbell 1921). Most jobs to be done were "woman's work," but women pitched in at other work because getting a job done was more important than who did it.

The traditional patriarchal family structure of Appalachian families required that the husband have the leadership role and make decisions in the economic, social, and familial spheres of their lives (Schwarzweller et al. 1971). Consequently, marriage was almost mandatory. For women who did not marry, an awkward life of dependency upon married kin was to be expected (Campbell 1921).

Contemporary Appalachian women have followed similar patterns. Marriage is still valued as the future role. Motherhood is expected, and most labor force participation is in traditionally gender-typed jobs, such as secretary, cook, waitress, and beautician (Beaver 1979). Adolescence and the subsequent courting period are times when women have special significance and attention. Marriage may also be an escape from the responsibilities of their parents' home. Early marriage may prevent women from completing their education or from receiving adequate work experience and training. Many husbands discourage their wives from working because of their pride as the traditional wage earner and head of the household and because of the importance of children in the family. These women may devote their lives to their families to the exclusion of their own education, skill development, and ability to provide a living when they are widowed or divorced or to provide for a disabled husband.

Labor-force participation has changed dramatically over the past thirty years for Appalachian women. A greater proportion of women are working outside the home, in some cases because of a weakening economy in which the husband cannot earn a sufficient wage to support his family, and in other cases encouraged by a changing occupational structure that includes women in nontraditional jobs. Women are now working in the coal mines, strip mines, on railroads, in lumbering and construction, as well as in traditional jobs as teachers, nurses, and hairdressers.

Appalachian migrant women, however, away from the familiar surroundings of the mountains, have had to adjust their roles to acclimate to an urban society. Their estrangement from the mountains is not tempered with a greater social affiliation and interaction with natives of northern cities (Schwarzweller et al. 1971). Their social isolation from those in the cities and their apparent desire to remain there and not return to the mountains leaves Appalachian women stuck between a "rock and a hard place": stuck without the social and emotional support needed to reduce the strains of changing roles, to smooth her way into the opportunities offered by the urban environment and to maintain the cultural contacts necessary for positive self-identity as women and Appalachians (Miller 1978). Mostly, these women came with their husbands or parents, or joined other relatives who came to industrial cities in search of jobs and a better life. Appalachian women brought with them to the cities of the North, East, and West the same cultural heritage as their sisters who stayed behind; however, migration forced changes in the culture. While Appalachian culture requires that women serve the traditional roles of homemaker and mother, the urban setting demands some transformation in decision-making roles, in employment, and in marital relationships.

Harriet Arnow's *Dollmaker* provides a vivid, although fictional, account of the stress and hardships that Gertie Nevel experienced in leaving her beloved land and adjusting to the urban life of Detroit. Trevino (1978) considers it a sensitive portrayal of Gertie and her family, who face prejudice, insensitive institutions, and disadvantages for attempts to maintain a unique identity.

The occupational roles of women have received some attention in the scientific literature. Eighty-three percent of Appalachians in northern Kentucky believe that women should not work to support the family, compared with 50 percent of other migrants and 42 percent of long-term residents (Traina 1980). These attitudes reflect cultural beliefs and behaviors in the Appalachian family. Beliefs that women should remain in the home and not participate in the workforce linger among Appalachian migrants; however, situations have necessitated that they alter their behavior to conform to the changing circumstances of the economy and customs in the new setting. While more Appalachian migrant women than Appalachian women in the mountains are among the employed workforce, substantially fewer Appalachian migrant women than urban women work outside the home.

Empirical studies show that Appalachian migrants have a low status in the stratification hierarchy in urban areas. Their occupational status is lower than that of other groups, either other migrants or natives. They are concentrated in unskilled or semiskilled jobs; few hold professional or managerial positions (Philliber 1981a, 1981b; Photiadis 1981; Schwarzweller et al. 1971; Schwarzweller 1981). In addition, Appalachians are found to receive the lowest income attained for concomitant increases in occupational status (Philliber 1981b). Studies on Appalachian employment status indicate that, in general, Appalachians are able to find jobs and are willing to accept lower-status jobs (Philliber 1981b; Photiadis 1981; Schwarzweller et al. 1971). Most studies of migration find that few Appalachian women, compared with their urban counterparts, worked outside the home (Philliber 1981a; Powles 1978), although a greater number are employed when compared with Appalachians who remained in the mountains (Schwarzweller et al. 1971). About one-third of women in the Beech Creek study worked outside the home in teaching and clerical positions, but most held semiskilled or unskilled jobs (Schwarzweller et al. 1971). One study indicated that Appalachian women are not disadvantaged in the urban occupational structure (Watkins and Trevino 1982).

The occupations of some well-known Appalachian women include writers (Mildred Haun, Harriet Arnow, Wilma Dykeman, Mary Lee Settles, and Lee Smith), poets (Muriel Dressler, Bennie Lee Sinclair), musicians (Elizabeth Cotten, Hazel Dickens, Sara Ogan Gunning, Jean Ritchie, Loretta Lynn, Dolly Parton, and the Judds), and community organizers (Aunt Molly Jackson, Mother Jones, Granny Hager, Widow Combs, Florence Reese, and the Brookside Women's Club). The heterogeneity of women exemplified here does not explain the negative stereotypes applied to Appalachian women. The Daisy Mae, Mammy Yokum, and, more recently, Dolly Parton images invoked when the derogatory term "hillbilly woman" is mentioned have placed Appalachian women in a position that necessitates their defending or obscuring their heritage. Kathy Kahn (1972) and Sharon Lord (1979) described women who further exemplify positive role models and the heterogeneity of Appalachian women: Granny Hager's struggle to obtain black-lung benefits and her subsequent advocacy of those rights for others; a college professor's ambitions to become a college president; the socialization of an Appalachian feminist; and the Wilson and Chandler women's efforts to adjust to the confinements and abuses of city life.

The consequences of work-role changes in Appalachian culture may result in greater opportunities for Appalachian women, especially unmarried women who may be less confined by the patriarchal family structure. Married women, on the other hand, may begin to experience greater authority within the family unit as a result of their roles as wage earners. Women in high-status and nontraditional occupations who function as role models may assist in diversifying the traditional occupational status of Appalachian women in the future. However, the status of women within the culture may place additional restrictions on future opportunities.

*H. Virginia McCoy*
*Diana Gullett Trevino*

## Bibliography

Arnow, Harriet. 1954. *The Dollmaker*. New York: Macmillan.
Beaver, P.D. 1979. "Hillbilly Women, Hillbilly Men: Sex Roles in Rural-Agricultural Appalachia." In *Appalachian Women*, edited by S.B. Lord and C. Patton-Crowder. Newton, Mass.: Education Development Center.

Campbell, J.C. 1921. *The Southern Highlander and His Homeland*. Lexington: University Press of Kentucky.

Kahn, Kathy. 1972. *Hillbilly Women*. New York: Doubleday.

Lord, Sharon B., and C. Patton-Crowder. 1979. "Appalachian Women: A Learning/Teaching Guide." Newton, Mass.: Education Development Center.

McCoy, C.B., and Virginia M. Watkins. 1981. "Stereotypes of Appalachian Migrants." In *The Invisible Minority*, edited by W.W. Philliber and C.B. McCoy. Lexington: University Press of Kentucky.

Miller, T. 1978. "Urban Appalachian Ethnic Identity: The Current Situation." In *Perspectives on Urban Appalachians*, edited by S. Weiland and P. Obermiller. Cincinnati: Ohio Urban Appalachian Awareness Project.

Philliber, W.W. 1981a. "Accounting for the Occupational Placement of Appalachian Migrants." In *The Invisible Minority*, edited by W.W. Philliber and C.B. McCoy. Lexington: University Press of Kentucky.

———. 1981b. *Appalachian Migrants in Urban America*. New York: Praeger.

Photiadis, J.D. 1981. "Occupational Adjustments of Appalachians in Cleveland." In *The Invisible Minority: Urban Appalachians*, edited by W.W. Philliber and C.B. McCoy. Lexington: University Press of Kentucky.

Powles, W.E. 1978. "The Southern Appalachian Migrant: Country Boy Turned Blue-Collarite." In *Perspectives on Urban Appalachians*, edited by S. Weiland and P. Obermiller. Cincinnati: Ohio Urban Appalachians Awareness Project.

Schwarzweller, H. 1981. "Occupational Patterns of Appalachian Migrants." In *The Invisible Minority: Urban Appalachians*, edited by W.W. Philliber and C.B. McCoy. Lexington: University Press of Kentucky.

Schwarzweller, H., J.S. Brown, and J. Mangalam. 1971. *Mountain Families in Transition*. University Park: University of Pennsylvania Press.

Traina, F.J. 1980. *The Assimilation of Appalachian Migrants in Northern Kentucky*. Cincinnati: Urban Appalachian Council, Working Paper No. 12.

Trevino, D. 1978. "Appalachian Women." In *Teaching Mountain Children*. Boone, N.C.: Appalachian Consortium.

Watkins, V.M., and D.G. Trevino. 1982. "Occupational and Employment Status of Appalachian Migrant Women." In *Critical Essays in Appalachian Life and Culture*, edited by R. Simon. Proceedings of the Fifth Annual Appalachian Studies Conference, Appalachian Consortium.

## Greek Ethnic Women in the U.S.

Women have been essential to the establishment of Greek diaspora communities throughout the world. They have maintained the home and family, socialized the children into the Greek culture, volunteered their work in ethnic organizations, and assumed positions in the paid labor force. Major differences among Greek ethnic women are shaped by generation—that is, migrant as opposed to native-born subsequent generations—time of migration, and structure of the dominant society in which the ethnic community is located.

### The Early Immigrants: The Pioneers

Most Greeks migrated to America at the turn of the century. By 1962, however, America had become the third choice of destination; Germany was the most popular and Australia/New Zealand the second most popular (Kayser et al. 1964). Far fewer in number than their male counterparts, those first Greek immigrant women came to America, Australia, and New Zealand married to marry Greek men who had migrated. They left their villages in Greece to live in the towns or cities of the new lands. While the material possessions of the early migrants were few, the arrival of the women made Greek family life possible and with that the beginning of an ongoing ethnic community with its own institutions, the most important of which was—next to the family—the Greek Orthodox Church.

With respect to the family, the work of the women consisted of the set of expectations associated with the Greek term *nikokepa*—that is, woman of the house—and those associated with retaining the Greek culture. A "good nikokepa," through her work, took care of her family, her husband, and her children. Her work typically consisted of cooking Greek dishes, keeping a neat and tidy house, and adhering to the highly prescribed expectations of Greek hospitality. This included preparing and storing a traditional Greek sweet to serve when visitors dropped by unannounced and cooking food for a large number of guests who would come to the house to celebrate the "name day" of her husband, as well as providing hospitality to Greek immigrant men traveling through the country in search of work.

As was expected of them, the vast majority of the early migrant women had children—some as many as eight or nine. The women socialized them into the Greek Orthodox religion, making sure that they observed holy days, including fasting periods, in the appropriate manner. They spoke to them in Greek and, when afternoon Greek school classes were established, made sure that their children attended, thus encouraging the maintenance of the Greek language. They monitored their children's friendship patterns with an eye to ensuring that they would marry other Greek ethnics, and they guided them in countless other ways in hopes of fostering the retention of Greek culture.

The women contributed much time to building and maintaining the ethnic community. Though names of the first Greek women immigrants do not appear among those of the early presidents of Greek Orthodox churches in the new lands, the women performed a number of essential duties for the newly born Greek community. In America, they established various women's organizations, such as the church-affiliated Philoptochos, the Daughters of Penelope, and the Maids of Athens. Through them, they further ensured the maintenance of the Greek culture, fostered a sense of community, helped those in economic need, cared for the sick and aged, and raised money to provide relief for those they had left behind in Greece.

These "pioneers" in a new land were discouraged from seeking higher education and working outside the home, particularly outside the family for non-Greeks. To have a wife, sister, or daughter working was considered a poor reflection on a man's ability to provide for his family. It appears that only a minority of Greek women worked outside the family and home at that time (Abbott 1909). In America, the greatest proportion of Greek working women thus employed tended to be single, working in the New England textile and shoe factories. In addition, in the American West, many married Greek women ran boarding houses for Greek workers (Papanikolas 1989). In the 1920s, a small number of Greek women arrived in America as a result of the expulsion of Greeks from Turkey. Because they emigrated from cities and were of a middle-class background, these women tended to be better educated than those who had come earlier: They took positions in the Greek community as the first teachers in afternoon Greek schools.

Both in Australia and the United States, where many of the early male migrants eventually opened small businesses such as a cafe or confectionery, Greek sisters, daughters, and wives worked in the store or shop, cooking, waiting on customers, dipping chocolates, and doing whatever was needed to keep the business going. Perhaps because it was considered inappropriate for women to work out-side the house or because effort put into the store was considered part of a woman's contribution to the family, little attention has been paid to these women's experi-ences; thus, to a certain extent, this work has been hidden. Often, it was not even considered "work" by the women themselves (Chapin 1991). Other "work" un-dertaken by women within the Greek ethnic community and outside of the fam-ily consisted of healing the sick or those in pain and providing midwife services (Papanikolas 1989).

### The Later Migrants

In contrast to their earlier counterparts, those Greek women who came to America in the post–World War II years came to a society already industrialized and to an established Greek community. Their numbers equalled those of their male coun-terparts, and, from 1961 to 1965, immigration by Greek females exceeded that of Greek males. Expected to take care of the family and home, many of these women also entered the labor force. Many went into light factory work; those relatively few with higher levels of education tended to go into teaching. They were more likely than Greek immigrant men to work in Greek-owned establishments. Those with higher education also worked for pay in Greek ethnic enclaves in the United States; Greek migrant women with at least sixteen years of schooling worked as teachers in the Greek day schools.

### Native-Born Greek Ethnic Women

Compared with the early immigrant women, the lives of second- and third-gen-eration Greek ethnic women are less circumscribed by patriarchy. However, as is true of earlier Greek ethnic women, those of the second and third generations are expected to take greater responsibility for the home and family and the mainte-nance of Greek ethnicity than are men.

Second- and third-generation women are assuming positions of leader-ship in the Greek ethnic community and pushing for further attenuation of patri-archy. Within the church, for example, they are serving on the Archdiocesan Coun-cil, the highest lay group in the church, and assuming elected positions such as president of the community. Although the Greek Orthodox Church has remained adamantly against the ordination of women, it is among these second- and third-generation Greek ethnic women that a movement is developing for greater involve-ment in the sacred rituals of the church.

With respect to the paid labor force, both second-generation Greek American women (with a median of 12.5 years of education) and Greek-Ameri-can men (with a median of 12.8 years) have a higher level of educational attain-ment than either American women or American men, who average 12.1 years of education (Demos 1989). The pattern of paid employment of Greek ethnic women and men follows the pattern of the general American population, with men hav-ing positions of higher prestige and salary. The occupations of second-generation Greek-American women tend to be in clerical areas, while those of their male coun-terparts tend to be in the areas of professional and technical work as well as in managerial and administrative areas (excluding farming) (Demos 1989). Second- or third-generation Greek-American women who have achieved a great deal of success in the greater society include the actress Olympia Dukakis, Maria Callas (who at one time in her operatic career was considered the world's leading soprano); Matina Souretis Horner, acclaimed psychologist and former president of Radcliffe College; Olympia Bouchles Snowe (R.-Maine), who in 1978 was the youngest woman elected to the House of Representatives; and Helen Boosalis, mayor of Lincoln, Nebraska, in the 1970s.

*Vasilikie Demos*

### Bibliography

Abbott, Grace. 1909. "A Study of the Greeks in Chicago." *American Journal of Sociology* (15):379–93.

Anderson, Joan. 1987. "Migration and Health: Perspectives on Immigrant Women." *Sociology of Health and Illness* 9:410–38.

Anthias, F. 1983. "Sexual Division and Ethnic Adaptation: The Case of Greek-Cypriot Women." In *One Way Ticket: Migration and Female Labor*, edited by A. Philzacklea, pp. 73–94. London: Routledge and Kegan Paul.

Bottomley, Gillian. 1979. *After the Odyssey: A Study of Greek Australians.* St. Lucia: University of Queensland Press.

Callinicos, Constance. 1990. *The American Aphrodite.* New York: Pella.

Chapin, Helen G. 1979. "From Sparta to Spencer Street: Greek Women in Hawaii." *Hawaiian Journal of History* 13:136–56.

———. 1991. "The Greeks of Hawaii." In *New Directions in Greek American Studies*, edited by Dan Georgakas and Charles C. Moskos, pp. 55–72. New York: Pella.

Demos, Vasilikie. 1989. "Maintenance and Loss of Traditional Gender Boundaries." *Journal of the Hellenic Diaspora* 15:77–93.

———. "Marital Choice, Gender and the Reproduction of Greek Ethnicity." In *Ethnic Women: A Multiple Status Reality.* New York: General Hall (forthcoming).

Kayser, Bernard, Kenneth Thompson, Roger Baternelle, and Basil Conkis. 1964. *Economic and Social Atlas of Greece.* Athens: National Statistical Service of Greece.

Kourvetaris, George A. 1983. "The Early and Late Greek Immigrant: A Comparative Sociological and Socio-Psychological Profile." *Hellenic/Etudes Helleniques* 1:23–32.

———. 1976. "The Greek American Family." In *Ethnic Families in America*, edited by Charles H. Mindel and Robert W. Habenstein, pp. 168–69. New York: Elsevier.

Labelle, Micheline, Deirdre Meintel, Genevieve Turcotte, and Marianne Kempineers. 1987. "A Comparative Study of the Conditions of Immigrant Working Women in Montreal." *Resources for Feminist Research* 16:34–35.

Moskos, Charles C. 1991. *Greek Americans: Struggle and Success.* New Brunswick, N.J.: Transaction.

Papanikolas, Helen Zeese. 1987. Aimilia-Georgios = *Emily-George.* Salt Lake City: University of Utah Press.

———. 1989. "Greek Immigrant Women in the Intermountain West." *Journal of the Hellenic Diaspora* 16:17–35.

Scourby, Alice. 1984. *The Greek Americans.* Boston: Twayne.

Topping, Eva Catafygioutu. 1987. *Holy Mothers of Orthodoxy.* Minneapolis, Minn.: Light and Life.

U.S. Bureau of the Census. 1973. *Census of the Population: 1970 Subject Reports.* Final Report PC(2)-1A, National Origin and Language. Washington, D.C.: U.S. Government Printing Office.

Veglery, Anna. "Differential Occupational Integration of Recent Greek Male and Female Immigrants to New York City." In *Ethnic Women: A Multiple Status Reality.* New York: General Hall (forthcoming).

Victorian Ethnic Affairs Commission. 1988. "Greek Women—Issues and Priorities." In *Aestraliotes Hellenes: Greeks in Australia*, edited by A. Kapadaris and A. Tamis, pp. 247–60. Melbourne: Seine.

## Women and Work in the South after the Civil War

Although slavery was officially abolished after the Civil War, a different form of "coerced labor" in the form of sharecropping developed, resembling in many aspects the former system. Agriculture with the emphasis on cotton cultivation was still predominant, which provided the developing textile industry with the necessary raw materials. Until recently, little research has been done concerning the issue of women and work in the South. Due to the concentration of blacks in the South, racial segregation was the main factor in determining employment possibilities for women, further limiting the already narrow choices posed by agriculture or the textile industry. A division of labor along gender lines put a "double burden" on women, making them responsible for the household, child care, and working in the fields or textile mills.

With the end of the Civil War in 1864 came the end of slavery. Black women now had more power over decisions of how to allocate their time; however, the character of the tasks women had to perform did not change substantially. Women's labor in the fields and cotton mills was still necessary for a family's survival. Although slavery was legally abolished, the economic system underlying the system of slavery was not altered. The plantation system, with its cultivation of cotton and tobacco, did not entirely disappear. A unique system of land ownership developed in its place. Tenant farming resembled, in many aspects, the former system of coerced labor under slavery. Men, women, and children were required to work in the fields.

At the turn of the century, labor markets throughout the U.S. were racially segregated, resulting in different employment possibilities for black and white women (Wright 1986). Because blacks were concentrated in the South until 1914, racial discrimination played a major role in keeping Southern labor markets segregated. In addition, compared to the industrial variety of the Northern states of the U.S., the economic structure of the South remained rather lopsided until the middle of the twentieth century, further limiting the employment possibilities for women. Furthermore, the labor force in the South was rather homogeneous, considering that the hiring of immigrant labor was not successful because of the Southerners' prejudices toward other nationalities (Hall-Dowd et al. 1987).

While the textile industry expanded after the Civil War, becoming the main employer for white women and children (U.S. Bureau of Labor Statistics 1916), black women were excluded from this industry because of racial segregation. Thus by 1900, 93.7 percent of white women worked in cotton mills compared with 1.2 percent of black women in all Southern states (U.S. Bureau of the Census 1907). Southern cotton mills developed certain characteristics that could be found only in the South, for example the family wage, a very paternalistic management philosophy, and hiring decisions based on race.

Despite the development of the cotton industry after the war, the South remained mainly agricultural. Former plantation owners still held large properties that had to be cultivated with cotton, tobacco, or sugar (Jones 1985). They rented their land to freedmen or impoverished white farmers who paid their rent in cash or in portions of their crop. Thus, sharecropping became the dominant form of rent arrangements (Ransom and Sutch 1977). Most farmers lacked the financial means to operate a farm independently and were dependent on credit and equipment provided by the landowner. Usually, these tenancy contracts were signed under the assumption that the farmer brought his whole family to work. Landowners and merchants, who were often the same person, profited from these contracts by asking for outrageous interest rates for the credit given. These high interest rates made it very difficult for families to break the cycle of debt despite the unpaid work of the wife and children (Ransom and Sutch 1977). Therefore, families moved frequently to change landowners and to start anew with the hope of finding better working conditions.

Although one of the immediate consequences of emancipation was that black women withdrew part of their labor force from the fields, their labor was still needed on the farms operated by their families. It was not unusual to see women plowing or hoeing the field, or picking cotton during the harvest season. However, black women had more freedom to allocate their time between child care, household chores, and agricultural work, a freedom they were not given during slavery. Considering that black women were forced to work eleven to thirteen hours a day during slavery, estimates show that their labor supply declined by one-quarter to one-third compared with the hours worked during slavery (Ransom and Sutch 1977). Black men and women often decided together how much time women spent in the fields of white planters. They preferred having women spend more time with their own families, and to limit the contact between white men and black women, which, during slavery, often resulted in physical and sexual abuse (Jones 1985). Black and white women worked in the fields, took care of the children, and performed domestic chores under difficult conditions. Most tenant households lacked many household items, possessing only basic cooking utensils or furniture. Children were considered economic assets, increasing the family's chance to get a piece of land to cultivate (Jones 1985). Black women frequently took care of the children of relatives or their neighbors, thus increasing their already "double burden." Inadequate housing conditions made the housekeeping tasks of women even more difficult; houses often had no water, overcrowding was common, the stove was often not more than a fire, and the walls of the houses often consisted of a single layer of boards (Lumpkin-Dupre et al. 1937). Thus, compared with their husbands, women worked both in the house and in the field.

In the period between 1865 and 1900, Northern and Southern entrepreneurs became interested in expanding the textile industry. The Southern cotton industry counted as the most important employer for women and children (U.S. Bureau of Labor Statistics 1916). The textile industry relied almost exclusively upon white labor, using the threat of employing black labor in the mills as a means to keep wages low (Stokes 1977). A particular characteristic of the Southern cotton mills was the family-wage system, which allowed employers to rely on multiple members of a single family but to pay them one family wage instead of individual wages (Wright 1986). Thus, women often worked side by side with their children and husbands. The mill villages of the South, including churches and schools, were often built and controlled by the mill owners. Families had to work in the mills, especially if housing or schooling was contingent on the labor-force participation of the whole family (U.S. Bureau of Labor Statistics 1916).

In addition to working in the mill, women were responsible for the domestic work and child care. A strict division of labor between the sexes could be found in this regard. Women also took in laundry or sewing tasks to supplement the family income (Hall-Dowd et al. 1987). Although many whites favored the idea of a woman's staying at home, economic necessity and the greater freedom for women connected with employment caused women to work in the mills. Single, divorced, and widowed white women and their children were welcomed as cheap labor, whereas black women were excluded from the mills. Single, divorced, or widowed black women frequently moved with their children to the Southern cities, finding employment as domestic servants, laundresses, cooks, or sometimes in the tobacco or oyster industry (Jones 1985). However, domestic service offered the most employment possibilities for black women. For example, in 1900 in North Carolina 75.9 percent of the 21,395 servants and waitresses were black women. In South Carolina, 93.5 percent of all servants and waitresses were black, as were 93.8 percent in Mississippi, 81.5 percent in Louisiana, and 92.2 percent in Georgia (U.S. Bureau of the Census 1907). Domestic service in the South closely resembled the former slave-mistress relationship, exposing black women to the racism of their white mistresses (Jones 1985). However, with emancipation black women refused to live in the houses of their employers and left in the evenings to stay with their families.

In summary, after the Civil War the South showed many characteristics that could not be found in other regions of the U.S. While at the turn of the century labor markets throughout the U.S. were racially segregated, employment decisions based on race became especially important in the South, where blacks were concentrated until 1914. A limited job structure and racial prejudice limited the employment possibilities for blacks, channeling black women—outside of sharecropping—into domestic or laundry services. The reliance on white labor in the cotton mills was predominant until the 1960s, and although blacks were not employed until then in large numbers, employers used them as a threat to keep wages low (Stokes 1977). Although white families could easily find employment in textile mills, compared with Northern mills at the time, Southern textile mills frequently controlled the social, moral, and intellectual development of their workers by controlling education, housing, and even churches (U.S. Bureau of Labor Statistics 1916). A strict division of labor by gender put a double burden on the women—household chores and field or mill work—and child care had often to be performed under conditions of extreme poverty.

*Sabine Rieble*

## Bibliography

Hall-Dowd Jaquelyn, James Leloudis, Robert Korstadt, Mary Murphy, Lu Ann Jones, and Christopher B. Daly. 1987. *Like a Family. The Making of a Southern Cotton Mill World*. Chapel Hill and London: University of North Carolina Press.

Jones, Jaqueline. 1985. *Labor of Love, Labor of Sorrow*. New York: Basic Books.

Katzman, David M. 1978. *Seven Days a Week*. New York: Oxford University Press.

Lumpkin-Dupre, Katherine, and Dorothy Wolff Douglas. 1937. *Child Workers in America*. New York: McBride.

Ransom, Roger L., and Richard Sutch. 1977. *One Kind of Freedom*. Cambridge: Cambridge University Press.

Stokes, Allen Heath, Jr. 1977. "Black and White Labor and the Development of the Southern Textile Industry, 1880–1920." Ph.D. dissertation, University of South Carolina.

U.S. Bureau of the Census. 1907. *Statistics of Women at Work*. Washington, D.C.: Government Printing Office.

U.S. Bureau of Labor Statistics, Bulletin 175. 1916. *Summary of the Report of the Conditions of Women and Child Wage Earners in the U.S.* Washington, D.C.: Government Printing Office.

Wright, Gavin. 1986. *Old South. New South*. New York: Basic Books.

## Women in the Civil Rights Movement

Typically, our conception of work is limited to paid employment and ignores "unpaid work" or volunteer work. This narrow view of work often leads us to downplay the achievements of women and their involvement in social movements. The civil rights movement of the 1950s and 1960s serves as an example in which the participation of women was crucial to success but is generally ignored.

Most research suggests that civil rights movement activities were largely organized and executed by black and white men. Even those organizations that were supportive of women's participation allegedly assigned women to clerical work and excluded them from the decision-making process (McAdam 1988; Rothchild 1982). Contrary to these myths, black and white women belonged to a variety of organizations, in which they held positions of varying importance and visibility (Crawford et al. 1990). In organizations controlled by men (such as the NAACP or the Southern Christian Leadership Conference [SCLC]), women were usually excluded from influential positions; however, they did the majority of the bureaucratic and organizational footwork (Morris 1984). On the other hand, projects administered by the Student Nonviolent Coordinating Committee (SNCC) or the Congress of Racial Equality (CORE), such as the Citizenship and Freedom Schools or other local projects, were frequently run by women (Carson 1981; Crawford et al. 1990; Robinson 1987).

Preexisting "movement halfway houses" (Morris 1984) also provided an important training ground for movement leaders. Such halfway houses included the Southern Conference Education Fund (which produced Anne Braden, a white activist), and the Highlander Folk School, which, starting in the 1940s, held interracial training seminars on how to challenge segregation. Among others, Septima Poinsette Clark (SCLC and NAACP activist who designed the Citizenship School program) and Rosa Parks (NAACP activist whose arrest triggered the Montgomery bus boycott in 1955) attended Highlander's training seminars (Clark 1986). Local civic and political groups also produced leaders such as Jo Ann Robinson, an instrumental organizer of the Montgomery bus boycott and leader of a women's group (Montgomery Improvement Association) and Daisy Bates, who led the Arkansas NAACP chapter during desegregation efforts in Little Rock. SCLC's citizenship schools in turn trained future civil rights leaders such as Fannie Lou Hamer, who later on became one of the Mississippi Freedom Party's leaders (Crawford et al. 1990; McAdam 1988; Robinson 1987).

To summarize, black and white women were active in virtually all civil rights movement organizations and halfway houses. But the scope of their activities was more diverse (and the division of labor less determined by gendered) in the SNCC than in other organizations (CORE, SCLC, NAACP, Black Panthers). Black and white women typically held different positions in civil rights movement organizations.

Most black women activists were directly involved in community work (voter registration) or coordinated other grass-roots efforts, especially educational programs, which have historically been an important avenue for black women's social activism. For instance, Dorothy Cotton and Septima Clark were in charge of SCLC's Citizenship Education programs, which existed throughout the South. Ella Baker was instrumental in founding the SCLC in 1957 but was soon frustrated by its hierarchical and male-dominated structure. Consequently, she became the intellectual founder of SNCC in 1960. SNCC operated Freedom Schools throughout the South to teach black citizens how to pass voter registration tests (Clark 1986; Morris 1984; Robinson 1987).

In addition to voter education, SNCC organized voter registration drives. Ruby D.S. Robinson and Diane N. Bevel occupied important posts in SNCC from its initiation. Bevel organized the famous "freedom rides" in 1961, and Robinson, executive secretary of SNCC in 1966, was highly critical of Stokely Carmichael's leadership. Due to its decentralized structure, SNCC had few executive positions, most of which were held by black men (Carson 1981; McAdam 1988). But during the 1964 "freedom summer," the majority of SNCC activists and volunteers worked as voter registrars or freedom school teachers, or organized and mobilized local communities. In SNCC, black and white women alike held teaching jobs, but black women also held other community positions and even leadership positions. Men typically were voter registrars or held executive positions. White women generally worked as freedom school teachers or held clerical positions as volunteers (McAdam 1988; Rothchild 1982).

Most white women did not enter the movement until the "freedom summer" of 1964, which also explains their concentration in SNCC and in local Mississippi projects administered by SNCC and CORE. They were new in the movement and their participation was usually temporary and limited to a few summer months. In addition, most of them were from the North and may have had skills that influenced their job assignments in SNCC projects (McAdam 1988). These individual-level factors of lack of seniority, lack of local ties, and having different work skills because of their college backgrounds, may be part of the reason why white women were assigned to jobs dealing with organizational maintenance, rather than to leadership or community positions involving the political organization and mobilization of the community (Evans 1976; McAdam 1988).

In sum, women activists in all civil rights movement organizations, including SNCC, were usually responsible for activities that contributed to organizational maintenance (coordination of activities, fund-raising, book keeping, and so forth), and men were usually responsible for executive and leadership positions. But women and men alike—especially in SNCC—organized and mobilized the indigenous black population.

Women's volunteer contributions, of course, have not been limited to the civil rights movement. Many women's rights activists of the 1960s and 1970s started as volunteers in the civil rights movement and continued their volunteerism in the 1970s women's rights movement. Moreover, volunteers have played an important role in galvanizing support for a variety of issues, such as the focus of women's groups on reproductive rights, economic and political issues (ERA, comparable worth, gender-related violence), and other social movements throughout the 1980s and 1990s.

*Regina E. Werum*

## Bibliography

Blumberg, Rhoda. 1980. "Careers of Women Civil Rights Activists." *Journal of Sociology and Social Welfare* 75:708–29.

Carson, C. 1981. *In Struggle: SNCC and the Black Awakening of the 1960s*. Cambridge: Harvard University Press.

Clark, S.P. 1986. *Ready from Within: Septima Clark and the Civil Rights Movement*. Navarro, Calif.: Wild Tree.

Crawford, V., et al., 1990. *Women in the Civil Rights Movement: Trailblazers and Torchbearers, 1941–1965*. Brooklyn, N.Y.: Carlson.

Evans, S. 1976. *Personal Politics*. New York: Knopf.

King, M. 1987. *Freedom Song: A Personal Story of the 1960s Civil Rights Movement*. New York: Morrow.

McAdam, D. 1988. *Freedom Summer*. New York: Oxford University Press.

Morris A. 1984. *The Origins of the Civil Rights Movement*. New York: Free Press.

Raines, Howell. 1977. *My Soul Is Rested: Movement Days in the Deep South Remembered*. New York: Putnam.

Robinson, J.A. 1987. *The Montgomery Bus Boycott and the Women Who Started It: The Memoir of Jo Ann Robinson*. Knoxville: University of Tennessee Press.

Rothchild, M. 1982. *A Case of Black and White: Northern Volunteers and the Southern Freedom Summers, 1964–1965*. Westport, Conn.: Greenwood.

Swift, Jeannine. 1991. *Dream and Reality: The Modern Black Struggle for Freedom and Equality*. New York: Greenwood.

# Economic Aspects of Women's Labor-Force Participation

## Gender and Earnings

Despite major increases in women's labor-force participation, the gap between men's and women's earnings remained relatively constant for three decades (1950 to 1980), with women employed full time earning only about 60 cents for every dollar earned by men employed full time. Over the last decade, the earnings gap narrowed gradually. Current estimates suggest that women earn about 72 percent of the wage rate of men. The size of the earnings gap indicates that women have significantly less purchasing power than men, and results in patterned differences in the material standard of living of women and men. The gender gap in pay contributes to a phenomenon referred to as the feminization of poverty. Estimates indicate that well over a third of the female-headed, single-parent families today have incomes below the poverty line. Earnings are not only important for their ability to command goods and services—they are also key determinants of other valued social rewards such as prestige and power. For this reason, the gender gap in earnings is a critical dimension of gender inequality.

In recent years, much empirical work in the social sciences has been devoted to explaining differences in earnings between the sexes (Marini 1988). Human-capital research in economics and status-attainment research in sociology have focused on productivity-related differences between individual women and men (such as level and type of education, experience, effort, hours worked) and assessed their contribution to the gender gap in pay. Because these perspectives emphasize worker characteristics assumed to be related to productivity, they can be classified as supply-side approaches to explaining the earnings gap between women and men. These explanations deemphasize the role of structural factors in the wage determination process and suggest instead that individuals are responsible for their wage level. Human-capital theorists attempt to explain pay differences between the sexes in terms of the voluntary choices of women. They argue that the gender-based division of labor in the home results in women intentionally limiting their human capital, and as a result their earning power (Mincer and Polachek 1974).

Research suggests that supply-side (human-capital) variables account for no more than 50 percent of the differences in earnings between men and women (Corcoran et al. 1984). Differences between women and men in terms of educational attainment and work experience have eroded over the last several decades. Today women and men have comparable levels of educational attainment and women spend far fewer years out of the labor force as a result of child-rearing, yet these changes have done little to narrow the gap in earnings. Supply-side explanations of the gender gap in earnings have become less influential as the human-capital investments of men and women have become more similar.

Discriminatory practices in the labor market also contribute to the gender gap in earnings. Studies focusing on discrimination as the key explanatory variable in understanding the wage gap are classified as demand-side explanations. These studies attempt to quantify the effect of labor-market discrimination on wages utilizing a "residual approach." This involves estimating, via multiple regression, the proportion of the gender gap in pay that is the result of the productivity-related characteristics of men and women workers, and allocating the residual to discrimination. This approach can be problematic in that the failure to specify and appropriately measure all of the productivity-related variables will result in overestimating the effect of discrimination on wages. Research suggests that as much as 50 percent of the earnings gap may be attributed to discrimination. Due to problems associated with the residual approach however, caution should be taken when drawing conclusions about the link between discrimination and differences in earnings between men and women.

Gender-segregated employment patterns can also be linked to differences in earnings between the sexes (England 1992). Occupational segregation refers to the concentration of women and men in different occupations that are predominantly of a single sex. Just as the gender gap in pay has remained relatively stable for decades, so has the overall degree of occupational segregation. The majority of women work in a small number of occupations, particularly in occupations in which the workers are predominantly women. These occupations tend to be lower paying than male-dominated occupations. In fact, research has shown that the higher the percentage of women in an occupation, the lower the average wage. The gender composition of jobs often appears to have an effect of wage level, even after all relevant productivity-related characteristics have been controlled for. Research indicates that more than a third of the gap in earnings between men and women is associated with differences in their occupational distributions (Treiman and Hartmann 1981).

An important question arises when examining the contribution of gender segregation in the workplace to the earnings gap: Why are occupations dominated by women paid at lower rates than occupations dominated by men? One explanation is that women cluster in sex-typed occupations as a result of gender-role socialization and discrimination, resulting in an artificially high supply of workers for such occupations. According to the laws of supply and demand, the oversupply of workers then results in lower wages. Another possible explanation for the lower wages associated with traditional women's occupations is the presence of "comparable worth discrimination." This form of discrimination occurs when the gender of the average incumbent of an occupation is taken into consideration when setting wage rates (England and Dunn 1988). Proponents of comparable worth legislation argue that wage hierarchies are not objectively determined on the basis of skill level, experience, and other relevant factors, but rather that gender biases influence the development of pay scales (England 1992). Comparable worth legislation would require that job evaluations be conducted to measure the intrinsic worth of jobs in order to eliminate the systematic undervaluing of work typically performed by women.

A final explanation of wage differentials between the sexes is offered by the structuralist perspective, which borrows heavily from theories of economic and labor-market segmentation (Coverman 1988). These theories focus on how the structure of labor markets may affect men's and women's earnings. Specific characteristics of firms and markets as well as industrial structures have been found to affect the distribution of rewards to women and men. Most structuralist theories conceptualize a dual economy, consisting of an advantaged and a disadvantaged segment. The presence or absence of economic advantage is thought to affect the level of wages paid by firms. Some research suggests that women are concentrated in the disadvantaged industries where wages are lower, and that a part of the gender gap in pay is the direct result of this differential placement of men and women across industries.

The gender gap in earnings serves as an indicator of the extent and persistence of gender inequality in the workplace. Gender stratification theorists suggest that women's economic role in society is a primary determinant of their overall status. Women's economic role is linked to the power and status they have in both the family and the public sector. The gap in earnings between men and women, then, is considered by many sociologists to offer much insight into the overall degree of inequality between the sexes. Explanations of differentials between the earnings of men and women are necessary in order to develop policies to enhance women's overall status and reduce the level of gender inequality.

*Dana Dunn*

## Bibliography

Corcoran, M., G.J. Duncan, and M. Ponza. 1984. "Work Experience, Job Segregation, and Wages." In *Sex Segregation in the Workplace: Trends, Explanations and Remedies*, edited by B.F. Reskin, pp. 171–91. Washington, D.C.: National Academy.

Coverman, Shelley. 1988. "Sociological Explanations of the Male-Female Wage Gap: Individualist and Structuralist Theories." In *Women Working: Theories and Facts in Perspective*, edited by Ann H. Stromberg and Shirley Harkess, pp. 101–15. Mountainview, Calif.: Mayfield.

England, Paula. 1992. *Comparable Worth: Theories and Evidence*. New York: Aldine De Gruyter.

England, Paula, and Dana Dunn. 1988. "Evaluating Work and Comparable Worth." *Annual Review of Sociology* 14:227–48.

England, Paula, George Farkas, Barbara Stanek Kilbourne, and Thomas Dou. 1988. "Explaining Occupational Segregation and Wages: Findings from a Model with Fixed Effects." *American Sociological Review* 53:544–58.

Kilbourne, Barbara Stanek, Paula England, and Dorthea Weir. 1990. "Skill, Compensating Differentials, and Gender Bias in Occupational Wage Determination." Paper presented at the annual meeting of the American Sociological Association. Washington, D.C.

Marini, Margaret Mooney. 1988. "Sex Differences in Earnings in the United States." *Annual Review of Sociology* 15:343–80.

Mincer, J., and S. Polachek. 1974. "Family Investments in Human Capital: Earnings of Women." *Journal of Political Economy* 82:76–108.

Stevenson, Mary Huff. 1988. "Some Economic Approaches to the Persistence of Wage Differences between Men and Women." In *Women Working: Theories and Facts in Perspective*, edited by Ann H. Stromberg and Shirley Harkess, pp. 87–100. Mountainview, Calif.: Mayfield.

Treiman, D.J., and H.I. Hartmann. 1981. *Women, Work and Wages: Equal Pay for Jobs of Equal Value*. Washington, D.C.: National Academy.

Ward, K.B., and C.W. Mueller. 1985. "Sex Differences in Earnings: The Influence of Industrial Sector, Authority Hierarchy, and Human Capital Variables." *Work and Occupations* 12:437–63.

## Income Inequality

Surveys of recent trends and historical patterns of income distribution reveal that women on average still earn less than men. From 1955 to 1990 the earnings of women working full time increased only a few percentage points, as income rose from 64 to 67 percent of male wages. Researchers addressing the persistence of this income gap disagree about the status of gender as a variable in income determination models. Traditional economic-based explanations view any difference between men's and women's income as a consequence of gender-neutral mechanisms (Becker 1975; Gordon et al. 1982; Wright 1979). Feminists posit an alternative that considers gender's effect on income independent of and in interaction with other variables (Coverman 1983; Hartmann 1981; Kessler-Harris 1990).

Traditional explanations of income inequality have emphasized either individual or structural characteristics (Marini 1989). The individual income determination models (that is, human capital, status attainment, culture/socialization) attribute the primary source of income inequality to individual supply-side attributes such as unequal endowments (skills) (Becker 1975). Such models explain gender differences in terms of the different investment choices men and women make in order to maximize their respective comparative advantages: Men invest mainly in human capital that raises their market efficiency and thereby yields higher returns to paid employment; women invest mainly in human capital that raises household efficiency, especially the bearing and rearing of children. Women earn less than men because they acquire less human capital (that is, less skill, education, and labor market experience) or choose jobs that do not interfere with domestic and child-care labor and, as a result, pay less than men's jobs (part-time work, or jobs that allow intermittent attachment) (Polachek 1981).

Shifting the emphasis to demand-side and class characteristics of production, structural-determination models (that is, dual economy, segmented labor market, and class models) derive income from the differentiation of conditions in economic sectors (competitive or monopoly economic sectors), labor markets (primary or secondary labor market), or class positions (worker or managerial class) (Gordon et al. 1982; Wright 1979). The structural model explains income differences between men and women as the consequence of women's concentration in the lower-paying subordinate positions of the competitive economic sector (that is, a large number of firms competing for market shares), the secondary labor market (low wages, job insecurity, truncated job ladders), or the working class. This distribution may be the result of either women's choice to balance domestic and child-care responsibilities with employment demands or employers' exploitation of the gender-based sexual division of labor. Most of these models remain silent on the mechanisms by which women and men get distributed into different structural positions.

Many feminists reject the traditional models' assumptions that markets or job structures operate gender-neutrally, and that income inequality can be explained solely by individual differences between men and women. Instead, gender is viewed as a socially constructed process that is reproduced through multiple institutions. Men and women are socialized and segregated into a variety of tasks labeled either masculine or feminine, where masculinity receives greater social rewards than femininity. Such an approach seeks to integrate ideological (that is, gender socialization, use of gender stereotypes, gendered organizations) and relational dynamics (that is, relational struggles between men and women at home, between men and women at work, and between employers-men-women at work) to account for the gender-based division of labor both in the workplace and in the household. Such gender dynamics affect the income determination process and create the different income profiles for men and women.

While feminist frameworks share a use of feminism as a mode of analysis, a method of approaching life and politics, and a way of asking questions and searching for answers, they emphasize different ways of examining as well as different aspects of women's oppression. Feminist research on income inequality focuses on either supply-side characteristics (human capital or domestic labor), demand-side characteristics (labor-market segmentation or occupational segregation), or both (dual-systems analyses). A number of feminists have tested and found little empirical support for the individual determination model's assumption that income inequality is caused by women's lower human capital and choice of jobs. For example, after controlling for hours worked, the human capital differences between men and women largely become nonsignificant (England 1984), yet women continue to earn less than men. These studies identify other weaknesses inherent to the human-capital model by showing the disparity between the human-capital model's expectations and the conditions of employment. The literature points out that men receive higher starting salaries than women; that single and married women work in a similar array of jobs; that female-concentrated jobs exhibit depreciation time horizons identical to those in male-concentrated jobs; and that women who spend a long time out of the labor force are no more likely than continuously attached women to be employed in female-concentrated occupations (England et al. 1988).

Several studies also have estimated the importance of the gender division of labor in the household on men and women workers' economic attainment (Calasanti and Bailey 1991; Coverman 1983). Women's involvement in the family is incompatible with the demands of market work, especially the emphasis of firms on profit maximization and competition that mandate a reward structure promoting continuous employment and long and relatively inflexible working hours. Women's responsibility for household labor influences the number of hours worked in wage-labor and the position in occupations, both of which reduce women's income. Generally, women lose in income as a result of their gender-role assignment and participation in domestic labor more than men, who have little or no such gender role.

These studies highlight the importance of improving measures of household labor to include factors such as the level of responsibility, control over resources, and the emotional labor performed by women. As Coverman suggests, most indicators of domestic labor time result in a conservative estimate of women's work load because they leave out intangibles like maintenance of family members' well-being, consumption, and status production. For these studies, the principal mechanism reducing women's income is the time burden of domestic labor on women's labor-force participation. Such a focus, however, ignores male domination as the basis for an unequal gender division of labor in the household and in the wage-labor force.

Feminists adopting a structural perspective attribute the lower wages earned by women to either a sex-segregated labor market in which women have become relegated to secondary labor-market positions (for example, low wages, job insecurity, truncated job ladders) (Barron and Norris 1976) or a sex-segregated occupational structure in which women have been restricted to jobs at the lower end of the occupational hierarchy (such as para-professionals, clerical workers, sales) (Reskin and Hartmann 1986). In the secondary labor market, the employer hires women either because women make up a reserve army of labor that can be pulled into production or pushed out depending on fluctuations of the market, or because women possess personal characteristics (such as dispensability, social differentiation, low interest in acquiring on-the-job training, and lack of solidarity) desired by secondary labor market employers. Consequently, women are concentrated in lower-paying jobs that offer little upward mobility, whereas men are concentrated in higher-paying jobs with greater opportunities, creating an income gap.

A slightly different feminist structural approach links the different earning capacities between men and women workers to occupational sex-segregation. As such, the unit of analysis shifts from the larger units of labor-market segments to the smaller units of occupational categories. The segregation of men and women into different occupations creates an income gap because of the lower wage structures in female-typed occupations, compared with male-typed occupations. Women not only experience an economic disadvantage because of the segregation across (horizontal segregation) occupations, but they also earn less than men within (vertical segregation) every occupational category for full-time wage workers. Adding part-time work to these figures would further skew the income gap, given that women perform the bulk of part-time work (Beechey 1987). These feminist structural models explicitly consider the interaction between household and employer practices, while the structural model (discussed above) almost exclusively focuses on economic conditions facing employers and workers.

Other feminists criticize labor-market studies (segmented labor market and occupational segregation) for focusing on characteristics of individuals or of jobs, examining outcomes rather than the process of filling economic positions (Beechey 1987), and failing to explain the gender division of labor. Recent studies examine and identify factors facilitating the gender differentiation of this filling process, including factors such as employers, unions, ideologies, and workers—both individually and collectively—through which women's work is devalued (Acker 1988; Cockburn 1991). For example, studies suggest that employers and recruiting personnel treat women differently than men in job recruitment and placement (Bills 1990). The resulting gender segregation of this filling process is further magnified by differential wage structures, which define women's work as less skilled than men's. These studies identify a male bias in the control over and social definition of skill (Cockburn 1991; Gottfried 1992).

Theoretically, some feminists posit a dual-systems analysis, which specifies multiple bases and intersecting systems of oppression, particularly capitalist and patriarchal systems, to explain income inequality by gender. This approach identifies patriarchal social relations within the household as the major constraint on women's options in the capitalist economy (Hartmann 1981). Men attempt to preserve their control over women's labor power in the household by reinforcing the unequal gender division of labor within the home and at work. These constraints may be ideological (the assumption of a male breadwinner) or material (the trade-off between home requirements and employment opportunities, sexual harassment and violence, exclusionary practices by employers and male workers, and so forth). Dual-systems analyses conclude that to reduce the relationship to women's direct involvement in wage labor would miss the importance of the indirect effect of women's dependence on the distribution of resources and power between men and women.

At issue in dual-systems analyses is how the asymmetrical sexual division of labor in the household disadvantages women in the economy. Gender relations should not be reduced to a technical efficiency argument in which the budgeting of time becomes the central mechanism constraining women's economic activity in the wage-labor force. Further, the dual-systems analysis approach criticizes class analysis for failing to explain the gender composition of classes, and instead argues that the configuration of the family, dependence on men, and domestic labor mediates women's relationship to the class structure. Yet the dual-systems analysis privileges the family and household as the primary site of gender formation. In doing so, it views gender as analytically outside of other systems and impinging on those systems only at certain points rather than as being a constitutive element of economic processes and relations (Acker 1988). A more complete explanation should include ideological and relational dynamics that reproduce gender at many institutional levels and settings, and result in a gender division of labor both in the economy and in the home. This integrated approach seeks to move beyond compensatory or unidimensional analyses of women's oppression by shifting to a multifocal lens through which new insights can come to light.

*Heidi Gottfried*
*David Wright*

## Bibliography

Acker, Joan. 1988. "Class, Gender and the Relations of Distribution." *Signs: Journal of Women in Culture and Society* 13:473–97.

Barron, R., and G. Norris. 1976. "Sexual Divisions and the Dual Labor Market." In *Dependence and Exploitation in Work and Marriage*, edited by D. Barker and S. Allen. London: Longman.

Becker, G. 1975. *Human Capital: A Theoretical and Empirical Analysis, with Special Reference to Education*. 2nd ed. New York: National Bureau of Economic Research.

Beechey, V. 1987. *Unequal Work*. London: Verso.

Bills, D. 1990 "Employer's Use of Hob History Data for Making Hiring Decisions: A Fuller Specification of Job Assignment and Status Attainment." *Sociological Quarterly* 31:23–36.

Calasanti, T., and C. Bailey. 1991. "Gender Inequality and the Division of Household Labor in the United States and Sweden: A Socialist-Feminist Approach." *Social Problems* 38:34–53.

Cockburn, C. 1991. *In the Way of Women: Men's Resistance to Sex Equality in Organizations*. Ithaca, N.Y.: ILR.

Coverman, S. 1983. "Gender, Domestic Labor Time and Wage Inequality." *American Sociological Review* 48:623–37.

England, P. 1984. "Wage Appreciation and Depreciation: A Test of Neoclassical Economic Explanations of Occupational Sex Segregation." *Social Forces* 62:726–49.

England, P., G. Farkas, B. Kilbourne, and T. Dou. 1988. "Explaining Occupational Sex Segregation and Wages: Findings from a Model with Fixed Effects." *American Sociological Review* 53:544–58.

Gordon, D., Edwards, R., and M. Reich. 1982. *Segmented Work, Divided Workers: The Historical Transformation of Labor in the United States*. New York: Cambridge University Press.

Gottfried, H. 1992. "The Impact of Skill on Union Membership: Rethinking Gender Differences." *Sociological Quarterly* 33:99–114.

Hartmann, H. 1981. "The Family as the Locus of Gender, Class and Political Struggles: The Example of Housework." *Signs* 6:366–94.

Kessler-Harris, A. 1990. *A Woman's Wage: Historical Meanings and Social Consequences*. Lexington, Ky.: University of Kentucky Press.

Marini, M. 1989. "Sex Differences in Earnings in the United States." *Annual Review of Sociology* 15:343–80.

Polachek, S. 1981. "Occupational Self-Selection: A Human Capital Approach to Sex Differences in Occupational Structure." *Review of Economics and Statistics* 63:60–69.

Reskin, B., and Hartmann, H., eds. 1986. *Women's Work, Men's Work: Sex Segregation on the Job*. Washington, D.C.: National Academy.

Wright, E.O. 1979. *Class Structure and Income Determination*. New York: Academic.

## Occupational Skill, Gender, and Earnings

Women incur a double disadvantage in paid work. This double reduction in women's earnings results, in part, from the concentration of women into "female" occupations. Predominantly female occupations often require a substantial amount of social/nurturant skill, a requirement that is not necessarily recognized as skill by many employers. In fact, occupational requirements for social/nurturant skill are inversely related to earnings. Likewise, the higher the percentage of females employed in an occupation, the lower the wages. These two occupational attributes explain approximately 16 percent of the gender earnings gap.

Female labor-force participation has increased dramatically throughout the last thirty years. Since 1980, more than half of all women over sixteen years of age have been either working for pay or seeking such work. Occupational distribution patterns for women greatly differ from those of men during comparable time periods. Although increasing numbers of women began to penetrate predominantly male occupations in the 1970s and the 1980s, sex segregation proved quite resistant to change. According to one index of occupational segregation, roughly 40 percent of all working women would need to change occupations to achieve an occupational distribution similar to that of men (Jacobs 1989). Compared with predominantly male jobs, predominantly female occupations often require a different set of skills or subject workers to a different set of on-the-job conditions.

Much of the gender gap in earnings is a direct consequence of occupational sex segregation. Women's earnings are subjected to a double reduction. Women lose earnings indirectly through a devaluation of the types of skills associated with female jobs, particularly social/nurturant skill. In addition, they lose earnings through the perception that women, generally perceived as secondary wage earners, deserve lower earnings, so that any job filled primarily by women is assigned a wage lower than those of men's jobs requiring comparable amounts of education and skill.

### Gender Differences in Demands for Occupational Skill

Current research (Kilbourne et al. 1990) shows that occupations containing mostly women provide less on-the-job training than is provided in "men's" occupations (see also England et al. 1982). The more women employed in an occupation, the less likely it is that the occupation involves hazardous or onerous working conditions. On the other hand, predominantly female occupations require more demands for social/nurturant skill. Even women working in occupations requiring high levels of cognitive or physical skill are still required to bring relatively higher levels of social/nurturant skill to their jobs. (For a more complete description of these findings, see Kilbourne et al. 1990; England et al. 1982.)

What is a social/nurturant skill? This skill entails the ability to deal with people, specifically, the ability to deal with one's own emotions in order to effectively deal with the behavior and feelings of other people. Hochschild (1983) calls this skill emotional labor. Although Hochschild focuses primarily on flight attendants, this skill is evident in many "women's" occupations. For example, it is required of teachers, counselors, and social workers, many of whom are women.

Why are women disproportionately concentrated in occupations requiring social/nurturant skill? The disparity results from women's choices and from discriminatory constraints women face. Employers slot women into jobs requiring interpersonal skills to capitalize on the way sex role socialization hones these skills in women (Hochschild 1983; Steinberg 1990). Women's access to predominantly male occupations is often subtly (or not so subtly) barred (Reskin and Roos 1990) by male workers. There is also evidence that sex-role socialization results in a propensity for women to select jobs requiring extensive interpersonal contact (Marini and Brinton 1984).

## Social/Nurturant Skill and Earnings

Social/nurturant skill not only goes unrewarded, but workers in occupations that require high levels of this skill actually suffer a wage penalty. Higher demand for social/nurturant skill in an occupation lowers wages. These negative effects persist even after statistically netting out the direct bias resulting from the percentage of women in an occupation and controlling for cognitive and physical skill (Kilbourne et al. 1990). (For similar findings, see Steinberg 1990; Steinberg et al. 1984.) Kilbourne et al. (1990) find that the concentration of women in occupations that require social/nurturant skill, and the wage penalty that accompanies this skill, explain approximately 6 percent of the gender gap in earnings.

Cultural feminist theory offers a compelling explanation for the indirect sort of gender bias seen in the devaluation of social/nurturant skill. Traditional Western thought divides activities into two spheres. Activities in the male sphere are seen as rational, intellectual, autonomous, and active. Activities in the female sphere are considered emotional, intuitive, connected, and reactive. Social/nurturant skill clearly falls into the latter sphere. This female sphere is seen as more connected with nature (largely because of women's role in biological reproduction) in a metaphysics that valorizes rationality and devalues nature. As long as social/nurturant skill is considered natural, it is not considered a skill. A reevaluation of the concept of skill is necessary if we are to move toward closing the wage gap between men and women workers.

## Percentage of Female Workers and Earnings

The higher the percentage of women in an occupation, the lower the wages in that occupation. This effect persists despite statistical controls for occupational skill demands and working conditions (England et al. 1988; Kilbourne et al. 1990). Kilbourne et al. (1990) find that the negative relationship between the percentage of women in an occupation and wages explains roughly 10 percent of the gender gap in earnings. Perceptions of appropriate gender roles result in this type of direct gender bias in earnings. Historical research shows that when the first "family wages" were paid in the early 1900s, women were not seen as entitled to these wages (May 1987), even if they were unattached to a capable male breadwinner. Men were, and still are, perceived as deserving sufficiently higher wages to support their families. This idea persists despite dramatic changes in both female labor-force participation and in household structure. Thus, more than a million women are currently the sole support of children (Reskin 1988) and could certainly use a "family wage." Women are also perceived as exerting less effort at, or being less committed to, paid work because of their responsibilities to home and family. Despite evidence that women work just as hard as men and are just as committed to their jobs (Bielby and Bielby 1984), the biased perception that women deserve less reward remains, and is reflected in lower wages in predominantly female occupations.

## Conclusions

In sum, women's earnings suffer from gender bias. One type of bias is direct: If a job is predominantly female, employers provide low wages. A second type of bias is indirect, through a devaluation of social/nurturant skill required in many predominantly female occupations. Combined, both types of gender bias explain 16 percent of the gender earnings gap. These issues raised by campaigns for "comparable worth" or "pay equity" are unlikely to go away, and will likely take on increased importance in the future. Shifts toward a postindustrial economy mean more employment in jobs requiring social/nurturant skill. A concentration of women in these new, low-wage jobs will exacerbate increasing income inequality in this country, with women and children once again the losers.

> *Barbara Stanek Kilbourne*
> *Paula England*

## Bibliography

Bielby, Denise D., and William T. Bielby. 1988. "She Works Hard for Her Money: Household Responsibilities and the Allocation of Work Effect." *American Journal of Sociology* 93:1031–59.

Bielby, Denise D., and William T. Bielby. 1984. "Work Commitment, Sex Role Attitudes, and Women's Employment." *American Sociological Review* 49:234–47.

England, Paula, Marilyn Chassie, and Linda McCormack. 1982. "Skill Demands and Earnings in Female and Male Occupations." *Sociology and Social Research* 66:147–68.

England, Paula, George Farkas, Barbara Stanek Kilbourne, and Thomas Dou. 1988. "Explaining Occupational Sex Segregation and Wages: Findings from a Model with Fixed Effects." *American Sociological Review* 53:544–58.

Hochschild, Arlie. 1983. *The Managed Heart: Commercialization of Human Feelings.* Berkeley: University of California Press.

Jacobs, Jerry. 1989. *Revolving Doors: Sex Segregation and Women's Careers.* Stanford: Stanford University Press.

Kilbourne, Barbara Stanek, Paula England, and Dorthea Weir. 1990. "Skill, Compensating Differentials, and Gender Bias in Occupational Wage Determination." Paper presented at the 1990 annual meeting of the American Sociological Association, Washington, D.C.

Marini, Margaret M., and Mary C. Brinton. 1984. "Sex Typing in Occupational Socialization." In *Sex Segregation in the Workplace: Trends, Explanations and Remedies,* edited by Barbara F. Reskin, pp. 192–232. Washington, D.C.: National Academy.

May, Martha. 1987. "The Historical Problem of the Family Wage: The Ford Motor Company and the Five-Dollar Day." In *Families and Work,* edited by Naomi Gerstel and Harriet Gross, pp. 111–31. Philadelphia: Temple University Press.

Reskin, Barbara F. 1988. "Bringing the Men Back in: Sex Differentiation and the Devaluation of Women's Work." *Gender and Society* 2:58–81.

Reskin, Barbara F., and Patricia A. Roos. 1990. *Job Queues, Gender Queues: Explaining Women's Inroads into Male Occupations*. Philadelphia: Temple University Press.

Steinberg, Ronnie J. 1990. "The Social Construction of Skill: Gender, Power, and Comparable Worth." *Work and Occupations* 17:449–82.

Steinberg, Ronnie J., Lois Haignere, Carol Possin, Donald Treiman, and Cynthia Chertos. 1984. *The New York State Pay Equity Study: A Research Report*. Albany, N.Y.: Center for Women in Government.

## Gender and Race Impacts on Occupational Segregation, Prestige, and Earnings

How do race and gender affect people's fates in the American labor force? The effects of gender on various occupational characteristics are widely discussed (Blumberg 1978; England and McCreamy 1987; Glenn 1987; Marini 1989; Sokoloff 1987). Of special interest are three classic focuses of labor-force analysis: segregation, wages, and prestige. Although explanations differ, it is agreed that gender affects occupational segregation (see, for example, Tienda et al. 1987), earnings, and prestige (Bose and Rossi 1983). Race effects on occupational characteristics have an even more venerable standing in the literature.

However, although everyone can be characterized in terms of both a sex and a race, relatively little research explores the effects of the two factors simultaneously on people's work fates. With respect to the joint impact of race and gender on occupational segregation, Glenn (1987, p. 72) highlights the impacts of race on what are often in the literature called racial ethnic (nonwhite) women. Sokoloff emphasizes both race and gender, suggesting that black women work in the bottom strata of female-stratified jobs (1987).

Concerning earning differentials, Blumberg argues, "Sex is a greater penalty than race when it comes to earnings" (1978, p. 105). Marini agrees, stating, "There is a large sex difference in earnings in all racial groups" (1989, p. 345). Sorensen too emphasizes gender, reporting that occupational segregation by race is not a significant factor influencing earnings except for white men (1989). Baron and Newman (1990) find strong negative effects of both gender and race occupational composition on pay: Higher percentages of women and minorities are associated with lower pay. Oddly, higher percentages of nonwhite women are not independently associated with lower wages in this study. Kilbourne et al. find a great complexity of race-gender effects in their research on gender and differences in earnings between blacks and whites.

Studies on occupational prestige tend to examine gender more often than race. Findings often indicate that the gender composition of occupations has a significant effect on prestige ratings (for example, Bose and Rossi 1983). Few researchers investigate gender-based and race-based prestige differences simultaneously among racial ethnic and white women (Sullivan 1984).

Thus, despite a plethora of analyses of race and gender effects separately, it remains unclear what results race and gender have when their joint impacts are examined on different characteristics of the same occupations (Mason 1986). The idea of "double jeopardy"—a doubled impact of race and gender on nonwhite women's occupational fates—is often invoked but rarely examined. In a widely cited assessment, King (1988) argues that the idea is overly simple because it assumes that the relationships among the various discriminations are merely additive, and she calls for research on it. Glenn too considers an additive approach overly simple and reports that in American nineteenth- and twentieth-century domestic and nursing work the effects of the two factors can be seen to be "inextricably intertwined" (1992, p. 33).

Besides a lack of sufficient research about the joint impacts of race and gender, extant studies are often limited to a small set of specific racial comparisons, such as white versus black (for example, Kilbourne et al. 1992), or white vs. black or Hispanic (Marini 1989; Tienda et al. 1987). Asian American women are mainly not included in race-gender analyses of segregation, of earnings, or of prestige. Nor are the various race/gender combinations usually contrasted with a single comparison group. Too, research usually restricts itself to single characteristics of occupations (Xu and Leffler 1992).

Three recent studies underline the need to examine race and gender together in order to understand the American occupational structure. Baron and Newman (1990) analyze them jointly as instances of "ascription" (as opposed to achievement) in the labor force, also asking whether factors like unionization, employment growth, ambiguous performance criteria, and how old or unusual the job is affect the impact of ascription on pay. This issue, the relative strength of ascription, cannot be examined unless more than one kind of ascription is studied simultaneously.

Kilbourne et al. (1992) scrutinize several widely believed generalizations about gender and race pay differentials in order to examine whether each is true only within one gender or race. They find that some are. For instance, while educational differences can be used to explain some pay differences between blacks and whites, they have no impact on pay differences between women and men. Occupational gender segregation costs black women more than white women. Marital status advantages men in general and black women but not white women. Job experience affects pay across both race and gender, especially influencing earning differentials between white women and men. Clearly it is unwise to assume that explanations of inequities between women's and men's pay can be generalized across blacks and whites, or, similarly, that explanations of inequities between blacks' and whites' pay can be generalized across women and men.

Finally, Wu and Leffler (1992) examine race and gender effects on several occupational characteristics in selected occupations. They report that with respect to occupational segregation, earnings, and prestige, the effects of race and gender on blacks, Asian-Americans, Hispanics, and whites differ. For instance, race more than gender affects the likelihood that a worker will occupy a high-prestige job, with black and Hispanic men experiencing the lowest occupational prestige and white men the highest. Segregation, on the other hand, shows stronger gender effects than race effects: From 70 percent to 73 percent of each racial group of women would need job changes in order to mirror the job distribution of white men. Earnings too exhibit stronger gender effects, with men in the four racial groups earning from 84 percent to 94 percent of white men's wages, compared with women's spread of 66 percent to 77 percent. With respect to all three occupational characteristics, both gender and race effects can be discerned, but in each case one has a more powerful impact than the other. However, when segregation and prestige are examined jointly, strong dual effects of race and gender become clear.

In their introduction to a special issue of *Gender and Society* on "Race, Class, and Gender," Wilkinson et al. (1992) note that the simultaneous consideration of several stratifiers can challenge not only the empirical data but also the theoretical paradigms that result when only one is considered. The examples of work by Baron and Newman (1990), Kilbourne et al. (1992), and Xu and Leffler (1992) illustrate that examining gender and race simultaneously can provide a more complete picture of the occupational situations of various work subgroups (black women, white men, and so forth). The first two articles also illustrate how the joint examination of gender and race can illuminate theories proposed to explain the occupational effects of each separately. To consider either factor alone would be to overlook ways in which each factor affects the American occupational structure, as well as ways in which they link differently to exhibit different joint impacts on different occupational characteristics.

*Ann Leffler*

*Wu Xu*

## Bibliography

Baron, James N., and Andrew E. Newman. 1990. "For What It's Worth: Organizations, Occupations, and the Value of Work Done by Women and Nonwhites." *American Sociological Review* 55:155–75.

Blumberg, Rae Lesser. 1978. *Stratification: Socio-Economic and Sexual Inequality.* Dubuque, Iowa: William C. Brown.

Bose, Christine E., and Peter H. Rossi. 1983. "Gender and Jobs: Prestige Standings of Occupations as Affected by Gender." *American Sociological Review* 48:327–28.

England, Paula, and Lori McCreamy. 1987. "Gender Inequality in Paid Employment." In *Analyzing Gender: A Handbook of Social Science Research*, edited by Beth B. Hess and Myra Marx Ferree, pp. 286–320. Newberg Park, Calif.: Sage.

Glenn, Evelyn Nakano. 1992. "From Servitude to Service Work: Historical Continuities in the Racial Division of Paid Reproductive Labor." *Signs: Journal of Women in Culture and Society* 18:1–43.

———. 1987. "Racial Ethnic Women's Labor: The Intersection of Race, Gender, and Class Oppression." In *Hidden Aspects of Women's Work*, edited by C. Bose, R. Feldberg, and N. Sokoloff with the Women and Work Research Group, pp. 46–73. New York: Praeger.

Kilbourne, Barbara, Paula England, and Kurt Beron. 1992. "Effects of Changing Individual, Occupational and Industrial Characteristics on Changes in Earnings: Intersections of Race and Gender." Unpublished manuscript.

King, Deborah. 1988. "Multiple Jeopardy, Multiple Consciousness: The Context of a Black Feminist Ideology." *Signs: Journal of Women in Culture and Society* 14:42–72.

Marini, Margaret Mooney. 1989. "Sex Differences in Earnings in United States." In *Annual Review of Sociology*, edited by W.R. Scott and J. Blake, pp. 343–80. Palo Alto, Calif.: Annual Reviews.

Mason, Karen Oppenheim. 1986. "The Status of Women: Conceptual and Methodological Issues in Demographic Studies." *Sociological Forum* 1:284–300.

Sokoloff, Natalie. 1987. "What's Happening to Women's Employment: Issues for Women's Labor Struggles in the 1980s–1990s." In *Hidden Aspects of Women's Work*, edited by C. Bose, R. Feldberg, and N. Sokoloff with the Women and Work Research Group, pp. 95–115. New York: Praeger.

Sorensen, Elaine. 1989. "Measuring the Effect of Occupational Sex and Race Composition on Earnings." In *Pay Equity: Empirical Inquiries*, edited by R.T. Michael, H.I. Hartmann, and B. O'Farrel, pp. 46–69. Washington, D.C.: National Academy.

Sullivan, Teresa A. 1984. "The Occupational Prestige of Women Immigrants: A Comparison of Cubans and Mexicans." *International Migration Review* 18:1045–62.

Tienda, Marta, Shelley A. Smith, and Vilma Ortiz. 1987. "Industrial Restructuring, Gender Segregation, and Sex Differences in Earnings." *American Sociological Review* 52:195–210.

Wilkinson, Doris, Maxine Baca Zinn, and Esther Ngan-Ling Chow. 1992. "Guest Editors' Introduction." *Gender and Society* 6:341–45.

Xu, Wu, and Ann Leffler. 1992. "Gender and Race Effects on Occupational Prestige, Segregation, and Earnings." *Gender and Society* 6:376–92.

## Comparable Worth and the Labor Market

Census figures for 1988 showed that for full-time wage and salaried employees, women's median weekly earnings were about 70 percent that of men's (U.S. Department of Labor 1990). Among the factors contributing to the pay gap between men and women is sex segregation in the labor market—that is, the tendency of men and women to work in different occupations and jobs (England 1992). Comparable worth (also known as pay equity) refers to a policy that compares pay levels of jobs done disproportionately by men with pay levels of jobs done disproportionately by women and tries to adjust pay so that the women and men who work in female-dominated jobs are not penalized because their jobs are done disproportionately by women. The policy presumes that jobs can be ranked objectively according to requisite skill, effort, responsibility, and working conditions. After such a ranking, pay is adjusted so that equivalently ranked male and female-dominated jobs receive equivalent pay (Hartmann et al. 1985; Blum 1991, p. 2).

Economic roots of comparable worth are found in sex-segregated labor markets. Notwithstanding the post-1970 influx of women into traditionally male jobs (England 1992, p. 15), the extent of sex segregation remains high (Baron and Bielby 1985; Committee on Women's Employment and Related Social Issues 1986, pp. 18–36). England (1992) notes that in 1980, only 87 out of 503 detailed census occupations contained between 30 percent and 50 percent women. Because the labor market as a whole is now about 40 percent female, England considers only occupations that hover loosely around that figure (that is, from about 30 to 50 percent female) to be integrated. The 1989 *Current Population Survey* provides insight into the content of occupations that remain segregated. In 1989, jobs that were over 80 percent female included secretary, child-care worker, hairdresser, cashier, book keeper, telephone operator, receptionist, typist, elementary-school teacher, librarian, and nurse. Jobs that were over 80 percent male included doctor, lawyer, dentist, taxi driver, plumber, electrician, carpenter, firefighter, auto mechanic, machinist, and truck driver (U.S. Bureau of the Census 1989).

A complete explanation of the male/female gap in earnings is beyond the scope of this essay (for overviews, see Rosenfeld and Kalleberg 1990; England 1992; Blau and Ferber 1986). Most relevant to arguments for comparable worth, however, is the relationship between the gender composition of an occupation or job and its earnings. Analyzing 1980 census data and examining pay for women and men separately, England (1992, pp. 125–87) finds that both women and men are directly disadvantaged by employment in an occupation that is predominantly female. "After adjusting for cognitive, social, and physical skill demands, amenities, disamenities, demands for effort, and industrial and organizational characteristics, jobs pay less if they contain a higher proportion of females" (England 1992, p. 181). England estimates that when an all-male and an all-female occupation are equivalent or "comparable" on all pay-relevant factors other than sex composition, the effect of changing from the all-male to the all-female occupation is a loss of between forty cents and one dollar per hour. She interprets this as "direct wage discrimination against predominantly female occupations" (1992, p. 181).

Legal roots of comparable worth are found in the failure of traditional equal-employment-opportunity policies to remedy this type of discrimination. Both the Equal Pay Act of 1963 and Title VII of the Civil Rights Act of 1964 prohibit discrimination in wages on the basis of gender. But, because these acts have been interpreted to mandate equal pay for equal—that is, the same—work, they do not apply to men and women who work in different jobs (see England 1992, pp. 225–40; Chamallas 1986, pp. 737–49). In 1981, in *County of Washington v. Gunther*, the Supreme Court appeared amenable to claims under Title VII of sex-based wage discrimination resulting from the lower earnings of female-dominated, as compared with comparable but not equivalent, male-dominated jobs. However, the *Gunther* Court never ruled directly on any comparable-worth claim. When lower courts have faced such claims under Title VII, in general they have sided with the employer (England 1992, pp. 232–41). In perhaps the most well known lower-court case (*AFSCME v. State of Washington*, 1985), the United States District Court for the Western District of Washington found that Washington had discriminated against predominantly female jobs by paying them less than predominantly male jobs deemed comparable according to the state's own comparable-worth study. The Ninth Circuit Court of Appeals reversed this district-court decision, arguing that Washington was protected by a "market defense" (Chamallas 1986, p. 765). The appeals court ruled that because the state based its compensation system on market prices, Washington could not be held liable for sex discrimination under Title VII.

If traditional equal-employment-opportunity legislation does not support direct claims of the wage discrimination at issue in comparable worth, neither can such discrimination effectively be attacked indirectly through affirmative action. Empirical studies suggest that although affirmative action can help reduce wage disparities between men and women by hiring and promoting women into traditionally male-dominated jobs, affirmative-action policies do not eliminate either gender segregation or the wage gap between male-dominated and female-dominated jobs (Rosenbaum 1985; Blum 1991, pp. 31–34). In his study of a Fortune 500 company employing between ten and fifteen thousand employees between 1962 and 1975, James Rosenbaum (1985) found that despite an aggressive affirmative-action program instituted by the firm during this period, gender segregation at the firm remained high. The company's all-female jobs paid only about three-quarters of what the all-male jobs paid. Even taking into account the part of this difference due to greater education and on-the-job experience associated with male-dominated jobs, the higher the percentage of female workers in the job, the lower the job's pay.

Against this joint backdrop of persistent devaluation of female-dominated occupations and jobs and the failure of traditional remedies, all but a few U.S. states and more than seventeen hundred localities have instituted comparable-worth policies for public-sector employees (Blum 1991, p. 2). Both legislation and public-sector collective bargaining have been used to achieve comparable worth. In the European Economic Community, comparable worth exists for the private, as well as the public, sector (McCrudden 1986).

Implementing comparable worth raises a host of technical, political, and economic issues (for overviews, see Blum 1991; England 1992; Evans and Nelson

1989a; Hartmann et al. 1985; Steinberg 1990). One important set of issues revolves around job evaluation—the technical process that reduces male- and female-dominated jobs to an underlying common denominator of skill, effort, responsibility, and working conditions so as to compare and rank them independently of the race and gender of job incumbents. Effective implementation requires that job evaluation be free from gender bias. If skill, effort, responsibility, and working conditions are the "compensable factors" (Hartmann et al. 1985, p. 9) that allow wages for different jobs to be compared and then realigned free of discriminatory elements, then gender bias can not enter into the choice of these factors: how the factors are defined and measured (including the collection of information on what people actually do in their jobs), and how these factors are combined to yield the overall "worth" (and so equitable wage rate) of the job. Substantial research (for example, Steinberg 1990; England 1992, pp. 189–223) shows just how difficult such gender-neutral assessments are. For example, empirical research shows that evaluation of the skill it takes to do a job is "shaped and confounded" by the gender of the job incumbent (Steinberg 1990, p. 452). Similarly, once men and women know which jobs are predominantly male and which are predominantly female, they tend to attribute to them the job content that best fits with gender stereotypes (Steinberg 1990).

Some economists have argued that comparable worth is inflationary and will cause wage losses and unemployment for some (disproportionately women) because of benefits enacted for others (England 1992, pp. 73–76). On the other hand, some feminists fear that comparable worth reinforces gender stereotyping rather than breaking down gender barriers at work (see Blum 1991, p. 18). Empirical studies of impact suggest that enacting comparable worth decreases, but does not eliminate, the gender gap in wages for covered male and female employees (Orazem and Mattila 1989 for Iowa; Evans and Nelson 1989b, p. 218, for Minnesota; Gregory and Duncan 1981 for Australia). In Australia, a substantially narrowed gender gap in wages was coupled with some disemployment for women in the private sector. Research on the politics of comparable worth shows wide variation across cases. Where Evans and Nelson (1989a, p. 13) paint a picture of comparable worth as an "elite-dominated" and "technocratic" reform in Minnesota, Blum's California case studies (1991, pp. 180–81) show a more overtly politicized and radicalized process, with grass-roots involvement of low-wage women. As for wage realignment, whereas in some cases only the lowest-paid job classes received raises as a result of comparable worth, in other cases raises were given to job classes at various levels of the pay hierarchy (Blum 1991, p. 176). Illustrating the link between politics and economics, the Iowa case shows how the pay gap between men and women in the public sector might have been reduced further if pay cuts for job classes deemed overvalued by the state's comparable worth study had not been politically untenable (Orazem and Mattila 1989, pp. 179–81, 197).

Regardless of what is shown by longer-term evidence on the economic, political, and technical impact of comparable-worth policies, debates over comparable worth have highlighted fruitful avenues of social-science research. One of the important legacies of comparable worth has been renewed appreciation for the politics of apparently technical decisions, including the "social construction of skill" (Steinberg 1990; see also Blum 1991; Evans and Nelson 1989a). As Blum (1991, p. 17) indicates, debates over comparable worth have "reveal[ed] that what [work] society deems valuable is in fact part of a field of social conflict, determined not by intrinsic value, natural merit, or abstract market forces but by power relations."

    *Robin Stryker*

## Bibliography

Baron, James, and William T. Bielby. 1985. "Organizational Barriers to Gender Equality: Sex Segregation of Jobs and Opportunities." In *Gender and the Life Course*, edited by A. Rossi, pp. 233–51. New York: Aldine.

Blau, Francine D., and Marianne A. Ferber. 1986. *The Economics of Women, Men and Work*. Englewood Cliffs, N.J.: Prentice-Hall.

Blum, Linda M. 1991. *Between Feminism and Labor*. Berkeley: University of California Press.

Chamallas, Martha. 1986. "Women and Part-Time Work: The Case for Pay Equity and Equal Access." *North Carolina Law Review* 64:709–75.

Committee on Women's Employment and Related Social Issues. Commission on Behavioral and Social Sciences and Education, National Research Council. 1986. *Women's Work, Men's Work: Sex Segregation on the Job*, edited by B.F. Reskin and H.I. Hartmann. Washington D.C.: National Academy.

England, Paula. 1992. *Comparable Worth: Theories and Evidence*. New York: Aldine de Gruyter.

Evans, Sara M., and Barbara J. Nelson. 1989a. *Wage Justice: Comparable Worth and the Paradox of Technocratic Reform*. Chicago and London: University of Chicago Press.

———. 1989b. "The Impact of Pay Equity on Public Employees: State of Minnesota Employees' Attitudes toward Wage Policy Innovation." In *Pay Equity: Empirical Inquiries*, edited by R.T. Michael, H.I. Hartmann, and B. O'Farrell, pp. 200–21. Washington, D.C.: National Academy.

Gregory, Robert G., and Ronald C. Duncan. 1981. "The Relevance of Segmented Labor Market Theories: The Australian Experience of the Achievement of Equal Pay for Women." *Journal of Post-Keynesian Economics* 3:403–28.

Hartmann, Heidi I., Patricia A. Roos, and Donald Treiman. 1985. "An Agenda for Basic Research on Comparable Worth." In *Comparable Worth: New Directions for Research*, edited by H.I. Hartmann, P.A. Roos, and D.J. Treiman, pp. 3–33. Washington, D.C.: National Academy.

McCrudden, Christopher. 1986. "Comparable Worth: A Common Dilemma." *Yale Journal of International Law* 11:396–436.

Orazem, Peter F., and J. Peter Mattila. 1989. "Comparable Worth and the Structure of Earnings: The Iowa Case." In *Pay Equity: Empirical Inquiries*, edited by R.T. Michael, H.I. Hartmann, and B. O'Farrell, pp. 179–99. Washington, D.C.: National Academy.

Rosenbaum, James E. 1985. "Jobs, Job Status and Women's Gains from Affirmative Action: Implications for Comparable Worth." In *Comparable Worth: New Directions for Research*, edited by H.I. Hartmann, P.A. Roos, and D.J. Treiman, pp. 116–36. Washington, D.C.: National Academy.

Rosenfeld, Rachel A., and Arne L. Kalleberg. 1990. "A Cross-national Comparison of the Gender Gap in Income." *American Journal of Sociology* 96:69–106.

Steinberg, Ronnie J. 1990. "The Social Construction of Skill: Gender, Power and Comparable Worth." *Work and Occupations* 17:449–82.

U.S. Bureau of the Census. 1989. *Current Population Survey*. Machine-readable data file. Conducted for the Bureau of Labor Statistics. Washington D.C: Bureau of Labor Statistics. (Printout from data file courtesy of Lisa Cubbins, University of Washington.)

U.S. Department of Labor. Women's Bureau. 1990. "Earnings Differences between Women and Men." *Facts on Working Women* 90–3 (October):1–7.

## Gender-Related Differences in Pension Coverage

In the United States, the percentage of employees covered by pension plans is lower among women than men. In 1988, the percentage of workers covered by a pension was 73 percent for men and 58 percent for women. There are several explanations for the gender difference in coverage for the current work force, the reasons that the gap narrowed during the 1980s, and why the gender gap in pensions is larger among the nonemployed elderly than the employed population.

    In order to understand why women have lower pension coverage than men, it is important to know why employers and workers might prefer to have part of compensation paid in the form of a pension. First, pension plans provide a tax-advantaged method for saving for retirement. The taxes on both the contributions and the interest earned are deferred until the worker receives benefits at retirement. Second, pensions can be used by the employer as an incentive device to reduce worker turnover or shirking.

Given the tax advantage of pensions, competition will force some firms to offer pensions. For example, suppose that firms A and B are competing for the same workers. Firm A offers thirty thousand dollars in salary and no pension; Firm B offers twenty-eight thousand dollars in salary and contributes two thousand dollars to a pension. Both are paying thirty thousand dollars in total. If workers prefer the package offered by B because of the tax advantages of pensions, firm A cannot compete with firm B for workers unless it offers a pension plan or increases total compensation above thirty thousand dollars. Thus, competition will force firms to offer pensions in order to attract workers at the lowest possible cost.

The incentive effects of pensions will depend upon the particular design that the firm chooses. Several design options are important. First, most pension plans require that workers have a minimum number of years with the firm before they are "vested." Prior to vesting, if the worker quits, she will receive only some fraction (perhaps none) of the pension contributions made previously on her behalf. Thus, prior to vesting, quitting imposes a penalty on the worker. A second important consideration is whether the plan is a defined benefit or a defined contribution plan. In the defined benefit plan, the worker's retirement benefits are typically tied to number of years of service and salary history. For example, a common formula sets the annual benefit equal to some fixed percentage of the employee's final salary for each year of service with the firm. In the defined contribution plan, the contributions to the pension are specified. The benefits that the worker receives at retirement are determined by the rate of return earned by the pension-fund manager. Thus, except for the vesting and tax considerations, the defined contribution plan is much like a private savings account.

In defined benefit plans, the pension plan can be designed to penalize workers for quitting, even beyond the vesting period. A study by Allen, Clark, and McDermed (1989) shows that a worker hired at age twenty-five for twenty-five thousand dollars in a "typical" defined benefit plan loses $105,000 in pension benefits if she quits at age fifty-five. Ippolito (1985) shows that these quit penalties emerge because, early in their careers, workers contribute more to the pension plan than they will receive upon quitting. This is offset later in the career when pension benefits rise faster than contributions. This "deferred compensation" has a least two desirable effects from the employer's perspective. First, since workers that quit prior to retirement are penalized, the pension can be used to reduce turnover. This is particularly important when the employer is faced with substantial hiring or training costs for a new employee. Second, the deferred compensation may reduce employee shirking (Lazear 1979). Workers who shirk and get caught can be fired, and the loss of the pension makes the dismissal more costly to the worker. Thus, the ability of defined benefit pension plans to defer pay makes the pension a potentially useful incentive device for the employer.

The causes of the gender gap in pension coverage and recent trends can now be described in the context of the reasons that pensions are formed. To illus-

TABLE 1   Percentage of Workers with Pensions by Gender*

| | Year | |
|---|---|---|
| | *1979* | *1988* |
| *21–36 Year Olds* | | |
| Males | 61.8 | 52.7 |
| Females | 46.3 | 46.7 |
| Gender Gap | 15.8 | 6.0 |
| *37–54 Year Olds* | | |
| Males | 75.8 | 72.8 |
| Females | 54.0 | 58.2 |
| Gender Gap | 21.8 | 14.6 |

*Statistics are based upon 1979 and 1988 May Current Population Survey data on employed nonagricultural workers aged 21 to 54.

trate the size of the gap and trends, data from the 1979 and 1988 May Current Population Surveys are exploited. The sample was restricted to nonagricultural workers aged twenty-one to fifty-four. The relevant statistics are presented in Table 1 for two age groups (21–36 and 37–54). The data are presented separately for the young and middle-aged because the labor market characteristics of the two groups differ substantially.

Consideration of the data in Table 1 reveals several interesting points regarding the gender gap in coverage. First, the gender gap in coverage is smaller among younger workers. In 1979, the difference in male and female pension coverage rates was 15.5 percentage points among young workers and 21.8 among middle-aged workers. Second, the gap in coverage diminished in the 1980s. Between 1979 and 1988, the gap fell from 15.8 to 6.0 for the young, and from 21.8 to 14.6 for the middle-aged.

There are several possible explanations for this gap in coverage. First, women have lower average earnings than men. Blau and Beller (1988) report that, among full-time workers, women had weekly earnings averaging 71 percent of men's in 1987. Given the tax advantages of pensions and the progressive nature of the U.S. income tax system, women will benefit less from a pension, as they are subjected to a lower marginal tax rate. Hence, firms are less likely to offer a pension plan to attract female employees. Second, women have more intermittent careers than men. Mincer and Polachek (1974) describe how career interruptions make women more likely to choose jobs that facilitate exit and entry. For example, women will choose jobs that have training that is general instead of specific to a particular employer. In the case of pensions, if women are more likely than men to leave the firm prior to retirement, they will benefit less from a pension and be less attracted to such jobs. Third, compared with men, women are less likely to unionize and more likely to work part time. This also contributes to lower coverage for women, as nonworkers and part-time workers are less likely to be covered by a pension.

The gap in coverage is smaller among the young because young men and women are somewhat similar in terms of labor-market behavior. O'Neill and

Polachek (1993) demonstrate that more recent cohorts of female workers are moving into traditionally "male" jobs, that they are less likely to drop out of the labor market, and that their earnings are more similar to men's. Moreover, the convergence in labor-market behavior of men and women has accelerated in the 1980s, thus causing the gap in pension coverage to narrow.

The gender difference in pension receipt among retirees is substantially larger than the gap in coverage among the work force. According to data in Woods (1988), the percentage of the nonemployed elderly (over age fifty-two) receiving a pension from previous employment was 53 percent for men and only 24 percent for women, implying a gap of 29 percent. The gap in the percentage that receive benefits could be greater than the gap in coverage among workers for several reasons. First, the labor-force participation rate of women is lower than that for men. Thus, even if coverage rates were identical for male and female workers, women will be less likely to receive a benefit because they are less likely to convert into pension receipt at retirement. This is because women are more likely to quit prior to vesting, and are more likely to take a lump sum distribution upon departure (Andrews 1990; Woods 1988). Third, the gender gap in pension coverage among employees has narrowed over time. Thus, when the current retirees were employed, the gender gap in coverage was likely larger than it is today.

In summary, pension coverage is lower among women than men for several reasons. They have lower incomes, more intermittent careers, and are more likely to have part-time and nonunion jobs. During the 1980s, the gender gap in coverage narrowed as women entered traditionally "male" jobs, and reduced the frequency and duration of career interruptions. This reduced gender gap in pension coverage will play an important role in making women financially secure at retirement in the twenty-first century. This is especially important given the growing numbers of single women and the cloud of doubt surrounding the viability of the Social Security System in the United States.

*William E. Even*

*David A. Macpherson*

## Bibliography

Allen, Steven, Robert Clark, and Ann McDermed. 1989. "The Pension Cost of Changing Jobs." National Bureau of Economic Research Working Paper No. 2935. Cambridge, Mass.

Andrews, Emily. 1990. "Retirement Savings and Lump Sum Distributions." Mimeographed.

Blau, Francine D., and Andrea H. Beller. 1988. "Trends in Earnings Differentials." *Industrial and Labor Relations Review* 41(4):513–29.

Employee Benefits Research Institute. 1990. *Fundamentals of Employee Benefit Programs*, 4th ed.

Even, William E., and David A. Macpherson. 1990. "The Gender Gap in Pensions and Wages." *Review of Economics and Statistics* 72(2):259–65.

Ippolito, Richard. 1985. "The Labor Contract and True Economic Pension Liabilities." *American Economic Review* 75(5):1031–43.

Lazear, Edward P. 1979. "Why Is There Mandatory Retirement?" *Journal of Political Economy* 87(6):1261–84.

Mincer, J., and S. Polachek. 1974. "Family Investments in Human Capital: Earnings of Women." *Journal of Political Economy* 82:46–110.

O'Neill, June, and Solomon Polachek. 1993. "Why the Gender Gap Narrowed in the 1980s." *Journal of Labor Economics* 11:205–28.

Turner, John A., and Daniel J. Beller. 1989. *Trends in Pensions*. U.S. Department of Labor Pension and Welfare Benefits Administration.

U.S. Bureau of the Census. 1988. *Current Population Survey*. Washington, D.C.: U.S. Department of Commerce.

————. 1977. *Current Population Survey*. Washington, D.C.: U.S. Department of Commerce.
Woods, John R. 1988. "Retirement-Age Women and Pensions: Findings from the New Beneficiary Survey." *Social Security Bulletin* 51(12):5–16.

### Income Possession in Couples

How money earned from employment is managed is an important consideration for working women. The way money is handled can affect the amounts that are spent for different purposes, and thus the benefits that are derived from women's earnings (Brannen and Moss 1987). Money-management style can also affect the extent to which women participate as active agents in the construction of their own lives. In North America today, women's increased occupational involvement as wage earners is helping to increase their economic agency.

Increased hours of employment is associated with nontraditional marital sex-role orientations among wives (Krausz 1986). Irrespective of the type of sex-role attitude held by their husbands, women who possess more modern sex-role orientations often transform financial decision-making activities that were previously husband-dominated into a more egalitarian process (Kim and Lee 1989). This process can take one of two forms—either more joint decision-making or the separation of financial tasks. In families where wives work for financial reasons, there is a higher probability that certain decision tasks will be made by the wife and husband separately (Rosen and Granbois 1983).

The earnings that women derive from their work are important for many reasons. Wages potentially provide women with personal financial resources, and they also enable them to make valuable contributions to the well-being of their families. Not surprisingly, earning money is a significant reward that most women derive from their work (Walker 1990). The money earned at work is sometimes valued for the opportunity it provides for women who are married or cohabiting to have some financial autonomy from their partners (Blumstein and Schwartz 1983). In fact, financial autonomy is not an inevitable consequence of paid employment. This is partly because of the power that men may exercise over women, and partly because personal autonomy is not every woman's principal goal.

Perhaps the most basic issue in household money management is the extent to which partners' incomes are pooled or held separately. It has been generally assumed that within marriage a couple will share almost everything and that the resources of adult earners will be pooled as "family money" used to sustain the family as a group. Blumstein and Schwartz (1983) report that a majority of couples assume that when they marry they should pool all of their property and financial assets. Working wives, and wives with high incomes, prefer to pool just as much as do full-time homemakers. Similarly, the overwhelming majority of wives state that when a wife works her salary should be considered family income in the same way that a husband's salary is (Smith and Reid 1986a).

Despite this apparent uniformity of opinion about money management, there is often considerable behavioral variation that may reflect differences in class position. Zelizer (1989) reports that in the United States in the period 1870–1930 the wages of working-class women were usually merged into the family's housekeeping money. On the other hand, the wages of middle-class women were more likely to be regarded as "pin money" to be used on extras and luxuries, which wives might be able to reserve for their own use.

In today's economy women are most likely to be able to retain control over their earnings when they have their own bank accounts. In practice, financial arrangements in couples can be very diverse (Smith and Reid 1986b). A couple may pool all of their income in one joint account. They may put most of their income into a joint account and have small separate accounts, or they may have individual control over most of their personal income and have only a minimal joint fund. Or they may have no joint banking arrangements whatsoever. The relative frequency of these different money-management practices varies according to the pattern of wives' employment. Wives who are employed full time are more likely to have separate bank accounts (Treas 1991).

A study of married and cohabiting couples in Canada provides further details on this point (Cheal 1991). Couples were divided into breadwinner/homemaker families (husband employed and wife keeping house), dual-earner families (husband in regular, full-time employment and wife employed part time or only marginally attached to the labor force), and dual-career families (husband and wife equally involved in occupational careers). All three family types make extensive use of joint bank accounts. However, they differ in the prevalence of separate personal accounts. Personal accounts range from a low of 0.5 per person in breadwinner/homemaker families to a high of 1.2 per person in dual-earner families. Furthermore, the extent of reliance upon different accounts is not the same in families of different types. In a clear majority of breadwinner/homemaker families, the only account with a financial institution is a joint account. In contrast, maintaining only joint accounts is practiced by less than half of dual-earner or dual-career families. Clearly, individual financial autonomy must be easier for women in dual-earner families and dual-career families than it is for women in breadwinner/homemaker families.

Financial autonomy for wives is probably most frequent among women with high incomes. In a sample of high-earning, dual-career couples in Chicago it was found that half pooled their incomes and half maintained separate accounting systems (Hertz 1986). Blumstein and Schwartz (1983) report that in both married and cohabiting couples in America women with high incomes have more financial independence. The higher a woman's income, the less likely she is to discuss her personal spending money with her partner. Also, women with large incomes are the most likely to have personal savings accounts to which their partners have no access—33 percent of wives who earned less than ten thousand dollars at the end of the 1970s had a personal savings account, as compared with 40 percent of those earning between ten and thirty thousand dollars and 57 percent of those who earned more than thirty thousand dollars (Blumstein and Schwartz 1983, p. 554). It follows from this, as Hertz (1986) found, that when wives earn as much as or more than their husbands, couples tend to employ separate accounting systems. Pooled accounting systems are more common when wives earn less than their husbands.

The results of the studies described here enable us to make a tentative prediction about future patterns of money management. If present trends continue, it appears that when women in paid employment succeed in raising their incomes through occupational advancement, we can expect to see them shift toward more independent styles of money management.

*David Cheal*

## Bibliography

Blumstein, Philip, and Pepper Schwartz. 1983. *American Couples: Money, Work, Sex*. New York: William Morrow.

Brannen, Julia, and Peter Moss. 1987. "Dual Earner Households: Women's Financial Contributions after the Birth of the First Child." In *Give and Take in Families*, edited by Julia Brannen and Gail Wilson. London: Allen and Unwin.

Cheal, David. 1991. "Family Finances: Money Management in Breadwinner/Homemaker Families, Dual Earner Families, and Dual Career Families." Winnipeg Area Study Report No. 38. Sociology Department, University of Manitoba.

Hertz, Rosanna. 1986. *More Equal than Others*. Berkeley: University of California Press.

Kim, Chankon, and Hanjoon Lee. 1989. "Sex Role Attitudes of Spouses and Task Sharing Behavior." In *Advances in Consumer Research Vol. 16*, edited by Thomas Srull. Provo, Utah: Association for Consumer Research.

Krausz, Susan. 1986. "Sex Roles within Marriage." *Social Work* 31:457–64.

Rosen, Dennis, and Donald Granbois. 1983. "Determinants of Role Structure in Family Financial Management." *Journal of Consumer Research* 10:253–58.

Smith, Audrey, and William Reid. 1986a. "Role Expectations and Attitudes in Dual-Earner Families." *Social Casework* 67:394–402.

Smith, Audrey, and William Reid. 1986b. *Role-Sharing Marriage*. New York: Columbia University Press.

Treas, Judith. 1991. "The Common Pot or Separate Purses?" In *Gender, Family, and Economy*, edited by Rae Lesser Blumberg. Newbury Park, Calif.: Sage.

Walker, Karen. 1990. "Class, Work and Family in Women's Lives." *Qualitative Sociology* 13:297–320.

Zelizer, Viviana. 1989. "The Social Meaning of Money." *American Journal of Sociology* 95:342–77.

## Economics of Housework

A substantial amount of time is spent on housework, and there are striking differences by gender in the amount of time spent on housework. While estimates vary widely depending on the sample examined and the methods used to generate the information, representative values of housework time range around six to fourteen hours per week for men and twenty to thirty hours for women. Housework is central to explanations of gender differentials in earnings, since gender differences in work history and occupations are often assumed to derive from gender differences in household responsibilities. In addition, the exclusion of time spent on home production from GNP statistics understates official measures of women's contribution to the economy.

Although a substantial amount of output is produced through home production, the value of home production time is not included in the official measures of national output, such as GNP. For instance, the value of material inputs into home maintenance is included in official measures of GNP, but the value of the homeowners' time spent on repairs is not included. The exclusion of highly labor-intensive home production activities such as housecleaning and child care particularly understates the value of output produced. In part, this exclusion of home production reflects the general difficulty of quantifying the value of non-market time. Time spent in the labor market is valued at the wage rate, but the value of time spent on home production is not so easily measured. Extended accounting systems that value home production time typically use either a cost-based concept, in which the value of home production is estimated by the cost of purchasing the equivalent goods or services in the market, or by an opportunity-cost method, in which time spent on home production is valued at the individual's wage rate (or predicted wage rate for nonmarket participants), net of income tax. Extended national income measures estimate the value of home production to be about one-third of conventional GNP (Eisner 1988).

Economists explain time allocation by assuming households choose the quantity of time to allocate to the market, to nonmarket production, and to leisure time in order to maximize satisfaction, which economists refer to as "utility." This process implies nothing about how housework time will be shared among members of the household. The primary economic explanation of the intrahousehold time allocation decision is based on human capital theory, but more recent bargaining models can also help explain the observed time-use patterns within households. Human capital theory treats the acquisition of skills as an investment decision. Individuals choose to acquire skills based on the cost of acquisition and the expected return from the possession of these skills. Within a household, gains from specialization and exchange will lead to one member of the household specializing in home production and the other specializing in market work. Human capital theory alone does not imply that women will specialize in home production. The controversial aspects of the use of human capital theory derive from the assumptions made by a number of its practitioners concerning natural or innate differences in the costs of acquiring different sorts of skills. Since only women bear children, it is argued (for example, by Gary Becker) that even if a husband and wife initially have equal market ability, childbearing will lead to development of different skills, making it optimal for women to specialize in home production and men to specialize in market work. Bargaining models examine how decisions are made in a long-term relationship in which transaction costs are high. The bargaining power of each spouse is related to his or her next best alternative. Since husbands typically have higher market wages than their spouses, their next best alternative to marriage may be to purchase in the market many of the services provided by a wife. The next best alternative to marriage for women may be a relatively low wage job, especially for women who have specialized in home production. Thus, the argument goes, men will tend to have stronger bargaining positions than women, which may lead to the observed greater share of housework time of women.

The greater share of household responsibilities borne by women appears to negatively affect their market wages relative to men. The effects of housework on market wages are both indirect and direct. The indirect effect works through the effect of household responsibilities on human capital accumulation. If women anticipate shorter working lives because of greater home responsibilities, human capital theory predicts that women will undertake less human capital investment, such as specialized education, and may seek jobs providing less firm specific training, as they expect fewer years in which to reap the benefits of their investments. In addition, employers may be less likely to hire or promote women whom they expect to have shorter or discontinuous working lives, and may have less incentive to invest in firm specific training of women workers. Since wages are higher for workers with more years of work experience, training, and job seniority, the weaker performance of women in the labor market relative to men can be traced to differences in household responsibilities.

The direct effect of housework on earnings is due to the reduction in the amount of energy and effort available for performing market work, as well as to restricting the types and locations of jobs compatible with heavy household responsibilities. Married women with children spend more than twice the time on housework as married men with children. Although men average more hours than women in paid employment, full-time employed women spend more total time on housework and market work than do men. In addition to physical fatigue induced by greater total work hours, the timing of household responsibilities, such as meal preparation and arranging doctors' appointments for children, makes schedules less flexible, so that market work may be disrupted. Women may restrict their job search to jobs close to home and with greater flexibility in scheduling or limited travel or overtime. One interpretation of occupational segregation is that men and women select employment in occupations that are compatible with their household responsibilities (for example, see Gary Becker).

A vast amount of empirical evidence indicates that only about half of the gap between men's and women's earnings can be explained by women's lower average values of human capital characteristics, particularly years of total work experience and job seniority. There is empirical evidence that housework has an independent, negative effect on the earnings of both men and women, after controlling for human capital characteristics and working conditions. However, since women average far more time on housework than do men, housework has a greater negative impact on their wages. Inclusion of time on housework substantially reduces the unexplained component of the gender wage gap.

*Joni Hersch*

## Bibliography

Becker, Gary S. 1985. "Human Capital, Effort, and the Sexual Division of Labor." *Journal of Labor Economics* 3(1, part 2):S33–S58.
———. 1981, 1991. *A Treatise on the Family*. Cambridge, Mass.: Harvard University Press.
Blau, Francine D., and Marianne A. Ferber. 1992. *The Economics of Men, Women, and Work*. 2nd ed. Englewood Cliffs, N.J.: Prentice Hall.
Eisner, Robert. 1988. "Extended Accounts for National Income and Product." *Journal of Economic Literature* 26(4):1611–84.
Gronau, Reuben. 1986. "Home Production—A Survey." In *Handbook of Labor Economics*, edited by Orley Ashenfelter and Richard Layard. Amsterdam: North Holland.
Hersch, Joni. 1991. "The Impact of Nonmarket Work on Market Wages." *American Economic Review Papers and Proceedings*. 81(2):157–60.
———. 1991. "Male-Female Differences in Hourly Wages: The Role of Human Capital, Working Conditions, and Housework." *Industrial and Labor Relations Review*. 44(4):746–59.
Juster, F. Thomas, and Frank P. Stafford. 1991. "The Allocation of Time: Empirical Findings, Behavioral Models, and Problems of Measurement." *Journal of Economic Literature* 29(2):471–522.
Mincer, Jacob, and Solomon Polachek. 1974. "Family Investments in Human Capital: Earnings of Women." *Journal of Political Economy* 82(2, part 2):S79–S108.
Shelton, Beth Anne. 1992. *Women, Men, and Time: Gender Differences in Paid Work, Housework, and Leisure*. New York: Greenwood.

# Gender-Based Division
# of Labor in the U.S.

## Occupational Sex-Typing

Occupational sex-typing is the process by which jobs are designated as male or female. Occupational sex segregation, the degree to which men and women are concentrated in distinctive jobs, has been extraordinarily constant. Despite the rise of antidiscrimination laws and changes in gender norms, occupational sex-segregation declined only slightly between 1950 and 1981 (Reskin and Roos 1990). There are at least five major theories of occupational sex-typing: Sex-Role, Labor Supply, Status Segregation, Buffering from Labor Costs, and Political Process. Historical evidence has cast doubt on the usefulness of the first two while supporting and validating the continued importance of the last three. Most discussions of women's work use all five, with no author being particularly associated with any one position.

Orthodox sex-role theory argues that women are allocated to jobs on the basis of the traditional sex-role ideologies that are pervasive in the society. Thus women are teachers because of their association with children, and waitresses because of their serving of food in the household. This theory has suffered from the large number of exceptions of men dominating relatively attractive "female-traited" positions. Thus, although women are traditionally linked to nurturing and emotion, most doctors and clergymen are men. Although women are associated with fine motor skills, few of them are surgeons or diamond-cutters. Although women do most of the food preparation in households, a majority of commercial cooks and bakers are men. It is hard to find a standard cultural pattern that provides a clear differentiation between male and female jobs.

Labor-supply theory argues that the gender composition of jobs is determined by the relative willingness of men and women to work in those occupations. A credible version of this argument comes from Strober (1984), who argues that jobs such as teaching have "feminized" when the conditions of work de-valued, making men less willing to apply for these positions. Otherwise sexist employers had little choice but to hire women. A more common but more questionable claim is that the increasing percentage of women in some jobs is due to increasing female labor-force participation, combined with a greater willingness for women to aspire to high-level positions. Oppenheimer (1970) has shown that increased female willingness to work has virtually nothing to do with the increases in female labor-force participation that occurred throughout the twentieth century. The increasing percentage of women in the American labor force was wholly the product of greater employer willingness to hire women. Epstein (1983) has shown that the increase of women in law resulted purely from changes in law school admissions policies; many of the women who attended law school during the feminization of law in the 1970s were women with traditional gender values who would have attended in previous decades had openings been available. Even in the Victorian period, when conservative gender ideology was widespread, employers such as the British Post Office found twelve women for every vacancy when they were offering highly paid, secure jobs (Cohn 1985).

Status segregation refers to the concentration of women in low-status jobs. Women are more likely to appear in jobs that are poorly paid, jobs that have few promotion prospects, and jobs with relatively minor control over human and financial resources. Not only are women on the bottom of most organizational hierarchies, but the worsening of occupational prospects is frequently associated with feminization. Reskin and Roos (1990) report that the occupations that showed the greatest rates of feminization during the 1970s tended to be those that were undergoing very significant de-skilling and economic devaluation. While there is little empirical dispute about women's low economic status, there is substantial ambiguity concerning its explanation. Human capital theorists have attempted to account for this in terms of women's higher propensity to quit their jobs, an explanation for which there is some negative evidence (see *Human Capital Theory*). Another approach is to invoke patriarchy, the general concern of men with maintaining superiority over women. Heidi Hartmann's (1976) dual-systems theory argues for the importance of both patriarchy and capitalist rationality, but acknowledges that the presence of dual-causal dynamics leads to indeterminate predictions of actual sex types. A third approach is to argue that the exclusion of women from good occupations is a defensive reaction by current male job holders to restrict the supply of potential competitors. Discrimination by male unionists is a special case of this phenomenon (Reskin and Roos 1990).

Labor-cost buffering theory argues that women are more likely to appear in jobs that are forced to economize on labor costs. The most distinctive feature of women workers is that their wages are lower than those of men. This wage differential is partially a product of overt pay discrimination and partially a product of being excluded from many employment possibilities by occupational sex-typing. Gary Becker (1957) has argued that by the logic of market competition, the wage differential should lead to employers' preferring women workers over men because of the potential for salary savings. Such considerations are less germane to firms for which reductions in labor costs are not especially important for organizational survival. An important category of firms that are buffered from labor costs are firms that are capital intensive. Firms that allocate a substantial proportion of their budget to raw materials and machinery can manage their cost-cutting through reduction of the supply budget, making it less important to obtain cheap labor. The most important application of labor-cost buffering theory is in explaining why women are concentrated in white-collar jobs, while men are concentrated in blue-collar jobs. Blue-collar occupations are substantially more capital intensive than white-collar occupations, making discrimination more economically feasible. The same logic explains why women are more concentrated in light rather than heavy manufacture, and particularly in labor-intensive, unfeminine, "sweatshop" settings. Cohn (1985) has documented the centrality of labor intensity in explaining the timing and pattern of the feminization of clerical work; Bridges (1982) has statistically documented the importance of labor intensity in determining the gender of American occupations.

More recently, a set of very promising models have been developed that view occupational sex-types as being the result of political processes. Baron et al. (1991) argue that the percentage of female workers in many jobs depends on the relative strength of internal and external political factions within organizations and the particular policy agendas being put forward by these groups. Using evidence from the California Civil Service, they argue that the feminization of public jobs was facilitated by external affirmative-action initiatives, the relative legal incapacity of employers to insulate themselves from affirmative action enforcers, turnover in agency leadership, which allowed new elites to reformulate local policies, the percentage of women both in the workforce and in leadership, and the extent to which bureaucratic procedures facilitated meritocratic rather than arbitrary promotion. Reskin and Roos (1990) report similar political factors affected female employment in insurance, real estate, bartending, and a number of other industries.

Overall, occupational sex-typing seems to be determined by a large number of factors, involving economics, organizational politics, and gender dynamics. Future developments in the field may involve developing more parsimonious accounts of this process.

*Samuel Cohn*

## Bibliography

Baron, James, Brian Mittman, and Andrew Newman. 1991. "Targets of Opportunity: Organizational and Environmental Determinants of Gender Integration within the California Civil Service 1979–85." *American Journal of Sociology* 96:1362–401.

Becker, Gary. 1957. *Economics of Discrimination*. Chicago: University of Chicago Press.

Bridges, William. 1982. "Sexual Segregation of Occupations: Theories of Labor Stratification in Industry." *American Journal of Sociology* 88:270–95.

Cohn, Samuel. 1985. *Process of Occupational Sex-Typing: Feminization of Clerical Labor in Great Britain*. Philadelphia: Temple University Press.

Epstein, Cynthia Fuchs. 1983. *Women in Law*. Garden City, N.Y.: Anchor.

Hartmann, Heidi. 1976. "Capitalism, Patriarchy and Job Segregation by Sex." *Signs* 1:137–70.

Oppenheimer, Valerie Kincaide. 1970. *Female Labor Force in the United States: Demographic and Economic Factors Governing Its Growth and Changing Composition*. Westport, Conn.: Greenwood.

Reskin, Barbara, and Patricia Roos. 1990. *Job Queues, Gender Queues: Explaining Women's Inroads into Male Occupations*. Philadelphia: Temple University Press.

Strober, Myra. 1984. "Toward a General Theory of Occupational Sex-Typing." In *Sex Segregation in the Workplace: Trends, Explanations, Remedies*, edited by Barbara Reskin, pp. 144–56. Washington, D.C.: National Academy.

## Sex Type and Prestige of Occupations

Research in sex differences over the past two decades has revealed that different occupations are associated with women and men (Albrecht et al. 1977; Evans-Rhodes et al. 1990; Schein 1973, 1975; Shinar 1975). Two major explanations of occupational sex-typing found in the literature are (1) the personality characteristics that are differentially attributed to men and women, and (2) the proportion of women to men currently employed in an occupation (Shinar 1975).

The personality characteristics explanation has two components. The first is based on the finding that descriptors such as aggressiveness, bravery, daring, and independence are closely associated with men, while descriptors such as timidity, sensitivity, and submissiveness are closely associated with women (Albrecht et al. 1977). The second is based on the perception that the occupations that require certain characteristics are associated with the gender that is perceived to possess those characteristics. Schein found that characteristics used by men (Schein 1973) and women (Schein 1975) to describe an ideal manager were similar to those characteristics used to describe an adult man but were quite dissimilar to those characteristics used to describe an adult woman. Therefore, based on these findings, the sex type for the occupation of manager is likely to be better described as "masculine" than "feminine" or "neutral." Studies in which the occupation of manager has been found to be masculine are consistent with this conclusion (Panek et al. 1977; Shinar 1975).

The proportion explanation claims that the perception of an occupation as masculine, feminine, or neutral is based on the proportion of men to women in a given occupation, such that a masculine job employs a greater proportion of men, a feminine job employs a greater proportion of women, and a neutral job favors neither women nor men. Shinar (1975) found that when not given a specific criterion for rating the sex type of an occupation, 86 percent of the raters used the proportion of women to men currently employed in the occupation as either their first or second choice for a judgment criterion.

The status of an occupation is determined by two objective measures: the education level required and the amount of compensation received for an occupation. In comparison, the prestige of an occupation is determined by many subjective measures and is the perception of the status of an occupation (Chartrand et al. 1987). Despite the subjective nature of the assignment of prestige to an occupation, prestige ratings have been consistent for over sixty years (Fossum and Moore 1975). Not only are these ratings consistent over time but also across different geographic locations (Fossum and Moore 1975).

Studies that have been conducted to explore the relationship between sex type and prestige suggest that occupations traditionally associated with women have yet to achieve the prestige level of occupations traditionally associated with men. Not only are fewer occupations considered to be feminine, but these occupations are lower in prestige.

Evans-Rhodes and her colleagues (1990) conducted a study using undergraduate students as subjects. The subjects rated the sex type and prestige of twenty-two occupations. Their findings suggest that both male and female students possess gender stereotypes about occupations. In addition, subjects rated masculine occupations as higher in prestige than neutral and feminine occupations, and neutral occupations as higher in prestige than feminine occupations.

A similar study was conducted by the authors in 1991 and used male and female managers as subjects (including human-resource department managers). The subjects rated 126 occupations, which were based on Shinar's list of occupations (1975). In general, the masculine occupations received higher prestige ratings than the feminine occupations. In addition, the mean ratings of prestige revealed that the prestige ratings of the feminine occupations have a very small range (that is, from lowest to highest rating). The difference in the ranges of prestige scores for masculine and feminine occupations suggests that masculine occupations are distributed from very high to very low prestige, while feminine occupations are distributed from moderate to very low prestige only.

Many of the studies of gender stereotyping have used college students (for example, Evans-Rhodes et al. 1990; Panek et al. 1977; Schein et al. 1989; Shinar 1975). Others that have examined issues more specific to the gender stereotyping of managerial jobs (Brenner et al. 1989; Schein 1973, 1975) have used adults in managerial positions as subjects. It could be argued that, while the occupational stereotypes held by college students may influence their career choices, the stereotypes held by adults in the workplace may have a greater influence on the important decisions regarding selection, promotion, and compensation.

This review suggests that college students as well as contemporary managers, including those charged with important human-resource decisions, continue to associate gender stereotypes with occupations, and, in doing so, view most occupations as being masculine. In addition, those occupations considered as feminine are perceived to be less prestigious than those occupations considered as masculine. These findings are disturbing, as they suggest a tendency to devalue occupations associated with women.

*Annette M. Girondi*

*David F. Bush*

## Bibliography

Albrecht, S.L., H.M. Bahr, and B.A. Chadwick. 1977. "Public Stereotyping of Sex Roles, Personality Characteristics and Occupations. *Sociology and Social Research* 61:223–40.

Brenner, O.C., J. Tomkiewicz, and V.E. Schein. 1989. "The Relationship between Sex Role Stereotypes and Requisite Management Characteristics Revisited." *Academy of Management Journal* 32(3):662–69.

Chartrand, J.M., T.E. Dohm, R.V. Dawis, and L.H. Lofquist. 1987. "Estimating Occupational Prestige." *Journal of Vocational Behavior* 31:14–25.

Evans-Rhodes, D., A. Murrell, and B. Dietz. 1990. *Gender Stereotyping of Occupations: Is Women's Work Still Women's Work?* Poster presented at the Eastern Psychological Association Conference, Philadelphia.

Fossum, J.A., and M.L. Moore. 1975. "The Stability of Longitudinal and Cross-Sectional Occupational Prestige Rankings." *Journal of Vocational Behavior* 7:305–11.

Girondi, A., D. Bush, and A. Nader. 1991. *Gender Stereotypes of Occupations: Does Women's Work Have Prestige Yet?* Poster presented at the Eastern Psychological Association Conference, New York.

Panek, P.F., M.C. Rush, and J.P. Greenawalt. 1977. "Current Sex Stereotypes of 25 Occupations." *Psychological Reports* 40:212–14.

Schein, V.E. 1973. "The Relationship between Sex Role Stereotypes and Requisite Management Characteristics." *Journal of Applied Psychology* 57(2):95–100.

———. 1975. "Relationships between Sex Role Stereotypes and Requisite Management Characteristics among Female Managers." *Journal of Applied Psychology* 60(3):340–44.

Schein, V.E., R. Mueller, and C. Jacobson. 1989. "The Relationship between Sex Role Stereotypes and Requisite Management Characteristics among College Students." *Sex Roles* 20(1–2):103–10.

Shinar, E.H. 1975. "Sexual Stereotypes of Occupations." *Journal of Vocational Behavior* 7:99–111.

## Gender-Segregated Occupations

Despite the rapid influx of women into the labor force over the last few decades, most continue to work in a rather narrow range of traditional female occupations. The term "occupational segregation" is used to refer to this concentration of women in occupations that are predominantly female. During the 1980s there was a slight decrease in the level of segregation in the workplace (Jacobs 1989), yet it is still the case that almost half of all employed women today work in occupations that are more than 75 percent female. Examples of occupations dominated by women include librarian, health technician, secretary and typist, nurse, data-entry worker, bank teller, bookkeeper, telephone operator, sewer and stitcher, child-care worker, and dental assistant.

The index of occupational dissimilarity is commonly used to measure the overall amount of occupational segregation in the workplace. This measure gives the percentage of one group—either men or women—who would have to change jobs in order for the occupational or industrial distributions of the two groups to be the same. Its value is 0 in the case of complete occupational integration and 100 if all occupations are completely segregated by gender. Research indicates that more than 50 percent of employed women would have to change occupations for women to be distributed in the same manner as men (Abrahamson and Sigelman 1987).

Over the last few decades, a number of white-collar occupations have become more occupationally integrated. Women have made progress in terms of entry into lower-level managerial and professional occupations. Further change is likely. Women now constitute the majority of the college student population, a critical preparatory role for entry into management and the professions. Women's participation in business, economics, law, accounting, and medical programs has undergone striking increases. These changes bode well for women's entry into the more elite, traditionally male occupations in the coming years. But a focus on professional and managerial positions tends to obscure the fact that only a minority of men and women are employed in such jobs. Similar progress has not been made, nor is it anticipated, in the skilled trades and other manual, blue-collar occupations. Women are dramatically underrepresented in these occupations. As recently as 1988, women accounted for only 9 percent of the skilled precision production, craft, and repair workers and 26 percent of machine operators, fabricators, and general laborers. Gender segregated employment remains the norm for the majority of occupations—particularly those that employ the majority of workers.

Gender segregation in the workplace is thought to be a leading contributor to the gender gap in pay (England 1992). Because women are concentrated in the lower paying occupations, they earn only about 72 cents for every dollar men earn. The single largest employment category for women, clerical work, is often referred to as the "pink collar ghetto" as a result of the typically low wages. This employment category contains more than one-third of all employed women. The second largest employment category for women, service work (such as food service, health-care service, personal services, and private household-service occupations) is also associated with below-average wages.

It can be convincingly argued that female-dominated occupations are paid less simply because women hold these jobs. Sociological research shows that the low pay in many female jobs (such as nurse, teacher, and librarian) cannot be explained by their demand for skill or training. Proponents of the doctrine of comparable worth question whether the wages in mostly female jobs aren't lower than the value of the work to the employers. Some suggest that this type of systematic undervaluing of women's jobs is a prevalent form of pay discrimination that remains immune to existing pay-equity legislation (England 1992).

Three explanations have been offered as to why women continue to cluster in traditionally female-dominated occupations despite the wage disadvantages: gender-role socialization, family obligations, and workplace discrimination (Reskin 1984). Gender-role socialization is thought to contribute to workplace segregation by encouraging women to prepare for and pursue traditional women's occupations. Women's traditional role in the family may also serve to restrict their occupational choices and cause them to cluster in occupations that are more compatible with their child-rearing role. Workplace discrimination affects women's occupational distribution in that they face barriers to employment in certain jobs as a result of the preferences of employers or male employees. Although selective hiring on the basis of sex was made illegal by Title VII of the Civil Rights Act of 1964, such practices have not ceased to exist.

Despite socialization pressures to conform to gender-specific occupational schemes, a minority of women still venture into nontraditional occupations. While such women manage to obtain the jobs they desire and reap the higher economic reward associated with male-dominated jobs, they may still suffer from the existence of occupational segregation. Women in nontraditional jobs report feelings of isolation, as well as resentment from male co-workers. Harassment of nontraditional employees is also common, and runs the gamut from practical jokes to threats of violence and workplace sabotage. This type of work environment is certainly not conducive to the satisfaction and well-being of the women workers or optimum job performance.

Legislative and policy changes can prove useful in reducing the amount of gender segregation in the workplace. Advocates of comparable-worth legislation argue that employers should be prevented from considering the sex composition of a job when setting wage rates (England 1992). If female-dominated occupations were carefully evaluated with respect to the contributions they make and remunerated accordingly, the average wage for such jobs would climb markedly. Raising the wages associated with traditionally female jobs would encourage more men to enter the positions and, over the long run, lead to a reshuffling of workers and less workplace segregation. While no targeted legislation is in place currently to force private enterprise to set pay scales for male- and female-dominated positions in an equitable fashion, a number of states are in the process of voluntarily adjusting state government employee's pay scales for this purpose.

*Dana Dunn*

## Bibliography

Abrahamson, Mark, and Lee Sigelman. 1987. "Occupational Sex Segregation in Metropolitan Areas." *American Sociological Review* 52:588–97.

Bielby, William T., and James N. Baron. 1986. "Men and Women at Work: Sex Segregation and Statistical Discrimination." *American Journal of Sociology* 91:759–99.

England, Paula. 1981. "Assessing Trends in Occupational Sex Segregation, 1900–1976." In *Sociological Perspectives on Labor Markets*, edited by Ivar Berg, pp. 273–94. New York: Academic.

———. 1992. *Comparable Worth: Theories and Evidence*. New York: Aldine De Gruyter.

———. 1982. "The Failure of Human Capital Theory to Explain Segregation." *Journal of Human Resources* 17:371–92.

Hodson, Randy, and Paula England. 1986. "Industrial Structure and Sex Differences in Earnings." *Industrial Relations* 25:16–32.

Jacobs, Jerry A. 1989. "Long-Term Trends in Occupational Segregation by Sex." *American Journal of Sociology* 95:160–73.

Kilbourne, Barbara Stanek, Paula England, and Dorthea Weir. 1990. "Skill, Compensating Differentials, and Gender Bias in Occupational Wage Determination." Paper presented at the Annual Meeting of the American Sociological Association. Washington, D.C.

Reskin, Barbara F. 1984. *Sex Segregation in the Workplace: Trends, Explanations and Remedies.* Washington, D.C.: National Academy.

Reskin, Barbara F., and Heidi I. Hartmann, eds. 1986. *Women's Work, Men's Work: Sex Segregation on the Job.* Washington, D.C.: National Academy.

Wharton, Amy S. 1989. "Gender Segregation in Private-Sector, Public Sector, and Self-Employed Occupations, 1950–1981." *Social Science Quarterly* 70:923–40.

## Sex Segregation in the Workplace

Sex segregation in the workplace refers to women's and men's concentration in different occupations, industries, jobs, and levels in workplace hierarchies. More broadly, sex segregation constitutes a sexual division of paid labor in which men and women do different tasks, or the same tasks under different names or at different times and places. People's race and sometimes their ethnicity and age are also bases for differentiation at work, so workplaces are segregated by sex, race, and ethnicity, as well as other characteristics. The assignment of jobs based on workers' sex, race, and ethnicity is one of the most enduring features of work in industrialized societies and a mainstay in preserving larger systems of inequality.

Because the work that people do greatly influences their pay, sex segregation contributes substantially to the gap in earnings between women and men (England and McCreary 1987). Segregation also reduces women's fringe benefits and their access to medical insurance, pensions, and Social Security income. By disproportionately relegating women to jobs with short or absent career ladders, segregation lowers women's chances of promotion. Both task and rank segregation restrict women's likelihood of exercising authority at work (Reskin and Hartmann 1986). The effects of segregation extend beyond the workplace. Men's higher incomes, occupational status, and authority preserve their power over women in private and public realms.

Ever since the Industrial Revolution removed most productive work from the home, employers have segregated the sexes, reserving better jobs for men (Goldin 1990). We can gauge the extent of sex segregation across occupations, industries, or jobs by examining the index of segregation. (An occupation refers to a cluster of related work activities that constitute a single economic role—for example, baker. In contrast, a job refers to the specific tasks performed by one or more people in a specific work setting—for example, a production baker at Oroweat's Oakland plant, or a "bake-off" baker at the Ballard Safeway store.) The index of occupational segregation shows the minimum proportion of either sex that would have to change from a sex-typical to a sex-atypical occupation for the sexes to be distributed similarly across all occupations. If sex had no effect on people's occupation, the index of segregation would equal 0. If women and men never held the same occupation, the index would equal 100.

In the United States, the amount of occupational sex segregation fluctuated slightly between 1910 (69.0) and 1970 (67.6). The century's largest drop in segregation occurred during the 1970s—by 1980, the index was 59.8 (Jacobs 1989). Segregation continued to decline in the 1980s, but at a much slower rate. The 1990 index—calculated for employed workers in 477 occupations—was 4.5 points lower than the 1980 index, indicating that out of every one hundred women about fifty-five would have had to switch from predominantly female to predominantly male occupations for the labor force to be fully integrated across occupations. Of course, even such an improbable wholesale redistribution would not truly integrate America's places of work because women and men in the same occupation typically work for different employers in different industries and hence hold different jobs (Bielby and Baron 1986).

Occupational segregation by race has dropped sharply in the U.S. since 1940, when most blacks were still confined to a small number of occupations. As Table 1 shows, race segregation has declined more rapidly among women than men (King 1992). However, American women of African, Asian, and Hispanic descent as well as Native-American women continue to be overrepresented in the least desirable, traditionally female jobs (Smith and Tienda 1988). In sum, women are less segregated by race than are men, and as far as occupations are concerned, being female is a bigger obstacle among the employed than not being white.

In all industrialized countries, barriers restrict women's access to many jobs. The pattern of segregation for the United States resembles that in other industrialized countries, although the Scandinavian countries exhibit particularly high levels of segregation, partly because their family policies encourage women to work part time (Rosenfeld and Kalleberg 1991).

Contributing to sex segregation are the actions of employers and workers, as well as cultural and institutional forces. Occupational sex labels and sex-role stereotypes influence employers' decisions as well as workers' occupational expectations. The occupational and industrial structures (in other words, where the jobs are) set limits on the pace of integration. For example, the growth of managerial occupations during the 1980s facilitated women's entry into managerial jobs, but the explosion of service jobs involving traditionally female tasks has slowed integration.

TABLE 1. Trends in Sex and Race Segregation

|  | 1940 | 1950 | 1960 | 1970 | 1980 | 1988[a] |
|---|---|---|---|---|---|---|
| *Segregation between* | | | | | | |
| Black and white women | 0.618 | 0.649 | 0.640 | 0.474 | 0.326 | 0.293 |
| Black and white men | 0.383 | 0.415 | 0.439 | 0.362 | 0.313 | 0.293 |
| Black women and men | 0.772 | 0.738 | 0.697 | 0.694 | 0.532 | 0.609 |
| White women and men | 0.802 | 0.729 | 0.729 | 0.723 | 0.574 | 0.604 |

Source: King 1992.

[a] Indexes based on 159 occupations common to census classification systems between 1940 and 1980.

Workers' characteristics and employers' policies also affect the extent of segregation. The human-capital explanation for segregation holds that women's family obligations (1) keep them from investing in education and experience—thus reducing their qualifications for male jobs—and (2) incline them toward traditionally female occupations that supposedly are easy to reenter and do not penalize workers for work interruptions. This theory has little support (England and McCreary 1987). Considerable evidence shows the importance of employers' and male workers' actions—including discrimination and stereotyping—in segregating workers (Reskin 1993).

The small decline in segregation during the 1960s stemmed more from men's entry into customarily female "semiprofessions" than from the integration of traditionally male occupations (Reskin and Hartmann 1986). The 1970s brought the first large-scale movement by women into the predominantly male occupations (of which there are more than three hundred). The 1980s brought increased understanding of what factors maintain and reduce it (Reskin and Hartmann 1986). Three factors contributed to the post-1970 decline in sex segregation. The first was "structural" changes in American occupations. The growth of several integrated occupations and the shrinkage of some highly segregated occupations redistributed jobs from segregated to integrated occupations.

The second component of desegregation resulted from women's gradual entry into many sex-atypical occupations (for example, statistician, groundskeeper). Several factors fostered women's increasing share of many male occupations. The more egalitarian values popularized by the women's liberation movement, later marriage and more divorce, and a recessionary economy meant that more women supported themselves and their families. These changes paved the way for laws and regulations barring sex discrimination in educational institutions and the workplace. Changing attitudes, bolstered by new regulations, encouraged many large employers to adopt equal-employment policies. As women's opportunities expanded, they increasingly resembled men in college major, job aspirations, attachment to the labor force, and paid work experience. A growing number of women entered occupations that had been reserved primarily for men, and occupations' traditional sex labels weakened and became less binding on labor-market participants. These factors reinforced small to moderate increases in the representation of women—mostly white women—in many customarily male occupations. Rarely did men replace white women in traditionally female jobs; instead, shortages created opportunities for women of color, contributing to the decline in race segregation among women.

The third component of occupational desegregation stemmed from women's substantial headway into a few male occupations such as insurance adjuster and bank manager. However, their substantial shifts in sex composition did not necessarily produce integration. Instead, some traditionally male occupational specialties such as residential real-estate salesperson and public-relations specialist, became resegregated as women's work. Employers hired thousands of women for these occupations when doing so would save money. Regulations that barred discrimination or required affirmative action contributed to women's large inroads into broadcast reporting, bank management, and bartending (Reskin and Roos 1990). So too did enormous job growth in a few customarily male occupations that outpaced the supply of qualified male applicants. Finally, employers resorted to women for occupations that could not attract enough men because their earnings had declined or they had deteriorated in other ways. In other words, employers turned to women when they needed to cut costs and when a deteriorating occupation did not generate an adequate supply of men (Reskin and Roos 1990). Women flocked to these formerly male occupations because they offered better pay and opportunities than the traditionally female occupations open to equally qualified women.

At the beginning of the 1990s, the majority of both women and men still worked in jobs in which the other sex was underrepresented, if not completely absent. Nonetheless, the work force was less sex segregated than at any earlier time in the twentieth century. How much has occupational desegregation enhanced workplace equity? Although the wage gap has declined, employers still pay a premium to workers in male-dominated jobs, so men and women in customarily male occupations usually outearn women in predominantly female jobs. And job segregation in mixed-sex occupations ensures that women rarely earn as much as their male counterparts (Reskin and Roos 1990). Moreover, while the tens of thousands of women who entered occupations and specialties that men were abandoning averaged higher pay than they would get in "women's" jobs, few earn as much as their male counterparts, and their wage advantage is unlikely to last in occupations that resegregate as "women's work."

The stalled pace of sex integration has three crucial policy implications. First, enforcing existing current programs to bar discrimination and implement affirmative action in training and employment is essential for continued declines in segregation. Second, the prevalence of job-level segregation within nominally integrated occupations means that we must find other solutions to the economic disadvantage under which women labor. One possible solution is pay equity (comparable worth)—the policy of compensating workers for the skill, effort, and responsibility their jobs require rather than for the sex composition of their workforce. However, pay equity cannot eliminate the wage disparity between the sexes so long as women are disproportionately consigned to jobs that society defines as low skilled and denied the opportunity to exercise workplace responsibility. Finally, women's continued responsibility for most family work hampers their access to some jobs. A more egalitarian division of domestic work and family-work policies that takes into account employees' family roles is needed to redress this disadvantage.

To achieve these goals, women must return to the tactics that fostered the pro-equality political climate of the 1960s and 1970s: They must act politically, applying pressure on employers, politicians, and regulatory agencies. Without such action, we will begin the twentieth century with a workforce in which sex and race rather than talents continue to determine the jobs people do.

*Barbara F. Reskin*

## Bibliography

Bielby, William T., and James N. Baron. 1986. "Men and Women at Work: Sex Segregation and Statistical Discrimination." In *American Journal of Sociology* 91:759–99.

England, Paula, and Lori McCreary. 1987. "Gender Inequality in Paid Employment." In *Analyzing Gender,* edited by Beth Hess and Myra Marx Ferree, pp. 286–320. Newbury Park, Calif.: Sage.

Goldin, Claudia. 1990. *Understanding the Gender Gap: An Economic History of American Women.* New York: Oxford University Press.

Jacobs, Jerry A. 1989. *Revolving Doors: Sex Segregation and Women's Careers*. Stanford: Stanford University Press.

King, Mary C. 1992. "Occupational Segregation by Race and Gender." *Monthly Labor Review* 115: 30–37.

Reskin, Barbara F. 1993. "Sex Segregation in the Workplace." *Annual Review of Sociology* 19:241–70.

Reskin, Barbara F., and Heidi I. Hartmann. 1986. *Women's Work, Men's Work: Sex Segregation on the Job*. Washington, D.C.: National Academy.

Reskin, Barbara F., and Patricia A. Roos. 1990. *Job Queues, Gender Queues*. Philadelphia: Temple University Press.

Rosenfeld, Rachel, and Arne L. Kalleberg. 1991. "Gender Inequality in the Labor Market: A Cross-National Perspective." In *Acta Sociologica* 34:207–25.

Smith, Shelley A., and Marta Tienda. 1988. "The Doubly Disadvantaged: Women of Color in the U.S. Labor Force." In *Women Working*, edited by Ann Helton Stromberg and Shirley Harkess, pp. 61–80. Mountain View, Calif.: Mayfield.

## Full-Time Homemaker as Unpaid Laborer

It is estimated that 33 percent of women who maintain families are not in the paid labor force, most of them being single parents and married women whose homemaker roles are full time. While a minority of men may assume such roles, there is agreement in the literature that domestic labor consists of unpaid work undertaken by women in their own households (Williams 1988). A homemaker, therefore, is defined as a woman who works full time as an unpaid domestic laborer. While this core definition does not address marital status or parenting, most research on homemakers and their associated roles has been conducted on samples of married couples with dependent children. Much of this research would also suggest that the terms housewife and homemaker are interchangeable.

The contemporary homemaker is caught in the struggle to positively affirm her role at a time when women's paid labor-force participation is rapidly increasing. Her sense of well-being is conditioned by satisfaction with both her domestic sphere and how her new role is more broadly defined. Research indicates that the homemaker role is a devalued one because it is seen as "women's work" and does not carry the same prestige as any other type of work done by men (Lindsey 1994). And domestic labor, even for pay, is perhaps the most devalued of the kinds of work women typically perform. Second, the homemaker is on continuous call to the demands of her husband and children, with her needs given low priority. Most important, the homemaker role is not a paid role and carries the associated status of "nonwork." Since the family is considered sacrosanct in the United States, financial arrangements for familial support are determined by individual couples. Regardless of the myriad of ways the family's income is divided, she has not "earned" it in the same way he does. This contributes to the burden of dependency experienced by many homemakers.

The domestic consequence of unpaid household labor supports what is referred to as the "resource hypothesis," which maintains that undesirable work will be performed disproportionately by those lacking resources either to demand sharing of the burden or allowing for the purchase of substitutes (Spitze 1986). Since household resources are likely to be judged in terms of financial contributions of family members, the unpaid homemaker will take on virtually all domestic chores. This is also linked to the "relative power hypothesis," which suggests that the more powerful spouse will perform the least amount of domestic work (Coverman 1989). It is again the connection between money and power that puts the full-time homemaker in a disadvantaged position in terms of household chores. This can be extended to include investigations of family decision-making where both middle-class and working-class housewives consistently report that their husbands have greater influence in important decisions (Steil 1989). The status of full-time homemaker works against spousal equality.

On the other hand, recent sociological and economic analyses are questioning the dominant ideology that determines that "real work" is composed only of that which is exchanged for wages. This ideology essentially ignores the wide range of services performed by homemakers for their families and society. Using capitalist terminology, the homemaker's vital roles include the physical and social maintenance and reproduction of the labor force, including the domestic laborer herself (Collins and Gimenez 1990). The majority of household work, such as shopping, cooking, sewing, child care and cleaning, would be indicative of this. Other household tasks involve direct production, processing activities, and maintenance work. Gardening, canning, making clothes, and household repairs are examples. In addition, homemakers routinely participate in voluntary activities in the community. In fiscally conservative times, businesses, private voluntary organizations, and governmental agencies increasingly rely on unpaid homemakers to provide essential services, such as caring for the elderly, acting as classroom aides and lunchroom monitors, organizing fund-raising drives, and working as crossing guards.

Until recently, homemakers have been excluded in most occupational ranking scales because such scales routinely use wages as a key factor in the ranking. Another problem in determining a homemaker's rank involves the fact that when an occupation is made up almost exclusively of women, it often suffers in prestige, regardless of educational level or task performed. Variation in rating of housewives is also confounded by both gender and social standing of the respondents (Bose 1985). In confronting these methodological difficulties, most research incorporates a combination of criteria, such as estimating the replacement costs of services that would be required in the event of homemaker absence, providing respondents with formal occupational titles associated with homemaker tasks (such as chauffeur, chef, counselor, accountant, nutritionist), and using random samples on representative cross sections of the population. Based on such evaluations, a number of researchers have now determined that a housewife would receive a middle prestige score (Bose 1985; Dworkin 1981; Lindsey 1994).

Whereas this overview demonstrates that an economic assessment may help to mitigate the devaluation of homemaking, it does not address the ambiguity and role conflict many women experience when actually assuming the role. Most contemporary women expect to marry, have children, and pursue a job or career, yet many also choose to leave the labor force when their children are young. While paid employment does not ensure marital equality, it offers women some degree of autonomy within their domestic arena. In order to reduce the psychological dissonance experienced by many homemakers, broader social values that assert that achievement and success are possible only through activities outside the home must be altered. When these are combined with revised definitions of what is considered economically productive work, homemakers should be accorded the prestige associated with the vital roles they perform.

*Linda L. Lindsey*

## Bibliography

Blumberg, Rae Lesser, ed. 1991. *Gender, Family and Economy: The Triple Overlap*. Newbury Park, Calif.: Sage.

Bose, Christine E. 1985. *Jobs and Gender: A Study of Occupational Prestige*. New York: Praeger.

Collins, Jane L., and Martha Gimenez, eds. 1990. *Work without Wages: Domestic Labor and Self-Employment within Capitalism*. Albany, N.Y.: State University of New York Press.

Coverman, Shelly. 1989. Women's Work Is Never Done: The Division of Household Labor. In *Women: A Feminist Perspective*, edited by Jo Freeman. Mountain View, Calif.: Mayfield.

Dworkin, Rosalind. 1981. "Prestige Ranking of the Housewife Occupation." *Sex Roles* 7:59–63.

Lindsey, Linda L. 1994. *Gender Roles: A Sociological Perspective*. Englewood Cliffs, N.J.: Prentice-Hall.

Spitze, Glenna. 1986. "The Division of Task Responsibility in U.S. Households: Longitudinal Adjustments to Change." *Social Forces* 64(March):689–701.

Steil, Janice M. 1989. "Marital Relationships and Mental Health: The Psychic Costs of Inequality." In *Women: A Feminist Perspective*, edited by Jo Freeman. Mountain View, Calif.: Mayfield.

Waring, Marilyn. 1988. *If Women Counted: A New Feminist Economics*. San Francisco: Harper.

Williams, Colin C. 1988. *Examining the Nature of Domestic Labour*. Aldershot, England: Avebury.

# II

# Approaches to Analyzing Women and Work

## The Measure of Female Labor-Force Attachment

The measure of labor-force attachment (LFA) is a multidimensional, longitudinal measure of women's market work. The measure, first published in 1977 (Maret-Havens 1977) in application to a national data set, incorporates several dimensions of work activity into a single quantitative index.

The LFA index varies from 0, for no measurable labor-market participation, to 100 for continuous, full-time, and year-round participation. The LFA measure differs from the census measure of labor-force status, which looks only at women's labor-market status (in or out of the labor force) at a given point in time. The dimensions of market work included in the LFA index are the following: proportion of years worked since leaving regular school (continuity of work experience); number of hours worked per week (full-time versus part-time work experience); and number of weeks worked per year (year-round versus temporary employment).

A computing formula for the LFA measure is given below. As an example, the measure is applied to data from the mature-women cohort file of the National Longitudinal Surveys of Labor Market Experience, available from the Center for Human Resource Research of Ohio State University. It includes labor-force participation for women since leaving school through 1977. To compute LFA for mature women, the formula is: $LFA = [(PYW_{<67}) + (\Sigma HW_{67-77}/48) + (\Sigma WW_{67-77}/48)]*50$; where $PYW_{67}$ is the proportion of years worked at least six months between leaving regular school and 1967; $\Sigma HW_{67-77}$ is the sum of hours between 1967 and 1977 (categories for each year are $0 = 0$, 1 through $20 = 1$, 21 through $39 = 2$, 40 or more $= 3$); and $\Sigma WW_{67-77}$ is the sum of weeks worked per year for each of the eight survey years (categories for each year are $0 = 0$, 1 through $26 = 1$, 27 through 49 $= 2$, 40 or more $= 3$).

For this summary measure of women's lifelong labor-force investment, the 1967–1977 dimensions of work intensity are each divided by a constant equivalent to twice their maximum value. The reason for this procedure is that the model assumes that recent work experience (after 1967) and early work experience (prior to 1967) are of equal importance for the worklife history of these mature women. The maximum value for dimensions of work intensity between 1967 and 1977 is

1.0 (0.5 for HW and 0.5 for WW) and the maximum value for the dimension of work continuity prior to 1967 is also 1.0. The entire expression is multiplied by 50 to yield an index with the range of 0 (for women with no measurable labor market experience) to 100 (for women who have worked consistently since leaving school in 1977 and whose participation is full time and year round).

The multidimensional nature of the labor force attachment measure more closely approximates a measure of the "provider role" (Hood 1986) than does the simple synchronic (point-in-time) measure of labor-force status. The measure also corrects problems in research on women's economic activity that are based on current activity status rather than usual activity status (on this issue see United Nations 1984). At the same time, because the LFA measure is both longitudinal and multidimensional it can be applied only to older women who have had time to develop labor-market careers.

The measure of labor-force attachment allows questions about possible variation in patterns of labor-market work among women over time. The LFA measure does not assume that all women (or men) are alike in their work patterns. Instead of coding all women as "0" (for out of the labor force) or "1" (for in the labor force), the measure of labor-force attachment can take any value from 0 to 100. Women with very low LFA scores are low on all three dimensions of market work—their work tends to be discontinuous, part time and part year. On the other hand, women with high scores have a history of continuous, full-time, and year-round employment. Women with middle range scores tend to have a recent history of full-time and year-round employment, but worked only intermittently during the early years of marriage and child-bearing.

One of the most important findings from the use of the LFA measure is that there is considerable variation in the labor force attachment of mature American women. Women who have LFA scores between 80 and 100 are defined as having careers in the American labor force. In 1977, career women constituted 14 percent of the total sample. Women with no measurable labor-force experience (LFA = 0), most of whom are keeping house, represent another 5 percent of the sample. In other words, only 5 percent of the national sample of mature women had no measurable work experience in 1977. Between these two extremes of "career women" and "homemaker," 80 percent of the sample could be found. The majority of mature women (approximately 60 percent of the sample) could be found in the categories of "strong" (LFA = 60–79), "moderate" (LFA = 40–59), and "sporadic" (LFA = 20–39) labor-force attachment. The mean LFA score was 41 ("moderate") with a standard deviation of 29. These findings indicate tremendous variability in the market work patterns of American women into the late 1970s.

Among the most important independent variables (causes) of variation in women's labor-force attachment are previous wages; husband's attitude toward wife's working; and race (Maret 1983). Women with the previous experience of high wages are more likely than other women to have careers in the labor force. Married women whose spouses are strongly in favor of their working are more likely than other married women to have labor-force careers. Black women are more likely than nonblack women to have careers in the labor force.

*Elizabeth Maret*

## Bibliography

Chenoweth, Lillian, and E. Maret. 1980. "The Career Patterns of Mature American Women." *Sociology of Work and Occupations* 7:222–41.

Hood, Jane. 1986. "The Provider Role: Its Meaning and Measurement." *Journal of Marriage and the Family* 48(May):349–59.

Maret, Elizabeth. 1982. "How Women's Health Affects Labor Force Attachment." *Monthly Labor Review* 105(April):56–58.

————. 1983. *Women's Career Patterns*. Lanham, Md.: University Press of America.

Maret-Havens, Elizabeth. 1977. "Developing an Index to Measure Female Labor Force Attachment." *Monthly Labor Review* 100(May):35–38.

Shaw, Lois B. 1986. *Midlife Women at Work*. Lexington, Mass.: D.C. Heath.

United Nations Department of International Economic and Social Affairs. 1984. *Improving Concepts and Methods for Statistics and Indicators on the Situation of Women*. Studies in Methods. Series F, No. 33. New York: United Nations.

## Geographic Aspects of Women and Work

There are at least three ways of thinking about the relations between geography and women's work. First, there is geographical variation in the degree of occupational segregation and the gendering of jobs and skills. This provides a vivid demonstration of the extent to which skills and gender relations are socially constructed. Secondly, different environments offer varying opportunities to combine different types of work. A close examination of the ways that environments expand or contract these opportunities has important implications for regional and urban planning. Thirdly, women tend to be more spatially constrained; they tend to look for and find paid employment closer to home than do men. This means that many women are highly dependent on locally available employment opportunities, a factor that requires consideration when formulating policies aimed to eradicate sex-based occupational segregation.

What is defined as women's work is not only historically but also geographically variable; this is most often demonstrated at the regional scale. In an exemplary study, Parr (1990) describes the gendering of work in two Ontario manufacturing towns from 1880 to 1950. In Paris, the majority of the labor force was female, and women performed jobs that in other places were defined as male. In Hanover, less than one hundred miles away, few women worked outside of the home, reflecting the different industrial structures, histories of labor recruitment, and ethnic composition in the two towns. Variations in local traditions of occupational segregation also have implications for types and levels of local service provision, which, in turn, affect women's opportunities to work outside the home. Mark-Lawson et al. (1985) make this argument through a close study of three towns in the English midlands between the first and second world wars. In the town in which there was little occupational sex segregation, women also had a more effective political voice and were able to instigate a range of social services, including institutionalized child care. Variability in local service provisions no doubt reinforces existing local differences in the gender relations of work.

Local environments affect the ease with which women can combine different types of work. Middle-class, suburban environments, often with poor access to paid employment, public transportation, and social services, have been seen as particularly problematic contexts for women who wish to work outside of the home (Hayden 1984). Women who live in suburbs often must construct intricate webs of informal networks in order to combine paid and mothering work (Dyck

1990). In contrast, inner-city residence typically allows women access to a wider range of jobs as well as urban amenities and formal and informal services. The decision to live in the gentrifying inner city has been interpreted as a strategy on the part of middle-class women and men to remake gender relations so as to allow a more equitable distribution of paid and domestic work (Mills 1989) (often with detrimental effects for the working-class households that are displaced as a result).

At an even finer geographical scale, conventional house forms reflect and reinforce traditional assumptions about gendered divisions of labor. There have been many experiments aimed at reshaping the distribution of women's work through urban and architectural design. Hayden (1981) describes several developed through the nineteenth century, including kitchenless houses in which the tasks of meal preparation and clean-up were removed from the private home and shared at the neighborhood level. In Canada, several feminist cooperative housing developments have been designed to facilitate the blending of paid and domestic work within the home (Wekerle 1988).

In general, women are particularly sensitive to local context for employment opportunities. Journey-to-work studies comparing women's and men's work trips have repeatedly documented that women work significantly closer to home than do men (Hanson and Johnston 1985). This generalization does conceal significant differences among women. Women working in professional and managerial positions tend to travel farther to work than do those working in unskilled jobs, as do women in full-time as opposed to part-time jobs (Hanson and Pratt 1992). A spatial mismatch between segregated housing and labor markets forces low-income African-American women living in some inner city areas to commute long distances to low-waged, suburban jobs (McLafferty and Preston 1991). In general, however, women's work trips are shorter than men's, signifying labor markets that are smaller in their geographical extent for women than men.

There are a variety of reasons why most women tend to travel relatively short distances to paid employment. Domestic responsibilities lead many women to search for jobs close to home so that they can get home quickly in an emergency or so that they can minimize overall travel time. Given that many female-typed jobs are poorly paid, there is little incentive to travel long distances to paid employment. Women tend to have poorer access to automobiles than do men. (For a review of the various explanations, see Hanson and Johnston 1985). Women and men also tend to search for paid employment differently; women are more reliant on personal and neighborhood (typically female) contacts for information about jobs (Hanson and Pratt 1991).

The paid employment that a woman finds, therefore, is frequently conditioned by what is available in the neighborhood where she lives. For many women this dependence on local employment opportunities is better conceived of in terms of constraint rather than choice because, in dual-headed, heterosexual households, the family residence is infrequently selected with the woman's employment needs foremost in mind (Hanson and Pratt 1991).

Different neighborhoods provide different job opportunities. Hanson and Pratt (1988) document the uneven spatial distribution of different types of male- and female-typed jobs in Worcester, Massachusetts. Furthermore, the urban geography of occupational segregation is a dynamic process; employers are remarkably sensitive to women's spatial immobility and to variations in residents' class, race, and skills, and they tend to locate their businesses so as to "capture" certain types of female labor (Hanson and Pratt 1992).

Recognizing the geography of occupational segregation bears on strategies for change. The finding that women tend to search for jobs locally, through informal, women-centered networks, suggests that affirmative-action programs will be effective only if information about a wide range of jobs is actively filtered through them. Understanding women's existing spatial constraints also suggests the necessity of integrating an extensive range of job opportunities within each community (which implies virtually reworking the economic geography of cities and regions) or, alternatively, changing relations in dual-headed households so that it is not the woman who almost inevitably seeks paid employment close to home.

*Geraldine Pratt*
*Susan Hanson*

## Bibliography

Dyck, I. 1990. "Space, Time and Renegotiating Motherhood: An Exploration of the Domestic Workplace." *Environment and Planning D: Society and Space* 8:459–83.

Hanson, S., and I. Johnston. 1985. "Gender Differences in Worktrip Length: Explanations and Implications." *Urban Geography.* 6:193–219.

Hanson, S., and G. Pratt. 1992. "Dynamic Dependencies: A Geographic Investigation of Local Labor Markets." *Economic Geography,* forthcoming.

———. 1991. "Job Search and the Occupational Segregation of Women." *Annals of the Association of American Geographers* 81:229–53.

———. 1988. "Spatial Dimensions of the Gender Division of Labor in a Local Labor Market." *Urban Geography* 6:180–202.

Hayden, D. 1981. *The Grand Domestic Revolution: A History of Feminist Designs for American Homes, Neighborhoods, and Cities.* Cambridge: Cambridge University Press.

———. 1984. *Redesigning the American Dream: The Future of Housing, Work and Family Life.* New York: Norton.

McLafferty, S., and V. Preston. 1991. "Gender, Race, and Commuting among Service Sector Workers." *Professional Geographer* 43:1–15.

Mark-Lawson, J., M. Savage, and A. Warde. 1985. "Gender and Local Politics: Struggles over Welfare Policies, 1918– 1939." In *Localities, Class and Gender,* edited by Lancaster Regionalism Group, pp.195–215. London: Pion.

Mills, C. 1989. "Interpreting Gentrification: Postindustrial, Postpatriarchal, Postmodern?" Ph.D. dissertation, Department of Geography, University of British Columbia.

Parr, J. 1990. *The Gender of Breadwinners: Women, Men and Change in Two Industrial Towns 1880–1950.* Toronto: University of Toronto Press.

Wekerle, G. 1988. *Women's Housing Projects in Eight Canadian Cities.* Ottawa: Canada Mortgage and Housing Corporation.

## Human Capital Theory

Human capital theory is the traditional approach used in economics to explain both women's lower wages relative to men and their concentration in low-status jobs. This theory parallels the neoclassical theory of wages by arguing that wages are linked to productivity. However, unlike orthodox neoclassicism, human capital theory argues that wages are not determined by current productivity alone, but also by the cash returns to workers who have invested in increasing their work-related skills. "Human capital" refers to the knowledge workers acquire through the investment of time and money to become more productive. Like "ability," it can rarely be measured directly. However, human capital theorists argue that years of education and years of experience improve workers' capacities, and that employers reward employees for attaining such skills.

Human capital theory argues that women are more likely than men to quit their jobs prematurely. Because of this, firms are reluctant to hire them for positions that involve employer-financed training. Women become excluded from high-status positions because such positions customarily involve extensive training. Women receive lower pay because the intermittent nature of female careers lowers women's skill levels and, by implication, female productivity. Although there is some evidence supporting human capital theory, recent feminist scholarship has successfully challenged its main assertions on many points. As a result, there have been several attempts to revise human capital theory to take into account the most cogent of the criticisms.

Technically, human capital theory does not argue that women are excluded from all high-status positions, but merely from jobs that involve high levels of firm-specific skills. Firm-specific skills are those that are of use only to one employer—for instance, mastery of a firm's proprietary technology. Firm-general skills are those of use to many employers in the labor market—for instance, literacy. Human capital theorists argue that an employee would pay for firm-general training because it would be of use to many employers; employers must themselves pay for firm-specific training because outsiders would not finance such education voluntarily. As a result, employers do not want to lose workers with firm-specific training, for that represents lost training costs. If one assumes that women have higher turnover than men, they would be poor choices for jobs with high firm-specific skills. Most high-status jobs involve extensive amounts of employer-financed skill acquisition. This includes most artisanal, professional, and managerial occupations. Women become excluded from these positions because managers are concerned with conserving training costs.

An additional argument that is made is that women choose low-status jobs as a strategy for maximizing their income. Anticipating short careers, they supposedly select jobs that do not penalize interrupted participation, offering instead high initial salaries rather than low salaries that improve with training. By doing so, they avoid wage reductions associated with human capital acquisition.

The most important challenge to human capital theory has been over the issue of the supposedly natural rates of female turnover. There is an extraordinarily large body of studies estimating gender differences in turnover. Approximately one-third of the studies report women as being more likely to quit than men, one-third find men more likely to quit than women, and another third find no differences. At a bivariate level, male quit rates are generally lower than those of women. However, the addition of simple gender-neutral controls, such as age, usually makes the differences disappear. Typical results are reported in Viscusi (1980). Global rates of turnover were higher for women than for men. However, there were no significant gender differences in tenure-specific turnover rates. Furthermore, women were more likely to decrease their quit rates in response to organizational incentives such as promotion opportunities than were men. Two extensive reviews of the empirical literature conducted by Anderson (1974) and Price (1977) have concluded that there is little support for the argument that women have higher turnover than men.

Even if significant immutable gender differences in quit rates did exist, it does not at all follow that this would produce occupational sex-typing with women being placed in low-status jobs. First, high female turnover is primarily caused by the domestic pressures associated with child-bearing. Female labor-force participation is the lowest for women with children three years of age or younger in the home (Blau and Ferber 1986). Women aged forty and over are at reduced risk of becoming pregnant. A woman who is hired at age forty and works until retirement at age sixty-five will provide twenty-five years of continuous service, a figure far in excess of average job tenures. One would expect that if employers found turnover a problem, they would consider either men or older women for jobs with high firm-specific skills. However, sex-typing divides jobs into male versus female and not male and older female versus younger female.

There have also been significant challenges to the claim that women's low pay is the product of interrupted careers. Preliminary findings had shown a correlation between low pay and the number of years spent in non–job-related activities among women in certain age groups (Mincer and Polachek 1974). However, subsequent analyses have shown that these findings do not apply to samples of adult women that are unrestricted by age. Formal attempts to decompose the wage differential between men and women show that interrupted work histories, educational shortfalls, and training shortfalls account for substantially less than half of the gender gap (Corcoran 1979). These already negative findings are likely to overestimate the impact of human capital variables by not excluding female turnover that is a function of preexisting low pay and poor promotion opportunities, rather than domesticity and weak labor-force commitment per se. England et al. (1988) have shown that female occupations do not offer higher starting pay than male jobs, nor are they less likely to penalize for work interruptions. In general, the predictions of human capital theory on women's wages are not supported.

Recent attempts to revive human capital theory in the face of these objections have generally involved the concept of "statistical discrimination." This hypothesis, advanced by Phelps (1972), is that women do not really have lower turnover than men. However, employers can not predict the turnover of individuals whether they be male or female. To protect themselves against the potential of accidentally selecting a high turnover candidate, employers invoke statistical trends and hire men. However, for statistical discrimination to effectively reduce aggregate turnover at the global level, average levels of male turnover have to be lower than average levels of female turnover. This is precisely the flawed assumption that the theory was designed to avoid. Realizing this liability, Aigner and Cain (1977) have developed a model by which the mean levels of male and female turnover are equal, but female turnover has a higher variance. Because female career lengths are thus harder to predict, employers err conservatively and hire men. It is not clear that when employers have a choice between investments with equal mean payoffs but different variances, they choose the investment with the lower risk. If this were so, financial speculation would never occur. Furthermore, the differential variability of female careers remains to be demonstrated.

Human capital theory remains the most important economic explanation of the concentration of women in low-status jobs. An alternative model will probably need to be developed that is more consistent with the evidence.

*Samuel Cohn*

**Bibliography**

Aigner, Dennis, and Glen Cain. 1977. "Statistical Theories of Discrimination in the Labor Market." *Industrial and Labor Relations Review* 30:175–87.

Anderson, B.W. 1974. "Empirical Generalizations on Labor Turnover." In *Studies in Labor and Manpower*, edited by Richard Pegnetter, pp. 33–59. Iowa City: University of Iowa Press.

Becker, Gary. 1964. *Human Capital*. Chicago: University of Chicago Press.

Blau, Francine, and Marianne Ferber. 1986. *Economics of Women, Men and Work*. Englewood Cliffs, N.J.: Prentice-Hall.

Corcoran, Mary. 1979. "Work Experience, Labor Force Withdrawals, and Women's Wages: Empirical Results Using the 1976 Panel of Income Dynamics." In *Women in the Labor Market*, edited by Cynthia Lloyd, E. Andrew, and C. Gilroy, pp. 216–45. New York: Columbia University Press.

England, Paula, George Farkas, Barbara Kilbourne, and Thomas Dou. 1988. "Explaining Occupational Sex Segregation and Wages: Findings from a Model with Fixed Effects." *American Sociological Review* 53:544–58.

Mincer, Jacob, and Solomon Polachek. 1974. "Family Investments in Human Capital: Earnings of Women." *Journal of Political Economy* 82:S76–S108.

Phelps, Edmund. 1972. "A Statistical Theory of Racism and Sexism." *American Economic Review* 62:659–61.

Polacheck, Solomon. "Occupational Self-Selection: Human Capital Approach to Sex Differences in Occupational Structure." *Review of Economics and Statistics* 58:60–69.

Price, James. 1977. *Study of Turnover*. Ames: Iowa State University Press.

Rotela, Elyce. 1981. *From Home to Office: U.S. Women at Work*. Ann Arbor, Mich.: UMI.

Viscusi, K.P. 1980. "Sex Differences in Worker Quitting." *Review of Economics and Statistics* 62:388–98.

## The Interdependence of Housework and Paid Work

Differences between the time spent on household work by women and men are well documented, and these are associated with differences in both time spent on paid labor and earnings. Rather than assuming that women should be responsible for household labor, researchers have proposed a variety of explanations for gender differences in time spent working at home and in the labor market.

Because time is finite (there are only twenty-four hours in a day), hours spent in one activity must, to some extent, reflect a trade-off. The trade-off is most typically between forms of labor. Thus, the more time spent in household labor the less time available for paid labor. Spending less time in paid labor is associated with lower earnings. Consequently, the greater time women spend on unpaid household labor is, indirectly at least, associated with their lower earnings. There is an interrelationship among household labor time, paid labor time, and earnings.

### Household Labor

In recent years there has been increased interest in women's and men's participation in household labor. Most studies still indicate marked differences in the time women and men contribute to unpaid labor. Whether Pleck's argument (1985) that men are spending more time in domestic labor, or Coverman's and Sheley's (1986) that there has been no significant change in men's contributions to household labor is true, the fact remains that women continue to spend more time on household labor than men and that the responsibility for integrating paid work with home demands still falls more heavily on women than men (Pleck 1989). Furthermore, if the burden of household labor deters women from taking jobs requiring considerable expenditures of time, their wages may be lower than those without household responsibilities.

Attempts to explain why women retain primary responsibility for household labor have been less successful than descriptions of those responsibilities. There are at least three distinct categories of explanations for women's and men's household labor time. The explanation most supported by the data is variously referred to as time availability, demand/response capability, or situational view (Coverman 1985; England and Farkas 1986). This perspective sees household labor time as a function of household demands (such as children or an employed spouse) and constraints (such as paid labor time). In other words, men and women spend time on household labor to the extent that there are demands on them to do so and they are able to respond to those demands. An alternative explanation conceptualizes the division of household labor as a function of the relative resources of household members. The focus here is on household members' resources relative to one another. Those with more relative resources are expected to use them to avoid unpleasant and undervalued activities, in this case household labor (Ross 1987). Thus, wive's greater household labor time would be explained by their lack of resources (earnings) relative to their husbands. The New Home Economists, a group of economic researchers/theorists (Becker 1981), also see a relationship between resources and household labor, but for them the association is the result not of a power struggle but of a consensual decision-making process that maximizes the benefit for the household as a unit. Finally, other researchers argue that ideology or sex-role attitudes affect household labor time such that women with more liberal sex-role attitudes will spend less time on household labor than women with more conservative sex-role attitudes, while the reverse is expected for men (Huber and Spitze 1983).

Other researchers have attempted to provide a framework for understanding the division of household labor with less focus on accounting for variation in women's and men's household labor time. Fenstermaker Berk (1985) and West and Zimmerman (1987) attempt to understand household labor as a resource for the "production of gender." Household labor is not simply something associated with gender, but one of the ways in which men and women define themselves. That is, gender is not seen as a dichotomous set of categories that are learned but as something that is created through everyday activities (Ferree 1990; Potuchek 1992). For these researchers the important issue is to understand the meaning attached to particular activities.

Although the nature of the association between household labor time and paid labor time is complex, it is clear that no matter what the source of gender differences in household labor time, it results in what is typically referred to as the "double day" for women who do participate in the paid labor force.

**Household Labor Time and Paid Labor Time**
Many explanations for the division of labor in the household and women's greater household labor time rely on the gender difference in labor-force participation as a partial explanation. That is, women continue to participate in the labor force at lower rates than men, although there has been some convergence. In 1987, women's labor-force participation rate was 56 percent, compared with 76 percent

for men. This represents a reduction in the difference between women and men but captures only part of the picture. For example, of those who participate in the paid labor force, women are more likely to work part time than men.

Until recently, the impact of household labor time on this process was ignored. Although paid labor time clearly places some constraints on women's and men's ability to participate in household labor, household responsibilities also limit paid labor time, especially for women (Shelton and Firestone 1988). Inflexibility in employment options (such as no flex time, limited parental leave, few child care options) means that women's continued responsibility for household labor limits their participation in the paid labor force. Moreover, women's household labor time is often difficult to integrate with paid work demands, while men's household labor time may more easily be adapted to paid work. This difference in adaptability reflects both women's greater absolute household labor time compared with men as well as differences in the specific tasks performed by women and men (Berk 1985; Shelton 1990).

### Household Labor Time and Earnings

Recent data continue to document the difference in earnings between women and men—women continue to earn significantly less than men, even when comparing only women and men who are employed full time (Blau and Winkler 1989). Early explanations for the wage difference usually were based on one of two broad suppositions. First, differential investments in wage-enhancing human capital like education, training, and experience account for different wages for women and men based on their value to the employer. Second, discrimination against women within the labor market explains at least a portion of their lower wages. Until the early 1980s, few researchers used gender differences in women's and men's roles in the household to account for any part of the gap in earnings. Recent efforts suggest that the more time women and, in some studies, men, spent on household labor the less they earned (Coverman 1983). This association remained even after taking into account differences in the paid labor time of women and men, which indicates that the differences between women's and men's participation in household labor have implications for their labor-force participation and earnings.

### Integrating Paid and Unpaid Labor

Much of the research attempting to explain women's and men's participation in paid and household labor emphasizes differences between men and women. On the one hand, this is both important and informative for accurately describing the differential experiences of women and men. On the other hand, this obscures similarities that direct our attention to connections between home and market. For example, women's labor-force participation rates are becoming increasingly similar to those of men. And, judging from the time they are investing in schooling and other training, their commitment to paid work is also becoming stronger (O'Neill 1985). Also wages, in combination with household responsibilities, impact women's employment decisions (England and Farkas 1986; Firestone and Shelton 1990). This contrasts to earlier ideas suggesting that women's employment decisions were based on women's assumptions that their household labor was more valuable than their paid labor (Becker 1981).

In the past, men were expected to exhibit little choice with respect to employment decisions because of their role as primary provider for the family. As wives become more involved in producing income, husbands are increasingly able to take a break from formal employment, to change career fields, to turn down overtime, to refuse to travel, and to reject transfers (Nieva 1985). Moreover, household responsibilities appear to interfere with both women's and men's paid labor time (Pleck 1989). Thus, the centrality of the breadwinner role seems to combine with household responsibilities to impact men's employment decisions. Consequently, the employment and household experiences of women and men can be understood only by examining both paid and unpaid work demands.

## Conclusion

This brief review strongly supports the idea that the spheres of market and home are integrally related, and that the basic relationship between them may be similar for men and women. Individuals and households exist along a continuum of interdependence embedded in social relations historically defined as gendered. However, neither men nor women seem successfully able to compartmentalize paid work and household responsibilities. Meaningful analyses of paid and unpaid work must be conducted simultaneously—neither can be understood in isolation.

*Juanita M. Firestone*

*Beth Anne Shelton*

## Bibliography

Becker, G.S. 1985. "Human Capital, Effort, and the Sexual Division of Labor." *Journal of Labor Economics* 3:833–58.

————.1981. *A Treatise on the Family.* Cambridge, Mass.: Harvard University Press.

Berk, S.F. 1985. *The Gender Factory: The Apportionment of Work in American Households.* New York: Plenum.

Blau, F.D., and A.E. Winkler. 1989. "Women in the Labor Force: An Overview." In *Women: A Feminist Perspective,* edited by Jo Freeman, pp. 265–86. Mountain View, Calif.: Mayfield.

Coverman, S. 1985. "Explaining Husbands' Participation in Domestic Labor." *Sociological Quarterly* 26:81–97.

————. 1983. "Gender, Domestic Labor Time and Wage Inequality." *American Sociological Review* 48:623–37.

Coverman, S., and J.F. Sheley. 1986. "Change in Men's Housework and Child-Care Time, 1965–75." *Journal of Marriage and Family* 48:13–22.

England, P., and G. Farkas. 1986. *Households, Employment and Gender: A Social, Economic and Demographic View.* New York: Aldine.

Fenstermaker Berk, S. 1985. *The Gender Factory: The Apportionment of Work in American Households.* New York: Plenum.

Ferree, M.M. 1990. "Beyond Separate Spheres: Feminism and Family Research." *Journal of Marriage and the Family* 52: 866– 84.

Firestone, J.M., and B.A. Shelton. 1990. "Impact of Male and Female Wages on Labor Force Participation." *Sociology and Social Research* 74:127–36.

Huber, J.A., and G. Spitze. 1983. *Sex Stratification: Children, Housework and Jobs.* New York: Academic.

Nieva, V.F. 1985. "Work and Family Linkages." In *Women and Work: An Annual Review.* Vol. 1, edited by L. Larwood, A.H. Stromberg, and B.A. Gutek. Newbury Park, Calif.: Sage.

O'Neill, J. 1985. "Role Differentiation and the Gender Gap in Wage Rates." In *Women and Work: An Annual Review.* Vol. 1, edited by L. Larwood, A.H. Stromberg, and B.A. Gutek. Newbury Park, Calif.: Sage.

Pleck, J.H. 1989. "Family-Supportive Employer Policies and Men's Participation." Paper presented at the National Research Council panel on employer policies and working families, Committee on Women's Employment and Related Social Issues.

————. 1985. *Working Wives, Working Husbands.* Newbury Park, Calif.: Sage.

Potuchek, J.L. 1992. "Employed Wives' Orientations to Breadwinning: A Gender Theory Analysis." *Journal of Marriage and the Family* 54:548–58.

Ross, C.E. 1987. "The Division of Labor at Home." *Social Forces* 65:816–33.

Shelton, B.A. 1990. "The Distribution of Household Tasks: Does Wives' Employment Status Make a Difference?" *Journal of Family Issues* 11:115–35.

Shelton, B.A., and J.M. Firestone. 1988. "Time Constraints on Men and Women: Linking Household Labor to Paid Labor." *Sociology and Social Research* 72:102–5.

West, C., and D. Zimmerman. 1987. "Doing Gender." *Gender & Society* 1:125–51.

## The Sex Segregation of Occupations: Structural Approaches

The sex segregation of occupations is a prominent feature of labor markets in contemporary societies (Jacobs 1989a; Jacobs and Lim 1992). Sex segregation is responsible for much of the wage gap between men and women in the labor force. Incumbents in female-dominated occupations, both male and female, earn significantly less than their counterparts in male-dominated fields (England et al. 1988). Segregation has been criticized on the grounds of efficiency as well as equity, since it poses artificial barriers to the matching of individuals' interests and skills and the jobs for which they would be best suited. Efforts to reduce segregation and its effects include affirmative action legislation, pay-equity (comparable-worth) reforms, the expansion of professional and vocational training opportunities for women, and the expansion of child-care facilities and support for working women, among others.

Sex segregation is a persistent feature of the economic system of developing, industrial, and postindustrial countries (Hartmann 1976). There is no clear association between economic development and reduced sex segregation (Jacobs and Lim 1992). In the United States from 1900 through 1970, roughly two-thirds of women would have had to change occupations in order to be distributed in the same manner as men (Jacobs 1989a). The level of segregation is even higher across jobs, rather than occupations. Estimates of the economic cost to women of occupational segregation range from 20 to 40 percent of the gender gap in wages, while the segregation of job titles may be responsible for as much as 60 percent of the gender gap in wages (Sorensen 1989; Tomaskovic-Devey 1993). While some have suggested that such amenities as more pleasant working conditions and more flexible schedules offer nonmonetary compensation to incumbents in female-dominated occupations, in-depth investigations have not supported these hypotheses (Glass and Camarigg 1992; Jacobs and Steinberg 1990).

Explanations for the persistence of sex segregation include socialization, human capital investments, and labor-market discrimination. Structural approaches emphasize the fact that individual choices are shaped by available opportunities and tend to reinforce existing patterns, in the absence of external pressures for change. A key question from a structural viewpoint is, "How is the system of segregation reproduced over time?"

One main approach to this question has focused on explaining why individual occupations maintain their sex-typed identity (Jacobs 1992; Reskin and Roos 1990; Strober 1993). Studies of the relatively few occupations that have changed from male-dominated to female-dominated reveal that the occupations were in decline before women entered, men left or entered in reduced numbers, and women's entry confirmed and reinforced the declining position of the occupation. These studies have emphasized that men's preferences determine the sex type of an occupation, and only when they are no longer interested do occupations become "women's work."

The other main structural approach to studying the sex segregation of occupations has focused on the mobility of individual men and women between sex-typed occupations (Jacobs 1989b). Evidence from a variety of studies indicates that while individual men and women do move between male-dominated, sex-neutral, and female-dominated fields, the system of segregation remains in place. This research has challenged the socialization explanation on the grounds that individuals who aspire to sex-typed fields often pursue employment in a different sex-type category. Similarly, the human-capital explanation is criticized from this vantage point. The sex type of fields of study in colleges is not a fixed attribute linked to lifelong plans, but rather changes frequently during college students' undergraduate years. The human-capital explanation of segregation has also been criticized on the grounds that choosing a female-dominated field is not an effective strategy by which to maximize one's lifetime earnings, even for those anticipating interruptions in their labor-force participation. The conclusion of these studies of individual mobility is that the structure of segregation is reproduced by a system of social control exerted throughout individuals' lives and not at any single decisive moment during the life course.

Since 1970 the level of segregation has declined at a modest but steady pace. The indices of segregation have declined from roughly 67 to 55, indicating that 55 percent of women would still have to change occupations in order to be fully integrated with men (Jacobs 1989a). Segregation has declined most rapidly in the area of career aspirations, followed by notable declines in the segregation of college majors and more limited changes in the labor market. Women have made significant progress in several prominent fields, such as law, medicine, and management, although they have not attained parity in any of these areas. The economic impact of comparable-worth reforms has been quite limited to date in the United States, although in other countries comparable-worth reforms have been more comprehensive and consequential.

*Jerry A. Jacobs*

## Bibliography

Bielby, W.T., and J.N. Baron. 1984. "A Woman's Place Is with Other Women: Sex Segregation within Organizations." In *Sex Segregation in the Workplace: Trends, Explanations, Remedies*, edited by B.F. Reskin, pp. 27–55. Washington, D.C.: National Academy.

England, P., G. Farkas, B. Kilbourne, and T. Dou. 1988. "Explaining Occupational Sex Segregation and Wages: Findings from a Fixed Effects Model." *American Sociological Review* 53:544–88.

Glass, J., and V. Camarigg. 1992. "Gender, Parenthood and Job-Family Compatibility." *American Journal of Sociology* 98:131–51.

Hartmann, H. 1976. "Capitalism, Patriarchy, and Job Segregation by Sex." In *Women and the Workplace: The Implications of Occupational Segregation*, edited by M. Blaxwell and B. Reagan, pp. 137–70. Chicago: University of Chicago Press.

Jacobs, J.A., 1989a. "Long Term Trends in Occupational Segregation by Sex." *American Journal of Sociology* 95:160–73.

———. 1989b. *Revolving Doors: Sex Segregation and Women's Careers*. Stanford, Calif.: Stanford University Press.

———. 1992. "Women's Entry into Management: Trends in Earnings, Authority and Values among Salaried Managers." *Administrative Science Quarterly* 37:282–301.

Jacobs, J.A., and S.T. Lim. 1992. "Trends in Occupational and Industrial Sex Segregation in 56 Countries, 1960–1980." *Work and Occupations* 19:450–86.

Jacobs, J.A., and R.J. Steinberg. 1990. "Compensating Differentials and the Male-Female Wage Gap: Evidence from the New York State Comparable Worth Study." *Social Forces* 69: 439–68.

Reskin, B., and P. Roos. 1990. *Job Queues, Gender Queues.* Philadelphia: Temple University Press.

Sorensen, E. 1989. "Measuring the Effect of Occupational Sex and Race Composition on Earnings." In *Pay Equity: Empirical Inquiries,* edited by R.T. Michael, H.I. Hartmann, and B. O'Farrell, pp. 49–69. Washington, D.C.: National Academy.

Strober, M. 1993. *The Dynamics of Occupational Segregation.* Unpublished manuscript, Stanford University Graduate School of Education.

Tomaskovic-Devey, D. 1993. *How Come Everybody Looks like Me? The Causes and Consequences of Sex and Race Segregation at Work.* Ithaca, N.Y.: Industrial and Labor Relations Press.

## Dimensions of Sex Segregation in the Workplace

Sex segregation in the workplace refers to the differentiation of work between men and women. Occupational segregation has received the most scrutiny, but segregation may be studied across many different units: work activities within a job, job titles within an organization, firms within an industry, and industries within an economy. In general, the smaller the unit examined, the higher the level of segregation observed (Bielby and Baron 1984; Reskin 1988). Sex segregation is analogous in some respects to residential segregation of racial and ethnic groups, in that in both cases privileged groups attempt to restrict access to socially desirable positions.

A sizable component of the sex gap in pay has been attributed to the sex segregation of work. Recent research indicates that, in the U.S., job-level segregation explains more than half of the sex gap in wages (Petersen and Morgan 1993; Tomaskovic-Devey 1993). Legislation requiring equal pay for equal work has limited force because women so often do different work than men. Comparable worth, or pay equity, proposals have been advanced to reduce the gender gap in wages associated with the devaluation of work performed by women.

There are at least three distinct aspects of sex segregation. The principal dimension of segregation that is the focus of most research is the degree to which men and women are distributed unevenly across occupations (Jacobs 1993; Gross 1968; James and Taeuber 1985; Massey and Denton 1989). This concept is typically measured with the index of dissimilarity (D), which indicates the proportion of women who would have to change occupations to be distributed in the same manner as men. Recent studies of the U.S. economy indicate that over half of women would have to change occupations and over two-thirds would have to change job titles to be distributed in the same manner as men. The level of sex segregation has declined during the 1970s and 1980s after remaining largely unchanged for most of the century. Similarly high levels are observed in other industrial countries as well as developing countries (Charles 1992; Jacobs and Lim 1992).

A second feature of sex segregation is the crowding of women into a limited number of fields, thus artificially creating a large pool of women for a restricted set of employment channels. This aspect is not directly captured by the index of dissimilarity, and requires the use of specific indices of concentration, designated C, for concentration or crowding. It should be noted that studies of crowding may be biased by the tendency of official statistics to report the work of male-dominated fields in more detail than female-dominated fields. This pattern would cause women to appear to be more crowded than they actually are.

For example, in the United States, detailed occupational data classify machine operators into forty-nine different specialties, based on the type of machinery they operate, while secretaries are reported in a single classification and are not differentiated by industry or responsibility level. Reliance on such data will inflate the level of occupational crowding by sex that no doubt exists in the United States economy.

A third aspect of segregation is the degree of intergroup contact—in other words, the chances of men and women sharing a job or an occupation. Intergroup contact measures—designated P*—reflect both the level of segregation and the representation of each group (Jacobs 1993; Lieberson 1980). Moreover, women's chances of sharing an occupation with men differ from men's chances of sharing an occupation with women. One striking result of the growth in women's labor-force participation is that women's chances of sharing an occupation with men has declined (as working women's numbers increase, women's chances of sharing an occupation with another woman increase), while men's chances of sharing an occupation with women has increased markedly. The two groups thus differ in how they experienced the same changes, an aspect of segregation revealed by measures of intergroup contact (Jacobs 1993).

Studies of sex segregation in the workplace have stressed the durability of this phenomenon and have discussed a range of policy recommendations to counter it and its effects, including reforms in career counseling, education, training programs, hiring practices, workplace cultures, affirmative action, government antidiscrimination laws, and comparable-worth wage reforms (Bergmann 1986; Jacobs 1989; Reskin and Roos 1990).

*Jerry A. Jacobs*

## Bibliography

Bergmann, B. 1986. *The Economic Emergence of Women*. New York: Basic.

Bielby, W.T., and J.N. Baron. 1984. "A Woman's Place Is with Other Women: Sex Segregation within Organizations." In *Sex Segregation in the Workplace: Trends, Explanations, Remedies*, edited by B.F. Reskin, pp. 27–55. Washington, D.C.: National Academy.

Charles, M. 1992. "Accounting for Cross-National Variation in Occupational Sex Segregation." *American Sociological Review* 57:483–502.

Gross, E. 1968. "Plus ca change . . . ? The Sexual Structure of Occupations over Time." *Social Problems* 16:198–208.

Jacobs, J.A. 1989. *Revolving Doors: Sex Segregation and Women's Careers*. Stanford, Calif.: Stanford University Press.

———. 1993. "Theoretical and Measurement Issues in the Study of Sex Segregation in the Workplace." *European Sociological Review.* 9:325–30.

Jacobs, J.A., and S.T. Lim. 1992. "Trends in Occupational and Industrial Sex Segregation in 56 Countries, 1960–1980." *Work and Occupations* 19:450–86.

James, D., and K. Taeuber. 1985. "Measures of Segregation." *Sociological Methodology,* Vol. 15, edited by N. Tuma, pp. 1–31. San Francisco: Jossey Bass.

Lieberson, S. 1980. *A Piece of the Pie*. Berkeley: University of California Press.

Massey, D.S., and N.A. Denton. 1989. "The Dimensions of Residential Segregation." *Social Forces* 67: 281–315.

Petersen, T., and L. Morgan. 1993. "Occupation-Establishment Sex Segregation and the Gender Wage Gap." Unpublished manuscript, University of California, Berkeley.

Reskin, B.F., 1988. "Bringing the Men Back in: Sex Differentiation and the Devaluation of Women's Work." *Gender and Society* 2:58–81.

Reskin, B.F., and P. Roos. 1990. *Job Queues, Gender Queues*. Philadelphia: Temple University Press.

Tomaskovic-Devey, D. 1993. *How Come Everybody Looks like Me? The Causes and Consequences of Sex and Race Segregation at Work*. Ithaca, N.Y.: Industrial and Labor Relations Press.

## Women in the Professions: Assessing Progress

Women's participation in the professions has increased dramatically in the last half-century, although women have yet to achieve parity with men. Nevertheless, the establishment of "parity" as a broad, socially acceptable goal is a significant political achievement. Evaluating the extent to which women have achieved parity within some of the dimensions of professionalization draws on three issues identified by Alvarez's framework (1990): (1) sociological analyses of the professions; (2) the nature of women's labor and how it fits into the four dimensions of professional activity; and (3) the outcomes of political strategies used by professional women.

### A Conceptual Overview of the Professions

Sociological analyses of professions have typically been either "trait" or "process" oriented. Trait researchers seek to identify the essential characteristics of both activities and the people who perform them. When an activity possesses a high degree of characteristics such as an exclusive body of knowledge, selection for knowing and using that body of knowledge as a "calling" to do the work, and the ability to self-regulate standards for work, it is termed a "profession." Process researchers assume that these characteristics form a continuum with occupations at one pole and professions at the other, and that activities will move along this continuum at different points in time. They assume that occupational groups will struggle to become like the professions, while professional groups will defend and maintain their status and privilege as protected positions in society.

Yet the trait approach does not explain how a particular trait contributes to the social definition of an activity as a profession. Process theorists do not systematically identify a set of processes that explain how an activity or its practitioners acquire a trait characteristic of a profession. Both approaches disadvantage women because some traits may be more characteristic of "male standpoints" or of greater political strength, rather than of "professionalization" per se.

The scheme proposed by Alvarez (1990) makes problematic the level of power available to any group attempting to impact on each dimension of professionalization. This provides an avenue for understanding how women have become agents on their own behalf within each profession, and in turn how women have been enlisted in collective attempts by those professions for their own increased societal influence.

### Women's Labor within Some Dimensions of Professional Activity

Women's progress toward full professionalization can be assessed along three of the dimensions of professionalization proposed by Alvarez (1990): (1) a systematic body of knowledge over which professionals have a monopoly; (2) a population with distinctive training and other attributes; and (3) a political coalition of organizations that enforce performance standards for each other. These standards are consistent with societal policies and shape regulatory policies for that profession on behalf of society.

An analysis of women's progress toward full professionalization must also take into account two processes of occupational segregation that have operated to place women into lower status and lower-paying positions in the labor market:

(1) External occupational segregation is the tendency of men and women to hold different types of occupations; (2) Internal occupational segregation is the tendency of men and women to hold different positions or specialties within a particular occupational field. Both external and internal occupational segregation devalue women's labor regardless of the qualifications, training, or expertise they bring to the job. There is a tendency for a certain degree of "male standpoint" to become accepted as a "professional" ingredient in prestigious, more-powerful occupations and jobs, while others are viewed as "less professional" because they contain more of a "female standpoint," such as the expectation of nurturing by nurses or help-fulness by librarians.

The first dimension of professionalization is the creation of a body of specialized knowledge and a monopoly over its use. Professional knowledge does not exist independently of social construction, but rather is subject to "social closure," a process whereby power struggles among political actors determine who has access to what knowledge. Hence, those who win access also determine what constitutes knowledge and how it evolves (Alvarez 1990). As modern, male-dominated medicine emerged and received political sanction by the state, traditional domains of women's knowledge, (such as obstetrics and gynecology versus midwifery) were undermined or prohibited through legal requirements for certification and licensing. To counteract these restrictions, women struggled for access to knowledge monopolized by male professionals through political demands for increased admission to colleges and universities. Empowered by academic access and the legitimacy of conferred degrees, they could then legitimately seek certification by professional associations and licensure by state authorities. Therefore, armed with these credentials, they could mobilize politically to break the institutional web that locked out representativeness of women and the representation of "women's standpoint."

As women achieve both greater numbers and higher positions in previously male-dominated professions, professional knowledge may undergo transformations in meaning as women's singular experiences and perceptions are incorporated and may contribute to development of knowledge in some areas. As change occurs both in the nature of professional knowledge as well as in who monopolizes its creation and its dissemination, new political coalitions are made possible. Thus, fields of knowledge may become established or become of greater importance because of more evenhanded association with women's needs or the standpoint of female practitioners. Such previously downplayed or unattended issues include legal protection for children, medical research on women's health-care issues, and economical housing for single-parent families. Thus, knowledge domains traditionally ascribed to women are being transformed from liabilities to professional assets with increasing public-policy impact. This may reinvigorate the legitimacy society-at-large attributes to the profession and expand women's mandate for professional activity.

A second dimension of professional activity concerns the criteria for professional membership. Who is permitted to become a member of a profession can be a significant determinant of what areas of professional practice are deemed important, worthy of high remuneration (pay and benefits), and preparatory for advancement to higher professional office and determination of public policy.

Acceptance into the community of professionals has in the past (and continues to be) determined by individual traits such as gender, ethnicity, and personality (such as charisma or altruism), or by specialized training or educational credentials (Alvarez 1990). In spite of their accepted usefulness in specific areas of professional practice, women's physical characteristics, personality types, and credentials have typically been undervalued in assessments of professionalization. Historically, as biological "child bearers," women were ascribed primary responsibility for an array of undifferentiated "domestic" roles. Even today, when child "bearing" can be differentiated from child "caring," the "cult of domesticity" still attributes to women a "natural" disposition to nurture and support others (Geschwender 1991). "Beyond the hearth" applications of this might explain prior virtual restriction of women to fields like nursing, teaching, librarianship, and counseling. The "cult of domesticity" segregates women into roles associated with nurturing, rather than those associated with financial or narrowly defined traditional professional practice, thereby protecting or expanding men's professional dominance. An analysis of structured power relations (that is, who makes decisions, establishes rules, and determines promotion ladders), may provide a better explanation for the gender gap in pay and status than gender differences in education and credentials.

As recently as 1982, women still experienced severe external occupational segregation. Nationally, women constituted only 14 percent of all lawyers and physicians nationally, 95.6 percent of all nurses, and 83.4 percent of all librarians. There is cause for some optimism, however. Current events in law frequently forecast what will occur in other professions. A survey of lawyers in California in 1991 suggests a large leap toward parity in the near future. In California, 74 percent of lawyers are male, 26 percent female. White males constitute 93 percent of California lawyers in practice twenty years or longer, but only 49 percent of those in practice less than five years. Thus, while parity (regarding both internal and external segregation) is still a far-off goal, access into the legal profession appears to be improving.

The prospect of parity in the legal profession being achieved soon may be an optimistic bellwether of changes to come in other professional spheres and in society at large. There are hopeful signs suggesting that the "glass ceiling" to status, power, and financial rewards might also be increasingly penetrable. In 1991, among white male lawyers in California, 41 percent earned more than $125,000 annually, compared with 23 percent of women lawyers. It is reasonable to predict that when those who currently have been in practice for less then five years obtain twenty or more years of professional experience, an increase in the proportion of women senior law partners will occur, and, by extension, chief executive officers of corporations and other institutions.

The third dimension of professional activity involves political coalitions creating and maintaining what constitutes professional knowledge, enforcing standards of practice, and screening applicants for admission into schools and practice settings. Not only do such coalitions set standards internally for a profession, they actively engage in shaping regulatory policies for that profession on behalf of society. Professional persons occupying leadership positions within these organizations have disproportionate power as enforcers of standards. Professional spokespersons are disproportionately chosen from among the most prestigious and most remunerated professional sectors.

Within professional fields, women are disproportionately found in less prestigious specialties. Researchers find women's work is consistently undervalued; statistically, differences in education and credentials account for little of this disparity. Concentration of women in lower-paying, lower-prestige positions accounts not only for their lower earnings, but also for their scarcity among professional spokespersons. Until recently, women tended not to enter medical subspecialties with responsibility for adult health; women were more likely to become pediatricians than surgeons. In turn, the lower status of this specialty precludes it as a training ground for administrators of health-care organizations, or beyond that, as preparation to become professional spokespersons entrusted with formulation of medical and health-care policies at state and national levels.

Internal occupational segregation within organizations hampers women from developing strong coalitions in the profession-at-large. Reskin and Roos (1990) found that female physicians and pharmacists tend to hold salaried positions in governmental agencies and chain drug stores, while men tend to be in private practice. These disparities contribute toward formation of the "glass ceiling" many women face, whereby disparate job tracks limit women from acquiring lower-level professional experience deemed necessary to qualify for higher, more influential, prestigious, and well-remunerated positions within professional practice. This occurs, not by virtue of innate inability or lack of basic qualifications, but by not having the sponsorship of well-placed, powerful senior colleagues, mostly white males, to articulate the value of incorporating "women's standpoint" as a central feature of the profession. Conversely, sex segregation concentrates and tracks men early into starter positions providing experiences later interpreted to be excellent, if not essential, qualifications for higher professional positions (Reskin and Roos 1990). In turn, unless women can have demographic representativeness among influential professional policy-making positions, their ability to instigate internal reform is severely limited.

To combat such concentration, professional women have engaged in concerted political action to establish social policies, regulations, and laws closing the gender gap in status, pay, and benefits, as well as access to and participation in all sectors of professional practice. Political activity by women, however difficult or intense, has not been an unalloyed success. Some efforts, like the "comparable worth" movement, have had little success, while equal pay for equal work has been a winning political appeal.

Political coalitions need time, resources, and leadership to form and focus parity as a broad social value into specific, obtainable objectives. The larger women's movement has benefited women's professional attainment in many ways. In the first wave of feminism (from the 1840s to the 1920s), the broadening of women's civil rights allowed women to legally act as autonomous individuals to whom greater educational and professional opportunities were available. In the second wave of feminism (1960s and 1970s), legislation mandating equality as a goal for the workplace facilitated the entry of women into traditionally masculine occupations in the expanding economy of that period. In both prior periods of intense feminism, issues of representativeness (a demographic assessment of the presence of women) had a basic, simple, and broad political appeal. By the 1980s and mid 1990s, given the prospects of cracks in the glass ceiling and the exercise of significant power by women professionals, the much more difficult, complex, and subtle issues of representation (whether women's perspective and self-interests have been involved in defining valuable professional knowledge and practices) have come into play (Alvarez 1979). The extent to which both men and women in society-at-large will provide political support for incorporation of a distinctive women's standpoint in the professions is still an openly contested and highly controversial question.

## Ironic Outcomes and Conclusion

In seeking parity within professional labor markets, conflicting political tactics have sometimes been adopted. The social movement to achieve gender transformation within the professions has pursued two tactical objectives: (1) to increase demographic representativeness of women within all areas of professional activity as a means to ensure representation of women's unique viewpoints and contributions; and (2) to make the workplace gender-neutral in terms of both remuneration as well as ascendancy to the highest, most authoritative positions (the right to exercise power). The first goal is to incorporate women's experience and standpoints, and application of their perspectives in formulation of workplace policies. The second goal is to foster an environment that evaluates and remunerates workers in terms of technical competence and positional status with minimal reference to gender. Government regulations prohibiting discrimination by gender or ethnicity are intended to produce such an environment. Workplace policies that encompass obligations of workers and employers (both male and female) without being gender-specific, such as parental leaves (as opposed to maternity leaves) of absence are another example. Managerial initiatives to achieve these goals inevitably encounter criticism. In the face of historical practices to the contrary, efforts to institutionalize parity are likely to be interpreted by some as "reverse discrimination" by both those who prefer traditional practices and perspectives as well as by those who believe gender should not be an explicit consideration, even if they support parity as a goal.

Such anomalies along the way toward achievement of gender equality in the professions demonstrate the need to assess the degree of progress separately within each specific and conceptually distinct dimension of professionalization. Within each specific context, we can both see the tremendous progress that has been made in the last quarter-century, and more specifically locate the institutional areas where new transformative effort is needed.

*Rodolfo Alvarez*
*Leah Robin*
*Mia Tuan*
*Amily Shui-I Huang*

## Bibliography

Alvarez, Rodolfo. 1979. "Institutional Discrimination in Organizations and Their Environments." In *Discrimination in Organizations: Using Social Indicators to Manage Social Change*, edited by Rodolfo Alvarez, et al. San Francisco: Jossey-Bass.

———. 1990. "Organizations and the Professions: Four Dimensions for Sociological Analysis." Unpublished manuscript. Department of Sociology, UCLA.

Epstein, Cynthia Fuchs. 1983. *Women in Law*. Garden City, New York: Anchor.

Gerson, Kathleen. 1985. *Hard Choices*. Berkeley: University of California Press.

Geschwender, James A.C. 1991. "Ethgender, Women's Waged Labor, and Economic Mobility," *Social Problems* 39(1):1–16.

Lorber, Judith. 1984. *Women Physicians: Careers, Status, and Power*. New York: Tavistock.

Menkel-Meadow, Carrie. 1989. "Exploring a Research Agenda of the Feminization of the Legal Profession: Theories of Gender and Social Change." *Law and Social Inquiry* (14)Spring:289–319.

Phipps, Polly A. 1990. "Industrial and Occupational Change in Pharmacy: Prescription for Feminization." In *Job Queues, Gender Queues: Explaining Women's Inroads into Male Occupations*, edited by Barbara F. Reskin and Patricia Roos. Philadelphia: Temple University Press.

Reskin, Barbara F., and Patricia Roos. 1990. *Job Queues, Gender Queues: Explaining Women's Inroads into Male Occupations*. Philadelphia: Temple University Press.

Ward, Patricia A., Peter F. Orazem, and Steffen Schmidt. 1992. "Women in Elite Pools and Elite Positions," *Social Science Quarterly* 73(1):31–45.

## Sex Stereotypes: An Underlying Dimension

Sex stereotypes are beliefs about the personal characteristics of women and men. Generally, women are seen as more supportive, dependent, and emotional; men as stronger, more independent, and objective (Lueptow 1984, pp. 54–55). Research over four decades has shown consensus between the sexes on the stereotypic traits, stability in the content over the years (Bergen and Williams 1991; Lueptow and Garovich 1992), and universality across cultures (Williams and Best 1990). While the stability and universality of the trait descriptions point to biological predispositions, most researchers assume stereotypic traits result from socialization and are artifactual and changeable. Whatever their source, given the segregation of work, sex stereotypes have implications for both selection and recruitment and directly relate to the sex typing of work (Reskin and Hartmann 1986, chap. 3). Stereotypes also have implications for personal well-being. In spite of the great early enthusiasm for the concept of androgyny among feminist writers (see Kaplan and Bean 1976) and early conclusions that androgynous persons experienced better psychological adjustment (Bem 1974), more recent research has shown the effect to have been because of the fact that androgynous women possess masculine as well as feminine traits. Masculinity, not androgyny, is related to psychological adjustment in both sexes (Cook 1985).

Sex stereotypes are characteristics believed to be associated with one sex or the other. Research from the 1950s to the 1990s has assessed stereotypes by using college students to generate lists of adjectives or behavioral characteristics more often associated with women or with men. The content of these lists has been remarkably consistent (Lueptow 1984, pp. 51–57), the male stereotype being characterized by assertiveness and strength, independence, and objectivity, the female by expressiveness, support, and emotionality. For example, the seven most masculine traits on Williams's and Best's Sex Stereotype Index (SSI) are aggressiveness, adventurousness, dominance, forcefulness, strength, independence, and ambition; the seven most feminine are sentimentality, emotionality, affection, sympathy, soft-heartedness, talkativeness, and attractiveness. In all of this research there has been strong agreement between the sexes regarding the content of the stereotypes.

There has been less consistency regarding the favorability of the stereotypes. Early researchers found men were rated as superior and their traits evaluated more favorably (Broverman et al. 1972). However, in their American and cross-cultural research, Williams and Best (1990) found no relation between favorability and masculinity scores on the SSI and found that roughly half of the countries rated women more favorably and half rated men more favorably. More recently, Eagly et al. (1991) found that women were evaluated *more* favorably than men. While some of this change may reflect weakness in the early research, it also appears that there has been real change in the favorability ratings of women since the 1960s.

A major event of the 1970s research was the emergence of the concept of androgyny. Earlier research had focused upon the masculinity of males and the femininity of females, and some scales were bipolar in treating masculinity and femininity as opposite ends of a single dimension. In what became a series of landmark studies, Sandra Bem (1974) emphasized a scoring system (Bem Sex Role Inventory) encompassing both masculine and feminine traits that permitted the scoring of androgyny—that is, presence of both masculine and feminine characteristics in the same person. While her research was relatively limited methodologically and her findings not unequivocal, the concept had substantial appeal and dominated research interests of feminist scholars, who elaborated the advantages of flexibility and adaptability of the non–sex-typed personality (Kaplan and Bean 1976) and the psychological disadvantage of sex-typing (Franks and Rothblum 1983). However, as research on relations between androgyny, achievement, and well-being accumulated, it became clear that despite the intuitive validity of the concept, androgyny was not the advantage to mental health and achievement it had appeared to be. Rather, it was masculinity that was related to mental health. Androgyny was beneficial, especially for women, because it included masculinity, not because of the combination of femininity and masculinity (Cook 1985). Androgynous persons are better liked and have higher self-esteem, however.

In addition to the focus on androgyny, other approaches have questioned the direct conceptualization of the stereotypes as consisting of masculinity and femininity, as Bem (1974) supposed. Factor analysis of the BSRI often reveals four dimensions. One is sex and a second is feminine expressiveness. The masculinity dimension bifurcates into two obvious, but not always recognized, dimensions: dominance and aggressiveness on the one hand and independence and self-sufficiency on the other. This factor structure appears to be remarkably stable across time (Waters and Popovich 1986).

Another approach to multidimensionality has been in the examination of the structure of stereotypes, going beyond personality traits to include gender labels, sex roles, occupation, and physical characteristics (Deaux and Lewis 1984). Of these various dimensions, physical structure emerges as the strongest indicator of masculinity-femininity. Given a tall, sturdy person with broad shoulders, other masculine components are assigned whether the person is labeled man or woman. Not surprisingly, sex-differentiated physical characteristics seem to be central to the concept of the sex stereotype.

While no clear and consensual formulation has emerged to replace early concerns with the patently significant concepts of masculinity-femininity, recent writings have returned to the old instrumental-expressive distinction as substitutes for masculine/feminine and emphasized the lack of relationships between sex-role orientations and sex stereotypes (Gill et al. 1987; Spence and Helmreich 1980). Another formulation that has recently become common in the psychological literature is the use of Bakan's distinction (1966) between agency (masculinity) and communion (femininity) to express the basic dimensions of sex stereotypes. Whether these substitutions are meaningful remains to be seen.

The social reality of sex stereotypes has by now been demonstrated in a substantial number of studies that have clearly documented the nearly perfect stability of the conceptions in populations from the 1950s to the 1990s in the U.S. and across cultures. Women and men are perfectly clear about the differences between women and men, and these perceptions have not changed for over forty years (Bergen and Williams 1991; Lueptow and Garovich 1992) and are held in societies throughout the world (Williams and Best 1990). This is a remarkable and generally unevaluated social psychological fact, especially when considered in the light of changes in sex roles and in sex-role orientations that have occurred during that same period (Simon and Landis 1989). It is difficult to believe that such constancy and universality could occur without an important underlying base, either in socialization or biology.

Most gender researchers assume these gender differences are the results of socialization, either in childhood or in adult situations. In childhood it is assumed that parents train their children in terms of their own stereotypic perceptions. This view is held in spite of the strong contrary evidence in Maccoby and Jacklin (1974) and in spite of the fact that parents have changed their attitudes about appropriate gender roles quite dramatically over the forty-year period during which stereotypes have remained constant.

The classic situational explanation of the stereotypic content grew from Parsons's and Bales's exposition (1955) of the two leadership styles observed in small-group research: instrumental and expressive. Parsons extended this to the family, arguing that the father played the instrumental role, the mother the expressive. The personality characteristics required to perform adequately in these two roles are generally those observed in the male and female stereotypes. Thus, the stereotypes can be viewed as clusters of characteristics acquired by males and females in anticipation of their future allocations to instrumental or expressive roles. The marked contrast between role changes and stereotypic constancy also raises questions for this explanation, and it is no longer seriously considered. Another situational explanation has to do with the ubiquitousness of gender presentations in all media, especially television, where the portrayal of women and men has also not changed much over the past decades (Davis 1990).

The likelihood that the observed stability and universality of the stereotypic characteristics reflect biological underlays is not generally advanced. In exception to that point we can note that Williams and Best (1990) suggested that the universality reflected real differences between the sexes, probably resting on biological factors, and Kenrick (1987) has outlined how genetically determined patterns interact with the environment to produce observed differences.

The centrality of physical characteristics in the stereotype cluster is consistent with biological explanations, as are the persisting empirical findings on the importance to the opposite sex of physical attractiveness in women and dominance in men (Sadalla et al. 1987). As noted previously, the constancy of the trait clusters across forty years of change is also more consistent with biological than with social explanations.

The relevance of this to work issues lies in the relation between sex-typing of work and the sex stereotypes. What have been defined as women's jobs generally entail nurturing, assisting, or supporting activities. Jobs requiring strength, risk, and high levels of dominance and competitiveness have typically been men's jobs. Selection of occupational goals and recruitment are, to some degree, based upon stereotypic concerns, although they have of course been highly mitigated by structural shifts, affirmative action, and redefinition of jobs and occupations.

*Lloyd B. Lueptow*

## Bibliography

Bakan, D. 1966. *The Duality of Human Existence: An Essay on Psychology and Religion.* Chicago: Rand McNally.

Bem, S.L. 1974. "The Measurement of Psychological Androgyny." *Journal of Consulting and Clinical Psychology* 42:155–62.

Bergen, D.J., and J.E. Williams. 1991. "Sex Stereotypes in the United States Revisited: 1972–1991." *Sex Roles* 24:413–23.

Broverman, I.K., S.R. Vogel, D.M. Broverman, F.E. Clarkson, and P.L. Rosenkrantz. 1972. "Sex-Role Stereotypes: A Current Appraisal." *Journal of Social Issues* 28:59–78.

Cook, E.D. 1985. *Psychological Androgyny.* New York: Pergamon.

Davis, D.M. 1990. "Portrayals of Women in Prime-Time Network Television: Some Demographic Characteristics." *Sex Roles* 23:325–32.

Deaux, K., and L.L. Lewis. 1984. "Structure of Gender Stereotypes: Interrelationships among Components and Gender Label." *Journal of Personality and Social Psychology* 46:991–1004.

Eagly, Alice H., Antonio Mladinic, and Stacy Otto. 1991. "Are Women Evaluated More Favorably Than Men? An Analysis of Attitudes, Beliefs and Emotions." *Psychology of Women Quarterly* 15:203–16.

Franks, V., and E.D. Rothblum, eds. 1983. *The Stereotyping of Women: Its Effects on Mental Health.* New York: Springer.

Gill, S.J., J. Stockard, M. Johnson, and M. and S. Williams. 1987. "Gender Differences: The Expressive Dimension and Critique of Androgyny Scales." *Sex Roles* 17:375–400.

Kaplan, A.G., and J.P. Bean, eds. 1976. *Beyond Sex Role Stereotypes: Readings: Toward a Psychology of Androgyny.* Boston: Little Brown.

Kenrick, D.T. 1987. "Gender, Genes and the Social Environment: a Biosocial Interactionist Perspective." In *Sex and Gender.* Vol. 7. *Review of Personality and Social Psychology,* edited by P. Shaver, and C. Hendrick. pp. 1–43. Newbury Park, Calif.: Sage.

Lueptow, L.B. 1984. *Adolescent Sex Roles and Social Change.* New York: Columbia University Press.

Lueptow, L.B., and L. Garovich. 1992. "The Persistence of Sex Stereotypes amid the Reconstruction of Woman's Role." Paper presented at the annual meeting of the American Sociological Association, Pittsburgh, Pennsylvania, August 1992.

Maccoby, E.E., and C.N. Jacklin. 1974. *The Psychology of Sex Differences.* Stanford: Stanford University Press.

Parsons, T., and R.F. Bales. 1955. *Family, Socialization and Interaction Process.* Glencoe, Illinois: Free Press.

Reskin, B.F., and H.I. Hartmann, eds. 1986. *Women's Work, Men's Work: Sex Segregation on the Job.* Washington, D.C.: National Academy.

Rotter, N., S.J. Dollinger, and J.A. Cunningham. 1991. "Agency-Communion in Affective Sexual Memories." *Psychological Reports* 68:61–62.

Sadalla, E.K., D.T. Kenrick, and B. Vershure. 1987. "Dominance and Heterosexual Attraction." *Journal of Personality and Social Psychology* 52:730–38.

Simon, R.J., and J.M. Landis. 1989. "Women's and Men's Attitudes about a Woman's Place and Role." *Public Opinion Quarterly* 53:265–76.

Spence, J.T., and R.L. Helmreich. 1980. "Masculine Instrumentality and Feminine Expressiveness: Their Relationships with Sex Role Attitudes and Behaviors." *Psychology of Women Quarterly* 5:147–63.

Waters, L.K., and P.M. Popovich. 1986. "Factor Analysis of Sex-Typed Terms from the Bem Sex-Role Inventory: A Multiple Replication across Time." *Psychological Reports* 59:1323–26.

Williams, J.E., and D.L. Best. 1990. *Measuring Sex Stereotypes: A Multinational Study.* Revised ed. Newbury Park, Calif.: Sage.

## Women's Adult Development

Four sets of issues affect women's adult development and provide distinct disciplinary paths for approaching its study: (1) Structural/institutional concerns, well developed in the sociological literature, explore the impact of widespread institutional conditions, policies, and roles on women's options and development; (2) Cultural concerns, grounded in social psychological and anthropologically based research, examine how culture shapes images of women and defines roles and life choices at home and work; (3) Psychologically based developmental concerns explore the gender-specific ways that women see and intrapsychically make sense out of their world; and (4) Biologically based concerns focus on the impact of physiological differences between men and women. Each set of issues offers a unique explanation of and implicit prescription for encouraging women's cognitive, social, and emotional growth.

The sociologically grounded, structural/institutional concerns (for example, Epstein 1988; Rix 1990) explore how institutions and socially constructed roles, policies, and conditions affect observed gender differences in life and work choices over the course of an adult lifespan. How does, for example, the reality of the "glass ceiling" in organizations influence women's interests, life choices, and commitments? How do economic realities, long-term institutional inequities, and government policies limit women's opportunities, keep child care a personal problem, and channel women into low-level jobs?

Cultural theorists (such as Frieze et al. 1978; Rosaldo 1974) take a different slant. These anthropological and social-psychological researchers assert that cultural images of men and women shape roles and life choices at home, in marriage, and in the workplace; serve as socialization standards for "appropriate" gender behaviors; and play the critical role in influencing women's adult development. How do shifting definitions of masculinity and femininity, for example, affect life and career paths for women? What impact does a pan-universal asymmetry in cultural evaluations of the sexes have on women's views of self, other, and the external world? How does culture shape scientific knowledge and mask the androcentric focus of theories about human nature and gender-appropriate life and work options?

A third approach to women's development is psychologically oriented. It focuses on the individual and the gender-specific ways in which a woman perceives and defines her world. What, for example, is a woman's way of knowing (Belenky et al. 1986)? What does cognitive-moral-social maturity look like for women (Gilligan 1982)? What age-specific developmental tasks, achievements, and transitions do women face over the course of a healthy lifetime (Bardwick 1980)? How do women's views of self and the world affect career choices and options (Gallos 1989)?

This third perspective has grown, in large part, from recognition that women's adult development can no longer be understood as a logical derivative from explorations of male experiences and that what has been historically defined as the foundation for understanding development in adulthood (such as Kohlberg 1981; Levinson 1978) was research conducted by and about men, presented and widely accepted as insights into all human nature.

A fourth approach to women's development is biological (for example, Goy and McEwen 1980; Parsons 1980). From this perspective, genes, hormones, and physiological factors account for gender-based differences in capacities, preferences, and life choices for women. How do, for example, menstruation, childbirth and nursing, menarche, and female hormones—historical cornerstones for theorizing about women's development for centuries—influence women's life choices? In what ways do differential brain patterns and cerebral composition for men and women affect behaviors and options at work and at home?

Understanding women's adult development is not an easy task. The existence of four different perspectives for approaching the topic and the androcentric underpinnings of classic theories of adult development underscore its complexity. Each perspective provides a unique slant on women's lives, choices, needs, and preferences, and contributes one essential piece to the unfolding puzzle of understanding women's adult lives.

*Joan V. Gallos*

## Bibliography

Bardwick, J. 1980. "The Seasons of a Woman's Life." In *Women's Lives: New Theory, Research, and Policy,* edited by D. McGuigan. Ann Arbor: University of Michigan Center for Continuing Education of Women.

Belenky, M., B. Clinchy, N. Goldberger, and J. Tarule. 1986. *Women's Ways of Knowing.* New York: Basic.

Epstein, C.F. 1988. *Sex, Gender, and the Social Order.* New Haven: Yale University Press.

Frieze, I., J. Parsons, P. Johnson, D. Ruble, and G. Zellman. 1978. *Women and Sex Roles: A Social Psychological Perspective.* New York: Norton.

Gallos, J. 1989. "Exploring Women's Development: Implications for Career Theory, Practice, and Research." In *Handbook of Career Theory,* edited by M. Arthur, D. Hall, and B. Lawrence. Cambridge, England: Cambridge University Press.

Gilligan, C. 1982. *In a Different Voice: Psychological Theory and Women's Development.* Cambridge, Mass.: Harvard University Press.

Goy, R., and B. McEwen, eds. 1980. *Sexual Differentiation of the Brain.* Cambridge, Mass.: MIT Press.

Kohlberg, L. 1981. *The Philosophy of Moral Development.* San Francisco: Harper and Row.

Levinson, D. 1978. *The Seasons of a Man's Life.* New York: Alfred A. Knopf.

Parsons, J., ed. 1980. *The Psychobiology of Sex Differences and Sex Roles.* Washington, D.C.: Hemisphere.

Rix, S., ed. 1990. *The American Woman 1990–1992: A Status Report.* New York: Norton.

Rosaldo, M. 1974. "Woman, Culture, and Society: A Theoretical Overview." In *Women, Culture, and Society,* edited by M. Rosaldo and L. Lamphere. Palo Alto, Calif.: Stanford University Press.

## Integrated Women: A Conceptual Framework

The concept of integrated women is an ideal type that represents a woman who is oriented by a consciousness of the different alternatives—feminist, traditionalist, and androgynous—and who possesses the possibility of integrating these alternatives within a chosen lifestyle. An integrated woman is a career woman who has the opportunity to interplay the meanings of feminist, traditionalist or androgynous within her life by combining behaviors and attitudes from the different orientations. The concept of integrated women enables researchers to break through the limitations encountered in the labeling of women. It recognizes that while role strain has been the focus of research (Houseknecht and Macke 1981; Parelius 1975; Voydanoff 1988), there also is a need for research to explore the complementarities of roles.

Current research is coming to focus upon the dynamic interplay of the multiplicity of roles that a woman plays in contemporary society (Baruch et al. 1987; Lin 1990). An increasing number of college-educated women are attempting to combine a professional career with marriage and family roles. Recent studies are not only documenting the interest of college women in attaining careers, but moving beyond this to examine the motivation and the meaning of work and family to women workers. There seems to be a consensus among college students today that their jobs in the future will not come to interfere with the well-being of their families. Marriage continues to be overwhelmingly favored as a way of life, and motherhood continues to be a primary concern to working women. A majority of women students prefer a dual-career and egalitarian family pattern (Lin and Moore 1985).

Specifically, the concept of integrated women has been developed along three dimensions: attitudinal, behavioral, and cognitive (Lin and Moore 1983). The attitudinal dimension for integrated women has been analyzed by (1) identification with the Women's Movement; (2) the expectation of dual-career equality; (3) the expectation of sharing housework; and (4) the expectation of combining marriage, family, and career. The behavioral dimension has been analyzed by how women modify their roles. This dimension has been measured by (1) women's handling of financial needs and work situations; (2) women's responsibilities in household chores and participation in child-rearing; (3) women's response to career interruption; and (4) women's involvement in putting their husbands through school. The cognitive dimension for integrated women has been related to (1) perceptions of men's social status; (2) perceptions of women's status at work; (3) perceptions of women's status on loan and credit applications; and (4) perceptions of women's social, economic, and educational statuses.

The attitudes of college women today are positive toward combining marriage, family, and career. Since the 1960s the challenge of obtaining a definition of new sex roles for women has been concentrated in two major directions: the ideologies of free choice and equality. The idea of equality has dominated American values since the birth of this nation. Today, women expect to be treated equally in all aspects of their lives. Outside the home, women expect to receive equal pay for equal work; on the job, women expect to receive equal opportunity for promotion and recognition. Inside the home, women expect to achieve equal conjugal power; women expect to share equal family responsibilities. Today's integrated women expect to have the option of either pursuing a career or playing their traditional homemakers' roles. They expect to have the option of being married or remaining single, of bearing children or remaining child-free. They also expect to have the opportunity to combine family, marriage, and career.

The attitudes of women need to be studied in relation to their behavior since research shows that there may be a greater range in acceptable behavior than attitudinal reports reflect (Yogev 1981). Study of the behavioral dimension examines the range of women's work and family roles. It is found that women will develop mechanisms for coping with role strain when combining work and family life (Voydanoff 1987). According to Cummings (1977) there is a gap between what is tolerable and the consensual ideal, or, stated differently, there are a possible range of acceptable outcomes rather than only one. It may be in those situations defined as "acceptable" that researchers can locate the ways in which ideals are stretched or worked out in life. For example, women who work stress the positive effect on families when both parents are working (Baruch et al. 1987). Johnson and Johnson (1980) found in their study of dual-career families that among upper- and middle-class families, almost all mothers rationalized their busy schedules with the phrase "It's the quality of the time spent with children that counts and not the quantity." At the same time that values are stretched in situations, the expectation to integrate marriage, family, and career has an influence upon levels of tolerance for situations that would be defined as acceptable. For example, when expectations for integration or role-sharing are higher, tolerance for career interruption decreases (Lin and Moore 1985).

Research on the attitudes and behaviors of contemporary women needs to include an understanding of the cognitive dimension. What do women perceive as the structural constraints and opportunities facing them today? A study of college women found that a discrepancy exists between female students' career aspirations and their views on the sex discrimination in work. Although they recognized the existence of sex discrimination and occupational segregation, the female students continued to aspire to high- or middle-status professions (Ferree 1987; Lin and Moore 1985). One factor that may explain the findings of high aspirations coupled with the awareness of sex discrimination is the involvement of greater numbers of women in higher education. Women with college education have always had higher rates of participation in the labor force than women with less education (Cummings 1977). Research shows that women's higher achievements in education do not result in equal compensation in the labor market.

For most women work is both a choice and necessity: It is a source of financial security or independence, of personal accomplishment and fulfillment, and of professional growth and development. On the whole, this commitment to a career is accompanied by women's belief that their jobs will not interfere with the well-being of their families even though women show a moderate willingness to modify family roles to meet career demands. A sense of personal integration is found through the stretch between what is expected and what will be accepted in any particular situation. Instead of stopping at the crossroad of career versus family, and marriage, integrated women have the ability and opportunity to combine career, family, and marriage. They are career oriented without rejecting marriage or family.

*Phylis Lan Lin*

## Bibliography

Baruch, Grace K., Lois Beiner, and Rosalind C. Barnett. 1987. "Women and Gender in Research on Work and Family Stress." *American Psychologist* 42:130–36.

Cummings, Laurie Davidson. 1977. "Value Stretch in Definitions of Career among College Women: Horatio Alger as Feminist Model." *Social Problems* 25:65–74.

Epstein, Cynthis Fuchs. 1987. "Multiple Demands and Multiple Roles: The Condition of Successful Management." In *Spouse, Parent, Worker: On Gender and Multiple Roles*, edited by Faye J. Crosby, pp. 23–35. New Haven, Conn.: Yale University Press.

Ferree, Myra Marx. 1987. "She Works Hard for a Living: Gender and Class on the Job." In *Analyzing Gender: A Handbook of Social Science Research*, edited by Beth B. Hess and Myra M. Ferree, pp. 325–47. Newbury Park, Calif.: Sage.

Houseknect, Sharon K., and Ann S. Macke. 1981. "Combining Marriage and Career: The Martial Adjustment of Professional Women." *Journal of Marriage and the Family* 43:651–60.

Johnson, Colleen L., and Frank A. Johnson. 1980. "Parenthood, Marriage, and Careers: Situational Constraints and Role Strain." In *Dual-Career Couples*, edited by Fran Pepitone-Rockwell, pp. 143–61. Newbury Park, Calif.: Sage.

Lin, Phyllis Lan. 1990. "Working Women in America: Choice and Challenge." In *Proceedings of the International Symposium on Women Human Resources*, pp. 15–60. Taipei: Bureau of Labor.

Lin, Phyllis Lan, and Mary C. Moore. 1985. "Integrated Women: A Study of College Women's Views on Combining Marriage, Family and Career." *Proceedings of the Indiana Academy of the Social Sciences* 19:146–52.

———. 1983. "Integrated Women: College Students' Views on Marriage, Family and Career." Unpublished monograph. Indianapolis, Ind.: University of Indianapolis.

Parelius, Ann P. 1975. "Emerging Sex-Role Attitudes, Expectations and Strains among College Women." *Journal of Marriage and the Family* 37:146–53.

Voydanoff, Patricia. 1987. *Work and Family Life.* Newbury Park, Calif.: Sage.

———. 1988. "Work Role Characteristics, Family Structure Demands, and Work/Family Conflict." *Journal of Marriage and the Family* 50:749–61.

Yogev, Sara. 1981. "Do Professional Women Have Egalitarism Marriage Relationships?" *Journal of Marriage and the Family* 43:865–71.

## Flexible Conceptual Style: Its Implications for Cultural Redefinition

In grounding intertheory studies of cognitive performance, four cross-nationally reliable conceptual styles arose, one of them, the Flexible style, being dominated by women (Cohen 1989). Women's modes of cognition and derivative personalities, learned in recipient roles in gender-based relationships, their "self" concepts and "referent others," their value systems, and their concepts of power and justice differ systematically from the Analytic conceptual style used as the male industrial model. The historical dominance of services by women carriers of the Flexible style has defined service occupations according to that style. Given the emergence of postindustrial service industry dominance in the employment market, the characteristics of the Flexible style are seen, thus, in aggregate, as potent definers of the directions of postindustrial culture. These gender-based characteristics are outlined below; they are related to women's political and labor-market integration and its impact on the emergent American culture.

Studies of cognition find girls/women use a distinctive mode of selecting and organizing sense data called the "Flexible" conceptual style (Cohen 1989). Using standardized tests of intelligence and achievement as the basis for culturally required processes, it differs from the Analytic style—the dominant process in modern industrial countries—and also from the Concrete rural style, and a deviant style, the Relational. These styles are defined by two choices in each of two cognitive rule-sets, one of them using analytic or descriptive rules for selecting relevant information and the second extracting that information or embedding it in a large number of possible contexts and in relationships among communicators. Flexible style users (women) abstract the parts or characteristics of a stimulus in the fashion required by the Analytic cultural model but embed what they extract selectively—that is, according to the participants, their motivations, what is taking place, and the emotional tone of the processes.

These cognitive rule-sets are derived from early primary-group socialization into adopting a defined role as "activator" or "recipient" of interpersonal processes. Through socialization into a recipient social role, Flexible style users become multiple-process thinkers based on their multiple-recipient social roles; they hold in their minds all of those processes that might involve them, activating each as it is called forth by others. In her discussion of moral development in girls/women, Gilligan (1982) makes a similar observation, referring to girls' recipient roles as acting in "a different voice" (the passive voice verb form). A philosopher and a stage-development theorist of moral cognition, Gilligan's approach differs from those of researchers testing other social and behavioral theories; it is remarkable in its arts and humanities contribution to women's studies.

A wide range of individual characteristics develop from women's use of the Flexible conceptual style. Their brain hemisphere use (Bogen 1969; Fausto-Sterling 1985) is bilateral, moving from the left hemisphere's analytic, linear thought processes to the right hemisphere's global, affect-based, mood- and tone-relevant functions at will. Memory retrieval forms are embedded for activation by a dominant social stimulus, and these may vary from context to context. On such personality inventories as the Minnesota Multiphasic Personality Inventory (MMPI), Flexible style users reject general positions on issues; and their response style is characterized by embedding—that is, writing in the margins the conditions under which each answer is appropriate. Their standardized test and school performance scores are middle range, irrespective of their native ability, since they obtain scores by responding correctly to the analytic mode of abstraction subroutines but incorrectly to those subroutines that require extraction (for example, word problems in arithmetic). Flexible-style users also reject as irrelevant all school subjects that are content-free (nonembedded), such as mathematics and scientific fields that focus on highly abstract levels such as physics. They consider social rules that function impersonally—that is, without reference to the special conditions of the participants—to be unjust. Their "self" concept is the "individualized action mode" and their "referent others" are the "significant others" of Kuhn and McPartland (1954) . They reject standardization (a characteristic of embedders). Their "self" is, thus, an idiosyncratic, multiply embedded "self" that functions variously as required as the receiver's social roles as defined for them by others.

Among the four conceptual style users, Flexibles talk more than users of other styles; their language content is characterized by absorption with explanatory process themes and with the intents and motivations of others. Much information is carried in vocal inflections and body language, and its form varies by the social context in which it is used. Among those forms used are the linear Analytic form when communicating with Analytics, and shorthand forms when communicating with other Flexibles. This latter form consists of incomplete sentences, insider references to other Flexibles, and with what appear superficially to be non sequiturs but that are movements among the multiple themes available and from one level of discourse to others. Their multiple "selves" have special costumes; dress, communication styles, personality styles, and other manipulable "fronts" activate their "selves" as called upon by others or by distinct interpersonal roles. Language is often used to test new environments for cues as to what roles to play there.

The "value family" adopted by Flexible-style users is called by von Mering (1961) the Inclusive Interpersonal Value Realm. It is characterized by egalitarianism, mutuality, reciprocity, interdependence, interest identity, and friendly competition, and by differential sanctions and rewards. Some of these characteristics were observed in girls' (as opposed to boys') play by Lever (1978) and Chodorow (1978). As the result of this process of development in which concepts of justice rely upon the special participants and their conditions in conceptually separate circumstances (embedding), girls do not adopt concepts of the highest levels of "justice" defined by moral theorists (Kohlberg 1981). These impersonal standards are seen by Flexibles as abstractions to be applied equally from the outside rather than generated as specific to specific instances and characters from the inside.

Women as Flexible style users differ from other style users by living in a three-dimensional physical, as well as social, environment. Since their physical space has height as well as flat dimensions, they can live in, and function effectively in, smaller spaces than the others. However, they require high-stimulation environments or they become bored, withdrawn, or depressed. When choice is available to do so, they increase the stimulation of their environments by social contacts (such as calling friends on the telephone, shopping, interfering with the affairs of others, or by posing needs that require social interaction or attention). Occupationally, they choose work settings with high social content, whether the work itself focuses on these areas (Cohen 1989). They see power as the ability to do work rather than the ability to coerce others.

Since their mass entry into the occupational market of modern industrial nations, women have held unique roles. At the turn of the century, they entered the labor market doing women's work—that is, cooking or food service, sewing or manufacturing clothes, nurturing children or caring for the aged, ill, or indigent. Men did not compete with them for these positions, and new professions such as teaching, nursing, and social work came to be defined by and dominated by women. Wherever subordinate roles to men emerged in offices or in merchandizing, women assumed a similar, statistical dominance there, playing their "recipient" roles but remaining autonomous in carrying out their tasks. Entire units of major businesses arose in which common work was divided among men and women with some units being dominated by and defined by the women who occupied those positions (England and McLaughlin 1979). Gender specialization in the occupations also defined women as society's major consumers—that is, when industrial society's division of labor impacted urban families, sending men away from home to work, a division of labor between production and consumption was created in which men were the producers and women the specialized consumers.

These latter motifs, emergent from the turn of the century, did not become significant until 1956 when the female controlled service industries began to dominate the labor market and when their differential contributions began to impact the country's Gross National Product indicators. Since that time, primary and secondary industrial sectors, dominated by men and characterized by the three other conceptual styles, have progressively lost their relative participation, pressing even married women and mothers into the labor market and into the armed services so as to prevent family downward mobility. While women are still paid less than men, their sheer numbers have had an imposing aggregate impact on industry, life styles, and politics. This impact is based in the sum of individual choices to use the surplus wealth generated by the nation's industrial growth to purchase services—such as education, medicine, and social welfare—fields dominated by and defined by women. The influence of women's Flexible style and its related value system is found in common postindustrial themes such as multiculturalism, empowerment, school choice, and restructuring—major shifts in the standardization themes of industrial culture.

Increasing dominance of the labor force by the services—that is, those industries expanding most rapidly—has placed women as an aggregate in the forefront of social change. Women purchase and produce a wide array of consumer products as well, and they are viewed by manufacturers as major markets. Since women outlive men, they also provide the major market for gerontological materials and life styles. Their new economic importance is also reflected in the political realm. Although the first woman has run for the vice presidency and in an array of other countries women prime ministers have been elected, in the United States the movement into positions of political importance has been aggregate. Women mayors are twenty times more numerous than in 1970, and one-fifth of state legislators are women, the latter number having quadrupled in the past two decades. Two state governors were elected, and in some states (such as Texas) in which major industries have located their service units at the expense of moving their male-dominated manufacturing units to other countries, the 1990 census has provided for an increased number of federal congressional representatives. It can be predicted that these representatives will express the political will of those increasing numbers of employed women who dominate the service industries newly established there and that they will elect women in increasing numbers to represent their own unique interests.

In summary, this contribution examines the influence of women's conceptual style—a system of cognitive organization arising out of conditions of gender inequality—on defining the emergent character of postindustrial culture. A large body of research on different conceptual styles finds that women use the Flexible style. This style emerges from the recipient role played by women in most family structures, regardless of those learned by their male counterparts. Using this style produces a unique personal style, characterized by special cognitive skills, middle-range performance measures when Analytic (industrial male) standards are used, special forms of memory organization and brain hemisphere dominance, a multiple group-based concept of "self" and "referent others" and the rejection of standardization. Their language use is greater in volume content and form, and they play different games, which socialize them to transfer different play models to life experiences than those used by boys of similar age and background. They can tolerate living in small spaces because they are three-dimensional thinkers but require very high stimulation in their environments or withdrawal and depression may result. When women came into the labor market in large numbers, they concentrated in the service industries. In 1956, these occupations began to dominate the employment market, defining them in a fashion consistent with women's unique conceptual patterns and skills. While employed women still receive less salary for their work than men doing similar jobs, their aggregate numbers, combined with their dominance in the consumer market, have given them an aggregate position of importance in both producer and consumer markets. It is suggested that, given statistical dominance of service industry units dominated by women in those states that received enlarged representation in the U.S. Congress, their political significance will also increase and that the international movement of women into positions of political importance will emerge as a significant characteristic of postindustrial culture.

*Rosalie A. Cohen*

**Bibliography**

Bogen, Joseph. 1969. "The Other Side of the Brain II: An Appositional Mind." *Bulletin of the Los Angeles Neurological Society* 34.

Chodorow, Nancy. 1978. *The Reproduction of Mothering*. Berkeley: University of California Press.

Cohen, Rosalie. 1989. *Conceptual Styles and Social Change*. 2nd ed. Littleton, Mass.: Copley.

England, P., and S.C. McLaughlin. 1979. "Sex Segregation of Jobs and Male-Female Income Differentials." In *Discrimination in Organizations*, edited by R. Alvarez, K.G. Lutterman, et al. San Francisco: Jossey-Bass.

Fausto-Sterling, Anne. 1985. *Myths of Gender*. New York: Basic.

Gilligan, Carol. 1982. *In a Different Voice*. Cambridge, Mass.: Harvard University Press.

Kohlberg, L. 1981. *The Philosophy of Moral Development*. San Francisco: Harper and Row.

Kuhn, M.H., and T.S. McPartland. 1954. "An Investigation of Self-Attitudes." *American Sociological Review* 19:69–76.

Lever, Janet. 1978. "Sex Differences in the Complexity of Children's Play and Games." *American Sociological Review* 43:471–83.

von Mering, Otto. 1961. *Grammar of Human Values*. Pittsburgh, Penn.: University of Pittsburgh Press.

# III

# Women in Diverse Occupations

# Overview of Women's Occupational Diversity

## Women in High-Status, Nontraditional Occupations

During the last two decades, increasing numbers of women have entered higher-level, nontraditional occupations. These higher-status, higher-paying positions include middle- and executive-level management, professional jobs, and technical and scientific positions. However, there is evidence that women in these jobs are not progressing at the same rate as their male counterparts (Morrison et al. 1987).

Although women continue to receive career counseling that guides them into sex-segregated jobs (Betz and Fitzgerald 1987), women have been increasing in proportion as undergraduate, graduate, and faculty in nontraditional areas of study (such as business, engineering, and natural sciences) during the past two decades (Fuehrer and Schilling 1985). In 1972, women constituted only 17.6 percent, 0.8 percent and 10 percent of managerial/administrators, engineering, and physical scientists and chemists respectively. In 1983, these figures reflected a dramatic increase in the number of women in these fields. Percentages of women were 32.4 (managerial), 5.8 (engineering), and 20.5 (natural scientists), respectively. In 1989, these figures rose slightly to 39.8 percent female managers, 7.6 percent women engineers, and 26.9 percent female natural scientists (U.S. Bureau of the Census 1980, 1991). However, there is continuing evidence of bias and some concern that as more women enter these jobs the status, prestige, and pay associated with them will deteriorate.

### Problems Experienced by Women in High-Status, Nontraditional Occupations

Although there is evidence that women in traditionally masculine jobs have higher self-confidence than women in more traditional jobs, women continue to be segregated on the lower end of the pay and career ladder. The concept of the "glass ceiling" (Morrison et al. 1987) is perhaps more apparent for women in high-paying, high-status jobs than for women in traditionally feminine jobs. Women tend to progress until mid-level management positions or, in academe, until they obtain entry-level assistant professor positions, but they do not in proportional numbers move beyond mid-management or to senior professor ranks.

There are numerous reasons for the lack of upward progress. One key issue is that college-educated white males in such jobs serve as the standard of comparison or evaluation. Women are assessed on the extent to which they deviate from this norm or standard (Gutek and Larwood 1987; Tavris 1992). Further, successful women scientists are not viewed as making it on their own; rather, they somehow have acquired the right way or correct approach or answers from someone else, presumably a male (Rose 1983). Women's pay in such jobs (especially science and academe) is often based on nonperformance factors, including husband's salary, rather than on merit.

In general, across all types of occupations, gender effects on personnel decisions are small. However, in masculine jobs, differences between men and women do emerge in subjectively based personnel evaluations. Women are less likely to be hired, receive less initial salary and fewer subsequent pay raises, are viewed in more stereotypic terms, and are the target of more subtle forms of sexual harassment in such occupations (Betz and Fitzgerald 1987; Heilman 1983; Kanter 1977). Women in nontraditional jobs experience major work–family conflicts including time-based conflict, strain-based conflict, and behavior conflict (Moore 1986). They tend to be isolated with less access to primary sources of job-relevant information and resources and assistance.

## Understanding Such Unique Issues for Women in High-Status, Nontraditional Positions

Kanter (1977) and Heilman (1983) offer explanations for the negative treatment of women in some jobs (nontraditional) and not in others. First, Kanter indicates that one major reason women in nontraditional jobs encounter unique barriers is their status as the lone or token female in the workgroup. Kanter (1977) found that the lone or token status of women sets three processes in motion that result in increased likelihood of negative experiences for women. First, the woman, by virtue of her token status, is highly visible to others. Although visibility can be positive when a woman succeeds, it is devastating when she fails. Her failure is viewed as a reflection on her whole gender. Also, the woman's appearance tends to be emphasized or to receive a great deal of attention. A second process involved in token status is contrast, which exaggerates differences with the dominant culture. Contrast has the practical result of effectively isolating the woman from others. Assimilation is the third process, and it involves the use of stereotypes to characterize the woman or social type (Kanter 1977).

Heilman and her colleagues (1989) replicated a widely cited study in the 1970s by Schein (1973) on employees' perceptions of requisite managerial skills. She found evidence that, in the late 1980s, as in the early 1970s, the skills cited as associated with managerial success are also associated more with men than with women. Further, Heilman (1983) explained that, even if a woman is not the lone one in a group but simply does not fit the gender stereotype of the job, she will be perceived as lacking essential skills for success in that position. Heilman's lack-of-fit model suggests that we assess what is needed in a job and then, based on gender stereotypes, make a determination of whether a man or a woman possesses those characteristics. When the assessment reflects a lack of fit (for example, a woman applying for or occupying a masculine job), the result is a more negative outcome or decision (Heilman 1983). As with Kanter, the attribution is that the woman attained the job by some extraordinary effort or a stroke of luck rather than by an enduring set of excellent skills and competencies.

Further, Tavris (1992) and others (Crosby 1992) suggest that we should abandon attempting to explain differences between the pay and performance of men and women as a result of innate tendencies or potential but rather focus on real disparities in the political and economic power and opportunities between men and women in our society.

*Jeanette N. Cleveland*

## Bibliography

Betz, N.E., and L.F. Fitzgerald. 1987. *The Career Psychology of Women*. Orlando: Academic.

Crosby, F. 1992. *Juggling*. New York: Free Press.

Fuehrer, A., and K.M. Schilling. 1985. "The Values of Academe: Sexism as a Natural Consequence." *Journal of Social Issues* 41:29–41.

Gutek, B.A., and L. Larwood. 1987. "Introduction: Women's Careers Are Important and Different." In *Women Career Development*, edited by B.A. Gutek and L. Larwood, pp. 7–14. Beverly Hills, Calif.: Sage.

Heilman, M.E. 1983. "The Lack of Fit Model." In *Research in Organizational Behavior*. Vol. 5, edited by B. Staw and L.L. Cummings. Greenwich, Conn.: JAI.

Heilman, M.E., C.J. Block, R.F. Martell, and M.C. Simon. 1989. "Has Anything Changed? Current Characterizations of Men, Women and Managers." *Journal of Applied Psychology* 74: 935–42.

Kanter, R.M. 1977. *Men and Women of the Corporation*. New York: Basic Books.

Moore, L.L. 1986. *Not as Far as You Think: The Realities of Working Women*. Toronto: Lexington.

Morrison, A.M., R.P. White, E. VanVelsor, and Center for Creative Leadership. 1987. *Breaking the Glass Ceiling: Can Women Reach the Top of America's Largest Corporations?* Reading, Mass.: Addison-Wesley.

Rose, H. 1983. "Hand, Brain, and Heart: A Feminist Epistemology for the Natural Sciences." *Signs: Journal of Women in Culture and Society* 9:74–85.

Schein, V.E. 1973. "Relationship between Sex-Role Stereotypes and Requisite Management Characteristics. *Journal of Applied Psychology* 57:95–100.

Tavris, C. 1992. *The Mismeasure of Woman*. New York: Simon and Schuster.

U.S. Bureau of the Census. 1980, 1991. Statistical Abstract of the United States. U.S. Department of Commerce. Washington, D.C.

## Gender and the Scientific Professions

The area of gender and science is multifaceted, growing, and has undergone recent epistemological and theoretical changes. Traditional sociological studies of gender and science focus upon women and their careers in science and science-related fields. These studies document the sex differences in scientists' careers, employment opportunities, salaries, tenure, and publication rates. Recently, the study of gender and science has expanded to address issues related to gender, feminist thought, and the production of scientific knowledge and practice.

A major sociological concern about women scientists has revolved around the issue of why there are so few women scientists. Is this an indicator of stratification and blocked access or other cultural and social factors? Traditional studies of gender and science focused upon the historical and contemporary stratification in men's and women's scientific careers in order to answer these questions. Stratification studies have been essential in establishing sex differences in scientific careers and productivity. As a group, women's careers in science have differed from men's careers (see Zuckerman 1991 for a thorough review of gender stratification studies). Small cumulative disadvantages for women start as early as doctoral training programs. Long demonstrates how these disadvantages accumulate early in graduate training and provide the origins for later sex differences (1990). For example, women's opportunity to collaborate with a mentor is significantly decreased when they are married and have children. The same effect does not hold for male students. Early advantages for males are transformed into greater advantages over the course of a scientist's career.

As a group, women scientists have lower rates of employment, are overrepresented in nontenured positions, have lower salaries, lower publication rates, and fewer citations than male scientists (Cole and Zuckerman 1984; Fox 1991; Long 1990). Fox (1991) has shown how the organization and environment of scientific settings (resources, rewards, communications, collegial interaction) are responsible for productivity differences between male and female scientists. Promotion and tenure are also different. Male scientists are promoted and receive tenure more quickly than female scientists (Zuckerman 1991).

Government agencies also collect and publish information on women scientists and engineers. Recent demographic and documentary data on American women scientists and engineers is available from the National Science Foundation in three different publications: the annual volume *Science Indicators* from the National Science Board (NSB 1989), a special title *Women and Minorities in Science and Engineering* (NSF 1986), and *Women and Minorities in Science and Engineering* (NSF 1990). These publications document and provide data on the racial and sex differences among scientists in employment, educational attainment, and performance.

The issue of recruitment and retention of women scientists has also led policy-makers, educators, and feminists to focus upon new ways to make science more accessible to women and to recruit more women scientists for the future (Rosser 1990; Healy 1992). Sociological explanations have focused upon the role of the teacher, peer pressure, and blocked access within the educational system for girls to take math and science courses (Humphreys 1982). Changing the classroom environment to attract more women and minorities to careers in science and engineering is a major concern for educators, scientists, industry, and government officials as we approach the twenty-first century (U.S. Task Force on Women, Minorities and the Handicapped in Science and Technology 1989).

The recovery of women's contributions to the field of science (in spite of obstacles to their acceptance and the lack of structural academic and research positions) has helped influence and develop the research literature of women and science into more feminist-oriented topics and discussions. For example, historically the "great women" of science have been biographically portrayed as the exception to their sex. "In spite of the fact that they were women," great scientists such as Marie Curie managed to produce Nobel-Prize–winning research. Recent historical studies have recovered the lives of more common women or overlooked scientists and have documented the important role that gender plays in the production of scientific knowledge (Merchant 1980; Rossiter 1982; Scheibinger 1989). Feminist critiques and gendered studies of science have shifted from the "woman question in science," which has focused upon women scientists, to the "science question in feminism" and the gendered construction of scientific knowledge (Harding 1986). Some of the conclusions reached in feminist studies of science suggest that both the knowledge and organizational structures of science are racist, sexist, and class-biased (Bleier 1984; Keller 1985; Tuana 1989).

## Summary

The study of women and science has changed within the last ten years. Stratification and inequality studies continue to contribute new data on the numbers, careers, and publications of women scientists. However, recent shifts and developments have extended this field to include studies of the gendered development and nature of scientific thought, its relationship to the recruitment of women scientists, and the potential for changes in the way that science is conducted and constructed. The nature of the debate in this field has shifted from the question of why women are underrepresented in the sciences to a question of how gender affects the scientific enterprise and its products. Special note: The book by Rosser (1990) contains one of the most comprehensive and helpful bibliographies in this area.

*Anne E. Figert*

## Bibliography

Bleier, Ruth. 1984. *Science and Gender: A Critique of Biology and Its Theories on Women*. New York: Pergamon.

Cole, Jonathan, and Harriet Zuckerman. 1984. "Marriage, Motherhood and Research Performance in Science." *Scientific American* 256:119–25.

Fox, Mary Frank. 1991. "Gender, Environmental Milieu, and Productivity in Science." In *The Outer Circle: Women in the Scientific Community*, edited by Jonathan R. Cole, Harriet Zuckerman, and John T. Bruer, pp. 188–204. New York: W.W. Norton.

Harding, Sandra. 1986. *The Science Question in Feminism*. Ithaca, N.Y.: Cornell University Press.

Healy, Bernadine. 1992. "Women in Science: From Panes to Ceilings." Editorial in *Science* 255: 1333–34.

Humphreys, Sheila, ed. 1982. *Women and Minorities in Science: Strategies for Increasing Participation*. Boulder, Colo.: Westview.

Keller, Evelyn Fox. 1985. *Reflections on Gender and Science*. New Haven: Yale University Press.

Long, J. Scott. 1990. "The Origins of Sex Differences in Science." *Social Forces* 68(4):1297–1315.

Merchant, Carolyn. 1980. *The Death of Nature: Women, Ecology and the Scientific Revolution*. New York: Harper and Row.

National Science Board. 1989. *Science & Engineering Indicators—1989*. Washington, D.C.: U.S. Government Printing Office.

National Science Foundation 1990. *Women and Minorities in Science and Engineering*. Washington, D.C.: National Science Foundation.

Rosser, Sue V. 1990. *Female-Friendly Science: Applying Women's Studies Methods and Theories to Attract Students*. Elmsford, N.Y.: Pergamon.

Rossiter, Margaret. 1982. *Women Scientists in America: Struggles and Strategies to 1940*. Baltimore, Md.: Johns Hopkins University Press.

Scheibinger, Londa. 1989. *The Mind Has No Sex?: Women in the Origins of Modern Science*. Cambridge, Mass.: Harvard University Press.

Tuana, Nancy, ed. 1989. *Feminism & Science*. Bloomington and Indianapolis: Indiana University Press.

U.S. Task Force on Women, Minorities and the Handicapped in Science and Technology. 1989. *Changing America: The New Face of Science and Engineering*. Washington, D.C.: U.S. Government Printing Office.

Zuckerman, Harriet. 1991. "The Careers of Men and Women Scientists: A Review of Current Research." In *The Outer Circle: Women in the Scientific Community*, edited by Jonathan R. Cole, Harriet Zuckerman, and John T. Bruer, pp. 27–56. New York: W.W. Norton.

## Women in the Service Occupation Sector

The percentage of women in the labor force has grown systematically since 1900. At the turn of the century, 20 percent of women worked; in 1989, more than 57 percent of the labor force were women. Only 5 percent of married women were employed at the turn of the century, but at the beginning of World War II 15 percent were employed, and that has increased to more than 50 percent today. Current percentages are even higher for both married and divorced women with children. This period of time was also characterized by two major shifts in economic dominance—from primary industry dominance at the turn of the century (farming, fishing, ore gathering, logging) to secondary or multiple-process industry (smoke-stack industry) dominance. From there, the shift at mid-century was to the dominance of postindustrial, third-sector service industries and fourth-sector production of information and other intangibles such as creative art and music. While first- and second-sector industries were dominated by men, both in their productive aspects and administration, and while the male administration of business in the postindustrial enterprises has been the rule, women have statistically dominated the third sector of interpersonal-service industries. Despite their lower-paying reward structures (women still make only about two-thirds of the salary commanded by men), and despite their subordination to public control and oversight in most instances, the aggregate numbers of women providing these services has increased with the availability of national surplus wealth. In 1956, services were already providing more than 50 percent of the nonagricultural employment and more than half of the nonagricultural contributions to the Gross National Product. In aggregate, thus, employed women had come to dominate the expanding portions of the employment market, despite the low value placed on their work. This employment-market dominance has also been reflected in women's increasing impact on the dominant culture, even in the absence of rapidly increasing numbers in positions of political power. Their aggregate impact on the occupations they dominate has placed them, thus, in the forefront of social change.

According to 1989 and 1990 U.S. Bureau of Labor Statistics, the range of jobs held by women has been relatively narrow, falling predominantly into clerical and service fields. For instance, 80 percent of clerical workers are women, and from 95 to 99 percent of service workers are women, totally dominating such occupations as secretary, typist and receptionist, dental hygienist or assistant, preschool teacher and teacher's aide, child-care worker, and practical nurse. Contrarywise, 95 percent of craftsmen are men, and males predominate in work that is linked to income, power, and prestige. That is, about 90 percent of engineers and 80 percent of doctors and lawyers are men. And even in those service occupations dominated by women, men control the conditions under which they work: Women represent 74 percent of classroom teachers but only 2 percent are superintendents, and although they represent almost half of the labor force, only 5 percent are executives. Of the Fortune 500 companies, only two CEOs are women, one of whom inherited her position. And in *Forbes* magazine's 1989 list of the four hundred richest Americans, only 13.5 percent were women. This is the case in higher education as well. Although in 1989, 54.2 percent of all college students were women and they earned 52.6 percent of all higher-education degrees (Kroc 1989), this is not reflected in the awarding of the advanced degrees that provide access to higher-level positions. For instance, in that same year, men received about 65 percent of doctorates, 60 percent of law degrees, 68 percent of medical degrees, and 76 percent of dental degrees, according to the U.S. Center for Education Statistics. In addition, the American Council on Education reported in 1984 that only 39 percent of professors in higher education were women and that only 12 percent of university presidents were women, most of them in small, all-female institutions, and this disparity has not radically changed.

The disproportionate distribution of women in clerical and service occupations is reflected in lower pay scales as well. In 1988, women in full-time positions earned $18,545 per year, while men earned $27,342. And the U.S. Bureau of the Census reported in 1989 that only 25 percent of women earned more than $25,000 per year, while 50 percent of men did. Men made more money in the same positions as women, male nurses making 10 percent more than female nurses and male bookkeepers making 16 percent more than their female counterparts. This disparity has been resistant to political assaults under equal-pay legal provisions because women appear to be relegated to salary strata that they dominate rather than being distributed among the full range of higher-level positions. Even new positions listed as challenging new careers for women such as computer programmer, nurse practitioner, telecommunications manager, employee trainer, and ombudsman have no channels of mobility to top management positions, and they contribute to the increased concentration of women in women's work. Employers claim that interruptions for child-bearing and motherhood affect women's capacity to be selected for more responsible, more rewarding positions. Disparities not accounted for by types of jobs and motherhood interruptions were claimed by Pear in 1987 to result from overt discrimination in which the "glass ceiling" prevents women's selection into and promotion to higher-paying positions. These disparities are even more marked among minority women in all fields. A history of gender relationships in the United States is provided by historian Alice Kessler-Harris (1982) using as secondary sources the work of economists such as Michael Piore, Harriet Zellner, and Mary Stevenson and historians Joan Scott and Louise Tilly.

Labor-market segregation has figured in broader aspects of social change as well. One important dimension of change has been the post–World War II emergence of the service industries, into which women have been largely segregated, as the most important contributors to a changing culture. That is, the twentieth century has seen two major transitions from one form of economic dominance to another. At the turn of the century, economic dominance shifted from agriculture and other primary industries to secondary or heavy industry—both male-dominated economies with their supportive sciences. The post–World War II transition was from male-dominated secondary industry to third-sector, interpersonal services into which women had been segregated, however, and from male-dominated physical sciences to the development of social and behavioral sciences of those industries dominated by women. In 1956, the United States became the first country in the world in which more nonfarm labor was engaged in postindustrial, service-industry occupations, and in which services were the largest contributor to the Gross National Product; other industrial countries followed suit. This transition has provided, in aggregate, a large number of women segregated into the expanding segments of the labor force, earning salaries and providing important new markets for goods and services, while earlier segments that are dominated and controlled by men decline.

Since 1956, some service industries have expanded horizontally, with women moving within the service sector into new arenas. For instance, this horizontal service shift invaded the previously all-male military (Feather 1989). While there were no women military officers in the United States in 1973, there were forty thousand at the end of 1987, providing services in the military, with ten women in the junior level general or admiral ranks and another 14 percent ready to move up. Service businesses serving niche markets have been impacted by women entrepreneurs as well. In the 1980s, more than half of the graduates of business schools were women. And while in 1970 only 1 percent of business travelers were women, 35 percent of the frequent flyers on airlines were women at the end of the 1980s, using three million dollars of business flights yearly. Women's business subscriptions to American Express cards also increased, from seventy thousand in 1972 to more than five million by 1986 (Feather 1989). While in male-dominated, large technological businesses, women still experience suppression both in rank and earnings, they have been active entrepreneurs in the development and running of a multitude of small, service-centered businesses of their own, and they remain major markets for products produced and provided primarily by other women.

Women have also pioneered and activated the separation of information services (fourth-sector products) from interpersonal services and the integration of these new products into traditional service arenas. For instance, the integration of computers into elementary-school education is largely in their hands, as is the translation of traditional office work, library reference and retrieval, and medical and government data systems into computer-processing systems. The development and manipulation of information has been a major product of the service industries traditionally dominated by women, and it is now the fastest growing industry globally. Women have also pioneered and supported clean earth and alternative health systems, from nutrition to medical transformations, providing rapidly expanding markets for even those specialties in which they are not the major providers but in which they are major consumers (Feather 1989).

The postindustrial transition in modern countries from male occupations to those statistically, if not politically, dominated by women is global, and accompanying cultural changes are already taking place. Change is apparent, for instance, in the breakdown of many common cultural monoliths. The standardization of the industrial age has been replaced by the increasing value of multiculturalism and heterogeneity, its specialization by generalism, its synchronization by flexible time schedules, and its depersonalization by individual worth and interpersonal caring. And the male-dominated physical sciences have been impacted by the growth of the social and behavioral sciences relevant to third-sector fields. The services that women in statistical aggregate dominate, therefore, are in the process of redefinition in the direction of their female participants and markets rather than by their male power structures.

In summary, the percentage of women in the labor force has grown systematically since 1900. In settings dominated by men, however, their opportunity structure has been severely limited and their occupational reward systems have never exceeded two-thirds of those available to men. During this same period of time, economic dominance in modern industrial countries has shifted twice, from agriculture to heavy industry and from heavy industry to services, and it is in the process of a third shift from interpersonal service dominance to information development/manipulation/transmission services. While agriculture and manufacturing still resist the integration of women into roles occupationally equal to those of their male counterparts, the later developing service industries have traditionally been defined by women. The nation's economic dominance has shifted to these third- and fourth-sector settings, placing women, in aggregate, in a position of importance both as producers and purchasers of the services they produce. While the integration of women into the governing levels of male-dominated industries has been limited, the world around that process has been changing, and the employment characteristics of women as service producers in an emergent era of service dominance has yet to be explored.

*Rosalie A. Cohen*

### Bibliography

Cohen, R. 1989. *Conceptual Styles and Social Change.* 2nd ed. Littleton, Mass.: Copley.

Chafetz, J.S. 1984. *Sex and Advantage: A Comparative, Macro-Structural Theory of Sex Stratification.* Totowa, N.J.: Romann and Allanheld.

Feather, F. 1989. *G Forces: The 35 Global Forces Restructuring Our Future.* New York: William Morrow.

Goffman, E. 1979. *Gender Advertisements.* Cambridge, Mass.: Harvard University Press.

Kessler-Harris, Alice. 1982. *Out of Work.* New York: Oxford University Press.

Kroc, E. 1989. *Early Estimates, National Higher Education Statistics: Fall 1989.* Washington, D.C.: National Center for Educational Statistics.

Pear, R. September 4, 1987. "Women Reduce Lag in Earnings but Disparities with Men Remain." *New York Times,* pp. 1, 7.

U.S. Bureau of Labor Statistics. January 1989. *Employment and Earnings* 36:1. Washington, D.C: U.S. Government Printing Office.

U.S. Bureau of Labor Statistics. January 1990. *Employment and Earnings.* Washington, D.C: U.S. Government Printing Office.

U.S. National Center for Education Statistics. 1989. *Digest of Educational Statistics.* Washington, D.C.: U.S. Government Printing Office.

## Women in Blue-Collar Occupations

Women make and repair goods and equipment in a variety of blue-collar jobs. These manual labor occupations are divided into two groups, roughly equivalent to skilled and unskilled/semiskilled occupations. The unskilled/semiskilled group is the largest, and women in these occupations frequently work under poor conditions, for low wages, and with little job security. Such occupations are also a major source of employment for third-world women, whose working conditions and wages are far below those of American workers. The other category of blue-collar women is employed in occupations that are considered skilled and that pay relatively high wages. However, women are severely underrepresented in this category. The reasons for this include declining growth in skilled occupations, leaving little room for women newcomers, employer discrimination, and institutional barriers. In recent years, through lawsuits and legislation, women in both varieties of blue-collar jobs have fought to improve their employment opportunities and working conditions.

In 1992, nearly 16 percent of the nation's thirty million blue-collar workers were women. The large majority of blue-collar women (78 percent) held jobs of the semiskilled variety, usually low-wage operative jobs in the textile, apparel, and electronics industries. Eight percent of all working women can be found in this category of operator/fabricator. Most of these women are Euro-American, although 15 percent are African American and 12 percent are Hispanic. Women in these jobs endure difficult work conditions. Dexterity, speed, and the ability to withstand boredom are the chief skills required. These jobs usually require shift work, and they often expose workers to hazardous or toxic work conditions. The threat of unemployment is high, either because of temporary unemployment during downswings or because of permanent relocation of the jobs to lower-wage regions. About a third of women operatives are union members—a higher proportion than women's unionization in other occupations. However, unions in general have suffered dramatic declines and they have often given low priority to women workers' concerns in collective bargaining.

The remainder of blue-collar women (12 percent) are in skilled jobs that have traditionally been the domain of men, such as plumber, power-plant operator, or machinist. These women numbered slightly over one million in 1992, slightly over 2 percent of the female labor force. Women in these jobs enjoy relatively high wages and often find the jobs more interesting than the traditionally female jobs in which most had worked previously. Skilled blue-collar women are more likely than women in traditionally female jobs to be Euro-American, to have finished high school, and to be single heads of families. While job satisfaction for women who stay in such jobs is higher than for women in sex-traditional jobs, they nevertheless face obstacles in getting hired and retaining their jobs.

Table 1 shows a high degree of sex segregation in blue-collar jobs, such that women tend to be clustered in the lower-paying, lower-status occupations. In 1992, women were only 8.6 percent of the broad occupational category "precision production, craft, and repair," but they were 25 percent of the less skilled and lower-status category "operators, fabricators, and laborers." Similarly, subcategory percentages show that male blue-collar workers are much more likely to be in occupations such as truck driver, which pay well, whereas women are concentrated in occupations, such as sewing-machine operator, that pay poorly.

---

TABLE 1. Percentage Female and Earnings in Selected Blue-Collar Occupations, 1983 and 1992

*Earnings by Occupation\**

|  | *1983 percentage Female* | *1992 percentage Female* | *1992 Median Weekly Salary* |
|---|---|---|---|
| Precision Production, Craft, and Repair | 8.1 | 8.6 | $491 |
| Mechanics and Repairers | 3.0 | 3.3 | $490 |
| Carpenters | 1.4 | 1.0 | $425 |
| Mine Workers | 2.3 | 0.6 | $635 |
| Operators, Fabricators, and Laborers | 26.6 | 25.0 | $357 |
| Sewing-Machine Operators | 94.0 | 87.4 | $217 |
| Pressing-Machine Operators | 66.4 | 67.1 | $240 |
| Truck Drivers | 3.1 | 4.6 | $486 |

---

*Full-time workers only, both sexes.
Source: *Statistical Abstracts of the United States: 1993.* Table 644. Washington, D.C.: U.S. Government Printing Office, and *Employment and Earnings 1993.* Washington, D.C.: U.S. Department of Labor.

## History

America's first generation of wage-earning women were what today we would call blue-collar women. The women first entering factory labor in the early nineteenth century were farm workers recruited by employers to fill their lowest-paying and least-skilled jobs. In fact, depending on the industry and the region, women were more likely to work in the early factories than men. By 1840, women made up over half and sometimes more than 90 percent of workers in textile mills, shoe factories, or millinery (hat) factories. Despite the long hours and hard work, these women workers welcomed the opportunities these new jobs gave them to leave the farm for a period of time, earn a wage, and experience freedom from familial control. In newly industrializing countries today, many women express these same sentiments about moving into factory work. However, today as in the past, work conditions can become so dreadful that women have to fight to improve them. In the early New England factories, employers began to cut costs by speeding up the pace of the work and cutting wages—practices that are now common in developing countries. In both cases, working women have responded by fighting to establish unions to demand better treatment, with some limited successes. By the latter part of the nineteenth century, the composition of the blue-collar female labor force changed from native-born farm women to poorer women—African Americans, immigrants, and widows—as employers sought a more tractable workforce.

World Wars I and II were watersheds in the history of women in blue-collar jobs, as women replaced the men gone off to war. The government pressured employers to hire women into defense-plant jobs building airplanes, riveting battleships, and assembling tanks. For many women, this was their first taste of high-paying "men's work" and most left these jobs reluctantly at the war's end to return to lower-paying positions or the home. Not until the 1970s did women slowly begin to reenter traditionally male blue-collar jobs. Their gains have been slim, as Table 1 shows.

## Explanations of Women's Under-Representation

Women's underrepresentation in traditionally male, skilled, blue-collar jobs is important for two reasons. First, female poverty—which stems partly from the low pay of traditionally female jobs—is a growing social problem; integrating women without college degrees into fairly high-paying, traditionally male jobs would be a major step toward rectifying this problem. Second, to the extent that women's small numbers are the result of barriers in getting hired into these jobs, principles of fairness dictate the need to remove the barriers.

In the 1970s and 1980s, when women made impressive gains in many traditionally male fields, such as law, medicine, and management, their gains in skilled blue-collar jobs were the smallest among all the major occupational groups. What are the reasons behind women's underrepresentation in these occupations? Clearly, either women prefer white-collar employment or something is preventing their access to skilled, blue-collar jobs. Many people assume that occupational outcomes reflect workers' choices; in other words, that women choose jobs as file clerks (with 1992 median weekly earnings of $301) rather than as electricians (with 1992 median weekly earnings of $550). This assumption is reflected in explanations for occupational sex segregation put forward by many economists and social psychologists. Economists argue that work values and child-rearing decisions strongly influence a woman's choice between a sex-traditional or sex-nontraditional job. Many social psychologists arrive at the same conclusion—that women do not want sex atypical jobs—by arguing that gender differences in childhood socialization lead women to be uninterested in masculine jobs. These lines of argument explain women's underrepresentation in blue-collar jobs by focusing on problems in the supply of workers.

Sociologists tend to emphasize factors external to individual workers that constrain their choices, thus focusing on problems in the demand for workers rather than in their supply. For example, despite government regulations barring discrimination, research shows that employers frequently refuse to hire women into traditionally male blue-collar jobs. Co-worker harassment may make some women—especially those with other job options—decide that the jobs' rewards are not worth it. Unions, too, have been responsible for discriminatory practices, although many have improved their record and are now fighting for equal opportunity and comparable-worth legislation. Examples of institutionalized personnel practices that also present obstacles are the practice of recruiting new hires through employee referrals or high-school shop instructors, veteran-preference rules, protective labor rules that have barred women of child-bearing age from jobs that expose them to toxins, seniority rules that penalize transfers from white-collar jobs to blue-collar ones, and employers' assignment of women to so-called "light" rather than "heavy" work—a distinction often based more on stereotyped notions of sex appropriateness than job content. In sum, "supply" explanations are inadequate on their own; obstacles stemming from the workplace figure heavily into the underrepresentation of women in skilled blue-collar jobs.

## Conclusion

Future improvement in women's blue-collar employment depends on several factors. The decline of the manufacturing sector in this country and its expansion in lower-wage countries places downward pressure on job opportunities, wages, and working conditions in blue-collar jobs for both women and men. Social policy regarding trade agreements, job retraining, and plant closings can address these issues, and much depends on the outcome of the political debate. Government enforcement of existing legislation in regard to affirmative action, unionization, and job health and safety conditions has been lax in the recent past, although history shows that gains can be made when laws are enforced. These, too, are essentially political issues. Thus, blue-collar women need to fight the battle in the political arena, drawing on blue-collar men, unions, and advocacy groups as allies for progress.

*Irene Padavic*

## Bibliography

Cockburn, Cynthia. 1983. *Brothers: Male Dominance and Technical Change*. London: Pluto.
Deaux, K., and J. Ullman. 1983. *Women of Steel: Female Blue-Collar Workers in the Basic Steel Industry*. New York: Praeger.
O'Farrell, B. 1988. "Women in Blue-Collar Occupations: Traditional and Nontraditional." In *Women Working: Theories and Facts in Perspective*, 2nd ed., edited by A. Stromberg and S. Harkess, pp. 258–72. Mountain View, Calif.: Mayfield.

Padavic, I. 1992. "White-Collar Work Values and Women's Interest in Blue-Collar Jobs." *Gender & Society* 6:215–30.

Padavic, I., and B. Reskin. 1990. "Men's Behavior and Women's Interest in Blue-Collar Jobs." *Social Problems* 37:613–28.

Reskin, B., and I. Padavic. 1994. *Women and Men at Work*. Thousand Oaks, Calif.: Pine Forge.

Reskin, B., and P. Roos. 1984. "Institutional Factors Contributing to Sex Segregation in the Workplace." In *Sex Segregation in the Workplace: Trends, Explanations, Remedies*, edited by B. Reskin, pp. 235–60. Washington, D.C.: National Academy of Science.

Rosen, E. 1987. *Bitter Choices: Blue-Collar Women in and out of Work*. Chicago: University of Chicago Press.

Schroedel, J. 1985. *Alone in a Crowd: Women in the Trades Tell Their Stories*. Philadelphia: Temple.

Walshok, M. 1981. *Blue-Collar Women: Pioneers on the Male Frontier*. Garden City, N.Y.: Anchor.

Westwood, S. 1985. *All Day, Every Day: Factory and Family in the Making of Women's Lives*. Urbana, Ill.: University of Chicago Press.

# Women in Science and Medicine

## Women Physicians

Women constitute about 38 percent of graduating medical students and 15 percent of practicing physicians in the United States, a dramatic increase in two decades (Relman 1989). Asian and Asian American women have entered careers as physicians at high rates, but other women of color remain poorly represented. Women's influx into careers as physicians sparks considerable speculation about how women's presence in medical careers will alter medical practice in the United States. Will increasing proportions of women doctors bring a distinctively feminine, humanizing character to the practice of medicine, or will processes of selection, socialization, and allocation within a still male-dominated medical-care system perpetuate existing patterns, despite change in the gender composition of the profession (see Eisenberg 1989; Lorber 1991)?

### Women's Distribution in Medicine

Although there are more women doctors, women remain unevenly distributed across medical specialties and are concentrated in the lower-paid, lower-prestige specialties of family and general medicine, pediatrics, obstetrics/gynecology, anesthesiology, psychiatry, and public health (Bickel 1988; Silberger et al. 1987). They still are scarce in high-prestige specialties such as surgery, where they make up less than 7 percent of practicing physicians, and in medical teaching and administration and important health policy-making positions. As Judith Lorber (1991) has noted, women physicians' authority over patient care approximates that of men physicians, but women have considerably less control over the health-care system and the medical profession.

Women have entered medicine in greater-than-token proportions at a historic period, when doctors are losing prestige, autonomy, and income measured in real dollars. Government and third-party control over medical practice has led to diminished career satisfaction and spiraling concern over liability. Thus, as in many other professions, women have entered medicine as men have left for other careers.

### Practice Structures and Work Patterns

Women doctors are more likely than men to be in primary-care specialties, to practice in groups rather than solo, and to hold staff rather than self-employed posts

(Silberger et al. 1987). Self-employment usually is more lucrative. Women doctors choose staff positions for several reasons, including greater flexibility in work and on-call hours, freedom from the business management aspects of medical practice, and distaste for entrepreneurial activities needed to build a practice and for fee-for-service medicine. Women are less likely to be in rural areas but more apt to serve needy populations. The latter is particularly true for women physicians of color (Silberger et al. 1987).

Women doctors practice about fifty-two hours weekly, compared with men's fifty-eight hours, which partially accounts for income gaps (Weisman and Teitelbaum 1987). The income difference is accounted for primarily by the practice-hour patterns of women doctors who are parents, who practice about forty-one hours weekly, significantly less than childless women and men who are or are not parents (Grant et al. 1990; Weisman and Teitelbaum 1987). Gender differences in practice hours persist in the careers of women and men doctors, but narrows once women are beyond child-rearing years. Younger women and men doctors spend less time in practice and more time with family than doctors in earlier eras, suggesting that younger male physicians are adopting the work-hour patterns of women doctors. Women doctors see fewer patients per hour and earn less income per hour devoted to patient care than male physicians in the same specialties. These patterns might result from quality-of-care-related choices to devote more time to each patient, or they might reflect greater difficulty for women doctors in establishing a full patient load.

**Discrimination against Women Doctors**
Although past studies reported gender-based discrimination by patients against women doctors, more recent research indicates widespread acceptance and even preference for the services of women doctors in specialties such as pediatrics and obstetrics/gynecology (Bowman and Allen 1991). However, women doctors still face blatant and subtle discrimination in medical school and residency training, ranging from overt sexist remarks and harassment by medical faculty and peers to lack of mentoring by medical school and clinical faculty for entering high-status positions in medicine (Grant 1988).

Furthermore, medical careers are structured on a male career model, and women doctors often have difficulty combining work and family needs. For example, maternity leave policies vary widely across medical schools and residency programs and are nonexistent in some. Few institutions allow part-time or shared residencies, especially in the high-status specialties with few women (Bickel 1988; Levinson et al. 1989). Women receive less sponsorship for attaining the highest-status posts in medicine and, from medical school onward, experience what Lorber (1984) terms the "Salieri" effect: underrecognition for their accomplishments in comparison with male peers.

**Professional Orientations and Values**
Women begin medical school with value orientations similar to those of male peers, but are somewhat more concerned than male classmates with humanistic aspects of medicine, links between illness and socioemotional states, and social applications of medicine (Bowman and Allen 1991; Grant and DuRoss 1984; Leserman

1981). Women are also more amenable to working with nonphysician health professionals in collaborative relationships. They are less concerned than men with prestige and income derived from medicine, but attach more value to lifestyle-control issues. No differences appear, however, in women's and men's interest in patient care, or in research or medical school teaching (Weisman and Teitelbaum 1985). Over the course of medical training, the orientations and values of women and men tend to converge (Grant and DuRoss 1984; Leserman 1981).

Early-career women physicians show closer affinities in professional values to male doctors in their specialty areas than to women in other fields. Women doctors' treatment strategies are not markedly different from those of male doctors, despite some variations in attitudinal orientations, a pattern that may reflect either socialization of women doctors into predominant practices and ideologies within their specialties or a lack of influence on the part of relatively junior physicians usually working in group settings (Eisenberg 1989; Grant et al. 1986). Thus, to date, women physicians do not appear to have transformed the practice of medicine in major ways, although such a potential may exist as women doctors become more senior and more powerful in medical practice, medical education, and health-policy organizations.

### Personal-Life Values

Both women and men doctors place strong value on family life (Levinson et al. 1991). A majority of women and men doctors marry and have children, but men are slightly more apt to do so than women (Bowman and Allen 1991; Grant et al. 1990). Women doctors spend substantially more time on home and child care than do male counterparts and experience considerable stress over balance of work and family life when children are young (Grant et al. 1990; Weisman and Teitelbaum 1987). Nevertheless, most women doctors regard themselves both as effective physicians and successful parents and report satisfaction derived from both domains (Grant et al. 1990).

### Recent Developments

Recent programs seek to expand opportunities and influence for women physicians in the U.S. These include strong affirmative-action programs, women's liaison officers, sexual-harassment policies, and support groups at many American medical schools; publication of the *Women in Medicine* newsletter and sponsorship of professional development conferences for women doctors by the Association of American Medical Colleges, and initiatives by the National Institute of Health to expand research on women's health and research opportunities for women physicians.

*Linda Grant*
*Layne A. Simpson*

### Bibliography

Bickel, J. 1988. "Women in Medical Education. " *The New England Journal of Medicine* 319:1579–84.
Bowman, M., and D. Allen. 1991. *Stress and the Woman Physician*. 2nd ed. New York: Springer-Verlag.
Eisenberg, C. 1989. "Medicine Is No Longer a Man's Profession." *New England Journal of Medicine* 321:1542–44.

Grant, L. 1988. "The Gender Climate of Medical School: Perspectives of Women and Men Students." *Journal of the American Medical Women's Association* 43:109–19.

Grant, L., and D.J. DuRoss. 1984. "Expected Rewards of Practice and Personal-Life Priorities of Women and Men Medical Students." *Sociological Focus* 17:87–106.

Grant, L., N. Genero, P. Nurius, W.E. Moore, and D.R. Brown. 1986. "Gender and Time Variations in Medical Students' Value Development." *Sex Roles* 15:29–49.

Grant, L., L.A. Simpson, X.L. Rong, and H. Peters-Golden. 1990. "Gender, Parenthood, and Work Hours of Physicians." *Journal of Marriage and the Family* 52:39–49.

Leserman, J. 1981. *Men and Women in Medical School: How They Change and How They Compare.* New York: Praeger.

Levinson, W., S.W. Tolle, and C. Lewis. 1991. "Women in Academic Medicine: Combining Career and Family." *New England Journal of Medicine* 321:1511–17.

Lorber, J. 1991. "Can Women Physicians Ever Be True Equals in the Medical Profession?" *Current Research in Occupations and Professions* 6:25–37.

———. 1984. *Women Physicians: Careers, Status, and Power.* New York: Tavistock.

Relman, A.S. 1989. "The Changing Demography of the Medical Profession." *New England Journal of Medicine* 321:1540–42.

Silberger, A., W.D. Marder, and R.J. Willke. 1987. "Datawatch: Practice Characteristics of Male and Female Physicians." *Health Affairs* 6:104–9.

Weisman, C., and M.A. Teitelbaum. 1985. "Physician Gender and the Physician-Patient Relationship: Recent Evidence and Relevant Questions. *Social Science and Medicine* 20: 1119–27.

———. 1987. "The Work-Family System and Physician Productivity." *Journal of Health and Social Behavior* 28:247–57.

## Women in Science

Women are underrepresented in scientific occupations, constituting approximately 12 percent of the population of scientists and engineers in the United States (National Science Board 1985). The small proportion of women in science has been attributed to a successive filtering process that tends to lower the probability of women's being engaged in scientific research. This filtering process, described by Zuckerman and Cole (1975) as "the triple penalty," is based on three potential, albeit not mutually exclusive, barriers. First, science is culturally defined as inappropriate for women (Schiebinger 1987); second, women are led to believe that they are less competent than men; and third, women are discriminated against. Furthermore, those who survive the screening process find an internal labor market segregated along gender lines.

Women are concentrated in certain scientific disciplines and are underrepresented in others (Shenhav and Haberfeld 1992). Whereas women constituted almost 24 percent of those engaged in the sciences in 1983, their representation in engineering was very low—only 3 percent. Among the sciences, women were most likely to be found in psychology (approximately 40 percent of those working in the discipline) and other social sciences (30 percent), mathematical sciences (35 percent), and life sciences (20 percent). They were least likely to be found in the physical and environmental sciences (10 and 15 percent, respectively).

The extent of sex segregation across thirteen major categories of scientific disciplines (using the index of dissimilarity) changed only slightly between 1976 (55 percent) and 1983 (50 percent). This measure indicates that 50 percent of the scientists in 1983, either men or women, would have been required to change their field in order to equalize the gender composition of the scientific labor force.

Women in 1983 occupied approximately 30 percent of all positions in academia. However, while they held only 27 percent of full-time positions, women worked in 36 percent of part-time positions. In addition, the representation of women was lower in the top academic institutions. Approximately 45 percent of the full-time female faculty in tenure-track positions were found at the top American research universities, as compared with 60 percent of the male faculty. Similarly, only 10 percent of the full professors and 20 percent of the associate professors were women, whereas 35 and 52 percent, respectively, of assistant professors and instructors were women.

Studies examining the gender effect on the allocation of nonremunerative rewards (for example, research funding and grants) have produced inconsistent results. Whereas some studies concluded that discrimination against female scientists is insignificant (Cole and Cole 1973; Cole 1979), other studies have found differences in the allocation of rewards, managerial positions, and awards to male and female scientists (Bognanno 1987). Empirical results regarding gender-based wage gaps are clear cut. Surveys conducted in the 1970s and 1980s show a 10 to 20 percent earnings gap (Haberfeld and Shenhav 1990).

The most commonly used measures of scientific productivity, especially in academia, are the number of journal articles and books published. Of full, associate, and assistant professors, 48 percent of males published more than ten articles from the beginning of their careers, as compared with only 23 percent of females. Similarly, 23 percent of the male faculty published more than two books, as compared with 12 percent of the females. However, these differences, combined with differences in other determinants of earnings, such as scientific discipline and experience, cannot fully explain the gap in earnings of 10 to 20 percent between male and female scientists. Between one-half and two-thirds of this gap remains "unexplained" after accounting for these differences (Barbezat 1989). This "unexplained" portion is usually attributed to market discrimination. Most studies seeking to estimate the "unexplained" portion of the gap between the average salaries of male and female scientists that may be attributed to discrimination have been conducted in academic settings. Studies conducted at a single university have reported that discrimination accounts for a 7 to 9 percent difference in earnings (out of an earnings gap of 10 to 20 percent), as compared with 10 to 16 percent reported in studies based on aggregated samples of scientists.

There are a few signs that the scientific labor market is becoming more balanced with regard to gender composition. Whereas the number of doctoral degrees awarded to men has been declining steadily since the beginning of the 1970s (an 18 percent drop between 1970 and 1985), the number of degrees earned by women grew dramatically (an increase of 212 percent) during that period. Put differently, the share of women among the doctorates awarded increased from 13 percent in 1970 to 37 percent in 1985.

*Yehouda Shenhav*
*Yitchak Haberfeld*

## Bibliography

Barbezat, Debra A. 1989. "Affirmative Action in Higher Education: Have Two Decades Altered Salary Differentials by Sex and Race?" In *Research in Labor Economics*. Vol. 10, edited by Ronald G. Ehrenberg, pp. 107–56. Greenwich, Conn.: JAI.

Bognanno, Mario F. 1987. "Women in Professions: Academic Women." In *Working Women: Past, Present, Future*, edited by Karen S. Koziara, Michael H. Moscow, and Lucretia D. Tanner, pp. 245–64. Washington, D.C.: Bureau of National Affairs.

Cole, Jonathan R. 1979. *Fair Science: Women in the Scientific Community*. New York: Free Press.

————, and Cole, Stephen. 1973. *Social Stratification in Science.* Chicago: University of Chicago Press.

Haberfeld, Yitchak, and Yehouda Shenhav. 1990. "Are Women and Blacks Closing the Gap? Salary Discrimination in American Science during the 1970's and 1980's." *Industrial and Labor Relations Review* 44:68–82.

National Science Board. 1985. *Science Indicators: The 1985 Report.* Washington, D.C.: U.S. Government Printing Office.

Reskin, Barbara F. 1978. "Sex Differences and the Social Organization of Science." In *The Sociology of Science,* edited by Jerry Gaston, pp. 6–37. San Francisco, Calif.: Jossey-Bass.

Schiebinger, Londa. 1987. "The History and Philosophy of Women in Science: A Review Essay." *Signs: Journal of Women in Culture and Society* 12:305–32.

Shenhav, Yehouda, and Yitchak Haberfeld. 1992. "Paradigm Uncertainty, Gender Composition and Earnings Inequality in Scientific Disciplines: A Longitudinal Study 1972–1982." In *Research in the Sociology of Organizations.* Vol. 10, edited by Samuel B. Bachrach, and Pamela S. Tolbert, pp. 141–72. Greenwich, Conn.: JAI.

Zuckerman, Harriet, and Jonathan Cole. 1975. "Women in American Science," *Minerva* 13: 83–102.

Zuckerman, Harriet, Jonathan R. Cole, and John T. Bruer. 1991. *The Outer Circle: Women in the Scientific Community.* New York: Norton.

## Women in Nursing

Nurses constitute the largest occupational group in the contemporary U.S. health-care system, numbering over two million active employees (Loft and Kletke 1989). The role of nurses in the health-care system has changed dramatically in the past century or so, but nursing has always been overwhelmingly female.

Activities associated with nurses have historically been carried out by women for their own families, and often also for community members. Common diagnoses, recommendations for treatment, and day-to-day tasks necessary to recover from illness were carried out by women whose training was most likely to be from assisting and observing other women in these activities.

With the progression of the nineteenth century, societal changes prompted the transfer of these (and other) activities to nonfamily members; some women became private-duty nurses. These women hired themselves out to care for sick people in their homes. Training for this type of work was still informal. Some women also worked as nurses in hospitals, but this work was devalued—as were the hospitals themselves—in the nineteenth century (Aiken 1983).

Professional registered nurses have three educational paths: a four-year baccalaureate degree, a two-year associate degree, or a hospital diploma program. The latter training route is being phased out in favor of the associate and baccalaureate degrees as nursing leaders have campaigned for raising the professional status of nurses (Aiken 1983; Allen 1987). Increasingly, nurses are seeking advanced education at the master's level in a variety of specialty areas including clinical nurse, nurse practitioners, nurse midwives, and nurse anesthetists. The American Nursing Association (ANA) offers certification examinations attesting to the advanced clinical skills of these nurses. In recent years doctoral programs in nursing have developed and are preparing nurses as researchers and educators. Licensed practical nurses function under the direction of registered nurses. Nurses' aides are employed in many institutions to support care provided by the registered nurse and licensed practical nurse.

Nurses have traditionally been seen as subservient to physicians. In part, this perception has been rooted in the gendered nature of both the work and the workers: female nurses assisting and carrying out the orders of male physicians, providing comfort and support to patients, but under the supervision of physicians. In 1917, the author of an article in the *American Journal of Nursing* observed that "the first and most helpful criticism I ever received from a doctor was when he told me I was supposed to be simply an intelligent machine for the purpose of carrying out his orders" (Dock 1917, p. 394). This general orientation regarding nurse-physician relations persisted well into the twentieth century, and was described in the 1960s as the "doctor-nurse game" (Stein 1967). According to the rules of this game, nurses make recommendations for patient care and physicians act on these recommendations, but neither party overtly acknowledges that this actually takes place.

Nursing practice has changed in the past couple of decades: Nurses are likely to do much more technologically sophisticated work, and to engage in more independent work. Nursing work now encompasses such diverse tasks as maintaining paperwork on patients, patient assessment, monitoring patients' recovery, and so forth. As a result, the doctor-nurse game is far less common than it once was. Nurses and physicians still differ in their beliefs about the legitimate scope of nursing work, but their relations are less likely to be as dominant/subordinate, and more likely to be as colleagues. Some nurses diagnose, prescribe, and engage in other activities that have been monopolized by physicians for the past hundred years. Even nurses who are not in clinical specialty practice are assigned a wider variety of tasks now than previously. Even with these changes in the nature of nursing, the basic distinction between physicians as cure-oriented and nurses as care-oriented persists.

Nursing is likely to continue the trend toward more autonomy and to engage in more independent and collaborative work, as policy-makers recognize that nurses provide quality health care for less money than physicians. The national nursing organizations are mobilized to increase nurses' visibility and improve public perceptions of nursing work.

*Beth Rushing*

## Bibliography

Aiken, Linda. 1983. "Nurses." In *Handbook of Health, Health Care, and the Health Professions*, edited by David Mechanic, pp. 407–31. New York: Free Press.
Allen, David. 1987. "Professionalism, Occupational Segregation by Gender and Control of Nursing." In *The Politics of Professionalism, Opportunity, Employment, and Gender*, edited by Sarah Slavin, pp. 1–24. New York: Haworth.
Dock, Sarah E. 1917. "The Relation of the Nurse to the Doctor and the Doctor to the Nurse." *American Journal of Nursing* 17: 394–96.
Loft, John D., and Phillip R. Kletke. 1989. "Human Resource Trends in the Health Field." In *Handbook of Medical Sociology*. 4th ed., edited by Howard E. Freeman and Sol Levine, pp. 419–36. Englewood Cliffs, N.J.: Prentice Hall.
Stein, Leonard. 1967. "The Doctor-Nurse Game." *Archives of General Psychiatry* 16:699–703.

## Midwives

For most of human history, midwives have been the primary attendants at childbirth; midwifery is clearly one of the oldest occupations held by women. The term *midwife* means "with woman," illustrating exactly what midwives do and have done for centuries: They are with women during labor, the birth of the baby, and immediately following birth. Midwives also provide care and guidance during pregnancy, and some midwives are increasingly performing other women's health services, such as routine gynecological care and contraceptive advice. Attendance at childbirth, however, is the most common work that midwives have traditionally done.

Beginning in the seventeenth century, midwives in many European countries began to lose their expert status in their communities as physicians were called to attend the births of upper-class women. Louis XIV is reputed to have begun this trend. He hired a "man-midwife" to attend the birth of his mistress's child in 1663, and the practice was rapidly adopted by the European upper classes, whose members could afford to pay the higher fees of the man-midwife. Female midwives continued to be respected providers of maternity care for large portions of European society, but the employment of man-midwives by the aristocracy was a critical step in the transition of authority from midwife to physician, for it came to be perceived as the ideal for birth attendance. Nevertheless, midwives continued to provide maternity care (and sometimes abortion services) to the bulk of European women, as their Asian, African, South American, and North American counterparts did in their own communities.

## American Midwifery, 1650 to 1930

Midwives were very important members of society in early-American settlements; they provided vital services to their communities. Colonial records indicate that midwives were expected to assist the community in its efforts to maintain order (Wertz and Wertz 1977). Midwives' testimony was frequently required in legal proceedings surrounding questions of paternity, abortion, and infanticide. Sometimes civil authorities consulted midwives' casebooks in order to ascertain birth dates and other vital records. Further evidence of the importance of midwives lies in the fact that in many early settlements, midwives were given salaries, rent-free houses or lots, or other special privileges, in return for which the midwives attended the births of poor residents. The services of midwives were clearly perceived by early-American communities as important.

Thus the picture we have of early-American maternity care is one in which women are the primary birth attendants, and those women who attend births are often highly respected members of the community. A few men were beginning to make inroads into the provision of obstetric care during this period, particularly in the cities, where British and French obstetrical practices—including employment of accoucheurs, or men-midwives—were beginning to be adopted. The first American physicians to practice midwifery began in the 1750s. In Philadelphia, Dr. William Shippen began midwifery in 1756; within a few years, he was attending normal births, despite the customary practice of calling physicians only in abnormal births. But Shippen also offered a training course for midwives, which indicates the continuing importance of midwives as maternity-care providers during this period.

Historians estimate that physicians attended only about 5 percent of American births in the middle of the eighteenth century. Over the next one hundred years, however, that proportion increased to about 40 percent (Leavitt 1986). By 1900, midwives and physicians were each attending about half of American births. Physicians thus made steady gains in the proportion of births they attended, and many midwives lost their livelihoods. Midwives did not, however, disappear.

In the early twentieth century, in particular, most of the practicing midwives in the United States were foreign-born, and most of the midwives' clients were also foreign-born. The nationality of the practicing midwives mirrored that of the population in their communities. For instance, 26 percent of Minnesota midwives in 1923 were from Sweden and Norway, and 17 percent were from Germany; the majority of the foreign-born population in Minnesota at the time was from Scandinavia and Germany. The most frequent nationality of midwives in Chicago from 1915 to 1926 was Polish; in New York, Italian midwives predominated. Just as families of foreign extraction were more likely to call a midwife for a birth, the midwives themselves were more likely to be foreign-born. As immigration into the United States decreased, the percentage of births to foreign-born women decreased. This contributed to the disappearance of the midwife in these communities.

The evidence suggests that even after physicians began routinely attending births, American midwives attended the births of women who could either not reach or afford physicians, or who preferred midwives for cultural reasons. Physicians' fees were typically at least twice those of midwives, and midwives provided both childbirth attendance and postpartum nursing care. In addition, physicians were more likely than the rest of the American population to be located in urbanized areas: Many people lived in communities where there were no physicians. Finally, many midwives' clients preferred childbirth attendants who shared their language or cultural beliefs and practices. All of these factors—affordability, availability, and culture—contributed to the fact that both Southern African-American women and Southwestern Mexican-American women were much more likely to employ midwives, while Anglo whites were much more likely to employ physicians.

## Contemporary Midwifery in the United States

Today, there are two types of midwives practicing in the United States: certified nurse-midwives (CNMs) and lay midwives. Certified nurse-midwives are typically trained first as a nurse, practice in hospital or clinic settings, and then go on to specialized university training in nurse-midwifery: 63 percent of CNMs in 1988 had master's degrees (Lehrman and Paine 1990). They undergo certifying examinations by the American College of Nurse-Midwives, and are legally accepted practitioners in all U.S. states and territories. Lay midwives, on the other hand, do not usually have prior medical or nursing training (although some do), but are women who have learned through apprenticeship, self-training, or who have attended one of several lay midwifery schools. Lay midwives are not usually legally accepted health-care practitioners in the United States: Currently only ten states have legalized lay midwifery practice. In other states, midwifery is either clearly illegal (ten states) or its legal status is ambiguous. Where lay midwifery is legally recognized, the state typically requires a specific amount of training and experience, and all but one state require lay midwives to pass an examination to qualify for practice (Butter and Kay 1988). Despite the lack of legal recognition of lay midwifery, it remains a small but consistent component of the informal sector of the U.S. health-care system.

Both lay and nurse-midwives attend births and provide prenatal and postpartum care for low-risk childbearing women. However, lay midwives practice almost exclusively at home, while nurse-midwives typically practice in hospitals, physicians' offices, out-of-hospital birth centers, and clinics. Nurse-midwives do attend home births, but these do not represent a very large proportion of the work that nurse-midwives do. Indeed, many nurse-midwives do not even provide maternity care: Routine, well-woman gynecological care is an increasing component of nurse-midwifery.

Both lay midwifery and nurse-midwifery face opposition from the medical profession, though physicians oppose lay midwives to a greater degree. Studies of the development of midwifery suggest that physician opposition is one of the most significant barriers to the practice of midwifery. Other factors, such as legal recognition of midwifery and child-bearing women's preferences for birth attendant, have also played an important role in shaping the position of midwives in the health-care system. The future of both nurse-midwifery and lay midwifery, like their histories, depends on the complex interrelationship of physicians, the state, and the child-bearing public.

*Beth Rushing*

## Bibliography

Butter, Irene, and Bonnie Kay. 1988. "State Laws and the Practice of Lay Midwifery." *American Journal of Public Health* 78:1161–69.
Eakins, Pamela, ed. 1989. *The American Way of Birth*. Philadelphia: Temple University Press.
Leavitt, Judith Walzer. 1986. *Brought to Bed: Childbearing in America 1750 to 1950*. New York: Oxford University Press.
Lehrman, Ela-Joy, and Lisa L. Paine. 1990. "Trends in Nurse-Midwifery: Results of the 1988 ACNM Division of Research Mini-Survey." *Journal of Nurse-Midwifery* 35:192–203.
Litoff, Judy Barrett. 1978. *American Midwives, 1860 to the Present*. Westport, Conn.: Greenwood.
———, ed. 1986. *The American Midwife Debate*. Westport, Conn.: Greenwood.
Rothman, Barbara Katz. 1982. *Giving Birth*. New York: Penguin.
Sullivan, Deborah, and Rose Weitz. 1988. *Labor Pains: Modern Midwives and Home Birth*. New Haven: Yale University Press.
Wertz, Richard, and Dorothy Wertz. 1977. *Lying-In: A History of Childbirth in America*. New Haven: Yale University Press.

## Health-Care Professionals

Women have historically been the primary providers of health care, and women continue to be critical to the enterprise of health and healing. Within their own families, women have traditionally been the people who diagnose, treat, and refer to other health-care providers; this role has not changed substantially (Glazer 1990). In addition to this family health work, women have historically provided the bulk of community health care, as herbalists, midwives, nurses, and physicians (Ehrenreich and English 1978). This community role changed somewhat as healing became institutionalized, but women remain vital members of the health-care system.

As health care increased in complexity and diversity, the number and type of health-care workers increased. Adoption of sophisticated diagnostic and treatment technologies and therapies has been accompanied by employment of technologists and technicians, whose provision of services is typically directed by, but separate from, physicians (Backup and Molinaro 1984).

In addition, there has been a growing recognition that the health needs of substantial segments of the population are not being met. Rural and inner-city residents, in particular, are in need of primary health care. In response to this need, occupational groups like nurse practitioners, physician assistants, and certified nurse midwives emerged in the United States health care system. They provide services to groups that, for geographic or economic reasons, have less access to physicians' care.

Physicians dominate contemporary Western health-care systems only in terms of occupational power. Numerically, however, nurses, technicians, technologists, therapists, and other health-related occupations predominate in the division of labor in health care. Registered nurses are the single largest occupational group in the United States health-care system. Furthermore, women are disproportionately represented in these occupations: At least three-quarters of the total workforce in health care is female. For instance, registered nurses, licensed practical nurses, speech therapists, occupational therapists, dental assistants, dental hygienists, and dietitians are all over 90 percent female (Butter et al. 1987). In contrast, approximately 16 percent of physicians are female.

Despite women's prevalence in health-care occupations, women are more likely than men to be found in occupations that are lower in pay, prestige, and autonomy. These jobs also often involve more direct and sustained contact with patients, and are thus a central part of health-care work (Butter et al. 1987).

The health-care industry is likely to continue to be predominantly female. Women are increasingly entering health occupations that have been traditionally male. For instance, the percentage of women physicians has grown substantially in the past twenty years, and over one-third of new medical-school graduates are female. As women enter medical-school in greater numbers, the proportion of female practicing physicians will increase. While men are now entering nursing in greater numbers, women still predominate in the field, and are likely to continue to do so for the foreseeable future. Thus, the net effect of changes in the health-care industry is unlikely to change the sex composition of its constituent occupations.

*Beth Rushing*

## Bibliography

Backup, Molly, and John Molinaro. 1984. "New Health Professionals: Changing the Hierarchy." In *Reforming Medicine*, edited by Victor Sidel and Ruth Sidel, pp. 201–19. New York: Pantheon.

Butter, Irene, Eugenia Carpenter, Bonnie Kay, and Ruth Simmons. 1987. "Gender Hierarchies in the Health Labor Force." *International Journal of Health Services* 17(1):133–49.

Ehrenreich, Barbara, and Diedre English. 1978. *For Her Own Good: 150 Years of the Experts' Advice to Women*. Garden City, N.Y.: Anchor Press/Doubleday.

Glazer, Nona Y. 1990. "The Home as Workshop: Women as Amateur Nurses and Medical Care Providers." *Gender and Society* 4(4):479–99.

*Elizabeth Wheeler, only female piano tuner in New York City, 1979. Photograph © Bettye Lane, New York. Reprinted by permission.*

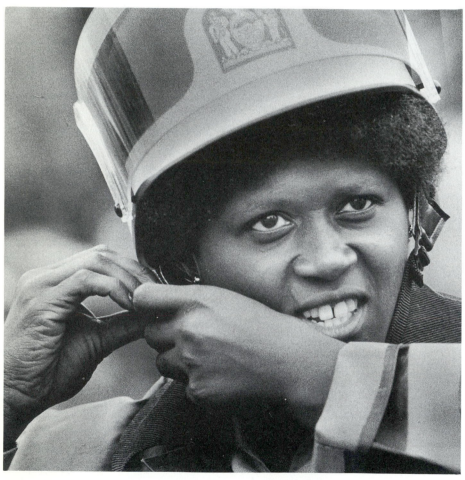

*One of the first women on the New York City Tactical Patrol Force, 1978. Photograph © Bettye Lane, New York. Reprinted by permission.*

*First female letter carrier in New York City, 1972. Photograph © Bettye Lane, New York. Reprinted by permission.*

*Asian American photographers. Both women have New York City press credentials.*
*Photograph © Bettye Lane, New York. Reprinted by permission.*

*National Park Service Rangers, Ellis Island, New York. Photograph © Bettye Lane, New York. Reprinted by permission.*

*New Mexico State Police. Photograph © Bettye Lane, New York. Reprinted by permission.*

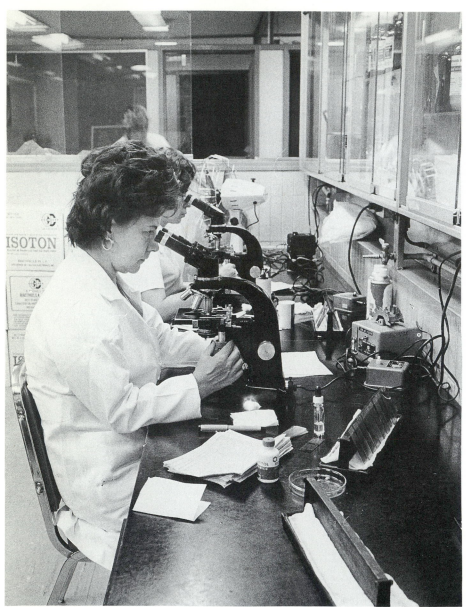

*Cell biologists in the research lab at Mexico City Medical Centre. Photograph © Bettye Lane, New York. Reprinted by permission.*

*Audio and video women. Photograph © Bettye Lane, New York. Reprinted by permission.*

*Irene Cornell, one of the first female network reporters, CBS Radio, New York City, 1979.*
*Photograph © Bettye Lane, New York. Reprinted by permission.*

*Anna Glauda, owner of construction company, Queens, New York. Photograph © Bettye Lane, New York. Reprinted by permission.*

*Medical doctors at Mexico City Medical Centre. Photograph © Bettye Lane, New York. Reprinted by permission.*

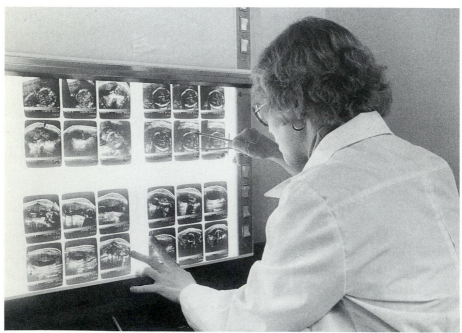

*Female radiologist viewing cat scan x-rays, Albert Einstein Hospital, New York City. Photograph © Bettye Lane, New York. Reprinted by permission.*

*Electrical technician trainee. Photograph © Bettye Lane, New York. Reprinted by permission.*

*Union carpenter in New York City, 1981. Photograph © Bettye Lane, New York. Reprinted by permission.*

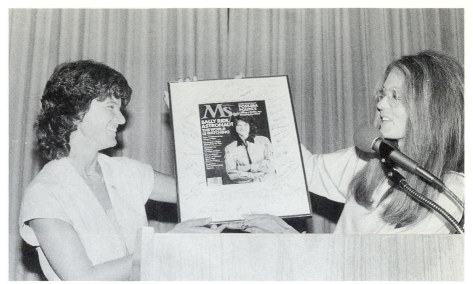

*Sally Ride, first woman astronaut, accepts MS magazine award at New York City hall from MS editor, Gloria Steinem. Photograph © Bettye Lane, New York. Reprinted by permission.*

*First television camerawoman to cover the Democratic Convention, 1976. Photograph © Bettye Lane, New York. Reprinted by permission.*

*Florence Adams teaches classes for women in electricity, plumbing, and car repair. Photograph © Bettye Lane, New York. Reprinted by permission.*

*First and only woman construction engineer to work on Roosevelt Island tramway, New York City. Photograph © Bettye Lane, New York. Reprinted by permission.*

*Construction worker trainee, New York City. Photograph © Bettye Lane, New York. Reprinted by permission.*

*Myrna Wright, the first woman to be hired as a bus driver in New York City. Photograph © Bettye Lane, New York. Reprinted by permission.*

*Business van in New York City. Photograph © Bettye Lane, New York. Reprinted by permission.*

*Architect Christine Benglia Bevington. Photograph © Bettye Lane, New York. Reprinted by permission.*

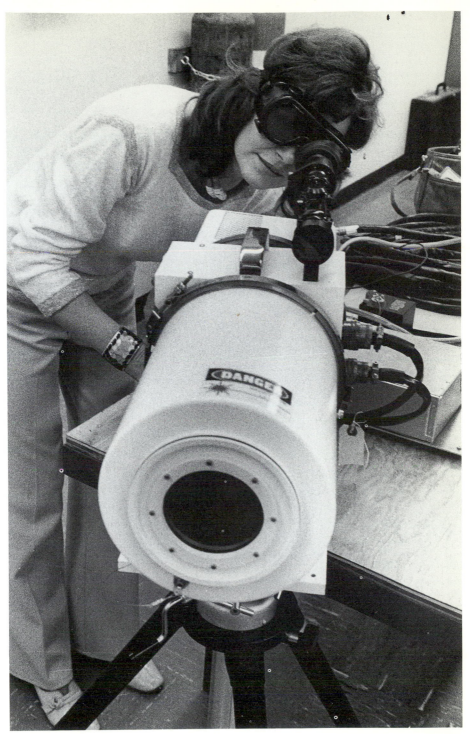

*Sylvia Hoyelle, electrical engineer working on laser beam equipment. One of the first women engineers hired at the White Sands Missile Range, Las Cruces, New Mexico. Photograph © Bettye Lane, New York. Reprinted by permission.*

*Ina Sookall was a member of the first class for women at the La Guardia Academy of Aeronautics, Helicopter Repair Division. Photograph © Bettye Lane, New York. Reprinted by permission.*

# Women in Education

## Women in Academia

Examination of the status of women in academia requires attention to two interrelated issues. The first is women's representation as students, faculty, and administrators in institutions of higher education. The second is the impact of scholarship by and about women on the curriculum and research in colleges and universities. Women have made dramatic gains as faculty and graduate students in academia in recent years and now earn more than half of all bachelor's and master's degrees. However, their influx has been uneven across types of institutions and academic disciplines. In academia, as in other occupational sectors, women encounter a "glass ceiling" blocking all but a few tokens from the highest leadership and policy-making positions. Feminist critiques and an explosion of new scholarship by and about women have appeared in numerous disciplines, but in most cases this scholarship has gained visibility only among women scholars and has not fundamentally transformed the knowledge base, methodological traditions, or pedagogical styles within academic disciplines (Kramarae and Spender 1992).

### Women's Representation in Academia

Women now constitute more than 40 percent of those in doctoral training in the United States and more than 30 percent of college and university faculty (Witt 1990), but are unequally distributed within academia. While women constitute greater than 50 percent of doctoral students in fields such as English, education, and psychology, they represent only 11 percent in biological sciences and only 2 percent in physics and astronomy (Sonnert 1990). Women are more apt than their male counterparts to be employed by undergraduate two- and four-year colleges rather than research universities and to hold part-time or non–tenure-track positions where pay, benefits, job security, and influence is minimal (Aisenberg and Harrington 1988; Fox 1989). From graduate school on, women often lack effective mentors who can aid their academic careers, and few have worked with female mentors who might serve as role models for handling issues specific to women, such as pregnancy, maternity leave, or sexual harassment (Fort et al. 1993). Minority women have an even harder time than white women finding mentors for academic careers; academic institutions employ few scholars of color and majority-race scholars are not always willing or effective mentors for women of color (Welch 1992).

Women faculty lag behind men in salary, academic rank, and appointment to top administrative posts (see, for example, Fox 1989). While in the past some variation could be explained based on less preparation and experience for women scholars, more recent cohorts of women and men scholars have similar training. Furthermore, a consistent literature shows gaps in women's salaries, even when experience and credentials are controlled for (Bentley and Blackburn 1992). Focusing on sociology, Roos and Jones (1993) show that women have entered academic posts only as men have left for more lucrative nonacademic jobs. Although a larger proportion of minority than white graduate students and faculty are women, minorities (except Asians) have enrolled in doctoral programs at declining rates during the 1980s, because of reduced financial support for graduate education and competition from other fields such as engineering and business, where careers do not require Ph.D.s (Pearson and Bechtel 1989).

### Gendered Divisions of Labor

When women and men faculty are located in similar institutions they frequently have different work assignments, owing largely to their differential placement in academia, which gives women more undergraduate teaching and advising than men (Kulis and Miller-Loessi 1992). Women of color are particularly apt to have heavy loads of advising and committee work (Brewer 1989). Their token status in most institutions puts them in great demand for formal and informal student advising and committee work. Also, many are cross-appointed in two departments, adding extra duties (Kulis and Miller 1988). Women are also more likely to hold temporary, non–tenure-track positions with heavy teaching loads and fewer resources for research (Fox 1989). These variations in formal and informal allocations of duties disadvantage women faculty, since rewards in academia accrue mostly for research productivity. Bielby (1991) concludes that despite rhetoric to the contrary, academic institutions are more similar to than different from other labor markets, embodying overt and subtle forms of gender inequities that can erode women's prospects over time.

### Women's Research Productivity

Studies prior to the 1980s based largely on natural and physical scientists suggest that women scholars publish less and receive fewer external research grants than men (Fox 1989). More recent research on a wider range of disciplines shows diminished gender differences in publication and research grant productivity when institutional locale, academic credentials, and year since degree are taken into account. In sociology, for example, women are overrepresented as authors of journal articles, relative to their proportions of faculty in departments with graduate programs (Ward and Grant 1985). Gender-linked differences in productivity occur mostly among the highly productive, mostly male "superstars." However, Cole (1987) reports that even when women's productivity equals men's, women garner fewer honorific awards and less national and international recognition, suggesting persistence of gender bias in reputational reward systems. Furthermore, universities still operate under what Hochschild (1975) terms "the clockwork of male careers," so that for women with children, the heaviest, pretenure productivity demands occur when they are most apt to have small children for whom they are primary caretakers. Universities have been slow to implement supports such as maternity leaves, flexible tenure calendars, or on-site day care that could help faculty balance work and family demands. These processes, in combination, might lead to cumulative disadvantages for women scholars over time.

## Scholarship by and about Women

The increase in scholarship by and about women in the past twenty years undoubtedly is linked to the influx of women at all levels of academia (DuBois et al. 1985; Kramarae and Spender 1992). Women's scholarship also has benefited from the expansion of women's studies programs and from journals and book publication series that provide outlets to an audience for feminist scholarship (Kramarae and Spender 1992). Feminist scholarship seeks not only to add to the knowledge base of various disciplines the overlooked experiences of women, but also to challenge the bases of scholarship in academic work by proposing distinctively feminist approaches to the creation of knowledge (Collins 1990). Whether a fundamental link exists between gender and genre is an issue in many disciplines. The feminist critique of prevailing theories and methods, in particular, provokes resistance from some scholars, who ignore, trivialize, or denigrate feminist scholarship (DuBois et al. 1985). Consequently, feminist scholarship might be ghettoized, confined to a primarily female audience but failing to transform research and teaching in fundamental ways (Stacey and Thorne 1985). Through mechanisms such as women's caucuses, curriculum transformation projects, funding programs for feminist research, and discipline-based groups on the status of women, women faculty and graduate students have become increasingly active in efforts to improve the status of women as students and workers in colleges and universities and to move feminist scholarship from the margins to the mainstream.

*Linda Grant*
*Kathryn B. Ward*

## Bibliography

Aisenberg, Nadya, and Mona Harrington. 1988. *Women of Academe: Outsiders in the Sacred Grove.* Amherst, Mass.: University of Massachusetts Press.

Bentley, Richard, and Robert Blackburn. 1992. "Two Decades of Gain for Female Faculty." *Teachers College Record* 93:697–709.

Bielby, William. 1991. "Sex Differences in Careers: Is Science a Special Case?" In *The Outer Circle: Women in the Scientific Community,* edited by Harriet Zuckerman et al., pp. 171–87. New York: Norton.

Brewer, Rose. 1989. "Black Women and Feminist Sociology." *The American Sociologist* 20:57–70.

Cole, Jonathan. 1987. *Fair Science: Women in the Scientific Community.* 2nd ed. New York: Columbia University Press.

Collins, Patricia Hill. 1990. *Black Feminist Thought: Knowledge, Consciousness, and Power.* New York: Routledge.

DuBois, Ellen, Gail Paradise Kelly, Elizabeth Laprovsky Kennedy, Carolyn Korsmeyer, and Lillian S. Robinson. 1985. *Feminist Scholarship: Kindling in the Groves of Academe.* Urbana: University of Illinois Press.

Fort, Deborah C., Stephanie J. Bird, and Catherine J. Didion, eds. 1993. *A Hand up: Women Mentoring Women in Science.* Washington, D.C.: Association for Women in Science.

Fox, Mary Frank. 1989. "Women and Higher Education: Gender Differences in the Status of Students and Scholars." In *Women: A Feminist Perspective,* edited by Jo Freeman. 4th ed. Palo Alto, Calif.: Mayfield.

Hochschild, Arlie R. 1975. "Inside the Clockwork of Male Careers." In *Changing Women in a Changing Society*, edited by Joan Huber. Chicago: University of Chicago Press.

Kramarae, Cheris, and Dale Spender, eds. 1992. *The Knowledge Explosion: Generations of Scholarship*. New York: Athene.

Kulis, Stephen, and Karen Miller. 1988. "Are Minority Women Sociologists in Double Jeopardy?" *American Sociologist* 19:323–39.

Kulis, Stephen, and Karen A. Miller-Loessi. 1992. "Organizations, Labor Markets, and Gender Integration in Academic Sociology." *Sociological Perspectives* 35:93–117.

Pearson, Willie, and H. Kenneth Bechtel, eds. 1989. *Blacks, Science, and American Education*. New Brunswick, N.J.: Rutgers University Press.

Roos, Patricia A., and Katharine W. Jones. 1993. "Shifting Gender Boundaries: Women's Inroads into Academic Sociology." *Work and Occupations* 20(4):395–428.

Sonnert, Gerhard. 1990. *Careers of Women and Men Postdoctoral Fellows in the Sciences*. Cambridge, Mass.: Project Access, Harvard University.

Stacey, Judith, and Barrie Thorne. 1985. "The Missing Feminist Revolution in Sociology." *Social Problems* 32:301–16.

Ward, Kathryn B., and Linda Grant. 1985. "The Feminist Critique and a Decade of Published Research in Sociology Journals." *Sociological Quarterly* 26:139–57.

Welch, Lynn Brodie, ed. 1992. *Perspectives on Minority Women in Higher Education*. New York: Praeger.

Witt, Stephanie. 1990. *The Pursuit of Race and Gender Equity in American Academe*. New York: Praeger.

## Women of Color in Academe

Women of color have made modest gains in their quest to join the faculty populations of higher-education institutions. Their numbers within all departments, fields of study, and professional schools have reached levels never before attained. Nevertheless, at 3 percent of all full-time faculty, they constitute a faculty population very much in need of institutional empowerment within all disciplines and professional schools. Even more than white women or men of color, women of color are severely disenfranchised compared with the white males who have traditionally dominated academe. Here, we attempt a close, systematic look at the structural, sociocultural, and psychological impediments to their incorporation, progression, and retention in academia. We conclude by suggesting the need for established senior faculty to be active, supportive members and for the creation of networks identifying and linking women of color within specific departments and whole institutions if academe is to be a more hospitable environment.

### An Overview of Women of Color in Academe

Faculty women of color have made discernible advances in the last two decades. Between 1975 and 1985, the number of women of color who were full-time faculty increased 23 percent from roughly twelve thousand to approximately sixteen thousand (Touchton and Davis 1991). Of this number, African-American women made up the largest share (9,230), followed by Asian women (3,781) and Hispanic women (2,404). This increase was due largely to three factors: (1) the concerted political action to create and implement national policy by overlapping constituencies of women, people of color, and white liberals; (2) the implementation of federal employment regulations such as those pertaining to affirmative action; and (3) a general increase in the number of minority women pursuing and receiving Ph.D.s. In 1985, women of color received 3.7 percent of conferred doctoral degrees, whereas they had received a mere 1.98 percent ten years earlier. After more than twenty years of intense political effort and legislative edict, parity with white men in academe was still a distant dream. To illustrate, while women of color experienced a 23 percent increase in number, their proportion of all full-time faculty remained steady at 3 percent between 1975 and 1985 (Touchton and Davis 1991). While data are not yet available, even if that rate of increase were doubled the following decade, in 1994, parity is still not in sight. Nevertheless, some encouraging advances have been made by Asian and African-American women in branching out to fields such as science and engineering; overall, however, women of color continue to be concentrated in traditionally "female" and "ethnic" specialties such as education and the social sciences (Chamberlain 1988). The few women of color in academe are overwhelmingly located in the academic "proletariat" —that is, part-time, temporary, or non–tenure-track positions (McMillen 1986). They typically advance more slowly than their white male counterparts, are concentrated at the lower rungs of academic ladders, and are disproportionately found at two-year community colleges rather than major research universities (Moore and Johnson 1989). Salary discrepancies further exacerbate their situations. In short, women of color have not found the door open to them in academe; rather, they remain marginal participants in most academic departments (Simeone 1987).

There is a paucity of systematic empirical research documenting women of color's experiences within academe; typically, they are made invisible as a distinct category of academic participants by being subsumed under either gender or minority categories in evaluation reports and demographic data-sets. Yet, they are not only differentiated by gender from the white males who dominate higher education institutions both statistically and in positions of power, but also from white academic women by ethnicity (Moses 1989; Hill Collins 1990). Their unique position in having dual salient identities, sexual and racial, however, merits special attention by researchers of academic institutions as a workplace. While sweeping generalizations about all women of color are misleading because of the peculiarities of any particular ethnicity, they share the experience of a unique kind of dual discrimination that may be doubly disempowering and thus qualitatively different from that experienced by white women or men of color; for this reason they may be viewed as a "double minority." Statistically, women of color in academe are more likely to come from a "class of origin" lower than the upper middle-class style within which most academics and professional persons function. Any comprehensive explanation of their experiences, then, must include a discussion of both active as well as passive forms of discrimination against people who are made vulnerable by virtue of being ascribed multiple group identities—that is, not only gender and racial, but class as well.

## Barriers Faced by Women of Color in Academe

The academic road is a precarious one for women of color. We now turn to the question of why: Why are women of color concentrated in lower-ranking non–tenure-track positions in the first place? Why are women of color more at risk of leaving academe than even men of color or white women? What are some of the personal, social, and structural impediments to their progression?

## Structural Barriers

One factor suggested for the dearth of women of color in academe is the shortage of qualified candidates coming through the pipeline of academic training (McMillen 1986). This analogy refers to the siphoning process whereby the pool of potential candidates is gradually narrowed until only the most qualified emerge out the other end. The implication here is that academic departments are eager to hire women of color, but few qualified candidates are procurable. The problem with this analogy, however, lies in its main assumption: If the pipeline can be filled with qualified candidates, the issue of representation will be solved. At issue, however, is not only representation generally, which usually means at the bottom of institutional structures, but of barriers to retention and to upward mobility. Few women of color acquire tenured positions, and fewer still reach full professor status. Thus, the problem is not only one of institutional failure to achieve representation at the point of entry, but also the subsequent effects the experience of double discrimination have upon the continued willingness by women of color to compete against entrenched forces, leading to premature job plateauing and early resignation.

A closer look at the formal and informal structures of academe may provide a fuller picture of the impediments to their advancement and retention. For instance, evidence suggests that women of color suffer from a lack of mentoring and encouragement from colleagues and senior faculty. Mentors function as "gatekeepers" to professional advancement by furnishing essential information such as guidelines for journal publication, potential funding sources, and crucial details about promotion/tenure procedures (Menges and Exum 1983). They also provide overviews of faculty departments and their internal dynamics, warn of potential political snares, and help link new hires to collegial networks. Information of this nature is conveyed informally—no official guidelines are handed out at the beginning of an academic career. The new hire who has the support of a mentor experiences greater ease in her incorporation into the hierarchy, while the one who does not is left to her own devices (and pitfalls).

According to Hall and Sandler (1983), women of color are less likely to be included in mentor relationships and collegial networks because of their outsider status. Members of "colleague systems" typically choose persons most like themselves as their protégés. Since available mentor pools largely consist of white males, forging relationships between women of color and white male mentors requires significantly more time and effort (Matclynski and Comer 1991). That women of color are concentrated in the academic proletariat may further contribute to their being unlikely candidates for mentoring by some white males who may not believe in the advancement of women. Moreover, frequently women's research interests fall outside traditional or "mainstream" areas that have been disproportionately characterized by the interests of white males and in which, therefore, they have a depth of expertise. Also both may be reluctant to become too involved with the other for fear of faculty gossip or perceived sexual relationships (Cordova et al. 1988). The informal, after-work meetings and casual gatherings that help transform a formal institutional relationship into a productive professional colleagueship, or even a supportive friendship, are, therefore, less likely to occur. Not surprisingly then, women of color are passed by in tenure proceedings when senior male faculty are insufficiently familiar with their professional work or do not know them well enough personally to assess whether they have the "prowess" for future academic success.

Additional departmental responsibilities may further add to the stress felt by women of color. Owing to their scarce numbers, they are typically called to serve upon boards that require female or minority representation; by their birthright they become "specialists" in these areas. Moreover, they typically have joint appointments in women's or ethnic studies simultaneous to their primary discipline. While these appointments account for much of the increase in women of color faculty, they may result in competing demands and expectations (Menges and Exum 1983). In short, women of color typically end up overloaded and overwhelmed because of their small numbers and high demand (Hall and Sandler 1983).

Further compounding matters, current fiscal crises and shrinking budgets in all institutions of higher learning have had a particularly detrimental impact on women of color. Having the least seniority and being overrepresented in the lower ranks, minority women are especially vulnerable to departmental layoffs ("last to be hired, first to be fired") during "retrenchment" periods (Menges and Exum 1983).

## Sociocultural Barriers

For all women, competing familial and career obligations intensify job stress. Social mores and expectations continue to dictate that women are the primary caretakers of children and the home. For women of color, these assumptions may be heightened by added cultural expectations and role conflicts. In many cases, they may be the first in their families to pursue an academic career; they may come from families or environments unable to understand or support, emotionally as well as financially, their academic ambitions. As Vasquez (1982) points out, traditional sex-role expectations that prescribe Latinas' roles as wives and mothers foremost combined with low socioeconomic status may account for the limited participation of Mexican-American women in higher education. In the face of these added pressures, women of color may end up having grave doubts about academia and their place within it.

## Personal and Psychological Barriers

It is important to recognize that the current generation of women of color faculty are establishing precedent; they are pioneers entering a world where few women of color have gone before. One consequence of this fact is the profound sense of social isolation these women feel (Cordova et al. 1988). So few women of color can be found campuswide, let alone within one's department, that the few who are present are indeed alienated. This alienation is further heightened by the reception they typically receive from their white male colleagues, as discussed above.

Issues of credibility also arise. There is a covert, if not overt, sense that rather than acquiring their position through professional merit, women of color are "filling two slots" because they are both female and a person of color. This stigma of tokenism places an extra burden on them to prove their academic worth to colleagues (Carroll 1973). Added scrutiny by the press and public because they are racial as well as sexual pioneers further exacerbates the pressures they feel to succeed. The social isolation from the buildup of these various factors places many women of color at risk of forgoing their careers. Academia is perceived as a less than hospitable environment, which appreciates neither their presence nor their contributions.

## Conclusion

In the past, academic success has demanded a great deal of intellectual conformity on the part of junior faculty, compliance to the ways and ideals of white males who are still the dominant constituency within academe. For women of color, this has typically meant leaving behind or at least compromising their own gender as well as ethnic perspectives in the selection, formulation, and conduct of intellectual projects. The need to conform to a preexisting academic orthodoxy in order to survive, however, perpetuates the very conditions that hinder them from full participation in the first place. To significantly alter the low participation and retention rate of women of color, serious efforts need to be taken to address the structural, sociocultural, and psychological barriers discussed above. Active mentors who provide advice on long-term career planning and collegial support for women of color in pursuit of tenure, thus fostering a sense of belonging in the profession, are essential. Local as well as national support networks identifying and linking women of color are also crucial. Successful examples of this include a recent conference held at MIT entitled "Black Women in the Academy: Defending Our Name" (Leatherman 1994). The need is great among women of color to find these networks, as evidenced by the unexpected turnout. Conference organizers expected five hundred women to participate; instead, two thousand women showed to share their experiences, forge collegial linkages and friendships, and, of course, commiserate with one another. Similar types of conferences, whether discipline-specific, ethnic-specific, or more broadly based, would likely draw similar showings. In short, then, women of color require a sense of place in academe, a place that legitimizes the importance of their contributions and scholarship.

*Mia Tuan*

*Leah Robin*

*Rodolfo Alvarez*

*Amily Shui-I Huang*

## Bibliography

Carroll, Constance. 1973. "Three's a Crowd: The Dilemma of the Black Women in Higher Education." In *Academic Women on the Move*, edited by A. Rossi and A. Calderwood. New York: Russell Sage.

Chamberlain, Marion K. 1988. *Women in Academe: Progress and Prospects.* New York: Russell Sage Foundation.

Cordova, Fred, et al. 1988. "Mentoring Women and Minorities in Higher Education." Psychology Department, Eastern New Mexico University. Portales, New Mexico.

Hall, Roberta, and Bernice Sandler. 1983. *Academic Mentoring for Women. Students and Faculty: A New Look at an Old Way to Get Ahead.* Washington, D.C.: Association of American Colleges.

Hill Collins, Patricia. 1990. *Black Feminist Thought: Knowledge, Consciousness, and the Politics of Empowerment.* New York: Routledge.

Leatherman, Courtney. 1994. "Black Women in Academe." *Chronicle of Higher Education.* 40(21):A17, A19.

Matclynski, Thomas, and Kelvie Comer. 1991. "Mentoring Women and Minorities: An Anecdotal Record." Dayton, Ohio: University of Dayton, Dept. of Education.

McMillen, Liz. 1986. "Women Flock to Graduate School in Record Numbers, but Fewer Blacks Are Entering the Academic Pipeline." *Chronicle of Higher Education* 33(2):1, 25

Menges, Robert, and William Exum. 1983. "Barriers to the Progress of Women and Minority Faculty." *Journal of Higher Education* 54:123–44.

Moore, Kathryn, and Michael Johnson. 1989. "The Status of Women and Minorities in the Professorate: The Role of Affirmative Action and Equity." In *Managing Faculty Resources*, edited by G.G. Lozier and M.J. Dooris. New Directions for Institutional Research No. 63. San Francisco: Jossey-Bass.

Moses, Yolanda. 1989. *Black Women in Academe.* New York: Ford Foundation.

Simeone, Angela. 1987. *Academic Women Working towards Equality*. South Hadley, Mass.: Bergin and Garvey.

Snyder, Thomas, and Charlene Hoffman. 1991. *Digest of Education Statistics*. Washington D.C.: National Center for Education Statistics.

Touchton, Judith G., and Lynne Davis. 1991. *Fact Book on Women in Higher Education*. New York: Macmillan.

Vasquez, Melba. 1982. "Confronting Barriers to the Participation of Mexican American Women in Higher Education." *Hispanic Journal of Behavioral Sciences* 4(2):147–65.

## Women as Teachers: A Historical Perspective (1830–1990)

In the mid nineteenth century, with the "feminization of teaching," women gained access for the first time to wage-earning work of a professional nature. Although teaching offered economic independence, social status, and an opportunity to travel, it also created limitations for women in terms of significantly lower pay than men and low status in a male-dominated educational hierarchy. In the early twentieth century some women teachers in urban areas, such as Chicago and New York, became politically active and organized to seek equal pay, tenure, and pensions (Hoffman 1981; Murphy 1990). By the 1950s, teachers nationwide achieved these provisions; thus, teaching became a career that allowed women to combine work and family responsibilities. The reform of teaching in the 1980s seemed to offer teachers greater opportunity but may raise questions of gender and equity.

Teaching has been considered "good work for a woman" since the mid nineteenth century, when Catherine Beecher recruited unmarried women to enter "woman's true profession" (Hoffman 1981). For the last 150 years, however, teaching has been filled with social, economic, and professional contradictions for women that simultaneously offer both opportunity and limitations, require sacrifice in return for rewards, and grant women teachers power while rendering them powerless (Apple 1985).

This "good work," like most traditional women's work, has always had its limitations: being one of the lower-paying occupations requiring higher education, being considered a "profession" primarily by teachers and not others, and being a one-step career for women who did not often advance into administration, a predominantly male domain after the 1930s (Richardson and Hatcher 1983).

In the late eighteenth century American education was extended to include girls, an idea considered radical by Europeans. Americans, however, wanted women to have some education so that they could teach their children at home as part of the moral and civic duty of virtuous "republican mothers." Thus teaching, considered natural for women, became an idealized role for the late-eighteenth-century homemaker (Spring 1986; Tyack 1974).

In the early nineteenth century, formalized school-teaching, especially of older children, was attractive as interim work for men who were preparing for other professions such as the ministry or law. Single women were accepted only as teachers of younger children, which extended the notion of feminine nurturing. As industrialization, immigration, and urbanization became influential social and economic factors in the nation's development in the nineteenth century, male civic leaders promoted the common school movement in the 1830s to provide free schooling for nonslave girls and boys. This expansion of educational opportunities at public expense created an increased need for teachers as well as a need to operate within a limited budget. These social and economic factors contributed to the creation of teaching as a new role for women (Hansot and Tyack 1988).

Men, who previously might have been teachers, now had work opportunities in business. Consequently, by 1870 unmarried women made up approximately 59 percent of this newly expanded teaching corps primarily because they worked for one-third to one-half the salary paid to men (Hoffman 1981). Although economically exploitive, this "feminization of teaching" offered social mobility and economic advantages to women whose paid work had previously been limited to such jobs as factory work, needle trades, domestic work, peddling, or prostitution. Limited to unmarried women, teaching became socially accepted wage work for women and was promoted as excellent preparation for marriage and child-rearing. Women teachers also had an opportunity for travel—they taught in urban and rural areas, in remote areas on the frontier, and in the South during Reconstruction. Propelled by idealism and independence, these women nevertheless endured hardship and isolation in these remote areas.

Teaching simultaneously promoted and sabotaged the interests of nineteenth-century women teachers, who were expected to motivate through affection while administering harsh discipline. Given power over their students' lives, they were powerless in relation to the male hierarchy. Placed in separate classrooms and usually working under a male principal whom they were to treat like their father, these unmarried women teachers were encouraged to be obedient and subservient (Grumet 1988; Strober and Tyack 1980).

Not all, however, remained this way. In San Francisco in 1870 Kate Kennedy, a suffragist, a teacher, and a member of the Knights of Labor, lobbied successfully with her colleagues for legislation that granted women equal pay. In the early twentieth century, when the women's movement supported suffrage, there were two women teachers' organizations in Chicago and New York, with memberships of approximately three thousand and fourteen thousand, that provided a strong exception to the standard of feminine passivity. Led by Margaret Haley and Grace Strachan respectively, these unions made teachers' issues into women's issues. Haley, herself a former elementary teacher, and the members of the Chicago Teachers Federation (CTF)—a union of female elementary teachers— militantly resisted the economic and ideological pressures to keep women teachers on a lower pay scale than men and to deny them financial security. In order to gain political influence for voteless women teachers, the CTF affiliated with labor. Haley and her "lady labor sluggers" battled the local corporate leaders and politicians at the community, city, and state levels. Consequently, the CTF was the first teachers' union to win and exercise power.

The CTF achieved some degree of financial security through the development of seniority, pension plans, and salary schedules for women teachers. Strachan's organization, the Interborough Women Teachers' Association (IWTA), however, stressed the single issue of equal pay for women teachers. Described by one historian as "woman power," this union militancy in the nation's two largest school systems led to changes for women teachers across the nation (Murphy 1990; Tyack 1974).

In the 1910s, women teachers, who came primarily from working-class families, could teach only if unmarried; thus, teaching was like a "contractual singlehood." By the 1920s, women teachers had gained some degree of economic and job security, as well as the right to remain in teaching after marriage; therefore, teaching became a long-term work option for women, who accounted for 86 percent of the public-school teaching force and almost 100 percent of all elementary positions.

Teaching changed dramatically in the next decades. The post–World War II baby boom created an increased demand for teachers; consequently, more married women remained in teaching. By the 1950s, women teachers came primarily from middle-class backgrounds and often considered teaching as "insurance" in case anything happened to their husbands. In the turbulent 1960s, teachers used strikes for the first time to achieve collective bargaining rights. Unlike the era of Haley and Strachan, in the 1960s teacher militancy tended to be gender-divided by roles and not issues, with males as leaders. The issue of pay was not gender-related, as schools had by then one pay scale for all teachers. Since the 1960s, women have tended to remain longer in teaching; however, some conflict for women teachers continues. The teaching schedule, that once conveniently enabled women to combine work and family responsibilities, has created a "triple day of work" for women teachers, who must juggle teaching, schoolwork at home, and family obligations. Women teachers in the 1970s who experienced "teacher burnout" were made to feel inadequate because they could not successfully manage all their responsibilities (Miller 1986; Biklen 1986; Freedman et al. 1982).

The 1980s reform and "professionalization" of teaching called for merit pay, career ladders, as well as increased teacher responsibility and autonomy. Once again, teaching offered women opportunity and limitations. With professional advancement through career ladders, teaching will no longer be just a "one-step career," and women will be able to advance professionally and financially while still remaining teachers. With additional duties, however, teaching will no longer be the "natural career" for women who want to combine work with ample family time. Women who do not want to fulfill the additional "professional" requirements for advancement on the career ladder will remain at a lower level.

Support for merit pay in the 1980s raises some subtle issues of financial and gender equity. In addition, merit pay and career ladders may reverse the economic gains achieved at the turn of the century, when salary schedules were created to provide financial security to women teachers. Merit pay, generally resulting in savings to the employer, tends to benefit a few outstanding employees and lessen the overall increases for the majority of workers. In teaching, women constitute the majority, holding a little over 70 percent of all public-school positions in 1987.

The issue of gender was generally considered a moot point after the 1950s, by which time school districts nationwide had uniformly adopted single salary schedules for all teachers, regardless of gender or grade-level responsibility. This prevailing notion of financial gender equity was challenged in the late 1980s by research indicating that women teachers tended to earn less because they had moved with their husbands and were often on the pay scale below their years of experience. In addition, the research found that women had fewer and less lucrative extracurricular activities available to them.

This example indicates that, although not a matter that is openly examined and discussed, gender inequity exists in the 1990s. Thus, it behooves women teachers to remain alert to the factors influencing their economic and professional status, lest they lose the gains won in the past.

*Susan R. Martin Macke*

## Bibliography

Apple, M. 1985. "Teaching and 'Women's Work': A Comparative Historical and Ideological Analysis." *Journal of Education* 86:455–73.

Biklen, S. 1986. "I Have Always Worked": Elementary Schoolteaching as a Career." *Phi Delta Kappan* 67:504–9.

Freedman, S., J. Jackson, and K. Boles. 1982. "The Other End of the Corridor: The Effect of Teaching on Teachers." *Radical Teacher* 23:12–13.

Grumet, M. 1988. *Bitter Milk: Women and Teaching.* Amherst: University of Massachusetts Press.

Hansot, E., and D. Tyack. 1988. "Gender in American Public Schools: Thinking Institutionally." *Signs: Journal of Women in Culture and Society* 13(4):741–60.

Hoffman, N. 1981. *Woman's "True" Profession: Voices from the History of Teaching.* Old Westbury, N.Y.: Feminist.

Miller, J. 1986. "Women as Teachers: Enlarging Conversations on Issues of Gender and Self Concept." *Journal of Curriculum and Supervision* 1:111–21.

Murphy, M. 1990. *Blackboard Unions: The AFT and the NEA, 1900–1980.* Ithaca, N.Y.: Cornell University Press.

Richardson, J., and R. Hatcher. 1983. "The Feminization of Public School Teaching: 1870–1920." *Work and Occupations: An International Sociological Journal* 10:81–100.

Spring, J. 1986. *The American School 1642–1985.* New York: Longman.

Strober, M., and D. Tyack. 1980. "Why Do Women Teach and Men Manage? A Report on Research on Schools." *Signs: Journal of Women in Culture and Society* 5:493–503.

Tyack, D. 1974. *The One Best System: A History of American Urban Education.* Cambridge: Harvard University Press.

Weiler, K. 1988. *Women Teaching for Change: Gender, Class & Power.* South Hadley, Mass.: Bergin and Garvey.

## Women in the K–12 Public School Superintendency

While women constitute two-thirds of all teachers in the United States, there are few women in public school administration. In 1991, 5.6 percent of the approximately eleven thousand K–12 superintendents—the highest position at the level of the local school district—were women (Bell and Chase 1993). In 1989, 12 percent of secondary principals and 29 percent of elementary principals were women (Schuster and Foote 1990). This sex-stratified system in which women teach and men manage is particularly striking because teaching experience is a prerequisite for most administrative positions. Furthermore, the superintendency is white- as well as male-dominated. African Americans, Asian Americans, Hispanics, and American Indians constitute 3.4 percent of superintendents; of this small group, 12 percent are women (Jones and Montenegro 1990). The sex and racial/ethnic stratification of public-school administration is generated and maintained by differential access to opportunities for advancement, white men's control over gatekeeping positions, and by subtle and blatant forms of sex and racial/ethnic discrimination.

The few women who do become superintendents tend to follow a different career path than men. This difference is largely due to sex segregation of jobs in public education. The historical pattern of women teaching young children and men teaching older students has persisted: In 1985, 83.5 percent of elementary-school teachers and 50 percent of high-school teachers were women (Shakeshaft 1989). Elementary teachers are less likely than secondary teachers to have access to opportunities through which vertical promotion occurs. Opportunities to perform extracurricular duties and entry-level administrative tasks such as directing special programs, coaching, and chairing departments exist primarily at the secondary level, where male teachers are concentrated (Wheatley 1981). Not surprisingly, women who do become superintendents often have longer teaching histories than men; Schuster and Foote (1990) found that more than three-fourths of women superintendents have taught more than five years, compared with less than two-thirds of their male counterparts.

Gaertner (1981) suggests that two career paths are most likely to lead to the superintendency. The path that men usually follow centers on school-building supervision, most often through the secondary assistant principalship and principalship. Only rarely do principalships at the elementary level—the administrative positions in which women are most likely to be found—lead to the superintendency. The other path is an instructional specialist pattern in which individuals move from instructional and curricular supervision to one or more central-office positions in instructional leadership, followed by a superintendency. Women are more likely to follow this route to the superintendency. Women of color in particular are often promoted into administrative positions in special instructional projects related to the needs of students of color (Ortiz 1982).

Many women superintendents report that their early aspirations were for traditional women's occupations such as teaching or nursing, and that they had no ambition for administrative positions even after they became teachers. Their aspirations for leadership developed either when they had the opportunity to watch closely as other administrators performed competently or incompetently, or when they were asked to do administrative tasks that they had not sought. In some cases, supervisors deliberately delegated tasks to them; in other cases, women held acting superintendencies during emergencies. For some women, the superintendent's incompetence or abdication of responsibilities left them doing the work without the pay or title (Bell 1990). These reports by successful women superintendents support the idea that ambition (or its absence) is explained by an individual's relation to the structure of opportunities and constraints in a particular occupational context (Kanter 1977).

Gatekeepers to the superintendency include not only superintendents who have clout at the local, state, and national levels, but also consultants who are hired by school boards to conduct superintendency searches, professors of educational administration who control access to internships and informal networks, and school-board members who have the responsibility of hiring and evaluating superintendents. The vast majority of these gatekeepers are men, although the number of women on school boards has increased in recent years. In 1990, 39 percent of school-board members were women (National School Boards Association 1990). Schuster and Foote (1990) found that only half of men but two-thirds of women superintendents worked in districts with two or more women on the school board.

Many women superintendents state that the support of powerful men has been pivotal to their success. Crucial forms of support range from encouragement (and time off) to finish dissertations, pressure to apply for administrative positions, introductions to other powerful men and influential informal networks, and collegiality with respect to the difficult problems faced on the job. However, women superintendents also report various forms of hindrance from men who have the power to shape their careers. Instances range from the benign neglect of not receiving help in finding internships or being ignored during their graduate education to blatantly sexist or racist attitudes and overt discrimination in hiring (Bell 1990, Chase, forthcoming).

Even when they have hired women superintendents, school-board members frequently report concerns about whether their communities would accept a woman leader and whether women could assert the authority necessary for the job. At the same time, they sometimes evaluate negatively the decisiveness and assertiveness of the women they hired. Women superintendents are not always aware of these gender-related concerns because they are usually raised behind closed doors (Bell 1988). Furthermore, even when school-board members and superintendency consultants express acceptance of women in positions of educational leadership, close analysis of the way gatekeepers talk about women reveals that their explanations of women's actions conceal relations of dominance in the contexts in which women superintendents work. In particular, the ideological discourses of individual achievement and gender neutrality turn attention away from inequalities structured into the occupation and onto the woman's successful performance as an individual (Chase and Bell 1990).

Women superintendents use a variety of leadership strategies that integrate what the massive literature on leadership calls "follower-focused" or "democratic" leadership on the one hand, and "task-focused" or "authoritarian" leadership on the other. Women superintendents make use of the authority vested in their position in a variety of ways: to delegate responsibility and foster autonomy in others; to encourage collaboration and teamwork; and to enforce adherence to their authority and to bureaucratic norms when they deem it necessary to do so (Bell and Chase 1989). Shakeshaft (1989) has identified overlap between effective educational leadership and women's school leadership. While superintendents in general have been described as ignorant of what goes on in classrooms and as misunderstanding teachers' perspectives, women's longer teaching histories combined with their greater experience in curriculum and instruction make them less likely to exhibit this learned administrative ignorance (Bell and Chase 1989).

*Susan E. Chase*
*Colleen S. Bell*

## Bibliography

Bell, Colleen S. 1990. "Gender and the Meaning of Professional Relationships for Women in the Superintendency." Paper presented at the annual meeting of the special-interest group Research on Women in Education, Milwaukee, Wis.

———. 1988. "Organizational Influences on Women's Experience in the Superintendency." *Peabody Journal of Education* 65:31–59.

Bell, Colleen S., and Susan E. Chase. 1993. "The Underrepresentation of Women in School Leadership." In *The New Politics of Race and Gender*, edited by C. Marshall and P. Zodhiates. 1993 Politics of Education Yearbook. London: Falmer.

Bell, Colleen S., and Susan E. Chase. 1989. "Women as Educational Leaders: Resistance and Conformity." Paper presented at the annual meeting of the American Educational Research Association, San Francisco.

Chase, Susan E. *Stories of Power and Subjection: The Work Narratives of Women Educational Leaders.* Amherst: University of Massachusetts Press, forthcoming.

Chase, Susan E., and Colleen S. Bell. 1990. "Ideology, Discourse, and Gender: How Gatekeepers Talk about Women School Superintendents." *Social Problems* 37:163–77.

Gaertner, Karen N. 1981. "Administrative Careers in Public School Organizations." In *Educational Policy and Management: Sex Differentials*, edited by P.A. Schmuck, W.W. Charters, Jr., and R.O. Carlson, pp. 199–217. New York: Academic Press.

Jones, Effie H., and Xenia P. Montenegro. 1990. *Women and Minorities in School Administration: Facts and Figures, 1989–1990.* Washington D.C.: American Association of School Administrators, Office of Minority Affairs.

Kanter, Rosabeth Moss. 1977. *Men and Women of the Corporation.* New York: Basic Books.

National School Boards Association. 1990. *Education Vital Signs*, a special supplement to the *American School Board Journal.* Alexandria, Va.: National School Boards Assn.

Ortiz, Flora Ida. 1982. *Career Patterns in Education: Women, Men, and Minorities in Public School Administration.* New York: Praeger.

Ortiz, Flora Ida, and Catherine Marshall. 1988. "Women in Educational Administration." In *Handbook of Research on Educational Administration*, edited by N.K. Boyan, pp. 123–41. White Plains, N.Y.: Longman.

Shakeshaft, Charol. 1989. *Women in Educational Administration.* Updated ed. Newbury Park, Calif.: Sage.

Schuster, Daphne J., and Tom H. Foote. 1990. "Differences Abound between Male and Female Superintendents." *School Administrator* 47:14–16, 18–19.

Wheatley, Margaret. 1981. "The Effects of Organizational Structures on Sex Equity in Education." In *Educational Policy and Management: Sex Differentials*, edited by P.A. Schmuck, W.W. Charters, Jr., and R.O. Carlson, pp. 255–71. New York: Academic.

# Women in Other Professions

## Women Clergy

The number of ordained women clergy, representing religious groups primarily from Christian and Jewish traditions, has increased sharply over recent decades. Women religious leaders historically have ranged from Hebrew prophets to founders of new religious groups. Although some evidence exists of women's ordination in Christian communities up to the eleventh century (Børresen 1993), women's ordination in contemporary denominations—with the same religious tasks and responsibilities as men—began only in the mid nineteenth century. Until the 1970s, women were a small fraction of all clergy. By the mid 1980s, most larger denominations, having removed gender restrictions to ordination, experienced a large female influx into seminaries and ordained positions. Women clergy continue to face challenges as accepted religious leaders in the United States and worldwide, from obtaining appointments to head congregations to denominational executive positions, and in equal opportunities for career advancement.

Women's religious leadership has fluctuated historically. Sociologist Max Weber observed that religious sects that arise in conflict with the prevailing religious tradition of a society's privileged class have tended to give greater equality to women. The Buddha admitted women to the Sangha (Order of Monks). Miriam and Deborah were important leaders—and prophets—among the ancient Israelites. Paul named women among the apostles and deacons of early Christian churches. In early Islam, women were counted among the religious scholars. But Weber also observed that as religious sects begin to institutionalize, taking steps for their self-preservation across future generations, women systemically have been marginalized from religious leadership. Institutionalization typically has coincided with women's religious activity, becoming privatized within the family or among women and children, through tasks conspicuously identified as "women's roles," or through sex-segregated religious orders. Alternatives have included missionary work, itinerant preaching and healing in small, often local religious sects, and founding new religious communities. Among women notable in founding or inspiring eighteenth- and nineteenth-century religious groups were Mother Ann Lee (American Shaker movement); Jemima Wilkinson (Universal Friends community); Barbara Heineman (Amana community); Phoebe Palmer (Holiness movement);

Aimee Semple McPherson (International Church of the Foursquare Gospel); Ellen White (Seventh-Day Adventist Church); and Mary Baker Eddy (Christian Science). Barriers to women clergy in many African-American denominations resulted in women founding most of the black spiritualist churches in the United States: for example, Mother Leafy Anderson (Eternal Life Christian Spiritualist Church); Sister Moore (Redeeming Christian Spiritualist Church); and Sister Wilma Stewart (St. Joseph's Spiritual Church) (Baer 1993). Of groups that survived, as they institutionalized men typically took charge of the organizational leadership.

Although women had preached in the United States for nearly two centuries, the first woman ordained was Antoinette Brown in the Congregational Church in 1853. Women soon were ordained in other congregationally oriented denominations such as the American Baptist, Unitarian, Universalist, and Christian (Disciples) Churches. Many of the first ordained women sought reforms for females both within organized religion and in society. Others subsequently sought ordination for pragmatic reasons, such as missionary work or a clergy discount when traveling with their ordained husbands. Overall, relatively few women were ordained during those years; in 1910, women clergy numbered fewer than seven hundred (U.S. Census).

Nearly a century later, women were finally granted ordination in another large group of U.S. denominations: the African Methodist Episcopal Church (1948), the United Methodist and United Presbyterian (U.S.A.) Churches (1956), the Presbyterian U.S. and Southern Baptist Churches (1964), and the Lutheran Church in America and American Lutheran Church (1970). A similar trend occurred in Europe and elsewhere: for example, in the British Methodist Church (1971), the Church of Sweden (1960), and the Presbyterian Church in Trinidad (1968). By 1970, seventy-two members of the World Council of Churches ordained women. Since 1970, women have been ordained to the rabbinate in Reform Judaism (1972), Reconstructionist Judaism (1974), and Conservative Judaism (1983); to the Lutheran pastorate in countries such as Malaysia (1986), Indonesia (1987), Hong Kong (1990), India (1991), and Tanzania (1991); and to the Anglican priesthood in locations such as Hong Kong and Kenya (1971), Canada (1976), the United States (Episcopal) and New Zealand (1977), Uganda (1983), Ireland (1990), the Philippines (1991), and Australia and South Africa (1992). The Church of England voted to ordain women priests beginning in 1994.

The Roman Catholic Church has remained firm against women's ordination. Although Vatican II (1963) increased opportunities for women's leadership, a strong grass-roots movement persists for Roman Catholic women's ordination. At least three women were ordained to the priesthood secretly in Czechoslovakia during Communist rule, and a woman was ordained to the priesthood in 1992 by a dissident African-American Catholic group, although the Vatican does not recognize these ordinations. Roman Catholic women also serve as lay pastors of congregations (Wallace 1992). Worldwide, none of the orthodox traditions—Christian or Jewish—ordain women, nor do some conservative Protestant and Anglican churches.

Several challenges face women clergy. The most far-reaching has been backlash against their presence, which, in some denominations, has extended to the reversal of women's ordination: for example, in the U.S. Southern Baptist Convention (1984), the Presbyterian Church of Australia (1992), and the Christian Reformed Church in America (1992). Backlash also has been expressed by church schism, such as that in the U.S. Episcopal Church (1977) over granting women access to all ordained orders.

Women have been disproportionately absent from positions of authority over large, affluent congregations and in denominational leadership (Carroll et al. 1983; Lehman 1985; Marder 1991; Nesbitt 1993), but this pattern is changing. The first woman bishop was Marjorie Matthews, elected by the United Methodist Church in 1980; the church since has elected seven more female bishops. In 1988 the first Anglican woman bishop worldwide, Barbara Harris, was elected in the U.S. Episcopal Church. Subsequently, Anglican churches have elected three more: one in New Zealand (1990) and two in the United States (1992, 1993). The first Lutheran woman bishop, Maria Jepsen, was elected in Germany (1992). Subsequently, Norway and the United States (1993) have elected two more. Women also are serving as religious organizational leaders: for example, Joan Brown Campbell, named executive director of the World Council of Churches (1985).

Women clergy still face difficulties in being accepted. Some congregations refuse to hire them; others hesitate to do so, especially for senior positions (Carroll et al. 1983), or if serious financial or managerial concerns exist (Lehman 1985). Where women are part of clergy couples, clergy wives are more likely than husbands to hold subordinate positions and to face issues similar to those faced by other dual-career couples, including multiple-role balance, conflation of work and family life, and greater responsibility for household tasks (Rallings and Pratto 1984). Studies on U.S. women clergy over the past two decades conclude that overall they aren't integrating well into the occupation beyond lower-level positions. They disproportionately hold assistant or associate positions, work part-time regardless of marital status, work in specialized positions less likely to lead to promotions, and have lower salaries than male colleagues (Carroll et al. 1983; Clark and Anderson 1990; Lehman 1985; Nesbitt 1993). A large proportion of women surveyed have experienced gender discrimination and sexual harassment (Clark and Anderson 1990).

Racism has compounded gender discrimination for many women clergy of color; in many African-American denominations and in congregations of multiracial Methodist and Baptist denominations, men have dominated the religious leadership and justified women's subordination partly in response to racism experienced in surrounding society (Baer 1993). Some denominations do have racially integrated women clergy from entry to denominational leadership levels: For instance, the United Methodist and U.S. Episcopal churches have both African-American and European-American women bishops, and women clergy of African, Asian, European, Hispanic, and Native-American ancestry. In countries with histories of missionary colonization, women clergy are being ordained primarily from the local population rather than the historical pattern of emigrating from the colonizing country.

Discrimination against women clergy continues on the basis of sexual orientation in most religious organizations. Heated debates on the topic, which developed in many mainline denominations during the 1970s, coincidentally as more women sought ordination, have yet to be resolved. In the United States, only Reform Judaism, Unitarian Universalism, the United Church of Christ, and Metropolitan Community Church formally allow openly lesbian women not committed to celibacy to be ordained.

Some religious leaders have expressed concern over occupational feminization of the clergy. As retiring male clergy are replaced increasingly by women, occupational feminization becomes likely over time. In 1992 the sex ratio in United States and Canadian Association of Theological School (ATS) seminaries was 30 percent female overall, with ratios in conservative evangelical seminaries somewhat lower and in moderate to liberal seminaries as high as 50 percent or more female. Jewish traditions that ordain women have had similar increases; for instance, nearly half of the applicants to Reform rabbinic programs have been female (Marder 1991). A similar trend has been reported in seminaries on other continents. Studies have identified occupational effects not unlike those in feminized secular occupations, such as job segregation with women concentrated in lower-level, newly created and truncated positions (Carroll et al. 1983; Lehman 1985; Nesbitt 1993). Although some women now hold leadership positions, men still dominate both occupational and organizational leadership.

Women clergy as religious leaders potentially could transform doctrines and traditions that historically have promulgated subordinate roles for women within both the family and society. Whether their ratio increases beyond token levels is problematic. But given their empowering, role-model effect on lay women (Carroll et al. 1983), women clergy over time may inspire a transformation of traditional gender arrangements among their adherents.

*Paula D. Nesbitt*

## Bibliography

Baer, Hans A. 1993. "The Limited Empowerment of Women in Black Spiritual Churches: An Alternative Vehicle to Religious Leadership." *Sociology of Religion* 54:65–82.

Børresen, Kari Elisabeth. 1993. "Women's Ordination: Tradition and Inculturation." *Theology Digest* 40:15–19.

Briggs, Sheila. 1987. "Women and Religion." In *Analyzing Gender*, edited by B.B. Hess and M.M. Ferree, pp. 408–41. Newbury Park, Calif.: Sage.

Carmody, Denise Lardner. 1979. *Women and World Religions*. Nashville, Tenn.: Abingdon.

Carroll, Jackson W., Barbara Hargrove, and Adair T. Lummis. 1983. *Women of the Cloth*. San Francisco: Harper and Row.

Clark, Juanne N., and Grace Anderson. 1990. "A Study of Women in Ministry: God Calls, Man Chooses." In *Yearbook of American and Canadian Churches*, edited by C.H. Jacquet, Jr., pp. 271–78. Nashville, Tenn.: Abingdon.

Lehman, E.C., Jr. 1993. *Gender and Work: The Case of the Clergy*. Albany: State University of New York Press.

———. 1985. *Women Clergy*. New Brunswick, N.J.: Transaction Books.

Marder, Janet. 1991. "How Women Are Changing the Rabbinate." *Reform Judaism* 19 (Summer): 4–8, 41.

Nesbitt, Paula D. 1993. "Dual Ordination Tracks: Differential Benefits and Costs for Men and Women Clergy." *Sociological Analysis* 54:13–30.

Rallings, E.M. and David J. Pratto. 1984. *Two-Clergy Marriages*. Lanham, Md.: University Press of America.

Ruether, Rosemary Radford, and Rosemary Skinner Keller, eds. 1981, 1982, 1990. *Women and Religion in America*. Three vols. San Francisco: Harper and Row.

Ruether, Rosemary Radford, and Eleanor McLaughlin, eds. 1979. *Women of Spirit: Female Leadership in the Jewish and Christian Traditions*. New York: Simon and Schuster.

Swatos, William H., ed. 1993. *Religion and Gender*. New Brunswick, N.J.: Transaction.

Wallace, Ruth A. 1992. *They Call Her Pastor*. Albany: State University of New York Press.

*The Woman's Pulpit* Vols. 68–71 (1990–1993). Philadelphia: Official Journal of the International Assn. of Women Ministers.

American Catholic Sisters played an important function in establishing the Catholic Church in America and were affected by the church's immigrant status. The church's need to address a rapidly expanding Catholic population and its adjustment to life in a new environment called for a shift in the lifestyle, roles, and needs of women in religious orders while the Catholic population grew (Misner 1988).

European congregations, such as the Benedictines, who led cloistered or semicloistered lives before migrating to the United States, had to abandon their previously secluded lifestyles for a more active role in relation to the faithful. Thus, newly formed religious communities together with immigrant congregations from Ireland, Germany, France, and the West Indies were primarily established for active service to the faith communities. The sisters' efforts were often more effective than those of the clergy in meeting the challenge of preserving and fostering faith within the newly arrived immigrants and in establishing credibility in the larger community. By the close of the nineteenth century, there were four times as many nuns as priests and the total population of sisters had grown to more than forty thousand; they also outnumbered male church workers in almost every diocese for which there are records (Ewens 1981).

Although during the nineteenth century sisters were subjected to prevailing gender ideology and were under male leadership, some authors argue that American Catholic sisters were among the most liberated women of the time. Despite limitations imposed by their institutional and gender status, they were self-supporting, well educated, and could own property (Kenneally 1990, p. 43). Even though neither secular society nor the Catholic Church expected women to act independently, the church's constant struggle to meet the basic needs of the expanding Catholic population placed women's religious communities in a position to manage their own finances and day-to-day activities without close clerical supervision. Their shift in lifestyle and roles, however, created tension with bishops who held on to notions developed in medieval Europe about the nature of women's religious congregations.

American sisters were not immune to the waves of anti-Catholic sentiment that erupted during the nineteenth century. Because of their attire and lifestyle, they became prime targets of abuse, forcing many to adopt contemporary dress. It was not until they proved their courage and dedication as military nurses during the Civil War and after nursing victims of the cholera and yellow-fever epidemics that these attacks subsided (Ewens 1981).

Although they established hospitals, orphanages, almshouses, and nursed in private homes, the sisters' chief occupation was teaching. They staffed elementary schools, academies, and night schools—industrial, parochial, private, and public ones. By 1900, there were 3,811 parochial schools in the United States, most of them run by sisters. There were also 663 girls' private academies run by religious orders of women, compared with 102 boy's academies run by religious orders of men (Ewens 1981).

The great migratory waves during the late nineteenth and early twentieth centuries had a significant impact on the sisters' work. The need to impart traditional Roman Catholic teaching in a society dominated by Protestant beliefs, plus the naturalization and assimilation needs of its newest members, forced the church to expand the parochial school system, thus creating a demand for large numbers of teachers. The church turned to the sisters, who were expected to work for low wages and were committed to a life of service.

As the nineteenth century drew to a close, a number of sisters, supported by the liberal segment of the church, became instrumental in the foundation of Catholic women's colleges to provide the necessary educational training for the full participation of Catholic women in society. Although some church leaders attempted to preserve traditional gender roles, these colleges produced an education comparable to men's and equal to that of the best secular institutions (Kenneally 1990).

But the leadership role in teaching and nursing played by the American Catholic sisters during the nineteenth century subsided in the first half of the twentieth. This occurred when a new Code of Canon Law—approved in 1917—severely curtailed religious women's public activities. Although teachers' and nurses' training during the early 1900s had advanced greatly in secular society, the new code did not allow the sisters to leave the convent to update their formal education; instead, their education was conducted by older sisters. "Works undertaken to serve the neighbor were defined as secondary, distinct, and separate from their religious identity" (Quiñonez and Turner 1992, p. 35). The sisters became isolated and confined to a "consecrated space," precluding any communication with other women, and assigned traditional gender roles (Weaver 1985). Sisters "were the incarnations of the 'eternal feminine,' chosen by God to be the brides of Christ" and perceived by the general population to enjoy a quasi-clerical status, as it was believed that "their austere but spiritually rich life was far superior to ordinary life" (Weaver 1985, p. 71). Thus, by the early 1950s they had lost some of the public regard and visibility that they had enjoyed as public servants.

The Second Vatican Council (1962–1965), a call to renewal in the Roman Catholic Church in response to the changes in the contemporary world, also called for change in the life of women's religious congregations. Although this mandate had deep implications for Catholic sisters worldwide, it was the Sister Formation Conference (SFC), established in 1953, that laid the groundwork for the radical change experienced by contemporary American sisters. A survey conducted in 1952 by the National Catholic Education Association (NCEA) had revealed the poor professional education received by the sisters. Thus, the SFC launched a national effort to train sisters to acquire professional skills equal to those of their secular colleagues (Ebaugh and Ritterband 1978). A grant from the Ford Foundation in 1956 allowed the creation of 150 formation and education centers nationwide.

The sisters responded enthusiastically to the challenges of formation and education. Although parish priests and bishops protested the program, the SFC enlisted the support of major superiors and college presidents and attracted scholars (theologians, sociologists, and psychologists) from Europe and the United States to teach the sisters at summer institutes. As a result, American sisters became the most educated group of sisters in the church and were among the most highly educated women in the United States (Quiñonez and Turner 1992).

Ideas about changes in religious life were also disseminated through the SFC and when the Second Vatican Council condemned every type of discrimination—including that of gender—and proclaimed women's rights to embrace a state of life or to acquire educational and cultural benefits equal to those recognized for men, no one took that mandate more seriously than the American sisters. Although immediate and visible changes occurred in dress, community formation, and areas of work and occupation, deeper transformations occurred around the meaning and mission of religious life. Thus, as renewal took place in the church, radical changes occurred in the personal and corporate lives of American sisters. By 1971, the Leadership Conference of Women Religious (LCWR), which had evolved from the Conference of Major Superiors of Women (established in 1956), shifted priorities to social justice and the empowerment of women and signaled "a public acknowledgement that their thinking about authority had changed" and that "their structural self-perception did not find its best expression in notions of 'superiors'" (Weaver 1985, p. 85). One of its presidents, Sr. Theresa Kane, greeting the pope in 1979, urged him to hear the appeal of women who believed all ministries should be open to them. Network, a Washington-based lobby focusing on social justice and feminist issues, was also founded in 1971 by a group of sisters. As new ministries emerged, LCWR endorsed the Equal Rights Amendment (ERA) and sponsored workshops on consumerism and economic justice, world hunger, and feminism.

Their activities eventually became controversial to official church authorities, who had previously regulated their congregations, as they democratized their religious orders, drafted new constitutions, established new living patterns, abandoned traditional dress, and instituted new ministries. As they established new relations with the laity, the clergy, and the hierarchy, they continued to expand their education and assumed responsibility and authority over their individual and communal lives.

After these two major structural changes, the number of women in Catholic religious orders began to fall rather sharply. Between 1960 and 1965 the number of women in religious congregations had grown from 168,527 to 179,954 (Ebaugh and Ritterband 1978), but by 1990 it had fallen to 128,000. Some predict a drop to 60,000 by the end of this century. This decline is partly due to the aging of this population, the number of women leaving religious life after the implementation of Vatican II, a new understanding about active ministry, and the decline in religious vocations. Because religious life is not attracting younger women at the present time, only 1 percent of the sisters are under thirty.

The second wave of feminism and the Vatican's declaration "On the Question of the Admission of Women to the Ministerial Priesthood" (1976), which denied women's access to ordination, also made an impact on American Catholic sisters. As a result, they founded or help to found several groups supporting women's issues. When the Women's Ordination Conference, a group advocating women's ordination to a renewed priestly ministry, met for the first time in 1975 to answer the question "Why cannot women be priests?" 90 percent of those present were sisters. Other groups, such as the National Conference of American Nuns (NCAN) and the National Association of Religious Women (NARW), were established by sisters to work for church renewal and social justice. Some congregations have sought to establish closer ties with women in secular society by starting chapters or comemberships through which these women can become part of the congregation without making simple vows or living in community.

During the last forty years, their traditional work in hospitals, in education, and for the homeless and the poor has been expanded to include a variety of occupations. In the church, sisters work as parish administrators, ministers (see Wallace 1992), canon lawyers, college and seminary professors, and spiritual directors; at diocesan levels, they occupy positions in marriage tribunals, as chancellors, auditors, and school superintendents. Sisters have also expanded their work for justice in Latin America; a request by the Vatican in the late 1960s that 10 percent of American sisters train to serve there resulted in over twenty thousand responding to the training. In spite of their contribution to the church, sisters share with the laity a lack of power in matters of doctrine and faith.

In society at large, American sisters are represented in the range of occupations open to other women. Congregations of sisters own and manage several hospitals throughout the United States and many have become involved in national and international grassroots movements helping the poor to fight for human rights.

The profound transformation experienced by American Catholic sisters from 1890 to the present has redefined their mission, work, and self-identity and changed their presence in the public arena and their relations with laity and clergy alike. It has also created tension with Vatican authorities, who conceive religious life as lived in convents, distinguished by religious dress and presided over by church authorities. American Catholic sisters have evolved into a highly trained and educated group engaged in a number of occupations and professional activities, leading lives of autonomy and self-determination. These changes can be traced to the creation of the Sisters Formation Conference (1953) and to the renewal mandated by the Second Vatican Council (1962–1965). Together with lay women, many American sisters experience the ambiguity of belonging to an institution that shares no power with the nonordained while maintaining an attachment to their religious values and enjoying the power and ability to choose and direct their own lives of faith.

*Silvia Cancio*

**Bibliography**

Donovan, Mary Ann, SC. 1989. *Sisterhood as Power*. New York: Crossroads.

Ebaugh, Helen, and Paul Ritterband. 1978. "Education and the Exodus from Convents." *Sociological Analysis* 39:257–64.

Ewens, Mary, O.P. 1981. "The Leadership of Nuns in Immigrant Catholicism." In *Women and Religion in America*. Vol. 1, edited by Rosemary Radford Ruether and Rosemary Skinner Keller. New York: Harper and Row.

Getz, Lorine M. 1986. "Women Struggle for an American Catholic Identity." In *Women and Religion in America*. Vol. 3, edited by Rosemary Radford Ruether and Rosemary Skinner Keller. New York: Harper and Row.

Kenneally, James K. 1990. *The History of American Catholic Women*. New York: Crossroads.

Leblich, Julia. 1992. *Sisters: Lives of Devotion and Defiance*. New York: Ballantine.

Misner, Barbara, SCSC. 1988. *Highly Respectable and Accomplished Ladies: Catholic Women Religious in America 1790–1850*. New York: Garland.

Quiñonez, Lora Ann, CDP, and Mary Daniel Turner, SNDdN. 1992. *The Transformation of American Catholic Sisters*. Philadelphia: Temple University Press.

Ruether, Rosemary Radford, and Rosemary Skinner Keller, eds. 1981. *Women and Religion in America*. Vol.1. New York: Harper and Row.

———. 1986. *Women and Religion in America*. Vol. 3. New York: Harper and Row.

Wallace, Ruth. 1992. *They Call Her Pastor: A New Role for Catholic Women*. Albany: State University of New York Press.

Weaver, Mary Jo. 1985. *New Catholic Women: A Contemporary Challenge to Traditional Religious Author-ity.* San Francisco: Harper and Row.

## Women in Journalism

The history of American women and journalism dates back to Colonial times, when women worked in family-run printing and publishing businesses (Beasley and Silver 1977; Beasley and Gibbons 1993). In fact, Mary Katharine Goddard was running the *Maryland Journal*, a prominent Baltimore newspaper founded by her brother, when the Continental Congress asked her to print the first copy of the Declaration of Independence in 1777.

Sarah Margaret Fuller became the first woman to work for a major newspaper in 1844, when Horace Greeley asked her to join the *New York Tribune* as a literary critic (Belford 1986; Edwards 1988). The following year she finished *Women in the Nineteenth Century*, a classic work on feminism that set the stage for the Seneca Falls convention on women's rights in 1848. The *Tribune* sent Fuller to Europe in 1846, making her the first female American foreign correspondent and, within a short time, the first female war correspondent.

By 1850 more than twenty-five magazines were being published in America, including many written for and edited by women (Beasley and Gibbons 1993). In contrast to most of the early women's magazines, which portrayed women in traditional roles, *Godey's Lady's Book* encouraged women to seek both education and a means to support themselves. This modern view clearly reflected the influence of Sarah J. Hale, an editor of the magazine for over forty years, who was widowed at a young age.

Up until 1850, women were not permitted to sit with men in the Senate press gallery (Beasley and Gibbons 1993; Belford 1986). Jane Swisshelm, a correspondent for Horace Greeley's *New York Tribune*, applied for a reporter's desk and was granted this right in 1850. But within thirty years, women were again effectively barred from the press galleries when a change in the rules entitled only the main representatives of newspapers to accreditation.

Between 1887 and 1895 Elizabeth Cochrane drew national attention to women reporters while working as a stunt journalist for the *New York World* (Beasley and Gibbons 1993; Belford 1986; Edwards 1988). Known to most Americans as Nellie Bly, she is remembered well for her attempt to break the fictional record of Phineas Fogg, the adventuresome character in Jules Verne's *Around the World in Eighty Days*. But Cochrane also wrote investigative pieces on social problems. In one case, she pretended insanity to gain entrance to a local insane asylum. Her stories led to an official investigation of the Blackwell's Island asylum and ultimately resulted in improved treatment for the insane.

U.S. census figures for 1880 show that only 288 of 12,308 journalists were women (Beasley and Gibbons 1993). By 1900, the number of journalists had risen to 30,098, of whom 2,193 were women. Most of the women employed by metropolitan newspapers worked on the women's and society pages, covering fashions, food, manners, and romantic relationships.

Jane Cunningham Croly, the first woman reporter to work on a daily basis at a desk in the city room, is credited with establishing the women's page format (Beasley and Gibbons 1993; Belford 1986). However, she is best remembered for establishing some of the earliest women's clubs. After she and other women journalists were barred from the New York Press Club's dinner honoring Charles Dickens, Croly established the first of these clubs, which she called Sorosis. In 1889 she established the Women's Press Club of New York City, serving as its president until her death in 1901.

World War I opened newsrooms to women as men set off for war (Beasley and Gibbons 1993; Edwards 1988). A 1918 graduate of Columbia University's school of journalism, Minna Lewinson, became the first woman to work for the *Wall Street Journal*. Her departure from the newspaper in 1923 marked a return to its former policy of hiring men only, which lasted until 1968. Columbia University had its own quota policy limiting the admission of women. Based on the argument that opportunities in journalism were limited for women, Columbia's policy remained in effect until the late 1960s.

From 1920 to 1930, the number of women editors and reporters increased from 7,105 to 14,786 (Beasley and Gibbons 1993). For the most part, however, opportunities for women remained limited to women's pages, magazines, and book publishing. The Depression hampered further increases in the number of women journalists, and by 1940 the number of women had reached only 15,890.

Nonetheless, women made history. In 1937, Anne Elizabeth O'Hare McCormick became the first woman to receive a Pulitzer Prize (Beasley and Gibbons 1993; Belford 1986; Edwards 1988; Robertson 1992). For most of her career, McCormick wrote almost exclusively for the *New York Times*, where she became the first woman on the *Times*'s prestigious editorial board. As a foreign correspondent, she interviewed Hitler, Stalin, Mussolini, Churchill, and most American political leaders, including Roosevelt.

When the war ended, women moved from city desks back to the women's pages. The number of women journalists employed by newspapers, magazines, and book publishers rose (Beasley and Gibbons 1993). But opportunities to cover hard news was still limited for women by rules that barred them from luncheon speeches by heads of state at the National Press Club. Nikita Khrushchev ended that practice in 1959 when he objected to the policy and insisted that women journalists attend his speaking engagement.

The women's liberation movement in the 1960s helped to transform the heretofore male-dominated world of journalism. Prominent feminist journalists like Betty Friedan and Gloria Steinem launched efforts to change the stereotyped roles of women in journalism (Beasley and Gibbons 1993). Recognizing that equality in the newsroom would happen only when women moved into news media positions traditionally held by men, women brought legal actions against some of the most respected news organizations in the United States: the *New York Times, Washington Post, Newsday, Readers' Digest,* NBC, and others (Beasley and Gibbons 1993; Beasley and Silver 1977; Robertson 1992). A 1971 ruling by the Federal Communications Commission, which held that women should be given equal opportunities in employment, opened the doors for a new generation of women journalists.

By the early 1970s, women represented one in five American journalists, and the number of women in journalism programs at American colleges and universities was growing (Johnstone et al. 1976; Weaver and Wilhoit 1991).

Women outnumbered men for the first time in 1977. And by the early 1980s, educational differences between men and women journalists disappeared (Weaver and Wilhoit 1992). In 1983 women were as likely as men to have completed college and majored in journalism. By 1988 studies showed that women had more education than and superior academic records to their male counterparts (Weaver and Wilhoit 1991).

The proportion of women working for the news media rose to one-third in 1983, suggesting that the FCC's 1971 equal-opportunity rule had been somewhat successful (Weaver and Wilhoit 1991). But nine years later the percentage of women journalists (33.4) seemed unchanged, despite the increasing enrollments of women in journalism programs. A different picture emerges, however, when years of experience are considered. Of those journalists with less than five years' experience, the percentage of women journalists is far higher, about 45 percent.

In 1992 the percentage of women in the various news media varied substantially, from about 25 percent in television and wire services to about 45 percent for weekly newspapers and news magazines (Weaver and Wilhoit 1992). Women constituted about one in three journalists working for radio and daily newspapers.

Female journalists earned 64 cents for each dollar earned by the average male journalist in 1971 (Weaver and Wilhoit 1992). By 1983 this figure had reached 71 cents. And by 1991 the median salaries for women stood at 81 percent of men's.

Overall, the gender gap in income tends to diminish with increasing years of experience (Weaver and Wilhoit 1992). In fact, in 1991 the gender gap in salaries for journalists with more than twenty years' experience actually favored women, whose median salary was $42,308 compared with $42,169 for men. With fifteen to nineteen years of experience the difference favored men, who made $41,333 compared with $40,000 earned by women. For journalists with five to nine years of experience the median salary of men was slightly higher than that of women—$26,696 versus $26,146.

The gender gap in income for journalists with four or less years' experience was slightly larger. Women made only $16,579, compared with men who earned $18,362. One explanation for this difference is that men tend to start out at larger organizations, which pay more, while women are more likely to begin at smaller news organizations, which pay less (Weaver and Wilhoit 1992).

The largest gender gap in income in 1991 showed up for journalists with ten to fourteen years of experience. It is not clear why women with this much experience earned $6,058 less than their male counterparts ($28,750 compared with $34,808).

Some types of news media pay more than others. But a 1988 survey of daily newspapers, television stations, and radio stations conducted by Jean Gaddy Wilson showed that women in higher positions earned significantly less than men in the same jobs, with the same experience, at the same size organization (Beasley and Gibbons 1993). The salary differences amounted to $9,704 in television, $7,793 in newspapers, and $3,323 in radio.

In 1985 women held only 6 percent of top media jobs and 25 percent of middle management positions (Wilson 1990). Wilson's 1988 survey showed a similar pattern. Women accounted for only 3 percent of general managers of television stations, 6 percent of newspaper publishers, and 8 percent of general managers of radio stations. And they were more likely than men to hold positions as beginning reporters and clerical staff.

The gains that women have made in the male-dominated field of journalism are perhaps no more evident than in their successful entry into sports lockerrooms, which occurred by the late 1970s. Today men still dominate sports reporting and editing, while women more often cover human-interest stories. But women continue to knock down the barriers faced by earlier generations of women journalists.

*Chris Von Der Haar*

## Bibliography

Beasley, Maurine H., and Sheila J. Gibbons. 1993. *Taking Their Place: A Documentary History of Women and Journalism.* Washington, D.C.: American University Press.

Beasley, Maurine, and Sheila Silver. 1977. *Women in Media: A Documentary Source Book.* Washington, D.C.: Women's Institute for Freedom of the Press.

Belford, Barbara. 1986. *Brilliant Bylines: A Biographical Anthology of Notable Newspaperwomen in America.* New York: Columbia University Press.

Edwards, Julia. 1988. *Women of the World: The Great Foreign Correspondents.* Boston: Houghton Mifflin.

Johnstone, John W.C., Edward J. Slawski, and William W. Bowman. 1976. *The News People: A Sociological Portrait of American Journalists and Their Work.* Urbana: University of Illinois Press.

Mills, Kay. 1988. *A Place in the News: From the Women's Pages to the Front Pages.* New York: Dodd, Mead.

Ricchiardi, Sherry, and Virginia Young, eds. 1991. *Women on Deadline: A Collection of America's Best.* Ames: Iowa State University Press.

Robertson, Nan. 1992. *The Girls in the Balcony: Women, Men and* The New York Times. New York: Ballantine.

Ross, Ishbel. 1936. *Ladies of the Press.* New York: Harper and Brothers.

Sanders, Marlene, and Marcia Rock. 1988. *Waiting for Prime Time: The Women of Television News.* Urbana: University of Illinois Press.

Weaver, David H., and G. Cleveland Wilhoit. 1991. *The American Journalist: A Portrait of U.S. News People and Their Work.* Bloomington: Indiana University Press.

Weaver, David H., and G. Cleveland Wilhoit. 1992. *The American Journalist in the 1990s: An Advance Report of Key Findings.* Arlington, Va.: Released at the Freedom Forum World Center.

Wilson, Jean Gaddy. 1990. "At Sea in a Sea of Change." *Quill* 78(1):31.

## Women in Broadcasting

It takes more than individuals who sit in front of a microphone or stand in front of a camera to produce a broadcast news program. There are also those who work as writers and those who operate cameras and soundboards and serve in other positions of technical support.

Like their counterparts in other occupations, a high proportion of women in broadcasting have been relegated to jobs different from jobs held by men in the industry. Gender differences in hiring practices, work assignments, promotion practices, and on-air standards of beauty have been documented by numerous studies of the broadcast news workforce (Beasley and Gibbons 1993; Fung 1988; Hosley and Yamada 1987; Sanders and Rock 1988; ). In fact, one often-quoted government report on the broadcast industry conducted in the late 1970s concluded that women and people of color provided little more than "window dressing on the set" (U.S. Commission on Civil Rights 1977).

In the 1990s, white women as well as women of color are more than "window dressing on the set." But research shows that women face more barriers in the broadcast industry than they do in some other segments of the mass media workforce. While women made up an estimated 29 percent of workers in radio newsrooms and 24.8 percent in television newsrooms in 1991, they made up an estimated 45.9 percent of weekly newspaper staffs and 33.9 percent of daily newspaper staffs. Woman fared less well in news service organizations (which faced particularly difficult economic challenges during the 1980s), making up 25.9 percent of those staffs in the early 1990s (Weaver and Wilhoit 1992, p. 5).

Weaver and Wilhoit's survey of U.S. journalists showed that the 1980s were difficult years for women in television newsrooms and that their representation declined from 33.1 percent in 1982 to 24.8 percent in 1991. However, other research using different sampling strategies has not shown the same decline in women's participation (*Media Studies Journal* 1993; Stone 1992, 1993).

Women, as well as people of color, have experienced in the broadcast television workforce what scholars Jannette Dates and William Barlow have called a "split image," meaning that they are considered good enough to be seen up front and on camera but not to be trusted with the reins of power (Dates and Barlow 1990). A 1992 survey of U.S. television stations found that women made up only 17 percent of the news directors (Stone 1993, p. 68).

Several factors appeared to work against women broadcasting during the 1980s, including a slow-down in the expansion of the broadcast news workforce and—during the Reagan presidency—less commitment on the federal level to affirmative-action policies (Beasley and Gibbons 1993; Lafky 1993).

Affirmative-action programs first gained momentum in the broadcast industry after the Federal Communications Commission in 1971 added women to an equal-opportunity rule that originally applied only to racial and ethnic minorities. This legislation required television and radio stations to file their affirmative action programs with the FCC and outline their efforts to provide equal-opportunity employment in their organizations. Under the Reagan administration, the FCC's commitment to affirmative action weakened.

Although women in recent years have been promoted to some highly visible positions in the broadcast news industry, very few women fill the top jobs in the field, such as producer or news director, or serve as a stand-alone anchor on a network news show (Sanders and Rock 1988). There are, of course, some high-profile exceptions to the rule, including Connie Chung, who joined Dan Rather as a permanent co-anchor of the *CBS Evening News* in 1993. Another exception is Diane Sawyer, who earns $7 million a year for her position as co-anchor of ABC's investigative news show, *Prime Time Live*, contributes to the show *Day One*, and anchors (on a rotating basis with Barbara Walters and Peter Jennings) on the TV news magazine *Turning Point*. Then there is ABC *World News Sunday* anchor Carole Simpson, an African-American journalist who was picked to moderate the first-ever presidential town hall debate at the University of Richmond during the 1992 presidential campaign. Simpson became the first African-American woman to anchor a network evening newscast when she sat in for two consecutive nights for ABC's Peter Jennings in 1989.

Just a few years earlier, pioneer television newswoman Marlene Sanders noted that women were facing barriers in the industry because it was believed that they did not have voices that were authoritative enough to hold the attention of the audience. The rating successes of many women in the industry suggest that those days are over.

Nevertheless, it is important to remember that Connie Chung, Barbara Walters, Diane Sawyer, and Carole Simpson are not typical women in the broadcast news industry. (Indeed, their successes are not typical of the majority of men in the field, either.)

It is also important to recognize the ways that gender-role socialization has an impact on the employment of women in broadcasting, including expectations from employers and members of the viewing and listening audiences about what is appropriate behavior for women.

The "packaging" of on-air television news staffs is just one example of the way that gender role expectations—expectations that are deeply embedded in the culture—influence the production of broadcast news. For example, it is rare in the United States, even on local news shows, to see all-female anchor teams, or for an older woman to be paired with a younger man on air. In fact, one joke in the broadcast industry is that male–female anchor teams resemble the second marriages of some men, with the mature, seasoned newsman paired with a younger, pretty TV "wife" (Fung 1988).

Much has been written about the need for women who appear in front of the camera to conform to rigid standards for what the dominant culture idealizes as female beauty (Wolf 1991), which is one reason why women of color who are successful in on-camera television work are often light-skinned. One exception to the age rule for television news is Barbara Walters, who is in her 60s but still is physically striking according to traditional standards of beauty.

One of the most publicized cases of a woman who spoke out against the gender bias she experienced in a television newsroom was newswoman Christine Craft, who filed a lawsuit after she was fired from an anchor position at a Kansas City television station for being "too old, too ugly and not deferential to men" (Craft 1988). Although a jury sided with Craft and awarded her $325,000, an appellate court struck down the decision.

Much can be learned about the barriers women face in the broadcast industry by examining the biographies and autobiographies of individual women who have worked their way into high-profile television jobs (see, for example, Ellerbee 1986; Sanders and Rock 1988). These stories show that the greatest successes have been achieved by women who have been photogenic and good looking in a rather traditional way. The successful women are also smart, hard working, and lucky enough to be in the right place at the right time. But great demands are made of women in the high-pressure world of broadcast news, and it takes more than being smart and beautiful to succeed.

*Sue A. Lafky*

## Bibliography

Beasley, M.H., and S.J. Gibbons. 1993. *Taking Their Place: A Documentary History of Women and Journalism*. Washington, D.C.: American University Press.

Craft, C. 1988. *Too Old, Too Ugly and Not Deferential to Men*. New York: Dell.

Dates, J.L., and W. Barlow. 1990. *Split Image: African Americans in the Mass Media*. Washington, D.C.: Howard University Press.

Ellerbee, L. 1986. *"And So It Goes": Adventures in Television*. New York: G.P. Putnam's Sons.

"A Field Guide for Women in Media Industries." 1993. *Media Studies Journal* 7(1-2):81–103.

Fung, V.M. 1988. "Sexism at the Networks: Anchor Jobs Go to Young Women and Experienced Men." *Washington Journalism Review* 10(8):20–24.

Hosley, D.H., and G.K. Yamada. 1987. *Hard News: Women in Broadcast Journalism.* New York: Greenwood.

Lafky, S.A. 1993. "The Progress of Women and People of Color in the U.S. Journalistic Workforce: A Long, Slow Journey." In *Women in Mass Communication.* 2nd ed., edited by P.J. Creedon, pp. 87–103. Newbury Park, Calif.: Sage.

Sanders, M., and M. Rock. 1988. *Waiting for Prime Time: The Women of Television News.* Urbana and Chicago: University of Illinois Press.

Stone, V.A. 1993. "Good News, Bad News." *RTNDA Communicator* 68–69.

———. 1992. "Little Change for Minorities and Women." *RTNDA Communicator* 26–27.

Thornton, L. 1990. "Broadcast News." In *Split Image: African Americans in the Mass Media,* edited by J.L. Dates and W. Barlow, pp. 389–418.

U.S. Commission on Civil Rights. 1977. *Window Dressing on the Set: Women and Minorities in Television.* Washington, D.C.: U.S. Commission on Civil Rights.

Weaver, D., and G.C. Wilhoit. 1992. *The American Journalist in the 1990s: A Preliminary Report of Key Findings from a 1992 National Survey of U.S. Journalists.* Arlington, Va.: Freedom Forum.

Wolf, N. 1991. *The Beauty Myth: How Images of Beauty Are Used against Women.* New York: Anchor.

## Women in Law

Between 1970 and 1990, the percentage of women lawyers in the United States rose from less than 3 percent to 22 percent. Women now constitute more than 40 percent of each law school graduating class. These figures represent a significant advance of women into a high-prestige profession. Yet, this decline in traditional entry barriers to the profession has highlighted barriers to women's advancement to the top ranks.

The American bar long sought to limit the supply of lawyers as a means of elevating lawyer incomes and social status. Starting at the turn of the century, bar associations increasingly limited bar admissions to graduates of bar association–approved law schools, ending the long, populist tradition of apprenticeship training. While these elite-sponsored reforms were designed to limit the access of ethnoreligious minorities to the bar, they had a significant impact on women, too (Abel 1989). A middle-class ideology of women's natural place being the "separate sphere" of domestic work was used to justify the exclusion of women from law schools. Unable to attend law school, women could not join the bar. For those few who attended law school, bar admission was a second, often insurmountable, hurdle (Menkel-Meadow 1989).

The admission of large numbers of women to law schools began in the late 1960s. From 1967 to 1983, the enrollment of women in American Bar Association–approved law schools increased 1650 percent. Women were about 3 percent of those admitted to the bar from 1945 to 1968. The percentage increased to 37.7 percent in 1983–1984 and to more than 40 percent by 1990–1991. While the profession as a whole was growing rapidly during the 1970s and 1980s (83 percent growth from 1970 to 1984), the percentage of female new members to the profession grew at a far higher rate (311 percent growth from 1970 to 1984). This wave of female lawyer admissions increased women's representation among the population of all lawyers. From 1950 to 1970, the percentage of female lawyers hovered around 2.6 percent of all lawyers. By 1980 women constituted 8.1 percent of lawyers, and in 1990 they were 22 percent of lawyers (American Bar Association 1992). In two decades, women gained access to this high-prestige occupation.

Yet, because women are overrepresented among the youngest lawyer cohorts, they are exposed to the restructuring forces transforming the legal profession. With access and entry to the profession now largely equalized, researchers have turned their attention to issues of gender segregation within the legal profession's three work sectors.

Most lawyers work in one of three sectors: professional private practice, government, or business. Each sector has distinctive organizational forms, types of work, professional time demands, career paths, and reward structures. Moreover, each sector is differently affected by the structural changes in the legal industry.

Private professional practice is the traditional lawyer role of independent professional counselor to clients. Private practice is divided into two "hemispheres"—the corporate hemisphere, with large firms serving the needs of the largest corporations and wealthy individuals, and the personal plight hemisphere, with small firms and solo practitioners serving the needs of small companies and middle-class individuals (Heinz and Laumann 1982). The large firms stand at the pinnacle of professional prestige and earnings. Generally, attorney income and prestige decline with firm size.

The structure of private practice is changing. Average firm size is increasing. Larger organizations mean greater hierarchical stratification and reduced autonomy for the youngest, subordinate professionals. Solo practice, though still common, is becoming increasingly uneconomical. Because women law graduates disproportionately go to very large firm and very small firm/solo legal practices, they are disproportionately exposed to the economic and career uncertainties prevalent in the bottom strata of both private practice hemispheres (Abel 1989; Hagan and Kay, 1995).

Government practice consists of local, state, and federal administrative agencies, prosecutors' offices, courts, and legal aid offices. Government jobs usually offer predictable work hours and civil service protections, which may explain the overrepresentation of women (and minorities) in this sector. Government employment varies in prestige, average income, and career advancement potential, with women conspicuously underrepresented in the prestigious federal judiciary and prosecutors' offices (Cook 1987).

Business is the fastest growing sector of legal employment, as corporations move much of their legal work "in-house" to reduce legal costs. These growing general counsels' offices are typically peopled by former large firm lawyers, though hiring directly from law school is increasingly common. While legal employment in business typically pays well and has predictable hours, these jobs offer less autonomy, career advancement potential, and job security.

Starting salaries vary widely by type of legal employer. In 1991, law graduates with first jobs in private practice on average earned 60 percent more than their classmates in government.

Women disproportionately find their first employment in the lowest paying legal sectors. For example, in 1991, male graduates found their first jobs in the highest paying legal sectors more often than their female classmates—in private practice (63.9 percent of men versus 57.5 percent of women) and in business (7.5 percent versus 6.2 percent, respectively). Whereas female graduates found more of their jobs in the lower paying government (29.7 percent of women versus 23.2 percent of men) and academic/public-interest positions (4.0 percent versus 2.0 percent, respectively). This results in women's starting salaries being lower than men's (median of $37,500 versus $40,000 in 1991). These sectoral income disparities increase with experience (Dixon and Seron, forthcoming).

Researchers offer competing theories to explain these sex-based employment differences. Human capital theorists argue that female attorneys "choose" not to invest in marketable job skills to the same degree as male attorneys. Hence male attorneys tend to cluster in the most demanding, best-paying legal positions, while women cluster in the less demanding, less lucrative legal sectors. Sociologists argue that social capital unrelated to work productivity, such as family background and gender, better explains the skewed distribution of men and women across legal sectors (Dixon and Seron, forthcoming; Hagan and Kay, 1995).

Because private practice is the legal sector with the highest prestige and earnings and large firms are the pinnacle of prestige and earnings within this sector, women's ability to succeed in the large, elite firms is a good measure of their overall access to the profession. The percentage of women entering the largest private-practice law firms increased dramatically in the 1980s, but a far lower percentage have advanced into the highest ranks of these firms. This ease of entry and difficulty with advancement has been termed a "glass ceiling."

The archetypal law firm consists of owner "partners" and employee "associates." Associates are hired directly out of law school to work for a multiyear trial period, after which they are made partners or fired. Economically, the partners charge clients more for associates' labor than they pay the associates. Partnership profits rise with increases in the number of hours associates bill to clients. This is achieved either by increasing the ratio of associates per partner or by making the associates work more billable hours. Firms used both strategies to increase partnership profits in the 1980s. This restructuring of private practice set a growing number of associates in competition for a small number of partnership positions. Billable hours is a central criterion in associates' partnership competition. High billable hours is thought to be an indication of professional "commitment" (Epstein 1993; Seron, forthcoming).

Yet, women's gender roles disadvantage them in this hours-based competition. Professionals are always on call. They demonstrate commitment through availability. Professional work is a "greedy institution" that requires long, often unpredictable hours. This model emphasizing temporal availability is based on the experience of middle-class professional men with full-time housewives caring for home and children. The generalized social expectation that women will care for home and children hinders their ability to display commitment in the form of complete work availability. Unlike men, women are subject to the time demands of a second "greedy institution"—their gender role (Epstein 1993; Seron, forthcoming).

The results of this role conflict are evident in women's retarded advancement in the private-practice sector. The first large cohort of female law graduates in the 1970s made partner at a significantly lower rate than their male classmates. Those who did make partner took several years longer, on average, than their male classmates. Taking parental leaves has a negative impact on women's partnership chances, whereas having children has a positive impact on men's partnership chances (Hagan and Kay, 1995). Other research found that in private practice, having children has a positive effect on male attorneys' incomes and a negative effect on female attorneys' incomes. Women without home and child care responsibilities fare better in the pursuit of lucrative partnerships (Dixon and Seron, forthcoming). In short, having children has a different effect on male and female attorneys' careers.

Moreover, there is evidence that the careers of women who forgo or postpone marriage and childbirth are also hindered by gender roles. Employers discount women's demonstrated professional commitment because of the expectation that they will "get married and pregnant, then quit." Within elite firms, women are overrepresented in the less prestigious, less lucrative "service" practices (Epstein 1993). Researchers debate whether this is a product of women's "choice" or institutionalized, sex-based segregation.

This unequal distribution of women across legal sectors and within the private-practice sector coincides with dramatic changes in the organization of legal work. Average law office size is increasing, furthering internal professional hierarchy. This restructuring of the profession may deepen the gender stratification of the profession (Abel 1989; Hagan and Kay, 1995; Seron, forthcoming).

Finally, the influx of large numbers of women has fomented debates about the "feminization of the profession." Already women's presence has spurred changes in laws on employment discrimination, family law, rape, domestic violence, and reproductive rights. Some argue that equality of opportunity within the profession is the positive goal. Other writers argue that the pursuit of this goal will inevitably transform the profession and legal organizations as women's different moral "voice" challenges the individualistic, hierarchical, and confrontational "male" form of legal work (Jack and Jack 1989; Menkel-Meadow 1985, 1989; Rhode 1988). Both the legal profession and theorists must move past this equality/difference dualism to avoid the creation of a permanent, two-tiered, gender-stratified, professional hierarchy.

*Daniel Poor*

## Bibliography

Abel, R. 1989. *American Lawyers*. New York: Oxford University Press.
American Bar Association. 1992. *Legal Education and Professional Development—An Educational Continuum*. Report on the Task Force on Law Schools and the Profession: Narrowing the Gap. Chicago: American Bar Association.
Cook, B. 1987. *Women in the Judicial Process*. Washington, D.C.: American Political Science Assn.
Dixon, J., and C. Seron. "Stratification in the Legal Profession: Sex, Sector, and Salary." *Law & Society Review* (forthcoming).
Epstein, C. 1993. *Women in Law*. 2nd ed. Urbana: University of Illinois Press.
Hagan, J., and F. Kay. 1995. *Gender in Practice: A Study of Lawyers' Lives*. New York: Oxford University Press.
Heinz, J.P., and E.O. Laumann. 1982. *Chicago Lawyers: The Social Structure of the Bar*. New York and Chicago. Russell Sage Foundation and American Bar Foundation.
Jack, R., and D.C. Jack. 1989. *Moral Vision and Professional Decisions: The Changing Values of Men and Women Lawyers*. New York: Cambridge University Press.
Menkel-Meadow, C. 1989. "Feminization of the Legal Profession: The Comparative Sociology of Women Lawyers." In *Lawyers in Society: Comparative Theories*. Vol. 3, edited by R.L. Abel and P.S.C. Lewis. Berkeley: University of California Press.
———. 1985. "Portia in a Different Voice: Speculations on a Women's Lawyering Process." *Berkeley Law Journal* 1:39–63.
Rhode, D. 1988. "Perspectives on Professional Women." *Stanford Law Review* 40(May):1163–1207.
Seron, C. *When Lawyers Go to Market: The Restructuring of Private Legal Practice* (forthcoming).

### Women in Organizational Communications and Public Relations

Both organizational communications and public relations, having emerged from different business disciplines, today share in common not only many occupational tasks and responsibilities but also a process of occupational feminization. In both occupations, the female sex ratio had reached 50 percent by 1982. Similarities between these and other female-predominant occupations include job segregation, with women disproportionately concentrated in lower-level technical positions (Dozier 1988; *Profile* 1981f), and lower salaries for women at every level of experience, area of expertise, and geographic region in the United States (Jacobson and Tortorello 1991; *Profile* 1981f). Although occupational feminization has been somewhat slower in Canada and other countries, similar trends have been evident (Scrimger 1989; *Profile* 1983f). Recent studies on student enrollment indicate that the high ratio of women entering these occupations will continue (Donato 1990; Dozier 1988).

Women have been part of public relations and organizational communications from the outset of these occupations. Public relations, dating back to an emergent distinction during World War I between advertising and publicity (Adams 1921), recognized women for their utility in interpreting a female viewpoint (Donato 1990). Organizational communications also grew in the wake of World War I, through the proliferation of "house organs"—employee publications conveying organizational information, activities, and policies with the objective of uplifting morale (Adams 1921). Women often entered these occupations through secretarial work, although some with journalism experience were hired directly into writing, editorial, and other professional positions. By 1950, women constituted 9.4 percent of all U.S. public relations practitioners (Donato 1990).

The 1960s brought new opportunities through an expanding economy, growth of media, and heightened political interest in public issues. During this decade, public relations and organizational communications were two of the fastest growing service occupations. The escalated demand, combined with increased numbers of newly college educated women, presented opportunities for increased recruitment and hiring of women as entry-level professionals. By 1970, public relations alone was 27 percent female (Donato 1990; Lukovitz 1989). Pressure for EEOC affirmative-action hiring during the 1970s further enhanced the female ratio (Donato 1990). By 1977, women constituted 50 percent of all organizational communications practitioners (*Profile* 1977f), and by 1982 they were 50 percent of all public relations practitioners as well (Dozier 1988).

In both organizational communications and public relations, gender-related differences are evident. First, women are younger than men; in public relations they represent over 75 percent of those under age thirty, and over 60 percent of all under age forty (Lukovitz 1989). Although the racial composition has been overwhelmingly European American (Toth and Cline 1989, *Profile* 1977f), a 1987 survey noted that two-thirds of minority practitioners were female and that the largest minority among women was African American (73 percent) (Kern-Foxworth 1989).

Women have been attracted to public relations and organizational communications for several reasons, such as flexible hours, especially for those with family and child-care responsibilities (Toth and Grunig 1991; Donato 1990); the transferability of liberal arts backgrounds into these occupations, areas where women disproportionately are represented; the high degree of job satisfaction within these occupations, in which the most critical factor has been the creative opportunities that constituent jobs hold; job freedom, professional development opportunities; and adequate salary, when compared with other female-dominant occupations (*Profile* 1981f). These factors not only concur with the kind of career investment that characterizes the history of women's occupational interests, but they also coincide with research identifying women's greater interest in intrinsic aspects of the job, in contrast to men's greater focus on the career (Cline et al. 1986). But in other research on public relations students, women as well as men have shown strong interest in management as an occupational goal (Lukovitz 1989).

## Issues Women Face

As these two occupations have expanded and diversified, job and organizational sex-segregation patterns have emerged. In the 1970s, the male-dominant, external-communication activities, concentrated in media and public relations, frequently held greater economic worth and organizational esteem than the internal, technical-communications positions that women more often held. Although by the 1980s women had penetrated external-communications fields, segregation has remained prevalent by level of position and type of employer organization. Men are concentrated disproportionately in highly paid industrial manufacturing and utilities organizations, while women are clustered in lower-paid transportation, entertainment, business services, financial/insurance, nonprofit, religious, and charitable organizations (Jacobson and Tortorello 1991; *Profile* 1975f). Women also more often hold technical or specialist positions, such as writing or editing, account coordination and supervision, while men hold managerial and decision-making positions (Wright and Springstein 1991; Dozier 1988). Even where women may hold a management title, they consistently earn less than men with similar titles (*Profile* 1981f).

The gender gap in salaries exists at virtually every level of experience, area of expertise, and in every region of the United States (*Profile* 1979f). Overall, according to a 1990 survey, the median public relations salary for men is 43 percent higher than for women, and men are more likely than women to receive salary bonuses (Jacobson and Tortorello 1991). Other studies also consistently indicate that gender is the most important variable in salary difference between men and women, even when controlling for factors such as education, experience, job title, and tasks (Dozier 1988; *Profile* 1981f; Toth 1988). Geographically, the U.S. salary gender gap is the most marked in New England, where men's wages are the highest (*Profile* 1979f; Wright and Springstein 1991). The gender disparity in salaries also increases with age and experience. Not only are women with less than five years' experience (or under age thirty-five), much more likely to earn within 90 percent of the salaries of their male counterparts (Jacobson and Tortorello 1991), but age seems to hold a negative value for women's opportunities relative to men's, peaking for women during their thirties (Lukovitz 1989; *Profile* 1979f). Although professionally accredited women earn substantially more than nonaccredited women (Wright and Springstein 1991), they also earn substantially less than professionally accredited men (*Profile* 1981f). Women's salaries are similar across racial groups (Kern-Foxworth 1989).

Despite a tendency toward salary parity in entry jobs, the gender gap widens substantially in higher-level, higher-paying positions where men typically outnumber women by two to one (Jacobson and Tortorello 1991, *Profile* 1979f). This pattern concurs with other evidence of limited upward occupational mobility for women. Women perceive more difficulty in reaching high-level positions, and have expressed stronger dissatisfaction than men with their opportunities for advancement (Jacobson and Tortorello 1991; Lukovitz 1989; Wright and Springstein 1991). Among women who are promoted, focus group and other research suggests that organizations have placed them as public-relations managers primarily to meet affirmative-action goals (Donato 1990; Toth and Grunig 1991), or to save money (Donato 1990; Lukovitz 1989). Many management titles that women hold may represent positions with little actual effect on organizational policy (Donato 1990; Dozier 1988), not unlike women's history within the banking occupation (Cline et al. 1986).

Some research has suggested that gender differences in these occupations result from passive factors such as women's socialization (Cline et al. 1986), lower aspirations, lower productivity and skill levels (Toth 1988), lower utilization of scientific research tools (Dozier 1988), lower use of male-dominant management styles considered normative in organizations, less aggressive negotiation of salaries (Lukovitz 1989), and a primary focus on job rather than career (Cline et al. 1986). Other research argues for structural causes such as institutional discrimination, metaphorically called a "glass ceiling" (Dozier 1988; Toth and Cline 1989) or a "velvet ghetto" (Lukovitz 1989; Cline et al. 1986), where women systemically are excluded from opportunities for high-level positions. For instance, in focus-group research, men consistently acknowledge that a "good-old-boy network" exists in these occupations, and that rewards tend not to be geared to performance (Toth and Cline 1989; Toth and Grunig 1991).

A strong response, or backlash, to occupational feminization has occurred in recent years, including concerns over feminization impeding growth in salaries and occupational prestige (Lukovitz 1989; Toth 1988), and that males are being hired or promoted over more qualified females to maintain a greater male sex ratio (Toth and Grunig 1991). Women have been hesitant to address gender issues within these occupations and in their workplace (Toth 1988; Cline et al. 1986). Jobs in these occupations over recent years have been vulnerable to organizational downsizing, resulting in a trend toward less long-term job security. The risk of forced job mobility combined with the competitive threat of younger women entering the occupation, and of a limited number of management jobs realistically available to women, may explain the tendency toward female conservatism in downplaying or denying occupational gender differences. A related factor is women's underlying dependency relationship upon a male management network for their career prospects. Gender issues are of less concern to younger women, who come the closest to salary parity in the lower-level positions they tend to hold (Cline et al. 1986).

Both public relations and organizational communications have encountered occupational encroachment, a tendency for the highest-level management tasks to be reassigned to another occupation. Since evidence of encroachment first appeared in both occupations prior to the female ratio reaching 50 percent (Dozier 1988), this suggests that feminization itself isn't responsible for diminished occupational authority, compensation, and prestige. This distinction is crucial for countering backlash arguments that have associated women with devaluation of these occupations.

*Paula D. Nesbitt*

## Bibliography

Adams, Elizabeth Kemper. 1921. *Women Professional Workers.* Chatauqua, N.Y.: Chatauqua Press.

Cline, Carolyn Garrett, Elizabeth Lance Toth, Judy VanSlyke Turk, Lynne Masel Walters, Nancy Johnson, and Hank Smith. 1986. *The Velvet Ghetto: The Impact of the Increasing Percentage of Women in Public Relations and Business Communication.* San Francisco: IABC Foundation.

Donato, Katharine M. 1990. "Keepers of the Corporate Image: Women in Public Relations." In *Job Queues, Gender Queues,* edited by Barbara F. Reskin and Patricia A. Roos. pp. 129–43. Philadelphia: Temple University Press.

Dozier, David M. 1988. "Breaking Public Relations' Glass Ceiling." *Public Relations Review* 14(3):6–13.

Jacobson, David Y., and Nicholas J. Tortorello. 1991. "Sixth Annual Salary Survey." *Public Relations Journal* 47(June):14–21.

Kern-Foxworth, Marilyn. 1989. "An Assessment of Minority Female Roles and Status in Public Relations." In *Beyond the Velvet Ghetto,* edited by Elizabeth Lance Toth and Carolyn Garrett Cline. pp. 241–86. San Francisco: IABC Research Foundation.

Lukovitz, Karlene. 1989. "Women Practitioners: How Far, How Fast?" *Public Relations Journal* 45(May):15–34.

*Profile* [Series of panel studies]. 1975–1991. San Francisco: International Association of Business Communicators.

Scrimger, Judith. 1989. "Women Communicators in Canada: A Case for Optimism." In *Beyond the Velvet Ghetto,* edited by Elizabeth Lance Toth and Carolyn Garrett Cline, pp. 219–40. San Francisco: IABC Research Foundation.

Toth, Elizabeth Lance. 1988. "Making Peace with Gender Issues in Public Relations." *Public Relations Review* 14(3):36–47.

Toth, Elizabeth Lance, and Carolyn Garrett Cline, eds. 1989. *Beyond the Velvet Ghetto.* San Francisco: IABC Research Foundation.

Toth, Elizabeth Lance, and Larissa A. Grunig. 1991. "Focus Group Participants Disagree on Gender Issues." *Public Relations Journal* 47(6):25.

Wright, Donald K., and Jeff K. Springstein. 1991. "PRSA Research Study: Gender Gap Narrowing." *Public Relations Journal* 47(June):22–24.

## Women in Public Accounting

The certified public account (CPA) credential is a mark of professionalism signifying that the holder has met the education, examination, and experience requirements. Like physicians and attorneys, public accountants offer their services to the public for a fee. In contrast, accountants employed by a firm, such as IBM, engage in private accounting. The focus of this article is on the progress women have made over time in attaining the CPA credential and in moving into upper level positions within public accounting.

Public accounting became a recognized profession with the passage of the first public accountancy laws in New York in 1896. Christine Ross became the first female CPA in 1899. Her certificate was withheld for a year while the Board of Regents debated whether a CPA license could be granted to a woman.

By 1910, thirteen women had become CPAs (Wescott and Seiler 1986). In contrast, 190,000 women made up 35 percent of the broad occupational category of bookkeepers, accountants, and cashiers. Conditions during the period from 1900 to 1925 suggest that women were able to obtain the classroom training required to pass the CPA examination but were unable to acquire the necessary experience to sit for the examination. As a general rule, public accounting firms did not hire women. Thirty-five years after the passage of the first CPA licensing laws there were just over one hundred women CPAs, compared with fifteen thousand men.

## World War II: Reluctant Acceptance

The shortage of labor created by World War II produced a vast need for female contributions on the home front. For the first time, women were actually encouraged to enter public accounting. According to statistics published by the War Manpower Commission, 8.4 percent of the accountants employed in 1943 by the public accounting firms were women. There is reason to believe that the figure was probably much higher, as roughly one-third of the men in public accounting went off to the war (Reid et al. 1987). However, doubts about the fitness of women for the more strenuous areas of public accounting, namely the audit, continued to exist.

## The Postwar Years: Prejudices Remain

During the postwar years women's representation in public accounting declined. When supply exceeded demand for accountants, males again were hired instead of females. Nonetheless, some women were able to retain their positions because they had been able during the war years to effectively demonstrate their competence and earn respect. This period was crucial for later developments because it enabled women to establish themselves as a small, but competent, minority, thus reducing earlier ideological resistance.

Beginning with the 1940 census, job classification became somewhat more specific. According to the Bureau of the Census, 18,265 women held positions as accountants and auditors in 1940, as compared with 55,660 holding these same positions in 1950—more than a 200 percent increase (Reid et al. 1987). Since census classifications are self-selected, there is no way of knowing the exact duties women had. An accountant designation can encompass a wide range of duties from clerical to controllership. The number of women CPAs increased from about 150 in 1940 to 600 in 1950. During the 1950s public accounting was among the most lucrative professions. The average salary of women CPAs in 1950 was $10,000, four times the national average for women workers. By 1954, 900 women had become CPAs out of a total of 52,000 certificates issued. This figure increased slowly but steadily to 1,500 by 1960.

## 1960 to 1970: Legislation and Discrimination

The Civil Rights Act of 1964 made it illegal to discriminate against women in hiring practices or educational opportunities. While laws do not immediately change practices and attitudes, civil rights policies did eventually influence hiring practices. Prior to 1964, certificates issued to women represented 3.4 percent of all CPA certificates issued since the inception of public accountancy laws. In the period 1964 to 1969, the percentage of new certificates issued to women increased only slightly to 4 percent. Once accounting was recognized as a career option for women, it took four years to obtain the degree and additional time for the requisite years of experience for certification. As these women met the requisite experience requirements, the number of new certificates issued to women increased dramatically. Women received 6.9 percent of new certificates issued in the period 1970 to 1974.

## 1970 to 1990: Greater Acceptance

The decade of the 1970s saw significant growth in the number of women accounting majors and of women hired by both small and large public accounting firms. The percentage of certificates issued to women has shown steady and substantial gains. Women received 14 percent of new certificates issued from 1975 through 1979 and 27.3 percent of new certificates issued from 1980 through 1984 (Meredith and Brown 1988).

American Institute of CPA (AICPA) figures show that the percentage of females graduating with bachelor's degrees in accounting was 28 percent in 1977. By 1989, 51 percent of the bachelor's degrees in accounting were granted to females. The percentage of female recruits, who represented only 24 percent of new public accounting recruits in 1977, increased to 47 percent in 1989 (Walsh and McInnes 1989).

In 1986, women occupied 17.2 percent of all mid-level public accounting positions, compared with 14.3 percent in 1983 and 4.7 percent in 1980 (Hooks and Cheramy 1989). In a 1990 survey, 43 percent of the public accounting firms reported that women now make up more than half of the professionals within their firms (*Accounting Today* 1990). Men continue to monopolize the upper-level positions in public accounting. However, the time required for a new recruit to attain partnership status is approximately ten to twelve years. Leaders of the big accounting firms note that "women represent roughly 10 percent of new partners being named— which was the percentage of new female employees 10 to 12 years ago" (Berg 1988). This is somewhat inconsistent with the Meredith and Brown study, which found 14 percent of new CPAs to be women in the 1975–1979 period (Meredith and Brown 1988). The percentage of females gaining partnership status is increasing but not quite keeping pace with the percentage of the qualified pool.

## Future Trends and Challenges

A special AICPA Upward Mobility of Women Committee (1989) was formed to study the problem and has released its report. Among the committee's conclusions:

> *The factors that affect upward mobility of women are not unique to accounting, but are, rather, universal obstacles confronting women in the general workplace. (AICPA 1989)*

Public-accounting firms are acutely aware of these problems. Gradually policies to accommodate two-career families are being adopted by many accounting firms. These include flex-and part-time schedules and parental leave. Similarly, some firms have begun to build greater flexibility in their career paths. Deloite Touche (a large international firm), for example, offers a four-day workweek for mothers who want to stay on the partnership track. It will take these women two to four years longer to become partners, but they will remain in the running. Two recent court cases should have a significant impact on the process of evaluating women for partnership in CPA firms. In *Hishon v. King & Spalding* (1984), the U.S.

Supreme Court ruled unanimously that partnership decisions fall under Title VII of the Civil Rights Act of 1964. The firm's attorneys argued that invitation of partnership changes an associate's status from that of "employee" to "employer"—thus, that advancement to partnership did not qualify as a term, condition, or privilege of employment. The court ruled against that argument, making the point that once a contractual relationship of employment is established, the provisions of Title VII attach and discrimination with regard to promotion to partnership is forbidden.

In *Hopkins v. Price Waterhouse* (1989), the U.S. Supreme Court reaffirmed that sexual stereotyping, judging the conduct of employees based on traditional gender stereotypes, falls under federal rules against sex discrimination. Price Waterhouse considered Hopkin's work to be good but evaluated her as being "overbearing" and "too assertive for a woman." The court ruled that this constituted sexual stereotyping and that employers have the burden of proving that they would have reached the same employment decision even if there had been no bias.

Projections suggest that accounting will remain one of the twenty fastest growing occupations at least through 1995 (Silvestri and Lukasiewicz 1985). Because women now represent 50 percent of the new hires in public accounting the profession cannot afford the lost training dollars, low employee morale, high turnover, and possibility of law suits associated with blocking the mobility of women CPAs. Hence it is likely that women will retain the positions they have gained and continue to advance within public accounting in upcoming years.

*Vicki Meredith*

*Sandra French*

## Bibliography

*Accounting Today.* August 27, 1990: 6.

American Institute of Certified Public Accountants. 1989. "Upward Mobility of Women, Special Committee Report to the AICPA Board of Directors." New York: AICPA.

Berg, Eric N. 1988. "The Big Eight: Still a Male Bastion." *New York Times.* July 11:15.

Hooks, Karen L., and Shirley J. Cheramy. 1989. "Women's Expanding Role in Public Accounting." *Journal of Accountancy* 167 (February):66–70.

Meredith, Vicki B., and Betty C. Brown. 1988. "Women at the Partner Level: What Does the Future Hold?" *Women CPA* 50(4):3–7.

Reid, Glenda E., Brenda T. Acken, and Elise G. Jancura. 1987. "An Historical Perspective on Women in Accounting." *Journal of Accountancy* 163(May):338–55.

Silvestri, George T., and John M. Lukasiewicz. 1985. "Occupational Employment Projections: The 1984–1995 Outlook." *Monthly Labor Review* 108:42–57.

Walsh, Marylou, and Mary McInnes. 1989. *The Supply of Graduates and the Demand for Public Accounting Recruits.* New York: AICPA.

Wescott, Shari H., and Robert E. Seiler. 1986. *Women in the Accounting Profession.* New York: Marcus Weiner.

# Women in Other Occupations

## Women Entrepreneurs

According to *Webster's Third New International Dictionary,* an entrepreneur is "the organizer of an economic venture, especially one who organizes, owns, manages and assumes the risks of a business." Almost one-third of the small businesses in the United States today are owned by women. Between 1980 and 1986, sole proprietorships owned by women rose from 2.5 million to 4.1 million—a 62.5 percent jump during a period when the receipts of male-owned businesses nearly doubled, from $36 billion to $71.5 billion (U.S. Small Business Administration 1986).

This marked increase in female entrepreneurs has produced during the past decade a substantial interest and documentation in both the academic and business fields. The following profile of the traditional female entrepreneur was gathered from collective studies by the U.S. Department of Commerce (1980).

The female entrepreneur is usually between thirty-five and fifty-five, formerly or still married, with a family, and more highly educated than the national average. Her immediate family members are also self-employed. She operates a relatively new, young firm, her first entrepreneurial effort, which is either service- or retail-oriented, with few employees. Personal savings or assets were the primary source of start-up financing. Employed for several years before starting her own business and probably with some managerial experience in her entrepreneurial field, she is motivated by a desire for money, independence, and a chance to use her skills and talents (Moore 1990).

However, research also indicates a division of female entrepreneurs into two groups: traditional and first generation. The traditional group (around 1945 to 1970) had a home and family orientation, focused on service- and retail-sector businesses, used personal sources for financing, obtained a liberal arts education, had a lack of expertise in business functions, and had difficulties in financing (Moore 1990). On the other hand, the modern group of entrepreneurs (1970 to the present) are career oriented, savvy in the business and technical skills needed to enter male-dominated businesses, knowledgeable in financial planning, and have attained previous corporate experience (Moore 1990). Most of the current research pertains to the "modern" female entrepreneur. Of particular concern is women's relative disadvantage to men in the area of small business.

Recent research has also shown that lower sales volumes and less income generated by female business owners is actually a reflection of the structural disadvantages they face (Loscocco, et al. 1990). Specifically, women business owners often face a lack of financial stability. Women have less access to financial capital and have more trouble finding banks to lend them the capital (Hisrich and Brush 1984). Moreover, because of women's economic dependence on men and women's past credit discrimination, women are less likely than men to have the fundamental resources to invest in their own businesses (Committee on Small Business 1988).

Another explanation for women's poor success rate as small-business owners pertains to the concentration of women in highly competitive, low-growth industries (Humphreys and McClung 1981; Loscocco and Robinson 1991). Furthermore, women's entrepreneurial adventures are newer and small, which definitely is reflected in their success rate (U.S. Small Business Administration 1986). In a questionnaire study of 1,742 members of the Smaller Business Association of New England (SBANE), researchers found that the typical woman has $1,346,900 in sales volume and takes home $51,340, while her male counterpart generates $3,414,300 in sales and receives an income of $95,240 (Loscocco et al. 1990). Men seemed to be in the business areas of services and manufacturing, while women were concentrated in the service areas.

Despite these problems, it is predicted that as women are beginning to feel more confident about their own skills, to build their own commercial networks, to establish credibility with customers, suppliers, and bank managers, and to start successful traditional and nontraditional businesses, the growth in the number and revenues of women-owned businesses will continue at a rate that will eventually reach 50 percent at the turn of the century (Birley 1989).

*Lynda L. Moore*

## Bibliography

Berney, K., and S. Nelton. 1987. "Women: The Second Wave—Starting Their Own." *Nation's Business* 75(5):18–27.

Birley, S. 1989. "Female Entrepreneurs: Are They Really Any Different?" *Journal of Small Business Management* 27:32–37.

Committee on Small Business. 1988. *New Economic Realities: The Rise of Women Entrepreneurs.* Washington D.C.: U.S. Government Printing Office.

Fried, L. 1989. "A New Breed of Entrepreneur—Woman." *Management Review* 78(12):18–25.

Hisrich, R.D. 1989. "Women Entrepreneurs: Problems and Prescriptions for Success in the Future." In *Women-Owned Businesses,* edited by O. Hagan, C. Rivchun, and D. Sexton, pp. 3–32. New York: Praeger.

Hisrich, R.D., and C. Brush. 1984. "The Woman Entrepreneur: Management Skills and Business Problems." *Journal of Small Business Management* 22(1):30–37.

Humphreys, M.A., and J. McClung. 1981. "Women Entrepreneurs in Oklahoma." *Review of Regional Economics* 6:13–21.

Loscocco, K.A., and J. Robinson. 1991. "Barriers to Women's Small Business Success in the United States." *Gender and Society* 5(4):511–32.

Loscocco, K.A., J. Robinson, R.A. Hale, and J.K. Allen. 1990. "Gender and Small Business Success: An Inquiry into Women's Relative Disadvantage." *Social Forces* 70(1):65–85.

Moore, D.P. 1990. "An Examination of Present Research on the Female Entrepreneur—Suggested Research Strategies for the 1990's." *Journal of Business Ethics* 9:275–81.

Stevenson, L. 1990. "Some Methodological Problems Associated with Researching Women Entrepreneurs." *Journal of Business Ethics* 9:439–46.

U.S. Department of Commerce. 1980. *Selected Characteristics of Women-Owned Businesses, 1977.* Washington, D.C.: U.S. Government Printing Office.

U.S. Department of Labor. 1989. *Facts on Working Women*. Washington, D.C.: U.S. Department of Labor Women's Bureau.

U.S. Small Business Administration. 1986. *The State of Small Business: A Report of the President*. Washington, D.C.: U.S. Government Printing Office.

## Women in the Military (1890–1990)

The participation of women in the work of the military over the last one hundred years has been characterized by changing policies, cyclical inclusion, internal stratification, and gradually increasing participation. Personnel demands determined their overall inclusion until the 1940s (that is, they were hired when there were not enough men to fill the needed positions). However, it took the changes of the 1970s to increase women's participation beyond 2 percent. Although today women are still stratified into certain jobs deemed acceptable for women (other than direct combat), military women command at various levels, serve throughout the world, and represent roughly 11 percent of the Armed Forces. Thus, women are a growing and important part of the work accomplished by the military.

Until the 1900s, women participated in the military by cooking, sewing, doing laundry, nursing soldiers, and even disguising themselves as men to fight (Enloe 1983; Rogan 1981). During the Spanish American War (1898), the army was confronted with an epidemic of typhoid fever and needed women nurses to fill nursing positions. Congress authorized the appointment of women as nurses—but as civilians, not military personnel. In doing their job, it was acknowledged how indispensable the nurses were to the army. Therefore, Congress established the Army Nurse Corps (ANC) in 1901 and the Navy Nurse Corps (NNC) in 1908 as auxiliaries to their respective branches. These nurses were given an officer's title and uniform but not full military status in terms of equal pay, benefits, or a commission (Holm 1982; Williams 1989).

During World War I, the navy used women "yeomanettes" in clerical duties, as draftsmen, translators, camouflage designers, and recruiters. The U.S. Marine Corps recruited women as "marinettes" for clerical duties to free men to fight. The army did not authorize a corps of women but did employ civilian women for clerical positions. A total of thirty-four thousand women served in the ANC, NNC, navy, marines, and coast guard during the war (Holm 1982).

With the entry of the United States into World War II, the services established women's auxiliaries because of the need for personnel. The Women's Auxiliary Army Corps (WAAC), navy WAVES (Women Accepted for Volunteer Emergency Service), and women reserves of the coast guard (SPARS) and marines were women's units distinct from the rest of the force. The WAAC did not offer as many benefits to its women as did the others. When WAAC women realized their lack of relative benefits, the army replaced the WAAC with the Women's Army Corps (WAC) to encourage them to remain. The WAC gave army women normal army rank and equal pay (Holm 1982).

Personnel shortages grew worse as World War II continued. Women began to move into nontraditional fields and soon served in almost every occupation outside of direct combat. By the war's end, over 350,000 women had served in the military (Holm 1982). Because of continued nurse shortages, women nurses were on the eve of being drafted and would have been, had the war not ended (Williams 1989).

Until the mid 1940s, women had been allowed in the United States armed forces only when personnel shortages existed and then only as part of auxiliary units. After each war they were dismissed. Thus, they were included cyclically—when demand necessitated. In 1947, this pattern began to change when the Army-Navy Nurse Act (P.L. 36-80C) established the Nurse Corps as a permanent part of the services. The next year Congress passed the Women's Armed Services Integration Act (1948), which established a permanent place for all women in the military. However, ceiling quotas still existed, women were still part of separate auxiliaries, discharged when pregnant, were primarily in administrative and medical positions, and their husbands had to be unemployed to have family member benefits.

The Defense Advisory Committee on Women in the Service (DACOWITS) was created in 1951 to advise and assist in the recruitment of women in the service. In spite of the work of the DACOWITS and the passage of Public Law 90-130 (1967), which removed the ceiling quotas and grade restrictions, the number of women remained under 2 percent of the force until 1972 (Binkin and Bach 1977). It took the changes in the 1970s to increase the number of servicewomen.

In the late 1960s and early 1970s, the modern women's movement was emerging in the United States. Demographic changes (longer life span, higher divorce rates, and reduced family size) coupled with the formation of women's rights groups (National Organization for Women, Women's Equity Action League, and the National Women's Political Caucus, to name a few) resulted in increased opportunities for women in the civilian world. These changes had an impact on the military.

During this time, it also appeared that the Equal Rights Amendment (ERA) would be ratified. The passage of the ERA through Congress made the Department of Defense realize that the ERA's impact on the services could, in fact, be profound. In addition, the draft ended in 1973, instituting the all-volunteer force. Now the Department of Defense had to fill voluntary positions (Holm 1982).

As a result of the aforementioned changes, women's roles in the military were reevaluated. In 1972, women were admitted to the Reserve Officer's Training Corps (ROTC). In 1976 (1) the first ROTC classes graduated women; (2) women were integrated into Officer Candidate School—a source of commission for qualified enlisted soldiers wanting to become commissioned officers; and (3) Congress ordered the service academies to begin admitting women as cadets and midshipmen.

In 1978, the last of the separate women's corps, the Women's Army Corps, was abolished, and women were admitted into the regular army (under the same promotion and personnel system as their male counterparts). In addition, women began to serve in roles more closely related to the military combat mission. Women joined missile crews, served on ships, and trained as pilots in the air force, navy, and army. However, they were still kept out of direct combat roles.

With the changes of the 1970s, the percentage of women in the military rose to 8.5 percent by 1980. In addition to changes in job availability and sources of commission, servicewomen's family members gained the same rights as servicemen's (1973), and women were no longer automatically discharged for pregnancy (1976).

Today, no longer segregated, military women make up roughly 11 percent of the force, command at various levels, and serve throughout the world. Despite the changes over the years, women in the early 1990s are still kept out of direct combat jobs because of the 1948 combat exclusion laws that emerged with the establishment of the air force and navy Women's Auxiliaries. Title 10 of the United States Code specifically prohibits women from serving on naval combat vessels and aboard combat aircraft of the navy, air force, and marines (except in certain professional support positions such as doctor, nurse, chaplain, and lawyer). The army is not covered in the code because at the time it was made law, WAC personnel served largely in administrative duties that did not involve combat; therefore, to have a combat exclusion law for the army would have been superfluous.

However, in 1977, with women being integrated into the regular army, a policy was established to keep them out of combat positions. Thus, women in all branches are theoretically kept out of direct combat jobs. This is a form of internal stratification—women working in predominantly male occupations yet more readily accepted and involved in some parts of those jobs than others. In the military, women are more readily accepted into nursing and administrative positions than combat-related positions. This reflects a preoccupation with gender differences on the part of some individuals and a felt need to keep the military (especially combat-related jobs) predominantly male (Hancock 1991).

Despite the effort to keep women out of combat, women have been exposed to combat situations in every major war in which this country has been involved (Rogan 1981). These have included (1) women disguised as men in the Revolution; (2) nurses in World War II who were forced to work under combat fire (two hundred of whom died); (3) eight women who died in Vietnam; (4) military police officers and helicopter pilots in the invasion of Panama in 1989; and (5) women in the Persian Gulf War, constituting 6 percent of the American forces—twenty-one of whom were wounded, five killed, and two taken prisoner.

Depending upon their theoretical proximity to combat, those career fields and positions that are open to women have changed and will probably continue to change. For example, in 1988, new standards for assessing combat risk were established, opening twenty-four thousand new jobs for women.

Women's roles in the military have slowly been increasing over the last one hundred years—from being employed only when personnel shortages existed to having a permanent place today. Though they are still stratified into certain branches and jobs deemed more appropriate for them, women in the military have become a visible part of the force (U.S. Department of Defense 1989). In addition, Department of Defense studies and statistics have consistently shown that women working in the military have performed their many responsibilities very well.

*Cynthia Riffe Hancock*

## Bibliography

Binkin, M., and S.J. Bach. 1977. *Women and the Military*. Washington, D.C.: Brookings Institution.

Enloe, C. 1983. *Does Khaki Become You? The Militarization of Women's Lives*. London: South End.

Hancock, C.R. 1991. *Women Officers at the United States Military Academy: A Study of Acceptance Patterns and Coping Mechanisms*. Unpublished doctoral dissertation, University of North Carolina, Chapel Hill.

Holm, J. 1982. *Women in the Military: An Unfinished Revolution*. Novato: Presidio.

Loring, N.H. 1984. *Women in the United States Armed Forces: Progress and Barriers in the 1980s*. Chicago: Inter-University Seminar on Armed Forces and Society.

*Minerva Quarterly Report on Women and the Military*. Minerva Center, 1101 South Arlington Ridge Road, #210, Arlington, Va.

Rogan, H. 1981. *Mixed Company: Women in the Modern Army*. Boston: Beacon.

Segal, M.W. 1982. "The Argument for Female Combatants." In *Female Soldiers: Combatants or Non-Combatants*, edited by N.H. Loring, pp. 267–90. Westport, Conn.: Greenwood.

Stiehm, J.H. 1989. *Arms and the Enlisted Woman*. Philadelphia: Temple University Press.

———. 1981. *Bring Me Men and Women: Mandated Change at the U.S. Air Force Academy*. Los Angeles: University of California Press.

Treadwell, M. 1954. *United States Army in World War II: Special Studies, The Women's Army Corps*. Washington, D.C.: Office of the Chief of Military History.

U.S. Department of Defense. 1989. *Military Women in the Department of Defense, Vol. VII*. Washington D.C.: Office of the Secretary of Defense.

Williams, C.L. 1989. *Gender Differences at Work: Women and Men in Nontraditional Occupations*. Los Angeles: University of California Press.

## Women Office Workers

Women's domination in clerical work reflects the sex-segregated nature of office work today. With women representing over 80 percent of the labor force in most clerical fields, it would appear that office work has always been "women's work." This was not always the case. Indeed, until the late nineteenth century clerical work was a male domain and was accorded a good deal of respect and status. The transformation of occupations in the office from "men's work" to "women's work" resulted primarily from several conditions: the expansion of industrial capitalism, advancements in technology, the education of women, and the unique fit of patriarchal ideology to the office setting. This article will briefly outline the entry of women into the office in the nineteenth century and the accompanying changes in ideology and in the status of office work created to accommodate increased numbers of women in the workforce. It will also briefly examine the twentieth-century office and women's role in it.

The men who dominated office work in the mid nineteenth century were well educated and middle class. As a white collar occupation, clerical work was prestigious and stood apart from manual labor. The work involved a range of skills in which the clerk was expert. The clerk's role in early industrial capitalism was to perform the full range of office duties necessitated by relatively small businesses of limited scope. These men had a close working relationship to their employers in which loyalty was often rewarded with promotions into management.

Industrial production grew as capitalism expanded. Both the economy and technology became increasingly complex and the workforce changed to meet the needs of the new economy. While the line between manual and office labor was clear cut, the interdependence of these two types of work for economic growth was central. For the economy to grow, not only was it necessary to expand production of goods, it was also necessary to develop a sophisticated system of record-keeping of profits and losses, with accompanying systems of files, correspondence, payroll, and other office functions vital to a modern business. The more complex the economy, the more sophisticated the nature of office work became. Thus, the demand for larger numbers of office workers grew, and with it a need for greater division of labor within the office. Once the size of the staffs grew and the work became more specialized, a loss of prestige followed. Clerks could no longer expect to be automatically promoted into management. Rather than having a per-

sonal relationship with their employers, clerks were organized in a more bureaucratic, depersonalized way. The increased complexity of the office also necessitated
specialization of labor to carry out office tasks, and concomitant loss of control over
office functions by workers followed.

In this environment of more specialized, less prestigious work, women
began to enter the labor force in greater numbers. There were several direct, significant factors affecting women's entry into the clerical labor force in the late nineteenth century. Increasing numbers of women were becoming well educated and
seeking jobs requiring those skills. Despite their education, women were excluded
from many types of professional work. But as the demand for clerical workers grew,
women gained entry into the office. This process was accelerated during the Civil
War, as men became less available for civilian jobs. By the time office work had
become de-skilled and no longer required well-educated workers, women had already gained a foothold. New technologies also played a significant role. The in-
vention of the typewriter and telephone in particular affected both the way office
tasks were performed and who performed them. These new technologies were
introduced without a sex specification, so women had opportunities to learn how
to use them as readily as men. Typewriting and telephone operating became acceptable work for women as they became a necessity in the modern office.

The prevailing patriarchal ideology that predated modern capitalism
served to protect men's position while allowing women's participation in the labor market in several ways. From an economic point of view, women were cheaper
labor than men. Employers chose economics over sex preference in hiring once
they saw the economic advantage of women's lower pay. Not only did this ideology protect men's wages (though it may have harmed family wages), it protected
their position in the occupational hierarchy. The general belief was that if women
had to enter the office workforce, they were at least significantly passive enough
to carry out their routine tasks without complaint and not threaten their male
supervisors by aspiring to rise above the lower clerical position into one of management. Hiring a woman protected a male manager's position better than hiring
a male clerk. While the capitalist economy gave women greater access to jobs, patriarchy preserved the better-paying, higher-status positions for men. Thus, capitalism and patriarchy became mutually reinforcing as women became full participants in the paid work world. Indeed, the idea of the female clerk or secretary as
a helpmate of her male boss became increasingly common in the early twentieth
century.

The feminization of clerical work continued into the twentieth century
as larger office staffs were required to maintain growing corporations. Work became even more specialized and the worker herself less skilled in a variety of tasks.
De-skilling contributed toward low pay, low prestige, and job insecurity. Office work
was beginning to take on characteristics of manual labor by creating routine jobs
tied to production demands and sophisticated machinery. In the early twentieth
century, some clerks unionized, particularly those in postal, retail, and railway
work. Some women's labor organizations were successful in organizing around
issues specific to women. For the most part, however, the majority of clerks did
not join unions, even when unions were organizing manual workers in record
numbers. Two factors contributed to this failure. First, despite the routine nature

of their work, clerks were distinctly separated from manual labor by their tasks and the lack of physical proximity, and they preferred to identify with management. They saw themselves as white-collar, middle-class employees, and superior to manual workers. Second, as office work became dominated by women, the prevailing patriarchal ideology had an impact on labor organizing, as it had on the office. Union organizers opposed organizing women on the grounds that they believed women did not deserve to earn higher pay and better jobs. Indeed, they did not want women competing for men's jobs. Women themselves often saw their jobs as stopgap measures prior to marriage, and thus not worth organizing for. Protective labor laws for women were often seen as all the protection women needed.

Through the twentieth century, women's increasing domination of office work belied the notion of women, and thus office clerks, as incidental workers. By the 1970s office workers were organizing around issues of pay and promotion and respect on the job, and began to gain respect from employers and unions alike. This early history of women's entry into office work lays the groundwork for studying office workers and their labor movement activities today.

*Roberta Goldberg*

### Bibliography

Berch, Bettina. 1982. *The Endless Day: The Political Economy of Women and Work.* New York: Harcourt Brace Jovanovich.

Davies, Margery. 1974. "Women's Place Is at the Typewriter: The Feminization of the Clerical Labor Force." *Radical America* 8:1–28.

Glenn, Evelyn Nakano, and Roslyn L. Feldberg. 1984. "Clerical Work: The Female Occupation." In *Women: A Feminist Perspective.* 3rd ed., edited by Jo Freeman, pp. 316–36. Palo Alto, Calif.: Mayfield.

Goldberg, Roberta. 1983. *Organizing Women Office Workers: Dissatisfaction, Consciousness, and Action.* New York: Praeger.

Hartmann, Heidi. 1976. "Capitalism, Patriarchy, and Job Segregation by Sex." *Signs: Journal of Women in Culture and Society* 1:137–69.

Lockwood, David. 1958. *The Blackcoated Worker: A Study in Class Consciousness.* London: Ruskin House, George Allen and Unwin.

## Women in Factory Work

Women working in factories is not a new phenomenon. Following the Industrial Revolution of the early 1800s, young women worked in textile, garment, and cigar-making factories in the United States. By the mid 1800s, northern-European immigrant women displaced many U.S.-born women in the textile mills of New England (Amott and Matthaei 1991; Kessler-Harris 1982). Eastern-European women as well as Italian and Jewish women moved into the garment industry during the late 1800s. It was not until labor shortages during World War II that African-American women moved into factory jobs in large numbers. Today, 17.7 percent of all manufacturing jobs in the United States are held by women (U.S. Bureau of Labor Statistics 1994).

Factory jobs are segregated by gender along industry lines and within firms. For instance, jobs in the steel industry are male dominated while the garment industry is female dominated. Within firms, men are more likely to work in skilled jobs such as mechanics, while women are more likely to work in lower-paying, semiskilled jobs such as assembly (see Juravich 1985 for a good example of gender segregation within a small manufacturing firm). This creates two tiers of factory work for women. The first is in male-dominated industries and firms, where the workforce is unionized, the pay is high, and the work is at least semi-skilled and relatively safe. The second tier is in female-dominated industries and firms. This type of work is usually low paying, low skilled, and typically not organized by unions.

Factory jobs also are segregated by race. While garment work is still female dominated, it no longer is done primarily by white women. Instead, Asian-American women, Latinas, and African-American women now are more likely to perform this work. Prior to World War II, when factory jobs were relatively good jobs in terms of wages and benefits, white women had a higher participation rate than women of color. By the 1980s, however, with manufacturing jobs and wages in decline, this trend reversed itself, as women of color now had higher participation rates than white women (Amott and Matthaei 1991). For the most part, this signifies white women's ability to move into higher-paid, less physically demanding professional and clerical jobs.

For women in female-dominated industries, such as textiles and tobacco, work conditions may be harsh and the pay low (see Pollert 1981 and Westwood 1985 for examples of female-dominated factory work). Often workers are paid according to a piece rate, where pay is based on how many pieces or parts a worker makes in a certain amount of time. Under the piece-rate system, women are not guaranteed a living wage and must work continuously with little time to rest in order to reach production quotas.

Traditionally male factory jobs offer women opportunities for higher wages. Primarily because of economic need, women will trade hard work and low status for the higher pay of male-dominated factory jobs (see Padavic 1991 and 1992 for studies of why women choose male-dominated plant jobs). In addition, women in these jobs have relatively high job satisfaction and may even have lower turnover rates than their male co-workers (Deaux and Ullman 1983). On the negative side, some women may be sexually harassed or isolated by a few male co-workers resentful of women's movement into these jobs (Harlan and O'Farrell 1982; for an analysis of the sexual harassment of women autoworkers, see Gruber and Bjorn 1982).

Resistance to work conditions such as abusive management or an unrealistic piece rate is well documented for male workers. Recent studies of women factory workers show that, as do men, women develop their own ways of resisting harsh conditions and building solidarity with each other (Cavendish 1982; Pollert 1981; Westwood 1985). Like men, women play games to speed up the day, such as racing co-workers to see who produces the most. Some of women's strategies are specifically gendered. For example, the women in a British garment factory participate in rituals surrounding the impending weddings of co-workers. To celebrate the occasion, workers dress up in risqué handmade costumes and stop work to party (Westwood 1985). These types of activities break up the exhausting and repetitive work day.

Women in factory work face the double burden of paid work and housework, as do other working women. For these women though, the burden may be especially acute. Factory work requires intense physical or repetitive labor leaving workers exhausted at the end of the work day (Cavendish 1982). In addition, due to cultural and gender-role norms of the working class, women factory workers often are partners in a traditional marriage where both the husband and the wife consider housework to be the woman's responsibility (Rosen 1987). Working-class women with families may be expected to work all day in the factory, then work all evening at home, leaving little free time of their own.

Currently, 8.9 percent of all women workers are employed in manufacturing jobs (U.S. Bureau of Labor Statistics 1994). As the U.S. economy continues to move away from a manufacturing-based economy to a service-based one, factory jobs for women will continue to decline. One example of this decline is the movement of manufacturing work out of factories and into workers' homes. Industrial homework, especially in garment and electrical component industries, is on the rise (Amott and Matthaei 1991). This work is typically not regulated and not unionized. While homework may offer one way to balance work and home constraints, it is usually low paying and offers little job security. At the same time though, a small number of women are making some gains in the higher-paying manufacturing jobs. Women's representation in male craft jobs, such as machine-making, is increasing. These two trends, industrial homework and women in male craft jobs, while offering women alternatives to service and clerical work, will continue the two-tiered system of factory work for women.

*Sandy Welsh*

## Bibliography

Amott, Teresa, and Julie A. Matthaei. 1991. *Race, Gender, and Work: A Multicultural Economic History of Women in the United States*. Boston: South End.

Cavendish, Ruth. 1982. *Women on the Line*. Boston: Routledge and Kegan Paul.

Deaux, Kay, and Joseph C. Ullman. 1983. *Women of Steel*. New York: Praeger.

Gruber, James E., and Lars Bjorn. 1982. "Blue-Collar Blues: The Sexual Harassment of Women Autoworkers." *Work and Occupations* 9(August):271–98.

Harlan, Sharon L., and Brigid O'Farrell. 1982. "After the Pioneers: Prospects for Women in Nontraditional Blue-Collar Jobs." *Work and Occupations* 9 (August):363–86.

Juravich, Tom. 1985. *Chaos on the Shopfloor: A Worker's View of Quality, Productivity, and Management*. Philadelphia: Temple University Press.

Kessler-Harris, Alice. 1982. *Out to Work: A History of Wage-Earning Women in the United States*. New York: Oxford University Press.

Padavic, Irene. 1991. "Attractions of Male Blue-Collar Jobs for Black and White Women: Economic Need, Exposure, and Attitudes." *Social Science Quarterly* 71(March):33–49.

———. 1992. "White-Collar Work Values and Women's Interest in Blue-Collar Jobs." *Gender and Society* 6(June):215–30.

Pollert, Anna. 1981. *Girls, Wives, Factory Lives*. London: Macmillan.

Rosen, Ellen. 1987. *Bitter Choices: Blue-Collar Women in and out of Work*. Chicago: University of Chicago Press.

U.S. Bureau of Labor Statistics. 1994. *Employment and Earnings* 41 (May). Washington, D.C.: U.S. Department of Labor.

Westwood, Sallie. 1985. *All Day, Every Day: Factory and Family in the Making of Women's Lives*. Urbana: University of Illinois Press.

## Women in the Garment Industry

The garment industry is particularly associated with women and work. On the production side, women form the backbone of the garment industry's labor force. On the consumption side, women are a targeted market segment because they are more likely the household purchasers of clothing. Furthermore, in the process of producing and marketing garments, this industry has played an important role in integrating women immigrants of various racial and ethnic backgrounds into

American society, and has served as a social context wherein important labor struggles have occurred. However, in the late twentieth century, the garment industry's use of production facilities and marketing networks organized on a global scale has meant that there are both increasing worker exploitation and greater challenges for labor organization.

## Historical Development of the Garment Industry

Textile and apparel production historically have been women's work (Chapkis and Enloe 1983). Preindustrial production of clothing was traditionally carried out in households and involved members of the household applying the skills they had acquired from elders. Women performed the various steps in the production process, from fiber preparation to weaving to final garment construction. While the primary objective of their work was to produce items that would be used by household members, aesthetic considerations were not ignored. Indeed, this was an arena wherein some women could excel and gain recognition for their skills. Any surplus they produced could also be bartered within the community or sold to generate cash for other necessary and desired household items.

While most men's clothing was purchased from traveling tailors in Colonial America, women's and children's clothing were generally produced in the household. Since hand-stitching techniques were used, sewing clothing was a time-consuming task; thus, clothing was generally produced with durability in mind. In the eighteenth century, entrepreneurs periodically scoured the countryside and purchased quantities of textiles from households, encouraging the development of small cottage-industry production oriented toward a market. Eventually, textile production became consolidated into factories such as the one in Lowell, Massachusetts, in the 1800s.

Young, unmarried, Euro-American women made up most of the work force of the early textile and garment factories. Labor recruiters favored daughters of farm families because girls were perceived to be the least necessary members for the operation of the households. Assurances of dormitory housing, religious study in their spare time, and the opportunity to earn cash for the family and for dowries served as incentives for families to send their daughters into factory work.

As Kidwell and Christman (1974) have noted in their work *Suiting Everyone: The Democratization of Clothing in America,* the availability of cheaper, factory-made fabrics and standardized patterns meant that people could purchase clothing and have more than the required two sets (one for everyday use, one for Sunday worship). Just as tailoring had been done earlier by skilled men, dressmaking emerged as an occupation in which skilled women could make a living. Finally, with the various innovations in the sewing machine taking place from the 1830s to the 1880s, the stage was set for mass production of clothing.

## Internal Organization of the Industry

The garment industry is often called a "sweated" industry because the production of clothing takes place within two kinds of firms: manufacturers and contractors. Manufacturers are involved in the entire process of garment production, from design to wholesaling. Remuneration and working conditions in manufacturing firms, called "inside" shops, are generally much better than those in contracting firms ("outside" shops), which usually perform only specific operations. This arrangement goes back to the nineteenth century, when dressmakers and tailors performed the skilled work of design, cutting, and final construction of the garment in their shops and used low-paid, "unskilled" seamstresses to sew straight pieces or do preparation work in their homes. Most of these seamstresses had family responsibilities; thus, taking in stitching work was their way to earn income without violating the prevailing Victorian ideals of domesticity.

The rationalization of clothing production began around the middle of the nineteenth century. Some tailors and dressmakers, anticipating future orders from their middle- and working-class clientele, began producing and stockpiling clothing or parts of clothes in various sizes. The Civil War further encouraged this practice because mass production of military uniforms in standardized sizes was required. Finally, tailoring and dressmaking techniques, which had relied on hand stitching, had placed limits on production levels; the standardization and proliferation of sewing-machine technology made mass production of clothing increasingly possible.

Rising inflation in the post–Civil War years, incorporation of sewing machine technology, and a flood of new European immigrants in the later nineteenth century modified the contracting arrangement between the tailor/dressmaker and seamstress. Italian, Jewish, and other Eastern-European contractors employed newly arrived immigrants from their home countries to fill the orders taken from the better capitalized and established manufacturing firms. Labor contractors competed among themselves for these orders (or parts of orders); thus, manufacturers could command the lowest price for their orders and maximize their profits. In order to make profits on low job bids, the contractors would cut their costs of production by further subcontracting portions of their orders to other labor contractors. The result was a complex chain of successively cheaper wages, longer hours, and more hazardous working conditions. Lacking both English-language skills and familiarity with their new society, most newly arrived immigrants had little choice but to work in these sweatshops. This "sweating" pattern was replicated on the West Coast with Asian and Mexican immigrant workers.

Within the industry, the category of apparel, gender, and ethnicity or race were, and continue to be, related to job assignments, which are in turn related to wage levels and working conditions. Men have generally occupied laying and cutting jobs, which, because they are considered "skilled," enjoy more autonomy and are better paid. In 1905, for example, male cutters earned $41^1/_2$ cents per hour. Women dominated sewing in power-machine operator jobs and earned $13^1/_2$ cents per hour. Working conditions and pay were also better in firms producing men's wear than they were for women's or children's wear. Generally, women were and continue to be found in piece-work jobs like sewing or embroidery, which are paid less, are externally paced, and enjoy less autonomy. Finally, Victorian social mores of domesticity in the late nineteenth and early twentieth century meant that married women were more likely to be doing piece work in their homes, and young single women were likely to be employed in the shops.

## Labor Organizations

Garment workers, especially women workers, were among the most militant of industrial workers in the early twentieth century and in this period, known as the Great Uprising, were repeatedly involved in strikes and other work stoppages. The relative homogeneity of the garment industry's workforce (primarily immigrants and young unmarried women) and their shared experience of horrible working conditions encouraged labor organization. The Triangle Shirtwaist Factory Fire of 1911 probably contributed most to dramatize these working conditions to the larger society and to legitimize the labor movement.

Jewish and Italian immigrant women progressively moved into leadership positions in several labor organizations. Four labor organizations emerged in this period: the United Garment Workers of America (UGWA), the International Ladies Garment Workers Union (ILGWU), the Amalgamated Clothing Workers of America (ACWU), and the Industrial Workers of the World (IWW). Each of these unions represented different segments of garment workers, and each held varying ideological orientations. The ILGWU and the ACWU continue to represent garment workers today.

While the unions were not totally successful in abolishing the "sweating system," they were successful in gaining collective bargaining on wages, benefits, and certain working conditions. As of 1990, according to the Bureau of Labor Statistics, the average hourly earnings of garment production workers was $6.57, substantially higher than the minimum wage of $3.85. Their success, however, has produced a new set of problems, most critical of which are the "runaway shops" and the resurgence of the illegal practice of "homework."

## Internationalization of Capital and Labor

Garment manufacturers have responded to the collective bargaining successes of labor unions by moving south into the less unionized Sunbelt states and overseas to take advantage of nonunion or cheaper sources of labor and lax workplace regulations. Runaway shops, often called "off-shore sourcing" sites, are set up in Free Trade Zones (FTZs) in various newly industrializing countries (NICs) to provide profitable production arrangements. For example, *Maquiladora*, unique sets of factories, have sprouted along many United States–Mexico border towns in order to take advantage of low-wage Mexican labor. The initial phases of design, laying, and cutting are performed in the United States. The labor-intensive sewing that historically had been performed by contracting shops now occurs in factories on the Mexican side of the border. Final assembly takes place in the United States with the import tariff based only on the low price of labor added while the pieces were in Mexico. While jobs are generated along the United States–Mexico border by this global assembly-line, wages are considerably lower than those in the traditional centers of the industry, and unionized jobs are being eliminated in those centers.

Another trend is occurring in the traditional garment industry centers of New York, Chicago, the Northeast, California, and even areas like Hawaii. A new international migration of labor and capital is taking place. Some of the labor immigration is legal, but much of it is undocumented, a fact that makes these workers prime candidates for exploitation. They cannot count on much legal protection and, like earlier immigrants, are hampered by their lack of familiarity with American society, its laws and language. It is not surprising, then, that undocumented workers are increasingly found in the reemerging sweatshops of these major metropolitan areas. Homework, a practice outlawed during the labor-reform period, is reemerging as well. Initially, garment-industry labor unions saw these new immigrants, especially the undocumented immigrants, as threats to unionized workers. There are indications that this may be slowly changing as unions realize that organization rather than exclusion may be in their best interests.

## Conclusion

The garment industry has undergone many changes, but in many ways it remains virtually unchanged. It continues to employ mostly women and, in particular, immigrant women. It continues to be a "sweated" industry, one that relies on subcontracting arrangements for squeezing the greatest amount of work from workers for the least pay in order to turn a profit. Labor organization in industrialized countries has prompted an increasingly global search by garment manufacturers for ever cheaper and more flexible labor. However, in the process, it has created the conditions for further global immigration and a new immigrant labor force, mostly women of color, and the conditions for new labor organizing struggles.

*Joyce N. Chinen*

**Bibliography**

Abbott, E. 1910. *Women in Industry: A Study of Economic History*. New York: Appleton.

Chapkis, W., and C. Enloe. 1983. *Of Common Cloth: Women in the Global Textile Industry*. Washington, D.C.: Transnational Institute.

Chinen, J.N. 1989. "New Patterns in the Garment Industry: State Intervention, Women and Work in Hawaii." Ph.D. dissertation, University of Hawaii.

Enloe, C. 1990. *Bananas, Beaches, and Bases: Making Feminist Sense of International Politics*. Berkeley: University of California Press.

Hillsman, S.T., and B. Levenson. 1982. "Job Opportunities of Black and White Working-Class Women." In *Women and Work: Problems and Perspectives*, edited by R. Kahn-Hut et al. New York: Oxford University Press.

Jensen, J.M., and Davidson, S. 1984. *A Needle, A Bobbin, A Strike: Women Needleworkers in America*. Philadelphia: Temple University Press.

Kessler-Harris, A. 1982. *Out to Work: A History of Wage-Earning Women in the U.S.* New York: Oxford University Press.

Kidwell, C.B., and M.C. Christman. 1974. *Suiting Everyone: The Democratization of Clothing in America*. Washington, D.C.: Smithsonian.

Lamphere, L. 1987. *From Working Daughters to Working Mothers: Immigrant Women in a New England Industrial Community*. Ithaca, N.Y.: Cornell University Press.

Nee, V.G., and B. Nee. 1972. *Longtime Californ': A Documentary Study of an American Chinatown*. New York: Pantheon.

Seidman, J. 1942. *The Needle Trades*. New York: Farrar and Rinehart.

Sumner, H. 1910. *History of Women in Industry in the United States*. Vol. 9 of the *Report on the Condition of Women and Child Wage Earners in the United States*. 61st Congress, 2nd Session, Senate Document #645. Washington, D.C.

U.S. Bureau of Labor Statistics. *Supplement to Employment and Earnings, United States, 1909–90*. 1991. Washington, D.C.: U.S. Department of Labor.

———. 1907. *Wages and Hours of Labor in the Clothing and Cigar Industry, #161*. Washington, D.C.: Department of Commerce and Labor.

Waldinger, R. 1979. *Through the Eye of the Needle: Immigrants and Enterprise in New York's Garment Trades*. New York: New York University Press.

## Prostitution

Prostitution is the exchange of sexual activity for payment. While not "the oldest profession," prostitution certainly has been one of the more controversial. In most of the United States and in many places throughout the world, prostitution is illegal. At the same time, prostitution not only persists, but it is the only job other than modeling in which women within the occupation are generally paid more than men. While most but not all prostitutes are women, those who purchase sex are primarily men. Thus, understanding prostitution entails confronting both gender differences in the social construction and control of sexuality and the economic contexts that make the commercial sale of sex possible.

Understanding prostitution has been difficult because of the underground nature of the work and the biases that exist on the part of mainstream society. The stigma against prostitution has been used in patriarchal societies to distinguish "good" girls from "bad" girls, to control, dissuade, punish, and alienate women that step outside the bounds of socially acceptable behavior. Studies of prostitution sometimes reinforce these biases and often emphasize psychological explanations for the existence and persistence of prostitution, or view the prostitute as deviant. Research has found a high incidence of previous sexual abuse (50 percent of adult prostitutes report having been sexually abused as children) and predominant drug use, especially among street prostitutes (James 1977). At the same time, many women with no history of sexual abuse become prostitutes, and many abuse survivors never become prostitutes. More recently, prostitutes have been scapegoated for spreading sexual diseases, especially AIDS, even though few studies implicate prostitutes as a major source of transmission (Alexander 1987; Jenness 1990).

Prostitution has alternately played sacred, respectable, and important roles in society. In *The Creation of Patriarchy* (1986), author Gerda Lerner argues that prostitution as we know it became institutionalized alongside the growth of class privilege and private property. In societies that considered fertility sacred, what we now label prostitution may have reflected religious leadership and the power of women. The people of ancient Mesopotamia considered ritualized sex with temple priestesses beneficial. When slavery became institutionalized in later societies, owners rented female slaves for sexual use, and sexual slaves became symbols of power for propertied men. In medieval Europe up until the industrial revolution, prostitution moved from an independent and informal cottage industry in the fourteenth century to be regulated in certain "red light" districts and finally confined to brothels owned by city officials (Otis 1985). With industrialization and migration to the cities, women unable to find wage labor in new factories turned increasingly to prostitution (see, for example, Hobson 1987).

Prostitution played an important role in the settling of the American West. Prostitutes were not only the earliest female settlers in many towns, but brothels and saloons provided an economic focal point, as men were engaged in the transient work of mining, herding, and trapping (Goldman 1981).

While prostitution in Western societies has been stigmatized, it has only recently been illegal. Interestingly, it is during times when women have most actively fought for rights that higher restrictions have arisen against prostitutes. Feminist reformers in the late nineteenth and early twentieth century saw prostitution as the leading symbol of male sexual coercion and saw antiprostitution platforms as important in ending the subjugation of women (Hobson 1987). When women were winning the right to vote in England the Contagious Diseases Acts was passed, which allowed suspected prostitutes to be arrested and taken for "treatment" at local hospitals. In the United States, feminist reformers in the late 1800s focused criticism on economic pressures forcing women into prostitution. Progressive Era reformers fought for laws to prevent what they saw as the widespread sale of white women into sexual slavery. After the passage of the White Slave Traffic Act (1910), almost every state in the union passed antiprostitution legislation. Although there is little evidence of widespread entrapment of women, these reformers' focus on the dangers of women's sexual freedom enforced the view of prostitutes as victims.

Modern prostitution is highly stratified, and the conditions of work vary greatly depending on the setting. The most dangerous, lowest status, and least paid is street prostitution. Yet street prostitution draws the most attention and is the most studied group. About 10 to 20 percent of prostitution involves street work, and around 60 percent of street prostitutes use pimps. Street prostitutes often pay pimps a percentage of their earnings for protection and help in finding johns (customers). In many cases, pimps are voluntarily chosen by women and provide emotional support that is difficult for prostitutes to acquire otherwise. On the other hand, pimps are sometimes a source of violence against prostitutes and can often take as much as 90 percent of profits. Street prostitutes often have very little control over the johns and do get the least desirable customers (Alexander 1987).

Work in massage parlors and brothels is more regulated and often involves de facto legalization. Massage parlors and brothel employees are usually required to obtain licenses from police departments, and activity is confined out of public view. Outcall or call-girl and escort services allow the most independence and control by prostitutes. These operations are progressively safer, higher paid, and bring in more high-class customers. Some high-class call girls can earn as much as $100,000 per year (Delacoste and Alexander 1987).

Research consistently shows that the majority of prostitutes enter the field for economic gain (James 1977). In spite of the turn-of-the-century fear that white women were being sold into sexual slavery, fewer than 10 percent of American prostitutes reported being coerced into prostitution (Alexander 1987). Nonetheless, prostitution is difficult work, and the few studies available show that most women rarely remain working as prostitutes beyond five years (Potterat et al. 1990).

While the relative respectability and freedom of prostitutes has varied over time, prostitution has always been dangerous work. Prostitutes, especially street walkers, are subject to violence by customers, and there is little legal protection. Prostitutes are easy victims for a variety of sexually transmitted diseases, including AIDS. Rape of prostitutes is rarely taken seriously when reported.

Police enforcement of antiprostitution laws has often considered prostitution a victimless crime, hence police reinforce laws to the extent required to legitimize "clean-up" campaigns. Some studies show that police will ignore "strolling" so long as women cooperate during crackdowns so that the police can make their quotas of arrests.

During the 1970s and 1980s, prostitutes were increasingly defending their profession as a rational choice over dependency on men through marriage or low-income jobs. Organizations of prostitutes and former prostitutes such as COYOTE (Call Off Your Old Tired Ethics) and affiliated organizations, the National Task Force on Prostitution, the International Committee for Prostitutes Rights, the U.S. Prostitutes Collective (PROS), and the related English Collective of Prostitutes all work against the stigmas that define prostitutes' work, and the poverty of women that sometimes spurs it. Margo St. James, one of the key organizers of COYOTE, works for better working conditions and civil rights for prostitutes. On the other hand, prostitutes and former prostitutes in WHISPER (Women Hurt in Systems of Prostitution Engaged in Revolt) believe that prostitutes are victims of an institution created by patriarchy to control and abuse women (see Jenness 1990 for a good discussion of COYOTE).

The contemporary feminist debate on prostitution is split between a critique of prostitution as reproducing patriarchal constructions of sex (and the objectification and danger that goes along with that) (see, for example, MacKinnon 1982) and the right of all women to define sexuality as they please (Delacoste and Alexander 1987; Pheterson 1989). The increasingly vocal debate between feminists and sex workers themselves (Bell 1987) calls for a more complex understanding of prostitution. The specific historical forms of capitalism and patriarchy that commodify all forms of service work (not just sex), work the sexual division of labor that makes prostitution such an economically lucrative alternative for women, the objectification of women, and the very real sexual slavery that exists in many third-world countries all must be considered when examining prostitution.

*Barbara G. Brents*
*Gayle Morris*
*Lisa Licausi*

## Bibliography

Alexander, P. 1987. "Prostitution: A Difficult Issue for Feminists." In *Sex Work: Writings by Women in the Sex Industry*, edited by Frederique Delacoste and Priscilla Alexander, pp. 187–214. Pittsburgh, Penna.: Clies.

Bell, L., ed. 1987. *Good Girls/Bad Girls: Sex Trade Workers and Feminists Face to Face*. Toronto: Women's Press.

Delacoste, F., and P. Alexander. 1987. *Sex Work: Writings by Women in the Sex Industry*. Pittsburgh, Penna.: Clies.

Goldman, M. 1981. *Gold Diggers and Silver Miners: Prostitution and Social Life on the Comstock Lode*. Ann Arbor: University of Michigan Press.

Hobson, B. 1987. *Uneasy Virtue: The Politics of Prostitution and the American Reform Tradition*. New York: Basic Books.

James, J. 1977. "Women as Sexual Criminals and Victims." In *Sexual Scripts: The Social Construction of Female Sexuality*, edited by Judith Long Laws and Pepper Schwartz. Hinsdale, Ill.: Dryden.

Jenness, V. 1990. "From Sex as Sin to Sex as Work: COYOTE and the Reorganization of Prostitution as a Social Problem." *Social Problems* 37(3):403–20.

Lerner, G. 1986. *The Creation of Patriarchy*. New York: Oxford University Press.

MacKinnon, C. 1982. "Feminism, Marxism, Method and the State." *Signs* 7:515–44.

Otis, L.L. 1985. *Prostitution in Medieval Society: The History of an Urban Institution in Languedoc*. Chicago: University of Chicago Press.

Overall, C. 1992. "What's Wrong with Prostitution? Evaluating Sex Work." *Signs* 17(4):709–24.

Pheterson, G., ed. 1989. *A Vindication of the Rights of Whores*. Seattle, Wash.: Seal.

Potterat, J.J., D.E. Woodhouse, J.B. Muth, and S.Q. Muth. 1990. "Estimating the Prevalence and Career Longevity of Prostitute Women." *Journal of Sex Research* 27(2):233–43.

# IV

# Factors Influencing Career and Occupational Choice

## White Women's Higher Education: Coeducation and Gender Role Expectations, 1870–1890

Throughout most of the 1800s, women's educational opportunities were limited, mostly to the elementary level. Middle-class white women had more opportunities to attend secondary schools and colleges than other women. Before 1850, "female seminaries" presented the most common type of higher education available to (white) women (Sklar 1976; Solomon 1985). While Oberlin was the first college to admit female and black students, coeducation at the secondary level did not become common until about 1900, and coeducation at the college level developed even more slowly. By 1900, 98 percent of all public high schools were coeducational, and the percentage of coeducational colleges doubled between 1870 and 1910 (from 29 to 58 percent) (Tyack and Hansot 1990). Similarly, the number of (mostly white) women attending college increased substantially between 1870 and 1900 (from eleven thousand to eighty-five thousand), and women's percentage of all college students enrolled increased from about 20 percent in 1870 to almost 37 percent in 1900. By 1900, twice as many women were enrolled in coeducational colleges as in women's colleges.

Nonetheless, only a small percentage of women (less than 3 percent of women age eighteen to twenty-one) attended college in 1900. Black women's college enrollments did not increase until the turn of the century. While some Northern colleges such as Oberlin (coed) and Radcliffe (women only) had enrolled black women as early as the 1860s, other prestigious white women's colleges (Vassar, Mount Holyoke) did not admit black women until well into the twentieth century (Solomon 1985). After the Civil War, black women's higher education in the South took place mostly at private black women's colleges (Spelman, Hartshorn) and "normal" (teacher-training) schools. Before 1900, only a few black women attended coeducational black schools (Fisk, Howard, Atlanta University) at the college level.

Between about 1870 and 1900, a public debate raged over coeducation in high schools and colleges. This debate was restricted to white women, because black women's educational opportunities were restricted to the elementary or at most secondary level (Smith-Rosenberg 1985; Tyack and Hansot 1990). For white women, the debate was not about whether they should receive secondary education, but rather whether they should be educated separately from men. During this heyday of Victorianism, opponents of coeducation at the secondary and higher levels used physiological and moral arguments to promote sex-segregated education and separate gender spheres (Clarke 1874, 1873; Smith-Rosenberg and Rosenberg 1973). Only white, middle-class families could afford to send their daughters to high schools and female academies, because they did not depend on a supplement to the family income. Frequently, such education served as quasi-vocational training to prepare young women for becoming wives and mothers. Physicians and educators alike surmised that women's sexuality and classical education might "unsex" women by failing to prepare them for motherhood (Clarke 1874, 1873).

Within this controversy, people debated whether coeducation meant identical education. Some argued in favor of identical coeducation; others favored coeducation (in time and place) but opposed identical education (curriculum) for women and men. Those who believed that the purpose of educating (white) women was to prepare them for motherhood and not for paid employment objected to identical education. In addition, social Darwinism and a view of women as "mothers of the race" were used to reject women's higher education entirely. Those who favored educating women countered that keeping girls in school during puberty would help channel their sexuality and preserve their morality.

E.H. Clarke, professor at Harvard University, published *The Building of a Brain* (1874) and *Sex in Education; or, A Fair Chance for Girls* (1873). He opposed higher education for women for four reasons: women's moral obligation toward society, psychological instability, intellectual inferiority, and physical inability to endure hard study. In fact, he claimed women's uteruses would atrophy if they studied. Women's moral obligation, according to Clarke, was to pursue motherhood. Motherhood was viewed as women's most noble occupation because only by bearing children could women secure the survival of the race. Mingling the spheres of the two sexes (such as via coeducation) could only lead to a decline in the number of middle-class babies. Clarke suggested that the white race would deteriorate because educated women of the middle and upper classes were increasingly unable to bear children, which meant that the "American race" would be "propagated by its inferior classes." Subjecting adolescent girls to a rigid education modeled after boys' capabilities would "unsex women," while adapting the system to girls' capabilities would "emasculate boys."

Many opponents of co- and identical education stressed the close connection between issues of morality and the separation of spheres (gender roles). They feared that male students' bad manners might damage young women's innate moral purity. Thus, separate education served two purposes: It upheld social standards of morality and prepared male and female students for their specific roles in society (Kerber 1986; Smith-Rosenberg 1985). Upholding academic standards at traditionally male schools was another concern of coeducation opponents, who feared that admitting women would lower such standards. When coeducational schools became more common despite Victorian appeals to issues of morality and proper gender spheres, the focus shifted to the perceived dangers identical education would pose to the survival of the (white) race.

Supporters of coeducation consisted mainly of teachers, school principals, and feminists like Julia W. Howe, Mary Terhune, Elizabeth Cady Stanton, and Thomas W. Higginson. They argued that coeducation would improve the morality and academic discipline of both sexes and that women's feminine character would improve men's manners and discipline. Men's presence would prevent women from developing a romanticized ideal of men, thus preparing them better for their future responsibility as wives (Howe 1972).

Paradoxically, arguments pertaining to women's roles as mothers, wives, and guardians of "racial" purity also were used to support women's secondary and higher education. Supporters, who agreed that women's primary role was motherhood, argued that women's femininity and fertility would be preserved and even amplified if they received proper education. Catharine Beecher and others insisted that education (including courses on hygiene, diet, and exercise) improved women's health. By combining intellectual with outdoor, physical activity, women would be strengthened and prepared to be "better" mothers who would bear healthy children and raise them to become responsible citizens ("Republican Motherhood") (Kerber 1986; Sklar 1976).

Despite the influence that Clarke's books had during the 1870s, by 1900 the public debate about coeducation at secondary and higher levels was settled—until recently. By 1900 almost all public high schools were at least nominally coeducational (Tyack and Hansot 1990). Coeducation at the college level also progressed steadily, but more slowly. While gender ideology considered being a good mother inseparable from being a good homemaker, women's role as mothers and "socialization agents" did not require them to obtain a liberal arts education. Coeducation did not (and does not) mean identical education. While coeducation gained practicability in the late 1800s, identical education continued to contradict the goals of those who argued in favor of gender-specific roles and occupations. Thus, the physiological debate of the 1870s left its imprint in the widespread notion that women and men are different and that education should therefore prepare both sexes for gender-specific occupations.

After 1900, gender differences in educational performance and attainment started to be attributed to socialization rather than inherent biological differences. Nonetheless, Victorian gender-role ideology continued to influence gender-specific curricula. Women's education was generally designed to prepare them for domestic duties as wives and mothers. Vocational (industrial) education for white women did not become prominent in secondary schools until the early 1900s but had been practiced at black schools since the 1870s. Of course, industrial education was de facto gender segregated.

*Regina E. Werum*

## Bibliography

Clarke, E.H. 1874. *The Building of a Brain*. Boston: Osgood.
———. 1873. *Sex in Education; or, A Fair Chance for Girls*. Boston: Houghton Mifflin.
Giddings, Paula. 1984. *When and Where I Enter: The Impact of Black Women on Race and Sex in America*. New York: William Morrow.
Howe, J. 1972. *Sex and Education. A Reply to Dr. E.H. Clarke's "Sex in Education."* New York: Arno.
Kerber, L. 1986. *Women of the Republic: Intellect and Ideology in Revolutionary America*. New York: Norton.
Rury, J. 1991. *Education and Women's Work: Female Schooling and the Division of Labor in Urban America, 1870–1930*. Albany: State University of New York Press.

Sklar, K. 1976. *Catharine Beecher. A Study in American Domesticity.* New York/London: Norton.
Smith-Rosenberg, C. 1985. *Disorderly Conduct: Visions of Gender in Victorian America.* New York: Oxford University Press.
Smith-Rosenberg, C., and C. Rosenberg. 1973. "The Female Animal: Medical and Biological Views of Woman and Her Role in Nineteenth Century America." *Journal of American History* 60:332–56.
Solomon, B. 1985. *In the Company of Educated Women. A History of Women and Higher Education in America.* New York: Yale University Press.
Tyack D., and E. Hansot. 1990. *Learning Together: A History of Coeducation in American Public Schools.* New Haven: Yale University Press.

## Gender Ideology in Early-Twentieth-Century Black Educational Reform

Historically, schools have provided women and men with gender-specific vocational training. This helps explain why women still work predominantly in a few occupations. Gender ideology in education has had distinct consequences for how women of different racial/ethnic backgrounds or socioeconomic classes have been taught.

Black women's education in the early twentieth century was shaped by racial ideology and by gender role expectations within the black community. Unlike white middle-class women of the time, all black women were expected to play an active, public role in shaping their communities (Harley and Terborg-Penn 1978; Neverdon-Morton 1989). Black women were expected to work, but faced severely limited job opportunities. Those who were literate or had some secondary education often became elementary school teachers or dressmakers. Most black women, however, worked as laundresses or domestic servants (Anderson 1988; Lerner 1972).

The black reform movement itself was based on middle-class assumptions about gender roles. Giddings (1984) notes that black reform organizations, such as the NAACP and the National Association of Colored Women/NACW, did not question the superiority of middle-class, Victorian values. Most black male reformers, including political progressives such as W.E.B. Du Bois, said little about whether and how black women should be educated (Meier 1963). The majority of reformers who supported equal (and identical) education for black men and women were women (Loewenberg and Bogin 1976). Many articles on black education appeared in prominent black newspapers, such as the *Colored American* and the *Voice of the Negro*. The former was controlled by Booker T. Washington and thus was more conservative than the *Voice*, which published more articles endorsing liberal arts instruction for women (Culp 1969; Mayo 1892).

Black educational reformers disagreed over the content and purpose of educating black women. Although they agreed that black women's duty was to elevate all African Americans, they disagreed over how black women were to do this. Some reformers supported teaching black women industrial skills, arguing that some female-dominated occupations required special training (dressmaking, millinery, laundressing). Receiving industrial education in some form was the norm for black women in the early twentieth century, even at prestigious liberal arts colleges such as Spelman College in Atlanta, Georgia. Because education was gender-specific, schools at the secondary and higher levels were often de facto segregated by gender.

Many black reformers supported industrial education for black women because of its potential economic benefits ("skilled workers get better wages"). Some argued that industrial education would improve black women's morality by teaching thrift and discipline and by preparing them for motherhood. Booker T. Washington, for instance, considered marriage and motherhood black women's highest duty. Since black women were to elevate the race, they had to be taught those skills necessary to become successful homemakers: mainly housekeeping and sewing. Other supporters of industrial education for black women stressed that homemaking and domestic work were professions. Mary C. Terrell fought for public recognition of black women's vocational skills and for black women's economic independence in general. She believed that training black women to become skilled domestics could help them and the black community gain economic independence (Loewenberg and Bogin 1976; Neverdon-Morton 1989).

A second group of reformers lobbied for combining academic and industrial education because it would prepare black women for a range of domestic and public responsibilities. They even promoted classical education for black women with vocational aspirations. For instance, Nannie H. Burroughs, who founded the National Training School for Girls in Washington, D.C., included liberal arts and industrial courses in the curriculum. The school introduced science into home economic courses and considered domestic work and home keeping true professions. Similarly, Lucy Laney believed that it was necessary to train black women in intellectual as well as occupationally related subjects. In an 1899 speech, she stated:

> The educated Negro woman . . . is needed . . . not only in the kindergarten . . . [but] in high school . . . and the college. . . . Not alone in the classroom can [she] lend a lifting hand, but as a public lecturer she may give advice . . . [that will] start [our] people on the upward way. (Loewenberg and Bogin 1976, pp. 299–300)

The third group of black educators supported expanding academic instruction for black women at all educational levels. They argued that schools were the only place where black women could learn languages, math, and philosophy. Skills they needed as domestic servants could easily be learned on the job. By supporting an academic curriculum, this group also wanted to widen black women's occupational opportunities. Educators in this group include Lucy Laney, who founded Haines Normal and Industrial Institute in Augusta, Georgia, in 1886. Her school became known as the training ground for future generations of black educational reformers, such as Mary McLeod Bethune. Bethune herself lobbied for black women's higher education, became president of the NACW in 1924, and headed the Division of Negro Affairs of the National Youth Administration—a federal relief program during the New Deal that improved black educational and work training opportunities.

W.E.B. Du Bois—who is generally considered a radical reformer because he endorsed classical education for black men—was conservative with respect to black women's education. He said little about whether black women should receive academic instruction (Meier 1963). But others in this group, such as Mary McLeod Bethune and Anna Julia Cooper, pointed out that academic education increased black women's occupational opportunities. In 1902, Sarah Pettey described black women's most important roles as teachers, social reformers (temperance, education), and social workers (for example, in settlement houses) and stated:

"Our educated women should organize councils, federations, societies of social purity and the like. These would serve as great mediums in teaching the masses" (Culp 1969, pp. 183–85).

In sum, black reformers debated the content of black women's education (that is, industrial or liberal arts education) as well as its purpose: which roles black women should hold; how education could prepare them to "lift as they climb"; whether black women's occupational opportunities and their social and political responsibilities should be broadened.

*Regina E. Werum*

## Bibliography

Anderson, James D. 1988. *The Education of Blacks in the South, 1860–1935*. Chapel Hill: University of North Carolina Press.

Culp, D.W. 1969 [1902]. *Twentieth Century Negro Literature or A Cyclopedia of Thought on the Vital Topics Relating to the American Negro*. New York: Arno.

Giddings, Paula. 1984. *When and Where I Enter: The Impact of Black Women on Race and Sex in America*. New York: William Morrow.

Harley, Sharon, and Rosalyn Terborg-Penn. 1978. *The Afro-American Woman: Struggles and Images*. Port Washington, N.Y.: Kennikat.

Hull, Gloria, Patricia B. Scott, and Barbara Smith. 1982. *But Some of Us Are Brave: All Blacks Are Men, All Women Are White*. Old Westbury, N.Y.: The Feminist.

Lerner, Gerda. 1972. *Black Women in White America*. New York: Pantheon.

———. 1979. *The Majority Finds Its Past. Placing Women in History*. New York: Oxford University Press.

Loewenberg, Bert J., and Ruth Bogin. 1976. *Black Women in Nineteenth-Century American Life. Their Words Their Thoughts Their Feelings*. University Park: Pennsylvania State University Press.

Mayo, A.D. 1892. *Southern Women in the Recent Educational Movement in the South*. Washington, D.C.: Government Printing Office.

Meier, August. 1963. *Negro Thought in America, 1880–1915. Racial Ideologies in the Age of Booker T. Washington*. Ann Arbor: University of Michigan Press.

Neverdon-Morton, Cynthia. 1989. *Afro-American Women of the South and the Advancement of the Race, 1895–1925*. Knoxville: University of Tennessee Press.

Scruggs, L.A. 1893. *Women of Distinction: Remarkable in Works and Invincible in Character*. Raleigh: Scruggs Publisher.

Solomon, Barbara Miller. 1985. *In the Company of Educated Women: A History of Women and Higher Education in America*. New Haven: Yale University Press.

## Contemporary College Women's Career Plans

Since the early 1970s in the United States, the percentage of female college students has risen dramatically to more than half of the college student population (National Center for Educational Statistics 1991). When contemporary women enter college, virtually all of them say that they plan to prepare for a career during college and to pursue it upon graduation. During their college years, women choose majors in a wide range of fields. They expect that their course experiences in the major will prepare them for good jobs in the work force. They make good grades, and they graduate more quickly and in higher numbers than men (Adelman 1991). Yet, many contemporary college women continue to make career decisions and choices that lead them into traditionally female roles in the work force. Since the 1970s, there have been only minor changes in the sex segregation of college majors (Meece and Eccles 1993). Overwhelmingly, women still choose to major in the humanities, education, library science, or foreign languages. Although women select college courses of study in science, mathematics, and engineering in larger numbers than ever before, women are concentrated in social sciences, biological sciences, and psychology. Further, regardless of college major, many college women do not pursue a career of their own, at least not without interruption, after graduation (Holland and Eisenhart 1990). Most of these women work outside the home, but they do so in lower-paying, traditionally female jobs, often with little or no prospect of advancement (Okin 1989). Once in the work force, women are dramatically underrepresented in high status, high-paying occupations, particularly those that require expertise in mathematics or science (National Science Foundation 1990). Within occupational category, women earn salaries consistently below men's. Something is happening to women as they attempt to translate their successful educational experiences in college into occupational success. Something is happening to women as they try to achieve the careers they plan in college.

Many studies of women and their career plans attempt to identify the background variables, such as mother's career experiences or high-school course work, that best predict women's choices of college majors or jobs. However, studies of predictors cannot explain why women make the choices they do.

There are three major explanations for why contemporary college women make traditionally female career plans. One explanation is that women choose female-dominated majors and occupations because they have been taught (socialized) from birth to do well in activities traditionally associated with females (Eccles 1987). For example, parents and teachers often encourage girls to be polite, quiet, nurturing, and to develop their verbal skills; boys, in contrast, are encouraged to be aggressive, boisterous, and to develop mathematical skills. Socialization pressures on children to behave in traditional, gender-appropriate ways are pervasive in families, neighborhoods, and schools. As children grow up, their opportunities to participate in nontraditional activities are few and easily overwhelmed by pressures to behave in gender-appropriate ways. When children behave in gender-appropriate ways, they receive praise and support from family and friends; when children behave inappropriately for their gender, praise and support may be withheld. As a consequence, young women and men grow up perfecting different skills and aptitudes. By the time students select courses and degree programs in high school and college, they have felt these socialization pressures for many years and from many people. Thus, they are likely to choose college majors and careers in which they can use and further develop the skills and aptitudes they have previously acquired. For women, this means choosing majors and planning careers in which they can rely upon gender-appropriate skills and aptitudes. If college women make traditionally female career plans, it is because their parents, their schools, and U.S. society have taught women to believe that they are most capable of and best suited for these careers.

A second explanation is that women plan for jobs that will not interfere with close personal relationships and family life (Richardson 1981). Whereas boys and men expect to find satisfaction in competitive activities and at work, girls expect that their greatest source of satisfaction will be their friendships, their romantic relationships, and their children. Socializing agents, such as parents and teachers, contribute to these different expectations. Parents tend to have lower occupational aspirations and higher domestic expectations for their daughters than their sons. School counselors are more likely to advise women to choose majors and occupations that will allow them to be happy in their lives. In contrast, counselors are more likely to advise men to choose majors and occupations in which they can make money. Consequently, when women complete college and go to work, they choose jobs that will not interfere with the rewards they hope to obtain from close relationships and family life. They select jobs with regular hours, little or no over-time, and part-time options. Often, these jobs are also low paying and without benefits or opportunities for advancement.

A third explanation addresses the specific question of why so few young women pursue advanced course work, majors, and careers in mathematics and science. The explanation is that the teaching of mathematics and science in school discourages girls and young women from pursuing or continuing in these fields (Hall and Sandler 1982). In-class activities that stress individual competition, uni-versal rules, and the accomplishments of men create unsupportive, "chilly climates" for girls and young women. Many girls and young women who express interest in mathematics and science eventually switch out of these classes and majors be-cause they find the subject matter and the way it is taught to be too impersonal, irrelevant, and inflexible.

The three explanations stress the conservative effects of socialization and institutional pressures that begin in early childhood. These pressures affect girls and women's thinking about their careers throughout their lives. They guide young women to make traditionally female career plans.

However, these pressures do not explain why many academically talented and ambitious college women suddenly scale back their career commitments or show little interest in pursuing their fields of study as college graduation ap-proaches. Three other explanations have been offered for this trend.

One theory is that college friendship groups exert special pressure on women to take traditional positions in society (Holland and Eisenhart 1990). At least on residential campuses, college friendship groups award high prestige and status to women who succeed in romantic relationships with men. Campus friend-ship groups pay virtually no attention to individual women's academic success or career plans. When friends and boyfriends ask women to participate in social ac-tivities, they encourage women to take time away from their course work and preparations for a career. Friends encourage women to invest time and energy in social and romantic relationships instead. By the time women graduate, they have developed commitments to romantic relationships that take priority over the women's own career commitments. Thus women college graduates often decide to support their boyfriends' career plans rather than their own.

A second explanation for college women's scaled back career plans is that women face blatant and subtle discrimination when they try to move into majors, jobs, or careers that have traditionally been the provinces of men (Vetter 1992). Forms of gender discrimination that are carefully monitored and regulated in el-ementary and secondary schools still flourish on college campuses. Women in mathematics, science, and engineering majors continue to be subjected to deni-als, taunts, jokes, and innuendo from male professors and peers that prevent or discourage women's continued participation in these majors. Women who retain nontraditional career interests through college may find that they are not hired into the jobs for which they prepared in college. These women may turn to tradi-tionally female occupations simply to find a job.

A third and final explanation is that when young women actually begin to look for a job, they realize that their chances of success are better in some fields than others (Gaskell 1992). Young women may purposely choose work in fields dominated by women because they feel more confident that they can find a job, keep it, and feel safe and appreciated in it. In other words, whatever their college majors, women may make career-related decisions based on their assessment of the best opportunities available to them in the work force at the time they enter it.

Although women are well-represented in colleges, do well in college, and increasingly consider majoring in nontraditional fields such as mathematics or science, most college women still make traditionally female career plans or scale down their career plans during or immediately after college. The explanations for this pattern include: socialization pressures on women to develop and pursue gender-appropriate skills and aptitudes; the chilly climate for girls and women in mathematics and science classes; the disinterest shown by family and friends toward women's careers; gender discrimination in the work force; and women's realistic assessment of their chances of obtaining a job and securing the kind of lifestyle they want. No single explanation is sufficient to cover all women's experiences; however, as a group, the explanations suggest why so few college women plan nontraditional careers and why so many different women do not achieve the careers they plan in college.

*Margaret A. Eisenhart*

**Bibliography**

Adelman, Clifford. 1991. *Women at Thirtysomething: Paradoxes of Attainment*. Washington, D.C.: U.S. Department of Education.
Belenky, Mary, Blythe Clinchy, Nancy Goldberger, and Jill Tarule. 1986. *Women's Ways of Knowing: The Development of Self, Voice, and Mind*. New York: Basic Books.
Eccles, Jacquelynne. 1987. "Gender Roles and Women's Achievement-Related Decisions." *Psychology of Women Quarterly* 11:135–72.
Gaskell, Jane. 1992. *Gender Matters from School to Work*. Philadelphia: Open University Press.
Hall, Roberta, and Bernice Sandler. 1982. *The Classroom Climate: A Chilly One for Women?* Washington, D.C.: Association of American Colleges, Project on the Status and Education of Women.
Holland, Dorothy, and Margaret Eisenhart. 1990. *Educated in Romance: Women, Achievement, and College Culture*. Chicago: University of Chicago Press.
Meece, Judith, and Jacquelynne Eccles. 1993. "Introduction: Recent Trends in Research on Gender and Education." *Educational Psychologist* 28(4):313–19.
National Center for Educational Statistics. 1991. *Digest of Education Statistics, 1991*. Washington, D.C.: Office of Educational Research and Improvement, U.S. Department of Education.
National Science Foundation. 1990. *Women and Minorities in Science and Engineering*. Washington, D.C.: National Science Foundation.
Okin, Susan. 1989. *Justice, Gender and the Family*. New York: Basic Books.
Richardson, Mary Sue. 1981. "Occupational and Family Roles: A Neglected Intersection." *Counseling Psychologist* 9(4):13–23.
Vetter, Betty. 1992. *What is Holding up the Glass Ceiling? Barriers to Women in the Science and Engineering Workforce*. Occasional Paper 92–3. Washington, D.C.: Commission on Professionals in Science and Technology.

## Computer Language Effects on Educational/Career Choices of Women

Computer technology has permeated all aspects of contemporary life. Understanding educational and career choices of women requires an understanding of technology and how it was developed. Design of this technology was and is rooted in the overwhelmingly male fields of math and science. Information-age technology is mediated by communication. The differences in educational choices between males and females begin as early as elementary school. The awarding of degrees in computer and information sciences is overwhelmingly to men and the awarding of degrees in business and office technology is overwhelmingly to women. The effects of computer technology on careers is different because of the clustering of the sexes in different career categories. The communication design of the computer information age interacts with career clusters to enhance traditional sex differences in the power structures involving educational and career choices.

## Design and Development of Computers

Technology has changed the shape of life today. Computerization is pervasive in home, leisure, school, and work life. Human-computer research is in its infancy and has explored many directions. Man-machine research techniques proved inadequate to research the human-computer relationship. Some research has attempted to define attitudes toward computers. No major difference between the sexes has been found in their attitudes toward computers. Other research looked at the amount of use of computers. No difference was found in amount of use. But the sexes used the computer for different purposes. Further research has defined the qualities of the human-computer interaction and how the human behaves when interacting with a computer. According to Martin, in Fulton (1985) there are differences in the logic between the human and the computer. "The human is adaptable, observes patterns, detects relevance and can invent questions. . . . The computer . . . is accurate, fast, has a vast memory reached through special retrieval routes, and can deal with complex, massive, logical problems that are sequential" (p. 370). According to Fulton (1985), the interaction is a social interaction mediated by language. The human treats the computer as though it were an ideal male with male language and perceived power. The social cognitive mode of computer technology sets it apart from machine technology and the interaction is qualitatively different. The computer "talks" to the human.

Males design the majority of computers and computer systems today. Programmer and system analysts positions are 80 percent male. The design of programs and systems is created from the inside out. Computer language has a mathematical/logical base. Computers are designed by and for the mathematical and scientific communities. Packages were generally designed for the work or educational space or job as it already existed.

Human language patterns are an integral part of the computer user and the salient feature interacted with on the computer. Language contains a gender/power stereotype that is adopted by most at a very young age. This natural language has a power/social component established by the dominant group in a society. The male/power stereotyped language is more precise and objective than the female stereotyped language. Computer language is even more precise, economical, and powerful than male language. It is formed at the machine level using mathematics following the rules of logic.

System designs have therefore enhanced rather than reorganized or redistributed the job design status quo. This is due to the low number of females in science or math careers and to the low power of the positions that females do occupy in careers or academics. Females were not in decision-making positions in great numbers, and still are not, when most information-age designs were created.

## Women's Education/Employment Choices in the Information Age

Diffusion of any new idea or technology takes time and affects all aspects of a culture. The system already in place has power structures. A new technology will be manipulated and structured as it becomes integrated into the system. Traditionally, gender roles have had a major impact on the educational and career choices guiding the females into stopping education at a lower level and choosing careers that are more language oriented and service oriented.

The American Association of University Women (AAUW/1991) nationwide poll studied self-esteem of adolescents and its relationship to education in math and science. Sex differences take a dramatic turn in adolescence as girls' confidence in their ability in math and science and their liking for math and science drop from elementary school ratings. This drop is related to a drop in self-esteem for adolescent girls. In addition, the study found that gender stereotypes still shape career choices of adolescents.

This early educational choice of opting out of computer classes is discussed in Williams (1987). It was reported that in a statewide high school contest on computer programming only one out of forty competitors was a female. She further reports a precipitous drop in the percentage of girls taking computer programming classes each year. However, girls greatly outnumber boys in word processing classes.

The confidence of the student for these areas has an influence on future educational choices. The Digest of Educational Statistics of 1990 demonstrates the difference in women's educational choices. In computer and information sciences, 32 percent of the B.S. degrees, 26 percent of the M.S. degrees, and 11 percent of the Ph.D.s were awarded to women. In contrast, in the category of business and office degrees, 75 percent of the B.S. degrees and 47 percent of the M.S. degrees were awarded to females. No Ph.D.s were awarded in this area.

It was reported by Savage (1990) that the number of degrees in computing received by women at the bachelor's level and above has been declining after a peak in 1986. This strongly indicates that although a trend for women to work outside the home continues, the career choices of women are following traditional patterns. Attitudes about appropriate choices for the sexes also exert an influence and enhance technological designs that support traditional educational and career choices for females.

*Margaret Anne Bly*

## Bibliography

American Association of University Women. (The Analysis Group, Inc.). 1991. *Shortchanging Girls, Shortchanging America*. Washington, D.C.: AAUW.

Arthur, W.D. Hart. 1987. "Empirical Relationships between Cognitive Ability and Computer Familiarity." *Journal of Research on Computing Education* 22(4):457–63.

Eberts, R.E., A. Majchrzak, P. Payne, and G. Salvendy. 1989. "Integrating Social and Cognitive Factors in Design of Human-Computer Interactive Communication." *International Journal of Human-Computer Interaction* 2(1):1–27.

Fulton, M.A. 1985. "Research Model for Studying the Gender Power Aspects of Human-Computer Communication." *International Journal of Man-Machine Studies* 23:369–82.

Gutek, B.A., and T.K. Bikson. 1985. "Differential Experiences of Men and Women in Computerized Offices." *Sex Roles* 13(3/4):123–36.

Hartman, H., R. Kraut, and L.A. Telly, eds. 1986. *Computer Chips and Paper Clips: Technology and Women's Employment*. National Research Council. Washington, D.C.: National Academy.

Postman, N. 1992. *Technopoly*. New York: Alfred A. Knopf.

Savage, J. 1990. "Women Losing Ground in IS." *Computerworld* 24(47):117.

Siann, G., A. Durndell, H. Macleod, and P. Gibson. 1988. "Stereotyping in Relation to the Gender Gap in Participation in Computing." *Educational Research* 30(2):98–102.

Snyder, T.D., and C.M. Hoffman. 1991. *Digest of Educational Statistics, 1990*. (NCES 91–660). Washington, D.C.: National Center for Education Statistics.

Temple, L., and H.M. Lips. 1989. "Gender Differences and Similarities in Attitudes towards Computers." *Computers in Human Behavior* 5:215–26.

Weizenbaum, J. 1976. *Computer Power and Human Reason*. San Francisco: W.H. Freeman.

Williams, J.H. 1987. *Psychology of Women: Behavior in a Biosocial Context*. 3rd ed. New York: W.W. Norton.

## Women, Work, and Religion

Previous research on women, work, and religion has taken different approaches in addressing the interconnections between them. Recently, social historians have reexamined the roles that women have occupied in religious institutions and social movements, rather than relegating them solely to their other historical roles in home and family (Sheils and Wood 1990). Sociologists, too, have considered linkages between women's work and religion. On one hand, investigators have explored religious involvement as a predictor of labor-force participation either as an extension of Weber's work ethic thesis or as an attempt to specify causal relationships between religious orthodoxy, gender-role attitudes, and employment. On the other hand, work has been used to predict church attendance, religious intensity, and religious orthodoxy. Before examining these studies of women and nonreligious work, however, let us turn to some other areas involving women's work roles within organized religion.

Historically, the Judeo-Christian tradition has upheld the importance of women's work role within the home as housewife and mother for Protestants and Catholics, alike. Housework carried with it ideological significance because the home was the domain of women's calling, and, by serving their families, they fulfilled their God-given roles (Hunter 1987). Those women who didn't hold to this ideal were viewed "as a danger to social order and to the welfare of future generations" (Oates 1989, p. 82). However, it has been suggested that, until recently, this glorified account of women's place in the social order was a possibility only for middle- and upper-class white women who could afford the luxury of remaining in the home (Andersen 1988). Working-class women, especially Catholic women, on the other hand, have worked outside the home, either in factories or in domestic service, in addition to the responsibilities of their own housework and child care, in order to make ends meet. It is this latter group of women who have been required to choose between the expectations of religious ideals and the material requirements of their class position and survival.

Judeo-Christian ideologies, though disseminated and controlled by men, have been used not only to strengthen the power of men over women but, in some cases, to challenge that power relationship. The institutional church remains one source for the ideological legitimation of gender roles, in that it often reinforces the rightness or naturalness of them. However, to focus solely on a legitimation thesis would be to overlook the dynamic nature of gender-role definition and redefinition within religious institutions. In this sense, religious traditions, narratives, and images may be appropriated by women to challenge existing gender relations as well as to provide a moral context for mobilizing collective action aimed at social reform. Religiously motivated women have been at the forefront of many social movements, such as the Abolitionist movement, the trade-union movement, the Civil Rights movement, antinuclear campaigns, and so forth. Thus, while being kept out of the central arenas of ecclesiastical power, women have been segregated into their own semiautonomous institutional spheres within which gender-based, oppositional ideological impulses could develop and gain momentum.

Today, women are moving into the realms of ecclesiastical authority. Among most mainline Protestant denominations (American Baptists, Episcopalians, some Lutherans, Presbyterians, United Church of Christ, United Methodists, and Unitarians) women are formally allowed to hold positions as priests and pastors. However, having achieved this structural position does not seem to be enough to ensure equality. Women in the pastorate often find themselves in less desirable and rural parishes. Few are senior pastors or head large and influential congregations, and more often than not they still are given charge of overseeing educational, charitable, or other "nurturing" ministries (Hargrove 1983). Despite formal recognition within Protestant churches, women's roles as minister maintains a rather tenuous legitimacy.

Theoretically, gender-role definitions are not monolithic in their effects; rather, they are contested and indeterminant. In other words, there may be some divergence between ideal gender roles as defined by church doctrine and the reality of roles as they are negotiated by church members in their daily lives. Women have used the images created about them (for example, that women are innately pious and have a superior moral sense compared with men) to legitimize their own roles in movements aimed at social change (Kenneally 1990). However, challenges to extant gender relations also have generated countermovements within particular denominations to block reforms considered detrimental to traditional roles and to structures perceived as divinely instituted. Current statements from Southern Baptist, Nazarene, and even Roman Catholic church hierarchies affirm the appropriate roles for women to be those in the domestic sphere and oppose secular legislation that would contribute to their corrosion (Hargrove 1983). Few recent studies investigate discrepancies between officially held religious dogma and everyday practice of believers. The impact of the growing tension between traditional religiously based attitudes toward women's work and the increasing economic necessities of having a dual-income household on religious institutions and their members, for example, has received little scholarly attention.

As the requirements of women's work change, the influence of religion as a source of gender-role legitimation also changes. Over the last three decades, the feminist movement has polarized denominations over the roles of women in church and society. Wuthnow (1988, p. 228) suggests that "religious conservatives began to see feminism as part of a more general ideological package to which they needed to voice opposition, while religious liberals increasingly saw it as a matter of moral and theological urgency." In examining the ongoing struggles over gender and access to religious power and resources, it remains crucial to explore the ways these struggles have resulted in coalition formation, disintegration, and reformation within religious bodies. While it is possible to focus on denominational differences (such as Episcopalian versus Southern Baptist attitudes toward women clergy), these struggles are occurring on a congregation by congregation level, where intraparish groups are in conflict over the direction in which both the local and national church should move on women's issues (D'Antonio 1983; Wuthnow 1988). Moreover, it is on the microstructural level, where individuals negotiate between their religious worldview and economic and political demands of their own lives, that we see the contested nature of gender roles played out.

### Religion, Gender, and Labor-Force Participation

Census data indicates that approximately 55 to 60 percent of women work for wages outside of the home, and most studies of gender differences in religious involvement suggest that women have higher rates of involvement than men (D'Antonio 1983). These two pieces of information have formed the basis for studies focusing on gender differences in the relationship between religious affiliation and labor-force participation. Hertel (1988) found female apostates to be more likely to be employed outside the home than women who were more involved religiously. This finding, for women, has been attributed to the high correlation between being single and employed as well as the correlation between educational attainment and the likelihood of working or lacking a religious identity. Drawing on Weberian theory, Hertel argues that labor-force participation is a matter of choice that ultimately reflects values. What is lacking in this study however is an understanding that for many women, working outside of the home is not a choice but a structural necessity.

On a slightly different track, Bainbridge and Hatch (1982) test the hypothesis that religion (Christianity) keeps women out of high-status jobs because of its inherently antifemale bias. These authors suggest that when religion is "established and monolithic" (that is, state-sanctioned), as in Canada for instance, it is more likely to act as an oppressor to particular groups. However, these authors assert that in a religiously pluralistic society like that of the United States, no one set of religious values can be imposed on the general populace. This argument is problematic because, in the case of the United States, a plurality of denominations that share to a large degree similar ethics is not the same as a plurality of religions that actually have divergent social values. Bainbridge and Hatch also restrict their analysis to the effect of religion on the entry of women into elite careers, specifically banking, law, medicine, and industrial management. It is unclear how generalizable their arguments would be if they had broadened the study to include more generally the entry of women into traditionally male occupations at all levels of the occupational hierarchy.

Perhaps the most complex attempt to model the relationship between religion and women's work was done by Morgan and Scanzoni (1987). In a study of 318 female college seniors, these authors found their measures of religious devotion to have both direct and indirect effects on their decisions to enter the paid labor force. Religion affects women's labor-force participation by shaping their images of women's roles. Women with high religious devotion tended to see themselves in more nurturing and supportive roles, which, in turn, was highly correlated to their selection of female-dominated majors. Women who were less religiously devout were also less likely to see themselves as nurturing and passive and were more likely to choose nontraditional college majors. They were more likely to expect to enter the paid labor force upon completion of their degree. In going beyond determining statistical relationships between measures of religion and work, Morgan and Scanzoni take steps toward specifying how day-to-day decisions and mechanisms give rise to these arithmetic relationships.

Labor-force participation also has been used to predict differences in church attendance for women. Ulbrich and Wallace (1984) test this relationship using numerous independent variables derived from econometric models of time allocation and its relationship to religious participation. They found that church attendance varies by employment status because of the indirect effects of age, religious intensity, and having a spouse of the same denomination. Working and nonworking women who are similar in these respects showed similar church attendance patterns. De Vaus (1984) also suggests that it is not employment status or lack thereof that explains women's high church attendance; rather, gender differences in attendance are statistical artifacts arising from the comparatively low church attendance of men in the full-time labor force.

In conclusion, scholars have begun to bring women back onto the historical stage in multiple social roles and to explore the relationships between the work and church-related aspects of women's lives. At a time when debates between and within various denominations rage over the appropriate social roles for women, researchers would make important contributions to our knowledge in this area by investigating a number of related issues. First, how do women make sense of their labor-force participation and their continued roles as housewives and mothers in light of their religious beliefs? Second, if women with low income and educational levels have always been in some way connected to the labor force, how does their higher membership in denominations that reinforce traditional gender roles affect how they view themselves and their work role? Finally, will the ideological stances of religious institutions regarding women's roles change as the number of women entering more visible structural positions in the church increases? Pursuing these questions will add to our understanding of how women make sense of their lives in the home, the church, and the workplace.

*William A. Mirola*

## Bibliography

Andersen, Margaret L. 1988. *Thinking about Women: Sociological Perspectives on Sex and Gender*. New York: Macmillan.

Bainbridge, William S., and Laurie R. Hatch. 1982. "Women's Access to Elite Careers: In Search of a Religion Effect." *Journal for the Scientific Study of Religion* 21(3):242–55.

D'Antonio, William V. 1983. "Family Life, Religion, and Societal Values and Structures." In *Families and Religions: Conflict and Change in Modern Society*, edited by William V. D'Antonio and Joan Aldous, pp. 81–108. Beverly Hills, Calif.: Sage.

de Vaus, David A. 1984. "Work Force Participation and Sex Differences in Church Attendance." *Review of Religious Research* 25(3):247–56.

Hargrove, Barbara. 1983. "Family in the White American Protestant Experience." In *Families and Religion: Conflict and Change in Modern Society*, edited by William V. D'Antonio and Joan Aldous, pp. 113–40. Beverly Hills, Calif.: Sage.

Hertel, Bradley R. 1988. "Gender, Religious Identity, and Work Force Participation." *Journal for the Scientific Study of Religion* 27(4):574–92.

Hunter, James Davidson. 1987. *Evangelicalism: The Coming Generation*. Chicago: University of Chicago Press.

Kenneally, James J. 1990. *The History of American Catholic Women*. New York: Crossroads.

Morgan, Mary Y., and John Scanzoni. 1987. "Religious Orientation and Women's Expected Continuity in the Labor Force." *Journal of Marriage and the Family* 49(May):367–79.

Oates, Mary J. 1989. "Catholic Laywomen in the Labor Force." In *American Catholic Women*, edited by Karen Kennelly, pp. 81–124. New York: Macmillan.

Sheils, W.J., and Diana Wood, eds. 1990. *Women in the Church*. Papers read at the 1989 summer meetings and the 1990 winter meeting of the Ecclesiastical History Society. Cambridge, Mass.: Basil Blackwell.

Ulbrich, Holley, and Myles Wallace. 1984. "Women's Work Force Status and Church Attendance." *Journal for the Scientific Study of Religion* 23(4):341–50.

Wuthnow, Robert. 1988. *The Restructuring of American Religion*. Princeton: Princeton University Press.

## Role Models and Occupational Choice

Same-sex role models are thought to increase the number of persons willing to make nontraditional occupational choices. However, the rapid increase in the number of women in such fields as law, pharmacy, medicine, veterinary medicine, and business management implies that most of these occupational choices were not influenced by same-sex role models. There were very few women professionals available in these fields when the upsurge began, suggesting that those influencing choice were not female professionals within the field. More broadly, many women (and men) may be responding to new opportunities without concern for the sex of influencer or the sex of people in the field.

The literature on occupational choice contains two approaches to the sex of occupational influencer. The role model approach emphasizes the sex structure of an occupation and asserts that nontraditional choice is increased when same-sex models are available to the novice (Betz and Fitzgerald 1987). In the role-model approach, sex-role socialization is thought to engender a concern for sex-appropriate work, and same-sex influencers presumably increase nontraditional choice by demonstrating "appropriate gender role behaviors" (Weishaar et al. 1981). Supporters of the role-model approach (such as Betz and Fitzgerald 1987; Douvan 1976; Tidball and Kistiakowski 1976) contend that female students making nontraditional choices feel more confident when encouraged by another female, especially one who is in the field. Some analysts further contend that same-sex influencers intensify commitment to complete a specific course of study and to enter the field.

The opportunity structure approach to occupational choice asserts that men and women respond similarly to available opportunity. Therefore, the presence of same-sex models and a concern for sex appropriateness will not be salient factors in the choice process (Kanter 1977). This approach implies that women and men will have similar influencers in regard to both sex and occupation. The sex composition of the occupation chosen is expected to determine largely the sex of influencers for both males and females.

Research tends to support the opportunity structure approach showing little importance to the sex of influencers and the number of same-sex people in the field. In general, women choosing nontraditional occupations report males as most influencing or supporting their selection (Betz and O'Connell 1992; Hackett et al. 1989). (See Betz and O'Connell for a review of relevant studies.) A number of studies that assert a positive effect by same-sex role models are not valid because they either fail to control for occupation (Basow and Howe 1979; Saltiel 1985), look at issues other than occupational choice, or attribute to the presence of female professors the positive effects of attending elite women's colleges (Tidball and Kistiakowski 1976).

One overlooked possibility is that males rely on same-sex models more than females. When Betz and O'Connell (1992) asked male and female students in engineering and nursing who most influenced their choice, they found that female engineers were as likely as male engineers to cite males. However, male nurses were more likely than female nurses to cite males as influencers.

The above findings are tentative, however, since the available studies have small or unrepresentative samples. Moreover, the studies do not focus on what influencers do to encourage nontraditional choice, and researchers often ignore the social relationships between influencer and chooser (for example, father/daughter, teacher/student, husband/wife), an unfortunate fact because studies that look at relationships (Saltiel 1985) find that parents and teachers are especially influential. It appears that support from significant others, especially those in a position to know the demands of a field and the abilities of a novice, greatly increases nontraditional choice.

The effect of same-sex models on occupational choice appears to be slight, but the effect of same-sex models on other aspects of the career process may be great (such as mentors, sponsors, colleagues). Long-term relationships with same-sex supervisors and colleagues may facilitate career advancement. Hence, further research on the effects of role models should separate career choice issues from career advancement issues so researchers can assess how same-sex versus opposite-sex relationships in the workplace affect careers and promotions.

*Michael Betz*

*Lenahan O'Connell*

## Bibliography

Basow, Susan A., and Karen G. Howe. 1979. "Model Influence on Career Choices of College Students." *Vocational Guidance Quarterly* 27:239–43.

Betz, Nancy, and L.F. Fitzgerald. 1987. *The Career Psychology of Women*. New York: Academic.

Betz, Michael, and Lenahan O'Connell. 1992. "The Role of Inside and Same-Sex Influencers in the Choice of Nontraditional Occupations." *Sociological Inquiry* 62:98–106.

Douvan, Elizabeth. 1976. "The Role of Models of Women's Professional Development." *Psychology of Women Quarterly* 1:5–20.

Hackett, Gail, Donna Esposito, and Sean O'Halloran. 1989. "The Relationship of Role Model Influences to the Career Salience and Educational and Career Plans of College Women." *Journal of Vocational Behavior* 35:164–80.

Kanter, Rosabeth M. 1977. *Men and Women of the Corporation*. New York: Basic Books.

Plas, Jeanne M., and Barbara S. Wallston. 1983. "Women Oriented Toward Male Dominated Careers: Is the Reference Group Male or Female?" *Journal of Counseling Psychology* 30:46–54.

Saltiel, John. 1985. "A Note on Models and Definers as Sources of Influence in the Status Attainment Process: Male-Female Differences." *Social Forces* 63:1069–75.

Tidball, M. Elizabeth, and Vera Kistiakowski. 1976. "Baccalaureate Origins of American Scientists and Scholars." *Science* 193:646–53.

Weishaar, Marjorie E., Barbara J. Green, and Linda W. Craighead. 1981. "Primary Influences of Initial Vocational Choices for College Women." *Journal of Vocational Behavior* 18:67–68.

## Sex, Gender Stereotypes, and Work

The majority of occupations in the U.S. labor force are segregated by sex, but after many decades there has been some evidence that desegregation is occurring (Bianchi and Rytina 1986). When desegregation occurs, it is generally due to women entering male-dominated occupations rather than to men entering female-dominated occupations. Women often cite higher wages as a major reason for entering a male-dominated occupation (Lillydahl 1986). The higher relative prestige of male-dominated occupations provides another incentive for women (Bose 1985). A women who enters a male-dominated occupation increases her status, whereas, a man who enters a female-dominated occupation suffers a decline in status. In addition to economic concerns, most men do not consider entering a female-dominated occupation because they fear being labeled effeminate (Williams 1989). Consequently, occupational segregation allows men to maintain their masculinity in contradistinction to femininity, which, in turn, serves to reinforce the belief that there are fundamental social and psychological differences between the sexes. Nevertheless, few published studies have investigated sex and gender differences in personality and work-value correlates relative to occupational choice and job satisfaction in male-dominated and female-dominated occupations.

### Sex, Gender Stereotypes, and Occupational Choice

Men and women who cross over into nontraditional occupations are expected to possess, or assume, the personality traits of the opposite sex. There is evidence that psychological masculinity exhibits a major influence on occupational choice. A synthesis of the research findings demonstrates that persons in male-dominated career fields score higher in masculinity than persons in female-dominated career fields (Elton and Rose 1987; Lemkau 1984). Notably, the majority of these studies compare either men or women—mostly women—in male-dominated and female-dominated occupations.

There is also some evidence that gender differences in work values may constitute an important aspect of occupational choice. Bridges (1989) found that female psychology students were just as likely as their male counterparts to hold masculine work values (such as desire for high income and authority), but traditional sex/gender differences in feminine work values (such as a desire to help others) continued to persist. Comparative analyses of women in male-dominated and female-dominated occupations have yielded similar results (Greenfeld et al. 1980).

Here it is important to note that most of the research that has been done on occupational values is based on student surveys conducted prior to 1980, and, to a lesser extent, on general population studies that failed to control for type of occupation (See Lueptow p. 283 this vol.). Less than a handful of studies have compared the work values of men and women employed in male-dominated and female-dominated occupations. No study has investigated the relationship between work values and occupational choice for men employed in male-dominated and female-dominated occupations, or for men and women employed in female-dominated occupations.

Studies involving intersex occupational value comparisons in male-dominated occupations have produced conflicting results. Kaufman and Fetters (1980) found no difference in the work values of male and female accountants. In contrast, Brenner et al. (1988) found traditional sex and gender differences in the occupational values of men and women in middle management. This discrepancy in findings appears to be related to the methodology of the two studies. Specifically, Kaufman's and Fetters's work excluded an important feminine occupational value—the desire to help others.

## Sex and Job Satisfaction

Few studies have done same-sex or intersex comparisons of job satisfaction in male-dominated and female-dominated occupations. The information that does exist suggests that more women than men are satisfied with their jobs (Agassi 1982), that women in male-dominated occupations tend to be more satisfied with their work than women employed in female-dominated occupations (Golding et al. 1983), and that males employed in male-dominated occupations are more satisfied than their female counterparts (Jagacinski 1987).

## Gender Stereotypes, Sex-Typing of Work, and Job Satisfaction

There is limited evidence that gender differences in job satisfaction are related to personality traits. According to Jagacinski (1987), masculine and androgynous persons in male-dominated occupations are more satisfied with their work than feminine or undifferentiated persons in male-dominated occupations. No study has examined the relationship between personality traits and job satisfaction for men and women employed in female-dominated occupations, for men employed in male-dominated and female-dominated occupations, or for women employed in male-dominated and female-dominated occupations.

Even less is known about the effects of work values on the job satisfaction of men or women employed in sex-typed and sex-atypical occupations. Greenfeld et al. (1980), for example, found that women in male-dominated occupations held more masculine work values than women in female-dominated jobs. They also found, contrary to others, that women in female-dominated occupations were more satisfied with their jobs than women in male-dominated occupations. However, these researchers failed to consider that gender congruency or incongruency in work values and occupational choice may affect job satisfaction. For instance, do women who score high in masculine work values tend to be more satisfied in male-dominated occupations than women who score low on masculine work values? No study has examined this issue.

## Concluding Remarks

Gender differences in personality traits and work values may facilitate entry into and job satisfaction in female-dominated and male-dominated occupations. However, at this point in time, such an interpretation must remain tentative. Further research is needed to access the relative contribution of personality traits and work values to the differential career choices of men and women in female-dominated and male-dominated occupations.

Importantly, there are several problems with the existing research that future studies need to address. First, women are more often studied than men. If only women in male-dominated occupations are studied, gender differences may be exacerbated. Hence, intra- and interoccupational comparisons of same-sex and intersex variations in gender orientation and job satisfaction would prove especially interesting. Second, the majority of studies focus on one or two sex-typed occupations. No study has simultaneously and systematically investigated the gender-role orientation and psychological well-being of men and women in a wide range of sex-typed occupations. Third, most studies use only one measure of gender-role orientation (for example, personality traits). Multiple measures of gender-role orientation—personality traits in combination with work values and attitudes toward gender roles, for example—would strengthen the validity of research findings. Fourth, sex-typed occupational studies have focused almost exclusively on examining self-report, personality, and behavioral correlates to paper-and-pencil measures of gender-role orientation (such as the BSRI and PAQ scales). Interpreting and classifying an individual's gender-role orientation based on item endorsements on an inventory diverts critical attention away from the fact that gender roles are situationally determined. Fifth, the direction of the relationship for personality traits and occupational choice is problematic. For example, do women in male-dominated occupations acquire masculine personality traits prior or subsequent to entering such occupations? Finally, the majority of studies fail to consider that occupational desegregation does not necessarily result in the diminution of gender differences. Despite occupational desegregation, men and women are still segregated in their duties (Reskin and Roos 1990). "Internal stratification" is not only the result of external pressures exerted on individuals in sex-atypical occupations, but of internal pressures as well. Williams (1989), for example, found that male nurses and female marines actively construct their own gender by redefining their activities in terms of masculine and feminine traits. Consequently, official policies, informal practices, and the redefinition of work by men and women in sex-atypical occupations all function to maintain gender differences within desegregated occupations.

*Aleta Esther Geib*
*Lloyd B. Lueptow*

## Bibliography

Agassi, J.B. 1982. *Comparing Work Attitudes of Women and Men*. Lexington, Mass.: Lexington Books.
Bianchi, S.M., and N. Rytina. 1986. "The Decline in Occupational Sex Segregation during the 1970s: Census and CPS Comparisons." *Demography* 23:79–85.
Bose, C.E. 1985. *Jobs and Gender: A Study of Occupational Prestige*. New York: Praeger.
Brenner, O.C., A.P. Blazini, and J.H. Greenhaus. 1988. "An Examination of Race and Sex Differences in Managerial Work Values." *Journal of Vocational Behavior* 32:336–44.
Bridges, J.S. 1989. "Sex Differences in Occupational Values." *Sex Roles* 20:205–11.
Elton, C.F., and H.A. Rose. 1987. "Significance of Personality in the Vocational Choice of College Women." *Journal of Counseling Psychology* 14:293–98.
Golding, J., A. Resnick, and F. Crosby. 1983. "Work Satisfaction as a Function of Gender and Job Status." *Psychology of Women Quarterly* 7:286–90.
Greenfeld, S., L. Greiner, and M.M. Wood. 1980. "The 'Feminine Mystique' in Male-Dominated Jobs: A Comparison of Attitudes and Background Factors of Women in Male-Dominated versus Female-Dominated Jobs." *Journal of Vocational Behavior* 17:291–309.
Jagacinski, C.M. 1987. "Androgyny in a Male-Dominated Field: The Relationship of Sex-Typed Traits to Performance and Satisfaction in Engineering." *Sex Roles* 17:529–47.
Kaufman, D., and M.L. Fetters. 1980. "Work Motivation and Job Values among Professional Men and Women: A New Accounting." *Journal of Vocational Behavior* 17:251–62.
Lemkau, J.P. 1984. "Men in Female-Dominated Professions: Distinguishing Personality and Background Characteristics." *Journal of Vocational Behavior* 24:110–22.
Lillydahl, J.H. 1986. "Women in Traditionally Male Blue-Collar Jobs." *Work and Occupations* 13:307–23.
Reskin, B.F., and P.A. Roos. 1990. *Job Queues, Gender Queues: Explaining Women's Inroads into Male Occupations*. Philadelphia: Temple University Press.
Williams, C.L. 1989. *Gender Differences at Work: Women and Men in Non-Traditional Occupations*. Berkeley: University of California Press.

# V

# Legal Factors Affecting Women's Work and Opportunity

**Protective Legislation in American Courts**

Protective legislation in American labor history refers to the efforts of the federal and state governments to prohibit child labor and to ameliorate the terms and conditions of employment for both male and female workers. The intervention of Congress and of state legislatures in contractual relations between employers and employees was based on the realistic assumption that workers and owners were not equal in bargaining power and that, therefore, the former needed the protection of government.

Although the genesis of protective legislation can be traced back to the Colonial period in American history, it was not until the 1840s and 1850s that ten-hour legislation was enacted in eight states. President Martin Van Buren by executive order established a ten-hour day for federal employees, and in 1857 Ohio and Wisconsin extended the same daily limits for state workers (Kessler-Harris 1982). But laws restricting hours and other attempts to improve working conditions did not fare well in the post–Civil War period. In 1885 the New York Court of Appeals *In Re Jacobs* held for the first time in American history that a state statute that prohibited the manufacture of cigars in tenement dwellings deprived a workingman of "personal liberty by driving him out of his own shop to work in a factory." The Illinois Supreme Court in 1895 in *Ritchie* v. *People* declared an eight-hour law for women a violation of freedom of contract, and the same year the highest tribunal in Colorado in an advisory opinion condemned an eight-hour law for both men and women as "class legislation" and violative of "the right of parties to make their own contracts" (Forbath 1991).

Initially, the United States Supreme Court had a different view of protective legislation. Although in 1890 it had read into the due process clause of the Fourteenth Amendment the concept of "liberty of contract," three years after the Illinois court decided the *Ritchie* case, the federal tribunal in *Holden* v. *Hardy* sustained the constitutionality of a Utah law establishing a ten-hour day in the state's mines and smelters. The employer's "defense," said Justice Henry Brown with a touch of irony, "is not so much that his right to contract has been infringed upon, but that the act works a particular hardship to his employees, whose right to labor as long as they please is alleged to be thereby violated. The argument would certainly come with better grace and cogency from the latter class" (169 U.S. 386 [1898]).

The Supreme Court changed its collective mind in 1905 in *Lochner* v. *New York*. Although the facts of *Holden* and *Lochner* were analogous, Justice Rufus Peckham could not see any relationship between the state's police power to protect the health of its constituents and a ten-hour law for bakers. There was ample evidence, cited in Justice John Marshall Harlan's dissent, that long hours spent in a bakery led to bronchial and lung diseases and shortened bakers' lives. But the majority insisted that there was no difference between the working conditions under which bakers labored and those of a "printer, a tinsmith, a locksmith, a carpenter, a cabinet maker, a dry goods clerk, a bank's, a lawyer's or a physician's clerk." The New York statute, the court held, was an example of "meddlesome interference" (198 U.S. 45 [1905]).

In 1908 the court did approve of a ten-hour law for women, and nine years later for both men and women in *Bunting* v. *Oregon*. But it joined these opinions with a persistent refusal to uphold the Congressional attempts to prohibit child labor in 1917 and 1922, declaring that the federal legislation violated the reserved powers of the states in the U.S. Constitution's Tenth Amendment, and in 1923 struck down a Congressional statute establishing a minimum wage for women in *Adkins* v. *Children's Hospital*.

The 1930s depression, labor-management violence, and the Roosevelt "revolution" led the Supreme Court to a more sympathetic reception of protective legislation. In 1938 Congress passed the Fair Labor Standards Act, abolishing with certain exceptions child labor under the age of sixteen, and providing initially for a minimum wage of 25 cents an hour and a work week of forty-four hours to be reduced by October 24, 1940, to forty. Three years later the Supreme Court had before it the case of *United States* v. *Darby*. Fred Darby, a lumber mill owner in Georgia with an extensive interstate business, refused to pay his workers the minimum wage prescribed by the standards act. From the Federal District Court in Savannah, where the judge held that Congress had gone beyond its delegated power to regulate interstate commerce, the case was appealed to the Supreme Court where, in a unanimous decision, Mr. Justice Harlan Fiske Stone overruled the lower court and sustained the constitutionality of the federal law and its application to the Darby Lumber Company (312 U.S. 100 [1941]).

The last example of federal protective legislation was the passage by Congress of the Occupational Safety and Health Act in 1970. The broad design of the law had as its purpose the safeguarding of workers from industrial accidents and occupational diseases. Enforcement of the standards established by the Labor Department was given in 1971 to the Occupational Safety and Health Administration (OSHA). But as one expert summarized the results fifteen years later, "OSHA has set few new standards. The Agency's inspectorate is small. Its programs have had little measurable impact on working conditions" (Nobel 1986).

*David L. Sterling*

## Bibliography

Forbath, William E. 1991. *Law and the Shaping of the American Labor Movement*. Cambridge, Mass.: Harvard University Press.

Kessler-Harris, Alice. 1982. *Out of Work: A History of Wage-Earning Women in the United States*. New York: Oxford University Press.

Nobel, Charles. 1986. *Liberalism at Work: The Rise and Fall of OSHA*. Philadelphia: Temple University Press.

Phelps, Orme. 1939. *The Legislative Background of the Fair Labor Standards Act*. Chicago: University of Chicago Press.

Stern, Robert J. 1946. "The Commerce Clause and the National Economy, Part II." *Harvard Law Review* 59(July):883–97.

### Relevant Cases

*In Re Jacobs,* 98 N.Y. 98 (1885)

*Ritchie* v. *People,* 155 Ill. 98 (1895)

*Holden* v. *Hardy,* 169 U.S. 386 (1898)

*Lochner* v. *New York,* 198 U.S. 45 (1905)

*Bunting* v. *Oregon,* 245 U.S. 428 (1917)

*Adkins* v. *Children's Hospital,* 261 U.S. 525 (1923)

*United States* v. *Darby,* 312 U.S. 100 (1941)

## Women's Work and Protective Legislation

Protective legislation refers to state intervention in labor-management relations for the purpose of ameliorating the terms and conditions of employment. The rapid growth of American industry after the Civil War and the presence of laboring women in it spurred efforts to safeguard their health and morals by new state laws. In 1890 there were approximately four million women in the American labor force. Working in factories, laundries, department stores, and as domestic servants, they represented 17 percent of those employed and 18.2 percent of the female population of the United States. Their jobs were most often unskilled, segregated, dead end, and mind numbing. Their pay was most often below subsistence; their work week averaged fifty-four hours. In the factories and sweatshops of American cities, the noise level was often deafening, the machinery dangerous, and the building poorly lighted and ventilated and unsanitary. In old and new buildings, women's work was speeded up by payment for piece goods and menaced by fire.

The most dramatic industrial disaster of the early twentieth century was the Triangle Shirtwaist fire in March of 1911, during which 146 young immigrant women, many of whom jumped from the ninth-floor windows, lost their lives. "Down came the bodies," one observer wrote, "in a shower, burning, smoking, flaming bodies with disheveled hair trailing upwards. These torches, suffering ones, fell inertly." The New York State Factory Inspection Committee, established after the fire and led by Robert S. Wagner, Sr., and Alfred E. Smith, held hearings and heard testimony about deplorable factory conditions, toilets in disrepair, dust-filled and dirty washrooms, crippling machinery, and working children (Stein 1962).

For many Americans, enamored by the Victorian cult of domesticity, the Shirtwaist fire was a graphic example of why the factory was no place for women; for others, committed to the improvement of conditions in the workforce, the remedy to poor pay and long hours was to encourage women to join unions. But American women would not leave the economy nor would they, except in the garment industry, join labor organizations in appreciable numbers. The solution to their plight appeared to be the passage of one-sex protective legislation; some lawmakers believed that special labor acts, restrictive in nature, would cause employers to replace women with male workers; others were concerned about young women laboring in unsavory and "immoral" work environments. Still others and their supporters, like Florence Kelley, were genuinely concerned with eliminating the harsh and unequal terms and conditions of female employment (Blumberg 1966).

The result was basically two kinds of protective legislation: those that attempted to confer benefits upon women workers, such as maximum hours, minimum wages, and mandatory rest periods, and those that denied employment to women and were clearly discriminatory, such as night-work regulations and outright prohibition of jobs in mining, bartending, pool rooms, and other occupations. (Ohio, for example, excluded women from eighteen job categories.) In 1890, thirteen states had laws on their statute books regulating hours for women in factories; by 1923, fourteen states, the District of Columbia, and the territory of Puerto Rico had passed minimum-wage laws. (Only one, Massachusetts, was an industrial state.)

The first legal challenge to the protective legislation in the United States Supreme Court came during the "Progressive" period, in 1908. Curt Muller, the owner of a laundry in Portland, Oregon, was convicted of violating the state's ten-hour law for women in manufacturing, laundries, and mercantile establishments. His conviction, sustained in the Oregon tribunals, was appealed to the Supreme Court of the United States. On the state's side, the services of Louis D. Brandeis, Harvard law graduate and Boston attorney, were secured by Florence Kelley and Josephine Goldmark on behalf of the National Consumers League (Mason 1946).

The brief that Goldmark researched and Brandeis submitted to the Supreme Court was unusual. There were only three pages of legal precedents and more than one hundred of medical and scientific data attesting to the deleterious impact of long hours of labor upon women's health; the purpose of these materials was to demonstrate a relationship between the state's police power to protect the health of women and maximum hour legislation. "Liberty of Contract," a concept that the Court had read into the due process clause of the Fourteenth Amendment to the Federal Constitution, could be restricted if there were a rational basis for the maximum-hour statute, a nexus between the state's authority to protect health and the law at issue.

In 1908, when *Muller* v. *Oregon* was decided by the Supreme Court, the tribunal was composed primarily of social conservatives averse to state interference in business. The Court, however, unanimously upheld the constitutionality of the Oregon maximum-hour law. "Her physical structure," wrote Justice David Brewer, "and a proper discharge of her maternal functions—having in view not merely her own health, but the well-being of the race—justify legislation to protect her from the greed as well as the passion of men" (208 U.S. 412 [1908]).

The minimum-wage legislation did not fare as well in the Supreme Court. The state statutes that regulated women's wages were often either unenforced or ineffective, partly because of concerns that these laws interfering with liberty of contract could not be justified on the basis of health or morals. In 1923, after the passage of the woman's suffrage amendment, the District of Columbia statute came before the Court in *Adkins* v. *Children's Hospital*. In a 5 to 4 opinion written by Justice George Sutherland, the Supreme Court held that the minimum-wage law for women violated liberty of contract in the due process clause of the Fifth Amendment (the Fifth Amendment applies to the federal government, while the Fourteenth pertains to the states). Sutherland could see no linkage between wages and women's health or morals. He sympathized with the employer who must pay an "exaction for the support of a virtually indigent person for whose condition rests upon him no peculiar responsibility and therefore in effect, arbitrarily shifts to him a burden which if it belongs to anybody belongs to society as a whole. . . . Morality," he continued, "rests upon other considerations than wages; and there is, certainly, no such prevalent connection between the two as to justify a broad attempt to adjust the latter with reference to the former" (261 U.S. 525 [1923]).

The *Adkins* decision was reversed a decade later; the opinions in *Radice* v. *New York* and *Goesaert* v. *Cleary* were more enduring. In *Radice* in 1924, the Court, speaking again through Mr. Justice Sutherland, upheld the constitutionality of a New York statute that prohibited women from being employed from 10 P.M. to 6 A.M. in restaurants in New York City and Buffalo. "The loss of restful night's sleep," Sutherland explained, "cannot be fully made up by sleep in the daytime, especially in busy cities, subject to the disturbances incident to modern life. The injurious consequences were thought by the legislature to bear more heavily against women than men; and considering their more delicate organism, there would seem to be good reason for so thinking" (264 U.S. 292 [1924]). A quarter century later in *Goesaert*, the Court approved a Michigan law that confined the employment of female bartenders to the wives and daughters of male owners. "Michigan," said Mr. Justice Felix Frankfurter, "evidently believes that the oversight assured through ownership of a bar by a barmaid's husband or father, minimizes hazards that may confront a barmaid without such protective oversight." The fact that a male owner may never actually be present and available in the bar did not appear to concern the Court's majority (335 U.S. 464 [1948]).

It was the exclusionary aspect of one-sex protective labor legislation that divided American women in the period after World War I. In 1923 the National Women's Party was able to secure the submission of a proposed Equal Rights Amendment to the United States House of Representatives. The party's leadership conceded that, if the amendment were added to the Federal Constitution, protective labor legislation for women could be placed in serious legal jeopardy. One-sex labor legislation favoring women might be ruled by state and federal courts to discriminate against men, and, therefore, violate the terms of an equal rights amendment. But the party argued that such state laws limited and denied women occupational opportunities; they were not worthy of women's support. Most of the other women's organizations, including the League of Women Voters, the Women's Trade Union League, and the YWCA, dissented; on state as well as federal levels, their representatives testified against equal rights bills, contending that women especially, because of their physical and economic vulnerability, needed the protection afforded by one-sex labor legislation (Lemons 1973).

To some degree the argument over the ERA was neutralized by the passage by Congress in 1938 of the Fair Labor Standards Act. The Fair Labor Standards Act established a minimum wage (initially twenty-five cents an hour) and maximum hours (initially forty-four a week) for both women and men, but excluded farm and domestic workers.

Before it was approved by Congress in 1972, the Equal Rights Amendment was seriously debated in 1946, 1950, 1953 and 1970. On each occasion except for the last, the conflict between the sex equality proposal and protective legislation for women, along with the issue of military service, proved detrimental to the amendment's enactment. In 1964, however, Congress passed an important civil rights act that as a general policy included in Title VII a ban on sex discrimination in employment. Enforced by the Equal Employment Opportunity Commission (EEOC), the new law ultimately undermined the legal viability of one-sex protective labor legislation.

Three cases came before the federal courts in the late 1960s. In *Rosenfeld* v. *Southern Pacific Co.* in 1968, the complainant was the employee with the most seniority to apply for the position as agent-telegrapher; she had been rejected on grounds that, according to California law, she would not be able to work the hours or lift packages above twenty-five pounds, as required by the job. The federal district court in ruling that South Pacific violated Title VII, held that the pertinent state protective laws were invalid under the 1964 Civil Rights Act (293 F.Supp. 1219 [C.D.Cal. 1968]). Again in *Weeks* v. *Southern Bell Telephone and Telegraph Co.*, the Court of Appeals for the Fifth Circuit held that a company policy that disqualified women from positions requiring the lifting of packages over thirty-five pounds violated Title VII (408 F2d. [5th.Cir. 1969]). And finally in *Bowe* v. *Colgate-Palmolive Co.* in 1969, the respondent-company could retain a thirty-five-pound weight-lifting limit, but it would have to be applied to all employees irrespective of sex. "It is best," stated the Seventh Circuit Court of Appeals, "to consider individual qualifications and conditions such as physical capacity and physiological makeup of an individual, climatic conditions, and the manner in which the weight is to be lifted" (416 F.2d. 711 [7th.Cir. 1969]).

The language of these cases, as well as of contemporary EEOC guidelines and decisions, made it clear that Title VII prohibited "stereotyped characterization of the sexes." Under this rubric the state protective laws for women that were in many ways archaic and that either barred them from economic opportunities or conferred upon them benefits not available to men were preempted by the terms of Title VII of the Civil Rights Act of 1964.

*David L. Sterling*

## Bibliography

Blumberg, Dorothy R. 1966. *Florence Kelley, The Making of a Social Pioneer* New York: A.M. Kelly.
Cott, Nancy F. 1987. *The Grounding of Modern Feminism*. New Haven: Yale University Press.
Landau, Eliot A., and Kermit L. Donahoo. 1971. "Sex Discrimination in Employment: A Survey of State and Federal Remedies." *Drake Law Review* 20(June):417–527.
Lemons, J. Stanley. 1973. *The Woman Citizen*. Urbana: University of Illinios Press.
Kessler-Harris, Alice. 1982. *Out of Work*. New York: Oxford University Press.
Mason, Alpheus T. 1946. *Brandeis, A Free Man's Life*. New York: Viking.
Stein, Leon. 1962. *The Triangle Fire*. New York: Carroll and Graff/Quicksilver.
Tentler, Leslie W. 1979. *Wage-Earning Women*. New York: Oxford University Press.
Urofsky, Melvin I. 1981. *Louis D. Brandeis and the Progressive Tradition*. Boston: Little Brown.

## Relevant Cases

*Muller* v. *Oregon*, 208 U.S. 412 (1908)
*Adkins* v. *Children's Hospital*, 261 U.S. 525 (1923)
*Radice* v. *New York*, 264 U.S. 292 (1924)

*Goesaert* v. *Cleary,* 335 U.S. 464 (1948)

*Rosenfeld* v. *Southern Pacific Co.,* 293 F.Supp. 1219 (C.D.Cal. 1968)

*Weeks* v. *Southern Bell Telephone and Telegraph Co.,* 408 F.2d. 228 (5th.Cir. 1969)

*Bowe* v. *Colgate-Palmolive Co.,* 416 F.2d. 711 (7th.Cir. 1969)

## Women's Rights in the Labor Market

"The full-fledged entry of women into the labor market represents one of the most important social changes in the American economy" (National Organization for Women 1985, p. 59). Today, of the fifty-five million workers, 44 percent are women, according to Mary Murphy of the U.S. Women's Bureau, speaking at the Fourth International Interdisciplinary Congress on Women, in New York, June 1990. The makeup of the workforce is constantly changing. Within the next decade a major portion of the workforce will be composed of women, minorities, and immigrants, and highly technological skills will be required.

The first official move toward the legal recognition of women's rights in the labor market was the appointment by President John F. Kennedy of the President's Commission on the Status of Women in 1963. First proposed in 1946, the commission was finally named by Kennedy at the request of Eleanor Roosevelt, one of the prime movers of the struggle for women's legal rights in the workforce. Thanks to the work of this commission, women's rights in the workforce became enacted into law.

The Equal Pay Act of 1963 was the first federal law designed to prevent sex discrimination by forbidding unequal pay for women and men who work in the same place and whose work requires equal skill, effort, and responsibility. Title VII of the Civil Rights Act of 1964 was a major legislative achievement to guarantee equal employment opportunity for women. It prohibits discrimination based on sex, race, color, religion, or national origin in hiring or firing; in wages and fringe benefits; in classifying, referring, assigning, or promoting employees; in facilities; in training, retraining, or apprenticeships; or in any other terms, conditions, or privileges of employment. The Equal Employment Opportunity Commission (EEOC) has responsibility for the enforcement of Title VII. A labor union is considered a person under Title VII and can file a charge on behalf of itself or one of its members. There is only one condition under which Title VII permits job distinction by sex: that is, when gender constitutes a "bona fide occupation qualification" (BFOQ) for a job. The two unquestioned BFOQs are wetnurse and sperm donor. The sex of an employee is rarely a BFOQ, however, and women may no longer be excluded from applying for jobs as fire fighters and police officers, nor may men be prohibited from applying for positions as flight attendants (Biskupic 1991).

There were several roadblocks to women's equal treatment under the law: so-called "protective legislation"; the lack of a common voice; and societal norms that kept women invisible. For example, the custom of a woman's giving up her identity after marriage in accepting "Mrs. John Smith" as her name, and the custom of a woman's surrendering her economic independence in her absence from the pages of the telephone directory, now corrected (in Wisconsin, for example) through the dual listing of both the husband's and wife's first names without charge. This loss of women's identity in marriage may be traced to the law of coverture, in which the woman and man after marriage become one: the man. The influence of this law of coverture may still be seen in our views of women and work. Along with this assumption was the perception that married women did not have to work, a fallacy that has now been overridden by the presence of married women as 60 percent of women in the work force, mandating their equal treatment under the law (Wisconsin Women's Council 1989).

The increase in college education among women produced a growing recognition that the labor market was somehow unfair to women. Through their increasing participation in unions, women have been making their voices heard. There has been a rapid unionization of the public sector (female, black, and white-collar workers). In 1984 women made up nearly half of all public-sector unions. In the teaching profession, whereas only one-quarter of all teachers were unionized in 1974, more than half were in 1980, and they have shown their power to effect legal changes in the labor market. For example, a landmark case was the one against Colgate Palmolive, recorded in "Jane Crow and the Law" by Mary Eastwood (1974). The issue of equal pay for work of comparable value can create a powerful organizing issue by raising women's expectations, self-esteem, and bargaining skills. Claims about the undervaluation of female-dominated jobs helped unionize clerical and technical staff, mobilize a strike, and secure substantial raises as a consequence. National journals and congressional reports have recorded the mounting concern for correcting existing bias in the workplace regarding sexual harassment, pregnancy, fetal vulnerability, hiring termination policies, age discrimination, and handicap discrimination. A landmark decision by the Supreme Court was handed down in the *Auto Workers* v. *Johnson Controls, Inc.* (March 20, 1991): Title VII as amended by the Pregnancy Discrimination Act forbids sex-specific fetal protection policies. The Court said that the respondent's professed concerns about the welfare of the next generation do not suffice to establish a BFOQ of female sterility. Title VII mandates that decisions about the welfare of future children be left to the parents who conceive, bear, support, and raise them rather than to the employers who hire these parents or the courts. Cases of women who underwent sterilization in order to keep their jobs are recorded by Susan Faludi in her investigation of the biases against women in the workforce (Faludi 1991).

Despite the equal-opportunity legislation of the past twenty-five years, women's status in the workplace remains far from equal. Women workers earn 65 percent of the annual salary of men workers, the same as in 1955 (Rohde 1991).

Sexual harassment in the workplace has been recognized as sex discrimination in employment under Title VII of the Civil Rights Act of 1964 and the Equal Protection clause of the Fourteenth Amendment (MacKinnon 1979, p. 6).

National networks for working women, such as the Congress of Labor Union Women (CLUW) and Nine to Five, are working to effect needed changes in such areas as comparable worth, occupational health and safety, job training and placement, firing and unemployment insurance, and social security and pension laws. By greater involvement in unions and by such networking in nationwide coalitions, women may in the future effect a real change in the distribution of income, as well as in their self-identification as independent persons regardless of their marital status.

*Mary Ann Rossi*

## Bibliography

Ariel, Joan, Ellen Broidy, and Susan Searing. 1985. *Women's Legal Rights in the United States: A Selective Bibliography*. Pp. 22–25. Chicago and London: American Library Association.

Biskupic, Joan. 1991. "The 'Civil Rights and Women's Equity' Act . . . A Look at Its Major Provisions." *Congressional Quarterly Weekly Report* (June 8)49:1500–01.

Chaison, Gary N., and P. Andiappan. 1989. "An Analysis of the Barriers to Women Becoming Local Union Officers" in *Journal of Labor Research* (Spring)10:149–62.

Drogin, Bob. 1984. "Comparable Worth at Center of Yale Strike" *L.A. Times,* November 18:I, 5.

Eastwood, Mary. 1974. "Jane Crow and the Law." *George Washington Law Review.*

Faludi, Susan. 1991. *Backlash: The Undeclared War against American Women.* New York: Crown.

Goldin, Claudia Dale. 1990. *Understanding the Gender Gap: An Economic History of American Women.* New York: Oxford.

MacKinnon, Catherine. 1979. *Sexual Harassment of Working Women: A Case of Sex Discrimination.* New Haven: Yale University Press.

National Organization for Women, Legal Defense and Education Fund, and Dr. Renee Cherow-O'Leary. 1985. *The State-by-State Guide to Women's Legal Rights.* New York: McGraw-Hill.

Rohde, Deborah L. 1991. "The 'No-Problem' Problem: Feminist Challenges and Cultural Change." *Yale Law Journal* 100:1731–93.

Wisconsin Women's Council and State Bar of Wisconsin. 1989. *Wisconsin Women and the Law.* Milwaukee Bar Assn. Foundation.

## Relevant Cases

*Autoworkers* v. *Johnson Controls, Inc.* In *U.S. Supreme Court Bulletin 1990–1991 Term.* Vol. 1 (Commerce Clearing House, Inc.: Chicago, 1991), B 1159 ff.

## Affirmative Action

As women have become more actively involved as members of the workforce, governments have enacted legislation (for example, Title VII of the Civil Rights Act) to prohibit sexual discrimination in selection, promotion, and other personnel decisions. In addition, to remedy inequities and to increase the employment opportunities for women (as well as other targeted groups), governments have also promoted Affirmative Action Programs (AAPs). Within the context of organizational practices, AAPs may result in targeting recruitment efforts at females, developing special selection procedures, providing special training opportunities, as well as setting goals and timetables to increase the participation of women within the organization. In spite of the worthy social goals of AAPs, they may have a number of negative consequences. Essentially, the negative consequences stem from the fact that AAPs create circumstances wherein people conclude that personnel decisions have been based on sex as opposed to merit (Crosby and Clayton 1990; Kleiman and Faley 1988). This article reviews the research results concerning the consequences of sex-based personnel decisions in terms of how they influence the way people view a woman and the job she does, and how women who benefit from sex-based selection may suffer in terms of how they view themselves. In addition, the review will examine research regarding factors that may serve to counter the negative effects of AAPs. The results of these studies are important for organizations and working women because they provide information that can be used in developing and implementing AAPs to their best advantage. The interested reader should consult Blanchard and Crosby

(1989) for discussions of other aspects of AAPs (such as AAPs and the courts, the justice of AAPs) and Carr-Ruffino et al. (1991), which provide a thorough overview of AAPs from a legislative perspective.

### Observers' Responses to Sex-Based Selection

One focus of AAP research has examined the influence of sex-based preferential selection on observers' perceptions of both the benefactor's job and the beneficiary. For example, when information indicated that female managers had secured their positions because of legal requirements to place more women in the position, the job the women held was devalued, viewed as less interesting, and less prestigious by others, especially males (Heilman and Herlihy 1984; Johnson 1990). Another study examined the influence of sex-based preferential selection on the reactions of the subordinate (Jacobson and Koch 1977). It was found that, when sex was the basis for appointing a woman as the leader, male subordinates blamed the woman more for failure and gave her less credit for success. In contrast, when male subordinates thought the woman was made leader on the basis of her qualifications, she was blamed less for failure and given more credit for success. Thus, the work women do and their performance as leaders is denigrated by others when they believe that the women have benefited from sex-based preferential selection.

### Sex-Based Selection and the Beneficiary

Other studies have examined the influence of sex-based selection on women themselves. In particular, Madeline Heilman and her associates have undertaken a series of studies examining the influence of sex-based selection on women's self-perceptions. In a laboratory experiment, Heilman et al. (1987) created a situation where women were selected as leaders either because of merit or because they were female. Subsequently, after overseeing the work of a subordinate, women who were selected on the basis of their sex rated themselves lower in their leadership abilities. These women also gave themselves lower performance ratings in comparison to women who thought they had been selected as leaders on the basis of merit. As well, preferentially selected women were less interested in persisting in the leadership role. Corroborating results were obtained in a follow-up study (Heilman et al. 1990). Thus, when women believe that they have been selected as leaders because they are females they develop less favorable images of themselves in terms of their competence as leaders.

Heilman et al. (1991) examined how the negative self-perceptions of sex-based selection can influence important behaviors. In this study they found that when given the choice of engaging a challenging versus unchallenging task, women assigned to be managers because they were female selected the less challenging task. This is an important finding because it indicates that preferential selection on the basis of sex may encourage women to shy away from the types of tasks and assignments that would be important for establishing their credentials and competence.

Finally, the results of field studies have provided results that parallel the laboratory findings (Chacko 1982; Heilman et al. 1992). For instance, Chacko studied women who felt that they had obtained a managerial position because they were female. These women experienced a number of negative reactions. In particular, the women reported less satisfaction with their work as well as less satisfaction with their supervisors and their co-workers. These women also reported more role conflict and role ambiguity, and they were less committed to their organizations.

## Counterbalancing Factors

Thus, sex-based preferential selection, as may be seen to occur with AAPs, may produce a number of negative consequences. Specifically, others (that is, observers and subordinates) may think less well of women who benefit from sex-based selection, and the women themselves may think less well of themselves. However, research indicates that these negative outcomes can be offset if merit is also highlighted as a reason for selecting a woman. For instance, as noted previously, Jacobson and Koch (1977) found that male subordinates gave a female leader credit for success and did not blame her excessively for failure when they thought she had been selected on the basis of merit. Similarly, Heilman et al. (1990, 1991) found that the negative consequences of sex-based preferential selection are mediated by a woman's self-confidence. For instance, when a woman was selected to be a leader on the basis of her sex, but, at the same time, it was made apparent that she was also well qualified for the position (in terms of her aptitude for leadership), then there was no evidence of the negative effects associated with being selected solely on the basis of sex.

Other research has found that people were less opposed to AAPs when the program involves "removing obstacles" versus providing "preferential treatment" (Tougas and Veilleux 1988, 1989). In a similar way, favorable reactions to AAPs are also more likely when people feel AA is fair or involves procedures that are fair (Nacoste 1987, 1989). Thus, AAPs may not inevitably have negative effects. Information on a woman's qualifications and feeling that the AAP is just or fair, in that it does not make preferential treatment salient, may curtail the potential for negative effects.

Therefore, in summary, AAPs and sex-based preferential selection may result in negative consequences. This would seem to be most apt to occur if sex is seen as the primary reason for the decision. However, a number of factors may mitigate the potential for negative consequences. Specifically, by emphasizing the role of merit and the fairness of the procedure, a woman who benefits from an AAP, and those with whom she must work, may be less likely to react negatively to actions stemming from the AAP. Subsequent research must begin to examine ways to engineer the public image of AAP decisions in order to minimize the perception that a woman's sex was the primary reason for a decision in her favor.

*Russel J. Summers*

## Bibliography

Blanchard F.A., and F.J. Crosby, eds. 1989. *Affirmative Action In Perspective*. New York: Springer-Verlag.

Carr-Ruffino, N., J.E. Baack, C. Flipper, K. Hunter-Sloan, and C. Olivolo. 1991. "Legal Aspects of Women's Advancement: Affirmative Action, Family Leave, and Dependent Care Law." In *Womanpower: Managing in Times of Demographic Turbulence*, edited by U. Sekaran and F.T.L. Leong, pp. 113–57. Newbury Park, Calif.: Sage.

Chacko, T.I. 1982. "Women and Equal Employment Opportunity: Some Unintended Effects." *Journal of Applied Psychology* 67:119–23.

Crosby, F., and S. Clayton. 1990. "Affirmative Action and the Issue of Expectancies." *Journal of Social Issues* 46:61–79.

Heilman, M.E., C.J. Block, and J.A. Lucas. 1992. "Presumed Incompetent? Stigmatization and Affirmative Action Efforts." *Journal of Applied Psychology* 77:536–44.

Heilman, M.E., and J.M. Herlihy. 1984. "Affirmative Action, Negative Reaction? Some Moderating Conditions." *Organizational Behavior and Human Performance* 33:204–13.

Heilman, M.E., J.A. Lucas, and S.R. Kaplow. 1990. "Self-Derogating Consequences of Sex-Based Preferential Selection: The Moderating Role of Initial Self-Confidence." *Organizational Behavior and Human Decision Making* 46:202–16.

Heilman, M.E., J.C. Rivero, and J.F. Brett. 1991. "Skirting the Competence Issue: Effects of Sex-Based Preferential Selection on Task Choices of Women and Men." *Journal of Applied Psychology* 76:99–105.

Heilman, M.E., M.C. Simon, and D.P. Repper. 1987. "Intentionally Favored, Unintentionally Harmed? Impact of Sex-Based Preferential Selection on Self-Perceptions and Self-Evaluations." *Journal of Applied Psychology* 72:62–68.

Jacobson, M.B., and W. Koch. 1977. "Women as Leaders: Performance Evaluation as a Function of Method of Leader Selection." *Organizational Behavior and Human Performance* 20:149–57.

Johnson, R.D. 1990. "The Influence of Legal Mandates on the Acceptance of Women as Professionals." *Journal of Social Psychology* 130:39–46.

Kleiman, L.S., and R.H. Faley. 1988. "Voluntary Affirmative Action and Preferential Treatment: Legal and Research Implications." *Personnel Psychology* 41:481–96.

Nacoste, R.W. 1989. "Affirmative Action and Self-Evaluation." In *Affirmative Action in Perspective*, edited by F.A. Blanchard and F.J. Crosby, pp. 103–9. New York: Springer-Verlag.

———. 1987. "But Do They Care about Fairness? The Dynamics of Preferential Treatment and Minority Interest." *Basic and Applied Social Psychology* 8:177–91.

Tougas, F., and F. Veilleux. 1988. "The Influence of Identification, Collective Relative Deprivation, and Procedure of Implementation on Women's Response to Affirmative Action: A Causal Modeling Approach." *Canadian Journal of Behavioral Science* 20:15–28.

Tougas, F., and F. Veilleux. 1989. "Who Likes Affirmative Action: Attitudinal Processes among Men and Women." In *Affirmative Action in Perspective*, edited by F.A. Blanchard and F.J. Crosby, pp. 111–24. New York: Springer-Verlag.

## Sexual Harassment

The results of surveys suggest that sexual harassment is not an unusual experience for working women. A review of the results of several surveys reported that 42 to 90 percent of working women surveyed reported that they had encountered some form of sexual harassment on the job. This situation is unacceptable because the presence of sexual harassment on the job serves to create a working environment that is intimidating and inhospitable to women. Thus, organizations are concerned with eliminating sexual harassment because of the detrimental effects it has on those who are the victims. However, organizations must also be concerned with eliminating sexual harassment because it is illegal. Organizations that permit sexual harassment in the workplace face the possibility of legal action that may be costly and potentially damaging to the organization's public image (Terpstra and Baker 1988). This article outlines the research themes of the sexual harassment literature. For this, research is reviewed in relation to explanatory models of sexual harassment, decision-making regarding complaints and incidents of sexual harassment, and victim reactions.

### Models of Sexual Harassment

From the larger conceptual perspective, several explanatory models of sexual harassment have been proposed. For instance, the biological model suggests that sexual harassment is unintentional because it is simply the outcome of the biologically based sexual attraction between people. In contrast, the organizational model contends that sexual harassment occurs because of the nature of organizations in terms of their climate, hierarchical relationships, and the differences in power among organizational members. In essence this model suggests that sexual harassment occurs because the opportunity is provided by the structural characteristics of organizations. Finally, the sociocultural model proposes that sexual harassment is a reflection of the fact that society values men more than women and bestows upon men a superior position in terms of power and status. In this model sexual harassment occurs when men attempt to maintain their dominance over women. The interested reader should consult Tangri, et al. (1982) for a succinct review of these three models of sexual harassment as well as an analysis of the support for each of the models based on data from a survey conducted by the U.S. Merit Systems Protection Board (1981).

However, the sexual harassment model with greatest currency within the field of organizational behavior is the sex-role spillover model (Gutek and Dunwoody 1987; Gutek and Morasch 1982). This model suggests that sexual harassment occurs when men fail to separate a woman's role as a worker from her sexual role. In other words, the model proposes that the sex-role "spills over" into the work situation. Although sex-role spillover may occur for various reasons, the male-female sex ratio in a work situation has been singled out as particularly important. The sex ratio is important because, when the ratio is skewed in favor of men (that is, few women co-workers), it is less likely that men will have the opportunity to interact with a woman as a co-worker, and, as a result, it is more likely that women workers will be conceptualized and treated in accordance with traditional, stereotypic notions that will include the sex role. Alternatively, if a particular occupation is dominated by women it is also likely that there will be sex-role spillover. In this case it occurs because the work will be viewed, by men and women alike, as the type of work that a "typical" woman would do. When the notion of a typical woman is invoked it inevitably includes the sex role.

Considerable evidence has been obtained to support the sex-role spillover model (see Gutek 1985; Gutek and Morasch 1982; Konrad and Gutek 1986). For example, Gutek (1985) found that, in comparison to the average working woman, women employed in nontraditional jobs, where most workers are males, were more apt to feel that sexual harassment was a problem. This is in agreement with the model because it suggests that male co-workers' interactions with female co-workers included behaviors that were based upon sex-role expectations. These behaviors would be noticed by female co-workers because they would be aware of the fact that they were being treated differently relative to their male co-workers. Gutek also found evidence to support the prediction that there would be sex-role spillover in traditionally female occupations. Women in these occupations indicated higher levels of sexual talk and joking in their work situations, but, at the same time, reported somewhat lower levels of sexual harassment. This finding also agrees with the model because it indicates that these women accepted the sexualization of the work environment. They would accept it because they accept the sex role as part of their work role because their work is classified as women's work.

The development and testing of explanatory models is useful because it helps to identify the causal factors involved in sexual harassment. As a result steps may be taken in attempting to deal with the problem. For example, the sex-role spillover model suggests that to eliminate the problem more women need to be integrated into nontraditional workplaces. Then male co-workers will become more familiar with women as individuals and co-workers as opposed to thinking of them in stereotypic terms. As a result, sexual harassment should be less likely. However, another approach to eliminating sexual harassment has focused on more short-term concerns relating to judging complaints of sexual harassment.

### Judging Complaints of Sexual Harassment

Research concerning the process of judging sexual harassment is related to the problem of defining sexual harassment. One of the findings of this research is that many factors can influence people's interpretations of social-sexual behavior. The most important of these seems to be the sex of the judge. For example, Konrad and Gutek (1986) found that 67 percent of the males surveyed but only 17 percent of the females surveyed said they would be flattered by sexual overtures at work. Not surprisingly, men were also more likely (54 percent) than women (44.7 percent) to agree with the suggestion that women who are sexually propositioned at work probably did something to bring it about. This research served as a basis for investigations of the processes involved in making decisions in regard to complaints/incidents of sexual harassment.

This area of research has sought to identify the factors that influence judgments of the responsibility of the people involved in a complaint of sexual harassment (see Popovich et al. 1986; Pryor and Day 1988). In addition, more recently, this research has examined the consequences of these judgments (that is, guilt, innocence) as determinants of decisions concerning discipline (Summers 1991; Thomann and Wiener 1987). For instance, Thomann and Wiener (1987) found that decision-makers' judgments of the responsibility of the perpetrator were determined by their assessments of the extent to which they were certain that sexual harassment had physically taken place and, also, the extent to which the harassment had been intentional. Subsequently, these judgments were important in determining the level of discipline suggested. This information can be used in training decision-makers to be sensitive to the sort of biases that may come into play in processing complaints of sexual harassment, and ensure that an organizational response acts as a deterrent (Gutek 1989).

### Victim Responses to Sexual Harassment

Finally, a third aspect of the sexual harassment research has dealt with victims' responses to the harassment. One approach has focused on the negative consequences that victims experience. For instance, Crull (1982) studied the emotional reactions of women who had experienced sexual harassment at work. It was found that women who had been the victims of workplace sexual harassment subsequently experienced negative stress reactions. Similarly, Jensen and Gutek (1982) found that women who had experienced sexual harassment at work reported negative emotional reactions. However, these researchers also found that these negative emotional reactions had negative implications for work behavior. In particular, they found that the victims of sexual harassment were less motivated in relation to their work and experienced difficulties in concentrating on their work responsibilities. For a thorough overview of the impact sexual harassment has on victims in terms of their emotional, cognitive, and behavioral dispositions the interested reader should consult Paludi's work (1991) on sexual harassment in universities. And, although not specifically dealing with sexual harassment, Schroedel's text (1985) on the experiences of women in the trades provides singularly rich descriptions of how women feel when they are the target of sexual harassment.

A complementary focus to this research theme has centered on coping responses to sexual harassment. This stream of research is best typified by the work of Baker and Terpstra et al. (1990). The strategy of these researchers is to present people with examples of sexual harassment and ask them to indicate how they would respond to the situation if they were the person harassed. This line of research has been pursued because of the feeling that understanding how people would react to sexual harassment provides information that can be used in training. Thus, knowing that sexually propositioning a woman may encourage her to make a formal complaint of sexual harassment may serve to discourage men from doing so. By being aware of the negative consequences of various types of sociosexual behavior at work men may be more circumspect in their actions.

In summary, organizations are concerned with sexual harassment because of the negative effects that it produces, for both the organization and the victim. Research on sexual harassment has focused on three areas: (a) models of sexual harassment; (b) decision-making relating to complaints or incidents of sexual harassment; and (c) people's reactions to being sexually harassed. The information gained from these research efforts is useful in understanding the issues surrounding sexual harassment. However, the shortcoming in the literature to date is that little research has focused on the application of research findings. In other words, there is little information pertaining to what is effective in making people more sensitive to the issues surrounding sexual harassment or the deterrent effect of particular policies. Although there are suggestions for what organizations must do to deal with sexual harassment (Gutek 1989; Powell 1988), there is little empirical research to confirm these suggestions. It is hoped that future research will address this gap in the literature.

*Russel J. Summers*

## Bibliography

Baker, D.D., D.E. Terpstra, and K. Larntz. 1990. "The Influence of Individual Characteristics and Severity of Sexually Harassing Behavior on Reactions to Sexual Harassment." *Sex Roles* 22:305–25.

Crull, P. 1982. "The Effects of Sexual Harassment on the Job: Implications for Counselling." *American Journal of Orthopsychiatry* 52:539–43.

Gutek, B.A. 1985. *Sex and the Workplace.* San Francisco: Jossey-Bass.

———. 1989. "Sexuality in the Workplace: Key Issues in Social Research and Organizational Practice." In *The Sexuality of Organization,* edited by J. Hearn, D.L. Sheppard, P. Tancred-Sheriff, and G. Burrell. London: Sage.

Gutek, B.A., and V. Dunwoody. 1987. "Understanding Sex in the Workplace and Its Effects on Women, Men, and Organizations." In *Women and Work: An Annual Review.* Vol. 2, edited by A.H. Stromberg, L. Larwood, and B.A. Gutek. Newbury Park, Calif.: Sage.

Gutek, B.A., and B. Morasch. 1982. "Sex-Ratios, Sex-Role Spillover, and Sexual Harassment of Women at Work." *Journal of Social Issues* 38:55–74.

Jensen, J.W., and B.A. Gutek. 1982. "Attributions and Assignment of Responsibility in Sexual Harassment." *Journal of Social Issues* 38:121–36.

Konrad, A.M., and B.A. Gutek. 1986. "Impact of Work Experiences on Attitudes toward Sexual Harassment." *Administrative Science Quarterly* 31:422–38.

Paludi, M., ed. 1991. *Ivory Power: Sexual Harassment on Campus.* Albany: State University of New York Press.

Popovich, P.M., B.J. Licata, D. Nokovich, T. Martelli, and S. Zoloty. 1986. "Assessing the Incidence and Perceptions of Sexual Harassment Behaviors among American Undergraduates." *Journal of Psychology* 120:387–96.

Powell, G.N. 1988. *Women and Men in Management*. Newbury Park, Calif.: Sage.

Pryor, J.B., and J.D. Day. 1988. "Interpretations of Sexual Harassment: An Attributional Analysis." *Sex Roles* 18:405–17.

Schroedel, J.R. 1985. *Alone in a Crowd: Women in the Trades Tell Their Stories*. Philadelphia: Temple University Press.

Summers, R.J. 1991. "Determinants of Judgments of and Responses to a Complaint of Sexual Harassment." *Sex Roles* 25:381–94.

Tangri, S., M.R. Burt, and L.B. Johnson. 1982. "Sexual Harassment at Work: Three Explanatory Models." *Journal of Social Issues* 38(4):55–74.

Terpstra, David E., and Douglas D. Baker. 1988. "Outcomes of Sexual Harassment Charges." *Academy of Management Journal* 31:185–94.

Thomann, D.A., and R.L. Wiener. 1987. "Physical and Psychological Causality as Determinants of Culpability in Sexual Harassment Cases." *Sex Roles* 17:573–91.

U.S. Merit Systems Protection Board. 1981. *Sexual Harassment in the Federal Workplace*. Washington D.C.: Office of Merit Systems Review and Studies.

## Sexual Harassment: Legal and Policy Issues

Research over the past twenty years indicates that sexual harassment is a frequent problem in work organizations and that it can have debilitating physical, emotional, and economic effects on its victims (Terpstra and Baker 1991). In spite of the serious negative effects of sexual harassment, there was a very limited legal foundation outlawing it until the passage of the Civil Rights Act of 1964 (MacKinnon 1979). Even with that legislation, it was not until 1977 that a court found sexual harassment to be actionable under Title VII of the law (Coles 1985). Since that time the Equal Employment Opportunity Commission (EEOC)(1980) has issued a definition of sexual harassment and the courts have attempted to clarify the types of behaviors that are considered to be illegal. In spite of this evolution of the law, there has continued to be confusion over what constitutes sexual harassment and what is a justifiable defense for employers (Cohen 1987). In 1986, the Supreme Court heard its first sexual harassment case and upheld the legality of bringing such a suit under Title VII, but left open the question of what constitutes a reasonable defense for employers (Hauck and Pearce 1987). In this increasingly litigious environment many employers have instituted policies banning harassment in the workplace. The effectiveness of such policies and the legal precedence for sexual harassment cases are discussed below.

Based upon Title VII, the EEOC (1980) defined sexual harassment as: "Unwelcome sexual advances, requests for sexual favors and other verbal or physical conduct of a sexual nature when submission to such conduct is made either explicitly or implicitly a term or condition of an individual's employment; submission to or rejection of such conduct by an individual is used as the basis for employment decisions affecting the individual; or such conduct has the purpose or effect of unreasonably interfering with an individual's work performance or creating an intimidating, hostile, or offensive working environment."

In an unusual sequence of events, the EEOC issued these guidelines sixteen years after the Civil Rights Act of 1964 was enacted into law and three years after the first courts had upheld the application of Title VII to sexual harassment cases. The guidelines contain two general categories of sexual harassment (Faley 1982). The first is often referred to as the Tangible Benefits Theory and deals with situations in which victims suffer direct employment repercussions from the offensive behaviors. The second category refers to the Atmosphere of Discrimination Theory, in which victims suffer psychological harm from the harassing work climate. In spite of the guidelines, there have continued to be questions about what constitutes sexual harassment under the Atmosphere of Discrimination Theory.

In 1986 the U.S. Supreme Court clarified some of these issues when it decided its first sexual harassment case, *Meritor Savings Bank* v. *Vinson*. This was a complex case in which the plaintiff experienced a sexually harassing work environment, but the company argued that Vinson had voluntarily had sexual intercourse with the employer's representative on numerous occasions. The Court decided for the plaintiff, upholding the application of Title VII to sexual harassment cases, including those in which the plaintiff had not suffered direct economic loss. Thus, the Court found that an intimidating, hostile, or offensive work environment constitutes sexual harassment. Further, the Court found that the determination of whether sexual harassment occurred is not based on whether the plaintiff voluntarily tolerated sexual advances, but on whether these advances were welcome or not (Hauck and Pearce 1987). However it was left unclear as to what the employer's liability is in such cases.

Before complainants take sexual harassment cases to the Federal Courts, they must first pass over a number of procedural hurdles. First, a complaint must be made to an EEO agent. The agent then meets with the complainant and counsels the individual as to what might be done. If the facts merit proceeding, a charge is filed and the agent holds a fact-finding conference with the involved parties. If no settlement can be reached at this point, the EEOC may file a lawsuit in Federal District Court (a relatively rare occurrence) or issue a "Right to Sue Letter" that allows the plaintiff to file a lawsuit on his/her own behalf.

Subsequent research indicates that only a small proportion of these cases are won by the complainants, either in state level EEO agencies or the federal courts. For example, of the cases filed with the Illinois Department of Human Rights over a two-year period, only 29 percent were settled in favor of the complainants (Terpstra and Baker 1988). Similarly, Terpstra and Baker's investigation (1992) of federal court cases indicates that 38 percent were decided in favor of the complainants. For complainants to have a high probability of winning, the sexual harassment needed to be severe, management needed to have been notified of the incident(s), subsequently taking no action regarding the problem, and the complainants needed to have had documents and witnesses to support their complaints. Even if complainants do win such cases, the settlements are often quite meager. For example, the average award by the Illinois Department of Human Rights was $3,234 (Terpstra and Baker 1988). Because of the effort involved in these many procedural steps and the limited resulting relief, many harassment victims have felt pursuing such avenues of redress are not worth the trouble (U.S. Merit Systems Protection Board 1981).

To prevent the need for the invocation of such procedures and to prevent the related suffering of sexual harassment victims, organizations need to develop written policies for acceptable work behavior and issue them to all existing and new employees (Powell 1988). Further, training programs should be offered to managers as to what is considered sexual harassment, how individual and situational factors may affect its occurrence, and what should be done if it should arise. However, Jensen and Gutek (1982) argue that just illustrating the types of forbidden behavior to employees may not be sufficient because of individuals' ingrained belief systems. They suggest that changing workers' fundamental sex-role attitudes may ultimately be necessary to eliminate harassment. Although such attitude change may be difficult in practice, Tangri et al.'s research (1982) suggests that the organizational climate and a responsible management can influence the frequency of harassing behaviors.

If sexual harassment does occur, clear policies need to exist to deal with it. Powell (1988) suggests a five-step process whereby the organization's actions are measured against the severity of the harassment. The first step is to interview the parties involved, including any witnesses that may have relevant information. Next, personnel files should be checked to see if the parties had conflicted in the past or their work performance had recent discrepancies. Based upon this information, the severity of the offense should be determined. In addition, the probability that the offense actually occurred should be determined. If, after following the preceding four steps, it is determined that a severe case of harassment has occurred, strong actions, such as dismissal or suspension, should be taken. If a mild form of harassment occurred, less drastic steps should be applied, such as a verbal warning.

As many harassment studies indicate, most individuals are reluctant to report sexual harassment incidents and invoke a formal procedure as described above, even when they are familiar with the organizational policies. Typically, individuals attempt to deal with the harassment themselves by ignoring the behavior. However, as the findings from the U.S. Merit Systems Protection Board (1981 and 1988) studies indicate, there are other, more effective responses. One of the best mechanisms may be simply to ask the harasser to stop the behavior. Rowe (1981) suggests a slightly more assertive response in which a victim, accompanied by a witness, delivers a letter to the harasser detailing the offensive behavior and stating what needs to be done to rectify the situation.

Unfortunately, there is very limited empirical evidence to suggest what types of reactions are most effective in stopping various types of harassing behaviors under varying circumstances (U.S. Merit Systems Protection Board 1981). Further, the U.S. Merit Systems Protection Board's survey (1988) found that government sexual harassment training programs had no effect on the rates of harassment. Thus, harassment continues to be a common organizational problem in which serious harm is done to victims. In turn the victims and employers are faced with an arduous and uncertain legal landscape.

*Douglas D. Baker*
*Dana L. Stover*

## Bibliography

Cohen, Cynthia. 1987. "Legal Dilemmas in Sexual Harassment Cases." *Labor Law Journal* (November) 38:681–88.

Coles, Frances S. 1985. "Sexual Harassment: Complainant Definitions and Agency Responses." *Labor Law Journal* (June) 36:369–76.

Equal Employment Opportunity Commission. 1980. "Discrimination Because of Sex under Title VII of the Civil Rights Act of 1964, as Amended; Adoption of Interim Interpretive Guidelines." *Federal Register* 45:25024–25.

Faley, R.H. 1982. "Sexual Harassment: A Critical Review of Legal Cases with General Principles and Preventive Measures." *Personnel Psychology* 35:583–600.

Hauck, Vern E., and Thomas Pearce. 1987. "Vinson: Sexual Harassment and Employer Response." *Labor Law Journal* (December):770–75.

Jensen, I., and B. Gutek. 1982. "Attributions and Assignment of Responsibility in Sexual Harassment." *Journal of Social Issues* 38(4):121–36.

MacKinnon, Catharine. 1979. *Sexual Harassment of Working Women: A Case of Sex Discrimination*. New Haven: Yale University Press.

Powell, Gary N. 1988. *Women and Men in Management*. Newbury Park, Calif.: Sage.

Rowe, M.P. 1981. "Dealing with Sexual Harassment." *Harvard Business Review* 59(3):42–46.

Tangri, S., M.R. Burt, and L.B. Johnson. 1982. "Sexual Harassment at Work: Three Explanatory Models." *Journal of Social Issues* 38(4):55–74.

Terpstra, David E., and Douglas D. Baker. 1992. "The Outcomes of Federal Court Decisions on Sexual Harassment." *Academy of Management Journal* 35(1):181–90.

———. 1988. "Outcomes of Sexual Harassment Charges." *Academy of Management Journal* 31:185–94.

———. 1991. "Sexual Harassment at Work: The Psychosocial Issues." In *Vulnerable Workers: Psychosocial and Legal Issues*, edited by M.J. Davidson and J. Earnshaw. Chichester, England: John Wiley and Sons.

U.S. Merit Systems Protection Board. 1981. *Sexual Harassment in the Federal Workplace: Is It a Problem?* Washington D.C.: U.S. Government Printing Office.

———. 1988. *Sexual Harassment in the Federal Government: An Update*. Washington D.C.: U.S. Government Printing Office.

### Relevant Cases

*Meritor Savings Bank v. Vinson,* 106 SCt. 2399 (1986).

## Family Support Act

The Family Support Act (FSA) of 1988 has been described as the most significant change in the American welfare system in the past fifty years. Changes in lifestyle choices and concerns about persistent poverty and welfare dependency led to this effort to transform the welfare system into a program to help families on public assistance to become self-sufficient, rather than simply to provide cash assistance. At the same time, however, it represents yet another attempt to improve the system through incremental, not large-scale, change.

FSA changes the existing Aid to Families with Dependent Children (AFDC) program, established by the Social Security Act of 1935 to provide cash welfare payments to single-parent families. As originally designed, AFDC provided widowed mothers with benefits so that they could stay at home to raise their children. In time, however, the primary recipients became families in which the mothers were separated, divorced, or never married (Smith et al. 1990, pp. 45–46).

By the mid 1980s, a combination of forces created a climate for change. With more than one-half of all married women with children under six employed outside the home, many Americans found it less acceptable for mothers on public assistance to be at home while other mothers worked. Interest in welfare-to-work programs grew and became a factor behind passage of the Family Support Act in 1988. The Omnibus Budget Reconciliation Act of 1981 had offered states the opportunity to develop programs emphasizing job search and work experience for AFDC recipients (Burkhart 1991). The Work Incentive Program (WIN), a forerunner of the current program, required most AFDC recipients with children over the age of six to register for the program.

At the same time, the public welfare system was widely criticized for creating long-term dependence and offering recipients few opportunities to become economically self-sufficient. FSA also emerged because government representatives, policy analysts, and activists could not agree on what to do about the steady increase in the number of children growing up in poverty, especially in families headed by single parents. According to the Census Bureau, the poverty rate for children rose to 20.6 percent in 1990, compared with 16.6 percent in 1967. These numbers translate into huge, long-term costs for government at the federal, state, and local levels. The country's need for a productive workforce and the potential pool of labor represented by unemployed welfare recipients were other forces for changing the welfare system.

### Provisions of the Family Support Act

The FSA redefines the relationship between the welfare system and families as one of "mutual obligations." A major goal is to foster self-sufficiency. The Job Opportunities and Basic Skills Training Program (JOBS) provides educational and employment-related activities and supportive services to AFDC recipients who need them. In return, public assistance recipients are expected to work toward economic independence, either through employment or participation in educational or training activities. Government's role is to provide the incentives and services to enable participants to find and retain jobs.

Concerns about the rising proportion of children growing up in poverty led to the second major thrust of FSA, the requirement that noncustodial parents assume some responsibility for their children's well-being and contribute to their support. The underlying premise is that both parents should play a role in child support, whether or not they live in the same household (Burkhart 1991, p.13). These child-support provisions have far-reaching effects, since they cover all children in families eligible for child support, not just AFDC children.

Moreover, the act represents a move toward assisting two-parent families with an unemployed adult member. In the past, states were permitted to provide benefits to two-parent families with incomes under the eligibility levels set by states for families in which the principal earner is unemployed. They now are required to do so under FSA.

These two major concerns, having noncustodial parents assume responsibility for the economic security of their children and fostering economic self-sufficiency of participants, are reflected in the first two titles of the act. Title I deals with child support and establishment of paternity, while Title II contains the provisions of the JOBS program. Title III deals with supportive services for families, and Title IV contains related AFDC amendments, including the requirement that all states set up an AFDC-Unemployed Parent (UP) program by October of 1990. Title V is concerned with demonstration projects, ranging from encouraging innovative education and training for children to funding between five and ten programs to expand the number of job opportunities available to poor families (Smith et al. 1990, pp.47–53).

### Child Support and Establishment of Paternity

This title of FSA extends preexisting amendments to the Social Security Act with regard to child-support payment collection. To summarize its major points briefly: In 1984, legislation had required all states to develop guidelines for setting child-support awards. These amendments also required states to withhold income for child support when a one-month lapse in payments had occurred. In November of 1990, states were required to begin wage withholding in child support orders for all cases handled by the Office of Child Support Enforcement. By 1994, states were to require immediate wage withholding for all support orders, with exceptions made only for good cause or alternative arrangements agreed to by both parties (Smith et al. 1990, p.47). The 1984 guidelines are binding in determining child-support award amounts, unless a written finding states that these would be unjust or inappropriate.

As regards paternity, starting in fiscal year 1991 states are penalized for not establishing paternity in a given proportion of cases of children born out of wedlock who receive AFDC or Title IV-D services. Paternity action can be taken up to a child's eighteenth birthday. The federal government will assume 90 percent of state costs involved in laboratory tests to establish paternity. However, AFDC recipients do not profit from the child-support payments collected, since they must assign all but fifty dollars monthly to the states. They receive monthly or quarterly notices of the amount collected.

**Job Training**

Title II of the act requires that all states establish a JOBS program to provide education, training, and needed support services for public assistance recipients with children. The focus is on the hardest to serve and those most likely to exhibit long-term dependency. The caretaker of a child over three years (or, at a state's discretion, over one year), is required to participate in the program, with some stated exceptions. Parents under twenty years of age who lack a high school diploma are required to participate in an educational program, unless considered inappropriate for them.

Within the overall AFDC population, groups targeted for the program are those receiving welfare for the last five years, those receiving welfare for three of the last five years, those lacking a high school diploma, and those with older children nearing the age when welfare will end. States are required to spend 55 percent of their funds on these target groups, unless other populations have a demonstrably greater need. In addition, states can serve eligible families with both parents present through the AFDC-UP program.

Sanctions are imposed on those who refuse to participate. In the early years of the program, however, minimum participation rates for states are low: 7 percent of the eligible caseload in 1990, rising to 20 percent by 1995. Since states are required to enroll volunteers first, participants in the early years may be drawn from those who want to be in the program.

**Assessment**

A state welfare agency's first activity is to assess each individual's education, skills, prior work experience, and employability. The agency also does an assessment of the participant's supportive service needs, including child care and transportation. Based on this assessment, the agency representative and the participant are to agree on an employability development plan that may include education, job training, and job readiness activities.

**Education and Employment Services**

States are required to provide job development and placement services, as well as job training and job readiness. In addition, they must provide at least two of the following: job search, on-the-job training, work supplementation, community work experience, or other approved work experience. States are given the flexibility of offering a variety of educational and training programs, including those offered through the Job Training Partnership Act (JTPA), community colleges, and community-based organizations. The options offered will be heavily dependent on existing programs and on Department of Social Services linkages with educational and training programs in an area.

Emphasis on education is an important aspect of FSA. For the first time, it becomes a required alternative for AFDC recipients who may be referred for activities ranging from basic skills remediation and high school completion to post-secondary education. States were given the option of defining the level of education allowed. For example, New York State limited job-related education to two years of college.

## Supportive Services

States are required to provide participants with services designed to help them achieve self-sufficiency. Access to child care is the most important, along with transportation and work-related expenses. Parents are permitted to choose the type of care they prefer, and states are reimbursed by the federal government for a share of total child-care costs. In some areas, there may not be enough slots for participants, especially if providers are paid less than market rates. The states must pay the market rate for child care or $175 per month for a child over two or $200 for a child under two years of age, whichever is less. Quality child care may not be available if providers are paid less than market rates.

## Transitional Services

States are required to provide child care and health-care assistance for all participants who need these services when they begin work. Child care is guaranteed for up to one year after participants are employed. However, states can establish sliding-scale fees for transitional child-care assistance. Medicaid assistance also must be continued for up to one year, with states given the right to establish income-related premiums to cover this extended coverage.

## Positive Aspects and Limitations of FSA for Women

The provisions of FSA can have both positive and negative implications for women. Access to education and training will enable some women on public assistance to move toward economic independence. The emphasis on education is an especially positive development. Mandated child care is an important and essential service if mothers with young children are to obtain training and enter the labor force. Additional support services can further increase the likelihood that participants will complete training and become employed.

The requirement that assessments be made of each participant's background, skills, and needs can be beneficial if they result in educational and employability plans leading to self-sufficiency. However, the scope of assessments will vary and, in some cases, will simply be used to screen participants for eligibility or to refer them to existing services.

Another positive component of FSA is the recognition that parents entering the labor force need help in making this transition. The extension of child-

and health-care benefits for one year is a move in the right direction. However, most new workers will not earn enough to be able to afford child and medical care. Many entry-level jobs either do not provide health care or offer family coverage at too high a cost for single parents.

The unemployed-parent provisions indicate a recognition that welfare-program requirements often have contributed to the breakup of two-parent families. However, the quality of the job training will be important. Moreover, only a small proportion of unemployed fathers will be served.

Experience with FSA also indicates some serious limitations and adverse effects for poor families. In addition to problems inherent in the act itself, other difficulties stem from how states interpret and put into practice its provisions. In some early implementation states, insufficient preplanning resulted in operational problems. States implementing the act later may have learned from these experiences.

Critics have especially singled out the FSA's coercive elements. Sanctioning will mean hardships for women who lose benefits. In addition, women are not allowed the option of staying at home with young children or of turning down training. Moreover, if job search and other inexpensive employment alternatives are emphasized, many participants will be placed in low-skill jobs rather than in job-training programs with the potential for increased skills and higher incomes.

Such practices have occurred in other job-training programs. The U.S. General Accounting Office (GAO) (1989) has criticized JTPA programs for their tendency to refer women and minorities to low-paying jobs while placing men in training programs to upgrade their skills. Women also were less likely to be trained for nontraditional jobs that were offering better salaries and more job security. Specific instances of racism and sexism by training providers were documented.

Another weakness is that FSA does not address how local or national economic conditions affect participants' ability to become self-sufficient. High unemployment rates result in more competition for job openings, and employers tend to hire those with more experience or skills. Moreover, changes in the nature of jobs, combined with the current economic downturn, have meant the elimination of many entry-level jobs. New jobs often require technical skills that JOBS participants lack or are poorly paid service jobs without benefits and security. The trend toward hiring part-time and contract workers puts new labor-force entrants at a disadvantage as well.

Research shows how difficult it is for single parents with limited skills to earn enough in entry level jobs to become economically independent. The Rockefeller Foundation's Minority Female Single Parent Program (1988–1990), directed by Phoebe Cottingham, funded programs in community-based organizations in Atlanta, San Jose, Providence, and Washington, D.C., during the 1980s. The program's goal was to determine whether comprehensive employability programs could make a difference in the economic self-sufficiency of single mothers. Only San Jose's Center for Employment Training led to significantly increased employment and wages, yet its participants' incomes were still low. (For additional research and evaluation on welfare-to-work issues, see Gueron and Pauly 1991; Zill et al. 1991.)

Health and child-care expenses eat up a large part of a minimum-wage worker's income. Even those women who are managing financially can be forced back on welfare by such events as a family member's illness or loss of inexpensive child care. Nor will the child-support provisions appreciably increase single-parent household incomes if absent fathers lack skills or earn only the minimum wage.

FSA's supporters applaud its efforts to end dependency and its improvements over previous programs. Its critics point out that FSA simply continues a long tradition of limiting welfare to the "deserving poor" (defined ever more narrowly) and of punishing recipients for being poor. To feminists, the legislation perpetuates the oppression of women and people by the patriarchal state (see Naples 1990). For many mothers, becoming employed means joining the ranks of the working poor and perhaps leaving their children worse off than on public assistance.

Consequently, some advocates for women and children focus on ensuring that the program works to the benefit of their constituencies. For example, a Children's Defense Fund report by Sherman and Ebb (1991) discusses the impact of FSA on teen parents and outlines the characteristics of a good JOBS program for this population. They also suggest how advocates can work in their communities for programs that meet the needs of young parents.

### Initial Experiences and Evaluation

It is still early to evaluate the effectiveness of FSA in meeting its goals. Some states have not yet had much experience. However, the recession has made it more difficult for states to meet participation rates. Case loads have increased at a time when states have less money for services, given flat federal government funding and tight state budgets (Wilson 1991). In many communities, high unemployment rates mean few jobs for entry-level workers.

These pressures may lead program administrators to place more emphasis on getting participants into the labor force quickly. "Creaming," that is, working with the most job-ready participants, may result. Job-search assistance may be favored over longer term training, although training would provide participants with better skills for achieving economic independence and have a more positive long-term impact on their lives.

An initial study of JOBS implementation in ten states (Maryland, Michigan, Minnesota, Mississippi, New York, Oklahoma, Oregon, Pennsylvania, Tennessee, and Texas) was conducted by the Nelson Rockefeller Institute of Government (Hagen and Lurie 1992). The authors found little evidence that the program was meeting a major objective: Changing the mission of public assistance from providing cash assistance to helping participants achieve economic independence. Moreover, many states expected to meet the federal mandate for participation and targeting but were less sure of successfully tracking and monitoring programs or of meeting federal reporting requirements.

Hagen and Lurie conclude that most of the states studied came closer to meeting the letter than the spirit of the law. Nationally, spending has been just under 50 percent of the federal money available. In the early 1990s, most states had not provided the necessary matching funds, in part because of the recession.

Their research also showed that the JOBS program offered a wide range of educational and training opportunities. However, problems were evident. As some critics predicted, child care was often insufficient and could lead to enrolling those with preexisting care arrangements, a new form of creaming. They also raised questions about giving preference to volunteers, about the reasonableness of the twenty-hour rule, and about a tendency to rely on low-cost options like job search and placement for the most job-ready. In general, state approaches ranged from emphasizing what was best for participants to making choices based on the scarcity of resources.

In-depth evaluation of FSA as a new social program clearly is needed. In addition to the Rockefeller Institute of Government study, the Manpower Demonstration Research Corporation, experienced in assessing welfare-to-work programs, has received an initial evaluation contract (Gueron and Pauly 1991).

Differences in state approaches and interpretations of FSA will make obtaining a national overview of the JOBS program more difficult (Greenberg 1990; Itzakovitz 1990). Federal reporting requirements are limited as well. There are no uniform reporting requirements on outcomes, sanctions, and supportive services. States do not have to report job-placement statistics, wage rates, retention rates, or educational attainment of participants. They also do not have to report the numbers receiving supportive services, the type of services provided, or how much. Educational activities of participants need not be reported by type; for example, the data will not indicate whether post-secondary education means college or vocational school.

To assess the program's effectiveness, researchers will need to do longitudinal studies, following participants over time to track their educational, job training, and employment histories. However, the data to be collected will provide only cross-sectional data on participants. For all these reasons, Greenberg (1990) concluded from a preliminary study of the JOBS program that few fundamental questions about the nature of programs could be answered. However, in-depth research will in time assess FSA's impact on poverty and evaluate its effectiveness in increasing the economic independence of women.

*Rosalie G. Genovese*

## Bibliography

Advisory Commission on Intergovernmental Relations. 1991. "Welfare Reform." *Intergovernmental Perspective* 17(2): entire issue.
Burkhart, Jo Anne. 1991. "The Family Support Act: Public Assistance for the 1990s." In "Welfare Reform." *Intergovernmental Perspective* 17:13,14,17.
Greenberg, Mark. 1990. "What's Happening in JOBS: A Review of Initial State Data." Washington, D.C.: Center for Law and Social Policy.
Gueron, Judith, and Edward Pauly. 1991. *Welfare to Work.* New York: Russell Sage.
Hagen, Jan L., and Irene Lurie. 1992. "Implementing JOBS. Initial State Choices." Nelson Rockefeller Institute of Government, State University of New York, Albany.
Itzakovitz, Gary. 1990. "Who Wins in Welfare Reform? It's Business as Usual." Paper presented at the 85th American Sociological Association annual meetings, Washington, D.C., August 11–15.
Naples, Nancy. 1990. "A Feminist Analysis of the Family Support Act of 1988." Paper presented at the annual meetings of the American Sociological Association, Washington, D.C.
*New Partnerships: Education's Stake in the Family Support Act of 1988.* n.d. A statement of the American Public Welfare Association, Center for Law and Social Policy, Center for the Study of Social Policy, Children's Defense Fund, Council of Chief State School Officers, Institute

for Educational Leadership, National Alliance of Business, and National Association of
State Boards of Education, and National Governor's Association, Washington, D.C.: WTG.

Rockefeller Foundation. 1988–1990. *Into the Working World*. New York: Rockefeller Foundation.

Sherman, Arloc, and Nancy Ebb. 1991. "The Family Support Act: How Can It Help Teen Parents?
An Introduction to the Family Support Act for Teen Parent Service Providers." Washington, D.C.: Children's Defense Fund.

Sherwood, Kay E., and David A. Long. 1991. "Jobs Implementation in an Uncertain Environment:
A Model That Helps Administrators Understand How Programs Might Unfold." *Public
Welfare* 49:16–27.

Smith, Sheila, Susan Blank, and James T. Bond. 1990. *One Program, Two Generations: A Report on the
Forum on Children and the Family Support Act*. New York: Foundation for Child Develop-
ment/National Center for Children in Poverty.

U.S. General Accounting Office. 1989. *Job Training Partnership Act: Information on Training, Placements,
and Wages of Male and Female Participants*. Fact Sheet for the chairman, Subcommittee on
Labor, Committee on Labor and Human Resources, U.S. Senate.

————. 1989. *Job Training Partnership Act: Service Outcomes for Participants with Differing Needs*. Report
to Congressional Requesters.

U.S. House of Representatives, Committee on Ways and Means. 1989. *General Explanations of the
Family Support Act of 1988*. Washington, D.C.: U.S. Government Printing Office.

Wilson, Benet. 1991. "States Barely Meet Participation Rate; HHS Guidelines Blamed." *Employment
and Training Reporter*, September 11.

Zill, Nicholas, Kristin A. Moore, Christine Winquist Nord, and Thomas Stief. 1991. *Welfare Mothers
as Potential Employees: A Statistical Profile Based on National Survey Data*. Washington, D.C.:
Child Trends (February 25).

## Job-Protected Leave For Family and Medical Reasons

When we examine management practice toward women in the workplace, we find
it adapts to circumstances. For example, despite the popularity of unpaid maternity leave during World War II, by 1964, 40 percent of employers had reverted to
the Depression-era tactic of simply terminating pregnant women (Kohl and
Greenlaw 1983). Today, by contrast, some large companies are starting to see the
development of women employees as "a business imperative" (Trost 1989). A 1992
survey reveals that 50 percent of responding companies' senior management regard work and family-benefit issues as more important today than two years ago
(Christine 1992). As women become integral parts of the workforce, a transition
is underway that brings work and family issues together in order to deal with problems and opportunities from a perspective of interdependent subsystems of society as a whole. A changing workplace is aided by legislative support. For example,
the U.S. Supreme Court (*Guerra* v. *California Federal Savings and Loan*, 55 U.S.L.W.
4077, 1987) upheld a California law requiring leave for new mothers (Nowlin and
Sullivan 1988). Justice Thurgood Marshall writing for the 6–3 majority said that
such legislation "promotes equal employment opportunity" because "it allows
women, as well as men, to have families without losing their jobs" (Press and
Wright 1987).

Job-protected leave for family and medical reasons, first introduced during the 99th Congress, was the first legislative issue to be taken up in the 103rd
Congress. Congressional leaders pledged to move with extraordinary speed on the
bill ("Family Leave Put on Congress' Fast Track" 1993). The Family and Medical
Leave Act of 1993 was signed into law by President Clinton on February 5, 1993.
The legislation requires employers with fifty or more employees to give workers
up to twelve weeks of unpaid leave after childbirth or adoption, to care for a seriously ill child, spouse, or parent, or in case of an employee's own serious illness.
While most of the media emphasis is on the family leave portion of legislation and

workplace policies, the medical leave portion of the legislation will impact 40 percent of the working men and women who have no job protection because of sickness ("Family Benefits Become Competitive Strategy" 1990). This compares to the 50 to 60 percent without job protection for childbirth (Worthington and Moss 1989).

It is easier to understand the changes currently taking place when we view them as a complex innovation that will diffuse over time and space. The process is gaining momentum because of changing demographics. "Nearly 50 percent of all mothers with children under one year and two-thirds of mothers with children under the age of three are now working outside the home. . . . Single working mothers have become a significant percentage of the workforce" (Clay and Feinstein 1987). When maternity leave is viewed as a women's issue, and one is a woman attempting to compete in a male-dominated workplace, the result is an attempt to conceal family life at work. Change occurs when both members of dual-career couples expect equitable treatment in the workplace for all, regardless of gender (Rogers and Rogers 1990).

Once the issue of leave for family responsibilities began to be considered in terms of federal legislation, conceptual development took place that first resulted in "parental leave"—that is, leave for either parent at the birth of a child—and then became more encompassing with the concept of "family and medical leave," covering both birth and adoption, and family illness, including that of employee, spouse, child, or parent. The point is that the innovation has not stood still but is evolving as dialogue continues. "The bill speaks to the concerns of workers who are young and old, male and female, married and single" (Clay and Feinstein 1987, p.67). Since innovations such as family-medical leave tend to diffuse, if you are an interested party, you should become involved in the design process.

The design process is aided by personnel specialists who observe that changing demographics are putting pressure on employers to accommodate the needs of the increasing numbers of working women with small children. "Job candidates are asking about work and family policies, such as parental leave and child care, during their initial interviews. To do this would have been unheard of just five years ago" (Meirs 1988, p.108). What was once considered a woman's issue is now being discussed in terms of "work and family," and articles are published that promote family-focused organization change (Hall 1990, p.21). A coalition is emerging in those organizations that view apathy as a threat to keeping and motivating duel-career employees. "The concept of 'maternity machismo' prevalent in the 1970s in which having a baby was thought to require no more than a brief career interruption, is now viewed as unrealistic and potentially harmful in terms of maternal/child welfare and family stability" (Samuels et al. 1988, p.750). Forces external to the organization, such as adolescent problems of drug use and dropping out of school, are resulting in a more systematic view of the relationships between home, school, work, and society in general.

The family-medical leave innovation is spread by the communication process of the media, which continues to outline the problems and call for solutions. A new behavioral norm is being created. For example, some organizations establish as a goal to make the list of best companies for working mothers, to be known in the future as the Working Mother 100. In seven years the number of companies featured increased from thirty to one hundred (Moskowitz and Townsend 1992), leading women to increase their expectations of employers. These expectations were documented in a recent survey by the International Foundation of Employee Benefit Plans, with 87 percent of responding companies reporting that their employees are increasing their demands for family benefits (Christine 1992).

Back at the state legislatures, there is a flurry of activity. Many states have either passed family-medical leave legislation or have pending legislation. For example, more than eleven hundred bills specifically related to children and families were passed during the 1987 sessions, double the number passed just five years earlier. An extensive legislative package in the state of Connecticut was labeled the "Family and Workplace Agenda" (Smith 1988). Legislation exists in twenty-four states and the District of Columbia. Benefits range from sixteen weeks in California, Connecticut, and the District of Columbia to four weeks in Hawaii (DiLieto 1992; "More States Adopt Family Leave Laws" 1992). The *Monthly Labor Review* reports annually (in the January issue) on state labor legislation enacted in the previous year. Competition exists between the states as some propose legislation with provisions that go beyond federal mandates, while others brag that business will not be hampered by such laws in their state. The communication process is fostered by such publications as *State Legislatures,* and the *Council of State Governments' CSG Backgrounder*. An article in *Governing* (Spivack 1988) reports that supporters of family-leave laws have carried the day in several states in recent years and calls these supporters a new coalition.

While support grows for family-medical leave, strong opposition continues. Congressional proponents could not find enough support to overcome presidential vetoes during the Bush administration. Then President Bush contended that a mandatory leave policy would reduce employer flexibility and undercut the competitiveness of U.S. employers in the global marketplace (Kulash and Sorensen 1991). A staunch opponent has been the National Federation of Independent Business, which says that thousands of workers will lose their jobs if family-medical leave is mandated (Dimeo 1992). A Gallup study of 950 firms conducted for the NFIB showed that employers would be less likely to hire young women, would reduce low-skilled jobs, cut benefits, and establish stricter personnel policies. Some small-business owners object to the arbitrary nature of a family leave rule: "The imposition of a federally mandated leave policy that encompasses all businesses without regard to specific needs of a particular industry would not only be unworkable, but potentially devastating to many small businesses and construction subcontractors in particular," says a Baltimore concrete construction subcontractor, noting additional expenses for benefits, salary, and training costs that legislation would bring ("Bills on Parental Leave Gaining" 1987). Recent research results are available from several sources that indicate that unpaid family-medical leave is less expensive than replacing employees who quit ("Unpaid Leave Easy and Inexpensive" 1991). Nevertheless, a federal mandate will not readily translate into positive action in many organizations. Each organization will need to integrate family-medical leave realistically into its environment. Benefit statistics can be found in publications by the U.S. Department of Labor, Bureau of Labor Statistics (1989, 1990, 1991).

Cultural factors play a significant role in determining how a particular country perceives family benefits in the view of Kathleen Westlock, a New York–

based international human-resources management consultant. "A big reason why family leave issues in the United States have largely been left up to the determination of employers and employees is because of our culture of rugged individualism. U.S. programs tend to be pragmatic, reflecting an every person for him- or herself attitude" (Christine 1992, p.79). Indeed pragmatism has been a part of the legislative debate for family-medical leave with revised proposals decreasing the maximum term of covered leave and increasing the number of employees for the exempt firm.

Progressive organizations put job-protected family-medical leave policies in place before federal passed legislation. In doing so they altered the competitive climate in the market for human resources. In terms of innovation diffusion terminology, these organizations were the early adopters. Those who fall far behind are the laggards. Businesses hoping to remain competitive cannot afford to be laggards (Rogers and Rogers 1990).

*Kathleen C. Brannen*

## Bibliography

"Bills on Parental Leave Gaining." 1987. *ENR.* (November 12):94.
Christine, Brian. 1992. "Grappling with Family Leave Legislation." *Risk Management* 39 (November):79–80.
Clay, William L., and Frederick L. Feinstein, 1987. "The Family and Medical Leave Act: A New Federal Labor Standard." *ILR Report* 25(Fall):62–69.
DiLieto, Patricia A. 1992. "Many Employers Face New State Family Leave Laws." *Journal of Compensation and Benefits* 7(March/April):16–24.
Dimeo, Jean. 1992. "Family Leave: A Campaign Issue Heating Up." *Pension World* 28(March):6.
"Family Benefits Become Competitive Strategy." 1990. *Omaha World-Herald.* June 24:1w.
"Family Leave Put on Congress' Fast Tract." 1993. *Omaha World-Herald.* January 22:3.
Hall, Douglas T. 1990. "Promoting Work/Family Balance: An Organization-Change Approach." *Organizational Dynamics* 18(3):5–18.
Kohl, John P., and Paul S. Greenlaw. 1983. "The Pregnancy Discrimination Act." *Personnel Journal* 31:752–56.
Kulash, Marjorie M., and Susan J. Sorensen. 1991. "Family Leave Controversy—A Clash of Philosophies." *Journal of Compensation and Benefits* 7(July/August):62–64.
Meirs, Margaret. 1988. "Parental Leave and the Bottom Line." *Personnel Journal* 36:108–12.
"More States Adopt Family Leave Laws." 1992. From the State Capitals 46(May 18):1–3.
Moskowitz, Milton, and Carol Townsend. 1992. "The 100 Best Companies for Working Mothers, 7th Annual Survey." *Working Mother* 15(October):33–42ff.
Nowlin, William A., and George M. Sullivan. 1988. "Legal Trends in Affirmative Action and Employee Rights." *Industrial Management* (January/February)30:26–28.
Press, Aric, A. McDaniel, and L. Wright. 1987. "A New Family Issue." *Newsweek* 107 (January 26):22–24.
Rogers, Fran Sussner, and Charles Rogers. 1990. "The Family-Friendly Corporation." *Harvard Business Review* 12(Summer):36–39.
Samuels, Linda B., Richard L. Coffinberger, and Susan C. Fouts. 1988. "Responding to Social and Demographic Change: Family and Medical Leave Proposals." *Labor Law Journal* 39:748–59.
Smith, Shelley. 1988. "Kids, Families and Politics." *State Legislatures* 14:26–30.
Spivack, Miranda S. 1988. "A New Coalition Is Winning on Family Leave." *Governing* 1 (September):66–70.
Trost, Cathy. 1989. "Firms Heed Women Employees' Needs." *Wall Street Journal.* November 22:B1.
"Unpaid Leave Easy and Inexpensive." 1991. *Employee Benefit Plan Review* 46(August):24–25.
U.S. Bureau of Labor Statistics. 1991. "BLS Reports on Its First Survey of Employee Benefits in Small Private Establishments." United States Department of Labor News, USDL 91-260. June 10.
——. 1989. "Employee Benefits in Medium and Large Firms, 1989." Bulletin 2363. Washington, D.C.: U.S. Government Printing Office.
——. 1990. "Employee Benefits in Small Private Establishments, 1990." Bulletin 2388. Washington, D.C.: U.S. Government Printing Office.
Worthington, E.R., and Shelly Osborne Moss. 1989. "The Impact of Federally Mandated Maternity/Paternity Laws on Small Business." *Journal of Business & Entrepreneurship* 1(March):58–70.

# VI

# Work Experiences and the Organizational Context of Work

# Women's Work Experiences

## Gender and Orientation toward Work

Drawing on earlier concerns with alienation (Seeman 1959), research on work orientations has distinguished between intrinsic and extrinsic aspects of the job (Centers and Bugental 1966; Herzberg et al. 1959; Rosenberg 1957). Intrinsic aspects refer to the work itself while extrinsic factors are things related, but not integral to, the job. One important extrinsic dimension has to do with people, working with or helping them; the other has to do with rewards such as salary, advancement, and job security (Rosenberg 1957). Studies of students (Herzog 1982; Lueptow 1980; Rosenberg 1957) have consistently shown strong female orientation toward the interpersonal factors and male orientation toward the other extrinsic rewards. When there are differences in intrinsic orientations, females generally hold stronger intrinsic values than males. These differences have persisted from the 1950s to the 1980s, in spite of changes in occupational preferences over that period (Herzog 1982; Lueptow 1980). Studies of working populations show fewer differences in values, but when they do occur, they are consistent with the differences observed in student populations.

Research on occupational values has distinguished between intrinsic and extrinsic aspects of work. This distinction rests upon powerful concerns in the writings of Karl Marx, Eric Fromm, and others about the way contemporary changes in work have operated to dehumanize workers (Seeman 1959).

These ideas emphasize the distinction between working because the work itself is interesting and related to the self and its growth and actualization—that is, meaningful to the worker—versus working because the work leads to money, security, recognition, or associations—things surrounding the job, but extrinsic to its actual performance and not controlled directly by the worker. This distinction was incorporated by Herzberg into his two-level theory of work motivation (Herzberg et al. 1959).

Even though mid-century concerns about alienation and meaning have given way to concerns for full employment, mobility, and equal opportunity, the intrinsic-extrinsic distinction has persisted in the study of occupational values and motives and been expanded with insights emerging from studies of sex differences.

Intrinsic orientations focus upon such things as interesting work involving the use of one's abilities and aptitudes where growth and learning lead to a sense of achievement or accomplishment. Extrinsic factors involve job commitments or conditions of work, income from work, chances for advancement, prestige, security, hours, and fringe benefits. Because of their relevance to sex differences, one set of extrinsic factors has come to be treated separately. These have to do with people orientation, valuing work because it involves interpersonal relations with co-workers, friendly management, or, most especially, the chance to help or serve others.

These two components of the extrinsic orientations reflect the substantial difference between the sexes regarding male concerns with self and autonomy and female concerns with relationships and response to the needs of others that appear in public conceptions of sex stereotypes and are seen as basic contrasts in the developing personalities of women and men (Gilligan 1982).

While some believe that males are more committed to work and to the intrinsic aspects of work, the bulk of the evidence shows that the major sex differences in orientation to work center around the extrinsic and people-oriented dimensions. These findings are clearest in the studies of high school and college students but appear also in studies of working populations and of the incumbents in jobs and professions.

Males emphasize the extrinsic factors of income and advancement most often, as well as such things as freedom, importance of work, leadership, and recognition. Females give preeminent value to helping others as well as being with others and having friendly co-workers or managers. In studies of working populations, working conditions and convenience of work also become important for females, but for school populations, the major factor is helping others. Both sexes emphasize such intrinsic factors as using abilities and aptitudes, having interesting work, and having a sense of personal accomplishment in work. However, when differences do occur, which is fairly often, it is females, not males, who have the stronger intrinsic interest in work. These patterns are very consistent with Veroff's argument (1977) that women are interested in achievement for its own sake, for the accomplishment itself, while men are interested in the impact achievement has upon their status, income, and recognition.

The specific content of these orientations is nicely illustrated in Table 4 of Herzog's study (1982) of national samples of high school students. While she does not use the intrinsic/extrinsic distinction itself, it is clear that males value status and money, job security, responsibility, and easy pace of work, while females value the intrinsic factors of stimulation in and mastery of work and the people-oriented values of altruism and contact with others. For example, the eight greatest differences, along with their regression coefficients, are female valuation of help people (0.39), meet others (0.39), be yourself (0.31), make friends (0.24), job worthwhile to society (0.22), and male valuation of much vacation (–0.34), no supervision (–0.23) and income (–0.22). Only three of the twenty-five values failed to show significant sex differences and only two of the significant differences failed to follow the pattern of male extrinsic, female intrinsic and people-oriented occupational values.

This pattern of sex differentiated occupational values has appeared in numerous studies of high school and college samples starting with Rosenberg's analysis (1957) of the Cornell values, Flanagan and Jung's analysis (1971) of 134 of the Project Talent High Schools, my own analysis (1980) in twenty Wisconsin high schools, and the limited but consistent data in the samples of over one thousand high schools in the national longitudinal study (Fetters et al. 1984). At the student level it appears that occupational values are consistent with sex-role stereotypes (see Lueptow p. 123, this vol.) and predispose youths toward sex-typed occupations (Reskin 1984, Chap. 11).

Three of these studies were longitudinal studies repeating the same value items over time: 1960–1970 (Flanagan and Jung 1971), 1964–1975 (Lueptow 1980), and 1976–1980 (Herzog 1982). In all cases the sex differences were essentially stable, except that differences in the values of leadership, promotion, and advancement increased in two of these studies between 1960 and 1975. Fetters et al. provide an exception to the above by observing a decrease in the sex differences between 1972 and 1980 in four of the five values they studied. Unanalyzed tables from the Monitoring the Future Project (Bachman et al. 1987) also indicate some change may have occurred, although the major differences persist. Taken overall, however, it appears that clear sex differences in orientations to work have persisted among student samples from the 1950s to the mid 1980s, although emerging evidence suggests that processes of change may be just starting.

Studies of more general populations of workers generally reveal fewer sex differences in occupational values than in student samples, but where differences are found they reflect traditional concerns, with males valuing self-expression (Centers and Bugental 1966), promotion, and advancement, pay, and security concerns (Agassi 1982; Jurgensen 1978; Neil and Snizek 1987) and females valuing people (Centers and Bugental 1966; Jurgensen 1978; Neil and Snizek 1987) and convenience (Agassi 1982; Walker et al. 1982). Studies of single occupations show value similarity in some cases and traditional differences in others (See "Sex, Gender Stereotypes, and Work," Geib and Lueptow, p. 243, this vol).

When occupational status is controlled for, many of the sex differences disappear (Walker et al. 1982; Agassi 1982; Brenner et al. 1988), suggesting they reflect either the motivational consequences of job circumstances or, more likely, the selection of the same jobs by persons with similar values and motives.

On the whole, there appear to be clear sex differences in work orientations that are most pronounced in student samples, and truncated but not eliminated in working populations. These differences are consistent with the stereotypic orientations of women and men, but qualified by the stronger female interest in the intrinsic aspects of work.

*Lloyd B. Lueptow*

## Bibliography

Agassi, J.B. 1982. *Comparing the Work Attitudes of Women and Men.* Lexington, Mass.: Lexington.

Bachman, J.G., L.D. Johnston, and P.M. O'Malley. 1987. *Monitoring the Future.* Ann Arbor: Institute for Social Research, University of Michigan.

Brenner, O.C., A.P. Blazini, and J.H. Greenhaus. 1988. "An Examination of Race and Sex Differences in Managerial Work Values." *Journal of Vocational Behavior* 32:336–44.

Centers, R., and D. Bugental. 1966. "Intrinsic and Extrinsic Job Motivations among Different Segments of the Working Population." *Journal of Applied Psychology* 50:193–97.

Fetters, W.B., G.H. Brown, and J.A. Owings. 1984. *High School and Beyond: A National Longitudinal Study for the 1980's; High School Seniors: A Comparative Study of the Classes of 1972 and 1980.* Washington, D.C.: National Center for Education Statistics.

Flanagan, J.C., and S.M. Jung. 1971. *Progress in Education: A Sample Survey (1960–1970)*. Palo Alto, Calif.: American Institute for Research.

Gilligan, C. 1982. *In a Different Voice: Psychological Theory and Women's Development*. Cambridge, Mass.: Harvard University Press.

Herzberg, F., B. Mausner, and B. Snyderman. 1959. *The Motivation to Work*. New York: John Wiley and Sons.

Herzog, A.R. 1982. "High School Seniors' Occupational Plans and Values: Trends in Sex Differences 1976 through 1980." *Sociology of Education* 55:1–13.

Jurgensen, C.E. 1978. "Job Preferences (What Makes a Job Good or Bad?)" *Journal of Applied Psychology* 63:267–76.

Lueptow, L.B. 1980. "Social Change and Sex Role Change in Adolescent Orientations toward Life, Work and Achievement: 1964–1975." *Social Psychology Quarterly* 43:48–59.

Neil, C.C., and W.E. Snizek. 1987. "Work Values, Job Characteristics, and Gender." *Sociological Perspectives* 36:245–65.

Reskin, B.F., ed. 1984. *Sex Segregation in the Workplace: Trends, Explanations, Remedies*. Washington, D.C.: National Academy.

Rosenberg, M. 1957. *Occupations and Values*. Glencoe, Ill.: Free Press.

Seeman, M. 1959. "On the Meaning of Alienation." *American Sociological Review* 24:783–91.

Veroff, J. 1977. "Process vs. Impact in Men's and Women's Achievement Motivation." *Psychology of Women Quarterly* 1:283–93.

Walker, J.E., C. Tausky, and D.O. Oliver. 1982. "Men and Women at Work: Work Values within Occupational Groups." *Journal of Vocational Behavior* 21:17–36.

## Gender Differences in Work Interests

In the three decades since passage of the 1964 Civil Rights Act, women have significantly increased their participation in a wide range of nontraditional occupations. Many social scientists assumed that the opening up of the job structure would eliminate or greatly reduce work-related differences between men and women (such as, differences in income, hours worked, occupation entered, and so on). Yet these and other differences remain large. Discrimination explains some but perhaps not all of these gaps, which may be caused in part by continuing differences in work-related concerns and interests. Researchers using representative national samples find men and women differ somewhat in regard to work interests or concerns. However, these differences may not occur when men and women are in the same occupation. To see if the sexes bring different work interests to their jobs, it is best to compare men and women in the same occupation.

### Two Theories of Gender and Work Interests

Some social scientists contend that work interest gender differences are primarily a function of opportunity structure. This social-structural approach asserts that present or anticipated work position shapes work interests by offering men and women the same rewards and experiences (Kanter 1977; Markham et al. 1985). Thus, it expects women and men in the same occupation (either gainfully employed or in occupational training) to exhibit similar interests in a wide range of occupational rewards. Proponents of the opportunity structure approach assert that differences observed in work interests and practices, which indicate a greater male concern for income and advancement and a greater female concern for helping people, are artifacts of gender segregation.

Advocates of the gender-socialization approach assert that women bring different values and traits to their work roles than men because of earlier gender training. These values and traits shape work-related interests, decisions, and practices (Lueptow 1981; Veroff 1977). Proponents of this approach also contend that men are socialized to be more aggressive and to exhibit a competitive interpersonal style, whereas women are taught to be less aggressive and to show a more relationship-oriented interpersonal style. In addition, men and women are expected to fulfill different adult roles; that is, males are expected to emphasize the work role as a primary breadwinner, and females are expected to emphasize interpersonal roles as wife/mother, even though they may be employed outside the home. The gender-socialization approach predicts two basic work interest patterns: a greater male concern for competitive dominance and a greater female concern for harmonious relationships.

### A Summary of Attitude Research Findings

There are ten commonly identified work interests and concerns in the work literature that are relevant to work-related gender difference. Eight of these dimensions of work address the rewards that influence selection of an occupation or anticipated work behavior (for example, income, the use of esteemed occupational skills, an opportunity to work independently, advancement into administration, and so forth). Two other issues pertain to preferred hours (part-time or full-time) and employment status (self-employment or employee).

Betz and O'Connell (1989) systematically combined twenty-two studies that controlled for occupation to compare the work interests of men and women in the same field. They obtained the patterned differences predicted by the gender socialization approach. Men stressed the concerns and interests related to competition and dominance and women stressed those related to social relationships. Men more than women were concerned about income, job security, and advancement into administration; wanted to avoid being supervised and to work independently; and were more likely to seek self-employment and to value the opportunity to exercise leadership. Women more than men were concerned with exercising esteemed occupational skills; wanted to help people and work with people; and preferred part-time hours and employee status. There were a total of 109 comparisons between the sexes in the twenty-two studies; the gender socialization approach predicted the sex with greater interest in 90 percent of the comparisons.

### Work Interests and Work Behavior

While gender differences appear to exist in the same occupation (a fact predicted by the socialization approach), they may not influence actual behavior in the workplace. Indeed, most attitude differences appear to be small (the gap between men and women—when measured in percentage and not rank order—is often less than 10 percent). Moreover, attitude measures often fail to predict behavior. However, the differences may be significant theoretically because: (1) work interest differences appear repeatedly despite the fact that interests are difficult to measure; (2) they take the pattern predicted by the socialization approach; and (3) the objective indicators of work interests (such as occupations and specializations entered, hours worked, self-employment, percentage working part-time) show large differences by sex that are consistent with, yet greater than, measured attitudinal differences.

Work interests are difficult to measure because most items on attitude surveys pertain to rewards—money, advancement, helping people, using skills—that are not mutually exclusive. (In fact, on Likert-type questions people can fall into response sets.) Respondents can mention all of them yet be motivated primarily by one. Moreover, people in a particular occupation acquire "a vocabulary of motives" they can use to explain their occupational choice. Thus doctors can say they entered medicine to help people when income or prestige was their primary concern. In sum, survey data on reasons for working in an occupation are only a rough estimate of an individual's work interests, concerns, and motivations.

The significance of attitudinal interest differences is underscored by work-related practices and behavior. For example, men are much more likely to focus on asocial, autonomous work with objects; men disproportionately enter engineering and work with tools as skilled craft workers (U.S. Bureau of the Census 1987, p.369). In a study of Wisconsin high school students, Lueptow (1981) found little female interest in blue-collar work.

Women tend to choose specialty areas that offer more harmonious personal relationships. In the field of nursing, women tend to be less interested than men in the more impersonal specialty areas of emergency room, industrial nursing, and nurse anesthetist (Williams 1989). Women in medicine disproportionately enter the specialty areas that involve more interpersonal contact or more work with children, such as pediatrics, psychiatry, public health, and obstetrics/gynecology (Wunderman 1980).

Men work more hours in a week outside the home than women. Shank (1988) reports that 27.7 percent of all male workers in the 25–54 age group work forty-nine or more hours per week, but only 10.4 percent of all women workers in that age group work that many or more hours per week. Twenty-seven and one-half percent of women age 25–54 work part time but only 4 percent of men in that age group do (U.S. Bureau of the Census 1987, p.369).

Men are much more likely to establish independent practices in areas such as law and medicine and start small businesses (U.S. Small Business Administration 1984, p.113). Haber et al. (1987) found that of all employed men in nonagricultural industries in 1983, 9.5 percent worked full time at their own noncasual business, but only 3.2 percent of all employed women worked full time at their own noncasual business. Men are also more likely to engage in white-collar crime (Steffensmeier and Cobb 1981), suggesting that males will use illegal as well as legal means to obtain money and recognition.

## Work Orientations and Discrimination

The empirical record strongly suggests that socialization into interpersonal styles and adult roles shapes the attitudes and behavior of men and women, producing different work interests in the same occupation. Work interest differences may contribute to lower female earnings and lower rank at work. But while women may be less concerned with money and rank, women do not want less money and rank. No doubt overt discrimination explains some of the gender gap in outcomes. Yet few instances of discrimination can be found by the Equal Employment Opportunity Commission (O'Connell 1991). Perhaps the dichotomy between discrimination and preference that generally frames the problem does not reflect the real nature of the discrimination process.

Interest differences and discrimination may interact. Women's relative preference for interpersonal harmony may impede their efforts to neutralize discrimination, thereby reducing their ability to maneuver in the workplace. Conversely, males may be advantaged by their emphasis on money and rank and their deemphasis on relationships. Males appear to be more willing than females when seeking pay raises and promotions to endure conflict and inflict costs on employers through sabotage, slowdowns, poor work, stealing, or quitting (Roy 1954). In addition, males are more likely to unionize (U.S. Bureau of the Census 1987, p.402). If management cannot easily replace a male worker or group of male workers, it may have to buy labor peace with pay raises and promotions.

Women can pursue four tactics historically used by other minorities facing discrimination to reduce, circumvent, or neutralize discriminatory intent: start their own professional practice or business, acquire technical skills, enter commission sales, or organize unions. Compared with men, however, women display less interest in these tactics (U.S. Bureau of the Census 1987, p.402).

## Conclusion

Socialization practices appear to produce gender-related work concerns, interests, and practices. We identified ten such concerns and interests, and connected them to two broad themes: a greater male concern for competitive dominance and a greater female concern for harmonious relationships. Yet the relationships among interests, gender, and income and occupational attainments are not established. Research is needed on the nature and size of these and other gender differences and their possible effects on attainment. One unexplored issue is the relative impact of skill and interest differences on occupational behavior. We suspect the impact of differential skills may not be as great as that of differential interests. For instance, math ability gender differences are relatively small while differences in the percentage of men and women in engineering are quite large. Another issue concerns the effects of family commitments on work interests and behavior. Previous gender socialization may not account for all differences in interests in the same occupation because women may take into account male unwillingness to perform domestic tasks when planning their careers.

Given the inherent difficulty of measuring interests and generally small connection between measures of attitudes and behavior, empirical work in specific organizations and occupations is needed to assess the relative contributions of interests and discrimination to differences in attainment. Interests are probably best measured by actual behavior (such as hours worked, self-employment, and willingness to incur conflict). Longitudinal studies that follow groups of females and males (such as the graduates of a law school class) might better uncover the factors that produce disparate career trajectories.

*Lenahan O'Connell*

*Michael Betz*

## Bibliography

Betz, Michael, and Lenahan O'Connell. 1989. "Work Orientations of Males and Females: Exploring the Gender Socialization Approach." *Sociological Inquiry* 59:318–30.

Haber, Sheldon E., Enrique J. Lamas, and Jules H. Lichtenstein. 1987. "On Their Own: The Self-Employed and Others in Private Business." *Monthly Labor Review* 110:17–23.

Kanter, Rosabeth. 1977. *Men and Women of the Corporation*. New York: Basic Books.

Lueptow, Lloyd B. 1981. "Sex-Typing and Change in the Occupational Choices of High School Seniors, 1964–1975." *Sociological Education* 54:16–24.

Markham, William T., Scott J. South, Charles M. Bonjean, and Judy Corder. 1985. "Gender and Opportunity in the Federal Bureaucracy." *American Journal of Sociology* 91:129–50.

O'Connell, Lenahan. 1991. "Investigators at Work: How Bureacratic and Legal Constraints Influence the Enforcement of Discrimination Law." *Public Administration Review* 51:123–30.

Roy, Donald F. 1954. "Efficiency and the Fox: Informal Intergroup Relations in a Piecework Machine Shop." *American Journal of Sociology* 60:235–56.

Shank, Susan E. 1988. "Women and the Labor Market: The Link Grows Stronger." *Monthly Labor Review* 111:3–8.

Steffensmeier, D.J., and M.J. Cobb. 1981. "Sex Differences in Urban Arrest Patterns, 1934–79." *Social Problems* 29:37–49.

U.S. Bureau of the Census. 1987. *Statistical Abstract of the U.S.: 1988.* 108th ed. Washington, D.C.: U.S. Government Printing Office.

U.S. Small Business Administration. 1984. *The State of Small Business: A Report to the President,* p.113. Washington, D.C.: U.S. Government Printing Office.

Veroff, Joseph. 1977. "Process vs. Impact in Men's and Women's Achievement Motivation." *Pyschology of Women Quarterly.* 1:283–93.

Williams, Christine. 1989. *Gender Differences at Work.* Berkeley: University of California Press.

Wunderman, Lorna. 1980. "Female Physicians in the 1970s: Their Changing Roles in Medicine." In *Profile of Medical Practice 1980,* edited by G. Glandon and R. Shapiro, pp. 51–66. Chicago: American Medical Assn.

## Women's Work Commitment

By the end of the 1970s combining paid work with family responsibilities became a viable lifestyle for the majority of women in the United States. Among all families, the proportion of dual-earner couples has nearly doubled since 1960 to about 55 percent, and the traditional family form of a married couple with children and with the wife not in the paid labor force declined to just 15 percent (Merrick and Tordella 1988). Over the same period, women's continuous participation in the paid labor force rose, particularly among mothers of young children, gender differences in levels of education declined, and the sex-role attitudes of women and men became more egalitarian. Furthermore, delay of age at first marriage, postponed onset of child-bearing, lower fertility, and increases in divorce and single-parent households suggested change in the organization and integration of work and family (Thornton 1989). By the 1980s, women were confronted with the balancing of commitments that follows changing involvements with the dual roles of paid work and family.

Commitments are associated with sustained lines of activity across situations. Commitment is typically conceptualized in one of two ways, one emphasizing behavior and the other emphasizing identity as the locus of individual action. According to the behavioral approach, commitment is conceptualized with respect to situational determinants. In this view, commitment is located in the process of retrospection that binds an individual to behavioral acts. To the extent that an individual's prior association with the line of activity has been explicit, irrevocable, public, and volitional, subsequent behavior will be more stable (Becker 1960).

According to the identity approach, commitment is conceptualized with respect to personal meaning (Burke and Reitzes 1991). Most recent scholarship on commitment to work and family adopts this definition. Commitment is seen as an attachment that is initiated and sustained by the extent to which an individual's identification with a role, behavior, value, or institution is considered to be central among alternatives as a source of identity. Research on work or family commitment typically emphasizes the measurement of identity by assessing an individual's "involvement," "central interest," or "orientation" with respect to a given activity or role.

Women's work commitment has been operationalized as "feelings about work or the 'meaning' it has for her" (Haller and Rosenmayr 1971, p.501), or as career salience with work a "central feature of adult life" (Almquist and Angrist 1971, p.263). Women's work commitment has also been defined as: "(a) the degree to which a woman is career motivated, (b) the degree to which an occupation is important as a source of satisfaction, and (c) the degree of priority ascribed to occupation among other sources of satisfaction" (Masih 1967, pp.653–54). Less often, work (or family) commitment is defined as plans, intentions, preferences, or aspirations for particular combinations of work and family roles.

Analysts are seldom explicit about the assumptions of their approach to definition and measurement and the implications for specification of models of work commitment. Even among those sharing the same conceptual approach to commitment, there is often little concern about appropriate measures. Seemingly valid measures are often assumed to be perfectly reliable although studies that empirically assess the quality of measurement find reliability to be generally low and variable across measures. Relying on multiple indicators and explicitly modeling the relationship between observable indicators and the underlying construct of commitment is one way to avoid significant bias due to unreliability of measurement (Bielby and Bielby 1984).

Overall, women and men in the paid labor force differ somewhat in their level of commitment to work and to family. Some research finds no gender differences in perceptions, absorption, or prioritizing in salience of work and family roles among dual-career couples, although wives perceived themselves to be less job involved than their husbands. When identity is measured in both spheres, women are found to be slightly more identified with family than with paid employment; the reverse is true for men. However, sex differences in relative identification with work disappear when women have work statuses and experiences similar to men's and have the opportunity to identify as strongly with the work role as do men. These findings from national samples have been replicated for women and men in blue-collar jobs and in a sample of U.S. Air Force personnel. Furthermore, overall sex differences in commitment to work are disappearing as women's commitment catches up with men's, which has remained relatively stable over the last three decades. Women's increased educational attainment and the expansion of job opportunities and rewards are associated with their increased attachment to the work sphere (Lorence 1987a; Loscocco 1990; Sekaran 1983).

Theoretical explanations for gender differences and change in commitment to work usually emphasize either consequences of gender socialization or effects of structural constraints in the labor market and features of the job. The "gender socialization" explanation emphasizes the consequences of engaging in prescribed gender-based roles and attitudes. This perspective is relevant to the allocation of commitments across the work/family interface, particularly when that allocation is associated with a normatively prescribed division of labor in household and child-rearing responsibilities (Moen and Smith 1986). The "structural" explanation attributes gender differences in work commitment to differences in workplace constraints and opportunities. This research consistently shows that work conditions and opportunities are the strongest determinants of work commitment and that marital and family status have little if any impact. Thus, these studies suggest that most of the difference between women and men in work commitment is due to their differential placement in work and opportunity structures (Lorence 1987b).

There is less research on family commitment and it is less conclusive. However, there is some evidence that a comparable "structural" explanation applies to family commitments. That is, differences between women and men in family commitment appear to be attributable to differences in family responsibilities and constraints. Investigators have found that when men have household responsibilities similar to women's, they are also as strongly committed to family roles as women. Overall, more research is needed on the determinants of gender differences in family commitment and on how structural location in the work sphere affects family commitment and vice versa.

How do work and family commitments interrelate? Scholars confirm the importance of including aspects of family support as well as job and economic factors to explain commitment to work. In a study of U.S. Air Force personnel, it was found that job commitment was best explained by the "fit" between the organization and self/family. Degree of "fit" was indicated by life satisfaction, perception of organizational responsiveness to families, the quality of the organizational environment as a child-rearing milieu, and spousal support for one's career. Results suggest that an organization that accommodates the familial concerns and constraints of its employees is able to sustain a higher level of work commitment among its labor force (Orthner and Pittman 1986; Pittman and Orthner 1989).

In research that directly examines the reciprocal effects between work and family commitment, no significant association was found between the two for men, and a negative relationship for the effect of family commitment on work commitment was found among women. Thus, data from the late 1970s suggest that married working women give precedence to family in balancing work and family identities. In contrast, married men may have the discretion to build commitment to both spheres without trading off one against the other. It may be that among couples subscribing to traditional gender-role norms, a husband strongly committed to work is perceived as simultaneously fulfilling his "provider" role within the family. Research also shows that traditional beliefs about a husband's provider role accounts for wives' greater reluctance to relocate for personal job advancement (Bielby and Bielby 1984, 1989). Finally, in a study of dual-earner couples in a Southern city, high levels of wives' work commitment contributed to perceptions of lower levels of marital adjustment among both spouses, while husband's work commitment had no such effect. Subscription to traditional gender-role beliefs and norms may account for the gender asymmetry in the link between involvement in the spheres of work and family. Moreover, shifts toward more progressive beliefs among husbands as well as wives should contribute to attenuation of those asymmetries.

Recent research suggests new accommodations between work and family may be emerging. Some report that women juggling multiple activities balance role enhancement against role conflict when combining work and family responsibilities. Findings on stress and coping indicate that dual-career couples who achieve a cognitive balance between parenthood and demanding jobs do not necessarily experience high levels of distress (Tiedje et al. 1990). Others observe that changes in conflict and stress at the work/family interface are associated with increased integration of work and family roles, not declines in involvement (Guelzow et al. 1991). Changes like these suggest that recent adaptations to balancing multiple roles and responsibilities may be redefining normative expectations about the interdependence of work and family life and thus the personal meanings assigned and identities derived from them.

With some exceptions, the study of work and family commitment is a field in which scholars have had little to say about policy issues regarding the balancing of commitment to work and family. Research on gender and work commitment indicates that gender differences disappear when women and men face similar career opportunities. While this would seem to belie employers' rationalizations that job segregation is the result of women's lower work commitment, the issue is rarely addressed in the empirical literature. Similarly, employers are just beginning to address women's and men's demands for new workplace policies that accommodate family involvement (Friedman 1987). However, one organizational response, the implementation of a "mommy track" or "daddy track," presumes that those who accommodate to family demands are incapable of sustaining a high level of work commitment. This presumption is inconsistent with much of the empirical research, but the issue as yet has not been addressed by those who study work and family commitment.

*Denise D. Bielby*

## Bibliography

Almquist, E. and S. Angrist. 1971. "Role Model Influences on College Women's Career Aspirations." *Merrill Palmer Quarterly* 17:263–79.

Becker, H. 1960. "Notes on the Concept of Commitment." *American Journal of Sociology* 66:32–40.

Bielby, D., and W. Bielby. 1984. "Work Commitment, Sex-Role Attitudes, and Women's Employment." *American Sociological Review* 49:234–47.

Bielby, W., and D. Bielby. 1989. "Family Ties: Balancing Commitments to Work and Family in Dual Earner Households." *American Sociological Review* 54:776–89.

Burke, P., and D. Reitzes. 1991. "An Identity Theory Approach to Commitment." *Social Psychology Quarterly* 54:39–51.

Friedman, D. 1987. "Family-Supportive Policies: The Corporate Decision-Making Process." *Conference Board* 897:1–47.

Guelzow, M., G. Bird, and E. Koball. 1991. "An Exploratory Path Analysis of the Stress Process for Dual-career Men and Women." *Journal of Marriage and Family* 53:51–64.

Haller, M., and L. Rosenmayr. 1971. "The Pluridimensionality of Work Commitment." *Human Relations* 24:501–18.

Lorence, J. 1987a. "Subjective Labor Force Commitment of U.S. Men and Women." *Social Science Quarterly* 68:45–60.

———. 1987b. "A Test of the 'Gender' and 'Job' Models of Sex Differences in Job Involvement." *Social Forces* 66:221–42.

Loscocco, K. 1990. "Career Structures and Employee Commitment." *Social Science Quarterly* 71:3–68.

Masih, L. 1967. "Career Saliency and Its Relation to Certain Needs, Interests, and Job Values." *Personnel and Guidance Journal* 45:653–8.

Merrick, T., and S. Tordella. 1988. "Demographics: People and Markets." *Population Bulletin*: 43:1–47.

Moen, P., and Smith. 1986. "Women at Work: Commitment and Behavior over the Life Course." *Sociological Forum* 1:24–38.

Orthner, D., and J. Pittman. 1986. "Family Contributions to Work Commitment." *Journal of Marriage and Family* 48:73–81.

Pittman, J., and D. Orthner. 1989. "Gender Differences in the Prediction of Job Commitment." In *Work and Family: Theory, Research, and Applications*, edited by E. Goldsmith, pp. 227–47. Newbury Park, Calif.: Sage.

Sekaran, U. 1983. "How Husbands and Wives in Dual-Career Families Perceive Their Family and Work Roles." *Journal of Vocational Behavior* 22:288–302.

Thornton, A. 1989. "Changing Attitudes toward Family Issues in the United States." *Journal of Marriage and Family* 51:73–93.

Tiedje, L., C. Wortman, G. Downey, C. Emmons, M. Biernat, and E. Lang. 1990. "Women with Multiple Roles: Role-Compatibility, Perceptions, Satisfaction, and Mental Health." *Journal of Marriage and Family* 52:63–72.

## Women and Job Satisfaction

Women report equal or greater job satisfaction than men in spite of objectively inferior jobs (Glenn et al. 1977). Women have been found on average to have less job autonomy, experience closer supervision, and have more limited promotional opportunities than men (Wolf and Fligstein 1979). This discrepancy between conditions and appraisals creates an anomaly that cries out for explanation. Researchers have had only limited success, however, in explaining this discrepancy. The major determinants of job satisfaction—job characteristics, family responsibilities, and prior expectations—operate in basically the same way for men and women. For example, it does not appear that women focus on different aspects of work (such as intrinsically rewarding aspects or time flexibility) in arriving at a given level of job satisfaction.

Women may arrive at a relatively high level of job satisfaction, however, by utilizing different comparison groups. For example, working women may compare themselves to nonworking women and be relatively pleased with the comparison. The possibility that men and women use different comparison groups suggests that women are not satisfied with inferior jobs because they have lower standards or lesser needs at work. Rather, women may report greater job satisfaction because they use different comparison groups. This insight suggests that as a greater proportion of women enter the labor force, women's reference groups for evaluating their jobs may shift and the reported job satisfaction of women and men may converge. We examine the possible explanations for women's higher job satisfaction in greater detail below.

### Job Characteristics

There has been a great deal of debate concerning the extent to which men and women give different weight to different aspects of work (see Agassi 1982). Most researchers find few differences in the consequences of gender-specific childhood socialization for job satisfaction. Nor do they find that job characteristics differentially affect the work attitudes of men and women. For instance, men and women appear to equally value or disvalue occupational prestige, earnings, training, job complexity, how closely the work is supervised, the level of authority exercised, job pressure, being held responsible for things outside one's control, how frequently one has to get dirty on the job, being underemployed, and workplace size. Where gender differences in work attitudes have been found, as in the analysis of Murray and Atkinson (1981), who find that women weigh relations with co-workers more heavily and men weigh advancement more heavily, these differences have been relatively small.

## Family Characteristics

Another possible explanation for women's relatively positive job attitudes is that women may rely on the family as an alternative source of satisfaction. This might enable women to put work-related concerns in a softer light. The role of children in moderating women's attachment to work has been a focus of much research, but tests of this hypothesis have met with mixed results. Working women with children under six are less satisfied than working women without young children. But single women and married women without children are less satisfied with their jobs than are married women with children. The greater reported job satisfaction of women with children may be because the problems and joys associated with children shift attention away from the job and toward the family. The relative dissatisfaction of women with young children is probably because of the added stresses associated with young children and the burdens of overlapping job and family responsibilities.

## Personal Expectations

Different expectations that men and women bring to the workplace provide a third possible explanation for women's relatively high job satisfaction. Complaints about work result not just from objective conditions at work, but also from the expectations that one brings to the workplace (Hodson 1989). Educated workers, for example, report greater dissatisfaction than less educated workers in the same job (Burris 1983).

These observations suggest that job attitudes are influenced by prior expectations as well as by objective conditions. What are the relevant expectations that workers bring to the job? Crosby (1982) reports that most workers compare themselves to someone of the same sex in appraising their jobs. Women's relative satisfaction with their jobs may be more easily understood if we are able to assume that at least some women workers compare themselves to other women rather than to men.

If women compare themselves to other women rather than to men, the employment situation of their mothers when they were growing up may provide a meaningful referent. If a woman's mother was not employed outside the home when she was growing up, her reference group may be more likely to be household employment. This reference point may make paid work outside the home seem relatively desirable, regardless of its limitations, because the income and status associated with paid work outside the home often compare favorably with unpaid household work. Conversely, if a woman's mother was employed outside the home when she was growing up, her reference point is more likely to be paid employment and her expectations for work may be higher. Women may also compare their situation with that of their sisters or female friends as relevant others. Again, comparisons with significant others who work at home may make women relatively satisfied with whatever paid work they have.

Once on the job, female workers may have little occasion for comparing their jobs with those of males because of occupational segregation. Occupational segregation may in this way indirectly contribute to the relatively high reported job satisfaction of women workers. In effect, women workers may not have full information on the extent to which they are underrewarded. Or, at least, their job situations may not provide daily reminders of these inequalities (Hodson 1989). A focus on reference groups leads to the hypothesis that women's relatively high job satisfaction can be understood in terms of the social comparisons they make at work.

An alternative to the reference group hypothesis for women's positive work attitudes focuses on differences in gender socialization to express discontent. To the extent that women are socialized to be more passive than men, women will be less likely to express their discontent at work, regardless of the extent to which they experience such discontent (Glenn and Feldberg 1977, p.60). However, other research has shown that women are not less likely than men to complain about illness or psychological distress.

## Conclusions

Women hold jobs that are on average inferior in many respects to those held by men. Yet women's attitudes toward their jobs are often more favorable than men's. Three possible explanations for this disparity have been considered by social scientists. First, men and women may have different appraisals of jobs because they value different characteristics of work. Second, women may be more satisfied because they focus on their roles as homemakers, rather than on their roles as workers, and derive additional satisfactions from this sphere. Third, men and women may have different expectations and utilize different comparison groups in arriving at evaluations of their jobs. For instance, women may compare themselves to other working women rather than to men and, thus, may not feel relatively deprived. Or, they may compare themselves to women engaged in homemaking and feel relatively satisfied with their employment situation regardless of its limitations.

The most significant explanation for women's relatively high levels of reported job satisfaction probably involves the reference groups to which women compare themselves. Solving the puzzle of greater female job satisfaction may thus be contingent on more precisely specifying the relevant reference groups that workers use when they evaluate their jobs. The solution to this puzzle may also have to include efforts to measure people's willingness to express discontent with their jobs. The problem of establishing reference groups seems solvable. The problem of measuring willingness to express discontent, as distinct from job satisfaction or from other specific attitudes, may present a more difficult research problem.

*Randy Hodson*

## Bibliography

Agassi, J.B. 1982. *Comparing the Work Attitudes of Women and Men*. Lexington, Mass.: D.C. Heath.
Burris, B.H. 1983. *No Room at the Top*. New York: Praeger.
Crosby, F. 1982. *Relative Deprivation and Working Women*. New York: Oxford.
Glenn, E.N., and R.L. Feldberg. 1977. "Degraded and Deskilled: The Proletarianization of Clerical Work." *Social Problems* 25:52–64.
Glenn, N.D., P.A. Taylor, and C.N. Weaver. 1977. "Age and Job Satisfaction among Males and Females: A Multivariate, Multisurvey Study." *Journal of Applied Psychology* 62:189–93.
Hodson, R. 1989. "Gender Differences in Job Satisfaction: Why Aren't Women Workers More Dissatisfied?" *Sociological Quarterly* 30:385–99.
Miller, J. 1980. "Individual and Occupational Determinants of Job Satisfaction: A Focus on Gender Differences." *Sociology of Work and Occupations* 7:337–66.
Mirowsky, J. 1987. "The Psycho-Economics of Feeling Underpaid: Distributive Justice and the Earnings of Husbands and Wives." *American Journal of Sociology* 92:1404–34.

Murray, M.A., and T. Atkinson. 1981. "Gender Differences in Correlates of Job Satisfaction." *Canadian Journal of Behavioral Science* 13:44–52.

Sekaran, U. 1985. "The Paths to Mental Health: An Exploratory Study of Husbands and Wives in Dual-Career Families." *Journal of Occupational Psychology* 58:129–37.

Voydanoff, P. 1980. "Perceived Job Characteristics and Job Satisfaction among Men and Women." *Psychology of Women Quarterly* 5:177–85.

Wolf, W.C., and N.D. Fligstein. 1979. "Sex and Authority in the Workplace: The Causes of Sexual Inequality." *American Sociological Review* 44:235–52.

## Women's Educational Leadership Experience

The fate of women within the administrative ranks of public education is a rather depressing one. Although in the early part of the century women were winning an increasing number of superintendencies and principalships, there has been a steep decline, particularly since World War II, in the numbers of women holding leadership positions in public education (Tyack and Hansot 1982).

New studies on the psychology of women (Chodorow 1978; Gilligan 1982; Lyons 1983; Miller 1976) articulate women's interpersonal orientation toward care and response to others and highlight relational strengths congruent with the needs of modern organizations. Several organizational psychologists, for example, Boyatzis (1982), envision future organizations as connected, interdependent communities of people based on trust, cooperation, and collaboration.

Researchers (Lortie 1975; Sarason 1971) have described the organizational climate of schools as loosely coupled, sometimes lonely work environments and the socialization of teachers as creating a sense of individualism. If schools, in particular, are to become innovative, creative organizations, research indicates that leaders with relational skills are needed, leaders who can foster collaboration and resolve conflicts.

The convergence of these factors raises several questions. Do women school managers differ from men in patterns of considerations used in decision-making and conflict resolution? Do women resolve professional dilemmas with different considerations based on their own value system developed out of their socialization as women? Does organizational level have an impact on patterns of considerations in decision-making and ratings of managerial style? Are women and men equally satisfied with their work in school management?

In keeping with earlier research on women school managers (see, for example, Biklen and Brannigan 1980; Tyack and Hansot 1982), research by Counts (1993) indicated that women superintendents and principals presented a demographic profile typical of women managers in general. The woman school manager was frequently the most educated member of her family of origin, the eldest child, less likely to be married and a parent than a man, older and having entered managerial ranks later, and more highly educated (twice as many women had completed doctoral programs as men).

Counts's research (1993) also found that there was a statistically significant difference between women and men superintendents and principals in patterns of decision-making considerations. Workplace dilemmas were analyzed according to a coding scheme conceptualized by Lyons (1983) based on "rights considerations" (referring to obligations, duties, rules) and "response considerations" (referring to the maintenance of relationships). Women were more likely to make decisions based on responding to others in order to maintain relationships than men. Also, principals used more "response considerations" than superintendents in decision-making. Relatedly, those administrators who were high in "response considerations" in resolving workplace dilemmas were also high on a relational scale for managerial style. Finally, among school managers, women superintendents were the least satisfied with their work.

More research is needed to understand both the values and valuable skills women bring to leadership positions. Women managers may, indeed, carry "the nurturant imperative" (Baruch et al. 1983) into the workplace. Even in jobs that require considerable assertiveness and leadership, the women administrators in Counts's study incorporate a considerable amount of response considerations into their decision-making process in the workplace. However, it is important to note that education is a nurturing profession, and career self-selection determines who chooses to become an educational practitioner.

It is important to note that the superintendency and principalship are very different jobs. A principal is head of a school, responsible to one individual, the superintendent, and enmeshed in daily relationships with teachers, students, and parents. Superintendents, on the other hand, are ultimately responsible for the functioning of a large hierarchically structured organization and report to a group of politically motivated members of the community, the school committee. The varied demands of these positions might, indeed, influence how principals and superintendents perceive themselves as leaders within their school and influence their decision-making.

How do women superintendents, in particular, fit into this analysis? It has been noted that considerations of response to others, although more prevalent in women, are less prevalent in women superintendents' workplace concerns than in women principals' decision-making. It could be inferred that women who assume the role of senior managers, or in this case superintendents, may make some accommodation in terms of their values as women with the responsibilities required of a managerial role. The evidence of the difficulty of the struggle may lie in the fact that women superintendents in Counts's research (1993) were the least satisfied with their work roles of the educational managers.

This process of reconciliation and integration for women managers is an interesting one and well worth further inquiry. It seems to reflect in part Miller's observations (1976) regarding women's psychological development. Women, "unlike other groups, do not need to set affiliation and strength in opposition . . . . We can readily integrate the two, search for more and better ways to use affiliation" (p. 96). In this study, although women managers did integrate the two, the effort seemed to increase with job level.

*Constance Counts*

## Bibliography

Baruch, Grace, Rosalind Barnett, and Caryl Rivers. 1983. *Lifeprints*. New York: New American Library.
Biklen, Sari K., and Marilyn Brannigan. 1980. *Women and Education Leadership*. Lexington, Mass.: D.C. Heath.
Boyatzis, Richard. 1982. *The Competent Manager*. New York: John Wiley and Sons.
Chodorow, Nancy. 1978. *The Reproduction of Mothering*. Berkeley: University of California Press.
Counts, Constance. 1993. "A Relational Managerial Model for Schools: A Study of Women and Men as Superintendents and Principals." *Proteus: A Journal of Ideas* 10(Fall):19–22.

Gilligan, Carol. 1982. *In a Different Voice*. Cambridge, Mass.: Harvard University Press.

Lortie, Dan C. 1975. *Schoolteacher: A Sociological Study*. Chicago: University of Chicago Press.

Lyons, Nona. 1983. "Two Perspectives: On Self, Relationships, and Morality." *Harvard Educational Review* 55(2):125–37.

Miller, Jean Baker. 1976. *Toward a New Psychology of Women*. Boston: Beacon.

Sarason, Seymour B. 1971. *The Culture of the School and The Problem of Change*. Boston: Allyn and Bacon.

Tyack, David B., and Elisabeth Hansot. 1982. *Managers of Virtue: Public School Leadership in America, 1920–1980*. New York: Basic Books.

## Women's Drinking and the Workplace

In American society excessive drinking and drinking-related problems permeate many aspects of contemporary life, including the workplace. Drinking problems may have some roots as well as consequences in the work setting. For this reason, work-based components of drinking problems and behaviors constitute an important topic of study. Furthermore, the past two decades have witnessed a significant influx of women into the labor force, suggesting that women may become subject to the same structural influences, in ways similar or dissimilar to men. Accordingly, this selection reviews the state of theoretical and empirical development of women's drinking and workplace influences by addressing three areas: (1) the importance of a separate focus on women's drinking; (2) research investigating structural sources of drinking problems in the workplace; and (3) research examining the impact of such factors specifically on women.

Before turning more specifically to work-related topics, it is important to clarify, indeed emphasize, the importance of a separate examination of women's drinking. As Ettorre (1992) demonstrates, women are not identical to men in their drinking-related characteristics. Furthermore, substance-abusing women are not a homogeneous grouping. (For literature reviews and empirical analyses regarding women's drinking in general, see Roman 1988; Wilsnack and Beckman 1984; and Wilsnack et al. 1991.)

In the interest of a more accurate understanding of women's drinking, Ettorre advocates challenging the masculinist views currently permeating both theory and research. At present, addiction studies in general are dominated by the medical field. Moreover, conflicts between natural and social sciences, as well as sociology's tendency to omit structural dimensions of gender, have encouraged stereotypical and stigmatized notions regarding women with drinking problems (for example, the disgrace associated with women's misuse of alcohol). Further, alcohol researchers generally interpret problems on an individual level. Because these images and orientations reinforce patriarchal relations and distort views of women, Ettorre proposes a feminist approach, or a "view from below," a perspective informed by women's awareness and struggles for equality.

Specifically addressing the work setting, it is important to review literature concerning structural factors connected to drinking problems, as well as the impact of these factors on women. Investigations during the last two decades have emphasized workplace correlates of drinking behaviors and problem consequences. Roman (1990) provides background regarding the salience of alcohol problems in the work setting. Responding to the lack of coordination and conceptual clarity in this body of literature, Trice and Sonnenstuhl (1990) observe that existing studies tend to form identifiable clusters: cultural, social control, alienation, and stress.

Research from the cultural perspective identifies the prominence of social norms in the workplace. Both administrative and occupational groups evolve generally agreed-upon standards of behavior. For example, tunnel and construction workers emphasize heavy drinking as a high priority, a common practice, and a functional behavior for generating group solidarity. The social control perspective posits that factors diminishing workers' integration into the workplace (absence of supervision and low visibility of performance) will encourage drinking problems. The alienation and stress perspectives are perceived as learned rationales for drinking. The alienation perspective proposes that certain job characteristics (such as boredom, low level of job complexity) generate a sense of dissatisfaction and powerlessness that workers relive through drinking; the work stress perspective examines work-based circumstances (such as role conflicts, overloads, or underloads) that serve to exacerbate already existing emotional distresses.

Other researchers have utilized a generalization perspective, positing that a person's experiences in the workplace are influential (that is, generalized) beyond that setting. Martin et al. (1992) extend the generalization model to examine job conditions that influence drinking behaviors. They report that the job characteristics derived from both alienation (levels of autonomy, extrinsic rewards, closeness of supervision), and stress (work overload, physical effort) were all found to have important direct and indirect effects on consumption, reasons for drinking, and escapist (self-medicating) drinking. In addition, these complex relationships between job characteristics and drinking variables differed for men and women.

Ames and Janes (1990) propose an environmental perspective, urging that greater research attention address the extent of on-the-job drinking and its integration into the workplace environment. Their research findings suggest that: (1) the workplace can be an enabling environment for heavy/problem drinking; and (2) combinations of personal and workplace risk factors distinguish moderate and heavy drinkers.

Both the generalization and environmental approaches view workplace problem drinking as caused by combinations of factors that go beyond the present cultural emphasis on the individual worker's pathology. Accordingly, Trice and Sonnenstuhl (1990) examine workplace risk factors within a more comprehensive framework of other risk sources. They perceive a complexity of risk factors generating alcohol use/abuse, including sociocultural, biological, and psychological aspects, as well as family dynamics and social class. In short, alcohol problems are caused by interactions of different categories of risk factors; the exact relationships involved are still in need of study. Based on available evidence, no single risk factor, whether biological or environmental, is capable of precipitating drinking problems.

Focusing on women, Wilsnack and Wilsnack (1992) review the theoretical state of work and alcohol issues. In particular, they critique the simplistic nature of available explanations, such as: (1) Is paid employment hazardous for women or protective of them? (2) Does employment generate role conflicts/overloads, convergence toward male drinking patterns, or perceptions of job stress precipitating problem drinking? Although some of these factors matter for some women, inconsistencies abound. Further, they conclude that women's drinking and employment are not spuriously related, because of youth or nontraditionality. Parallel to arguments presented regarding workplace influences in general, Wilsnack and Wilsnack propose more complex analysis, going beyond bivariate relationships. Further, they recommend a search for higher-order interactions, a recognition of the diversity in the female population, and greater clarification of employment concepts and measures.

Research from the generalization perspective reflects these suggestions. Parker and Farmer (1988), using a sample of employed men and women in metropolitan Detroit, examined the impact of job pressures on frequency of bar patronage, volume of consumption, symptomatic drinking, and alcohol abuse. They report some common effects for both genders but also some gender distinctions. For both men and women, greater job competition and lower work complexity tend to contribute to symptomatic drinking and alcohol abuse. Concerning structure in the workplace, job pressures increase both bar patronage and consumption volume. For men, however, job pressure takes the form of job competition; for women, it takes the form of time pressure.

In evaluating the current state of the generalization model, Martin et al. (1992), consistent with others cited, recommend large, representative samples, longitudinal data bases, standardization of job and social characteristics, hypothesized interactions, and studies of population subgroups. Regarding drinking behaviors, they argue for clarification of measures and question the validity of consumption as a major indicator of problem drinking.

In conclusion, conceptual and theoretical development of women's drinking and workplace influences is currently at an important transition point. Earlier literature has been inconclusive, controversial, and fragmented to date, but theoretically driven models are developing and directions for future undertakings abound. Research in this area has emerged and matured in recent years; more in-depth studies of employment factors influencing women's drinking can now be undertaken. This review examines major contributions to date, with an emphasis on specific findings as well as recommendations for future investigations.

*Susan M. Cunningham*

## Bibliography

Ames, G., and C. Janes. 1990. "Drinking, Social Networks, and the Workplace: Results of an Environmentally Focused Study." In *Alcohol Problem Intervention in the Workplace: Employee Assistance Programs and Strategic Alternatives*, edited by P. Roman, pp. 95–111. New York: Quorum.

Ettorre, E. 1992. *Women and Substance Use*. New Brunswick, N.J.: Rutgers University.

Martin, J., T. Blum, and P. Roman. 1992. "Drinking to Cope and Self-Medication: Characteristics of Jobs in Relation to Workers' Drinking Behavior." *Journal of Organizational Behavior* 13:55–71.

Parker, D., and G. Farmer. 1988. "The Epidemiology of Alcohol Abuse among Employed Men and Women." In *Recent Developments in Alcoholism*, edited by M. Galanter, pp. 113–30. New York: Plenum.

Roman, P. 1990. "The Salience of Alcohol Problems in the Work Setting: Introduction and Overview." In *Alcohol Problem Intervention in the Workplace: Employee Assistance Programs and Strategic Alternatives*, edited by P. Roman, pp. 1–16. New York: Quorum.

———. 1988. *Women and Alcohol Use: A Review of the Research Literature*. Rockville, Md.: U.S. Department of Health and Human Services.

Trice, H., and W. Sonnenstuhl. 1990. "On the Construction of Drinking Norms in Work Organizations." *Journal of Studies on Alcohol* 51:201–20.

Wilsnack, S., and L. Beckman. 1984. *Alcohol Problems in Women: Antecedents, Consequences, and Intervention*. New York: Guilford.

Wilsnack, S., A. Klassen, B. Schur, and R. Wilsnack. 1991. "Predicting Onset and Chronicity of Women's Problem Drinking: A Five-Year Longitudinal Analysis." *American Journal of Public Health* 81:305–17.

Wilsnack, R., and S. Wilsnack. 1992. "Women, Work, and Alcohol: Failures of Simple Theories." *Alcoholism: Clinical and Experimental Research* 16:172–79.

## Race and Sex Discrimination: A Comparison

Although social scientists believe all minorities confront similar obstacles and endure similar types of discrimination (Dworkin 1982; Zinn 1990), it is possible that the frequency of specific types and the overall incidence of discrimination varies by minority group. This entry explores possible differences in the discrimination experienced by African Americans and women by contrasting discrimination motivated by the victim's race with discrimination motivated by the victim's sex. African-American women, of course, can be victims of both race and sex discrimination but, when I contrast African-American experience to that of women, I am referring to the minority status that motivates the discrimination.

One likely difference is the frequency of discrimination. United States Equal Employment Opportunity Commission data (1990, p.20) show that African Americans are more likely to file race discrimination complaints than women are to file sex discrimination complaints. While black people are about 10.1 percent of the U.S. workforce (U.S. Department of Labor 1988), complaints alleging race discrimination represented 44.7 percent of all complaints filed with government agencies in 1988 (U.S. Equal Employment Opportunity Commission 1990). In comparison, women are 45 percent of the workforce but complaints alleging sex discrimination were only 30.1 percent of all complaints. The fact that blacks file race complaints more often than women file sex complaints suggests that African Americans face a somewhat different workplace environment than that faced by women.

The frequency of the specific types of complaints alleged also appears to vary by minority status. (Examples of types of discrimination include discrimination in promotion, conflict with co-workers because of race or sex, and different terms and conditions of employment.) Differences in the experiences of minorities are probably related to: (1) the resources that a minority group possesses; (2) the attitudes of majority group members toward the minority; (3) the history of the majority group's relationship to the minority group; and (4) the degree of threat the minority group poses to the more privileged members of the majority group.

Regarding resources, white men and women are more likely to possess college degrees (25.4 and 18.45 percent, respectively) while black men and women are less likely (11.6 and 11.9 percent, respectively) (U.S. Bureau of the Census 1991, p.138). Thus white women are more eligible than black men and women for promotions to higher levels in organizations.

Yet white women appear to face obstacles in translating their skills into career and income attainment. It appears therefore that they still confront barriers to advancement in the form of a "glass ceiling" that restricts the number of females who enter high-paying positions and the top levels in many occupations and organizations (Benokraitis and Feagin 1986). Thus, while black workers probably encounter race discrimination at all levels of organizations, white women may encounter relatively more sex discrimination at the upper levels. At upper levels they are more of a threat to the majority males because proportionately more white women than African Americans are qualified.

Equal Employment Opportunity Commission (EEOC) statistics (U.S. EEOC 1990, p.20) show that women are more likely than African Americans to file unequal pay complaints. However, women are not more likely to allege discriminatory denial of promotion. This latter fact may be due to the reluctance of mid-level employees seeking promotions to file complaints against their employers. African Americans, who have less education and are, therefore, more likely to occupy low level positions, may be more willing to file promotion complaints because they have less to lose. O'Connell's analysis (1992) of a sample of discrimination complaints found that women were more likely to be in mid-level career tracts where presumably they have much to lose by filing. However, O'Connell also found that women were more likely to file promotion complaints when complaints alleging pregnancy and sexual harassment discrimination (types of complaints unique to women and that rarely involve the issue of promotion) were removed from the sample.

As alluded to above, a significant proportion of the discrimination women encounter involves pregnancy and sexual harassment. The EEOC (1990, p.20) reports that 25 percent of all sex discrimination cases involve sexual harassment and pregnancy. While women appear to experience less sex discrimination at the entry level, women may face more resistance than black males at the entry level in one occupational category—skilled blue-collar jobs. Statistics show that women are more underrepresented in the craft occupations than African Americans. For example, women are 2.1 percent of all construction workers and blacks are 7.5 percent (U.S. Department of Labor 1988). Historically, both black men and white and black women were excluded from skilled blue-collar occupations, but black men may encounter less resistance today to entry than white and black women encounter because black males did physical labor in heavy industry and construction and skilled blue-collar work is sex stereotyped as male work.

Conflict between majority and minority is a common occurrence on the job; but blacks may encounter more conflict because historically they have faced more hostility than other racial minorities. Therefore, black-white relations in the workplace may be more prone to conflict than female-male relations. Conflict manifests itself in day-to-day interaction with co-workers and supervisors. The EEOC does not categorize cases by the presence of on-the-job conflict, but two conflict-related issues suggest greater black-white than female-male conflict. Blacks are more likely to file complaints alleging discriminatory discharge and discipline (U.S. EEOC 1990, p.20). One study of the content of complaints filed with a state agency (O'Connell 1992) found that race discrimination complaints are three times as likely as sex discrimination complaints to involve allegations of conflict on the job. In that study, women were more likely than African Americans to allege discrimination in hiring and promotion and those alleging such discrimination were more likely to obtain a cause finding while those alleging conflict with co-workers and supervisors were less likely. In fact, in O'Connell's study those filing sex discrimination complaints were six times as likely as those filing race discrimination complaints to obtain a cause finding.

## Conclusion

Currently, our knowledge of the distribution of types of discrimination experienced by minorities is very limited. But for historical and empirical reasons social scientists have reason to believe that minority groups will have differing relations with their respective majorities and will experience both different frequencies of the types of discrimination and different amounts of discrimination overall. Research sensitive to these differences is needed, especially those related to the more subtle processes that occur in the workplace. There are many unexplored issues. For example, to increase our knowledge of the workplace, research is needed on the amount and types of conflict-related discrimination different minorities encounter.

Separating discrimination motivated by sex from discrimination motivated by race can help researchers estimate the extent to which black women pay a double price for occupying two minority statuses. The fact that the black-female/white-female wage gap is now quite small despite greater white education suggests that race discrimination is less of an obstacle than sex discrimination. It appears that black women have advanced by gaining access to traditionally white female occupations (Blau 1984). However, Fullbright (1986) reports that black female managers have less upward mobility than either black males or white females. So the extent to which the oppression of black women is "interlocked" (Collins 1986) is an open question.

There are policy-related benefits to research on differences in victimization by minority status. Knowledge of discrimination differences will facilitate efforts to combat discrimination because law enforcement agencies can use such knowledge to concentrate on the types of discrimination a minority is more likely to encounter (for example, if women experience relatively more discrimination when seeking promotion to upper-level positions and blacks experience relatively more conflict with co-workers and supervisors, government officials can target these areas). At this time only 3 percent of discrimination complaints produce cause findings (U.S. General Accounting Office 1988). So research relevant to reform of the process is needed.

*Lenahan O'Connell*

## Bibliography

Benokraitis, Nijole V., and Joe R. Feagin. 1986. *Modern Sexism: Blatant, Subtle, and Covert Discrimination.* Englewood Cliffs, N.J.: Prentice Hall.

Blau, Francine. 1984. "Discrimination against Women: Theory and Evidence." In *Labor Economics: Modern Views,* edited by William Darity. Boston: Kluwer-Nijhoff.

Collins, Patricia Hill. 1986. "Learning from the Outsider within: The Sociological Significance of Black Feminist Thought." *Social Problems* 33:514–31.

Dworkin, Rosalind J. 1982. "A Women's Report: Numbers are Not Enough." In *The Minority Report,* edited by Anthony G. Dworkin and Rosalind J. Dworkin. New York: Holt, Rinehart and Winston.

Fullbright, Karen. 1986. "The Myth of the Double Advantage: Black Female Managers." In *Slipping through the Cracks: The Status of Black Women,* edited by Margaret C. Simms and Julianne Maluveaux. New Brunswick, N.J.: Transaction.

O'Connell, Lenahan. 1992. "Types of Discrimination and the Complaint Investigation Process: Why Subtle Discrimination is Difficult to Prove." Paper presented at the American Sociological Assn. meetings, Pittsburgh, 1992.

U. S. Bureau of the Census. 1991. *Statistical Abstract of the United States.* (111th ed.) Washington, D.C.: U.S. Department of Commerce.

U.S. Department of Labor, Bureau of Labor Statistics. 1988. *Employment and Earnings.* 36(January):183–88.

U.S. Equal Employment Opportunity Commission. 1990. *Combined Annual Report Fiscal Years 1986, 1987, 1988.* Washington, D.C.: U.S. Government Printing Office.

U.S. General Accounting Office. 1988. *Equal Employment Opportunity: EEOC and State Agencies Do Not Fully Investigate Discrimination Charges.* Washington, D.C.: U.S. Government Printing Office.

Zinn, Maxine Baca. 1990. "Family, Feminism and Race in America." *Gender and Society* 4:68–82.

## Sexual Harassment: Psychological and Behavioral Issues

Over the past fifteen years it has become apparent that sexual harassment is a common and serious problem in organizations (Gutek 1985; MacKinnon 1979). Individuals' perceptions of what constitutes sexual harassment may vary based on a number of situational factors such as the relative power of the harasser, group norms, and the type and frequency of the harassing behavior (Collins and Blodgett 1981; Konrad and Gutek 1986). Further, personal characteristics of the harassees, such as their race, gender, religion, marital status, sex-role attitudes, work experience, and self-esteem may influence perceptions of and reactions to potentially harassing behaviors (Baker et al. 1990; Gutek 1985). Estimates of the frequency of sexual harassment vary widely depending on the sample and research methods employed; however, a large-scale study done by the United States Merit Systems Protection Board (USMSPB) (1981) found that 42 percent of female and 14 percent of male federal government workers were victims of such behaviors. The occurrence of sexual harassment can have severe physiological and psychological effects on individuals and can lead to increased turnover and absenteeism (Crull 1982). Further, the climate and effectiveness of the work groups within which such incidents occur is often degraded, resulting in lowered productivity (USMSPB 1988).

A number of theories have been offered to explain why sexual harassment happens. For example, the occurrence of harassment may be affected by biological factors, sex-role socialization, group norms, and the status and power of the individuals involved (Tangri et al. 1982). There continues to be some confusion over what constitutes sexual harassment. Although legal definitions exist, they often contain ambiguities (MacKinnon 1979). Further, people's personal interpretations of harassing behaviors are affected by many individual and situational factors.

The most commonly reported forms of sexual harassment among federal workers were sexually related teasing, looks, gestures, and touching (USMSPB 1988). The board also found that more severe forms of harassment, such as demands for sexual relations and rape, occurred much less frequently. Similar results were found by Gutek (1985) in her study of a random sample of Los Angeles–area workers. Over half of the women she surveyed reported that they had been harassed with behaviors such as nonsexual touching and sexually related comments and gestures that were meant to be complimentary. While less frequently occurring, a sizable proportion (8 percent) of the women said that they had been asked to have sexual relations as a condition of their jobs. These two surveys also indicate that the majority of harassers are married, older than the harassee, and a co-worker or peer (as opposed to a supervisor).

Reactions to sexual harassment seem to be influenced by the implied or overt threat associated with the behavior (USMSPB 1981, 1988). When individuals are harassed by co-workers they tend to see few positive consequences for going along with the unwanted behavior and few negative consequences for refusing to comply. Thus, ignoring such behaviors is a common response to harassment. However, when immediate supervisors are the harassers, the victims do perceive that power may be used against them if they do not comply, and that they may receive rewards for going along. If the harasser is a supervisor higher in the organizational hierarchy than the victim's immediate supervisor, individuals have a lower fear of retribution for not complying with the behavior. Thus, it seems supervisors closest in the hierarchy and those with direct organizational power are most feared.

Subsequent research by Baker et al. (1990) indicates that for the more threatening behaviors, the most frequent reactions are to report the incident, leave the field or job, and physically resist. For the less threatening behaviors, harassees are more likely to ignore the behavior, avoid the protagonist, or alter themselves or the environment. Harassees are also more likely to directly confront the harasser regarding the less severe incidents. Baker et al.'s research (1990) indicates that the type of immediate reaction may also be influenced by the harassees' gender, religion, attitudes toward women, self-esteem, and locus of control.

As might be expected, many workers are deeply troubled by sexually harassing situations and seek advice from others. According to the 1981 USMSPB study, about half of the women and a third of the men discussed the harassment behavior with others. Typically, victims talk with co-workers, friends, or relatives. However, talking with such individuals seems to be relatively ineffective, as these people have little power to improve the situation. Even talking to individuals with some authority in the situation was not always helpful. For example, women who had suffered severe harassment, such as rape, found that talking with Equal Employment Opportunity Officers or union officials often had no effect or negative effects. The most effective methods for stopping sexually harassing behaviors were the assertive responses such as asking or telling the person to stop and reporting the behavior to a supervisor or other official.

Relatively few workers actually file formal complaints or contact someone in authority about the incident (Gutek 1985). Many of those who do not complain about sexual harassment worry that they might be blamed for the incident or that nothing will be done. Gutek also reported that many women did not report the incident because they feared that the harasser might be harmed by the action. Thus, the victims tended to keep quiet about the offensive behaviors in spite of their suffering.

Regardless of whether sexual harassment victims file charges and win their cases their careers may be negatively affected. Gutek (1985) reported that 9 percent of the women she surveyed had at some point quit their jobs because they were sexually harassed. Five percent of the women had been transferred and almost 10 percent had quit trying for a job because of sexual harassment. Another 7 percent had lost a job because they had refused sex. Even more dramatic findings were reported by Crull (1982), who found that 42 percent of the female sexual harassment victims in her study had resigned from their jobs because of the incidents. These are serious career hurdles that men do not typically have to overcome. For example, among Gutek's (1985) male respondents, only 1 percent had ever quit a job because they were sexually harassed and 0.2 percent had transferred because of harassment.

Given that women are the predominant victims of sexual harassment, some argue that it is a mechanism men use to keep women out of nontraditional jobs thereby protecting men's position of economic privilege (Farley 1978; Mac-Kinnon 1979). Even if such a control strategy is not consciously pursued by men, the effects of harassment on women are multifaceted and deleterious. In addition to the direct career problems caused by sexual harassment, many individuals suffer emotional harm and negative psychological consequences.

There is strong evidence that the effects of sexual harassment on individuals are very serious. For example, Crull (1982) found that of the sexual harassment victims she surveyed, 90 percent had suffered psychological problems, 75 percent had decreased work performance, and 63 percent experienced physical health problems related to the harassment. Similarly, Tangri et al.'s analysis (1982) of the 1981 USMSPB data indicates that 36 percent of the women and 19 percent of the men who were sexually harassed had decreased positive feelings toward their work. Similarly, 33 percent of the women and 21 percent of the men had negative emotional reactions. Further, 8 to 15 percent had a lower ability to work with others on the job, reduced time at work, and decreased quality and quantity of work. Gutek (1985) reports similar evidence. Of the harassment victims she surveyed, 38 percent had a deterioration in their feelings about work and 28 percent had reduced feelings about their relationships with others on the job. In addition, of these victims 80 percent experienced disgust, 68 percent anger, and 20 percent depression in response to the sexual harassment (Jensen and Gutek 1982).

In another study, Loy and Stewart (1984) assessed the emotional and physiological reactions to four types of sexual harassment: verbal commentary, verbal negotiation, physical manhandling, and physical assault. Emotional reactions were the most common response to all types of harassing incidents. Eighty percent of those who were harassed with verbal commentary suffered emotional reactions such as nervousness, irritability, uncontrolled anger, or loss of motivation. Twenty percent of those who had been harassed with verbal commentary suffered physiological problems such as uncontrolled crying, sleeplessness, weight loss, and stomach pains. For the more severe incidents of physical assault, a higher proportion of the victims suffered from physiological problems.

Another detrimental effect suffered by victims of sexual harassment, reported by Loy and Stewart (1984), dealt with problems of social stigmatization. Following the harassing incident 31 percent of the victims they studied were ignored by the harasser. Another third of the victims were not supported by their peers. Others have found that harassment victims often fear retaliation if they complain about the incident. Such social isolation is likely to compound the negative job and personal consequences for the victims.

In light of these many negative psychosocial effects, it is not surprising that individuals report lowered productivity, increased absenteeism, reduced commitment, and interrupted careers resulting from sexual harassment (Gutek 1985; USMSPB 1981). Sexual harassment can also negatively affect group work climate, ultimately leading to lowered organizational productivity. For example, the USMSPB (1988) estimates that reduced productivity resulting from sexual harassment cost the federal government at least $267 million (for the period from May 1985 to May 1987), not including the personal costs and grief the victims had to bear. To obtain compensation for the suffering caused by sexual harassment, individuals are increasingly seeking redress from state and federal equal employment opportunity commissions and courts, further increasing litigation and settlement costs for organizations (Waks and Starr 1982).

Because sexual harassment is such a complex problem, it does not lend itself to a simple interpretation and solution. To begin to understand the causes and effects of sexual harassment, we need to identify who is most vulnerable to such behaviors, what types of behaviors are perceived as harassing, and what the subsequent effects are in the short and long run. In turn, it is important to assess the effects of sexual harassment on the groups and organizations within which it occurs. Based upon this knowledge policies should be developed to reduce its occurrence and negative impact.

*Douglas D. Baker*

## Bibliography

Baker, D.D., D.E. Terpstra, and K. Larntz. 1990. "The Influence of Individual Characteristics and Severity of Harassing Behavior on Reactions to Sexual Harassment." *Sex Roles* 22(5/6):305–25.

Collins, E.G.C., and T.B. Blodgett. 1981. "Sexual Harassment: Some See It . . . Some Won't." *Harvard Business Review* 59(2):76–95.

Crull, P. 1982. "Stress Effects of Sexual Harassment on the Job: Implications for Counseling." *American Journal of Orthopsychiatry* 52:539–44.

Farley, L. 1978. *Sexual Shakedown: The Sexual Harassment of Women on the Job.* New York: McGraw-Hill.

Gutek, B.A. 1985. *Sex and the Workplace.* San Francisco: Jossey-Bass.

Jensen, I., and B.A. Gutek. 1982. "Attributions and Assignment of Responsibility in Sexual Harassment." *Journal of Social Issues* 38(4):121–36.

Konrad, A.M., and B.A. Gutek. 1986. "Impact of Work Experiences on Attitudes toward Sexual Harassment." *Administrative Science Quarterly* 31:422–38.

Loy, P.H., and L.P. Stewart. 1984. "The Extent of Affects of the Sexual Harassment of Working Women." *Sociological Focus* 17(1):31–43.

MacKinnon, C. 1979. *Sexual Harassment of Working Women: A Case of Sex Discrimination.* New Haven: Yale University Press.

Tangri, S., M.R. Burt, and L.B. Johnson. 1982. "Sexual Harassment at Work: Three Explanatory Models." *Journal of Social Issues* 38(4):55–74.

U.S. Merit Systems Protection Board. 1981. *Sexual Harassment in the Federal Workplace: Is It a Problem?* Washington, D.C.: U.S. Government Printing Office.

———. 1988. *Sexual Harassment in the Federal Government: An Update.* Washington, D.C.: U.S. Government Printing Office.

Waks, J.W., and M.G. Starr. 1982. "The Sexual Shakedown in Perspective: Sexual Harassment in Its Social and Legal Contexts." *Employee Relations Law Journal* 7:567–86.

# Factors Influencing Work Performance and Effectiveness

## Computers, Gender, and Elementary-School Teaching

Until recently, an underlying assumption in the literature on occupations has been that new technology would affect the work of men and women uniformly. Current research on occupational skilling, however, reveals that this is not necessarily the case, suggesting a need to examine more closely the experiences of women upon the introduction of new technology to their workplace (Wajcman 1991; Wright 1987). The consequences of computer technology on the work of elementary-school teachers offers an opportunity to consider this issue in greater depth. When effectively integrated into their work routines, computers offer teachers an important instrument with which they may develop relevant technical skills, enhance their teaching strategies, and expand their autonomy in the elementary-school setting (Evans-Andris 1991). Because of differences in computing styles, the introduction of computers in elementary schools does not affect the work of men and women in the same way. Even though men are more likely to possess technical computer skills (Kay 1992; Lewis 1987), among those teachers who demonstrate proficiency with computers, women are more likely to integrate the computer as a relevant teaching tool (Evans-Andris 1991; Lewis 1987). In an environment that traditionally has been characterized by relatively homogeneous skills and occupational rewards among workers, the introduction of computers may have critical implications for the structure of women's work at the elementary school level.

Previous studies examining the effects of technology on skill requirements generally argued that technology either uniformly upgraded worker skills or deskilled workers (Vallas 1990). These studies employed notions of skill that were narrowly defined and emphasized the technical competency of workers. Wajcman (1991) argues that traditional definitions of skill are gender biased and, in fact, promote male dominance in the workplace.

Recent evidence regarding computer technology and work suggest that men are more likely than women to possess technical computing skills (Lewis 1987). While women may possess lower levels of skills technically, they are not necessarily less proficient with computers. Research reveals, rather, that women and men use computers differently (Becker 1985; Kay 1992; Lewis 1987; Turkel

1984). Men tend to approach computers in a technical fashion, focusing on programming, computer manipulation, and graphic techniques as an end in themselves (Becker 1985; Lewis 1987). Women, on the other hand, are more apt to approach computers in a humanistic manner, using the equipment as a productive tool in their work and incorporating it into cooperative activities (Lewis 1987).

## Computing among Elementary-School Teachers

The two different computing styles are expressed by the utilization patterns among elementary-school teachers. In a study on computers and occupational dynamics in nine elementary schools, Evans-Andris (1991) found that a disproportionate number of men who were proficient with computers used computer class time to promote the technical aspects of computers among their students. Their lessons frequently included lectures on flow-charting, internal computer operations, technical terminology, and so forth. Moreover, these teachers most often presented their computer lessons in isolation from their other curricular agendas. On the other hand, female teachers with apparently similar levels of computer proficiency typically integrated computer applications into their regular working agenda. For example, a teacher might present a lesson on a particular topic and then guide her students to relevant software in order to exemplify or reinforce the learning concepts. Likewise, it was not uncommon for these teachers to assign special projects or reports for their students, which required the use of computers. Additionally, these teachers usually volunteered to train other teachers in their schools who lacked computer skills. Generally, female teachers who were proficient with computers applied the technology in creative ways that championed the idea of computer innovation in their schools, strengthened their teaching skills, and enhanced classroom lessons.

These different approaches to computer technology raise questions regarding the effects of the technology on the work of men and women. Under what conditions are elementary school teachers rewarded for their computing skills? Evans-Andris (1991) found that the acquisition of technical skills alone did not guarantee occupational rewards for teachers. The competent male teachers whose lessons focused on the technical aspects of computing went largely unrewarded for their expertise. Although they gained recognition because of their technical skills, other teachers often viewed those skills as irrelevant to the job of teaching. Women who were proficient with computers received important rewards for their skills. They attained high visibility in their school communities because of the popularity of their computing activities among students and because of their efforts to promote the idea of computer innovation among other faculty members. They exercised greater decision-making by coordinating and managing the computing activities in their schools. Finally, they reported that they increased their opportunities for occupational advancement because of their proficiency with computers.

The recognition of technical skill at the expense of other technology-related skills has produced a distorted view of the effects of technology in the workplace, particularly with regard to the work of women. Whereas previous evaluations of the effects of technology on work favored technically competent workers, the experiences of elementary-school teachers with computers reveal that the acquisition of technical skills does not automatically result in occupational rewards. Only those computer-proficient teachers who used the technology in ways relevant to elementary-school teaching gained important rewards in schools. This suggests a need to expand the concept of skill to reflect a broader level of proficiency with technology. This will promote a more accurate understanding of the effects of technology on the work of both men and women.

There may be critical implications for the structure of women's work as schools continue to introduce computer technology at the elementary level. Teachers should be encouraged to develop and integrate both technical and humanistic computing skills in the classroom so that they will be fully competent to engage the technology in ways that are most meaningful and relevant to their work. Teachers who demonstrate an integrated level of computer proficiency will be more likely to experience positive effects from the technology in their work. When teachers do this, they will increase their opportunities for occupational rewards. Additionally, through their experiences with computer technology they will inspire other teachers as well as students to model their innovative behavior.

*Melissa Evans-Andris*

## Bibliography

Becker, Howard J. 1985. "Men and Women as Computer Using Teachers." *Sex Roles.* 13(3/4):137–48.

Evans-Andris, M. 1991. "Computer Technology and Occupational Dynamics among Teachers in Elementary Schools." Unpublished doctoral dissertation, Department of Sociology, Indiana University.

Kay, Robin. 1992. "An Analysis of Methods Used to Examine Gender Differences in Computer-Related Behavior." *Journal of Educational Computing Research* 8(3):277–90.

Lewis, L. 1987. "Females and Computers: Fostering Involvement." In *Women, Work and Technology,* edited by B. Wright et al., pp. 268–80. Ann Arbor: University of Michigan Press.

Lockheed, Marlaine E. 1985. "Women, Girls, and Computers: A First Look at the Evidence." *Sex Roles* 13(3/4):115–22.

Turkel, S. 1984. *The Second Self: Computers and the Human Spirit.* New York: Simon and Schuster.

Vallas, S. 1990. "The Concept of Skill." *Work and Occupations* 17:379–98.

Wajcman, J. 1991. "Patriarchy, Technology and Conceptions of Skill." *Work and Occupations* 18:29–45.

Wright, B. 1987. *Women, Work and Technology.* Ann Arbor: University of Michigan Press.

## Male-Female Communication in the Workplace: Invisible Barriers to Upward Mobility

Women are joining the workforce in increasing numbers; presently more than 50 percent of all women work. They are better trained and educated than their predecessors yet they still are not achieving executive positions in the corporate hierarchy (Raynolds 1987). Among other factors such as sex-role stereotype, lack of mentoring, and career/family concerns (Ragins and Sundstrom 1989), women's communication style might be a subtle barrier to their success. Women communicate differently than men (Carli 1990; Lakoff 1975). As corporate America is male dominated and career potential is evaluated based on male behavior patterns, this difference in communication style could affect women's career success.

### The Male Managerial Model

Corporate America is a patriarchal society, a society that views and evaluates the world from the male frame of reference. Anything that differs from this perspective is considered deviant. Thus in organizations, it is male behavior that is the standard against which women are compared. It is masculine personality characteristics such as aggressiveness, competitiveness, directness, and ambition that are perceived as requisite characteristics for successful management careers (Powell 1988; Powell and Butterfield 1989; Schein 1975, 1978), and both men and women have indicated a preference for stereotypical male management behaviors. Women are perceived as too emotional, gentle, illogical, and sensitive to succeed in the corporate environment, and their use of "women's language" reinforces those perceptions.

### Male-Female Communications

According to Lakoff (1975), women use more hedges, "I think," "perhaps"; more tag questions, a question such as "isn't it" or "right?" following a declarative sentence; more polite and grammatically correct language and weaker expletives than men. Empirical evidence on the differences between men's and women's speech is limited, and existing research provides mixed results. Yet, it is generally agreed a gender difference does exist.

Women are discriminated against linguistically in two ways: how they are taught to use language and how language treats them. From childhood, they are taught to speak "like a lady" and, in today's world, when they do they place themselves in a no-win situation. If they comply, using linguistics that are perceived as submissive and powerless, "women's language," they are judged as unintelligent and lacking in the ability to participate in serious discussions. On the other hand, if they don't comply, they are criticized for lacking femininity and being "bitchy."

While women do most of the work in maintaining a conversation, it is generally men who control the interaction. Men decide what is appropriate or inappropriate in conversation. When women control conversations they are perceived negatively, as acting inappropriately (Fishman 1983). In a similar vein, men interrupt women more in cross-sex conversations and this is indicative of a power differential that exists between men and women in face-to face interactions in today's culture (West and Zimmerman 1983).

In addition to language usage, Henley (1977) explored the effects of women's nonverbal communications. She demonstrated that space, time, touch, expression, demeanor, and environment can be means of communicating power, status, and dominance between men and women. Women are taught to sit "properly, like a lady"; men can sprawl and command more space. Usually it is the less powerful who are kept waiting, and in corporate America women are the less powerful. Thus, women's communication style affects their ability to communicate effectively.

Networking and access to information is crucial to upward career mobility. The informal network is particularly important because that is how one forms alliances, obtains information, and learns the ropes. Yet women are frequently excluded from networks and sources of information or exclude themselves (Fairhurst 1985). Women tend to network with other women rather than with men. While establishing and maintaining networks within their organization, their profession, and their community will allow women to be heard and known to one another, in the corporate environment networking primarily with other women could be nonproductive for them, as they are excluded from the men's network, the dominant network.

## Impact of Gender-Role Stereotypes in the Workplace

Communication patterns support many of the existing stereotypes about men and women. From early childhood women are socialized to believe men are the bread-winners, women the homemakers. Men are strong, assertive, intelligent; women are weak, submissive, and flighty. Yet these stereotypes cannot be supported in today's world. There are men and women who are strong, assertive, and intelligent, just as there are men and women who are weak, submissive, and flighty. While some men have become homemakers, an ever-increasing number of women are becoming breadwinners (Hunsaker 1985). These stereotypical portrayals put working women in a double bind.

Women work for economic survival, yet their employment opportunities are restricted by tradition and stereotypical roles that have developed over the years, most notably since the Industrial Revolution. Although women adopt the role of businesswomen, they have trouble relinquishing the roles of housewife and mother. Women continue to assume principal responsibility for their home, family, and social life in addition to their career responsibilities (Hunsaker 1985).

While there tends to be a belief that family responsibilities are more equally shared between men and women in dual-career families, in *The Second Shift* Hochschild and Machung (1989) demonstrated that women still assume most of the responsibility for running the house. What confronts working women now is how to overcome and adapt their socialized beliefs that they are the principal care-takers of the home in order to survive and succeed in today's changing environment. They need to reformat their lives to equalize their career opportunities and constraints with those of their spouses (Hertz 1986).

Kanter (1977) noted it is not women's skills and abilities that limit their success; rather it is the roles in which they are placed within the organization that determines their effectiveness or lack of it. She also argued that women's scarcity in organizations, particularly in positions of power, affects their environment and performance. Women often find themselves alone among male peers, where they are perceived as "tokens," symbols of all women. As tokens, women are highly visible. This can be advantageous because it allows one to become known within the organization, but it can also be detrimental as one can be isolated and perceived as different.

Stereotypical perceptions of "women's work" still exist. For example, as women's numbers in a particular occupation increase, the prestige and pay scale of the position declines, implying it is the perception of a woman's role that carries the stigma of insignificance and not the occupation itself. However, research on the behavioral differences of males and females shows few differences between them. In fact, considerable evidence exists that male and female managers have similar traits, ambitions, values, and job-related skills and behaviors (Powell 1988).

## New Directions for Research on Male-Female Communications

In a study evaluating perceived career potential and co-worker attractiveness, Booth (1991) found respondents perceived males and females the same when they delivered the same message, using the same assertive language in the same office environment. Considerable research has focused on sex stereotypes and gender issues in recent years but little has been done to integrate the findings. Not only is it necessary to have a thorough understanding of the similarities and differences between men and women, it is also necessary to appreciate individual differences and utilize the resources that are available.

Women are a vital, valuable, and costly resource in organizations. To attract and retain them, it will be necessary for corporations to incorporate women into the system, provide them with challenging work, and reward them appropriately. New directions in research on gender and communications at work must incorporate women's values into the male-dominated system. Rather than forcing women to conform to the male system, perhaps it is better to adapt the system to be more flexible and tolerant of diversity.

*Rosemary Booth*
*Terri A. Scandura*

## Bibliography

Booth, R. 1991. *Power Talk: Perceptions of Women's and Men's Career Potential in Organizations.* Unpublished doctoral dissertation, University of Kentucky, Lexington.

Carli, L.L. 1990. "Gender, Language and Influence." *Journal of Personality and Social Psychology* 59(5):941–51.

Fairhurst, G.T. 1985. "Male-Female Communication on the Job: Literature Review and Commentary." In *Communication Research 9*, edited by R.N. Bostrom, pp. 83–116. Newbury Park, Calif.: Sage.

Fishman, P.M. 1983. "Interaction: The Work Women Do." In *Language, Gender and Society,* edited by B. Thorne, C. Kramarae, and N. Henley, pp. 89–101. Cambridge, Mass.: Newbury House.

Henley, N.M. 1977. *Body Politics.* New York: Simon and Schuster.

Hertz, R. 1986. *More Equal than Others.* Berkeley: University of California Press.

Hochschild, A., and A. Machung, 1989. *The Second Shift.* New York: Viking.

Hunsaker, J.S. 1985. "Work and Family Life Must Be Integrated." In *Women in Management.* 2nd ed., edited by B.A. Stead, pp. 68–74. Englewood Cliffs, N.J.: Prentice-Hall.

Kanter, R.M. 1977. *Men and Women of the Corporation.* New York: Basic Books.

Lakoff, R. 1975. *Language and Woman's Place.* New York: Harper and Row.

Powell, G.N. 1988. *Women and Men in Management.* Newbury Park, Calif.: Sage.

Powell, G.N., and D.A. Butterfield. 1989. "The 'Good Manager': Did Androgyny Fare Better in the 1980s?" *Group and Organizational Studies* 14(2):216–33.

Ragins, B.R., and E. Sundstrom. 1989. "Gender and Power in Organizations: A Longitudinal Perspective." *Psychological Bulletin* 105(1):51–88.

Raynolds, E.H. 1987. "Management Women in the Corporate Workplace: Possibilities for the Year 2000." *Human Resource Management* 26(2):265–76.

Schein, V.E. 1975. "Relationships between Sex Role Stereotypes and Requisite Management Characteristics among Female Managers." *Journal of Applied Psychology* 60(3):340–44.

———. 1978. "Sex-Role Stereotyping Ability and Performance: Research and New Directions." *Personal Psychology* 31:259–68.

West, C., and D.H. Zimmerman. 1983. "Interaction: The Work Women Do." In *Language, Gender and Society,* edited by B. Thorne, C. Kramarae, and N. Henley, pp. 102–17. Cambridge, Mass.: Newbury House.

## Successful Job Search and Informal Networks

Both researchers and the public have an interest in how interaction patterns between the sexes influence the job acquisition process and promotion opportunities of individuals. In the last twenty years or so, buzz phrases such as "old boy network," "new girl network," "networking," and most recently "sisterhood betrayal" reflect this interest. These nebulous, common-sense notions continue to characterize most people's understanding of informal recruitment processes. Yet recently, some empirical work on same-gender and cross-gender networks has contributed to our growing understanding of the relationship between informal recruitment (that is, employee and business referrals) and de facto sexual discrimination.

Mark Granovetter's groundbreaking research (1974, 1982) sparked a variety of research on informal information networks and occupational attainment. One line of research examined sex differences in access to informal job information and sex segregation. Research has revolved around three separate issues: (1) Are men and women equally likely to utilize personal networks in job search? (2) Are the sexes equally successful in gaining employment through personal networks? (3) Does a successful informal search produce similar outcomes for men and women?

In one review of the literature, Roos and Reskin (1984) conclude, "Studies suggest that the use of personal contacts in securing initial employment is more effective for men, which may explain men's greater propensity to use them" (p. 246). However, subsequent studies including statistical controls and larger representative samples challenge such conclusions (Campbell and Rosenfeld 1985; Marsden and Campbell 1990; Moore 1990). Women's personal networks, are the same size as male networks, and differences in network composition are considerably reduced when variables related to employment, family, and age are controlled (Moore 1990). Further, women do not appear to differ significantly in their disposition or successful use of informal networks in job search (Campbell and Rosenfeld 1985; Corcoran et al. 1980). Female job searchers use and find jobs through informal networks as often as male job searchers.

Kanter (1977) and more recently Moore (1990) advance a structuralist position to understand why informal networks do not produce the same outcomes for males and females. If women held the positions of power in work organizations that men presently hold, women's outcomes for informal search (that is, pay and mobility) would converge with those of their male peers. Moore (1990) argues that it is a lack of structural power and not women's psychological dispositions that hinders the use of instrumental networks.

While generally agreeing with the structuralist approach, we have contended that this position overestimates the primacy of employment relationships and at least underestimates the resiliency of the patriarchal family. Female and male behavior in the distribution of job information continues to be influenced by more than one hierarchy. Men and women may both seek and find employment through informal networks, but the information is tinged by sexist attitudes.

Our research (Marx and Leicht 1989) on 329 external hires in one major bank revealed that referrals are the predominant means by which job searchers acquired positions. Both men and women utilize this search strategy, but the gender networks operate in distinctive ways.

The traditional notion of the "old boy network" receives some support. Men are more likely to recommend male friends and business associates for positions. Further, men are more likely to directly influence the selection process for male referrals than for female referrals. Male contacts appear to be territorial in the referral process. They referred women for subordinate positions only and displayed a reluctance to recommend other males to positions with authority over themselves.

The results provide greater support for the notion of the "new girl network" than "sisterhood betrayal." Other women provide a valuable resource to female job searchers. Women provide female job searchers with employment information and influence the selection process in their favor. Unlike male contacts, female information sources often refer women to positions of equal or greater authority in the organization. While researchers such as Madden (1987) and Briles (1987) find large numbers of working women feeling they have been betrayed by female co-workers, our results suggest that many women promote the interests of other women. On a negative note, women and men direct female ties into sex-typed employment.

Since our research (Marx and Leicht 1989) examined only one organization with limited controls, our results must be interpreted with great caution. However, the findings do hint at the resiliency of patriarchal structures in job acquisition and point to the need for additional research on gender networks and occupational sex segregation.

*Jonathan Marx*
*Kevin T. Leicht*

## Bibliography

Briles, J. 1987. *Women to Women: Fom Sabotage to Support*. Fars Hills, N.J.: New Horizon.

Campbell, K.E., and R.A. Rosenfeld. 1985. "Job Search and Job Mobility: Sex & Race Differences." *Research in the Sociology of Work* 3:147–74.

Corcoran, M., L. Datcher, and G.J. Duncan. 1980. "Information and Influence in the Labor Market." In *Five Thousand Families—Patterns of Economic Progress*. Vol. 8, edited by Greg J. Duncan and James Morgan, pp. 1–38. Ann Arbor: Institute for Social Research, University of Michigan.

Granovetter, Mark S. 1974. *Getting a Job: A Study of Contacts and Careers*. Cambridge, Mass.: Harvard University Press.

———. 1982. "The Strength of Weak Ties: A Network Theory Revisited." In *Social Structures and Network Analysis*, edited by Peter V. Marsden and Nan Lin, pp. 105–30. Beverly Hills, Calif.: Sage.

Kanter, R.M. 1977. *Men and Women of the Corporation*. New York: Basic Books.

Madden, T.R. 1987. *Women vs. Women: Uncivil Business War*. New York: AMACOM.

Marsden, P.V., and K.E. Campbell. 1990. "Recruitment and Selection Processes: The Organizational Side of Job Search." In *Social Mobility and Social Structure*, edited by Ronald Brieger, pp. 59–79. Cambridge: Cambridge University Press.

Marx, J., and K.T. Leicht. 1989. "Successful Informal Job Search: A Gender Comparison of Network Structure." A paper presented at the 30th annual meeting of the Midwest Sociological Society in St. Louis.

Moore, G. 1990. "Structural Determinants of Men's and Women's Personal Networks." *American Sociological Review* 55 (October):726–35.

Roos, P.A., and B.F. Reskin. 1984. "Institutional Factors Contributing to Sex Segregation in the Workplace." In *Sex Segregation in the Workplace: Trends, Explanations, Remedies*, edited by Barbara F. Reskin, pp. 235–60. Washington, D.C.: National Academy.

## Human Resource's Challenge: The Work-Family Interface

The potential for conflict between work and family for most employed persons is great. While the issue of taking care of home-based situations has traditionally been viewed as a female concern, research suggests males have similar concerns. They are also challenged by attempts to balance career and family matters (Shellenbarger 1992). Men are relaxing their work commitments as family considerations are increasing in importance (Friedman 1987). As organizations strive to address work-family issues, human-resource (HR) professionals will be called upon to play a major role in developing and implementing work-family interface policies (Nollen 1989).

Research on the work-family interface has found: (1) general stereotypes about women and men and their traditional roles are often deeply held and resistant to change (Shellenbarger 1992); (2) both men and women tend to feel that home life gives them more satisfaction than career or other interests (Schultz et al. 1989); (3) women and men may view the importance of work-family issues quite differently (Covin and Brush 1991); and (4) work-family interface issues are associated with productivity (Fernandez 1986), job satisfaction (Wiley 1987), and intention to quit (Burke 1989).

Organizations have been slow to recognize the consequences of work-family interdependence (Shellenbarger 1992). While much attention has been paid to "family-friendly" firms, closer examination shows less activity in the work-family arena than anecdotal evidence suggests. A 1992 survey revealed two-thirds of respondents would never offer even minimal assistance to working parents (Shellenbarger 1992). Among employers who claim to offer family-friendly programs, most are very informal, with no written policy and limited coverage to a few employees.

Senior managers are frequently unaware of the daily issues confronting employees and are not inclined to address them as business priorities (Rodgers 1992). Further, work-family concerns may not be viewed as relevant to key decision-makers because they do not see them as impacting organizational outcomes. Anecdotal evidence suggests this realization precipitates managerial commitment to respond to work-family issues (Morgan and Tucker 1991). Morgan and Milliken (1992) found greater work-family responsiveness among companies where periodic surveys of employees and other information gathering mechanisms were used, and when HR executives viewed changing demographics as an issue affecting bottom line results.

If interest in work-family initiatives is likely to evolve, it seems likely to occur among HR professionals who are charged with being more aware of issues affecting the use of human resources than other policy-makers. Although gender has been shown to influence individuals' attitudes toward career and family issues (see, for example, Skeen et al. 1989), one would expect human-resource professionals would be more sensitive to issues arising from balancing career and family and more aware of the negative impact arising from conflict in this area on employee satisfaction and commitment.

To explore this, the authors examined attitudes of human-resource professionals with regard to a variety of career/family issues. Several significant differences in the attitudes of male and female HR professionals were found. Men were generally less supportive of asking corporations and government to take greater responsibility for child care. Men were generally more supportive of traditional child-care arrangements. This finding may be attributed to the fact that men tend to be less affected by issues related to child care (Aneshensel et al. 1981). Sekaran (1986), for example, notes women typically handle the bulk of family responsibilities even when both members of the couple have full-time jobs.

Consistent with previous research, women also disagreed more strongly than men with statements suggesting that career commitment for women might be less than that of men. Stereotypes regarding commitment are generally not supported by research. For example, a study by Powell et al. (1984) suggests women are more committed to their careers, as opposed to their family or home lives, than male managers of equivalent age, salary, education, and managerial level.

Perhaps the most notable finding of the Covin and Brush research was that gender-related differences do exist in attitudes toward work-family issues among human-resource professionals. For this reason, organizations must remember that the gender of a person contributing to policy decisions about work-family issues may affect the nature of decisions made or the degree of importance attached to such issues, regardless of position or background.

In sum, organizations would be well-advised to seek input from a broad-based, representative group of individuals when developing policies to address work-family concerns. They must create a corporate-wide discussion about work and family life.

*Teresa Joyce Covin*
*Christina Christenson Brush*

## Bibliography

Aneshensel, C.S., R.R. Frerichs, and V.A. Clark. 1981. "Family Roles and Sex Differences in Depression." *Journal of Health and Social Behavior* 22:379–83.

Burke, R.J. 1989. "Some Antecedents and Consequences of Work-Family Conflict." In *Work and Family: Theory, Research and Applications*, edited by E. Goldsmith. Newbury Park, Calif.: Sage.

Covin, T.J., and C.C. Brush. 1991. "An Examination of Male and Female Attitudes toward Career and Family Issues." *Sex Roles: A Journal of Research* 25(7–8):393–415.

Fernandez, J.P. 1986. *Child Care and Corporate Productivity: Resolving Family/Work Conflicts*. Lexington, Mass.: Lexington.

Friedman, D.E. 1987. "Work versus Family: War of the Worlds." *Personnel Administrator* (August):32(8):36–38.

Morgan, H., and F.J. Milliken. 1992. "Keys to Action: Understanding Differences in Organizations' Responsiveness to Work-and-Family Issues." *Human Resource Management* 31:227–48.

Morgan, H., and K. Tucker. 1991. *Companies That Care: The Most Family-Friendly Companies in America, What They Offer and How They Got That Way*. New York: Simon and Schuster.

Nollen, S. 1989. "The Work-Family Dilemma: How HR Managers Can Help." *Personnel* 60:25–30.

Powell, G.N., B.Z. Posner, and W.H. Schmidt. 1984. "Sex Effects on Managerial Value Systems." *Human Relations* 37:909–21.

Rodgers, C.S. 1992. "The Flexible Workplace: What Have We Learned?" *Human Resource Management* 31(Fall):183–99.

Schultz, J.B., Y.L. Chung, and C.G. Henderson. 1989. "Work/Family Concerns of University Faculty." In *Work and Family: Theory Research and Applications*, edited by E. Goldsmith, pp. 249–64. Newbury Park, Calif.: Sage.

Sekaran, U. 1986. *Dual Career Families*. San Francisco: Jossey-Bass.

Shellenbarger, S. 1992. "Lessons from the Workplace: How Corporate Policies and Attitudes Lag Behind Workers' Changing Needs." *Human Resource Management* 31:157–69.

Skeen, P., L.P. Paguio, B.E. Robinson, and J.E. Deal. 1989. "Mothers Working Outside the Home: Attitudes of Fathers and Mothers of Three Cultures." In *Work and Family: Theory Research and Applications*, edited by E. Goldsmith, pp. 373–82. Newbury Park, Calif.: Sage.

Wiley, D. 1987. "The Relationship between Work/Nonwork Role Conflict and Job Related Outcomes: Some Unanticipated Findings." *Journal of Management* 13:467–72.

# Gender's Influence on Organizational Structure and Culture

## The Stratification of Women within Organizations

Female labor-force participation has undergone a dramatic change in the past few decades, rising from approximately 30 percent of all women in the 1960s to over 50 percent by 1990. While women's work roles have changed dramatically over the past century, their workplace experiences do not mirror those of male workers. Extensive investigation of gender segregation in the workplace indicates women have not found job opportunities equivalent to those of their male counterparts (Reskin and Roos 1987). Not only is there a substantial degree of occupational gender segregation, with women becoming concentrated in a few occupations (Beller 1982, 1984), there are also gender-related distribution dynamics within occupations, or intraoccupational segregation (Bielby and Baron 1986, 1987). Such gender segregation is one of the major causes of the earning gap between men and women (Trieman and Hartmann 1981). This article will briefly discuss the segregation of women within organizations. First, the segregation of women within different types of organizations will be examined. Then, both the vertical and horizontal distribution of women within organizations will be discussed. Finally, major theories explaining gender segregation will be presented.

The degree of gender segregation occurring within an organization depends, among other things, upon the firm's type of ownership. Between the years 1950 and 1981, gender segregation declined the greatest amount in publicly owned organizations, compared to private-sector firms and the self-employed (Wharton 1989). Employment practices at public-sector organizations are strongly influenced by political pressures to hire disadvantaged groups. The state's role as guarantor of equal opportunity for disaffected social groups forces it to pursue more egalitarian hiring practices than private employers. Private-sector firms are more able to indulge in expressing a "taste for discrimination," though gender segregation even for these firms declined somewhat between 1950 and 1981 (Wharton 1989). Conversely, gender segregation among the self-employed has remained relatively stable during this period. The self-employed are especially vulnerable to stereotyped gender roles. Customers, financial institutes, and other organizations from whom the self-employed require support often view nontraditional occupational roles for women negatively. Thus, men and women will choose more "gender-appropriate" self-employment occupations, continuing the pattern of gender segregation within these roles.

### Vertical and Horizontal Segregation within Organizations

Within organizations, however, there are distribution dynamics occurring both vertically and horizontally, which contribute to gender segregation. Despite a number of advances, women still tend to be unequally distributed across hierarchical levels within organizations. Female representation within organizations declines at successively higher levels of job skill, status, responsibility, income, and authority (Fox and Hesse-Biber 1984; Morrison et al. 1982). For instance, a study of eight hundred of the largest U.S. industrial and service companies found that women constituted less than 0.5 percent of the 4,012 people listed as the highest ranking company officers and directors (Fierman 1990). Thus, while increasing numbers of women are gaining access to traditionally male occupations, these women are overwhelmingly located at lower levels in the occupational hierarchy. These female-typed jobs provide few promotional opportunities and provide little or no on-the-job training, often a requisite for upward mobility.

However, vertical distribution may not account for all the gender segregation occurring in organizations. Unequal horizontal distribution of women also occurs and may be a more subtle, but equally powerful, form of segregation. For any given occupation, women and men tend to be streamed into different areas or departments of organizations, regardless of their hierarchical level (Baron and Bielby 1985; Bielby and Baron 1986, 1987; Stover 1991). For instance, despite greater numbers of women entering managerial positions in banks, the majority of these women move into management positions in small branches, physically segregated from the main branches where major decisions are made (Reskin and Roos 1987). Stover (1991) found that, within universities, women were significantly more likely than men to manage departments that were less powerful (as measured by budgetary funding), and those that were declining in size. Similarly, Talbert and Bose (1977) found the horizontal segregation of clerks to be based on gender. Male clerks were significantly more likely than female clerks to be placed in high-status departments, departments with high-priced merchandise, to report less direction by a supervisor, and to receive greater work discretion.

The major empirical contribution on the horizontal distribution of male and female workers within firms has been from Bielby and Baron (1986, 1987; Baron and Bielby 1985). They investigated the distribution of men and women within several hundred California organizations and examined the jobs to which each were assigned. Within any firm there will be various occupations that are composed of both men and women. However, it was found that when an enterprise employs both sexes in the same occupation, men and women are usually assigned different job titles and are usually placed in different locations within the firm. For instance, in a publishing firm, men performing a certain set of tasks were given the title of assistant editor; women performing the exact same duties were titled researchers and located in a different organizational area. The job classification of researcher also possessed a much shorter promotion ladder than that of editor. Thus, men and women are segregated by job titles within work settings, channeling women into specific types of job classifications, typically those with shorter career ladders.

As suggested by the work of Bielby and Baron, the horizontal and vertical distributions within organizations are ultimately linked. Future opportunities for workers in less powerful or prominent organizational departments are often quite limited. Without jobs that offer opportunities to gain visibility and influence, women find it more difficult to advance within organizations. Thus, horizontal placement may have implications for future vertical placement within organizations.

## Theories Concerning Gender Segregation

There have been several theories advanced to account for gender segregation within organizations. Several individual-level, "supply side" models, such as human capital and socialization theories, have been offered. However, "demand side" explanations such as sex-role socialization, and more recently, institutionalization theory, have been advanced to account for organizational gender segregation. These latter models seek to identify how segregation is maintained by job-, organization-, and industry-level characteristics (Bielby and Baron 1986).

The theory of human capital has traditionally been used by economists to explain segregation (Polachek 1981). This theory points to the importance of the greater amount of education and training men have tended to acquire in preparation for, and in the course of, spending virtually all their preretirement years in the labor market. This is used to explain both men's choices of occupations that require more education and training and why they reach higher levels within organizations (Polachek 1981). While human capital theory has its staunch supporters, recent research casts doubt on it as a major explanation for gender segregation within organizations. Beller (1982), found human capital (as measured by education and experience) to have less of an impact on gender segregation within firms than the presence or absence of federal equal employment opportunity (EEO) programs in the workplace. Bielby and Baron (1987) found human capital (as measured by skills, training, and turnover costs) to explain less than 15 percent of the variance in sex segregation at the job level within firms. Similarly, Stover (1991) found significant horizontal segregation of male and female managers after controlling for such human capital as years of education and previous job experience. Thus, the usefulness of human capital to explain gender segregation within organizations is, at best, limited.

A second explanation of gender segregation views socialization practices as a main factor in which women and men become located within firms (Marini and Brinton 1984). Boys and girls are not raised with the same expectations, the same role models, or the same incentives. This influences later occupational aspirations and expectations. Thus, according to this theory, individuals "self-segregate" themselves.

Beyond these individual-level explanations, however, more structural factors may contribute to gender segregation within organizations. According to institutional theory, certain work roles and jobs within organizations become typified or institutionalized as belonging to either men or women (Zucker 1977). The division of positions between men and women becomes expected, accepted, and taken for granted. Work becomes defined as women's or men's work, and this institutionalization of past practices comes to affect the subsequent selection of position occupants. For example, Stover (1991) found that the best predictor of whether a man or woman would manage a department was the gender of the past departmental manager. Thus, gender segregation becomes part of a group's culture.

There is also a large body of literature suggesting that women, for a variety of reasons, are typically perceived as less competent than men for certain roles, particularly for executive/managerial roles (Heilman et al. 1989). A primary reason for such female devaluation includes reliance on sex-role stereotypes. Several studies have indicated that women are perceived as possessing fewer managerial skills and competencies than men and are assigned to less important tasks (Gerdes and Garber 1983; Taylor and Ilgen 1981). Role assignments, then, become based on gender rather than actual skills and abilities. Reliance on sex-role stereotyping can help explain why certain jobs are institutionalized as belonging to either men or women. It can also help explain why women are often routed to declining and less powerful departments in a firm. According to resource dependence theory (Salancik and Pfeffer 1974), powerful departments have the ability to request and receive those resources (including human resources) they perceive as most valuable, competent, and necessary to their task. Accordingly, more powerful departments are able to exercise a selection bias in favor of males, especially for crucial managerial and executive positions.

In conclusion, gender segregation remains a significant problem within organizations today. It is unarguable that the vertical segregation of women is occurring, with women significantly underrepresented at higher levels within firms. Yet, also occurring within organizations is the more subtle form of horizontal segregation, with women being streamed to less powerful or important areas of the firm. Not only does this distribution pattern affect subsequent career moves of women, but also salary levels.

*Dana L. Stover*

## Bibliography

Baron, J., and W. Bielby. 1985. "Organizational Barriers to Gender Equality: Sex Segregation of Jobs and Opportunities." In *Gender and the Life Course*, edited by A.S. Rossi. New York: Aldine.

Beller, A. 1982. "Occupational Segregation by Sex: Determinants and Changes." *Journal of Human Resources* 17:371–92.

———. 1984. "Trends in Occupational Segregation by Sex and Race, 1960–1981." In *Sex Segregation in the Workplace*, edited by B.F. Reskin. Washington, D.C.: National Academy.

Bielby, W., and J. Baron. 1986. "Men and Women at Work: Sex Segregation and Statistical Discrimination." *American Journal of Sociology* 91:759–99.

Bielby, W., and J. Baron. 1987. "Undoing Discrimination: Job Integration and Comparable Worth." In *Ingredients for Women's Employment Policy*, edited by C. Bose and G. Spitze. Albany: State University of New York Press.

Fierman, J. 1990. "Why Women Still Don't Hit the Top." *Fortune* (July) 122(3):46–60.

Fox, M.F., and S. Hesse-Biber. 1984. *Women at Work*. New York: Mayfield.

Gerdes, E.P., and D.M. Garber. 1983. "Sex Bias in Hiring: Effects of Job Demands and Applicant Competence." *Sex Roles* 9:307–19.

Heilman, M., C. Block, R. Martell, and M. Simon. 1989. "Has Anything Changed? Current Characterizations of Men, Women and Managers." *Journal of Applied Psychology* 74:935–42.

Marini, M.M., and M.C. Brinton. 1984. "Sex Typing in Occupational Socialization." In *Sex Segregation in the Workplace*, edited by B.F. Reskin. Washington, D.C.: National Academy.

Morrison, A., R. White, and E. Van Velsor. 1982. *Breaking the Glass Ceiling*. Reading, Mass.: Addison-Wesley.

Polachek, S. 1981. "Occupational Self-Selection: A Human Capital Approach to Sex Differences in Occupational Structure." *Review of Economics and Statistics* 58:60–69.

Reskin, B., and P. Roos. 1987. "Status Hierarchies and Sex Segregation." In *Ingredients for Women's Employment Policy*, edited by C. Bose and G. Spitze. Albany: State University of New York Press.

Salancik, G., and J. Pfeffer. 1974. "The Bases and Use of Power in Organizational Decision Making: The Case of a University." *Administrative Science Quarterly* 19:453–73.

Stover, D.L. 1991. "The Horizontal Distribution of Female Managers within Organizations." Unpublished manuscript, University of Idaho, Moscow.

Talbert, J., and C. Bose. 1977. "Wage-Attainment Processes: The Retail Clerk Case." *American Journal of Sociology* 83:403–24.

Taylor, M.S., and D.R. Ilgen. 1981. "Sex Discrimination against Women in Initial Placement Decisions: A Laboratory Investigation." *Academy of Management Journal* 24:859–65.

Trieman, D., and H. Hartmann. 1981. *Women, Work and Wages: Equal Pay for Jobs of Equal Value*. Washington, D.C.: National Academy.

Wharton, A. 1989. "Gender Segregation in Private-Sector, Public-Sector and Self-Employed Occupations, 1950–1981." *Social Science Quarterly* 70:923–39.

Zucker, L. 1977. "The Role of Institutionalization in Cultural Persistence." *American Sociological Review* 42:726–43.

## Organizational Culture

Organizational culture refers to an organization's "ways of doing things" as reflected in the regular activities of its members and the various artifacts that have come to symbolize the organization. Numerous factors serve to give an organization a particular feel and look, and these can include rites (such as Holy Communion in the Catholic Church), ceremonies (such as commencement at Harvard University), dress (such as the conservative blue suits of the IBM sales force), stories (such as the history of the founder that is imparted to the new Mary Kay recruits), symbols (such as McDonalds's golden arches), buildings (such as the distinctive style of mosques), slogans (such as At Ford, Service is Job Number One), expressed values (such as Rotary International's commitment to "service above self"), leadership style (such as that of Lee Iacocca), and various other aspects of an organization's operation. The culture of an organization is thought to shape the experiences of its members—how they feel about the organization and how they feel about themselves. The feminist contention that gender is a cultural phenomenon and that various elements of sexual discrimination are rooted in the culture of a society, has led feminists to examine the character of organizational culture and its part in the processes of sexual inequities.

The association of culture with the generation of values, a sense of belonging, commitment, and identity encouraged management to study the relationship between organizational culture and efficiency. North American and British management interest in organizational culture developed in the context of sharp competition from Japanese companies. Since 1980, numerous books and articles have been written on the subject, beginning with a focus on the differences between Japanese and American culture (Ouchi 1981) and subsequently ranging over a variety of issues concerning the nature of organizational culture. Most of these studies failed to deal with the issue of gender, presenting organizational culture as a nongendered phenomenon and, in the bargain, ignoring the dominant role of men in the construction of the cultures of organizations. Ouchi (1981), however, notes that the large Japanese corporations exclude women from their tenured ranks.

Feminist studies of organizational culture have revealed numerous links between an organization's "way of doing things" and sexual discrimination. The way that an organization is structured, for example, can influence the way that women experience the organization and feel accepted by it. A relative absence of women in the middle and upper levels of management can create a negative impression that discourages women from attempting to better themselves within the organization (Kanter 1977). Indeed, the very character of organization—with its stress on male-associated factors of formality, lack of emotion, instrumentality—acts as a barrier to female opportunity.

What an organization does and how it does it is closely associated with its system of production, with its technology. Attitudes to training, skill, production abilities, and knowledge can influence female opportunities and experiences of the workplace. The identification, by those responsible for organizational recruitment and promotion, of types of skill, physical strength, and knowledge as male attributes inhibit the chances of women to be allowed to undertake certain tasks (Stiehm 1981).

Organizational language, style, and system of communications can signal a sense of competence and acceptance to those involved. Women may feel less included in the organization where an overwhelming number of communications signal maleness. Examples of male-associated signs include dominant use of the male pronoun and other male references (such as chairman) throughout official documents, memos, and other communications; the use of motivational and other organizational metaphors that draw upon male-associated sports and military references; use of demeaning and derogatory terms for women (such as "a bitch of a machine," "the girls in the office"); little or no use made of positive (that is, active, authoritative) images of women in presentations of corporate image; male control of the communications system (that is, male chair persons); formal and informal dress codes that stress traditional male notions of femininity (such as pressure on women to wear dresses rather than slacks). The use of informal channels of communications and activities to conduct business is often detrimental to women where those channels are based on "old boys networks" and where the social activities of an organization are built around expectations of men only participation (such as golf).

Organizational culture at any point is an outcome of the activities of those involved. In the process women are far from simple recipients of cultural experiences. Women have responded in various ways to the problem of male-dominated organizations, including acquiescence, individual resistance, the development of female culture, and the establishment of separate women's organizations. Feminist research into organizational culture has generally been concerned to help women identify ways in which they can overcome and change cultural barriers to female opportunity.

*Albert J. Mills*

## Bibliography

Benson, S.P. 1986. *Counter Culture: Saleswomen, Managers and Customers in American Department Stores, 1890*. Urbana and Chicago: University of Illinois Press.

Crompton, R., and G. Jones. 1984. *White-Collar Proletariate: Deskilling and Gender in Clerical Work*. Philadelphia: Temple University Press.

Kanter, R.M. 1977. *Men and Women of the Corporation*. New York: Basic Books.

Lamphere, L. 1985. "Bringing the Family to Work: Women's Culture on the Shop Floor." *Feminist Studies* 11:519–40.

Martin, J. 1992. *The Cultures of Organizations.* Oxford: Basil Blackwell.

Mills, A.J. 1988. "Organization Acculturation and Gender Discrimination." In *Canadian Issues, X(I)—Women and the Workplace,* edited by P.K. Kresl, pp. 1–22. Montreal: Assn. of Canadian Studies/International Council for Canadian Studies.

Mills, A.J., and P. Tancred, eds. 1992. *Gendering Organizational Analysis.* Newbury Park, Calif.: Sage.

Morgan, G. 1986. *Images of Organization.* Chap. 6. Newbury Park, Calif.: Sage.

Morgan, N. 1988. *Women in the Canadian Federal Public Service.* Ottawa: Status of Women Committee.

Ouchi, W. 1981. *Theory Z.* Reading, Mass.: Addison-Wesley.

Pollert, A. 1981. *Girls, Wives, Factory Lives.* London: Macmillan.

Stiehm, J.H. 1981. *Bring Me Men and Women: Mandated Change at the U.S. Air Force Academy.* Berkeley, Calif.: University of California Press.

## Organizational Sexuality

Organizational sexuality refers to the relationship between organizational arrangements and the construction and manipulation of sexuality. Sexuality, at its most basic level, can be defined as a person's sexual self; those aspects of a person that make him or her sexually attractive to another. Despite the fact that sexual attractiveness can take various forms, dominant (male) images of heterosexuality persist, within which the creation and exploitation of female sexuality is a particularly pernicious aspect, but which also involves homosexual and lesbian harassment (Schneider 1982). Evidence of widespread sexual harassment in the workplace, and the exploitation of female sexuality (such as in advertising and sales techniques) has led feminists to examine the role of organizations in regard to sexuality.

Acts of sexual harassment are among the clearest examples of sexual behavior at work. At its most explicit, sexual harassment involves unwanted attention of a sexual nature, whether through acts of a physical, verbal, or otherwise suggestive nature: The overwhelming majority of cases involve the sexual harassment of a woman by a man. Studies of sexual harassment at work indicate that there is a relationship between the incidence and type of harassment and the character of the workplace itself. Some workplace environments, for example, either encourage or fail to discourage sexual harassment.

Power is a central issue in sexual harassment. Organizational arrangements create countless contexts or power inequities in which men occupy the majority or the only positions of power and authority. In many cases of sexual harassment organizational power is a factor, where the woman is bothered by an organizationally more powerful male or has to rely on a male power structure to intervene to prevent harassment. In several industrial counties the invidious character of sexual harassment has been recognized and legislation has been established to deal with it.

Less recognized as a problem is the manipulation by organizations of female sexuality. In addition to the clear and blatant use of female sexuality in advertising, numerous organizations utilize certain female looks, voice, style of dress, and behavior to sell their products or services. A prime example is the airline industry where various companies have required female flight attendants to present an image of attractiveness and attentiveness (Hochschild 1983). Other examples include the sexual imagery often expected of female receptionists, secretaries, and restaurant and other service-oriented positions that deal with the public. Not surprisingly, sexual attractiveness is frequently a factor in the recruitment practices of those organizations concerned with sexual imagery, but it can also influence the recruitment decisions of other organizations. Guteck and Cohen (1992), for example, found that, in certain cases, male recruiters are more likely to hire those female candidates who are perceived as attractive over those who are not.

Other ways in which sexuality intrudes into the workplace include the use of sexuality to achieve personal and organizational ends, sex-role spillover, sexual imagery, and sexual innuendo. In the context of a sexualized workplace—that is, an organization that encourages sexuality—some women learn to use sexuality to achieve certain ends. Female use of sexuality, however, has been overstressed in the literature and in practice through the use of innuendo that links female success with sexuality. A far greater problem is sex-role spillover where patriarchal relationships are reproduced in the workplace creating numerous situations where women are expected to service the needs of men within the organization—such as fetching coffee. Collinson (1988), Pollert (1981), and Sheppard (1989) draw attention to the ways in which male managers use sexuality to control the activities of female subordinates, through the use of language (such as referring to female employees as "love" or "sweetheart"), an insistence on narrow dress codes (such as requirements that women wear dresses as opposed to slacks), through the use of touching and body language (such as the male manager placing his arm around a female subordinate), and sexual harassment (such as the use of demeaning remarks and behavior to force compliance). Studies of male sexuality (Willis 1977) have drawn attention to the relationship between organizational arrangement and masculinity, in particular the expectations that many organizations have for macho (blue-collar) and competitive-aggressive (managerial) behavior for their male employees, which, as a result, contributes to the development of narrow, negative forms of masculinity, forms that are usually antiwomen in their outcomes.

A central and recurring theme of organizations is heterosexuality. Signs of sexual preference other than heterosexuality are rarely tolerated within organizations. Very little research has yet been done on homosexuality at work, but what evidence there is indicates that gay women and men are usually expected to conceal their sexual preferences from organizational view (Schneider 1982, 1984). Pressure to conform to heterosexual views of reality put additional strains on gay women (Hall 1990).

Debate on organizational sexuality is relatively new and as yet the concept is highly contested. At least four major ways of understanding organizational sexuality can be identified, as (1) a biological essence, or the reproduction of essential drives in organizational contexts; (2) the outcome of social roles, where relatively fixed sex roles become translated into organizational behaviors; (3) a fundamental political category, "an historical constructed collectivity of interest and community set within definite relations of power dominance" (Hearn and Burrell 1990, p.6); and (4) a communicative practice and discourse of power "maintained through the order of the discourse and the mutually reinforcing interventions of power, knowledge and pleasure" (Hearn and Burrell 1990, p.6). In any event, each of these perspectives shares a view of organizational sexuality as a barrier to equity at work.

*Albert J. Mills*

### Bibliography

Collinson, D.L. 1988. "Engineering Humour: Masculinity, Joking and Conflict in Shopfloor Relations." *Organization Studies* 9:181–99.

Davies, S. 1989. "Inserting Gender into Burowoy's Theory of the Labour Process." *Work, Employment & Society* 4:391–406.

Guteck, B.A., and A.G. Cohen. 1992. "Sex Rations, Sex Role Spillover, and Sex at Work: A Comparison of Men's and Women's Experiences." In *Gendering Organizational Analysis*, edited by A.J. Mills and P. Tancred, pp. 133–50. Newbury Park, Calif.: Sage.

Hall, M. 1990. "Private Experiences in the Public Domain: Lesbians in Organizations." In *The Sexuality of Organization*, edited by J. Hearn, D.L. Sheppard, P. Tancred-Sheriff, and G. Burrell, pp. 125–38. London: Sage.

Hearn, J., and G. Burrell. 1990. "The Sexuality of Organization." In *The Sexuality of Organization*, edited by J. Hearn, D.L. Sheppard, P. Tancred-Sheriff, and G. Burrell, pp. 1–28. London: Sage.

Hearn, J., D.L. Sheppard, P. Tancred-Sheriff, and G. Burrell, eds. 1990. *The Sexuality of Organization*. London: Sage.

Hochschild, A.R. 1983. *The Managed Heart*. Berkeley: University of California Press.

Pollert, A. 1981. *Girls, Wives, Factory Lives*. London: Macmillan.

Schneider, B.E. 1982. "Consciousness about Sexual Harassment among Heterosexual and Lesbian Women Workers." *Journal of Social Issues* 38:75–98.

———. 1984. "The Office Affair: Myth and Reality for Heterosexual and Lesbian Women Workers." *Sociological Perspectives* 27:443–64.

Sheppard, D.L. 1989. "Organizations, Power and Sexuality: The Image and Self-Image of Women Managers." In *The Sexuality of Organization*, edited by J. Hearn, D.L. Sheppard, P. Tancred-Sheriff, and G. Burrell, pp. 139–57. London: Sage.

Willis, P.E. 1977. *Learning to Labour*. Farnborough, England: Saxon House.

## Sexual Coercion in the Workplace

In recent years there has been an increase in the amount of attention given to sexually coercive behavior in the workplace, its origins, and the implications for relations between men and women working together. Part of the problem lies in early socialization patterns in the educational system, which emphasize socially constructed differences in men and women and offer distorted views of sexuality and sexual norms. Stereotypical gender socialization sets up interactive patterns between men and women that are conducive to date rape and sexual harassment. Furthermore, males and females often define sexual encounters differently and thus view sexual harassment in the workplace in the context of gendered expectations. The consequences for perpetrators and victims of sexual harassment are discussed, and the implications for interactive patterns between men and women in the workplace are addressed.

By the time children reach elementary school, they are engaging in sex-segregated activities and reinforcing traditional conceptions of masculinity and femininity (Thorne 1986). In childhood conversations, boys tend to negotiate for status while girls seek intimacy and connections in their interactions (Goodwin 1991). These differences are reinforced in adolescence in the separate activities through which high school and junior high school students seek status with their peers. Since very little information is given to children and adolescents concerning sexuality and sexual feelings, they often turn to each other to make sense of cultural messages (Corsaro 1985). In the process, they tend to reproduce sexually coercive attitudes and behaviors within their own peer interactions. Kanin (1984) found that peer-group socialization in high school was a critical factor in explaining the behavior of date rapists, in that these men had been a part of peer groups that viewed women as sexual conquests.

One important source for social messages about sexual interaction norms is the education system. Schools, from primary through the high school level, reinforce very narrow, opposing definitions of masculinity and femininity (Thorne 1986).

For example, athletic activities for adolescent boys enhance status for those participating (Eder and Parker 1987) and emphasize stereotypically male values such as achievement, athletic prowess, strength, and male authority. Simultaneously, athletics programs set men up for failure by undermining self-affirmation and intimacy through competition and winning (Messner 1987). It is little wonder that for men sexuality may be linked with achieving and status (Beneke 1982).

Young women, on the other hand, are taught to take care of men's sexual needs, to be supportive of men, and to ignore their own sexual urges (Fine 1988). They are ill equipped to face a potentially threatening situation when they begin working. Since rape is often associated with strangers, women may not even expect that a boss or coworker will be sexually coercive. Given that women regularly have to put up with intrusive male behavior in the form of catcalls, whistles, jokes, or unwanted touching (Stanko 1990), victims of harassment or coercion in the workplace may be confused about what constitutes an abusive situation. They may in fact normalize the situation because they need the job or they see no other choice (MacKinnon 1979).

According to a survey conducted by Goodchilds et al. (1988), by the age of fourteen both males and females think of nonconsensual sex as rape only when a certain level of force is used and if the attack involves two people who do not know each other. If the attack involves people who do know each other, forced sex was considered all right by males fourteen to eighteen depending on how long the two people were together, how aroused the male was, the amount of money the man spent on the woman, or on the condition of the woman: If she was intoxicated or indicated in any way that she wanted to have sex, forced sex was considered to be acceptable.

Among adults, there is a connection between gender ideology and the acceptance of sexually coercive behavior. People who endorse traditional gender stereotypes or who believe that heterosexual relationships are essentially adverserial are more likely to think that myths about rape are true (Burt 1980) and are more tolerant of sexual harassment (Reilly et al. 1992). While men and women tend to agree that rape involves unwanted sexual intercourse and the use of physical force, they disagree when there is a relationship between the attacker and the victim (Gordon and Riger 1989) in that men are more likely than women to accept rape myths, to be more tolerant of sexual harassment (Reilly et al. 1992), and to hold women responsible for their own victimization (Jensen and Gutek 1982). Women who hold traditional views on gender relations are also more likely to blame the victim than women who are more liberal (Jensen and Gutek 1982). This suggests that traditional gender ideology, which polarizes male and female roles, contributes to sexually coercive attitudes and behaviors that then reinforce gender inequality.

Indeed, the work world is divided by gender, with most women working in low-pay, female-dominated fields. These jobs tend to place women in the position of working for or with men who have more economic clout and power than they do. Moreover, they are in jobs that often require performing tasks that are supportive of men's jobs, and reinforce traditional conceptions of women's roles, which may include being sexually attractive to men (MacKinnon 1979). Even women in traditionally male-dominated fields are considered exceptions, and may be accused of "sleeping their way to the top" or getting ahead because of their sexual attractiveness. Regardless of the job, the structure of the workplace, like the educational system, is set up to reinforce traditional gender roles.

The polarization of heterosexual relations in the educational system and in the labor force institutionally lays the groundwork for miscommunications. Men and women work together in the context of economic inequality, and they are products of a school system that does not challenge traditional notions of what it means to be female or male in this culture. The resulting misunderstanding between men and women is highlighted by the fact that men view sexual harassment as normal sexual interaction, and therefore women should feel complimented by the attention (Jensen and Gutek 1982). So in reinforcing traditional gender definitions, the schools also normalize the implications: male dominance and male violence against women.

While guidelines to curb sexually coercive behavior in the workplace are important, it is essential that the education begin before women and men enter the labor force. This implies that the school system must examine the types of attitudes and behaviors that are reinforced in terms of gender, sexuality, and sexual coercion. This is not the only reform necessary, but an institutional response from the educational system is a prerequisite for beginning to change the environment in which men and women work.

*Lori K. Sudderth*

## Bibliography

Beneke, T. 1982. *Men on Rape: What They Have to Say about Sexual Violence.* New York: St. Martin's.

Burt, M. 1980. "Cultural Myths and Supports for Rape." *Journal of Personality and Social Psychology* 38:217–30.

Corsaro, W.A. (1985). *Friendship and Peer Culture in the Early Years.* Norwood, N.J.: Ablex.

Eder, D., and S. Parker. (1987). "The Cultural Production and Reproduction of Gender: The Effect of Extracurricular Activities on Peer-Group Culture." *Sociology of Education* 60:200–13.

Fine, M. 1988. "Sexuality, Schooling, and Adolescent Females: The Missing Discourse of Desire." *Harvard Educational Review* 58:29–53.

Goodchilds, J.D., G.L. Zellman, P.B. Johnson, and R. Giarrusso. 1988. "Adolescents and Their Perceptions of Sexual Interactions." In *Rape and Sexual Assault.* Vol. 2, edited by A.W. Burgess, pp. 245–70. New York: Garland.

Goodwin, Marjorie Harness. 1991. *He-Said-She-Said: Talk as Social Organization among Black Children.* Bloomington: Indiana University Press.

Gordon, M.T., and S. Riger. 1989. *The Female Fear.* New York: Free Press.

Jensen, I., and B. Gutek. 1982. "Attributions and Assignments of Responsibility for Sexual Harassment." *Journal of Social Issues* 38:121–36.

Kanin, E.J. 1984. "Date Rape: Unofficial Criminals and Victims." *Victimology.* 9:95–108.

MacKinnon, C. 1979. *Sexual Harassment of Working Women.* New Haven: Yale University Press.

Messner, M. 1987. "The Life of a Man's Seasons: Male Identity in the Life Course of the Jock." In *Changing Men: New Directions in Research on Men and Masculinity,* edited by M.S. Kimmel, pp. 53–67. Newbury Park, Calif.: Sage.

Reilly, M.E., B. Lott, D. Caldwell, and L. DeLuca. 1992. "Tolerance for Sexual Harassment Related to Self-Reported Sexual Victimization." *Gender and Society* 6(1):122–38.

Spreitzer, E., and M. Pugh. 1973. "Interscholastic Athletics and Educational Expectations." *Sociology of Education* 46:171–82.

Stanko, E. 1990. *Everyday Violence: How Women and Men Experience Sexual and Physical Danger.* London: Pandora.

Thorne, B. 1986. "Girls and Boys Together . . . But Mostly Apart: Gender Arrangements in Elementary Schools." In *Relationships and Development,* edited by W. Hartup and Z. Rubin, pp. 167–84. Hillsdale, N.J.: Lawrence Erlbaum.

# Gender-Based Bias
# and Discrimination

## Sex Discrimination at Work

With the passage of legislation aimed at ensuring equitable treatment of women in work settings, it was hoped that stereotypic views of women would gradually dissipate and that occupational sex discrimination would become an ill of the past. Unfortunately, research aimed at assessing current perceptions of women suggests that such unbridled optimism is unwarranted. In one study (Heilman et al. 1989), male managers were given an inventory, composed of ninety-two attributes—many of which are required to handle managerial level jobs successfully—and asked to describe one of seven target groups: men (in general, managers, or successful managers), women (in general, managers, or successful managers), or successful middle managers. Results demonstrated that men in general were perceived to possess many of the attributes required of successful managers, whereas women in general were not. For example, men were seen as assertive, logical, and emotionally stable, whereas women were seen as passive, reserved, and sentimental. And, when depicted as managers, women still were characterized as less similar to successful managers than were men. It was only when depicted as successful managers that this gap in the perceptions of men and women was bridged. Yet, even successful women managers were seen as lacking in one critical attribute—leadership ability. These results provide clear evidence that the field of management is still seen as stereotypically male. However, there has been one significant change—women managers no longer perceive women as less well suited for management positions than men (Brenner et al. 1989). It is also worth noting that the views of today's students—tomorrow's business leaders—have not evolved all that much. A survey of undergraduate management students revealed that men were described similarly to successful managers, whereas women were not (Schein et al. 1989). This difference, however, held for male but not female respondents. And, a longitudinal study of MBA students from 1975 to 1983 found that males had negative attitudes, and females positive attitudes, toward women executives (Dubno 1985).

Sex stereotypes have a profound effect on how women are treated in the workplace. Once triggered, these beliefs are translated into actions and, as a result, women often are accorded less favorable ratings than men when applying for a job ("access-bias") or when their work is evaluated ("treatment bias"). Consequently, women are hired and promoted at substantially lower rates than men (Cannings 1988; Olson and Becker 1983). Attempts to eliminate sex discrimination must first take into account two critical factors: (1) perceptions of a woman's relevant work attributes; and (2) perceptions of the requirements of the job. For it is the perceived inconsistency between women's attributes and the requirements of traditionally male jobs that give way to negative performance expectations. These negative expectations about women as a group, in turn, bias subsequent inferences about the likely ability and performance of an individual woman. The idea that stereotypic beliefs mediate discrimination in personnel decisions is instructive; it suggests that before bias can be eliminated this reliance on stereotypes must somehow be preempted.

Fortunately, a more optimistic note can now be sounded: Discrimination is not inevitable. Recent research demonstrates quite convincingly that there are a number of organizational factors that can help to undermine the use of sex stereotypes when making personnel judgments, thus, eliminating bias against women.

One factor believed to promote bias against women is their token representation in male-dominated organizations (Kanter 1977). A token woman, by virtue of her salience, is seen first as a "female," triggering negative stereotypes of women as generally less qualified than men. This reasoning suggests that women will be treated more equitably as their proportional representation in work settings increases. Indeed, there is evidence that male-female differences in personnel assessments abate when the sex composition is more balanced (Sacket et al. 1991). Such research findings support the general idea that bias is not inevitable and, more specifically, suggest that there are measures organizations can take to eradicate discrimination. One method would be to actively manage the sex composition of the applicant pool, striving to ensure that it does not become overly skewed toward men.

A second factor presumed to regulate the sex stereotype-sex discrimination sequence is the amount and type of information provided to decision-makers. Looking first at hiring decisions, it has been proposed that stereotypes will exert less influence when judgments are based on applicant qualifications that are directly relevant to job success. In this case the informational value of stereotypic beliefs is believed to be undermined; whereas when judging a job applicant whose credentials are somewhat ambiguous with regard to job success, the need to rely on sex-based performance expectations is heightened. Research designed to test this reasoning has found that the provision of objective evidence of high-performance ability is successful in eliminating bias against women in hiring decisions (Heilman et al. 1988). This same reasoning applies to work performance evaluations insofar as discrimination is less likely when ratings are based upon individuating, job-relevant behavior, and when clear performance standards are in effect. It should not be overlooked, however, that decision-makers must have the time, opportunity, and inclination to process this information carefully . If these conditions are absent, the likelihood of sex bias remains high (Martell 1991).

The significance of these findings is straightforward. Organizations that make selection decisions based on insufficient applicant information run the risk of making discriminatory judgments against women. The same is true if performance ratings are based only upon work products of ambiguous quality or little relevant work behavior and when ratings are made in the absence of clear performance standards. Fortunately, these factors often are under the control of organizations; given their role in the discriminatory treatment of women, they should be closely monitored.

Despite the obstacles placed before them, women slowly have made their way into many (though not all) male-dominated fields. This fact has been hailed by some as the ultimate solution to the problem of occupational sex discrimination. It is believed that with mere exposure to the competent performance of women in traditionally male domains, views of women will improve, ushering in the end of discrimination. This proposition was recently put to the test (Heilman and Martell 1986). First, the good news. Exposure to the successes of women in nontraditional occupations did eliminate sex discrimination in subsequent personnel decisions. Yet, the conditions under which this occurred were extraordinarily narrow. Biased assessments of women were eliminated only when: (1) decision-makers had previously been exposed to the successful work performance of women as a group (and not just a solo woman); and (2) there was a direct link between the occupation in which women were depicted as successful and the occupation for which the hiring decision was subsequently made. Apparently, the success of a token woman was easily dismissed as anomalous and decision makers were unwilling to extrapolate from the successes of women in one predominantly male field (such as criminal law) to the likely success of a woman in another (such as finance). These results are sobering, suggesting that mere exposure to successful women is unlikely to put an end to discrimination. Yet, in a more positive vein, there is a valuable message here for organizations. Making salient the successful work performance of women as a group in a heretofore male-dominated field may well enhance the treatment of other women in the same or closely related fields.

Finally, the role of motivation in reducing sex discrimination has received some attention. There is growing evidence that, when motivated to do so, decision-makers are quite capable of abandoning sex-based expectations, judging women solely on their merits (Fiske and Neuberg 1990). Research in this area holds much promise. It suggests that by stressing the importance of rendering unbiased and accurate personnel decisions, and by holding people responsible for their decisions, organizations can help to ensure more equitable treatment of women.

*Richard F. Martell*

### Bibliography

Brenner, O.C., J. Tomkiewicz, and V.E. Schein. 1989. "The Relationship between Sex Role Stereotypes and Requisite Management Characteristics." *Academy of Management Journal* 32:662–69.

Cannings, K. 1988. "Managerial Promotion: The Effects of Socialization, Specialization, and Gender." *Industrial and Labor Relations Review* 42:77–88.

Dubno, P. 1985. "Attitudes toward Women Executives: A Longitudinal Approach." *Academy of Management Journal* 28:235–39.

Fiske, S.T., and S.L. Neuberg. 1990. "A Continuum of Impression Formation, from Category-Based to Individuating Processes: Influences of Information and Motivation on Attention and Interpretation." In *Advances in Experimental Social Psychology.* Vol. 23, edited by M.P. Zanna. New York: Academic.

Heilman, M.E., C.J. Block, R.F. Martell, and M.C. Simon. 1989. "Has Anything Changed? Current Characterizations of Men, Women, and Managers." *Journal of Applied Psychology* 74:935–42.

Heilman, M.E., and R.F. Martell. 1986. "Exposure to Successful Women: Antidote to Sex Discrimination in Applicant Screening Decisions." *Organizational Behavior and Human Decision Processes* 37:376–90.

Heilman, M.E., R.F. Martell, and M.C. Simon. 1988. "The Vagaries of Sex Bias: Conditions Regulating the Undervaluation, Equivaluation, and Overvaluation of Female Job Applicants." *Organizational Behavior and Human Decision Processes* 41:98–110.

Kanter, R.M. 1977. "Some Effects of Proportions on Group Life: Skewed Sex Ratios and Responses to Token Women." *American Journal of Sociology* 82:965–90.

Martell, R.F. 1991. "Sex Bias at Work: The Effects of Attentional and Memory Demands on Performance Ratings of Men and Women." *Journal of Applied Social Psychology* 21:1939–60.

Olson, C.A., and B.E. Becker. 1983. "Sex Discrimination in the Promotion Process." *Industrial and Labor Relations Review* 36:624–41.

Sacket, P.R., C.L.Z. Dubois, and A.W. Noe. 1991. "Tokenism in Performance Evaluation: The Effects of Work Group Representation on Male-Female and White-Black Differences in Supervisory Ratings." *Journal of Applied Psychology* 76:263–67.

Schein, V.E., R. Mueller, and C. Jacobson. 1989. "The Relationship between Sex Role Stereotypes and Requisite Management Characteristics among College Students." *Sex Roles* 20:103–10.

## Discrimination against Married Women

Discrimination against older and married women has been quite widespread. It was primarily practiced during the early twentieth century. The most common form was a systematic preference for hiring young single girls, while avoiding older or married women. This preference has persisted despite the fact that younger workers are more likely to quit than older workers, making young girls relatively expensive in terms of training costs.

Another important form of discrimination were marriage bars. These were policies that stipulated that women were required to resign on the occasion of their marriage or the birth of their first child. Some firms allowed management the discretion of making exceptions. Others dismissed women universally. Such policies were particularly likely among white-collar employers.

In the early twentieth century, marriage bars were quite prevalent. The British Post Office, an aggressive user of such devices since the 1880s, not only had a mandatory bar but had a dowry program as well. Because so many of its women workers were choosing to stay single rather than leave their jobs, it instituted a dowry program by which women on the occasion of their marriage received a full month and a half of severance pay. In 1946, a study by the British government determined that nearly every non–civil-service public employer in Britain used bars; this practice was imitated by every large private sector employer examined. Marriage bars also existed in nearly every civil service in the Commonwealth. A 1960s report by the International Labor Office found that marriage bars were nearly universal in Japan, the Netherlands, Italy, and Ireland. Furthermore, most countries limited the employment of married women as teachers and airline stewardesses. More specific bans could be found in English, Belgian, Greek, Australian, and South African nursing, Portuguese textile manufacture, and Italian and Belgian chemicals (International Labor Office 1962). Currently, marriage bars are widely practiced in Japan and other East Asian nations, although in the Japanese case, formal specifications of bars in the employment contract is illegal.

The United States has made much less use of marriage bars than have other nations; this may be due to the greater labor scarcity that has generally distinguished the American labor market. The primary period of discrimination against married women in America was the Great Depression. There was a relatively minor use of marriage bars in the 1920s, although most employers strongly preferred to hire single girls. In the 1950s, there was an enormous increase in the hiring of married women that came with the soaring demand for clericals, teachers, nurses, and workers to fill other traditionally female jobs (Oppenheimer 1970). In the 1930s however, the looseness of the labor market encouraged policies that increased rather than decreased turnover. Contemporary surveys of employer practices report bar use ranging from 13 to 61 percent. (Best 1938; Shallcross 1940). In schoolteaching, the percentage of urban districts with marriage bars rose from 61 in 1927 to 77 in 1931 and 87 in 1941 (Scharf 1980).

One of the best sources of information on discrimination against married women in Depression-era America is the survey of office employment practices done in seven cities by the Women's Bureau of the Department of Labor. A reanalysis of the data in this study shows that 77 percent of all office employers discriminated against older or married women in some way. The most common practice was preferring to hire young, single women. Seventy-five percent of all employers had an explicit age preference in hiring. Only 27 percent of the firms had policies of firing women on marriage or child-bearing. Marriage bars were of substantially more importance in banking and insurance than in other industries, of more importance in small cities than in large ones, of more importance in large firms than in small firms, and ironically, more important where personnel departments rather than line managers set hiring policy (U.S. Women's Bureau 1931). Goldin (1990) has suggested that these bars came from employer perceptions of low productivity among older women.

One important explanation of this phenomenon is Cohn's theory (1985) of synthetic turnover. Synthetic turnover is a strategy for lowering labor costs by artificially increasing female quit rates, allowing the substitution of fresh, entry-level workers for relatively expensive veterans. Synthetic turnover usually takes the form of discrimination against older or married women. Because turnover rates are inversely correlated with age, any systematic bias for hiring younger workers over older workers will raise the quit rates of the resulting labor force. In many job settings, employers want to minimize turnover. However, there exists a particular configuration of circumstances under which it becomes economically advantageous for an employer to increase his quit rates: the co-existence of tenure-based salary scales, low productivity returns to worker experience, and an ample supply of replacement labor.

Many workers are paid on tenure-based salary scales, in which pay rates increase on an annual basis. Such pay scales are designed to motivate performance by making workers compete to obtain higher rather than lower raises. A consequence of such annual raises is that workers become increasingly expensive over time. These rising expenses are sustainable when they are matched by productivity increases. Since workers learn a great deal about their jobs in the first few years of their careers, their productivity rises markedly, and this finances the transition from probationary to full rates of pay. However, there exists a significant subset of jobs with limited returns to experience; in such occupations, the productivity of workers does not increase significantly over their careers. In clerical occupations, for example, the productivity of a one-year office worker can be similar to that of a veteran clerk who has been employed for fifteen years. If these two workers were both paid on piece rates, or paid a flat rate, the similarity of their output would be nonproblematic. However, if the veteran has a higher salary, due to her having received annual wage increases, then it would be advantageous for the employer to have her quit, so that she could be replaced with an entering recruit.

Increasing turnover is only viable if there is an ample supply of replacement labor. The costs of locating and retraining new workers is sufficiently nontrivial as to make most personnel managers attempt to minimize turnover. However, in a loose labor market, there may be sufficient candidates that these costs become minor.

Discrimination against older women becomes an effective device for artificially increasing turnover. Discriminating against all older workers is not practical, because in most organizations there is a core of skilled jobs with high returns to experience for which the firm would prefer longer careers. Firms engaging in synthetic turnover need a bifurcated labor force, with stable and unstable employees being divided by some objective demographic marker. Employers often chose to segment the labor force by gender because of the widespread historical acceptance of arguments claiming that women are secondary bread winners.

Evidence for the economic basis of discrimination against married women can be found in the following: (1) that marriage bars were most prevalent in the Great Depression, when supplies of replacement labor were ample; (2) that marriage bars were most prevalent in white collar work where tenure-based salary scales coincided with low levels of firm-specific skills; and (3) that discrimination against married women in advanced economies is particularly severe in Japan, where commitments to the life-time employment and salary increases for male workers encourages employers to use women to create turnover and a constant influx of entry-level workers.

*Samuel Cohn*

## Bibliography

Best, Doris. 1938. "Employed Wives Increasing." *Personnel Journal* 17:212–20.

Cohn, Samuel. 1985. *Process of Occupational Sex-Typing: Feminization of Clerical Labor in Great Britain.* Philadelphia: Temple University Press.

Erickson, Ethel. 1934. *Employment of Women in Offices.* United States Women's Bureau. United States Department of Labor. Bulletin # 120. Washington, D.C.: U.S. Government Printing Office.

Goldin, Claudia. 1990. *Understanding the Gender Gap: Economic History of American Women.* New York: Oxford University Press.

International Labor Office. 1962. "Discrimination in Employment or Occupations on the Basis of Marital Status." *International Labour Review* 85:368–89.

Oppenheimer, Valerie Kincaide. 1970. *Female Labor Force in the United States: Demographic and Economic Factors Governing Its Growth and Changing Composition.* Westport, Conn.: Greenwood.

Scharf, Lois. 1980. *To Work and to Wed: Female Employment, Feminism and the Great Depression.* Westport, Conn.: Greenwood.

Shallcross, Ruth. 1940. *Should Married Women Work?* New York: Public Affairs Pamphlet #49.

United States Women's Bureau. 1931. *Related Survey Material to Bulletin #120: Employment of Women in Offices.* Record Group 86, Records of U.S. Women's Bureau, National Archives, Washington, D.C.

## Sex Bias in Performance Evaluations

Two approaches for understanding sex bias in performance evaluations are the cognitive information processing approach, which explains bias in terms of the manner in which raters cognitively process information about ratees' performance, and the lack of fit model, which explains bias in terms of raters' perceptions of the "fit" between the characteristics of a ratee and those required of the job. These approaches provide a unique perspective for understanding sex bias in performance evaluations. Furthermore, based upon these approaches, recommendations for the design of unbiased performance evaluations can be made.

Accurate and effective performance evaluations are important to organizations for a number of reasons. For example, a variety of important personnel and human-resource decisions are based upon them (such as promotion and merit pay). In addition, performance evaluations often play a critical role in an organization's defense against charges of employment discrimination. For instance, they are frequently used to document performance problems. For these reasons, it behooves employers to design and administer performance-evaluation systems in the most effect manner possible.

Not surprisingly, a great deal of research attention has been devoted to understanding the factors that influence the fairness and accuracy of performance evaluations. A significant amount of this research has examined the effects of ratee sex on performance evaluations. Although some inconsistencies can be found, research conducted in laboratory settings suggests that males tend to be evaluated more favorably than females, especially when the job is traditionally male dominated (Kaolin and Hodgins 1984; Nieva and Gutek 1980). This pro-male bias occurs even when the performance of males and females is identical. The results of more recent research, which has utilized field methodologies, has produced conflicting findings. For example, some studies report that men are evaluated more favorably than are women (Day and Stogdill 1972); others have found that women are rated as more effective than men (Pulakos and Wexley 1983). Still others have failed to detect any differences between evaluations of men and women (Rice et al. 1984).

There are two alternative approaches for understanding sex bias in performance evaluation. The first, which can be referred as the cognitive information processing approach, suggests that discrimination results from biased cognitive processing of information about female ratees. The second approach, referred to as the lack of fit model, explains sex bias in terms of a rater's perception that there is incongruence (lack of fit) between the perceived characteristics of women and the characteristics perceived to be necessary for success in a particular job. Because these approaches rely upon different mechanisms to explain sex bias in performance evaluations, they suggest that different aspects of the rater and the rating context make sex bias more or less likely to occur. As such, each approach provides a unique explanation for the inconsistencies in previous research in this area. After reviewing these approaches, their implications for research and the development of unbiased performance evaluation systems will be described.

## Alternative Approaches to Understanding Sex Bias

The cognitive information processing approach to understanding sex bias in performance evaluations and other personnel actions relies heavily upon the psychological processes involved in social information processing. According to this orientation (Ashmore and Del Boca 1979; Dobbins et al. 1985; Feldman 1981; Fiske and Taylor 1991), most raters enter the performance-evaluation situation with well developed schemata of men and women. Schemata, which are commonly referred to as stereotypes, are cognitive structures that represent knowledge about a concept or type of stimulus. They include information about the typical attributes of a stimulus, in addition to the relations among the attributes. For examples, sex stereotypes link each sex with common behaviors and characteristics. Schemata have important effects on the processing of social information. Specifically, the observation, interpretation, storage, and retrieval of information about an individual tend to be biased toward the characteristics of stereotypes. In the context of performance evaluation, the effect of this biased processing of information is for raters to have a tendency to differentially evaluate the performance of men and women, even when their performance is identical.

The cognitive information processing approach can be seen in a recent study by Dobbins et al. (1988). They suggested that if stereotypes bias the processing of information, then individual differences in stereotypes of women should be related to evaluations of women's job performance. Specifically, individuals who hold traditional stereotypes of women (that is, those who associate femaleness with ineffectiveness) will have a tendency to overly attend to, encode, store, and recall examples of ineffective performance. On the other hand, individuals who hold nontraditional stereotypes of women should be less inclined to exhibit such biased information processing.

The cognitive information processing approach also recognizes that situational factors affect how individuals process information. Evidence suggests that inferences about an individual's characteristics are more biased by sex stereotypes in uncertain or ambiguous situations. Because predictions about an individual's future performance involve a substantial amount of uncertainty, Dobbins et al. (1988) predicted that individuals with traditional stereotypes of women would be more biased in their evaluations of women's performance when making ratings for research purposes.

In a laboratory study designed to test these predictions, Dobbins et al. (1988) found that the raters with traditional stereotypes of women were less accurate in their evaluations of female ratees than raters with nontraditional stereotypes of women. Furthermore, this difference occurred only when appraisals were made for administrative purposes (that is, promotions). In a follow-up field study, they found that students with traditional stereotypes of women were more harsh in their ratings of female professors than were students with nontraditional stereotypes of women.

To summarize, the cognitive information processing approach provides a theoretical framework for understanding how individuals process social information. In so doing, it offers insight into the factors that give rise to bias in performance evaluations.

An alternative approach to understanding sex bias in performance evaluations is presented by Heilman (1983). This approach, known as the lack of fit model, suggests that sex bias is a function of two factors, the first of which is sex stereotypes. The model suggests that individuals categorize others as being either female or male. As a result, characteristics associated with sex stereotypes are ascribed to these individuals. The second factor in the model involves the sex-typing of jobs. The lack of fit model suggests that there are common conceptions about the gender classification of different jobs, with jobs held predominantly by males classified as male-dominated (such as manager) and jobs held predominantly by females classified as female-dominated (such as secretary). Sex-typing of jobs is a function of the sex of the usual job-holder. According to the lack of fit model, sex bias occurs when there is a lack of fit between an individual's (rater's) perceptions about the characteristics of an individual (female) and the perceived requirements of the job (manager). This lack of fit results in expectations that the individual will fail and subsequent negative evaluations of his or her performance.

The lack of fit model can be seen in a recent study by Sackett et al. (1991). They demonstrated that the gender composition of the work group moderates the relationship between rate sex and performance evaluations. Specifically, they found that women were rated approximately one-half a standard deviation lower than their male counterparts when women made up less than 20 percent of the work group. However, when women made up 50 percent or more of the work group, they were evaluated more favorably than their male counterparts. These effects occurred even after controlling for female-male differences in cognitive ability, psychomotor ability, education, and experience.

**When Is Sex Bias Likely?**

The cognitive information processing approach and the lack of fit model provide unique explanations for sex bias in performance evaluations. More importantly, however, is that they both provide insight into the individual and situational factors that give rise to sex bias in evaluations. Specifically, they suggest that raters who hold traditional conceptions of women are more likely to provide biased evaluations of women's performance, especially when evaluations serve as the basis for promotional decisions. Bias is also more likely when raters have only a basic familiarity with the performance of their employees. Finally, when women make up only a small percentage of individuals in a particular job, their performance is more likely to be evaluated as less favorable than that of equally performing male counterparts.

Based upon the approaches reviewed here, a number of recommendations can be made for reducing the likelihood of sex bias in performance evaluations. First, raters should be trained about the characteristics associated with effective and ineffective performance. They should then be encouraged to use these schemata as a basis for categorizing their employees, rather than sex stereotypes. Second, raters should be trained in how to effectively observe, record, and integrate information about their employees' performance. Third, the dimensions upon which employees are evaluated should be clearly defined in specific, behavioral terminology. Finally, raters should evaluate employees on only those performance dimensions that they have an opportunity to observe directly. This is especially important when evaluations serve as the basis for promotion decisions. By following these recommendations, it may be possible to reduce bias against women in performance evaluations. By accomplishing this, organizations may more accurately evaluate employees' performance, thus facilitating the more effective use of their available human resources.

*Jeffrey D. Facteau*
*Gregory H. Dobbins*

## Bibliography

Ashmore, R.D., and F.K. Del Boca. 1979. "Sex Stereotypes and Implicit Personality Theory: Toward a Cognitive-Social Psychological Conceptualization." *Sex Roles* 5:219–48.

Day, D.R., and R.M. Stogdill. 1972. "Leader Behavior of Male and Female Supervisors: A Comparative Study." *Personnel Psychology* 25:353–60.

Dobbins, G.H., R. Cardy, and D. Truxillo. 1988. "The Effects of Purpose of Appraisal and Individual Differences in Stereotypes of Women on Sex Differences in Performance Ratings: A Laboratory and Field Study." *Journal of Applied Psychology* 73:551–58.

Dobbins, G.H., C. Stuart, E.C. Pence, and J.A. Sgro. 1985. "Cognitive Mechanisms Mediating the Biasing Effects of Leader Sex on Ratings of Leader Behavior." *Sex Roles* 12:549–59.

Feldman, J.M. 1981. "Beyond Attribution Theory: Cognitive Processes in Performance Appraisal." *Journal of Applied Psychology* 66:127–48.

Fiske, S.T., and S.E. Taylor. 1991. *Social Cognition.* 2nd ed. New York: McGraw Hill.

Heilman, M.E. 1983. "Sex Bias in Work Settings: The Lack of Fit Model." *Research in Organizational Behavior* 5:269–98.

Kaolin, R., and D.C. Hodgins. 1984. "Sex Bias and Occupational Suitability." *Canadian Journal of Behavioral Science* 16:311–25.

Nieva, V.F., and B.A. Gutek. 1980. "Sex Effects on Evaluation." *Academy of Management Review* 5:267–76.

Pulakos, E.D., and K.N. Wexley. 1983. "The Relationship among Perceptual Similarity, Sex, and Performance Ratings in Manager Subordinate Dyads." *Academy of Management Journal* 26:129–39.

Rice, R.W., D. Instone, and J. Adams. 1984. "Leader Sex, Leader Success, and Leadership Process: Two Field Studies." *Journal of Applied Psychology* 69:12–31.

Sackett, P.R., C.L.Z. DuBois, and A.W. Noe. 1991. "Tokenism in Performance Evaluation: The Effects of Work Group Representation on Male-Female and White-Black Differences in Performance Ratings." *Journal of Applied Psychology* 76:263–67.

## Persistent Gender Bias in Personnel Decisions

Gender bias in personnel decisions continues to limit women's upward mobility in organizations. Both subtle and explicit differences are found between men and women in such decisions as hiring/selection, performance appraisal, perceptions of leadership effectiveness, subordinate satisfaction with leader, and promotion recommendations (Benokraitis and Feagin 1986; O'Leary and Ickovics 1992). However, other research reveals no significant difference in the assessment of men and women at work (Pulakos et al. 1989; Thompson and Thompson 1985). Although research is equivocal regarding the existence of disparate decisions, there is unequivocal evidence that disproportionately few women had top-level executive positions in nonentrepreneurial organizations (Brown 1988; Morrison et al. 1987).

### Number of Women in the Executive Positions

Although there are record numbers of women graduating from top MBA programs and Ph.D. programs, there are few women proportionately who achieve the top-level corporate positions (Brown 1988; Morrison et al. 1987). For example, according to the *Wall Street Journal,* five hundred of the top sixty-seven hundred managers at IBM were women. Only twenty-six of the top 880 executives at AT&T were women, while at Chemical Bank, 15 percent of the more than one thousand vice presidents were women (cited in Morrison et al. 1987). These specific figures are illustrative of a much longer list of potential examples.

On the other hand, the popular press suggests that women can not handle the high-level executive positions and drop out in alarming rates (Dubois 1986), although the trend is that more and more women are entering the managerial ranks. Are women not qualified for responsible work positions? Further, are more negative decisions made regarding women at work?

## Actual Abilities and Work Behavior

The preponderance of evidence documents few actual differences between men and women in leadership or managerial potential. In both laboratory and field studies (Bass 1990), few significant differences are found between men and women in cognitive, verbal, and nonverbal competence, personality, value and interests, needs and motives, and so forth. Differences that occur include sex-role identification and self-confidence and are found in power and uses of power. Many of the differences that remain between men and women are based on differences in resources, power/status and expectations or stereotypic beliefs held by others, and society.

Despite few actual differences in leading potential and leadership style, the evaluation by others of women's success or effectiveness is different (Bass 1990). Even when men and women exhibit the same behavior, they are evaluated differently and the reasons for success (given by others) differ. Key situational factors that moderate the relationship between the gender of the manager and perceived success include the gender composition of the group and the gender type of the task.

Evidence is mixed regarding the performance of the group under male and female leaders. While some studies find few differences, numerous studies have found that employees prefer male managers. Confounding factors in these studies that could influence results include type of pay plan, duration of leader-subordinate relations, subordinate attitudes toward women, perception of supervisor's upward influence, and type of task (Bass 1990).

## Differences in Perceptions, Subjective Evaluations, and Personnel Decisions: Attitudes toward Women

Particularly in leadership positions, there is continued widespread belief among both men and women that men make better leaders than women in positions of authority (O'Leary et al. 1992). Recently, Heilman and her colleagues (1989) replicated Schein's study (1973) that found that characteristics associated with a successful manager were more similar to male characteristics than to stereotypic female characteristics. However, when male and female subordinates have had experience in working with a female boss, there is little difference in preference.

## Attributions and Evaluations of Performance of Women

The evidence of male-female difference in job performance is mixed, although differences tend to be small (Dobbins and Platz 1986; Smith 1986). However, the explanations for successful and unsuccessful performance of men and women differ markedly. Further, women give themselves lower performance assessments than men. Finally, the same behavior is evaluated differently depending on whether it is carried out by a man or a woman (O'Leary and Hansen 1985). That is, when successful, effort by men is viewed as an indicator of high ability. The same effort level by a woman on a similar task with success is perceived as a lack of ability, and the effort is viewed as compensating for the lack of ability (O'Leary and Ickovics 1992).

## Other Decisions

Recruitment bias and job placement bias continue to exist, with preferential treatment of males (Powell 1988). This bias is exacerbated in male-dominated jobs. A woman's average pay is 70 percent of a man's even in the same occupation. Further, the highest-paid jobs are those with predominantly male workers.

## Understanding Gender Biases at Work

There is no evidence of innate, biologically determined difference between men and women in ability of skill or predispositions that would account for the dearth of women in jobs and careers that pay well, have status and prestige, and so forth. Therefore, there must be other reasons. According to O'Leary, the bases for biased decision-making are connected with women's capacity to bear children and the subsequent and incorrect assumption that working mothers are less committed to work than men. Although women may differ in terms of the values they place on career and family (mommy track vs. career track), American work continues to be outdatedly organized and structured with the assumption that there is a full-time person at home tending to household and child-care responsibilities (O'Leary and Ickovics 1992). Others (Heilman 1983) believe that if the gender stereotype of the individual does not match the gender types of the job, more negative outcomes will result for the individual.

Persistent gender stereotypes of men, women, and a successful worker as found in both Schein (1973) and Heilman et al. (1989) are one barrier to women's progress at work. The acceptance and internalization of the feminine stereotype is one internal barrier for women especially at the initial stages of career choice (Betz and Fitzgerald 1987).

A number of experts, however, recommend that the focus of research and attention should be placed on external barriers to women's success at work (Betz and Fitzgerald 1987; Tavris 1992). These external barriers include the political structure of the United States, which to date has lacked a national child-care plan or a plan of research to investigate work-family conflicts experienced by millions of its productive workers. Further, organizations and the educational curricula provide limited, and encourage few, opportunities and activities for women to experience tasks that are instrumental to their success in the paid world of work. Finally, reflecting both the political and organizational structure/environment, a null environment (Betz 1989) exists for women because there is less family and societal support for women than for men who decide to combine career and family.

*Jeanette N. Cleveland*

## Bibliography

Bass, B.M. 1990. *Bass and Stogdill's Handbook of Leadership: Theory, Research and Managerial Applications.* New York: Free Press.

Benokraitis, N.V., and J.R. Feagin. 1986. *Modern Sexism: Blatant, Subtle, and Covert Discrimination.* Englewood Cliffs, N.J.: Prentice Hall.

Betz, N.E. 1989. "The Null Environment and Women's Career Development." *Counseling Psychologist* 17:136–44.

Betz, N.E., and L.F. Fitzgerald. 1987. *The Career Psychology of Women.* New York: Academic.

Brown, L.K. 1988. "Female Managers in the U.S. and in Europe: Corporate Boards, MBA Credentials and the Image/Illusion of Progress." In *Women in Management Worldwide*, edited by N.I. Adler and D.N. Izraeli, pp. 265–74. Armonk, N.Y.: M.E. Sharpe.

Dobbins, G.H., and S.J. Platz. 1986. "Sex Differences in Leadership: How Real Are They?" *Academy of Management Review* 11:118–27.

Dubois, J. 1986. "One in Three Management Women Drops Out." *USA Today.* July 31:1.

Heilman, M.E. 1983. "The Lack of Fit Model." In *Research in Organizational Behavior.* Vol. 5, edited by B. Staw and L.L. Cummings. Greenwich, Conn.: JAI.

Heilman, M.E., C.J. Block, R.F. Martell, and M.C. Simon. 1989. "Has Anything Changed? Current Characterizations of Men, Women and Managers." *Journal of Applied Psychology* 74:935–42.

Morrison, A.M., R.P. White, E. VanVelsor, and Center for Creative Leadership. 1987. *Breaking the Glass Ceiling: Can Women Reach the Top of America's Largest Corporations?* Reading, Mass.: Addison-Wesley.

O'Leary, V.E., and R.D. Hansen. 1985. "Sex as an Attributional Factor." In *The Nebraska Symposium on Motivation*. Vol. 32, edited by T. Sonderegger. Lincoln: University of Nebraska Press.

O'Leary, V.E., and J.R. Ickovics. 1992. "Cracking the Glass Ceiling: Overcoming Isolation and Alienation." In *Woman Power: Managing in Time of Demographic Turbulence*, edited by U. Sekaran and F.T.L. Leong, pp. 7–30. Newbury Park, Calif.: Sage.

Powell, G.N. 1988. *Women and Men in Management*. Newbury Park, Calif.: Sage.

Pulakos, E.P., L.A. White, S. Oppler, and W.C. Borman. 1989. "Examination of Race and Sex Effects on Performance Ratings." *Journal of Applied Psychology* 74:770–80.

Schein, V.E. 1973. "Relationship between Sex-Role Stereotypes and Requisite Management Characteristics." *Journal of Applied Psychology* 57:95–100.

Smith, J.E. 1986. *Women in Management (1979–1984): A Review of the Literature*. Paper presented at the American Psychological Assn., New York.

Tavris, C. 1992. *The Mismeasure of Woman*. New York: Simon and Schuster.

Thompson, D.E., and T.A. Thompson. 1985. "Task Based Performance Appraisal for Blue Collar Jobs: Evaluation of Race and Sex Effects." *Journal of Applied Psychology* 70:747–53.

U.S. Bureau of Census (1980, 1991). *Statistical Abstract of the United States*. U.S. Department of Commerce. Washington, D.C.

## Gender and Workplace Dispute Resolution

Conflict is a normal part of human activity, and disputes are everyday occurrences in public and private spheres. In the workplace, disputes can range from co-workers' short-term personality conflicts over work assignments to long-term union-management disagreements about wages, benefits, and hours. The means of resolving disputes can range from informal conversation to lengthy, bitter strikes. Resolving workplace disputes is in the interest of employers, unions, and workers, for it promotes fairness in treatment, organizational legitimacy, and production efficiency (Lewin and Peterson 1988; McCabe 1988; Westin and Feliu 1988).

Workplace dispute resolution refers to the formal and informal rules individuals and groups use to resolve problems in employment. Within organizations, such rules function "as a system of private law" (Thomson 1974). When effective dispute resolution is possible in the workplace, it protects employees against arbitrary and unjust authority and can provide for the systematic review of complaints and grievances.

Despite considerable interest in the study of industrial justice from the 1940s through the mid 1970s, the intraorganizational processes and consequences of dispute resolution are only now being updated to include the growth of female labor-force participation since World War II (Wertheimer and Nelson 1975). This growing body of empirical evidence on women's workplace disputes mainly concerns sexual harassment and sex differences in arbitration and dispute refereeing. This research suggests that patterns of gender differences in workplace disputes may have larger scale consequences for employment inequality more generally.

Workplace dispute resolution may, for heuristic purposes, be conceptualized in three components: origins, processes, and outcomes (Gwartney-Gibbs and Lach 1994b). Findings summarized below suggest that all three components are patterned by gender roles and, given the highly sex-segregated nature of employment, by sex types of jobs. That is, women and incumbents of sex-segregated jobs appear to have different types of disputes, different ways of dealing with them, and different outcomes in dispute settlement than men and those in sex-atypical jobs.

## Gender Roles and Workplace Dispute Resolution

The origins of women's and men's workplace disputes differ in ways consistent with gender roles. Women's typical roles in household and family responsibilities interfere with employment (Abel 1991; Berk 1985). But men's typical gender roles, particularly a greater propensity for aggressive behavior, appear to be associated with workplace disputes over insubordination, violence, and threats (Stockard and Lach 1989). Women workers show greater sensitivity to interpersonal relationship problems than men, often voicing disputes concerning personality conflicts (Gwartney-Gibbs and Lach 1994b). But they also described difficulty resolving personality conflicts through formal channels. Even in cases severe enough to be labeled "harassment," workers perceived that formal procedures were not designed to recognize or resolve interpersonal conflict (Stanko 1985).

Gender differences appear clearly in the processes used to resolve problems in the workplace. Women less often pursue workplace disputes to resolution because of several factors, including gender-role socialization, the lack of provision for female-typed issues in formal procedures, and a lack of sympathy or support on the part of "gatekeepers" (union stewards, supervisors) of formal procedures (Clark 1988; Gwartney-Gibbs and Lach 1993; Reskin and Padavic 1988). Women workers consistently use lateral transfers to move away from problems, while men more often use formal procedures provided by the company (Gwartney-Gibbs and Lach 1993, 1994b). Whether transfers to "solve" workplace disputes are part of a pattern of avoidance associated with women's gender roles, or due instead to opportunity structures associated with female-typed occupations or a lack of support from gatekeepers of dispute-resolution mechanisms, remains an open question.

Women's propensity to use lateral transfers instead of formal procedures to solve workplace disputes produces several outcomes. First, disputes that enter the formal processes are extreme, not representing the day-to-day conflicts women workers experience. Second, workers who use lateral transfers to solve workplace problems often lose union protections and human capital—that is, job-specific training and expertise. Employers more often train and offer promotional opportunities to employees who stay on the job. Men less often transfer to solve workplace disputes than women; likewise, men have longer average job tenure than women. High levels of turnover and labor-force intermittency have long been recognized as one explanation for lower earnings of women workers. To the extent that lateral transfers are associated with lower job-specific skills and training for women workers than men, turnovers internal to an organization may have a similar effect on the earnings of women who use lateral transfers to resolve conflict.

## Occupational Sex Segregation and Workplace Dispute Resolution

Sex segregation in employment is related to the origins, processes, and outcomes of workplace disputes for both women and men in sex-atypical jobs (tokens) and for women in sex-typical jobs (Kanter 1977a, 1977b; Segura 1989; Swerdlow

1989). Disputes originate for tokens in discrimination, harassment, and social isolation, and for women nontokens with "gender-role spillover" (Nieva and Gutek 1981).

Both men and women tokens experience harassment and discrimination from co-workers and supervisors. But these are generally mild rather than severe, and are often in the ambiguous realm of "personality conflicts." Few workers labeled their experiences harassment or discrimination, for they seemed unsure if it was really occurring or whether they were partly responsible (Gwartney-Gibbs and Lach 1993, 1994a; Roos and Reskin 1984; Segura 1989).

Token men clerical workers often report "no problems" in the workplace, yet they describe office situations very similar to those described by women workers as "hothouses," in which personality conflicts explode (Gwartney-Gibbs and Lach 1994a). One explanation may be that it is inconsistent with male gender roles to recognize disputes that are interpersonal in nature. "Gender-role spillover" suggests that persons in highly sex-segregated occupations will be treated on the basis of gender-role stereotypes in the workplace. This may become disputable if the stereotype is irrelevant to a worker's job requirements or personality. Women report being disciplined for not acting "nice enough" or not being "sensitive to the needs of co-workers"—expectations consistent with gender-role stereotypes and not with job descriptions. Such expectations are not imposed upon men in female-typed jobs; indeed, several described using their gender roles, especially interpersonal aggressiveness, to get their way (Gwartney-Gibbs and Lach 1994a).

Occupational sex segregation is related to processes of resolving workplace disputes in different ways for tokens and nontokens. For tokens, high visibility generates pressure to conform in order to gain acceptance from the dominant group; when disputes are voiced, little support comes from informal networks to pursue issues. For nontokens, greater support comes from networks to resolve disputes formally and informally (Gwartney-Gibbs and Lach 1994b).

Women tokens have great difficulty articulating their disputes, finding co-workers to talk with, and discovering what to do. Sometimes procedures take years, while problems worsen. In part, this is due to the nature of the issues—the mildness of social ostracism compared with a fistfight, and difficulty documenting ambiguous feelings of exclusion or isolation from men co-workers. But it is also because formal dispute-resolution mechanisms do not have provisions for, or experience with, types of disputes women tokens experience. Cases of employees who struggled to document discrimination and harassment became legends in corporate culture, serving to deter others from pursuing disputes. Thus, few tokens with disputes attempt to use formal procedures; rather, they live with the disputes, transfer to new jobs, or resolve them informally.

Men tokens less often report any problems at all. When they do, however, they describe using formal procedures successfully, and they mention managers sensitive to personal issues that created short-term problems (such as a wife unavailable for child care). Several men tokens describe being adopted, like mascots, by women co-workers and coached in resolving disputes over promotion, equipment, and personal space. Their disputes less often concern interpersonal difficulties, but when that happens, they do not conform to the passive and subordinate behavior typical of women (Gwartney-Gibbs and Lach 1994b).

One important outcome of these differential origins and processes of workplace disputes related to occupational sex segregation may be the persistence of sex-segregated workplaces. To the extent that sex-segregated workplaces are more conducive to settling everyday disputes, it makes sense for women to prefer to work among women and men to work among men (Gwartney-Gibbs and Lach 1994b).

## Conclusion

Gender differences are apparent in workplace disputes' origins, processes, and outcomes. Some of these differences are attributable to gender roles, but many gender differences appear to interact with sex-typed jobs. Thus, it is difficult to disentangle explanations that are based upon gender roles from explanations that give precedence to women and men workers' different structural positions.

Workplace dispute resolution is a topic largely neglected in research on gender and employment inequality. And gender is a topic largely neglected in research on workplace dispute resolution. But it appears that these intraorganizational processes underlie broader patterns of employment inequality well documented in census and survey data.

*Patricia A. Gwartney-Gibbs*
*Denise H. Lach*

## Bibliography

Abel, Emily K. 1991. *Who Cares for the Elderly? Public Policy and the Experiences of Adult Daughters.* Philadelphia: Temple University Press.

Berk, Sarah Fenstermaker. 1985. *The Gender Factory: The Apportionment of Work in American Households.* New York: Plenum.

Clark, Paul F. 1988. "The Role of the Steward in Shaping Union Member Attitudes toward the Grievance Procedure." *Labor Studies Journal* 13:3.

Gwartney-Gibbs, Patricia A., and Denise H. Lach. 1994a. "Gender Differences in Clerical Workers' Disputes over Tasks, Interpersonal Treatment, and Emotion." *Human Relations* 47(6):611–39.

———. 1994b. "Gender, Workplace Dispute Resolution, and Employment Inequality." *Law & Society Review* 28(2):501–31.

———. 1993. "Gender Differences in Grievance Processing and Its Implications for Rethinking Shopfloor Practices." In *Women Workers & the Labor Movement: Forging a New Partnership,* edited by Dorothy Sue Cobble, pp. 299–315. Ithaca, N.Y.: ILR.

Kanter, Rosabeth Moss. 1977a. *Men and Women of the Corporation.* New York: Basic Books.

———. 1977b. "Some Effects of Proportions on Group Life: Skewed Sex Ratios and Responses to Token Women," *American Journal of Sociology* 82:965.

Lewin, David, and Richard Peterson. 1988. *The Modern Grievance Procedure in the United States.* New York: Quorum.

McCabe, Douglas M. 1988. *Corporate Nonunion Complaint Procedures and Systems.* New York: Praeger.

Nieva, Vivian, and Barbara Gutek. 1981. *Women and Work: A Psychological Perspective.* New York: Praeger.

Reskin, Barbara F., and Irene Padavic. 1988. "Supervisors as Gatekeepers: Male Supervisors' Response to Women's Integration in Plant Jobs." *Social Problems* 35:536.

Reskin, Barbara F., and Patricia A. Roos. 1990. *Job Queues, Gender Queues: Explaining Women's Inroads into Male Occupations.* Philadelphia: Temple University Press.

Roos, Patricia A., and Barbara F. Reskin. 1984 "Institutional Factors Contributing to Sex Segregation in the Workplace." In *Sex Segregation in the Workplace: Trends, Explanations, Remedies,* edited by Barbara F. Reskin. Washington, D.C.: National Academy.

Segura, Denise A. 1989. "Conflict in Social Relations at Work: A Chicana Perspective." In *Estudios Chicanos and the Politics of Community,* edited by Mary Romero and Cordelia Candelaria. Boulder, Colo.: National Assn. for Chicano Studies.

Stanko, Elizabeth A. 1985. *Intimate Intrusions: Women's Experience of Male Violence.* Boston: Routledge and Kegan Paul.

Stockard, Jean, and Denise Lach. 1989. "Conflict Resolution: Sex and Gender Roles." *Annual Revue of Conflict Knowledge and Conflict Resolution* 1:69.

Swerdlow, Marian. 1989. "Men's Accommodations to Women Entering a Nontraditional Occupation: A Case of Rapid Transit Operatives." *Gender & Society* 3:373.

Thomson, A.W.J. 1974. *The Grievance Procedure in the Private Sector*. Ithaca, N.Y.: School of Industrial and Labor Relations, Cornell University.

Wertheimer, Barbara M., and Anne Nelson. 1975. *Trade Union Women: A Study of Their Participation in New York City Locals*. New York: Praeger.

Westin, Alan F., and Alfred G. Feliu. 1988. *Resolving Employment Disputes without Litigation*. Washington D.C.: Bureau of National Affairs.

# Management
# and Organizational Mobility

## Academic Mentors as Gatekeepers

Academia serves as a major gatekeeper to higher status occupational roles in society. The primary vehicle for this is the mentoring process, whereby the mentor provides sponsorship and informal training to his or her student.

The role of academic gatekeeper frequently begins during graduate training. Responsibilities of graduate students early in their programs are relatively clear cut. At the doctoral level, however, course content is more specialized, while the criteria for the evaluation of students are much less clear cut. Doctoral candidates are gaining expertise in their chosen specialties, and the number of faculty with expertise in a similar area is relatively small. Standards for evaluation are thus determined by a small group of experts, and these individuals become crucial as gatekeepers.

We view that mentoring as an advanced stage of gatekeeping that is particularly important in graduate education. Mentoring involves more than formal training and thus is not a required aspect of a professor's role. In examining mentoring, current research tends to focus on two issues: the criteria used by faculty in deciding whom to mentor, and the effects of mentoring on students' careers.

### Definition of Mentoring

Two aspects of mentoring have been distinguished in the literature, informal training and sponsorship. Zuckerman (1977) included the following as components of informal training: collaboration, role modeling, advising, informal teaching, and informal discussions. Long (1990) cited Zuckerman as noting that during informal training, mentors show students the "real world" of scientific professions by teaching "what really matters." Long (1990) cited Overington (1977) as finding that through this process, students are able to learn the "culture" and "grammar" of their fields. Dresselhaus (1987) described informal training as a process in which mentors show their students "the ropes" through inspiration and role modeling.

The second aspect of mentoring, sponsorship, was noted by Zuckerman (1977) to include introductions, nominations for awards, and recommendations.

Shapiro et al. (1987) described a continuum of mentoring called the "patron system." Sponsorship represented one extreme of the patron continuum. Dresselhaus (1987) included advocacy, providing leadership for student networks, and representing interests of women on faculty and national committees as broader and less individual-specific forms of sponsorship.

Hall and Sandler (1982) suggest that nominations for awards can be particularly important factors in women's career outcomes. Merit awards can certify the competence of women students, increasing their equality with men in their own eyes and in the views of peers and future evaluators. Awards can also sometimes help women gain entry into scholarly networks, from which they might otherwise be barred.

### Mentoring as a Selective Process

Mentoring involves informal training, but past research suggests that not all doctoral students receive it. Weiss (1981) reported that 33 percent of the students in her sample had no informal contact with faculty at any time during their graduate training, while only 20 percent had informal contact more than once a month. Additionally, Blackburn et al. (1981) found that only 20 percent of faculty in their study co-authored papers with dissertation students more than rarely. These two studies, then, suggest that only about 20 percent of faculty/student pairs engage in activities associated with informal training to a significant extent.

Two reasons for the lack of universality of informal training were noted by Long (1990): (1) men are sometimes reluctant to mentor women because of fears about connotations of the relationship; and (2) questions about career commitment among women with children. Also, Hall and Sandler (1983) noted that senior academicians tend to select persons like themselves as protégés. Because senior faculty are predominantly white and male, women and minorities tend to be underselected. Taken together, then, these pieces of research suggest the importance of considering criteria involved in decisions of faculty to mentor or not to mentor particular students.

### Effects of Mentoring

Past research suggests that effects of mentoring may vary, depending upon which aspect, sponsorship, or informal training is considered. Several researchers (Long et al. 1979; Long 1990; Reskin 1979) found sponsorship to be an important determinant of prestige of the first job. Indeed, the eminence of the mentor was more important than the productivity of either the mentor or the protégé. Nonetheless, this advantage is tied to mentors' retaining their protégés at their own universities; when protégés do not remain at their mentors' institution, the effect is nonsignificant (Long et al. 1979).

In contrast, past research suggests that informal training is likely to affect productivity of protégés. Long (1990) reported that aspects of informal training, such as collaboration, increase future publication rates of protégés. Reskin (1979) found a positive relationship between productivity of mentors and productivity of their protégés. Crane (1965) found that the performance and achievements of mentors and the closeness with which they work with their students influence their ability to impart advantages, such as knowledge, skills, and professional values. More specifically, two key factors in attainment of recognition in science are selection of good research topics and continuity of topic. Mentors are highly influential in the development of these traits. Particularly among protégés who are initially employed in minor universities, gains from high individual productivity are greater in cases where there is continuity in topic. Topical continuity increases the likelihood of becoming part of a network of scholars outside the institution of employment and hence of achieving recognition and opportunities for more prestigious employment.

Finally, Simeone (1987) found that women in male-dominated fields who have had female mentors are able to learn how to handle difficult job situations tied to tokenism more effectively than are those without female mentors. Further, Simeone (1987) cited Feldman as finding that women who had close relationships with faculty were more apt to have ambitious career plans. Finally, Simeone (1987), Richey et al. (1988), and Hall and Sandler (1986) suggested that same-sex mentors may be more beneficial than opposite-sex mentors as role models of professional conduct and career strategies.

Past research suggests that the effects of mentoring are twofold. First, sponsorship increases the likelihood that a protégé will attain an advantageous starting position. Second, informal training serves to increase quality and quantity of work and hence increases likelihood of recognition in further stages of the career. An important corollary of this distinction is that productive mentors at less prestigious universities can still aid their students through the gates to professional recognition by providing informal training. Thus, mentoring can occur in and affect careers of students regardless of the prestige level of the doctoral institution and the eminence of the mentor. Nonetheless, the degree of a mentor's effectiveness may be greater when the protégé is of the same sex. By working informally with and sponsoring some, but not all, of their doctoral students, mentors influence career outcomes.

Research by the authors sought to determine how mentors chose protégés and whether careers differed for protégés with a same-sex versus different-sex mentor. We surveyed a nationwide sample of academicians employed in doctoral-granting departments of English, sociology, and chemistry. We asked them about the frequency with which they engaged in mentoring activities and the student qualities that influenced their selection of protégés. Both male and female faculty indicated the following as the most important determinants of their willingness to engage in mentoring activities with a particular student: (1) student's motivation; (2) quality of the student's performance in courses taught by the respondent; and (3) performance in the graduate program generally.

In attempting to determine the effects of same-sex and different-sex protégé/mentor pairs, we examined publication records of sociology graduates. We determined if they had collaborated on publications with a faculty member at his/her dissertation institution. Such a publication was used as an indicator that the student had a mentor during graduate school. We expected that it would have a positive effect on a student's career productivity. We found that the publication rates of females and males were higher when they had collaborated on at least one piece with a female mentor than when they had done so with a male mentor or had no mentor. As such, our research is consistent with past research (Long 1990; Crane 1965) that collaboration with a mentor has a positive effect on protégés' publication rates. Our research, however, is inconsistent with contentions of Richey et al. (1988) that same-sex mentors may have more beneficial effects than opposite-sex mentors.

At the same time, Richey et al. (1988) and Hall and Sandler (1986) suggest that female mentors may place greater emphasis on equity, reciprocity, and cooperation as opposed to a more hierarchical system of authority. If so, perhaps the greater equality in female mentors' relationships with their protégés permits protégés earlier opportunities to explore strategies of their own choosing that subsequently enhance their ability to work independently as they enter their first jobs. In contrast, protégés of male mentors may learn more refined skills in particular aspects of research as members of their mentors' research teams, while less often acquiring a global view of the research process.

Overall, our research and previous research support the view that mentoring, as reflected in research collaboration, has a positive influence on protégés' professional performance. As such, it tends to confirm the importance of mentoring as a gatekeeping function that operates in academia, particularly in graduate training for professional degrees.

*Sandra French*
*Alice C. Wilson*

## Bibliography

American Sociological Assn. 1979. *Guide to Graduate Departments of Sociology.* Washington, D.C.: American Sociological Assn.

Blackburn, R.T., D.W. Chapman, and S.M. Cameron. 1981. "'Cloning' in Academe: Mentorship and Academic Careers." *Research in Higher Education* 15:315–27.

Crane, D. 1965. "Scientists at Major and Minor Universities: A Study of Productivity." *American Sociological Review* 30:699–714.

Dresselhaus, M.S. 1987. "Responsibilities of Women Faculty." In *Women in Scientific and Engineering Professions,* edited by V.B. Haas and C.C. Perrucci. Ann Arbor: University of Michigan Press.

Fox, M.F. 1985. *Scholarly Writing and Publishing: Issues, Problems and Solutions.* Boulder, Colo.: Westview.

Hall, R.M., and B.R. Sandler. 1983. "Academic Mentoring for Women Students and Faculty: A New Look at an Old Way to Get Ahead." *Project on the Status and Education of Women.* Washington, D.C.: Assn. of American Colleges.

Hall, R.M., and B.R. Sandler. 1986. "The Campus Climate Revisited: Chilly for Women Faculty, Administrators, and Graduate Students." *Project on the Status and Education of Women.* Washington, D.C.: Assn. of American Colleges.

Hall, R.M., and B.R. Sandler. 1982. "Women Winners." *Project on the Status and Education of Women.* Washington, D.C.: Assn. of American Colleges.

Long, J.S. 1990. "The Origins of Sex Differences in Science." *Social Forces* 68:1297–1315.

Long, J.S., P.D. Allison, and R. McGinnis. 1979. "Entrance into the Academic Career." *American Sociological Review* 44:816–30.

Overington, M. 1977. "The Scientific Community as Audience: Toward a Rhetorical Analysis of Science." *Philosophy and Rhetoric* 10:145.

Reskin, B.F. 1979. "Academic Sponsorship and Scientists' Careers." *Sociology of Education* 52:129–46.

Richey, C.A., E.D. Gambrill, and B.A. Blythe. 1988. "Mentor Relationships among Women in Academe." *Affilia* 3:34–47.

Shapiro, E.C., F.P. Haseltine, and M.P. Rowe. 1987. "Moving up: Role Models, Mentors and the 'Patron System.'" *Sloan Management Review* 19:51–58.

Simeone, A. 1987. *Academic Women: Working toward Equality.* South Hadley, Mass.: Garvey.

Weiss, C.S. 1981. "The Development of Professional Role Commitment among Graduate Students." *Human Relations* 34:13–31.

Zuckerman, H. 1977. *Scientific Elite: Nobel Laureates in the United States.* New York: Free Press.

**Influences on Women's Managerial Advancement**

Determinants of women's advancement into management roles are proposed to arise from work and home situations and present and past circumstances. Individual factors of personal dispositions and early family background have been proposed to influence women becoming managers (Lemkau 1979). More recently (Riger and Galligan 1980), however, the work situation has been stressed as more influential. The debate as to whether women's advancement into management roles is caused by situational or individual factors, or both, is important in understanding how that rare person, "the woman manager," arises. The correct relative emphasis on individual or situational factors is necessary in order to redress women's continued underrepresentation in management.

Social cognition theory (Bandura 1986) provides an integrative framework for the many background, personal, and environmental factors thought to influence women's career behaviors. From a social cognition view, the major influences on behavior are environmental, rather than background or personal. Personal dispositions are said to serve as the predominant influence only when situational constraints are weak, while relevant experience is thought influential for behavior through practice and mastery of skills. Hence, the most important influences on women's managerial advancement would be environmental (that is, work, home). Work-relevant experiences would be less (but moderately) influential, whereas women's attitudes and early background would be either weak or unimportant.

**The Work Environment: Development**

Of substantial importance to women's managerial advancement is the extent to which the work environment enables the development necessary for managerial work (Burke and McKeen 1992). Ragins and Sundstrom (1989) explained how training develops the knowledge, skills, credentials, and credibility, and thus expertise, for women to be promoted to powerful positions in organizations. Women managers receive less training and development than men (Tharenou and Conroy 1994). Training is positively related to women's managerial level, more strongly than are work structure, work-relevant experiences, home roles, attitudes, and early socialization (Tharenou and Conroy 1994). The less preventing attendance at training, the greater the promotion of women managers (Tharenou and Conroy 1994).

A second developmental influence in the work environment for women is the interpersonal support they receive for career advancement. Support from others is argued to be especially important for women to overcome their lack of integration into male networks, peer groups, and mentoring systems (Ragins and Sundstrom 1989; Riger and Galligan 1980). Women with mentors (as for men) advance further in terms of promotion and salary than those without (Ragins and Sundstrom 1989). Career encouragement from colleagues and more senior persons has also been shown to be important in assisting women to gain executive status (Morrison et al. 1987). Organizational career encouragement is positively related to women managers' promotion (Tharenou and Conroy 1994)—more strongly than are training, work structure, home roles, attitudes, and early socialization.

### The Work Environment: Structure

Sex-linked structural features of the work environment, such as internal labor markets and sex composition of managerial hierarchies, have been emphasized as resulting in women's lower incomes and lack of advancement compared with men's (Marini 1989). More female managerial hierarchies are associated with higher managerial levels for women (Tharenou and Conroy 1994), indicating that women's advancement occurs more where they are less of a numerical minority in the hierarchy (Kanter 1977). Visibility, isolation and entrapment are then reduced (Kanter 1977). Moreover, men have longer and more specified career ladders than do women (Marini 1989). Career ladders are associated with women managers' promotion (Tharenou and Conroy 1994), indicating that opportunity is required for advancement to occur. Moreover, public-sector employment is more associated than private with women's promotion to managerial level (Tharenou and Conroy 1994), perhaps because the public sector has led affirmative-action reform. Overall, the work situation's structure has been found to predict women managers' promotion and managerial level, consistently stronger than the home situation, attitudes, and early socialization (Tharenou and Conroy 1994).

### Work-Relevant Experiences

Work-relevant experiences in terms of the amount, diversity, and continuity of work experience enhance women's advancement in organizations. Such experiences enable the development of relevant work skills and thus assist preparation for progression to higher organizational levels. Greater work experience, education, and mobility have been consistently related to managers' level, promotion, and salary (Cox and Harquail 1991), including women managers (Tharenou and Conroy 1994). However, men's mobility and moves for advancement, but not women's, have been positively related to their managerial level.

The impact of work-relevant experiences is also consistent with human capital explanations for advancement. According to this view (Marini 1989), enhanced skill acquisition through work experience, mobility, education, and training is conducive to productivity improvement and thus is rewarded by advancement. However, men managers' human capital investments (such as work experience and education) have been shown to result in greater reward (Marini 1989) than those of women managers. Moreover, work-relevant experiences have been found less important for women's managerial level and promotion than the work situation's structure and development opportunities (Tharenou and Conroy 1994).

### The Home Environment

Home roles are thought to intrude more into women's work lives than men's. Ragins and Sundstrom (1989) proposed that a spouse and children interrupt women's work experience and thus reduce their promotion to powerful positions in organizations. Consistent with this view, women managers are more likely to be unmarried and childless than are men managers (Tharenou and Conroy 1994). Women are more likely to move from full- to part-time work because of young children (Felmlee 1984), and women managers may leave the workforce because of heavy demands with preschool children (Rosin and Korabik 1990). The increased career interruptions and role overload from home demands may result in unfavorable perceptions by the decision-makers who fast-track potential managerial candidates (Ragins and Sundstrom 1989). However, home responsibilities and work-home role compatibility have not been found associated with women's managerial level and promotion (Tharenou and Conroy 1994). This may be because women with home demands either do not take on managerial roles or because women managers develop extensive coping strategies to reduce the impact of family commitments on work.

## Attitudes

Consistent with a social cognition perspective, personal dispositions are thought to have weak effects on women's managerial advancement when work environment effects are strong. Traits such as lower self-confidence, success attributions to external unstable factors, lower power and achievement needs, and more feminine sex-role traits are argued to be poor explanations for women's lack of managerial advancement (Riger and Galligan 1980). Structural and social aspects of the work situation are thought to have more powerful effects (Riger and Galligan 1980). Moreover, if personality factors have effects, they are thought likely to do so only in interaction with the organizational situation (Fagenson 1990). When the relative importance of personality variables (self-confidence, success attributions) has been assessed for women's managerial level and promotion, their impact has been weak or nonsignificant (Tharenou and Conroy 1994). Much stronger effects occur for the work situation (development, structure) and work-relevant experience (Tharenou and Conroy 1994).

## Early Background

Early background factors, such as first-born status, maternal employment, parent education levels, parental encouragement for education, and close relationships with parents, are argued to be facilitating factors for the development of career salience and less feminine sex-role self-concepts in women (Lemkau 1979). Hence, they are thought to influence women to pursue sex-atypical employment, such as managerial jobs. However, early socialization factors have been found to be either weakly or nonsignificantly related to women's managerial levels and promotion and to be unimportant compared with the work situation and work-relevant experience (Tharenou and Conroy 1994).

## Conclusion

Overall, it can be argued that the work situation, especially through development and structure and work-relevant experiences, is more likely to determine women's managerial advancement than are personal dispositions and early background factors. Studies support a social-cognition view. Personalistic explanations for women's managerial advancement in the form of attitudes and early background are inadequate, in keeping with critiques (Riger and Galligan 1980). When women do not advance in the managerial hierarchy, it is more likely to be because of structural and social aspects of work environment than because of differential sex-role socialization and unfavorable personal dispositions. Home demands may result in women with responsibilities deferring managerial roles, perhaps permanently, or until less incompatibility occurs between family and work. Practical implications for organizations are that women's advancement into management will be improved by enhanced training and development, greater career encouragement, more gender-balanced hierarchies and greater internal labor markets, and more work experience and moves for advancement.

*Phyllis Tharenou*

## Bibliography

Bandura, A. 1986. *Social Foundations of Thought and Action: A Social Cognitive Theory.* Englewood Cliffs, N.J.: Prentice Hall.

Burke, R.J., and C.A. McKeen. 1992. "Women in Management." In *International Review of Industrial and Organizational Psychology,* edited by C.L. Cooper and I.T. Robertson, pp. 245–82. New York: Wiley.

Cox, T.H., and C.V. Harquail. 1991. "Career Paths and Career Success in the Early Career Stages of Male and Female MBAs." *Journal of Vocational Behavior,* 39:54–75.

Fagenson, E.A. 1990. "At the Heart of Women in Management Research." *Journal of Business Ethics* 9:1–8.

Felmlee, D.H. 1984. "The Dynamics of Women's Job Mobility." *Work and Occupations* 11:259–81.

Kanter, R.M. 1977. *Men and Women of the Corporation.* New York: Basic Books.

Lemkau, J.P. 1979. "Personality and Background Characteristics of Women in Male-Dominated Occupations." *Psychology of Women Quarterly,* 4:221–40.

Marini, M.M. 1989. "Sex Differences in Earnings in the United States." *Annual Review of Sociology* 15:343–80.

Morrison, A.M., R.P. White, and E. Von Velsor. 1987. *Breaking the Glass Ceiling.* Reading, Mass.: Addison-Wesley.

Ragins, B.R., and E. Sundstrom. 1989. "Gender and Power in Organizations." *Psychological Bulletin* 105:51–88.

Riger, S., and P. Galligan. 1980. "Women in Management: An Exploration of Competing Paradigms." *American Psychologist* 35:902–10.

Rosin, H.M., and K. Korabik. 1990. "Marital and Family Correlates of Women Managers' Attrition from Organizations." *Journal of Vocational Behavior* 37:104–20.

Tharenou, P., and D.K. Conroy. 1994. "Men and Women Managers' Advancement." *Applied Psychology: An International Review* 43:5–31.

## The Advancement of Women in Post-Secondary Educational Administration

Academic administration, much like its private-sector counterpart, business management, has been historically characterized by a clear sex-based division of labor. Women in senior administrative positions are still few, while, at the same time, they are overrepresented in lower-level support positions and within traditional fields for women. Recent literature recognizes that organizational factors create and reinforce the glass ceiling in academia. Moreover, the career paths of academic women, which often differ from those of male administrators, act as barriers to women's advancement. There is also a growing policy-oriented literature that develops and evaluates organizational strategies for equalizing the gender balance in higher educational administration. Women are now the majority of undergraduate students nationwide and are achieving numerical parity with men in master's-level graduate programs. That their representation among faculty and administration has not increased so dramatically is a cause for concern and further research.

Since the 1970s, women have made slow but steady progress into the ranks of institutional leadership. According to Kaplan and Tinsley (1989), 10 percent of chief executive officers in the approximately three thousand colleges and universities in the United States are women, including 6 percent of the CEOs of publicly supported institutions. Although this number is low relative to the proportion of men, it represents a doubling of women's representation over the past decade. Women most often attain chief executive positions in four-year liberal arts colleges, particularly private women's colleges. Senior women academic deans are primarily clustered in nursing, home economics, and the humanities. Women administrators in major support positions continue most often to be librarians, registrars, and student-affairs officers.

The total number of senior women administrators in the post-secondary edifice also nearly doubled between 1975 and 1983. The Decade of Change Project of the Office of Women of the American Council of Education tracked the progress of senior women administrators (at the level of dean and above), documenting a change in the average of 0.6 women per institution in 1975 to 1.1 in 1983 (Touchton and Shavlik 1984). These averages represent a 90 percent increase in the actual number of women, from 1,625 to 3,084. Increases were recorded in all types of institutions, with publicly controlled institutions able to achieve virtual parity with private institutions, formerly the employers of almost three-fifths of women administrators. Women and minorities continue, however, to be underrepresented in senior-level administrative positions and overrepresented in the lower levels of the hierarchy.

Human capital explanations are often used to explain gender differences in the occupational structure, and clearly personal investment and career mapping are critical for postsecondary administrators. In particular, education is a significant factor in the mobility of both male and female administrators. A series of successive positions is also crucial to upward mobility in administration. While these factors are significant for both men and women, empirical research suggests the existence of a double standard in both the application of standards and accessibility of the upward track. For example, research consistently shows that nearly half of men versus one-third of women administrators have achieved doctoral status. Yet, while 90 percent of women presidents and provosts hold the doctorate, this holds for only 80 percent of total incumbents (Kaplan and Tinsley 1989). Thus, there are clearly expectations regarding the credentials of senior administrative women that exceed those for senior men.

Advancement into top-level positions in academic administration generally proceeds through faculty lines, with the department chairship a critical rung on the ladder. However, department chairships do not appear to be as accessible to women as to men (Moore 1984). And despite nearly two decades of national efforts to recruit women into academic administration, recent expansion of the administrative hierarchy has appeared to disproportionately benefit white men. The proportion of white men who are the first to occupy a position far exceeds that of women and minorities, particularly at the senior level (Sagaria and Johnsrud 1987).

Human capital theory, then, can provide only a limited explanation for the patterns of women's participation in higher educational administration. Analysis of the organizational contexts within which academic administrators' work has been valuable in developing a more comprehensive understanding of the dynamics of postsecondary institutions. For a decade, research conducted by the Project on the Status and Education of Women of the Association of American Colleges has documented a "chilly climate" for women wherever they are located in the complex configuration of roles and statuses that compose academic institutions. Beyond overt gender-based discrimination and sexual harassment, both of which still flourish, researchers have documented the existence of subtle discrimination in individual behaviors and attitudes, as well as policies and practices of the organization (Hall and Sandler 1982; Pearson et al. 1988; Sandler and Hall 1986).

For women in administration, the differential treatment and exclusionary practices take on several forms beyond those experienced by women students, faculty, and staff members. Perhaps most problematic is the continuing perception that leadership is best exercised by men. The societal equation of masculinity to management capabilities continues to permeate the world of work, whether organizations are business oriented, educational, or agencies of the state. When women achieve leadership positions they are, more often than not, isolated from other women. This isolation heightens their visibility and performance pressures and may lead to the acceptance of negative stereotypes about other women.

Creating organizational cultures that are supportive of women administrators requires more than simply hiring more women, however. My own recent research among administrators in a national sample of doctoral-granting institutions suggests that the most hospitable organizational cultures are not necessarily found in institutions with more women administrators. Rather, those institutions in which concrete organizational policies regarding gender equity have been implemented, and formal and informal campus networks focused on gender issues advocate for change, are perceived as having more supportive cultures for women.

A history of extraorganizational efforts to identify and advance potential women administrators can be documented since the early 1970s. Between 1970 and 1980, the Ford and Carnegie foundations, along with a host of smaller foundations, sponsored many advancement projects such as the Project on the Status and Education of Women of the Association of American Colleges. The National Identification Project of the American Council on Education (ACE/NIP), established in the late 1970s, continues to sponsor state committees to facilitate networking among qualified women and those senior men and women who might assist in their recruitment (Tinsley 1985). The HERS/Bryn Mawr Summer Institute, an intensive, comprehensive, residential program for women seeking or currently developing administrative careers, has been in operation since 1976 (Kaplan and Tinsley 1989; Tinsley 1985).

In sum, women's history in postsecondary administration reflects their history in business management in many ways. Societal value for male leadership and the negative conditions for women working in a traditionally male domain have combined to restrict their access to the administrative hierarchy of the ivory tower. With continued research, as well as conscious organizational efforts to promote gender equity through creating hospitable cultures and structures of mobility, increasing numbers of women may enter and remain in career paths in higher educational administration.

*Laura L. O'Toole*

## Bibliography

Hall, Roberta, and Bernice Sandler. 1982. "The Campus Climate: A Chilly One for Women." Washington, D.C.: Project on the Status and Education of Women, Assn. of American Colleges.
Kaplan, Sheila, and Adrian Tinsley. 1989. "The Unfinished Agenda: Women in Administration of Higher Education." *Education Digest* 55(4):24–27.

Moore, Kathryn M. 1984. "Careers in College and University Administration: How Are Women Affected?" *New Directions for Higher Education* 45:5–15.

O'Toole, Laura L. 1992. *Gender and Culture in Higher Education Administration: A Cross-Organizational Analysis.* Doctoral dissertation, University of Delaware.

Pearson, Carol R., Donna L. Shavlik, and Judith G. Touchton, eds. 1988. *Educating the Majority: Women Challenge Tradition in Higher Education.* New York: Macmillan.

Sagaria, Mary Ann D., and Linda K. Johnsrud. 1987. "Administrative Intrainstitutional Mobility: The Structuring of Opportunity." Paper presented at the annual meeting of the Assn. for the Study of Higher Education, San Diego, California.

Sandler, Bernice, and Roberta Hall. 1986. "The Campus Climate Revisited: Chilly for Women Faculty, Administrators, and Graduate Students." Washington, D.C.: Assn. of American Colleges.

Tinsley, Adrian. 1985. "Upward Mobility for Women Administrators." *Journal of the National Association of Women Deans, Administrators, and Counselors* 49:3–11.

Tinsley, Adrian, Cynthia Secor, and Sheila Kaplan, eds. 1984. *Women in Higher Education Administration.* San Francisco: Jossey-Bass.

Touchton, Judy, and Donna Shavlik. 1984. "Senior Women Administrators in Higher Education: A Decade of Change, 1975–1983." Preliminary report, Office of Women in Higher Education, American Council on Education, Washington, D.C.

Welch, Lynne B., ed. 1990. *Women in Higher Education: Changes and Challenges.* New York: Praeger.

## Beyond the Stereotypes: Women in Leadership Roles

While the number of women in management positions is increasing, it is still a common assumption that men are better suited for leadership positions than are women. The importance and practical implications of this issue have inspired numerous research studies on sex differences in leadership. Typically, these studies have employed three major research methods—laboratory experiments, laboratory simulations, and field studies. Recent meta-analytic techniques have found few differences between male and female leaders in terms of initiating structure, consideration, subordinate satisfaction, and effectiveness. Recognizing that few sex differences in leadership exist, future research needs to identify barriers to upward career mobility for women.

As a result of legislation banning sexual discrimination, affirmative action programs, and shifts in cultural views, women represent an increasing percentage of the workforce. For instance, a U.S. Department of Labor report indicated that in 1990 women held 40 percent of the management/administrative positions as compared to 32 percent in 1983 (Marsh 1991). Furthermore, women are projected to continue to make rapid inroads in what have previously been considered male-dominated professions (Johnston and Packer 1987).

Nevertheless, many individuals still believe that men are better suited for leadership positions than are women. For instance, Schein (1973) asked managers to indicate the typical characteristics of men, women, and successful managers. She found that the characteristics of men and those of successful managers were highly related, but only a weak association existed between the attributes of women and successful managers. Moreover, these results were replicated in a recent study by Heilman et al. (1989).

These stereotypes could have serious consequences for women in terms of upward career mobility. Indeed, it is reasonable to suppose that gender stereotypes have always posed a barrier to women as they try to climb the corporate ladder. While women are entering the ranks of management in growing numbers, the number of women who have actually progressed to upper-management positions is disproportionately small (Russell, 1994). The advancement of women into upward management positions may be thwarted by what has been termed a "glass ceiling," a seemingly undetectable barrier to upward advancement (Morrison and Von Glinow 1990).

## Past Research

As noted above, one possible explanation for the "glass ceiling" phenomenon is that men are truly more effective leaders than are women. Not surprisingly, a large number of research studies focusing on sex differences in leadership have been conducted to test this hypothesis. Typically, these studies have employed three major research methods—laboratory experiments, laboratory simulations, and field studies. Furthermore, much of the research in this area has focused on four outcome variables: leader effectiveness, subordinate satisfaction, initiating structure, and consideration. Leadership effectiveness and subordinate satisfaction are important outcome variables because of their practical value and conceptual contributions to the field. Initiating structure and consideration are salient criteria because of their prominence in past leadership research and in theoretical models. Initiating structure is the extent to which a leader structures, organizes, and prescribes how the work is to be accomplished. Consideration is the extent to which a leader demonstrates interest in the well-being of the subordinates (such as being supportive and receptive to subordinates' ideas).

The typical laboratory study has examined leadership differences between males and females by presenting subjects with a vignette, videotape, or a narrative summary of a male or female leader. After watching a videotape or reading a description of the leader, the subject is asked to rate the leader on the following dimensions: initiating structure, consideration, or effectiveness. On the other hand, the laboratory simulations have assessed differences in male and female performance by asking subjects to be leaders of contrived work-related tasks. Examples of these simulated exercises are solving puzzles or constructing paper airplanes. The third commonly used method for comparing the leadership performance of males and females is the field study. In these studies, the research setting is an actual organization as opposed to a laboratory. The general methodology employed in field studies is for subordinates to rate their managers on initiating structure, consideration, and effectiveness. They are also asked to rate their satisfaction with the leader.

In summary, a large body of research has been conducted examining sex differences in leadership. However, both within and across the research methodologies, the findings of these studies have been inconsistent and often contradictory. That is, some studies found sex differences in leadership, whereas other studies found no differences between male and female leaders.

## Meta-Analysis

While consistent patterns of findings may not be detectable with the traditional narrative review, they may be revealed with meta-analytic review procedures. Meta-analysis was developed to overcome the difficulties of the narrative review. It allows a quantitative cumulation of results across studies, even when the construct of interest is assessed with different measures. Research indicates that the conclusions of meta-analysis are more accurate than conclusions reached with the narrative review even when as few as seven studies are summarized (Cooper and Rosenthal 1980).

Meta-analytic techniques have recently been used to analyze sex differences in leadership. For example, Dobbins and Platz (1986) examined the dependent variables of initiating structure, consideration, subordinate satisfaction, and leadership effectiveness. Their study included the results of seventeen studies having a combined total sample size of 5,990 subjects. Interestingly, this study revealed no differences between male and female leaders with respect to initiating structure, consideration, and subordinate satisfaction. Effectiveness was the only variable that distinguished the performance of males and females as leaders, with male leaders being rated more effective than female leaders. However, these differences were present in laboratory studies but not in the field studies. These effects may have occurred in the laboratory because laboratory studies take place during a relatively short time interval, resulting in limited opportunities to observe and assess the effectiveness of leaders. Consequently, this may have created an ambiguous situation for subjects to appraise performance, and raters may have relied on gender stereotypes when rating leadership effectiveness. Once again though, it is much more meaningful to note that these differences did not hold in an actual organizational setting. The results from this meta-analysis strongly suggest that little difference exists between male and female leaders with respect to these four criteria.

## Future Research

Although this meta-analysis indicates that few differences exist between men and women with respect to four predominant leadership outcome variables, it does not eliminate the need for future research on gender issues in this area. Now that we have evidence to indicate that men and women have the ability to perform equally well in leadership positions, one future avenue of research is to identify situations that may serve as barriers preventing women from advancing up the corporate ladder.

For instance, it is becoming clear that the psychological impact of preferential selection (which is frequently associated with affirmative-action programs) can adversely affect women managers. Heilman et al. (1990) found that women who were preferentially selected and provided with no information about their ability perceived themselves more negatively than did women who were selected by virtue of their merit. However, there were no differences between males who were selected preferentially and males selected on their merit. Other work has shown that women, unlike men, were less likely to choose a demanding task if they believed they were selected preferentially as opposed to being selected based on merit (Heilman et al. 1991).

Preferential selection programs may also adversely affect women trying to move into high-level managerial positions because such programs may cause others to devalue women's performance. One of the major findings in social psychology is that observers attempt to explain the behavior and performance of others (Fiske and Taylor 1991). When a male is promoted into an upper-management position, observers attribute his promotion to his skills, abilities, and motivation. When a woman is promoted into an upper-management position, on the other hand, the presence of an affirmative-action system provides observers with another reason for the promotion (she was promoted because the organization needed a woman). Thus, her subordinates may not believe that she is as competent as a man would be. In essence, the presence of affirmative-action systems may provide an alternative explanation for the success of women, which in turn makes it more difficult for them to be perceived as successful and ascend in the organizational hierarchy.

Numerous implications of these studies exist. First, if a woman thinks she has been preferentially selected for a position, she may perceive herself as less competent. Consequently, she may be reluctant to assertively pursue the demanding assignments that could provide her with high visibility and distinguish her as a high performer. Ultimately, this reluctance could hamper a woman's chances for skill development and serve to offer support for the rival hypothesis that she holds her managerial position because of the organization's affirmative action program. Accordingly, this chain of events has the potential to close the doors for women in terms of upward mobility.

## Summary

Despite the fact that women have made great strides to assume leadership roles in the workforce, there is evidence to indicate that their progress has been limited, especially in terms of achieving upper-level management positions. Until recently, research on the existence of sex differences in leadership was inconclusive. However, it now appears that there are few differences between men and women in terms of four predominant leadership outcome variables: effectiveness, subordinate satisfaction, initiating structure, and consideration. Thus, future research needs to identify other factors in the workplace that may pose barriers to the upward mobility of women in leadership positions.

> Stephanie D. Myers
> Gregory H. Dobbins

## Bibliography

Cooper, H.M., and R. Rosenthal. 1980. "Statistical versus Traditional Procedures for Summarizing Research Findings." *Psychological Bulletin* 87:442–49.

Dobbins, G.H., and S.J. Platz. 1986. "Sex Differences in Leadership: How Real Are They?" *Academy of Management Review* 11:118–27.

Fiske, S.T., and S.E. Taylor. 1991. *Social Cognition* 2nd ed. New York: McGraw-Hill.

Heilman, M.E., C.J. Block, R.F. Martell, and M.C. Simon. 1989. "Has Anything Changed? Current Characterizations of Men, Women, and Managers." *Journal of Applied Psychology* 74:935–42.

Heilman, M.E., J.A. Lucas, and S.R. Kaplow. 1990. "Self-Derogating Consequences of Sex-Based Preferential Selection: The Moderating Role of Initial Self-Confidence." *Organizational Behavior and Human Decision Processes* 46:202–16.

Heilman, M.E., J.C. Rivero, and J.F. Brett. 1991. "Skirting the Competence Issue: Effects of Sex-Based Preferential Selection on Task Choices of Women and Men." *Journal of Applied Psychology* 76:99–105.

Johnston, W., and A. Packer. 1987. *Workforce 2000: Work and Workers for the Twenty-First Century.* Indianapolis, Ind.: Hudson Institute.

Marsh, B. 1991. "Women in the Work Force." *Wall Street Journal.* October 18:B3.

Morrison, A.M., and M.A. Von Glinow. 1990. "Women and Minorities in Management." *American Psychologist* 45:200–208.

Russell, J.E.A. 1994. "Career Counseling for Women in Management." In *Career Counseling for Women,* edited by W.B. Walsh and S.H. Osipow. Hillsdale, N.J.: Lawrence E. Erlbaum Associates.

Schein, V.E. 1973. "The Relationship between Sex Role Stereotypes and Requisite Management Characteristics." *Journal of Applied Psychology* 57:95–100.

## The Upward Mobility of Women in Organizations: Directions for Future Research

Despite increased representation of women in the workforce (U.S. Department of Labor 1989), their progress into upper management has been negligible (U.S. Department of Labor 1991). Fagenson (1986) notes that fewer than 0.1 percent of the chief executive officers of Fortune 1300 companies are women. Research has indicated that women face barriers not found in traditional male careers (Nieva and Gutek 1981; Ragins and Sundstrom 1989). Existing models of career mobility are based upon predominantly male samples and do not consider issues that may be important in women's careers (Dipboye 1987; Terborg 1977). These issues include sex role socialization, career paths, interpersonal processes such as mentorship (Ragins and Sundstrom 1989) and family responsibilities (Hunsaker 1985).

Research on women's upward mobility is diverse, representing a variety of theoretical domains (Gutek and Larwood 1987; Scandura and Stewart 1992 for reviews). Nieva and Gutek (1981) suggest four explanations for the lack of women's mobility: (1) structural, (2) sex roles, (3) intergroup, and (4) individual. Structural explanations focus on labor market and organization characteristics such as level of bureaucratization (Buzzanell and Goldzwig 1991), career paths (Larwood and Gattiker 1987), access to positions (Tickamyer and Bokemeier 1984), internal labor markets (Felmlee 1982) and labor market sex segregation (Bielby and Baron 1986). Sex role explanations attribute the lack of women's upward mobility to career-family conflicts (Hunsaker 1985) and the reluctance of men to accept women in management because of stereotypes. Intergroup constraints on women's upward mobility include gender-based discrimination and sexual harassment (Ragins and Scandura 1992), and subtle processes such as women's exclusion from powerful male networks. Individual level explanations focus on male-female trait differences deemed necessary for managerial success (Schein 1973), women's career expectations and career choice (Vogel et al. 1970), and human capital models that include age, experience, tenure, education, and training (Terborg 1977).

### Directions for Future Research

Research must recognize the complexity of the issue of women's upward mobility. The literature is fragmented, and more comprehensive models would enable comparison of competing explanations of the inability of women to reach top management. Samples of women and men might be examined comparatively to assess differences in career attitudes, human capital, career paths, mentoring, and family responsibility. Women's careers are different than men's (Gutek and Larwood 1987), and those differences that influence upward mobility may provide the best explanations for the lack of female representation in top management. The following research summary is offered as an example of how diverse approaches might be integrated (Scandura and Stewart 1992).

### A Study of Factors Associated with Women's Upward Mobility

A survey of female executives containing measures of career attitudes, career histories, organizational policies, and mentorship was conducted. The objective of the survey content was to represent various domains in the literature on women's upward mobility (structural, sex-roles, intergroup, and individual). Potential respondents were mailed surveys and 176 returned them in postage-paid envelopes (14.1 percent). Of those, eighty identified a male peer who completed and returned an identical survey in a separate, postage-paid envelope.

Eighty percent reported that their current position was within three decision levels to the top of their organization. About half (47 percent) of the respondents were employed by service organizations and 30 percent were employed by manufacturing companies. Eighty-seven percent were employed by organizations having five hundred employees or fewer. Demographic characteristics included 77.2 percent married with 44 percent having children under eighteen living at home. The average age of the respondents was forty-four years. The sample was 95 percent white and 71.6 percent held bachelor's or master's degrees.

While the initial female respondent sample was randomly drawn, it is possible that respondent and nonrespondent differences existed. To address this, a step in the data collection included a postage-paid business reply postcard that requested participation (participation was voluntary, and complete confidentiality was assured), the number of levels between the female executive's job and the top level of the organization, the number of persons supervised, and the type of organization (government, service, manufacturing, small business). Nonresponse bias was evaluated by comparing responses of those who completed the survey (N=176) with those who did not wish to participate (N=538). No statistically significant differences were found between these two groups.

## Sex-Role Socialization
Gender differences existed in attitudes toward women and men as equals (sex-role egalitarianism) in the matched sample of female and male respondents (Beere et al. 1989). Women reported that they perceived women and men as equal across a variety of life and work situations to a greater degree than their male peers. Future research should determine this concept across organizational levels, since this was a high-ranking sample.

## Career Paths
Demographic information indicated that the female executives had attained high organization levels. They held positions equal in rank, budgetary and managerial authority, and responsibility to those of their male peers, supporting the peer-matching strategy for the study. Most respondents were employed in line, rather than staff, positions, consistent with previous research (Larwood and Gattiker 1987). Fifty percent of the respondents were presidents of their own businesses, which reflects a national trend of growth in female entrepreneurs (Bowen and Hisrich 1986).

## Career Attitudes
Women were as satisfied with their jobs as their male peers, as assessed by the Minnesota Satisfaction Questionnaire (Weiss et al. 1967). Women were also equally committed (loyal) to their organization as measured by the Organizational Commitment Questionnaire (Mowday et al. 1979). Women reported no more job stress (Rizzo et al. 1970) than men and there were no significant differences in intentions to quit. Statistically significant differences in career progress expectations were

found. Women and men differed on their perceptions of their own career potential. Examples of questions from this measure included "I expect that I will attain a higher level in this organization," and "I expect to be promoted at a rate faster than my peers" (men were more likely to agree than women). Hence, perceptions of future career mobility were higher for males.

**Career-Family Issues and Family Policy**

The female executive sample was examined by comparing women who reported having children under eighteen living at home and those who did not. Results of this analysis indicated that women with dependent children reported lower career expectations and higher levels of job stress and thoughts of quitting, and were less likely to report having a mentor than women without dependent children. Respondents indicated whether their organization offered organizational policies associated with managing family concerns at work. Promising areas were employee personal loans, parental-leave policies, and flexible working hours.

**Mentoring and Career Development**

In addition to formalized policy, many organizations encourage formal or informal mentoring relationships, which are developmental relationships between senior executives and junior executives (Kram 1985). With respect to mentoring in the survey, 65 percent indicated that they had experienced a mentoring relationship in their career (50 percent currently had mentors). And women were just as likely as men to report having had a mentor at some point in their career.

Since this was a high-ranking sample, respondents were also asked to indicate whether they had ever mentored other individuals. Fifty-two percent of the respondents indicated that they had been a mentor. Again, women were just as likely as men to report being a mentor. Women were equally likely to have intentions to be a mentor; however, women reported that they were more interested in mentoring women than their male counterparts. Women executives were also more willing to mentor "someone of the opposite sex" than their male counterparts. These results, taken together, indicate that perhaps women are more willing to serve as mentors than men.

**Factors Affecting Women's Upward Mobility and Career Plateaus**

A career plateau is defined as "the point from which employees are unlikely to be further promoted or given positions of increased responsibility" (Feldman 1988, p. 136). Career plateaus are relevant to women's upward mobility because women are not represented at upper management levels, and this may represent one definition of restricted upward mobility. Using the previously mentioned female executive sample, sex-role socialization, career paths, mentoring, and family responsibility variables were regressed onto the career plateau variable, controlling for human capital variables (age, race, experience, organization tenure, and education) using hierarchical regression analysis procedures. The number of months since the respondents' last promotion was used as an indicator of career plateau.

This model included factors suggested by Nieva and Gutek (1981) to explain women's lack of mobility: structural factors (line versus staff), sex-role factors (sex-role socialization and family responsibility), intergroup factors (mentoring), and individual factors (human capital variables and career attitudes). Results of this investigation indicated that sex role socialization, internal career paths, and mentoring were significantly and negatively associated with career plateaus of female executives.

## Summary

Career issues for women encompass aspects of the individual, the family, and the organization. This research summary offers an example of a more comprehensive approach to the study of women's upward mobility in which multiple explanations for the inability of women to reach upper-level management positions are considered simultaneously. It is hoped that this review encourages future studies that take into account multiple perspectives on the complex issue of the upward mobility of women in management.

*Terri A. Scandura*

## Bibliography

Beere, C.A., D.W. King, D.B. Beere, and L.A. King. 1989. "The Sex-Role Egalitarianism Scale: A Measure of Attitudes toward Equality between the Sexes." *Sex Roles* 10, 563–76.

Bielby, W.T., and J.N. Baron. 1986. "Men and Women at Work: Sex Segregation and Statistical Discrimination." *American Journal of Sociology* 93:1031–59.

Buzzanell, P.M., and S.R. Goldzwig. 1991. "Linear and Nonlinear Career Models: Metaphors, Paradigms and Ideologies." *Management Communication Quarterly* 4:466–505.

Dipboye, R.L. 1987. "Problems and Progress of Women in Management." In *Working Women*, edited by K.S. Kozara, M. Moskew, and L.D. Tanner, Washington, D.C.: Bureau of National Affairs.

Fagenson, E.A. 1986. "Women's Work Orientations: Something Old, Something New." *Group and Organization Studies* 11:75–100.

Feldman, D.C. 1988. *Managing Careers in Organizations*. Glenview, Ill.: Scott Foresman.

Felmlee, D.H. 1982. "Women's Job Mobility Processes within and between Employers." *American Sociological Review* 47:142–51.

Gutek, B.A., and L. Larwood. 1987. "Introduction: Women's Careers Are Important and Different." In *Women s Career Development*, edited by B.A. Gutek and L. Larwood, pp. 7–14. Newbury Park, Calif.: Sage.

Hunsaker, J.S. 1985. "Work and Family Life Must Be Integrated." In *Women in Management*. 2nd ed., edited by B.A. Stead, pp. 68–74. Englewood Cliffs, N.J.: Prentice-Hall.

Kram, K.E. 1985. *Mentoring at Work*. Segregation, Ill.: Scott Foresman.

Larwood, L., and U.E. Gattiker. 1987. "A Comparison of the Career Paths Used by Successful Women and Men." In *Women's Career Development*, edited by B.A. Gutek and L. Larwood. Newbury Park, Calif.: Sage.

Mowday, W.H., L.W. Porter, and R.M. Steers. 1979. "The Measurement of Organizational Commitment." *Journal of Vocational Behavior* 14:224–47.

Nieva, V.F., and B.A. Gutek. 1981. *Women and Work: A Psychological Perspective*. New York: Praeger.

Ragins, B.R., and T.A. Scandura. 1992. "Antecedents and Correlates of Sexual Harassment: A Test of Competing Hypotheses." Paper presented at the Society of Industrial and Organizational Psychology, Montreal, Canada.

Ragins, B.R., and E. Sundstrom. 1989. "Gender and Power in Organizations: A Longitudinal Perspective." *Psychological Bulletin* 105:51–88.

Rizzo, J.R., R.J. House, and S.I. Lirtzman. 1970. "Role Conflict and Ambiguity in Complex Organizations." *Administrative Science Quarterly* 15:150–63.

Scandura, T.A., and K.A. Stewart. 1992. "The Glass Ceiling: A Critical Review of the Literature on Women's Upward Mobility and Directions for Future Research." Proceedings of the Southern Management Assn., New Orleans, Louisiana.

Schein, V.E. 1973. "The Relationship between Sex Role Stereotypes and Requisite Management Characteristics among Female Managers." *Journal of Applied Psychology* 57:95–100.

Terborg, J.R. 1977. "Women in Management: A Research Review." *Journal of Applied Psychology* 62:647–64.

Tickamyer, A.R., and J.L. Bokemeier. 1984. "Career Mobility and Satisfaction of Women Administrators in Postsecondary Education: A Review and Research Agenda." *Sociological Spectrum* 4:335–60.

U.S. Department of Labor. 1989. "Outlook 2000: The Labor Force." *Occupational Outlook Quarterly* 33:4–11.

———. 1991. *A Report on the Glass Ceiling Initiative*. Washington, D.C.: Secretary's Office, U.S. Department of Labor.

Vogel, S.R., I.K. Broverman, D.M. Broverman, F.E. Clarkson, and P.S. Rosenkrantz. 1970. "Maternal Employment and Perception of Sex Roles among College Students." *Developmental Psychology* 3:381–84.

Weiss, D.J., R.V. Dawis, G.W. England, and L.H. Lofquist. 1967. *Manual for the Minnesota Satisfaction Questionnaire*. Minneapolis, Minn.: Industrial Relations Center, University of Minnesota.

# Programs and Strategies
# for Change

## Resistance in the Workplace

Feminists view resistance as vital both as an organizing concept for rereading women's histories and as a mode of action creating possibilities for the transformation of the conditions of women's oppressions. Taking gender struggle as an orienting framework, feminists have criticized the gender-neutral conceptualizations of labor resistance developed in class analysis or models of organizational control (Ferguson 1984; Kaplan 1982; Milkman 1985; Sacks 1988; Westwood 1984). This chapter illustrates the importance of resistance for feminist studies of women and work.

Most generally, resistance invokes a sense of force and counterforce; the dictionary defines resistance as "the act or power of withstanding, striving against or opposing" (OED 1989, p. 717). While there are physical applications of this dynamic (as in electrical or mechanical resistance), the use of the term with regard to persons implies agency in the context of relations of domination and oppression. Agency involves taking action, whether that is done as a coming to awareness (consciousness) or as an embodied operation; whether the action taken is determined by prevailing conditions and institutions or by the person's understandings and experiences (that is, structurally or subjectively determined); and whether there is an individual or a collective effort. The concept of resistance has become an important focus for social analysis as researchers explore questions of when, how, and why the oppressed might take action to counter forces of domination.

Feminist treatments have complicated the concept of resistance. For example, feminist analyses have called into question the dichotomies characterizing common-sense understandings of social life—public/private, impersonal/intimate, objective/subjective, active/passive, masculine/feminine—that constitute the context for social control and resistance. Consequently, this critique blurs the line between accommodation or adaptation and resistance. Women's resistance takes up forms and opportunities emerging from experiences of women's oppression that can not be categorized in accord with traditional distinctions. For example, resistance among women in many female-dominated occupations (such as sales clerks or clerical workers) is exercised through informal networks rooted in the routines of women's everyday lives. Women often weave domestic rituals and celebrations of women-centered events (such as marriages, the birth of a child) into an ensemble of practices, thereby constituting an oppositional culture to resist management control (Westwood 1984). Such an ensemble is an aspect of women's resistance within household/domestic work contexts as well as in the waged workplace. In both indirect and confrontational ways, women resist oppression of a gendered division of 'private sphere' labor that assigns them primary responsibility for 'second shift' work (such as child care, household maintenance, emotional labor) (Luxton and Rosenberg 1986). Through enticement and withdrawal, argument and threats of divorce or separation, women get men to share in second shift responsibilities (Hochschild 1989). Women-centered practices that integrate home and work blur taken-for-granted distinctions like "private"/"public" and constitute women's resistance as complex and multifaceted.

Contemporary feminist analyses further complicate resistance by setting it within a nexus of power relations so as to trace linkages among multiple oppressive relations (such as race, age, gender, ethnicity, and world position). The context of women's resistance involves linkages both within and between such oppressive relations. For example, working-class women have struggled against male domination in both the workplace and the union. Female automobile workers opposed Ford Motor Company and the United Auto Worker's Union because both had refused to honor their seniority after World War II (Milkman 1987). The women's resistance was set within a context linking gender discrimination with different dimensions of class oppression.

The complexities of oppressive relations contextualize the "multiple jeopardy" and diversified consciousness that characterize the work experiences of minority women (King 1988). This complexity casts doubt on the assumption that women's resistance can be organized around common experiences of gender oppression. Rather, a diversity of lived experiences, legacies, and possibilities inform resistance practices among women, practices that do not necessarily affirm the solidarity of sisterhood. For example, black women doing domestic work have a legacy of resistance to their mistresses (Jones 1986; Rollins 1985) that includes boycotting those who mistreated their domestic workers (Kessler-Harris 1982). In summary, contemporary feminist analyses complicate the concept of resistance when they contend that collective action (whether formal or informal) and communality are configured by difference, conflict, and otherness (Spelman 1988).

Finally, feminist scholarship itself implies resistance not only to established disciplinary territories and protocols within the academy (as in dilemmas faced by women's studies programs), but to the scholarly mandate of self-bifurcation that alienates women as academics from their identities as women. The emergence of feminist research for women resists the tradition of research about women. Research for women not only engages women as active subjects rather than objects of research, but also locates researchers and subjects on the same critical plane (Smith 1987). Research for women starts from women's everyday experience with and practical knowledge of social relations and calls into question the dominant orders structuring those relations in ways that subordinate, marginalize, and oppress women. Doing research for women can be viewed as part of the practice of resistance, not only because it refuses to embrace theoretical conventions and brings into awareness the conditions and experiences of women's everyday lives but also because it articulates and shares in women's active confrontation with structures and practices of oppression. In so doing, feminist research becomes a part of the practice of resistance that it motivates.

We turn now to specific examples of the importance and complexities of women's resistance in studies of women and work. Our discussion is organized around categories intrinsic to the literature on paid labor and resistance. In class analyses and conventional organizational and industrial relations studies, resistance has been developed as a political concept with a focus on institutional-level struggle among (formally or informally) organized collectivities. The emphasis has been on the structural dimensions and institutional relations characterizing the resistance of labor to economic and political control and exploitation (Glenn and Feldberg 1979), sometimes examined in terms of worker recalcitrance, opposition, and non-compliance. Local or individual forms of worker resistance are located within the framework of larger public struggles. An example that reframes class analysis within a perspective drawn from women workers' experiences is the schema developed by Gottfried and Fasenfest (1984) to account for propensities toward unionization and collective resistance among women clerical workers and telephone operators. They relate various relations in production with the technical or nontechnical nature of the labor process to account for propensities among clerical workers for formal (union) or informal forms of collective action in the workplace.

Other contemporary theories of resistance have taken a "bottom up" perspective and a focus on the cultural significance of everyday acts of resistance. Following in the tradition of ethnographic studies of underclass groups (such as University of Chicago urban sociology) and cultural studies of workers' cultures and subcultures (such as British cultural studies), this research explores the ways workers blur the distinction between accommodating and resisting oppressive workplace conditions and relations. Researchers identify the myriad tactics of survival through which workers refuse assimilation, incorporation, or inculcation even at the cost of remaining in manual labor jobs (Willis 1974). Adopting this perspective to analyze women's accommodation and resistance, Valli (1986) shows how women becoming clerical workers reproduce a culture of idealized femininity to resist the impositions of wage labor. But in doing so, they inadvertently consent to and confirm their own subordination, preparing themselves for unskilled, low-paid, and unpaid domestic labor. From a slightly different point of view, Ferguson (1984) argues that the survival strategies of the bureaucratically powerless provide resources for an alternative form of empowerment, one drawing on the personal relations and the connectedness of nurturing experiences characteristic of women's lives.

Another distinction evident in the study of resistance can be mapped on a continuum marked at one end by forms of worker resistance that take place on a local, immediate, and often informal level. These everyday forms of resistance include covert and subtle forms like restriction of output and rule violations, or more illicit, subterranean forms like sabotage and theft (Jermier 1988). Among such resistance tactics common to secretaries are the many ways they find to reappropriate control over space, movement, and time (such as taking extra time in the bathroom, misfiling, forgetting to correct typos) to deny and disrupt organizational structures and routines (Judith 1970).

On the other end of the continuum is institutionalized labor conflict, which involves more expansive relations of capital and labor, definitive forms of organization, and manifest conflict at both the institutional and shopfloor level. Workers' strikes, both official and unofficial, are examples of resistance as labor conflict. While studies of worker strikes have taken the experiences of male, blue-collar workers as exemplary, feminist scholars have asserted a qualitative difference between women's and men's experiences with formally organized resistance activities. Kaplan's concept (1982) of a life-nurturing orientation as the instigating and organizing principle in women's political, collective action develops an important counterpoint to the male-dominated assumptions about large-scale labor resistance. In her recent account of a hospital worker's campaign to certify a union at Duke Medical Center, Sacks (1988) identifies women's community and family-based networks, especially among black women workers, as primary sources of collective solidarity. Suggesting a more complex understanding, Costello (1984) finds women's labor solidarity to be fragmented and subverted by class affiliations as well as familial and domestic responsibilities and expectations. Her study of a strike by women clericals at an insurance company follows the emergence of their collective consciousness of domination, their experience of solidarity during the strike, and the ambivalences that fragmented the group after the strike.

Finally, contemporary theories of resistance are beginning to develop alternative conceptualizations. Traditionally, resistance has been thought of as reactive, a reflexive response to the exercise of power or force, or a position defined in opposition to another. In this sense, resistance implies antagonistic struggle in which resistance by the oppressed is not just accommodated but can be anticipated and effectively neutralized. But resistance also can be regarded in terms of an interactive process rather than antagonistic positions. In this sense, resistance is more than reaction.

Resistance as interactive process is not determined by but engages the context of power relations to open possibilities for different linkages within and among those relations (Sotirin 1992). For example, the gossip and chit-chat that goes on among women in the office are everyday practices of resistance that articulate an alternative relational logic based on emotional-connective rather rational-instrumental relationships. Admittedly these practices appropriate and reproduce elements of their context of bureaucratic and male/masculine domination (such as ideals of femininity, routinized discrimination), but they also assert connections (familial, sexual, domestic) that open up different workplace realities and possibilities—for instance, the naming of sexual harassment and the demand for pregnancy provisions. It is in such conceptual moves beyond resistance as reaction that feminist thought and studies of women wage workers advance theories of resistance.

The ubiquity and importance of resistance in the experiences of women wage workers invites a tendency to find resistance everywhere (Milkman 1985) and celebrate it unreflectively (Gottfried and Fasenfest 1984). Contemporary conceptualizations must consider the ambivalence of resistance, including its dialectic relation to accommodation and its potential to fragment as well as unite women workers.

*Patricia Sotirin*
*Heidi Gottfried*

## Bibliography

Costello, C. 1984. "Working Women's Consciousness: Traditional or Oppositional?" In *To Toil the Live-long Day: America's Women at Work, 1780–1980*, edited by C. Groneman and M.B. Norton, pp. 284–302. Ithaca, N.Y.: Cornell University Press.

Ferguson, K. 1984. *The Feminist Case against Bureaucracy*. Philadelphia: Temple University Press.

Glenn, E.N., and R. Feldberg. 1979. "Clerical Work: The Female Occupation." In *Women: A Feminist Perspective*. 2nd ed., edited by Jo Freeman, pp. 313–38. Palo Alto, Calif.: Mayfield.

Gottfried, H., and D. Fasenfest. 1984. "Gender and Class Formation: Female Clerical Workers." *Review of Radical Political Economics* 16:89–103.

Hochschild, A. 1989. *The Second Shift: Working Parents and the Revolution at Home*. New York: Viking.

Jermier, J. 1988. "Sabotage at work: The Rational View." In *Research in the Sociology of Organizations*, edited by S. Bacharach and N. Ditomaso, pp. 101–34. Greenwich, Conn.: JAI.

Jones, J. 1986. *Labor of Love, Labor of Sorrow: Black Women, Work and the Family, from Slavery to the Present*. New York: Vintage.

Judith, Ann. 1970. "The Secretarial Proletariat." In *Sisterhood is Powerful: An Anthology of Writings from the Women's Liberation Movement*, edited by R. Morgan, pp. 94–110. New York: Vintage.

Kaplan, T. 1982. "Female Consciousness and Collective Action: The Case of Barcelona, 1910–1918." *Signs* 7:545–66.

Kessler-Harris, A. 1982. *Out to Work: A History of Wage-Earning Women in the United States*. Oxford: Oxford University Press.

King, D. 1988. "Multiple Jeopardy, Multiple Consciousness: The Context of a Black Feminist Ideology." *Signs* 14:42–72.

Luxton, M., and H. Rosenberg. 1986. *Through the Kitchen Window: The Politics of Home and Family*. Toronto: Garamond.

Milkman, R. 1987. *Gender at Work: The Dynamics of Job Segregation by Sex during World War II*. Urbana: University of Illinois Press.

Milkman, R., ed. 1985. "Women Workers, Feminism and the Labor Movement since the 1960s." In *Women, Work and Protest: A Century of U.S. Women's History*, pp. 300–22. Boston: Routledge and Kegan Paul.

*Oxford English Dictionary*. 1989. Clarendon Press; New York: Oxford University Press.

Rollins, J. 1985. *Between Women: Domestics and Their Employers*. Philadelphia: Temple University Press.

Sacks, K.B. 1988. *Caring by the Hour: Women, Work and Organizing at Duke Medical Center*. Urbana: University of Illinois Press.

Smith, D. 1987. *The Everyday World as Problematic*. Boston: Northeastern University Press.

Sotirin, P. 1992. "Rearticulating Resistance: Gender, Power, and Meaning in Pink Collar Office Work." Ph.D. dissertation, Purdue University.

Spelman, E. 1988. *Inessential Woman: Problems of Exclusion in Feminist Thought*. Boston: Beacon.

Valli, L. 1986. *Becoming Clerical Workers*. Boston: Routledge and Kegan Paul.

Westwood, S. 1984. *All Day, Every Day: The Factory and the Family in the Making of Women's Lives*. Urbana: University of Illinois.

Willis, P. 1974. *Learning to Labor: How Working Class Kids Get Working Class Jobs*. New York: Columbia University Press.

## Corporate Programs for Preventing Sexual Harassment

Despite attempts by many organizations to prohibit sexual harassment via corporate policy statements, complaint procedures, and disciplinary systems, harassment continues to be a problem in the workplace. This is because continued power imbalances inherent in male-female interaction provide a springboard for sexual harassment to occur on the job. In order to prevent rather than merely react to harassment, organizations should conduct gender-communication training programs that involve employees in the collective creation of an organizational culture free of sex-role conditioned behavior, gender-based misunderstandings, and interactional power differences. Such training should occur in conjunction with standard prohibitions and disciplinary sanctions against sexual harassment.

Since the Equal Employment Opportunity Commission published its Guidelines on Sexual Harassment in November of 1980, many organizations have developed policy statements, complaint procedures, and disciplinary codes regarding sexual harassment (Bryson 1990; Howard 1991; Waxman 1990). While these measures constitute a necessary first step in dealing with sexual harassment, they are insufficient to prevent or reduce incidents of harassment. Despite these measures, sexual harassment is still prevalent in the workplace. Surveys have estimated that anywhere from 25 to 90 percent of working women have been victims of sexual harassment (Koen 1989).

Sexual harassment continues to be a problem in workplace organizations because corporations, for the most part, have taken a reactive rather than a proactive or preventive approach to the problem. While policy statements that define and prohibit sexual harassment as well as complaint procedures and disciplinary actions are strategies necessary to limit a company's liability in sexual harassment cases, these steps do not reduce or prevent the incidence of sexual harassment in workplace organizations. A more complete and effective program would alter the workplace culture to create more equitable relationships between male and female employees. Lewis and Johnson (1991) argue that sexual harassment will not be eliminated without change in the organization's culture.

Organizational behavior literature calls for training to create workplace climates free of sexually harassing behavior. Spann (1990) articulates the need for employers to move beyond policy statements and complaint procedures to problem prevention through work-climate alteration. Stringer et al. (1990) suggest that organizations use training to articulate expected behaviors and suggest rules for the new roles created when women enter a predominantly male department, organization, or occupation. Waxman (1990) calls for training programs to help the sexes discuss and confront issues of sexuality on the job.

A workplace culture in which sexual harassment is rare or nonexistent must have at its core equal power distribution between women and men throughout the organization. This is because power is the major factor contributing to sexual harassment. The literature on sexual harassment consistently points to power differences between women and men resulting from society's traditional sex-role socialization as a major cause of sexual harassment (Betz and Fitzgerald 1987; Collins and Blodgett 1981; Tangri et al. 1982). Stringer et al. (1990) assert that a culture that attributes more power to men than to women provides males with natural gender power to harass and deprives females of the power to resist or report harassment. Popovich (1988) attributes the higher incidence rates of sexual harassment of females rather than of males to women's less powerful job positions and to the unequal distribution of power between the sexes in society. Gutek (1985) explains that whether sexual harassment is viewed from an organizational, legal, or feminist perspective, unequal power relationships between women and men rooted in cultural conditioning spill over to work contexts and provide a foundation by which sexual harassment is legitimized in the workplace.

If power differences between the sexes are the main cause of sexual harassment, then corporate programs for preventing sexual harassment must seek to equalize power between male and female employees. There are various sources of organizational power that can be altered to create more symmetrical power distributions between male and female employees. Power equalization may be achieved through the equitable distribution of formal roles and salaries (Stringer et al. 1990), through balanced ratios in the numbers of male and female employees (Kanter 1979), and through structural changes that replace hierarchies with decentralized structures to spread power (Kanter 1983). Another strategy for altering the power dynamics in organizations is to change the culture of communication to replace interaction rules which linguistically position men as more powerful and women as less powerful in organizational interactions. Gender-communication training, which changes the power imbalances inherent in male-female interaction, offers organizations a proactive or preventative way to deal with sexual harassment.

Research has shown that men and women communicate differently on a number of dimensions (Arliss 1991; Pearson et al. 1991; Tannen 1990). Communication style differences between women and men include distinctions in self-disclosure, assertiveness and aggressiveness, interruptions, use of personal space and touch, and smiling. These differences can contribute to sexual harassment by creating and reinforcing power imbalances between women and men. Women's tendencies to disclose personal information, feelings, and attitudes, as one aspect of a typical female communication style, can be misinterpreted by male colleagues as flirtatious, intimacy-seeking, or signaling sexual interest. Men, who are conditioned by society to be verbally and sexually aggressive, may carry that behavior to their workplace interactions with women and inadvertently begin a harassing episode. Women, whose communication style typically includes nonassertive language, may not possess the skills to tell men forcefully when overtures are unwanted, intimidating, and interfering with job performance. Men, comfortable with interrupting and changing conversational topics, may redirect workplace communications to inappropriate sexual topics, and women, by virtue of their typical conversational roles, may not know how to disallow sexual topics at work. Women in the workplace may allow men to invade their personal space and to touch them. And men may believe that women find close interaction distances and touch comfortable in the workplace. Women, conditioned to smile in a variety of circumstances, even uncomfortable ones, may find that male colleagues are attributing sexual motives or acquiescence to their smiles.

Communication styles unique to women and men can provide the impetus for a chronically sexually harassing environment to emerge in an organization. The sex-role conditioned behavior typically manifested by men and women can predispose men to engage in harassing behaviors and deprive women of the strategies for assertively reacting to and preventing the escalation of harassment. Because men and women communicate in a different cultural arena, their interactions take on a cross-cultural quality and have implications for sexual harassment.

Male-female communication training as part of a sexual harassment prevention program can provide employees with an awareness of their stereotypical behaviors and can help employees develop gender-flexible communication skills. Such training can utilize assessment instruments that provide participants with profiles of their typical behaviors in such areas as self-disclosure or assertiveness, for example. Role-plays, which allow the sexes to practice new communication behaviors, can begin the process of expanding behavioral flexibility. Having trainees engage in behavior reversals can demonstrate the feelings of power or powerlessness associated with typical male-female communication styles. Workplace examples of misunderstandings of gender-related communication can provide the impetus for meaningful discussions about the motives and interpretations that men and women attribute to each other's behavior. Videotapes of mixed-sex interaction can provide powerful illustrations of habitual, though perhaps unconscious, sex-role conditioned communications.

The goal of such a training program is not for males to communicate in a feminine style or for females to adopt masculine behaviors. Rather, both sexes must be equipped with the skills of behavioral flexibility, the ability to monitor their own behaviors, and the capacity to clarify misunderstandings in male-female interactions. Training in male-female interaction dynamics is not meant to replace company policy statements, complaint procedures, and disciplinary measures regarding harassment. Rather, it is a way to complement standard human-resources practices by teaching employees to communicate in such a way as to prevent the occurrence of sexual harassment. Male-female communication training should not put responsibility on one sex for modifying its behavior while the behavior of the other sex remains unchanged. A key to the effectiveness of such training is that both males and females have responsibility for adjusting their behavior and contributing to new workplace communication climates. Since men and women are constrained by sex-role socialization, both sexes must work together to break free of conditioning, to overcome misunderstandings, to eliminate interactional power differences, and to create a workplace culture that is equitable, professional, and free of sexual harassment.

*Cynthia Berryman-Fink*

## Bibliography

Arliss, Laurie P. 1991. *Gender Communication.* Englewood Cliffs, N.J.: Prentice-Hall.

Betz, N.E., and L.F. Fitzgerald. 1987. *The Career Psychology of Women.* Orlando, Fla.: Academic.

Bryson, C.B. 1990. "The Internal Sexual Harassment Investigation: Self-Evaluation without Self-Incrimination." *Employee Relations Law Journal* 15:551–59.

Collins, E.G.C., and T.B. Blodgett. 1981. "Sexual Harassment: Some See It and Some Won't." *Harvard Business Review* 59:76–95.

Gutek, Barbara. 1985. *Sex and the Workplace.* San Francisco: Jossey-Bass.

Howard, S. 1991. "Organizational Resources for Addressing Sexual Harassment." *Journal of Counseling and Development* 69:507–11.

Kanter, R.M. 1983. *The Change Masters.* New York: Simon and Shuster.

———. 1979. *Men and Women of the Corporation.* New York: Basic Books.

Koen, Clifford. 1989. "Sexual Harassment: Criteria for Defining Hostile Environment." *Employee Responsibilities and Rights Journal* 2:289–301.

Lewis, K.E., and P.R. Johnson. 1991. "Preventing Sexual Harassment Complaints Based on Hostile Work Environments." *SAM Advanced Management Journal* 56:21–36.

Pearson, Judy C., Lynn Turner, and William Todd-Mancillas. 1991. *Gender and Communication.* Dubuque, Iowa: W.C. Brown.

Popovich, Paula M. 1988. "Sexual Harassment in Organizations." *Employee Responsibilities and Rights Journal* 1:273–82.

Spann, Jeri. 1990. "Dealing Effectively With Sexual Harassment: Some Practical Lessons from One City's Experience." *Public Personnel Management* 19:53–69.

Stringer, Donna M., Helen Remick, Jan Salisbury, and Angela B. Ginorio. 1990. "The Power and Reasons behind Sexual Harassment: An Employer's Guide to Solutions." *Public Personnel Management* 19:43–52.

Tangri, S.S., M.R. Burt, and L.B. Johnson. 1982. "Sexual Harassment at Work: Three Explanatory Models." *Journal of Social Issue* 38:33–54.

Tannen, Deborah. 1990. *You Just Don't Understand.* New York: William Morrow.

Waxman, Merle. 1990. "Institutional Strategies for Dealing with Sexual Harassment." *Employee Responsibilities and Rights Journal* 3:73–75.

## Remedying Gender-Based Wage Discrimination: The Comparable Worth Approach

Recent approaches to remedying gender-based wage differences have incorporated the notion that job categories, even though they may appear to differ substantially in terms of their duties and characteristics, can be evaluated and compared for the purpose of determining relative pay levels. Although they may differ significantly in form and outcome, these approaches are generically referred to as comparable worth strategies. A key element of a comparable worth approach to achieving gender-based pay equity is the selection and implementation of a method for assessing job content and determining the relative "worth" of the jobs performed within an organization. Since the late 1970s, pay equity advocates have borrowed extensively from the repertoire of traditional job ranking tools developed by compensation managers and salary administrators. These methods include job analysis, job description, job classification and job evaluation. These terms are defined below and some of the specific implications for the comparable worth approach to remedying gender-based wage inequities are highlighted.

### Job Content

This concept is used to represent the activities, tasks, and responsibilities associated with a specific job category; it may also include the structural or environmental features that determine the context in which these duties are performed. The term "job content" may be used to encompass a broad range of attributes and characteristics pertaining to the nature and scope of the tasks, duties, and responsibilities assigned to a particular job category. The process of job analysis is used to collect data on the content of the work performed by members of specific job categories. The job content associated with a particular position is frequently depicted in a "position profile" or job description. The process of job evaluation is used to assess and compare the job content of various positions in a particular organization. It should also be noted that in the literature on wage and salary administration, compensation systems, and other discussions of comparable worth policies, the term "job content" may be used to connote both a theoretical construct (that is, an abstraction or "ideal type") as well as a specific, empirically anchored summary of the job's content based on the concrete activities performed by current job holders.

### Job Analysis

This term refers to a set of activities that serve as a vital precursor to the process of job evaluation (see below for a more detailed discussion). Job analysis is a generic term that subsumes a variety of different methods used for the purpose of collecting data on job content. The objective of this process is to comprehensively and uniformly collect data on the nature and scope of the tasks, duties, and responsibilities assigned to a particular set of job categories. These methods may include such data collection techniques as surveys and questionnaires (both open-ended and closed-question formats); structured interviews with job incumbents and their supervisors or subordinates; participant observation; and "desk audits." Often, a comprehensive data collection strategy based on a combination of these activities is used in order to fully capture the content of the full range of jobs under consideration.

It is important to note that "job analysis," especially when it is used by compensation specialists and salary administrators, is a "term of art" narrowly applied to the process of collecting data concerning job content. As used in this context, it does not imply a direct or even indirect comparison among jobs (see instead, "job evaluation"). Thus, in the specific, technical usage of this term, job analysis is seen as distinct from the process of job evaluation; yet, the "end products" of job analysis (that is, the job descriptions generated by this process) usually constitute the set of data used in the subsequent process of job evaluation.

It is equally important to note that job analysis refers to the collection of data concerning the nature of the job itself, as distinguished from the characteristics of the person performing the work or the manner in which the work is performed by a specific employee (this is also the case for the processes of job evaluation and job classification). Thus in job analysis, the process of data collection is concerned with aspects of the work that transcend the specific performance of these duties by a particular individual. The specific performance of the duties, the level of competence of the employee, and the degree of mastery of the tasks (how well the employee does the job, and so forth) is usually assessed in the context of an individual's "performance appraisal," such as in a "merit pay" evaluation.

**Job Descriptions**

As indicated above, once the job content data have been collected, the next phase of the job analysis process results in the creation of "position profiles" or job descriptions. In general, the purpose of a job description is to identify, define, and locate the work within the complete range of tasks performed by members of the organization. In the context of a comparable worth approach to eliminating gender-based wage inequities, the emphasis has been on describing the work as it is actually being performed, as opposed to how it might be performed under idealized circumstances (that is, to move beyond generalized or highly generic position descriptions), and to capture actual as opposed to hypothetical relationships among jobs (that is, to identify elements of the organizational structure that actually affect relationships among jobs as opposed to relying on those "captured" and depicted on an idealized supervisory hierarchy or organizational chart). Job descriptions usually take the form of structured narratives that include the principle tasks and activities of the job; the circumstances or context in which the duties are performed, such as the specific structural or environmental factors; approximations of the requisite knowledge, skills, and previous experience needed to perform the work; and the relationship of this particular job to others in the organization in terms of the supervisory or other communication structures.

Key issues concerning the process of job analysis and the subsequent creation of job descriptions that are particularly relevant to the issues of remedying gender-based wage inequities include potential differences in the degree to which data collection methods fully capture the nature and scope of the work traditionally performed by women; the use of data collection strategies that may "undercount" the activities of female job incumbents; the use of stereotypic or "gender-loaded" language in the creation of the job description narratives (particularly the choice of "passive" versus "active" verbs and adjectives used to describe the work predominantly performed by women); and the use of traditional or gender-specific job titles such as "maid" versus "custodian," and so forth (Miller et al. 1980).

## Job Classification

Used as a term to indicate both a process and its outcome, job classification is a key element in understanding the relationships among various job titles in an organization. As a process, job classification refers to the procedures used to rank and sort various job titles into "job classes," also called "ranges" or "grades." As an end product, the term job classification, or more precisely, a "job classification system," refers to the hierarchical structure created when job categories are assigned to specific classification grades. The broadly defined "grades" used by various departments of civil service to rank public-sector jobs serve as illustrations of large-scale job classification systems. The best known example of these systems is the highly developed "General Schedule" (GS system) used by the U.S. federal government.

At least four aspects of job classification (as both a process and a set of structural relationships) can be identified as being of particular significance to understanding the relatively disadvantaged position of women in the workplace. First, past practices in implementing job classification systems often created separate job classification hierarchies on the basis of gender or race. Although court decisions have found the use of explicitly segregated job classification systems to be illegal in the U.S., some analysts suggest that the legacy of these early segregated classification systems may "live on" in some of the techniques and practices used to identify and structure the job classes and result in ongoing wage discrimination (Blumrosen 1979). Furthermore, the well-established practice of using specific language to create many narrowly defined job titles in male-dominated occupational fields compared with the tendency to use broadly based or generic job titles for the work performed predominantly by women has been linked to disparate classification outcomes for men and women (Miller et al. 1980).

Secondly, job classification systems usually determine the level of compensation associated with a job category. Minimum and maximum pay rates are directly tied to the grade level to which the job category has been assigned. The presence of a direct link between a job's classification grade and its corresponding wage range provides significant challenges to some of the traditional approaches used to explain wage differences among individuals. For example, "human capital theory" places a primary emphasis on an individual's traits and characteristics (that is, "human capital," such as a person's training, skills, and ambition) as "determining" the relative pay received by the individual. As such, interpretations of the source of wage differences between men and women that are based on human capital theory have traditionally ignored the structural position of the job category within the job classification system. Given the widespread use of job classification systems as the basis for anchoring minimum and maximum pay ranges for jobs, job classification provides a structural determinant of pay that may be immune to "human capital" factors (for discussion, see Stevenson 1978).

Similarly, job classification systems are often seen as providing the basis for creating "career ladders," or the pathways for promotion leading from one level of the organizational hierarchy to the next. As some analysts have suggested, job classification systems assert the presence of "natural" linkages among certain types of jobs, while overlooking the possible connections among others. This may create significant obstacles to the career development of women and other minorities in the workplace (Fox and Hesse-Biber 1984). Again, to the extent that the job classification system establishes career opportunities for some by linking their jobs to other positions in the hierarchy, it may also produce significant obstacles to the occupational mobility of others. The relationship between a job's location in the job classification system and the likelihood of opportunities for promotion also provides challenges to the validity of individually oriented explanations of career achievement.

Finally, job classification systems may enjoy a presumption of "rationality" which, on closer examination, may lack full justification or substantiation (Acker 1989; Barker 1986). The job classification system actually in place in an organization is likely to have emerged gradually, often over an extended period in which new jobs are created while others become obsolete. The actual structure of a job classification system is more likely to resemble a tattered patchwork of policies with significant exceptions and addenda than an internally consistent, comprehensive, and well-reasoned administrative system. Recent examinations of existing job classification systems used by various states and the federal government have suggested that these structures require significant overhauling to eliminate the most glaring inconsistencies, and vigilant oversight to maintain the internal consistency of these systems once they have been rectified (Acker 1989; Haignere and Steinberg 1984; Miller et al. 1980).

Yet, perhaps even more significant for feminist analyses of the position of women in the workplace has been the recent research that suggests that both gender and class bias have been built into the fundamental premises and processes of job classification. For example, preliminary work by Acker (1989) on the underlying values used in the processes of job evaluation and job classification (as well as other kinds of administrative policies and procedures) suggests the presence of significant gender bias in the construction of these systems. Created primarily by and for managers, these administrative structures often conform to and protect the value systems and interests of the male elites of the organization.

## Job Evaluation

Beginning in the late 1970s, the various methods of job evaluation (including job analysis and job classification) were used for the purpose of implementing comparable worth policies. However, prior to the 1970s, when "job evaluation" was still in its early stages of development as an administrative tool, the term was used as a generic label for a variety of different assessment techniques used for the purpose of examining and comparing job content. Some of these assessment methods were quite rigorous and formal, others fairly idiosyncratic and superficial. Over time, both the techniques and the term itself have become somewhat more precise. Today, job evaluation usually refers to the process of systematically identifying, analyzing, and comparing the knowledge, skills, tasks, duties, and responsibilities associated with the work performed by the individuals found in specific job categories.

Job evaluation usually occurs after some form of job analysis has taken place. Often, as the result of the job evaluation process, a new job classification system is created, or modifications are made in the existing job classification system. Since job classification systems usually (but not always) form the basis for determining wage and salary relationships among job categories, examining these systems and attempting to eliminate both race- and gender-based biases has been recognized as an important aspect of attempts to achieve pay equity.

Several broadly defined types of job evaluation methods have been identified; each type uses a slightly different process for comparing the jobs and arriving at a rank ordering of the job categories. The different types of job evaluation methods include simple ranking, job grading, factor comparison methods, and point factor comparison methods (for a full description of each type, see Treiman 1979).

Advocates of comparable worth have often recommended using point factor comparison methods as the preferred type of job evaluation method for establishing more equitable wage relations among job categories (Remick 1978, 1980; Treiman and Hartmann 1981). This type of job evaluation method is based on the selection of several specific "compensable factors." These are the specific traits or characteristics of the work that are recognized as being of value to employers and for which the employees presumably are compensated. Examples of compensable factors commonly used in standard point factor comparison methods include such characteristics as knowledge and skills, work experience, problem solving, responsibility for resources and materials, human relations skills, and work environment/job hazards. Additionally, in many cases these factors are weighted to give added influence to those characteristics or traits deemed most important for the determination of the relative value of the work performed.

Once the compensable factors have been selected, each is stated in terms of a factor definition. Furthermore, different degrees or levels of each factor are defined and numerical values are assigned to each of the levels of the factor, thus forming a point scale for each of the compensable factors. For example, the compensable factor identified as "physical effort" might be defined in terms of a set of degrees or levels ranging from "normal" to "moderate" to "considerable" to "extensive." Each of these levels would have a corresponding point value assigned to it (for example, "normal" = 5 points, to "extensive" = 50 points).

As the process of job evaluation proceeds, a description of the content of each job category is reviewed. Job evaluators, or "raters," either working in teams or alone, assess the job content in terms of the levels established for the compensable factors and assign a corresponding point value to the job. In many methods, the point score given to the job category is then multiplied by a weighting value that has been assigned to the compensable factor. When the scores for each of the jobs on each of the factors have been established and weighted accordingly, a total point score for each job category is calculated. This is the sum of the factor scores for each of the separate factors making up the job evaluation method. The total point score is then used to rank the job categories, clustering job categories with identical or similar point values into the "ranges" or "grades" that make up the job classification system. Later, these grades or point ranges are used for establishing the relative wage and salary levels of the jobs in the classification system.

FIGURE 1. "The Comparable Worth Process" as Implemented by the State of Oregon

1) JOB ANALYSIS
   • data gathering
   • job description

2) JOB EVALUATION
   • assess jobs for skill, effort, responsibility and working conditions

3) CLASSIFYING JOBS
   • build new job classes based on similar job descriptions and evaluation scores

4) COMPENSATION ANALYSIS
   • identify inequities in current compensation policies
   • select desired pay policy

5) IMPLEMENTATION
   • upgrade undervalued classes
   • implement new pay policy
   • implement revised classification plan

6) MAINTENANCE
   • monitor pay policy to maintain equitable relationships
   • keep classification system and job evaluation systems current

Source: Final Report and Recommendations: Task Force on State Compensation and Classification Equity to the Sixty-Third Legislative Assembly of the State of Oregon (1985, p. 12).

**Comparable Worth Processes**

Though the precise steps and stages of a comparable worth approach to eliminating gender-based pay inequities may vary considerably across the specific organizations in which this process is applied, there are common elements that are present in most implementations. These stages are illustrated in Figure 1: "The Comparable Worth Process."

A cornerstone of the comparable worth strategy is to "pay comparable wages to jobs of comparable worth." The intermediate processes of job analysis, job description, job evaluation, and job classification provide the basis for making these comparisons among jobs. As used in the context of a comparable worth approach, the total point score derived for each job category during the job evaluation process becomes a measure of the relative "worth" of the job to the organization. Further analyses are then carried out to determine if jobs of similar worth are being compensated equivalently. Existing compensation levels are then modified or adjusted accordingly.

A number of authors have examined the practice of using job evaluation methods to assess and compare the content of the work performed by incumbents of different job categories (for a recent summary of this work, see England 1992). The issues these authors raise are worthy of attention whether or not the job evaluation method under consideration is being used explicitly to implement comparable worth policies. Some of the issues raised by the process of job evaluation include the reliability and validity of job evaluation scales (Schwab 1980); potential gender bias in the selection of compensable factors (Remick 1978, 1980, 1984); the "under-evaluation" of the content of the work traditionally performed by women (Blumrosen 1979); the use of a priori versus "policy-capturing" approaches for determining the relative weights assigned to the compensable factors (Haignere and Steinberg 1984; Remick 1984); the effect of unintended factor weights (Barker 1986; Treiman and Hartmann 1981); the process used for the conversion of job evaluation points into actual pay levels (Acker 1989); and the underlying values embedded in traditional methods of job evaluation (Acker 1987, 1989; Barker 1986).

In the early 1980s it was estimated that approximately 120 public sector jurisdictions had initiated reviews of their job classification and compensation systems using some form of comparable worth process. By 1987, through the advocacy efforts of feminists, labor unions, and other "pay equity alliances" the level of implementation, though still largely confined to the public sector, had expanded exponentially. For example, in the state of Minnesota, passage of two comprehensive pay equity laws resulted in the implementation of comparable worth pay adjustments in over sixteen hundred public sector jurisdictions (Evans and Nelson 1989). The use of comparable worth approaches to remedying gender-based wage inequities has now gradually moved into the private sector as well.

*Melissa A. Barker*

## Bibliography

Acker, Joan. 1989. *Doing Comparable Worth: Gender, Class, and Pay Equity*. Philadelphia: Temple University Press.
———. 1987. "Sex Bias in Job Evaluation: A Comparable Worth Issue." In *Ingredients for Women's Employment Policy*, edited by Christine Bose and Glenna Spitze. Albany, N.Y.: SUNY Press.
Barker, Melissa A. 1986. "An Organizational Perspective on Job Evaluation Methods: Implications for Comparable Worth Approaches to Pay Equity." Ph.D. dissertation, Department of Sociology, University of Oregon.
Blumrosen, Ruth G. 1979. "Wage Discrimination, Job Segregation and Title VII of the Civil Rights Act of 1964." *Journal of Law Reform* 12:399–502.
England, Paula. 1992. *Comparable Worth: Theories and Evidence*. New York: Aldine de Gruyter.
Evans, Sara M., and Barbara J. Nelson. 1989. *Wage Justice: Comparable Worth and the Paradox of Technocratic Reform*. Chicago: University of Chicago Press.
Fox, Mary Frank, and Sharlene Hesse-Biber. 1984. *Women at Work*. Palo Alto, Calif.: Mayfield.
Haignere, Lois, and Ronnie Steinberg. 1984. *Review of Massachusetts' Statewide Classification and Compensation System for Achieving Comparable Worth*. Report submitted to the Commonwealth of Massachusetts Special Committee on Comparable Worth. Albany, N.Y.: Center for Women in Government, Institute for Government and Policy Studies of the Rockefeller College, SUNY.
Hartmann, Heidi, ed. 1985. *Comparable Worth: New Directions for Research*. Washington, D.C.: National Academy.
Miller, Ann R., D.J. Treiman, P.S. Cain, and P.A. Roos. 1980. *Work, Jobs and Occupations: A Critical Review of the Dictionary of Occupational Titles*. Washington, D.C.: National Academy.
Remick, Helen. 1980. "Beyond Equal Pay for Equal Work: Comparable Worth in the State of Washington." In *Equal Employment Policy for Women: Strategies for Implementation in the United States, Canada and Western Europe*. Philadelphia: Temple University Press.
———. 1981. "The Comparable Worth Controversy." *Public Personnel Management Journal* 10:371–83.

————. 1984. "Major Issues in *a priori* Applications." In *Comparable Worth and Wage Discrimination: Technical Possibilities and Political Realities*, edited by Helen Remick. Philadelphia: Temple University Press.

————. 1978. "Strategies for Creating Sound, Bias-Free Job Evaluation Plans." In *Job Evaluation and EEO: The Emerging Issues*. New York: Industrial Relations Counselors.

Schwab, Donald G. 1980. "Job Evaluation and Pay Setting: Concepts and Practices."In *Comparable Worth: Issues and Alternatives*, edited by Robert E. Livernash. Washington, D.C.: Equal Employment Advisory Council.

Stevenson, Mary Huff. 1978. "Wage Differences between Men and Women: Economic Theories." In *Working Women*, edited by Ann H. Stromberg and Shirley Harkess. Palo Alto, Calif.: Mayfield.

Treiman, Donald J. 1984. "The Effect of Choice of Factors and Factor Weights in Job Evaluation." In *Comparable Worth and Wage Discrimination: Technical Possibilities and Political Realities*, edited by Helen Remick. Philadelphia: Temple University Press.

————. 1979. *Job Evaluation: An Analytic Review*. Interim report to the Equal Employment Opportunity Commission. Washington, D.C.: National Academy.

Treiman, Donald J., and Heidi Hartmann, eds. 1981. *Women, Work and Wages: Equal Pay for Jobs of Equal Value*. Washington, D.C.: National Academy.

# VII

# Issues Emerging from the Intersection of Work and Family

# Overview of Work and Family Linkages

## Work-Family Linkages in Early Industrialization: The Public-Private Split

From the beginnings of human history women have always worked. They have consistently contributed both to the economic production of their society and to the material subsistence of their kinship group. To understand the problems of women and work in contemporary societies, it is essential to trace the roots of these problems to historical changes in the social definitions of women's work. As an abundance of research testifies, the most critical redefinition of women's work in American society occurred during the period of early industrialization (late 1800s, early 1900s). At this time, the idea of a public-private separation, with men in the public (occupational) sphere and women in the private (family) sphere, laid the foundation both for structural segregation of women's and men's occupations (exclusion of women from many occupations or occupational segregation) and ideological changes (women equated with family) that continue to subordinate women's paid and unpaid work.

Much of the mainstream literature on early industrialization focuses on changes in men's occupations. Since the early 1970s, the burgeoning scholarship on gender, in a variety of academic disciplines, has extended the history of the public-private dichotomy by analyzing the experiences of women. The central question is: How was an economic division of labor by sex, in earlier times, transformed into an institutionally based and politically legitimized separation of public from private systems? The research underscores the significance of the public-private dichotomy in dictating the linkages between women's occupational and family commitments.

### Preindustrial Societies and the Division of Labor

In seeking to understand gender inequality inherent in the separation of public and private, gender scholars have had to overcome a persistent assumption that the family is a natural, biological, and universal unit existing in separation from other societal structures and processes. For example, it has often been argued that women's subordination in preindustrial societies is due to their role in reproduction (pregnancy, child-bearing), which caused a basic division of labor by sex that led to male dominance. But the work on gender in early societies underscores the fact that a direct relation of biological mothering to cultural subordination is not obvious (Petchesky 1979). Further, male dominance is not natural but is a social construction, varying in degree and form; it is therefore amenable to change. In short, there is no universal content or shape to gendered divisions of labor, "family," or male dominance (Rosaldo 1980).

Gender scholars have detailed the transformation of an economic division of labor in which the work of women and men was equally important into a division of labor with higher value placed on men's work, and a structural separation of public from private systems (Chafetz 1984; Osmond 1981). Centuries before industrialization, the private sphere of kinship/family became devalued and the public sphere (states and markets controlled by men) increasingly idealized; thus, prevailing ideologies legitimized a structural public-private division. The historical period of Athenian democracy, starting in the fifth century B.C., provides a vivid example of both the idealization of the public arena and the associated subordination of women (Kelly-Gadol 1987).

### Early Capitalist Industrialization

Comparative historical analyses indicate that in Western societies the second critical change in the conceptualization of public-private spheres and of women's status occurred at the time of early industrialization. Mainstream accounts describe a shift of economic production from family to factory, with men shifting to wage work and women staying home to care for house and children. This interpretation assumes that men and women began to inhabit separate but equal and complementary spheres. Marxist accounts emphasize social class as the most crucial dimension of capitalist industrialization; they acknowledge women's subordination, but define it as, at most, secondary. In contrast, gender analyses of the transition to capitalist industrialization place equal (and interactive) importance on changing arrangements of gender and of social class.

One of the distinguishing characteristics of capitalist industrialization in the United States and England was the development of sharp distinctions between a middle class whose wealth was based on business and industry and an industrial working class whose labor produced that wealth (Ehrenreich and English 1978). The experiences of women in these two classes clearly affected each other, but their lifestyles were starkly differentiated. For affluent women, the socially prescribed activities included motherhood, homemaking, and personifying the feminine virtues of piety, morality, and nurturance. In contrast, economic necessity frequently forced working-class women to join their husbands (and, often, their children) in earning money for sheer family survival. Because of these real differences in experiences, the literature on working-class women focuses primarily on their struggles with wage work; these struggles also affected work opportunities for middle-class women. The literature on middle-class women emphasizes changes in family ideology, changes which, in turn, influenced family norms and responsibilities of working-class women.

The development and entrenchment of a radically different type of public-private ideology affected the experiences of women in both social classes. In one of the most revolutionary changes in the history of the gendered division of labor, the nuclear family (the private sphere) became idealized, in sharp contrast to the devaluing of families/households in the eras preceding industrialization. Furthermore, women began to be equated with family. These changes had different implications for women and for men of different social classes.

**Working-Class Experiences**

The research of Heidi Hartmann (1979) explores the somewhat contradictory dynamics of capitalism and of patriarchy as they evolved historically. Hartmann points out that industrial capitalism posed a threat to patriarchal control in families, since women and children potentially could enter the labor force, earn their own wages, and become independent. Why did this not happen? Hartmann concludes that job segregation by gender (and the associated development of the family wage and protective legislation) perpetuated the traditional patriarchal subordination of women within capitalist industrial society. Hartmann cites historical evidence to support her thesis that working-class men, with the help of their unions, had a significant influence in removing working-class women from the factories (where they were viewed as a threat to men's jobs) or into low-paid, low-skilled jobs, and ensuring that women would continue to be responsible for the domestic labor in individual families (the greatest opposition was to married women doing factory work).

The history of early textile factories illustrates what were to become predictable trends in other industries. Initially, textile factories employed primarily women and children as cheap and malleable workers. Men had to be lured into factory work in higher-skilled jobs or managerial positions. By the mid 1800s, male factory operatives called for the regulation of child labor. Middle- and upper-class men elaborated this protest into moral outrage at the exploitation of women as well as children. The result was protective legislation that eliminated child labor and increasingly defined women's employment. While factory conditions were deplorable for all workers, unions did not support protective legislation for men. Corresponding to the emerging public-private ideology, unions sought to organize working-class men but to protect women workers. Protective legislation established a special legal status for women workers, restricting their freedom to work at some jobs and limiting the hours they could work at others. This legislation further reinforced the prevailing assumptions that all women were mothers (or potential mothers) and that women's "place" was in the home (Kessler-Harris 1982).

Demands that men's wages should be increased and paid on a family basis paralleled union arguments for protective legislation. The concept of the family wage was based on the argument that men should have an income advantage because of their family responsibilities. The corollary assumption was that since women are normally supported by men, their wages should be lower. The family wage was based on two premises: (1) survival for the working-class family (under the rationale that if all family members were in the labor force it would create lower wages for each individual); and (2) the assumption that men should be the family breadwinners. Thus, an economically dependent family became essential to the notion of "normal manhood," and, since it was also assumed that all women would, sooner or later, become wives, it legitimated the exclusion of women from the labor force. The belief that even working-class women should not work was so embedded in the ideology that proposals to help women in poverty were consistently framed in terms of "charitable aid" rather than higher wages in the labor market.

It is important to understand that the family wage was more ideology than reality—that is, the larger wage was actually awarded only in a few skilled or unionized sectors of the labor force. At the time, a family wage appeared beneficial. It is in hindsight that contemporary gender scholars can point out that the most enduring consequences of the family wage ideology were the constraints it placed on women's job and family activities.

### Social Class Differences in the Ideology of Public-Private Spheres

Women and men of different social classes had varying reasons for supporting the ideology of separate spheres as embodied in the specific issues of protective legislation and the family wage. Working-class women engaged in wage work out of necessity. Job experiences of women in factories and sweat shops were disagreeable and often hazardous, and in the 1800s most of their lives also included bearing and raising children. Then, as today, low-income family life required cooperation and sharing between the sexes and generations. Family was, and is, the primary defense against underclass oppression. Thus, to many working-class women it appeared extremely desirable for the family breadwinner to be the man. Working-class men endorsed the public-private ideology because they perceived the material advantages of being the family's "natural breadwinner" with the wife its "natural homemaker." Men often took spending money off the top of their wages; earning the wage was their only family responsibility, with home the breadwinner's place of rest and leisure away from work. The working-class male ideology of the private sphere was not simply adopted in imitation of the middle-class lifestyle but was linked more directly to the preindustrial image of masculinity as family head.

The nineteenth-century middle class offers the most vivid picture of both the structural separation of public-private spheres and the development of an ideology of "the family" that pronounced this separation as normative. Mainstream literature on this period has focused on the making of the modern American family, the conjugal family, the change from institution to companionship, the loss of family economic functions, and the complementary role patterns of husband and wife (Degler 1980). Gender scholars offer new insights by focusing on the power relations involved in the construction of two hierarchical, diametrically opposed images of male and female nature and prescribed activities. They question the assumption that family is somehow separate and exempt from power relations in the larger society. They argue that the public-private dichotomy is a balanced world seen through men's eyes. Women were not passive subjects (many reacted, some endorsed, a few rebelled), but women did not create nor were they ever allowed the power to experience the benefits of both public and private spheres.

While the idealization of women had precedents in preindustrial times, what appears unique about "the modern family" is the idealization of the private sphere and the "granting" of women's "dominion" over domesticity and child care. It is important to recognize two less positive developments that underlie this "modernization." First, the idealization of women was most exaggerated at exactly the time when women's competition in the public world was becoming a realistic possibility. For middle-class women, especially, it justified their separate and unequal education and their exclusion from the emerging professions and associated political institutions. Second, while the pedestal may have appeared to elevate women, they were not granted status as individuals; as a group, they were literally equated with home and family.

Why did middle-class women accept and some actively promote the ideology of domesticity? A basic reason is that they had no desirable alternatives, since marriage was economically and normatively imperative. The cult of domesticity appeared to offer middle-class women a purpose in life and a respectable status, and the idea of women's moral superiority was appealing. Women were attracted to the idea that they were not only different from men but "better." In essence, the rationale was why should women strive for equality when they had already been granted superiority? Finally, the middle-class was bombarded by articles, manuals, and books extolling "true womanhood" and the virtues of domesticity.

What were the consequences for middle-class women of this radical separation of public-private spheres? On the one hand, the ideology of extremely polarized gender differences created barriers for women and increased male dominance. Women lost the limited legal rights they held in Puritan times; they were excluded from the courts, lost their property rights, and were explicitly defined as legal dependents of their husbands (Easton 1976). On the other hand, the widely proclaimed assertion of women's moral superiority gave them the promise of a new role in society. Paradoxically, this new role served as a key to release some upper-middle-class women from the confines of the home. It led rather directly to the establishment of higher education for women and to their involvement in charitable community concerns. Subsequently, college-educated and socially active women expanded their issues to national movements around issues of slavery, temperance, and social welfare. These events culminated in the early women's rights movement in the United States.

What did the idealization of women, motherhood, and the home offer middle-class men? The public-private belief system promised a multifaceted solution to a complex dilemma men faced in a period of unprecedented social change: How to retain the stability and security associated with an agrarian past within the competitively hostile, urban world of early industrialization. "The home" was idealized as a haven of peace, safety, nurturance, warmth, and order in a chaotic world. Men created the ideology of hearth and home as an antithesis to a new masculine ideal of being hardhearted, tough, and realistic. Class-privileged men could preserve the qualities they valued and needed for balance (a well-ordered household and nurturant wife/mother) while enjoying advantages of a new era, which demanded allegiance to the sphere of work.

### Race Differences in the Experience of Public-Private Spheres

It is essential to underscore the dynamics of race, and the interaction of race with gender and social class, to complete the picture of the public-private separation. From slavery through early industrialization and to the present, African-American women's work has been crucial to the American economy (Amott and Matthaei 1991). Ironically, white men had little difficulty in discarding the ideology of female piety and fragility when money and sexual license were at stake. During slavery, both field and industrial work by African Americans showed little sex segregation. Not only was their physical labor expropriated, but African-American women also had no legal right to their sexuality nor to the children they bore. Demonstrating the flexibility of ruling men's power to define gender through law, church, and media, at the same time that middle-class white women's motherhood was extolled and their bodies protected, African-American women were stereotyped as promiscuous and they were sexually harassed, abused, and exploited (Higginbotham 1992).

After abolition, the majority of rural African-American women worked either as share croppers with their families or in personal and domestic service to whites. In urban areas, although black women greatly preferred the higher pay and shorter hours of factory work, white employers excluded African-American women as well as men from almost all jobs with the exception of the lowest of manufacturing operations, such as in canneries, tobacco stemming, and oyster shucking (Jones 1985). Skilled, white, working-class men, as noted previously, secured some protection and advancement through union organization. While many black men struggled to be admitted to labor unions, their battle was unsuccessful until the late 1960s. White workers protested vehemently when blacks were hired, fearing that their presence would drive wages down. White immigrants (numbering over thirty million between 1850 and 1920) were hired before blacks even in unskilled and domestic labor positions. In rural and in urban areas, blacks often served as a reserve labor supply to be called in only during periods of peak demand. They were also used as strike-breakers to threaten immigrant workers into conformity. The largest proportion of African-American women were servants for whites at wages so low that all but the lowest income householder could afford such help. Frequently, black servants could take care of their own children only after they had worked twelve hours or more in the home of a white family.

In short, the majority of African-American women were oppressed by a compounded hierarchy of class, gender, and race that marked them as the lowest of the low in power and in status. One consequence of this devaluation was that many African-American working-class women struggled simply to endure their wage work, and sought to derive their personal and community status primarily from their family work (Harley 1990). The idea of "separate spheres" increasingly described the separate lives of whites and blacks, men and women, white-collar and blue-collar workers. For African Americans, the 1896 Supreme Court decision on *Plessy v. Ferguson* resulted in the doctrine of "separate but equal" races. For middle-class white women this paralleled the establishment of "separate but complementary public-private spheres." These specific race and gender rules legitimated such extreme forms of discrimination that the next sixty years were punctuated with civil rights' and women's social movements.

## Conclusion

The public-private dichotomy (of the late 1800s, early 1900s) had both a material and an ideological base. The economic base reduced the threat of women's competition in the public world. The ideological base, however, explains why idealization of a public-private separation became so pervasive and persistent. The cultural embodiment of gendered, separate spheres allowed an apparent resolution to a contradiction in men's values between self-serving individualism and nurturant community.

In summary, sociohistorical scholarship from the perspective of *women's* experiences: (1) focuses on the organization of work within and outside of families as shaped both by a patriarchal gender system and by a classist, racist economic system; (2) refutes the family-linked stereotypes of the man as sole provider and breadwinner and the woman as dependent and economically unproductive, neither a useful ideal (it embeds women's subordination) nor a description of the actual lives of most people; (3) demonstrates that the locus of women's subordination is not just in the economy nor just in the family—that is, "separate spheres" do not exist in most women's daily experiences; and (4) recognizes a societal gender system that is autonomous with regard to any specific institution yet links all major institutions.

*Marie Withers Osmond*

## Bibliography

Amott, T., and J. Matthaei. 1991. *Race, Gender & Work*. Boston: South End.

Chafetz, J. 1984. *Sex and Advantage*. Totowa, N.J.: Rowman and Allanheld.

Degler, C. 1980. *At Odds*. Oxford: Oxford University Press.

Easton, B. 1976. "Industrialization and Femininity." *Social Problems* 23:389–401.

Ehrenreich, B., and D. English 1978. *For Her Own Good*. Garden City, N.Y.: Anchor.

Harley, S. 1990. "For the Good of Family and Race." *Signs* 15:336–49.

Hartmann, H. 1979. "Capitalism, Patriarchy, and Job Segregation by Sex." In *Capitalist Patriarchy and the Case for Socialist Feminism*, edited by Z.R. Eisenstein, pp. 206–47. New York: Monthly Review.

Higginbotham, E. 1992. "African-American Women's History and the Metalanguage of Race." *Signs* 17:251–74.

Jones, J. 1985. *Labor of Love, Labor of Sorrow*. New York: Basic Books.

Kelly-Gadol, J. 1987. "The Social Relation of the Sexes." In *Feminism and Methodology*, edited by S. Harding. pp.15–28. Bloomington: Indiana University Press.

Kessler-Harris, A. 1982. *Out to Work*. New York: Oxford University Press.

Osmond, M.W. 1981. "Comparative Marriage and the Family." *International Journal of Comparative Sociology* 22:169–96.

Petchesky, R. 1979. "Dissolving the Hyphen: A Report on Marxist-Feminist Groups." In *Capitalist Patriarchy and the Case for Socialist Feminism*, edited by Z.R. Eisenstein, pp. 373–90. New York: Monthly Review.

Rosaldo, M. 1980. "The Use and Abuse of Anthropology: Reflections on Feminism and Cross Cultural Understanding." *Signs* 5:389–417.

## Gender Segregation of Housework

Gender inequality in the United States is perhaps most apparent within the home. American women, even those employed full time, continue to work longer hours than do their husbands on household tasks, and there is little evidence that men's proportionate share of housework has changed much during recent decades (Coverman 1985; Gershuny and Robinson 1988; Hochschild 1989). But this focus on partners' hourly contributions to housework gives a rather incomplete picture of the household division of labor. Indeed, the concept of a household division of labor implies more than the simple arithmetic of relative shares of time devoted by each marital partner to domestic chores. It also implies that husbands and wives divide their available time among various tasks. The goal here is to illustrate a new measure of the gender division or segregation of household chores among American couples.

## Measuring the Household Division of Labor

As a concept, the division of household labor has two analytically distinct dimensions: number of hours and types of work tasks allocated to each spouse. But these separate dimensions are rarely reflected in empirical research. Instead, household labor has typically been operationalized as the hours of time allocated by each spouse to the maintenance, upkeep, and care of both the material household and the well-being of household members. Previous studies have drawn a single overriding conclusion: Women spend a disproportionate share of total family labor time on household chores (Thompson and Walker 1989).

That some partners spend many hours on domestic chores has no necessary connection, however, to whether housework tasks are segregated or shared. Some egalitarian couples (as defined by the husband's share of family labor) may in fact exhibit a highly sex-segregated division of labor. Partners may share housework but not specific tasks. There is overwhelming evidence that females continue to contribute disproportionately to household labor and that each spouse tends to "specialize" in certain chores (Berk 1985). But we know a good deal less about the extent and etiology of the latter than the former.

## Measuring the Gender-Based Segregation of Family Work

The index of dissimilarity (D) provides a useful summary measure of the gender segregation of household labor. D is used here to measure the extent of segregation in the distribution of time allocated by the husband and wife to various household tasks. For each couple, this measure is calculated as:

$$D = \frac{1}{2} \sum_{i=1}^{k} /w_i\text{-}h_i/$$

where $w_i$ is the proportion of the wife's total labor (measured in hours) that is devoted to task i, and $h_i$ is the proportion of husband's total time devoted to task i. D indicates the percentage of the husband's time that would have to be allocated to other tasks before equality was achieved in the husband's and wife's proportion distribution of time across all household tasks. A D of zero indicates that the percentage distribution of time across household tasks is equal for the husband and wife, while a D of 1.0 indicates complete segregation of family labor (that is, there is no overlap in the tasks that the man and woman do). Thus, as D increases, the distribution of the husband's and wife's family labor contribution becomes increasingly specialized or segregated.

Data from the 1988 National Survey of Families and Households (NSFH) (Sweet et al. 1988) can be used to illustrate the value of this new measure (see also Blair and Lichter 1991). Table 1 provides the percentage distributions of household labor time by sex. Consistent with previous research, females contribute approximately twice the amount of total household labor that males do (bottom line). Men work about fourteen hours per week, but spend roughly one-third of it on outdoor tasks (30.8 percent). Females, on the other hand, allocate most of their family work time to meal preparation (28.7 percent), cleaning dishes (17.1 percent), and cleaning house (22.8 percent). As these data indicate, comparisons of

| Household Tasks | Males | | Females | |
| --- | --- | --- | --- | --- |
| | hours/ week | percentage of total hours | hours/ week | percentage of total hours |
| Meal Preparation | 2.27 (3.19) | 15.7% | 9.49 (6.27) | 28.7% |
| Dishes | 1.73 (2.39) | 12.0% | 5.66 (4.32) | 17.1% |
| Ironing/Washing | 0.58 (1.27) | 4.0% | 4.11 (3.21) | 12.4% |
| Cleaning House | 1.48 (2.29) | 10.2% | 7.56 (6.05) | 22.8% |
| Outdoor Tasks | 4.45 (5.04) | 30.8% | 1.70 (2.85) | 5.1% |
| Auto Maintenance | 1.43 (1.76) | 9.9% | 0.14 (0.70) | 0.4% |
| Managing Bills | 1.19 (1.63) | 8.2% | 1.55 (1.85) | 4.7% |
| Shopping | 1.31 (1.63) | 9.1% | 2.89 (2.09) | 8.7% |
| TOTAL HOUSEHOLD LABOR | 14.44 (10.03) | 99.9% | 33.10 (16.84) | 99.9% |

(Adapted from Blair and Lichter, 1991; standard deviations shown in parentheses)

total hours devoted to particular tasks reveal very large sex differences during the late 1980s in the amount and type of household labor.

Of central interest here, however, is the degree of segregation or specialization of household labor. Using the task categories shown in Table 1, an index of dissimilarity is calculated for each couple (see equation). Remarkable variation in segregation is revealed (D range = 0–1.0), with an average index of dissimilarity of 0.61. Substantively, this means that the average male would have to reallocate 61 percent of his family work to other chores before gender equality was achieved in the percentage distribution of labor time across all domestic tasks. Clearly, household labor is highly segregated by sex, and the D provides an easily interpretable summary measure of sex-based patterns of family work.

Blair and Lichter (1991) found as well that family work segregation is more likely to characterize some couples than others. For example, the educational attainment of both males and females is highly associated with the sex-based allocation of tasks. Specifically, increases in education are associated with decreases in segregation. Among couples in which the female is highly educated (16+ years of formal education), D is 0.54, whereas the corresponding figure for couples in which the female has less than twelve years of formal education is 0.73. Nevertheless, despite the apparent gradient of segregation by education, household labor clearly is highly segregated even for highly educated couples.

At the same time, while the earnings of males do not greatly affect the sex specialization of household labor, the earnings of females reveals a strong inverse association with D. In addition, although high income among females apparently provides some leverage for attaining a more equitable sex distribution of labor across tasks, it does not ensure complete gender equality. For example, couples in which the woman earned over $35,000 annually still exhibit relatively high levels of segregation (see Blair and Lichter 1991).

Sex-role attitudes also were found to be highly associated with household labor segregation; couples with egalitarian sex-role orientations had a lower segregation index than those couples with traditional orientations. The results for family-role ideology reveal a similar trend. Relatedly, nontraditional couples, such as cohabitators, are slightly less segregated in work patterns than are married couples. And, as expected, couples in relationships of long duration were found to be more sex segregated in family work patterns than are newly formed couples.

The presence and age of children have only small effects on family labor segregation, and couples in which the wife worked forty or more hours have only slightly lower levels of segregation than do couples in which the wife worked less than twenty hours. Not surprisingly, household work is more highly sex segregated if the husband's labor-force hours are high (as opposed to low). In addition, couples in which the male is working a shift work schedule report slightly lower levels of task segregation in the household.

The spheres of domestic work activity in the late 1980s remain highly segregated by sex. Indeed, based on this measure of family work segregation, males would have to reallocate over 60 percent of their family work time to other tasks before sex equality in the division of labor was achieved.

The potential implications here are nontrivial. For example, the lack of sharing of housework is associated with poor mental health among married women, especially in the form of elevated levels of depression (Ross et al. 1983). Moreover, the gender segregation of domestic tasks presumably has implications for the sex-role socialization of children (Brody and Steelman 1985). The fact that some tasks come to be defined as "men's work" and others as "women's work" is likely to reinforce traditional gender roles among children in the home.

In conclusion, the index of dissimilarity used by Blair and Lichter redirects attention away from the uncritical reliance on hours of husbands' family work as the best (or sole) indicator of the division of household labor. Hours and tasks are conceptually distinct dimensions of household labor. Indeed, the singular focus on husbands' hours worked may be inappropriate or even misleading. The segregation measure presented here provides a point of departure for thinking more carefully about how husbands and wives divide or share family work.

> *Sampson Lee Blair*

## Bibliography

Berk, S.F. 1985. *The Gender Factory: The Apportionment of Work in American Households*. New York: Plenum.

Blair, S.L., and D.T. Lichter. 1991. "Measuring the Division of Household Labor: Gender Segregation of Housework among American Couples." *Journal of Family Issues* 12(1):91–113.

Brody, C.J., and L.C. Steelman. 1985. "Sibling Structure and Parental Sex-Typing of Children's Household Tasks." *Journal of Marriage and the Family* 45:265–73.

Coverman, S. 1985. "Explaining Husband's Participation in Domestic Labor." *Sociological Quarterly* 26:81–97.

Gershuny, J., and Robinson, J.P. 1988. "Historical Changes in the Household Division of Labor." *Demography* 25(4):537–52.

Hochschild, A. 1989. *The Second Shift*. New York: Viking.

Ross, C.E., J. Mirowsky, and J. Huber. 1983. "Dividing Work, Sharing Work, and In-Between: Marriage Patterns and Depression." *American Sociological Review* 47:198–211.

Sweet, J., L. Bumpass, and V. Call. 1988. "The Design and Content of the National Survey of Families and Households." Working paper NSFH-1, Center for Demography and Ecology, University of Wisconsin.

Thompson, L., and A.J. Walker. 1989. "Gender in Families: Women and Men in Marriage, Work, and Parenthood." *Journal of Marriage and the Family* 51:845–71.

## Career, Family, and Changing Life Course Patterns

Major historical events of the twentieth century have had a differential impact on women of different ages, altering the life course for successive cohorts. Demographically, changes in women's life course patterns are defined by changes in the rates at which women assume significant social roles (such as the roles of student, paid worker, spouse, or parent) and by changes in the timing, sequencing, and duration of these roles (Hess 1988; Huber 1988; McLaughlin et al. 1988; Riley 1988). Women's social roles, as well as their age cohort, affect their attitudes, aspirations, expectations, and values (Hess 1988; Riley 1988). This article focuses primarily on the changes in the typical life course pattern of white women in the United States during the twentieth century.

During the early decades of the twentieth century there was a gradual increase in women's labor-force participation, and employed white women were typically young and single (McLaughlin et al. 1988). Then in the 1940s the labor-force participation of married women began to increase rapidly as women were recruited into the workforce during World War II. During the war and immediate postwar period, the most notable increases in women's employment occurred among married mothers of school-age and grown children (Bianchi and Spain 1986, McLaughlin et al. 1988). Thus there was established a "bimodal pattern" of women's labor-force participation in which women entered the labor force prior to marriage, withdrew for marriage and child-rearing, and sometimes returned to paid employment when their heavy child-rearing responsibilities were completed (McLaughlin et al. 1988).

At the end of World War II, the marriage rate increased sharply, and the "marriage boom" continued throughout the 1950s (McLaughlin et al. 1988). Moreover, compared with their mothers' generation, the cohorts of young women who reached adulthood at mid century married at an earlier age and had more children, producing the "baby boom" generation born between 1946 and 1964 (McLaughlin et al. 1988).

As the oldest baby boomers began to reach adulthood in the late 1960s, women's life course patterns changed significantly. From the 1960s through the 1980s, women's educational attainment increased significantly (McLaughlin et al. 1988). Moreover, the labor-force participation rates of all women, but especially married women in their twenties and thirties, rose rapidly during the late 1960s and 1970s as young women began to establish a pattern of continuous labor-force participation throughout adulthood with little or no withdrawal from employment during the early child-rearing years (Bianchi and Spain 1986, McLaughlin et al. 1988).

Changes in family behavior accompanied changes in employment patterns: Women delayed marriage and child-bearing and had smaller families (Bianchi and Spain 1986; McLaughlin et al. 1988). Thus, for example, the average family size declined from over three children during the baby boom era to 1.8 children in 1976 (McLaughlin et al. 1988). Since the 1960s there have also been increases in divorce and in the proportion of women who remain single (Bianchi and Spain 1986; McLaughlin et al. 1988).

During the 1970s women's attitudes toward employment changed rapidly, bringing attitudes into alignment with emerging behavior patterns. Thus women became more supportive of a married mother's choosing paid employment, even when it conflicted with a husband's wishes or family responsibilities. Attitudinal changes supporting women's commitment to paid employment occurred among women of all ages, even though the changes occurred earlier and were more pervasive among younger women (McLaughlin et al. 1988).

College women's career attitudes also changed significantly. By the early 1970s, college women no longer anticipated withdrawal from the labor force for child-rearing. Moreover, during the 1970s and 1980s college women demonstrated increasing career orientation as reflected in their educational goals, their interest in individual achievement, and the importance they assigned to a career in their life plans (Komarovsky 1985; McLaughlin et al. 1988).

Yet, while young women have become increasingly career oriented, they have maintained a strong commitment to having a family as well. Indeed, although the proportion of college women who rated commitment to raising a family as "very important" declined somewhat during the early 1970s, this rate partially recovered and stabilized at a high level (McLaughlin et al. 1988).

Women's attitudes are affected not only by their age cohort or generation, but also by the social roles they occupy (Hess 1988; Riley 1988). Thus, for example, during the intense period of early child-rearing, a married mother's commitment to family tends to be strong, regardless of the mother's age or the level of her career commitment (Faver 1984).

Social structural changes and changes in the individual life course are reciprocal, interdependent processes. Just as changing social and economic conditions have altered the life course for women, so too the changing experience of successive cohorts has effected changes in social institutions including the labor force, the educational system, and the family (Huber 1988; McLaughlin et al. 1988).

Yet, changes in social norms and institutions have not proceeded as rapidly as changes in women's career aspirations and their desire to pursue career and family roles simultaneously. The resulting strain can be described by William Ogburn's (1964) concept of "cultural lag," which points to the discontinuities resulting from differential rates of change in societal norms, values, and institutions during a period of rapid social change (Bianchi and Spain 1986; see also Huber 1988).

For some women, cultural discontinuity is manifested in a discrepancy between career aspirations and opportunities to fulfill aspirations through paid employment. Indeed, despite women's increasing career orientation, structural constraints such as lack of adequate child-care facilities, relatively low wages for women, and the disproportionate allocation of household tasks to women continue to limit women's employment, especially during the early child-rearing years (Bianchi and Spain 1986). For women who are highly career oriented, the discrepancy between aspirations and opportunities for paid employment may be particularly frustrating (Faver 1984).

In sum, the typical life course pattern of women has changed significantly during the twentieth century. In recent decades women have increasingly valued and pursued simultaneous involvement in career and family roles. However, adequate adjustments in social institutions to accommodate and facilitate women's new life course pattern have yet to be achieved.

*Catherine A. Faver*

## Bibliography

Avioli, P.S., and E. Kaplan. 1992. "A Panel Study of Married Women's Work Patterns." *Sex Roles* 26:227–42.

Bergmann, B.R. 1986. *The Economic Emergence of Women*. New York: Basic Books.

Bianchi, S.M., and D. Spain. 1986. *American Women in Transition*. New York: Russell Sage.

Bielby, D.D. 1992. "Commitment to Work and Family." *Annual Review of Sociology* 18:281–302.

Faver, C.A. 1984. *Women in Transition: Career, Family, and Life Satisfaction in Three Cohorts*. New York: Praeger.

Hess, B.B. 1988. "Social Structures and Human Lives: A Sociological Theme." In *Social Structures and Human Lives*, edited by M.W. Riley, pp. 16–23. Newbury Park, Calif.: Sage.

Hochschild, A., and A. Machung. 1989. *The Second Shift: Working Parents and the Revolution at Home*. New York: Viking.

Huber, B.J. 1988. "Social Structures and Human Lives: Variations on a Theme." In *Social Structures and Human Lives*, edited by M.W. Riley, pp. 346–63. Newbury Park, Calif.: Sage.

Komarovsky, M. 1985. *Women in College: Shaping New Feminine Identities*. New York: Basic Books.

McLaughlin, S.D., B.D. Melber, J.O.G. Billy, D.M. Zimmerle, L.D. Winges, and T.R. Johnson. 1988. *The Changing Lives of American Women*. Chapel Hill: University of North Carolina Press.

Ogburn, W.F. 1964. *On Culture and Social Change*. Chicago: University of Chicago Press.

Rexroat, C. 1992. "Changes in the Employment Continuity of Succeeding Cohorts of Young Women." *Work and Occupations* 19:18–34.

Riley, M.W. 1988. "On the Significance of Age in Sociology." In *Social Structures and Human Lives*, edited by M.W. Riley, pp. 24–45. Newbury Park, Calif.: Sage.

Spenner, K.I., and R.A. Rosenfeld. 1990. "Women, Work, and Identities." *Social Science Research* 19:266–99.

Wenk, D., and P. Garrett. 1992. "Having a Baby: Some Predictions of Maternal Employment around Childbirth." *Gender & Society* 6:49–65.

## Working Women and Eldercare

The combination of women entering the labor force at an increasing rate, an increase in the number of single-parent families (mostly headed by women), and increasing longevity have created a dependent-care situation that continues to grow in intensity. The closeness of this relationship is more strongly felt by women than men because women tend to be the caregivers of dependents in our society. The dilemmas created by this relationship, therefore, are most strongly felt by women, specifically those with both home and work responsibilities.

That these responsibilities weigh more heavily upon women than men can be seen by looking at government data. Today, 64.8 percent of those mothers with children under nineteen years of age are working; 54.5 percent among mothers with youngsters less than six years old. The greatest increase in labor-force entrance has been among women under thirty-five with children under three years old. In 1987, about 59 percent of the country's fifty-two million children under the age of fifteen had mothers who were employed outside the home.

The fact that the dependency burden falls heavily on women is supported by other facts. A manager of a hospital's senior-service division claims that 87 percent of all caregivers are women (Clifford 1991). The number of forty year olds with at least one surviving parent increased from 70 percent in 1900 to 95 percent in 1985. The average woman today will spend seventeen years of her adult life as the mother of a dependent child and eighteen years as the daughter of an elderly dependent parent (Cordtz 1990).

Increasing longevity will continue to create problems for those who must care for the elderly. A growing portion of our labor pool is caring for frail, elderly relatives needing long-term care; a large proportion (70 percent) of our elderly rely mainly on relatives for these needs (Callahan and Wallack 1981). More than half the women caring for elderly relatives work outside the home and nearly 40 percent of them are still raising children of their own (England 1989). The Older Women's League reports that over half of the 1.8 million women who are caring for children and parents at the same time are in the paid labor force. This organization discovered that four-fifths of the caregivers of elders who were interviewed had children still living at home (Kuriansky 1991).

One of the consequences of this increase is that, with relatively few community-based alternatives to nursing homes and home care, a growing number of working women will be faced with reducing their employment in order to provide eldercare (England 1989).

### Consequences of Caregiving Responsibilities

Caregiving responsibilities can have adverse effects upon work performance. A survey conducted by the *New York Times* in 1989 revealed that 83 percent of employed mothers were torn by conflict between their work and home responsibilities (Bauer 1990). Emotional stress as a result of eldercare responsibilities was noted by over 50 percent of the respondents in a corporate survey conducted by Retirement Advisors of New York City (Creedon 1987, p.22). A 1991 interview series conducted by the Older Women's League of 305 caregivers in five communities revealed that 90 percent of the women caregivers had experienced some negative effect, such as stress, on their ability to work as effectively as they did before assuming eldercare responsibilities (Kuriansky 1991). Effects other than stress are absenteeism, tardiness, job-leaving, and reduction of productivity. For example, in 1984, two-thirds of the sixty-nine respondents to the New York Business Group on Health Care survey admitted to "excessive" nonbusiness telephoning at work, affecting productivity on the part of caregiving employees, and a large proportion of the respondents had noted signs of stress among caregiving employees (Crawford 1990). In a study conducted by the chairman of John Hancock Financial Services and *Fortune* magazine, 60 percent of the senior executives responding claimed awareness of specific work-related problems with elder-caregiving employees. Forty-five percent had noticed employee stress, 38 percent noted late arrivals and early departures, and 30 percent noted absenteeism among caregiving employees.

Regarding job-leaving, among 150 caregiving families of the elderly interviewed for a study done at the Philadelphia Geriatric Center, it was discovered that over one-quarter of the then nonworking women had left the labor force to care for their mothers. Another 26 percent of those still working had entertained the notion of quitting or, at least, cutting back on the hours they would work (Crawford 1990).

### Assistance for Caregivers

Various types of assistance programs targeted at working caregivers exist. While most are directed at child care, an increasing number of companies are addressing the issue of eldercare as well. Many companies offer information on caregiving such as referral services, networking, and seminars for employees.

A flexible benefits program, or cafeteria plan, is another option. A flexible spending account is designed to fit the needs of employees at particular phases of their lives and, therefore, provides flexibility as needs change in the form of interchangeability among benefit choices. Some of these choices are medical and dental benefits, income deferral and retirement programs, legal aid, unemployment assistance, and child care and other dependent care assistance.

Flextime scheduling and compressed work weeks are gaining in popularity (Martin and Hartley 1975). Types of rearranged work scheduling include staggered hours that are employer-assigned, unspecified staggered/flexible hours, the three- and four-day week, permanent part-time, and a task system arrangement (task completion is counted instead of work hours). Notably, some of these criteria are used in popular press surveys of "family friendly" or "female friendly" companies.

### Benefits of Employer Support

With the adoption of ways to accommodate the work-family connection have come positive outcomes. Personnel in a bank in Los Angeles discovered that for every three dollars spent in aiding employees in their dependent care responsibilities, four dollars were "saved" in reduced absenteeism and turnover and in increased productivity. Excel-Nyloncraft discovered that child-care concerns were at the root of high turnover, excessive absenteeism, and low employee morale; the company set up an on-site "learning center" in 1981.

The retention of valuable employees was found to be the result of flexible work scheduling. Sixty-eight percent of the respondent companies surveyed by Catalyst, a New York City-based research group, claimed this scheduling resulted in a positive effect on retention; 58 percent said it resulted in the same effect on recruitment, and 65 percent said that those working a flexible schedule sustained higher productivity. Increased job satisfaction leading to higher productivity has been reported by a majority of the employees who use a flexible work schedule at Pacific Bell. A report cited by Peterson (1980) documents that eight of eleven firms offering flextime reported a decrease in absenteeism, tardiness, and overtime costs, and an increase in worker morale and productivity.

*LouEllen Crawford*

**Bibliography**

Bauer, Gary L. 1990. "Congress Gets the Child-Care Issue Wrong." *Wall Street Journal*. October 10:A16.

Callahan, James, Jr., and Stanley S. Wallack, eds. 1981. *Reforming the Long-Term System*. Lexington, Mass.: D.C. Heath.

Clifford, Jane. 1991. "Children Who Serve as Caregivers Usually Ill-Prepared." *Gazette Telegraph*. May 19:E12.

Cordtz, Dan. 1990. "Hire Me, Hire My Family." *Financial World* 159(September 18):76–79.

Crawford, LouEllen. 1990. *Dependent Care and the Employee Benefits Package*. Westport, Conn.: Quorum.

Creedon, Michael A., ed. 1987. *Issues for an Aging America: Employers and Eldercare*. Southport, Conn.: Creative Services.

England, Suzanne E. 1989. "Eldercare Leaves and Employer Policies: Feminist Perspectives." In *Proceedings of First Annual Women's Policy Research Conference*, pp. 117–21. Washington, D.C.: Institute for Women's Policy Research.

Kuriansky, Joan. 1991. "Recognizing Caregiving Realities and Other Challenges for Congress." *OWL Observer* (May-June):2.

Martin, Virginia Hider, and Jo Hartley. 1975. *Hours of Work When Workers Can Choose*. Washington, D.C.: Business and Professional Women's Foundation.

Peterson, Donald J. 1980. "Flextime in the United States: The Lessons of Experience." *Personnel* (January–February):21–31.

Sullivan, Joyce. 1981. "Family Support Systems Paychecks Can't Buy." *Family Relations* 30(4):607–13.

# Providing for Children in the Work/Family Arrangement

### Planning to Combine Work and Child-Rearing

This article considers how women construct plans to combine work and family and factors that encourage or discourage them from matching their early plans. About two-thirds of all women create specific plans to combine employment and child-rearing by the time they are finished with school. Among the others, about two-thirds have general plans about an occupational career goal or desired family size but do not have strategies for achieving these goals; the rest have few plans and prefer to live day by day. When making plans, women report that they are more likely to change their choices about the number and timing of children to fit their career plans than to change their career plans to fit their childbirth desires. The extent of challenge, responsibility, and financial reward of early jobs; the support of job supervisors and husbands; personally valuing employment or home-making; and timing of marriage and childbirth are the factors most likely to influence women to maintain or to change their minds between their early plans and later actions.

### Plans for Integrating Employment and Child-Rearing

During the first half of this century, the most common role pattern among white upper- and middle-class women was to be either a single career woman or a mother so that plans to integrate these roles were rare. Many minority and lower-class women did raise children and work outside of their home, but documentation of their plans is anecdotal.

During the second half of the twentieth century, women have developed plans to combine employment and child-rearing in either a sequential or simultaneous pattern. For example, during the 1970s and 1980s, about one-third of white girls and two-thirds of black girls either planned to be or were employed within one year following childbirth, thus undertaking these roles simultaneously (Granrose and Cunningham 1988; Macke and Morgan 1978; Simms 1988). About half of the remainder planned to work after completing school, to leave the labor force at childbirth, and perhaps return to employment when the last child was independent, a sequential pattern. The rest had no specific plans. The most notable historical trend in these plans is an increase in the amount of time engaged in both roles simultaneously. This occurs because more women have planned to and have returned to employment sooner after childbirth in more recent years than in the past (Eggebeen 1988; Harmon 1989; Helson and Picano 1990; Sullivan 1992).

The strategies for combining employment and child-rearing most commonly included in these plans are working part time, waiting until after children are in school to return to work, hiring household help, placing children in day-care centers, and getting husbands to help. The most common threats requiring a change in plans that young women foresee are equally divided between financial need and employer policies (Granrose 1985).

Factors that influence women to select a more or less simultaneous plan include commitment to a career, the anticipated consequences of staying home or returning to work, normative expectations of friends and family, and maternal role models (Granrose and Cunningham 1988; Greenberger et al. 1988; Helson and Picano 1990; Hock et al. 1985). The factor most often playing a decisive role is the perception of what would be best for the child. Women who plan a more simultaneous pattern are more confident than women planning a less simultaneous or a sequential pattern that they will have enough time and skills to manage both work and family, and they anticipate fewer harmful effects to their children if they are employed.

Friends' opinions and women's expectations about their future husbands play a significant role in constructing plans for combining a career and child-rearing. Women who are members of a couple are more likely to develop more detailed and sophisticated work and child-rearing plans and to consider more alternatives if their first plans cannot be executed. Friends, parents, and spouses who support maternal work are likely to influence women to plan for a more simultaneous pattern (Baber and Monaghan 1988; Granrose and Cunningham 1988).

Women also commonly report adopting a plan based on what their mothers did or did not do. In some cases, mothers served as a positive role model that daughters wished to emulate; in other cases daughters learned what not to do from watching their dissatisfied mothers (Amstey and Whitbourne 1988; Granrose and Cunningham 1988). This negative role modeling is often reported by white daughters of bored, unemployed mothers and black daughters of mothers employed in difficult, low-paying, blue-collar jobs (Macke and Morgan 1978). If their mothers were absent or presented a model of what not to do, women report planning their lives after mothers of friends, older sisters, and grand-mothers.

The impact of career plans on child-bearing plans is more common than the reverse (Granrose 1985; Waite and Stolzenberg 1976). Many women plan to delay or reduce the number of children and a few would have their children further apart because of their career plans. A small minority say they would change careers or jobs because of the number or timing of children they plan to have. In the past, more white women than black women have planned to do less full-time work because of their child-bearing or child-rearing plans, even taking into consideration financial differences, but this racial difference is decreasing (Simms 1988).

## Stability or Change between Plans and Actions

Environmental circumstances in employment or maternity that conflict with plans set limits on the extent to which plans are implemented (Rexroat and Shehan 1984). For example, if a woman plans to combine employment and child-rearing simultaneously using a helpful spouse to assist in child care, but she fails to marry, to get pregnant or to hold a job, she cannot implement her previous plans. Evidence of stability between occupational aspirations and later behavior indicates a positive relationship between plans and behavior that is fairly strong ($r = 0.4$ to $0.5$) for shorter time periods but weakens ($r = 0.15$ to $0.2$) if the time period examined extends to as many as ten years, a common duration between occupational choice and child-bearing (Jacobs 1989; Sewell et al. 1980). The impact of child-rearing plans or experiences on these occupational changes is not fully understood, however.

If environmental constraints do not occur, the strongest factor that contributes to stability between plans, and actions is personal commitment to a career role for simultaneous plans, and commitment to the homemaker role and exclusive maternal care for sequential plans (Amstey and Whitbourne 1988; Hock et al. 1985). Those who are unsure which role they prefer when the plans are made are more likely to change their minds later.

In addition to personal commitment, a few specific life experiences are often found to influence a change in plans. Among those who plan simultaneous employment and child-rearing, those who change their minds are more likely to have experienced job supervisors and husbands who disapprove of maternal employment; jobs that they find unchallenging, unrewarding, and stressful; or more children, earlier children, or children born closer together than they expected. Among those who planned to leave the labor force for longer periods during child-rearing, those who later changed their minds were more likely to be more career oriented, to have supervisors and husbands who supported maternal work; more education; more interesting jobs; more aversion to fussy or difficult babies; or more financial need than they expected (Eggebeen 1988; Gerson 1985; Granrose 1992; Hock et al. 1985; Spitze and Waite 1980). Consistent with historical trends, women were more likely to spend more time in simultaneous roles of mother and employee that they had planned than the reverse (Harmon 1989; Granrose 1992).

In summary, a woman's personal preference for the worker or homemaker role and perceptions of what will benefit her child are the key determinants of the plans she constructs and the consistency between plans and actions. Support from others who are important to her and unexpected child-bearing patterns also play key roles in making and changing plans.

*Cherlyn Skromme Granrose*

## Bibliography

Amstey, F., and S. Whitbourne. 1988. "Work and Motherhood: Transition to Parenthood and Women's Employment. *Journal of Genetic Psychology* 149:111–18.

Baber, K., and P. Monaghan. 1988. "College Women's Career and Motherhood Expectations: New Options, Old Dilemmas." *Sex Roles* 19:189–203.

Eggebeen, D. 1988. "Determinants of Maternal Employment for White Preschool Children: 1960–1980." *Journal of Marriage and the Family* 50:149–59.

Gerson, K. 1985. *Hard Choices*. Berkeley: University of California Press.

Granrose, C. 1992. "Consistency and Change in Plans for Maternal Employment." In *Working Paper*. Philadelphia: Temple University Department of Human Resource Administration.

———. 1985. "Plans for Work Careers among College Women Who Expect to Have Families." *Vocational Guidance Quarterly* 34:284–95.

Granrose, C., and E. Cunningham. 1988. "Postpartum Work Intentions among Black and White College Women." *Career Development Quarterly* 37:2149–64.

Greenberger, E., W. Goldberg, T.J. Crawford, and J. Granger. 1988. "Beliefs about the Consequences of Maternal Employment for Children. *Psychology of Women Quarterly* 12:35–59.

Harmon, L. 1989. "Longitudinal Changes in Women's Career Aspirations: Developmental or Historical?" *Journal of Vocational Behavior* 35:46–63.

Helson, R., and J. Picano. 1990. "Is the Traditional Role Bad for Women?" *Journal of Personality and Social Psychology* 59:311–20.

Hock, E., K. Morgan, and M. Hock. 1985. "Employment Decisions Made by Mothers of Infants." *Psychology of Women Quarterly* 9:383–402.

Jacobs, J. 1989. *Revolving Doors: Sex Segregation and Women's Careers*. Stanford: Stanford University Press.

Macke, A., and W. Morgan. 1978. "Mother's Employment and Daughter's Work Orientation: A Test of Alternative Socialization Processes for Blacks and Whites." *Social Forces* 57:187–204.

Rexroat, C., and C. Shehan. 1984. "Expected versus Actual Work Roles of Women." *American Sociological Review* 49:349–58.

Sewell, W., R. Hauser, and W. Wolf. 1980. "Sex, Schooling and Occupational Status." *American Journal of Sociology* 86:551–83.

Simms, M. 1988. "The Choices that Young Black Women Make: Education, Employment, and Family Formation." *Working paper No 190*. Wellesley, Mass.: Wellesley College Center for Research on Women.

Spitze, G., and L. Waite. 1980. "Labor Force and Work Attitudes: Young Womens' Early Experiences." *Sociology of Work and Occupations* 7:3–32.

Sullivan, S. 1992. "Is There a Time for Everything? Attitudes Related to Women's Sequencing of Career and Family." *Career Development Quarterly* 40:234–43.

Waite, L., and R. Stolzenberg. 1976. "Intended Childbearing and Labor Force Participation of Young Women: Insights from Nonrecursive Models." *American Sociological Review* 41:235–52.

## Employment and Child Care

In recent years the need for child care has increased tremendously. In 1987, 55 percent of women with children age three years or under were employed, compared with less than 25 percent in 1967 (Shank 1988). Unfortunately, adequate policies regarding child care are lacking in the United States as is research on child-care needs (Scarr et al. 1989).

Parents also lack the information necessary to make adequate judgments about child care. Three quarters of the mothers surveyed by Rabinovich et al. (1988) indicated that they had received conflicting information about whether, how often, or with whom to leave their infants. Seventy-five percent of these mothers also reported they needed more information about the issues of mother-infant separations and substitute care.

The type of child care that parents use varies tremendously. The child may be cared for in his or her own home, in the caretaker's home, or in an institutional setting (day-care center). The caretaker may be a relative or a stranger. In a nationwide survey of employed mothers with children under one year, Klein (1985) found the majority of nonmaternal care was provided by a relative (father, grandparents, or other relative). Home-based care (infant's home or caregiver's home) by a nonrelative was the next most frequent type of care. Day-care centers were used by less than 6 percent of the employed mothers with infants. As children grow older the use of day-care centers increases (Hock et al. 1988), however relatives still provide a majority of the care (Hofferth and Phillips 1991).

The availability of day-care centers and licensed day-care homes has increased dramatically (Hofferth and Phillips 1991). Since 1976 the number of centers has tripled and the number of licensed day-care homes has increased by a third. However, a relatively large percentage (40 percent) of women report that finding substitute caregivers was difficult (Rabinovich et. al. 1988). The availability of day-care centers may vary by geographic area and the cost may make them prohibitive to parents. Currently, low-income parents may pay 20 to 25 percent of their income for child care.

The type of care chosen for use by parents is influenced by many different factors. Two of the most important factors are cost and availability of care (Hock et al. 1988). Other factors that influence the parental decision include location, flexibility, number of hours of operation, relation of the caregiver to the family, curriculum, number and ages of children, mother's and father's income, hours of maternal employment, parental education, parental experiences in day care, and mother's anxiety about separation from the infant (Hock et al. 1988; Lehrer 1983).

The type of child care parents can afford may have an influence on the quality of care the child receives (Hofferth and Phillips 1991). Quality of child care is enhanced by the education and training of the caregivers, small child-to-staff ratios, and staff stability. All of these characteristics may be directly related to the cost of the care. Currently, parents spend an average of sixty-three dollars per week for the care of their preschool children. This relatively low cost is made possible by low wages for the caregivers and large child-to-staff ratios (Hofferth 1992).

Parental satisfaction with child-care arrangements may be influenced by many different factors, including difficulty in obtaining care and the quality of the care. Bradbard and Endsley (1986) have developed a model that describes the different factors and their interaction that may influence the mother's satisfaction with child-care arrangements. Included in the model is the mother's self-concept, her ability to competently adapt to her many roles. Equally important are family influences such as the support of the spouse and the child's reactions to the child-care arrangement. Community influences such as social networks, extended family members, employers, and expert information as well as society's view of mothers who are employed and utilize child care all have an influence on the mother's satisfaction with child care.

Satisfaction with child-care arrangements may have an impact on both the mother and infant. Mother's satisfaction with child care has a positive relationship to her work satisfaction (Harrell and Ridley 1975), and the fewer types of child-care arrangements the mother must rely on (the more "hassle" free ) the greater her satisfaction with her roles (that is, being employed and a parent).

Mother's satisfaction with child-care arrangements also has an impact on the infant. Weinraub et al. (1988) found mothers who were satisfied with child-care arrangements more likely to have infants who were securely attached. Stable alternate child-care arrangements also influence infant-parent attachment. The instability in caregiving arrangements was associated with a greater likelihood of at least one insecure attachment to the parents (Goldberg and Easterbrooks 1988).

By 1995 it is predicted that 66 percent of children under the age of six will have mothers in the workplace (Hofferth 1992). Child care is an important factor in a mother's ability to function adequately in the workforce. Presently, parents in the United States are faced with a lack of good, low-cost child care and support for their use of child care.

*Diane E. Wille*

## Bibliography

Bradbard, M., and R. Endsley. 1986. "Sources of Variance in Young Working Mothers' Satisfaction with Child Care: A Transactional Model and New Research Directions." *Advances in Early Education and Day Care* 4:181–207.

Goldberg, W., and M.A. Easterbrooks. 1988. "Maternal Employment when Children Are Toddlers and Kindergartners." In *Maternal Employment and Children's Development,* edited by A. Gottfried and A. Gottfried, pp. 121–54. New York: Plenum.

Harrell, J., and C. Ridley. 1975. "Substitute Child Care, Maternal Employment and the Quality of Mother-Child Interaction." *Journal of Marriage and the Family* 37:556–64.

Hock, E., D. DeMeis, and S. McBride. 1988. "Maternal Separation Anxiety: Its Role in the Balance of Employment and Motherhood in Mothers of Infants." In *Maternal Employment and Children's Development,* edited by A. Gottfried and A. Gottfried, pp. 191–229. New York: Plenum.

Hofferth, S. 1992. "The Demand for and Supply of Child Care in the 1990s." In *Child Care in the 1990s: Trends and Consequences,* edited by A. Booth. Hillsdale, N.J.: Lawrence Erlbaum.

Hofferth, S., and D. Phillips. 1991. "Child Care Policy Research." *Journal of Social Issues* 47:1–13.

Klein, R. 1985. "Caregiving Arrangements by Employed Women with Children under 1 Year of Age." *Developmental Psychology* 21:403–6.

Lehrer, E. 1983. "Determinants of Child Are Mode Choice: An Economic Perspective." *Social Science Research* 12:69–80.

Rabinovich, B., M. Zaslow, J. Suwalsky, R. Klein, and N. Gist. 1988. *Mothers' Feelings about Separations and Substitute Care: A Descriptive Study.* Paper presented at the meeting of the International Conference on Infant Studies, Washington, D.C.

Scarr, S., D. Phillips, and K. McCartney. 1989. "Dilemmas of Child Care in the United States: Employed Mothers and Children at Risk." *Canadian Psychology* 30:126–39.

Shank, S. 1988. "Women and the Labor Market: The Link Grows Stronger." *Monthly Labor Review* 111:3–8.

Weinraub, M., E. Jaeger, and L. Hoffman. 1988. "Predicting Infant Outcome in Families of Employed and Nonemployed Mothers." *Early Childhood Research Quarterly* 3:361–78.

## Shift Work and Child Care

Today, over half of all married couples with children have both spouses work to support the family, and one-third of full-time, dual-earner couples with children have at least one spouse who works other than a regular day shift (Presser 1987). Approximately 18 percent of the 80.5 million full-time employees have work schedules that differ from the regular daytime pattern according to the U.S. Bureau of Labor Statistics (1992). One out of every six working mothers and one out of every five fathers with children under fourteen holds an evening or night job or a rotating shift, according to Harriet Presser (1987). As a result, one out of every six two-income couples with children under the age of six has work hours that do not overlap at all (McEnroe 1991).

Presser's 1988 study of young parents with a child under age five found that when mothers worked a fixed, nonday shift, child care was provided by the father 28 percent of the time and by other relatives 31.5 percent of the time. When mothers worked part time, fathers provided child care 42.9 percent of the time and other relatives 35.6 percent of the time. When fathers worked fixed, nonday shifts, mothers provided care 42.4 percent and other relatives provided care 38.3 percent of the time. Approximately one-fourth of the child care is provided by a grandmother, although one-third of them are working full time (Presser 1988).

One reason parents work these shifts is that employers need or require this type of work. Shift work is less common in the higher-paid sectors of the economy, with only 11 percent of professionals (other than health care) and only 9 percent of managerial personnel working these hours. Shift work is most prevalent among workers in service occupations, where 42 percent work these hours, according to the U.S. Bureau of Labor Statistics (1992). This is the fastest-growing sector of the economy and a sector that hires a large number of women. Although these are lower-paid fields, employers often pay higher wages to those individuals willing to work evenings and weekends. Some parents are willing to work those shifts in order to get more money or because they are the only jobs available. Another advantage is that the couple can enjoy a dual-income without the added cost of child care. According to McEnroe, on the average child care uses up approximately one-sixth of the family income. For low-wage earners, child care, especially for more than one child, may cost close to the earning capacity of the parent, making work economically profitable only if a relative can provide free child care.

Other working parents choose to work nonoverlapping shifts because they feel that parental care should not be substituted for or that their children are best cared for by family members.

While some parents find this arrangement preferable or the only one economically feasible, there are some disadvantages. In essence, this means that parents working split shifts are both full-time workers and full-time primary caregivers. They are similar to single parents with two incomes (McEnroe 1991). This arrangement leaves parents little leisure time to rest, be together, or even sleep. Parents with more traditional gender-role expectations may be dissatisfied with the wife's working outside the home and the husband's performance of domestic duties. More egalitarian couples may see this as an advantage.

The increase in shift work creates new child-care problems for parents who do not have spouses or other relatives who provide child care. When these parents work nontraditional shifts because it is the best or only employment available, they find few child-care centers open at the times that they need them. They are often left with few viable child-care alternatives. Parents that work rotating shifts have even greater problems adjusting family life and arranging child care.

The growing number of shift-work jobs available affords a workable child-care arrangement for some families; however, shift work poses additional child-care problems and stresses for other families.

*Allie Funk*

*Margaret McLean Hughes*

## Bibliography

Herta, R., and J. Charlton. 1989. "Making Family under a Shift Work Schedule: Air Force Security Guards and Their Wives." *Social Problems* 36:491–507.

McEnroe, J. 1991. "Split-Shift Parenting." *American Demographics* 13(February):50–52.

Presser, H.B. 1986. "Shift Work among American Women and Child Care." *Journal of Marriage and the Family* 48:551–63.

———. 1988. "Shift Work and Child Care among Young Dual-Earner American Parents." *Journal of Marriage and the Family* 50: 133–48.

———. 1987. "Work Shifts of Full-Time Dual-Earner Couples: Patterns and Contrasts by Sex of Spouse." *Demography* 24:99–112.

U.S. Bureau of Labor Statistics. 1992. *Workers on Flexible and Shift Schedules* (USDL 92-491). Washington, D.C.: U.S. Government Printing Office.

## Maternal Role Conflict

Though the employed mother is a norm today (Zill 1991), many mothers are in conflict concerning their roles as worker and mother. Historically, women have participated in productive labor concurrently with child-bearing and child-rearing (Rossi 1977). It is only recently that the Industrial Revolution has created an economy that allows some women to be full-time mothers. In contemporary American society, women feel pressure to stay at home and raise their children and to enter the labor force (McCartney and Phillips 1988). This return to the labor force, after the birth of their infant, is often compelled by a financial need (Owen and Cox 1988).

Though employment may create conflict for the mother, it also has the potential to have positive effects (Hoffman 1989). Mothers who are employed report a higher level of personal life satisfaction. Employment has also been found to act as a buffer against stress from family roles. However, the dual roles of worker and mother may be stressful for women. Best (1988) suggests that the stress felt by mothers of young children may be due to role overload rather than role conflict. The increase in participation of women in the workforce has not been met with an increase in participation by males in child care and housework (Managhan and Parcel 1990).

One important aspect of the mother's role conflict is her feelings about separation from her infant. The basis for these feelings may be cultural or biological. Currently, in our culture mothers are considered to play the most important role in the lives of their infants. The biological components of the mother's need for closeness to her infant is emphasized by the ethological theory (Bowlby 1969).

Hock et al. (1989) recently developed a scale to assess the mother's anxiety about separation from her infant and her perception of separation effects on the infant. Infant characteristics appear to have an impact on maternal separation anxiety. Mothers are more concerned about the effect of separation with their first-born infants (Pitzer 1984), and separation anxiety decreases as the child matures (Hock et al. 1988; Hock and Schirtzinger 1992).

A relationship is also found between maternal employment and anxiety about separation from the infant (McBride 1990; McBride and Belsky 1988). Mothers who are employed report lower levels of employment-related separation anxiety. Higher levels of separation anxiety were associated with a return to work later in the infant's life and working fewer hours per week.

Maternal employment preference may also have an impact on the mother's separation anxiety and perception of the impact of separation on the infant (Hock et al. 1988). Mothers who prefer employment were less anxious about separation and less concerned about the effects of separation on their infant. Mothers who prefer employment may be less invested in the role of mother. For these individuals, motherhood is one of their many roles that they must balance and integrate. Low levels of separation anxiety are associated with mothers who are less traditional in their sex-role behavior (Hock and Schirtzinger 1992). The mother's role preference rather than employment, per se, may have a greater impact on the mother's psychological well-being. Hock and DeMeis (1990) investigated the link between maternal preference for employment and depression and stress. Homemakers who preferred employment outside of the home had higher levels of depression symptomology than women whose preference and employment matched (homemakers who preferred to stay home and women working outside of the home who preferred this) and women who were employed who preferred to stay home.

Employment has been found to have both positive and negative effects on mothers. The negative effects center upon role overload, which may be alleviated by the spouse's level of involvement in child care and housework (Baruch et al. 1983). Role stress may also be associated with the mother's anxiety about separation from her infant. This anxiety is interrelated with the mother's employment preference and may influence her level of involvement in the workforce. The mother's role preference rather than employment or role stress may have a greater impact on her psychological well-being.

*Diane E. Wille*

## Bibliography

Baruch, G., R. Barnett, and C. Rivers. 1983. *Lifeprints.* New York: McGraw-Hill.

Best, M. 1988. *Conflict Experienced between Roles in Employed Mothers of Infants.* Paper presented at the meeting of the International Conference on Infant Studies, Washington, D.C.

Bowlby, J. 1969. *Attachment and Loss.* Vol. 1: Attachment. New York: Basic Books.

Hock, E., and D. DeMeis. 1990. "Depression in Mothers of Infants: The Role of Maternal Employment." *Developmental Psychology* 26:285–91.

Hock, E., S. DeMeis, and S. McBride. 1988. "Maternal Separation Anxiety: Its Role in the Balance of Employment and Motherhood in Mothers of Infants." In *Maternal Employment and Children's Development,* edited by A. Gottfried and A. Gottfried, pp. 191–229. New York: Plenum.

Hock, E., S. McBride, and M. Gnezda. 1989. "Maternal Separation Anxiety: Mother-Infant Separation from the Maternal Perspective." *Child Development* 60:793–802.

Hock, E., and M. Schirtzinger. 1992. "Maternal Separation Anxiety: Its Developmental Course and Relation to Maternal Mental Health." *Child Development* 63:93–102.

Hoffman, L. 1989. "Effects of Maternal Employment in the Two-Parent Family." *American Psychologist* 44:283–92.

Managhan, E., and T. Parcel. 1990. "Parental Employment and Family Life: Research in the 1980s." *Journal of Marriage and the Family* 58:1079–98.

McBride, S. 1990. "Maternal Moderators of Child Care: The Role of Maternal Separation Anxiety." *New Directions for Child Development* 49:53–70.

McBride, S., and J. Belsky. 1988. "Characteristics, Determinants, and Consequences of Maternal Separation Anxiety." *Developmental Psychology* 24:407–14.

McCartney, K., and D. Phillips. 1988. "Motherhood and Child Care." In *The Different Faces of Motherhood,* edited by B. Birns and D. Hay. New York: Plenum.

Owen, M., and M. Cox. 1988. "Maternal Employment and the Transition to Parenthood." In *Maternal Employment and Children's Development,* edited by A. Gottfried and A. Gottfried, pp. 85–119. New York: Plenum.

Pitzer, M. 1984. *A Study of Maternal Separation Anxiety in Working Mothers of Second-Born Infants.* Doctoral dissertation, Ohio State University.

Rossi, A. 1977. "Biosocial Perspectives on Parenting." *Daedalus* 106:1–31.

Zill, N. 1991. "U.S. Children and Their Families: Current Conditions and Recent Trends, 1989." *SRCD Newsletter* 1–3.

## Maternal Occupational Conditions and Children's Family Environments

As the prevalence of employment among American mothers of young children has risen, much research has considered possible effects of maternal work experiences on children's lives. Early studies of such effects typically contrasted employed with nonemployed mothers on various cognitive and social child outcomes, with largely inconclusive results (Hoffman 1989). More recent studies have expanded this line of research in two important ways. First, studies have begun to focus more directly on the patterns of family interaction that mediate the effects of maternal employment on child outcomes (Menaghan 1991). Second, as the proportion of mothers who are employed has increased, attention has turned to variation in the occupational conditions that employed mothers experience and to theoretical arguments linking occupational conditions to family interaction and home environments.

Children's family environments are an important influence on child outcomes. Prior research treating home environments as an independent variable has shown that the quality of children's family environments is positively related to their later academic achievement and emotional well-being (Bradley et al. 1988; Parcel and Menaghan 1990; Rogers et al. 1991). Yet relatively little is known about how social factors, including maternal work, affect the quality of the young child's family environment. Early research on determinants of family environments has emphasized the effects of individual parental attributes, particularly maternal educational attainment and intellectual capacities, and household composition, including the number of children and father's presence, as well as total family economic resources (Belsky 1984; Bradley 1985). Occupational and economic factors have received relatively little attention. In the interest of expanding our understanding of work-family linkages, this brief entry reviews theoretical arguments positing relationships between maternal working conditions and family environments; it also summarizes some empirical evidence on the role that maternal working conditions play in shaping the home environments that working mothers are able to provide their young children.

Occupational effects on children's family environments are produced in several ways. Clearly, earnings from jobs are crucial in providing needed material resources for children. But in addition, the character of work experiences affects adult outcomes and thus family interaction. The substantive demands of occupations increase adults' own intellectual functioning, as reflected in more complexity and flexibility in cognitive processes. Second, parental occupations influence the values and beliefs that parents hold, and these values and beliefs are important determinants of parental child-rearing behaviors. Third, work conditions also affect individual emotional distress. In turn, parents' intellectual functioning, beliefs, and values, and level of emotional distress affect parent-child interaction.

Social structure and personality theorists have been influential in developing theoretically expected relationships between occupational conditions and adult psychological functioning. Both cross-sectional and longitudinal studies have shown that more substantively complex work, which provides greater opportunities to exercise self-direction and independent judgment, enhances intellectual flexibility (Kohn et al. 1983).

Experiences on the job also shape individual beliefs and values, including parents' child-rearing values; job incumbents come to value the characteristics demanded on the job more generally, for themselves and for their children. Kohn and his colleagues have documented that parents with jobs that permit greater occupational self-direction place a greater value on their children's autonomy as well, with somewhat less concern with strict conformity to parental demands. Luster and his colleagues (1989) show that such occupation-linked values affect observed parent-child interaction: Parents who value conformity are more concerned with parental control and more fearful of spoiling their children; accordingly, they are less warm and involved and restrict their young children's actions more frequently.

Work stress research has shown that the conditions of work that are more common in less desirable jobs—routinization, low autonomy, heavy supervision, and little demand or opportunity for substantively complex work—exacerbate psychological distress and reduce self-esteem and personal control. To the extent that work experiences leave parents feeling uncertain of their own worth and emotionally distressed, they are less able to be emotionally available to their children or to provide them with responsive, stimulating environments (Belsky and Eggebeen 1991; Menaghan 1991). Such effects may be exacerbated by other difficult family conditions, such as absence of a spouse or high marital discord.

Occupations offering less desirable working conditions also tend to offer fewer extrinsic benefits as well. Low wages and few benefits are distressing in their own right, and the concomitant psychological distress affects parent-child interaction (Conger et al. 1984; Siegal 1984). Low wages also make it more difficult for parents to provide needed material resources to children, and homes are more impoverished in terms of play materials, children's books, newspapers, and magazines. In addition, low-wage jobs often further compromise children's home environments because more total work hours are needed to accumulate sufficient family income, thus reducing time and energy for satisfying interaction (Nock and Kingston 1988).

Much of the empirical work related to these arguments has focused on characteristics of fathers' jobs rather than mothers' or has been concerned with total family income without isolating effects of maternal wages. Recent work on maternal occupational conditions and family environments provides more direct support for these arguments (Menaghan and Parcel 1991). This work utilizes data from the mother and child data sets collected as part of the National Longitudinal Survey of Youth (NLSY), a longitudinal study of youth born between 1958 and 1965 and their children. Employed mothers are likely to differ from unemployed mothers in ways that represent selection effects into employment as well as causal effects of employment. Menaghan and Parcel therefore controlled for maternal age, socioeconomic status of mother's family of origin, maternal cognitive achievement and educational attainment, and sense of mastery and self-esteem, as well as child gender and health.

Family environments were assessed using a combination of maternal report and interviewer observation, using a set of items derived from the Home Observation for Measurement of the Environment (HOME) (Bradley 1985). These tapped three major aspects of family environments: cognitive variables, including language stimulation, provision of a variety of stimulating experiences and materials, and encouragement of child achievement; social variables, including responsiveness, warmth, and encouragement of maturity; and physical environmental variables, including amount of sensory input and organization of the physical environment.

Three aspects of maternal working conditions were considered: occupational complexity, wage levels, and usual hours worked per week. Occupational measures use data from the U.S. Dictionary of Occupational Titles. This approach to measurement of occupational conditions is noteworthy as it provides a means to attach more detailed information regarding maternal work than is typically collected in many studies of family environments, so long as sufficient information has been collected to code occupation by U.S. Census codes.

Menaghan and Parcel found that the mother's occupational complexity contributed to home environment, even when maternal background characteristics and current family circumstances were controlled. Having higher numbers of children in the family, however, detracted from the home environment, presumably because parental energies must be diffused among more children. Maternal characteristics were also of major importance. Mexican-American and black mothers scored lower than whites and other Hispanics on the home measure. Older mothers and those who had completed more years of schooling also provided better home environments. In addition, mothers with a stronger internal locus of control and high self-esteem created stronger home environments for their children than mothers whose locus of control was more external and who had lower self-esteem.

The finding that the complexity of current maternal occupation exerts a significant effect on a child's family environment lends further support to social structure and personality frameworks that argue that the working conditions parents face on the job influence parental values and behaviors relevant to parenting. Home environments in turn have a major impact on child verbal knowledge (Parcel and Menaghan 1990), suggesting that mothers' occupational complexity, operating in part through home environments, influences critical cognitive resources that their children will use in the achievement of their own occupational outcomes. Home environments are also important predictors of early childhood behavior problems (see Rogers et al. 1991), suggesting that the effects of maternal occupational experiences are socioemotional as well as cognitive.

Prior research and theory had suggested that the conditions adults experience at work affect their own cognitive functioning, their attitudes and values, and their emotional well-being; it is increasingly clear that when these adult workers are mothers these conditions have intergenerational repercussions on children's lives as well. Additional study of the processes by which employed women's working conditions come to shape their children's daily life and future prospects is needed to fulfill the potential of these investigations. In particular, current cross-sectional studies must be augmented by studies of stability and change in both maternal occupational circumstances and children's family environments. For children in dual-earner families, more understanding is needed regarding the relative and joint impact of paternal and maternal occupational experiences. Given the multiple theoretical arguments linking occupational experiences to adult and child outcomes, it is not surprising that empirical investigations along these links are increasing.

*Elizabeth G. Menaghan*

## Bibliography

Belsky, Jay. 1984. "The Determinants of Parenting: A Process Model." *Child Development* 55:83–96.

Belsky, Jay, and David Eggebeen. 1991. "Early and Extensive Maternal Employment and Young Children's Socioemotional Development: Children of the National Longitudinal Survey of Youth." *Journal of Marriage and the Family* 53:1083–1110.

Bradley, R.H. 1985. "The HOME Inventory: Rationale and Research." In *Recent Research in Developmental Psychopathology*, edited by J. Lachenmeyer and M. Gibbs, pp. 191–201. New York: Gardner.

Bradley, R., H.B. Caldwell, and S.R. Rock. 1988. "Home Environment and School Performance: A Ten-Year Follow-up and Examination of Three Models of Environmental Action." *Child Development* 59:852–67.

Conger, Rand D., J.A. McCarty, R.K. Yang, B.B. Lahey, and J.P. Kropp. 1984. "Perceptions of Child, Child-Rearing Values, and Emotional Distress as Mediating Links between Environmental Stressors and Observed Maternal Behavior." *Child Development* 55:2234–47.

Hoffman, Lois W. 1989. "Effects of Maternal Employment in the Two-Parent Family." *American Psychologist* 44:283–92.

Kohn, M.L., C. Schooler, and J. Miller. 1983. *Work and Personality: An Inquiry into the Impact of Social Stratification*. Norwood, N.J.: Ablex.

Luster, T., K. Rhoades, and B. Haas. 1989. "The Relation between Parental Values and Parenting Behavior: A Test of the Kohn Hypothesis." *Journal of Marriage and the Family* 51:139–47.

Menaghan, E.G. 1991. "Work Experiences and Family Interaction Processes: The Long Reach of the Job?" *Annual Review of Sociology* 17:419–44.

Menaghan, E.G., and T.L. Parcel. 1991. "Determining Children's Home Environments: The Impact of Maternal Characteristics and Current Occupational and Family Conditions." *Journal of Marriage and the Family* 53:417–31.

Nock, S.L., and P.W. Kingston. 1988. "Time with Children: The Impact of Couples' Work-Time Commitments." *Social Forces* 67:59–85.

Parcel, T.L., and E.G. Menaghan. 1990. "Maternal Working Conditions and Child Verbal Facility: Studying the Intergenerational Transmission of Inequality from Mothers to Young Children." *Social Psychology Quarterly* 53:132–47.

Rogers, S.J., T.L. Parcel, and E.G. Menaghan. 1991. "The Effects of Maternal Working Conditions and Mastery on Children's Behavior Problems: Studying the Intergenerational Transmission of Social Control." *Journal of Health and Social Behavior* 32:145–64.

Siegal, M. 1984. "Economic Deprivation and the Quality of Parent-Child Relations: A Trickle-Down Framework." *Journal of Applied Developmental Psychology* 5:127–44.

## Maternal Working Conditions, Childcare, and Cognition

The dramatic increase in paid employment among mothers of young children prompts questions concerning the impact of such employment on child outcomes. Certainly given the demonstrated links between cognition and school performance, and between school performance and adult occupational and economic outcomes, the impact of paid maternal employment on child cognitive outcomes is a topic of major concern. This question, however, cannot be addressed in isolation from the issue of the impact of alternative care arrangements on children of working mothers. Although not always addressed simultaneously, the questions are closely intertwined: The need for child care varies with the demands of employment, and the arrangements a mother can afford may vary importantly with income derived from her labor. Literature on both of these topics has progressed from studies of whether alternative care or maternal employment influences child outcomes to analysis of whether variations in maternal employment or child-care arrangements influence children positively, negatively, or not at all.

Initially, researchers contrasted children of employed and nonemployed mothers and found few consistent differences as well as conflicting findings (see Hoffman and Nye 1974 for a summary). Many of these early studies used small samples, concentrated on reported tests of statistical significance at the expense of parameter estimation, failed to test hypotheses on statistical interaction even when theories suggested that the effects of employment might vary by child or family characteristics, and as a group failed to use common theoretical and empirical strategies, thus hampering cumulation of findings. With a few exceptions, the studies were cross-sectional, as opposed to longitudinal in design, thus hampering confident assessment of causality. More recently researchers have turned to studies that investigate how variations in employment experiences influence maternal well-being and intellectual flexibility, resources likely to influence parent-child interaction and, potentially, child outcomes. For example, Miller et al. (1979) demonstrate that occupational self-direction and job pressures affect employed women's well-being, self-evaluation, intellectual flexibility, and sense of efficacy. Other research links maternal outcomes with mother-child interaction and suggests that mothers with a stronger internal locus of control and higher psychological well-being display more attentive and stimulating parental behavior.

Similarly, Belsky (1984) distinguishes two waves of day-care research. The first contrasted day-care/non-day-care children and was subject to two flaws: Most studies used university-based, high-quality day-care settings not typical of the arrangements of children in nonmaternal care, and most failed to control for preexisting differences likely to characterize "home" and "day-care" children even before variation in care was experienced. Few significant or consistent differences were found. Two, however, are noteworthy. In contrast to cultural expectations regarding the superiority of home care, enrollment in high-quality day care seemed to prevent the decline in cognitive functioning from infancy through age six that has been observed among economically disadvantaged home-reared children. Most recent work, however, suggests that enrollment in unstable or poor-quality day care prior to age one increased emotional and social problems in subsequent years, provoking renewed concern with negative effects. Some studies also suggest that effects vary by gender of the child, with more positive effects observed for girls than boys.

The second wave of day-care research began to identify linkages between social-structural features of care—such as group size, caregiver-child ratios, and caregiver training—and children's everyday experiences, and between those experiences and child outcomes. Studies established the negative role of large group size and poor caregiver-child ratios: As these increased, scheduling became less flexible; caregivers engaged in less facilitative social stimulation, expressed less positive affect, and were more restrictive and negative. And children spent more time in solitary activities, were more frequently unhappy, and were less frequently involved in any sustained activity. In turn, less frequent and less positive adult-child and peer interaction was associated with lower cognitive and social competence. These findings are consistent with research on parental caregiving, suggesting that more sensitive, stimulating, and responsive care facilitates child development.

Most recently, Parcel and Menaghan (1990) have drawn on personality and social structure frameworks (Kohn and Schooler 1982, 1983) to argue that the working conditions mothers face on the job influence the values they hold more generally, for themselves and for their children. White-collar parents place more emphasis on self-direction and internalization of norms, whereas blue-collar parents stress conformity to externally imposed standards. The conditions of work that are more common in less well paid jobs—routinization, low autonomy, heavy supervision, and little demand or opportunity for substantively complex work—also erode intellectual flexibility and exacerbate psychological distress, thus providing reduced resources for child rearing.

Parcel and Menaghan (1990) use data from the 1986 National Longitudinal Survey of Youth's (NLSY) Mother-Child data set to investigate whether several dimensions of maternal working conditions—occupational substantive complexity, hourly wages, and work hours—influence a measure of receptive vocabulary

(Peabody Picture Vocabulary Test-Revised [PPVT=R]) among three- to six-year-old children of working mothers. They also consider the role of maternal and child-background characteristics such as maternal race/ethnicity, child gender, maternal mental ability, maternal schooling, maternal grandmother's schooling, and maternal age; the role of family characteristics such as marital status, number of children, and spouse's earnings; the role of the home environment and characteristics of the child's alternative care environment—that is, caregiver/child ratio and type of child-care arrangement (formal center/school, nonrelative care, relative care, other care).

They find that positive predictors of PPVT-R include maternal mental ability, having an older mother, having a maternal grandmother with higher level of schooling, maternal work hours that average twenty-one to thirty-four per week, and having a stronger home environment. Negative predictors include child of male gender, maternal race/ethnicity being black or Hispanic, having a mother who works more than forty hours per week and comes from a family with greater numbers of siblings. Characteristics of child care are not associated with PPVT-R scores in either bivariate or multivariate analyses. Additional analysis of these data revealed that there was regional variation in average PPVT-R scores such that children living in the South scored close to ten points lower than children in the North-Central region, and 8.8 and 6.6 points lower than children in the West and Northeast, respectively (Parcel and Geschwender 1991). Multivariate analyses reveal that these differences can be largely explained by regional variations in maternal race, mental ability, and family background, by variations in children's home environments including modes of discipline, and by variations in parental work hours. Taken together, these findings suggest that variations in maternal working conditions do influence cognitive functioning of young children, although home environments, maternal and child background characteristics, and family configuration are also important.

Other work using the NLSY Mother-Child data set documents that current maternal occupational conditions also influence additional measures of children's cognition, specifically the reading and arithmetic subscales of the Peabody Individual Achievement Test (PIAT), administered to the children at least five years of age, and on measures of verbal memory. Low maternal wage levels and long work hours have negative effects, and maternal education and mental ability have positive effects. Although these findings help to establish the external validity of the conclusions noted above for PPVT-R, additional research should consider whether paternal working conditions show differing or similar effects, whether other aspects of working conditions also affect child cognition, and whether these findings hold as children mature.

*Toby L. Parcel*

## Bibliography

Belsky, J. 1984. "Two Waves of Day Care Research: Developmental Effects and Conditions of Quality." In *The Child and the Day Care Setting: Qualitative Variations and Development*, edited by R.C. Ainslie, pp. 1–34. New York: Praeger.

Hoffman, L.W., and F.I. Nye. 1974. *Working Mothers*. San Francisco: Jossey-Bass.

Kohn, M.L., and C. Schooler. 1982. "Job Conditions and Personality: A Longitudinal Assessment of Their Reciprocal Effects." *American Journal of Sociology* 87:1257–86.

———. 1983. *Work and Personality: An Inquiry into the Impact of Social Stratification*. Norwood, N.J.: Ablex.

Miller, J., C. Schooler, M.L. Kohn, and K.A. Miller. 1979. "Women and Work: Psychological Effects of Occupational Conditions." *American Journal of Sociology* 85:66–94.

Parcel, T.L., and L.E. Geschwender. 1991. "Explaining Regional Variation in Verbal Facility among Young Children." Manuscript in preparation, Ohio State University, Columbus, Ohio.

Parcel, T.L., and E.G. Menaghan. 1990. "Maternal Working Conditions and Children's Verbal Facility: Studying the Intergenerational Transmission of Inequality from Mothers to Young Children." *Social Psychology Quarterly* 53:132–47.

## Maternal Employment and Children's Achievement

Of women in the labor force, mothers with children at home have been the fastest growing group in recent decades. These changes have prompted policy debate about the impact of maternal employment on children. A central concern is whether the relationships parents have with their children are affected by the employment status of the parents. This is important because parents' relationships with their children are considered crucial for the development and socialization of children extending into adolescence and for a range of outcomes from academic achievement to juvenile delinquency. Parent-child relationships take many forms, and some kinds of interactions and activities might be affected by maternal employment differently than others. Thus, the question of how maternal employment influences parent-child relationships is closely linked to whether maternal employment affects the child, because the relationships between parent and child are likely to intervene.

One policy concern about the effect of maternal employment is for children whose mothers are subject to programs requiring mothers to participate in work and training programs to qualify for welfare payments. These are sometimes referred to as "workfare." Also, interest in the effect of maternal employment on the achievement of children is not limited to researchers in the United States. As Dronkers (1989) points out, however, the political context of the debate is sharply different depending on the country. In the Netherlands, for example, the motivation of researchers is in response to government policy discouraging mothers with young children from working, and challenged by those who believe in a mother's right to work.

The research on the effects of maternal employment on the child indicate mixed results. In a review of research on maternal employment and children's achievement for the National Academy of Sciences, Heyns (1982) concludes that there are no measurable differences between children's achievement based on the employment status of their mothers. Another review, published two years earlier, found measurable differences in academic performance and other measures of the child's well-being depending on maternal employment status, and that girls, especially, benefit when mothers are employed (Hoffman 1980). Each has maintained and elaborated their positions since (Heyns and Catsambis 1986; Hoffman 1989).

Milne et al. (1986) entered the debate claiming to show negative effects of maternal employment for children in two-parent, white families. Once they accounted for the higher levels of income, education, educational expectations of parents, smaller family sizes, and activities of the child (like time spent doing homework and reading for pleasure), the differences between achievement of children by mother's employment status diminished but did not go away. Thus they conclude that performance differences among children depending on mother's employment status could, in part, be explained by differences in the child's family environment. Heyns and Catsambis (1986) reanalyzed some of the data used by Milne et al. (1986) and showed that many of their conclusions could be explained by the somewhat unusual methods they used to analyze the data. Moreover, they found that it was only employment of the mother before the child entered school that had a measurable effect on achievement. The conditions of the mother's employment and of her decision to work outside the home may explain the observed influence of maternal employment on the child.

Hoffman (1989) concurs about the importance of considering the circumstances under which the mother is employed in evaluating the effect of employment. Her conclusions, however, are different from those of Heyns and Catsambis (1986). In very low income families, Hoffman finds that employment has a positive effect on children, most likely because of the importance of the increase in available income from the mother's paid job. Maternal employment has a positive effect on girls' expectations and self-concept when accompanied by the mother's positive attitudes about self and job. There is no evidence, however, that these positive attitudes contribute to higher academic achievement of daughters of women in the labor force. Moreover, Hoffman finds a negative relationship between full-time maternal employment and achievement of boys. These results are corroborated by others (such as Desai et al. 1989). Hoffman stresses that differences in achievement of groups of children (boys and girls, middle income and low income) may be explained by differences in the relative need for income and parent-child relationships.

Underlying the debate about effects of maternal employment on children is the belief that relationships between mothers and their children must be different depending on whether a mother is in the labor force. Perhaps her job demands time that she would otherwise spend with her child, or perhaps it focuses her attention and interest away from her family and children. Or, more positively, perhaps it increases her human capital, which helps her children. Surely if maternal employment makes a difference to the child, it is likely to be exhibited in the relationships between parents and child and parents' involvement with the child.

Nock and Kingston (1988) do find differences in the amount of time parents spend with their child or children depending on maternal employment status, although the differences are most pronounced for parents of preschoolers. They distinguish between child-oriented activities of the parent with the child and other activities in which the child is present but not the center of attention, like homemaking activities. Among parents of preschoolers, they find large differences in the amounts of time parents spend with their child in non-child-centered activity when single-earner and dual-earner families are compared, but little difference in child-centered activity, mainly because parents of preschoolers engage in very little child-centered activity. Among mothers of school-age children, there are no differences in the amount of time spent on child-centered activity. In contrast, mothers employed outside the home spend much less time with their children while engaging in the routine chores associated with domestic life, like housekeeping, mainly because they spend less time engaging in those activities. They are more likely to use the time with their children on child-oriented activity.

Muller (1993) examined the relationship between mother's employment status, parents' involvement with their child's education, and the academic achievement of eighth graders. In general, children whose mothers are employed full time attain slightly lower test scores than those whose mothers are not in the labor force. The difference, however, can be explained entirely by differences in the amount of time the eighth graders were left unsupervised after school. When the mother is employed full time, parents are less involved in activities outside the home and particularly on activities that were more likely to require a fixed time for engagement, like volunteering at school, after-school supervision, maintaining friendships with other parents, and restricting the amount of weekday television watched. On activities that are less subject to time inflexibility (and probably conflict with work schedules less), parents do not have different levels of involvement when the mother works full time compared with mothers not in the labor force. This suggests that parents are not less interested in involvement when the mother is employed full time, but that certain kinds of activity are difficult. Among activities less constrained by external factors, the amount parents talked with their child about current school activities is an especially important predictor of the child's achievement. There were no differences in these levels of interaction depending on whether the mother was employed full time or was not in the labor force.

Muller (1993) also finds that parents tend to be most involved with their child's education when the mother is employed part time. In addition, their adolescents achieve higher test scores. Parental involvement does not explain the difference in performance. There may be something about the children, their parents, and families that contributes both to the mother's decision to work part time and to the ways parents are involved. Families that have more income, education, two earners, and a high priority in their child's education may be more able and likely to arrange for the mother to work part time outside the home. This allows parents to balance the needs of children with the needs of the family for the mother to be employed. These findings illustrate Heyns's and Catsambis's (1986) point that the relationship between maternal employment and the outcomes of the child are linked in very important ways to the circumstances of the mother's employment.

To summarize, maternal employment appears to make some difference in the ways parents are involved with their child. There is little evidence that different levels of parental involvement explain differences in achievement, in part because there is little evidence for differences in achievement depending upon the mother's employment status. In considering the impact of maternal employment on both parental involvement and on achievement, the circumstances of the mother's employment and the attitudes of the parents are crucial factors. Moreover, the effects may be influenced by the extent to which societal institutions, like employers and schools, provide flexibility and services to meet the needs of employed parents and their families.

*Chandra Muller*

## Bibliography

Desai, S., P.L. Chase-Lansdale, and R.T. Michael. 1989. "Mother or Market? Effects of Maternal Employment on the Intellectual Ability of 4-Year-Old Children." *Demography* 26:545–62.
Dronkers, J. 1989. "Working Mothers and the Educational Achievements of Their Children." In *The Social World of Adolescents: International Perspectives,* edited by K. Hurrelmann. Berlin: Walter de Gruyter.

Heyns, B. 1982. "The Influence of Parents' Work on Children's School Achievement." In *Families that Work: Children in a Changing World*, edited by S.B. Kamerman and C.D. Hayes. Washington, D.C.: National Academy.

Heyns, B., and S. Catsambis. 1986. "Mother's Employment and Children's Achievement: A Critique." *Sociology of Education* 59:140–51.

Hoffman, L.W. 1989. "Effects of Maternal Employment in the Two-Parent Family." *American Psychologist* 44:282–92.

———. 1980. "The Effects of Maternal Employment on the Academic Attitudes and Performance of School-Age Children." *School Psychology Review* 9:319–36.

Milne, A.M., D.E. Myers, A.S. Rosenthal, and A. Ginsburg. 1986. "Single Parents, Working Mothers, and the Educational Achievement of School Children." *Sociology of Education* 59:125–39.

Muller, C. 1993. "Parent Involvement and Academic Achievement." In *Parents, Their Children and Schools*, edited by B.S. and J.S. Coleman. Boulder, Colo.: Westview.

Nock, S.L., and P.W. Kingston. 1988. "Time with Children: The Impact of Couples' Work-Time Commitments." *Social Forces* 67:59–85.

## Maternal Working Conditions and Children's Behavior Problems

As mothers of young children work outside the home in increasing numbers, questions arise regarding the impact of maternal employment on the social and behavioral development of young children. Given that behavior problems in children are associated with academic and social hardships that continue to have negative consequences for their well-being and success as adults, this is an important question (Caspi et al. 1987). Research on the effects of maternal employment considers general categorizations or employment status as well as the impact of variations in the types of jobs mothers hold and the conditions in which they work. This paper will briefly discuss the theoretical arguments and empirical evidence regarding the impact of specific maternal working conditions on children's social development.

The effects of maternal employment have been studied by considering the effects of different employment statuses such as employed/not-employed or full-time employment/part-time employment. Research in this area may draw general conclusions suggesting, for example, that child outcomes vary when mothers are employed part time rather than full time, or when mothers are employed or are not employed. Research on the effects of maternal employment has also elaborated family conditions under which maternal employment has positive or negative effects. For example, effects are shown to vary depending on the number and age of the children in the household, the normative expectedness of employment given one's other social positions, both spouses' preference for wife's employment, and the extent to which household tasks are shared (Menaghan 1989; Rosenfield 1989; Ross and Mirowsky 1988; Ross et al. 1983).

The impact of maternal employment on children is also influenced by the specific conditions and experiences mothers face at work. Researchers have investigated how such variations in employment experiences affect parenting values and behavior, and ultimately, child outcomes. Kohn and his colleagues have demonstrated that the substantive complexity and opportunities for self-direction that are experienced at work affect parental child-rearing values and the kinds of behavior parents encourage in their children (Kohn 1977; Kohn and Schooler 1983). Occupations are conceptualized in terms of white- and blue-collar work, with white-collar work involving the use of ideas or symbols, interchange with peers, complex content, and greater independence. Blue-collar work is conceptualized as involving manipulation of tools or machinery, with more routinization and direct supervision of workers. They argue that individuals come to value and encourage in their children characteristics that are conducive to success in their own type of work. Parents in white collar jobs may attempt to foster self-direction and cooperation in their children, while parents in blue-collar jobs may place greater emphasis on conformity and obedience to authority in their children.

Occupations also vary in the extent to which individuals are required to work with things, as opposed to other people. Occupations involving work with things are more likely to be routinized and closely supervised. Workers in these types of jobs are likely to be controlled by the pace of the machinery or a supervisor. Mothers subject to this type of work experiences may be more likely to use parenting styles that echo their work experiences; these include closely supervising and limiting the autonomy of their children, emphasizing obedience to parental authority, and greater use of physical punishment.

In contrast, work involving interaction with people is likely to be performed under conditions in which workers are expected to internalize a set of rules and norms regarding work behavior and to work with less direct supervision. Mothers in this kind of work may be more likely to encourage their children to internalize norms of behavior rather than simply obeying parental authority. They may rely less on physical punishment, emphasizing explanations and reasoning so children are able to evaluate their own behavior and voluntarily comply with parental expectations, even without direct parental supervision.

Occupational demands for physical activity may also influence parenting styles and child behavior problems. Physically active jobs may be associated with blue-collar work, the conformity-oriented parenting style discussed above, and higher levels of child behavior problems. However, one could argue that physically active jobs permit mothers to exercise some degree of control over workplace activities, control that could be reflected in parenting that emphasizes child autonomy.

Maternal work hours and level of pay are also characteristics that differentiate the experiences of employed mothers and influence the effects of their employment on their children. Research indicates that long work hours are associated with higher levels of work/family conflict and strain among both women and men (Piotrkowski et al. 1987; Voydanoff 1987). Employed women may be particularly prone to these negative effects since they have greater responsibility for household work in addition to their work outside the home (Voydanoff 1987). Feelings of role strain and overload may make it difficult for mothers to provide guidance and intervention in their children's behavior.

Similarly, with financial resources stretched to the limit in providing adequate health care, nutrition, and housing, mothers may experience psychological distress, making positive and loving interactions with their children even more difficult (Conger et al. 1984). Under these circumstances, it may be very difficult for mothers to provide guidance to their children regarding the appropriateness of certain behaviors (Menaghan 1983).

Using data from the 1986 National Longitudinal Survey of Youth's Mother-Child data set, Rogers et al. (1991) argue that these different experiences of workplace control will be reflected in parenting styles and reports of child behavior problems, in the same way that Kohn and his colleagues have argued for connections between occupational complexity and parenting. In addition to considering occupational characteristics related to workplace control such as substantive complexity of work, work with things versus people, and requisite level of physical activity, they also consider the effect of maternal hours worked and level of wages, maternal sense of mastery, household composition, maternal marital history, the quality of the home environment, and maternal and child background characteristics on mothers' reports of their children's behavior problems.

Their results indicate that higher levels of behavior problems were reported by mothers whose work involves things rather than people. They argue that the direct form of control and lack of autonomy characteristic of these jobs may influence mothers' parenting style and thus, their reports of behavior problems in their children. Mothers who were either divorced or remarried in the previous year also reported higher levels of behavior problems in their children. Lower levels of child behavior problems were reported by mothers whose work required more physical activity, suggesting that greater physical activity on the job may promote a sense of autonomy and control over the work environment, which promotes a reasoning based parenting style and reports of child behavior problems. Lower levels of behavior problems were also reported by mothers with a greater sense of mastery, and those who had more adequate home environments.

These findings suggest that understanding the relationship between maternal employment and children's social development and emotional health requires greater attention to the complexity of mothers' work experience and occupational conditions. Conditions such as working with things rather than people, and the amount of physical activity required on the job, have implications for mothers' reports of child behavior problems. Rogers et al. (1991) suggest that this may be due to differing parental styles rooted in the forms of workplace control mothers experience. Future research must continue to investigate the effects of maternal employment on children in terms of the specific conditions of mothers' work and forms of workplace control they experience.

*Stacy J. Rogers*

## Bibliography

Caspi, Avshalom, Glen H. Elder, and Daryl J. Bem. 1987. "Moving against the World: Life-Course Patterns of Explosive Children." *Developmental Psychology* 23:308–13.

Conger, Rand D., John A. McCarty, Raymond K. Yang, Benjamin B. Lahey, and Joseph P. Kropp. 1984. "Perceptions of Child, Child-Rearing Values, and Emotional Distress as Mediating Links between Environmental Stressors and Observed Maternal Behavior." *Child Development* 55:2234–47.

Hoffman, Lois. 1989. "Effects of Maternal Employment in the Two-Parent Family." *American Psychologist* 448:283–292.

Kohn, Melvin L. 1977. *Class and Conformity, A Study in Values*. 2nd ed. Chicago: University of Chicago Press.

Kohn, Melvin L., and Carmi Schooler. 1983. "Job Conditions and Personality: A Longitudinal Assessment of Their Reciprocal Effects." *American Journal of Sociology* 87:1257–86.

Menaghan, Elizabeth G. 1983. "Individual Coping Efforts: Moderators of the Relationship between Life Stress and Mental Health Outcomes." In *Psychosocial Stress: Trends in Theory and Research*, edited by Howard B. Kaplan, pp. 157–91. New York: Academic.

———. 1989. "Role Changes and Psychological Well-Being: Variations in Effects by Gender and Role Repertoire." *Social Forces* 66:693–714.

Piotrkowski, Chaya S., Robert N. Rapoport, and Rhona Rapoport. 1987. "Families and Work." In *Handbook of Marriage and the Family*, edited by Marvin B. Sussman and Suzanne K. Steinmetz, pp. 251–83. New York: Plenum.

Rogers, Stacy J., Toby L. Parcel, and Elizabeth G. Menaghan. 1991. "The Effects of Maternal Working Conditions and Mastery on Child Behavior Problems: Studying the Intergenerational Transmission of Social Control." *Journal of Health and Social Behavior* 32:145–64.

Rosenfield, Sarah. 1989. "The Effects of Women's Employment: Personal Control and Sex Differences in Mental Health." *Journal of Health and Social Behavior* 30:77–91.

Ross, Catherine E., and John Mirowsky. 1988. "Child Care and Emotional Adjustment to Wives' Employment." *Journal of Health and Social Behavior* 29:127–38.

Ross, Catherine E., John Mirowsky, and Joan Huber. 1983. "Dividing Work, Sharing Work, and In-between: Marriage Patterns and Depression." *American Sociological Review* 48:809–23.

Voydanoff, Patricia. 1987. *Work and Family Life*. Beverly Hills, Calif.: Sage.

## Childbirth and Career Interruptions

Childbirth forces women to cease employment temporarily. The length of this career interruption varies considerably across women because of differences in their jobs, their financial status, and the cost and desirability of day care for their children. Many studies claim that the career interruptions associated with child-bearing are responsible for many of the gender-related differences in labor-market outcomes. It has been argued, for example, that women's greater frequency of career interruptions causes them to prefer certain occupations and may induce hiring discrimination against women by some employers. In the past few decades, women with young children have become much more likely to work and have also returned to work more quickly after childbirth. These changes have contributed to a reduction in the gender difference in earnings and a decline in occupational segregation. The effect of children on the employment decision can be described in the context of a simple theoretical model. Define a woman's reservation wage as the lowest hourly wage at which she would accept employment. If her offered wage rate exceeds her reservation wage, she chooses employment. The value of the reservation wage will be determined partly by the demand for her time in the home.

Numerous variables affect the offered and reservation wage. The wage rate a woman is offered will rise with her education and experience and will vary across occupations. An increase in the reservation wage can be caused by an increase in the demand for her time in the home. Since young children demand considerable amounts of time, they will increase the demand for the mother's time in the home and her reservation wage. Moreover, since younger children are more "time-intensive," the effect of children on the reservation wage is expected to fall as the children grow older.

An increase in the husband's income will increase the demand for all goods, including that for the wife's time in the home. Hence, women married to men with greater incomes are expected to have higher reservation wages and be less likely to be employed.

As the cost of substitutes for the woman's time in the home rises, the demand for her time increases. Hence, tax credits for day care and government subsidies aimed at lowering the cost of day care will lower reservation wages and increase employment of women with children (Heckman 1974).

Empirical work supports the notion that the positive effect of children on reservation wages declines as they age. Gronau (1973) estimates that an additional child under age three increases the mother's reservation wage by 14 to 26 percent; an additional child aged three to five results in an increase of only 7 to 14 percent. A child aged six to eleven results in an increase of 4 to 7 percent; and a child over age eleven has no significant effect on the reservation wage. Thus, younger children have a greater effect on the mother's willingness to be employed.

Even (1987) analyzes the determinants of the length of the career interruption following childbirth for a group of women that were employed during pregnancy. The results indicate that the career interruption is typically shorter for women who are younger, have more prior labor-market experience, have a professional or technical occupation, and have less spousal income. The probability of returning to work falls rapidly as the career interruption progresses. For example, the probability that a woman returns in the first six months following childbirth is approximately 35 percent. However, if she has not returned within the first six months, the probability that she returns within the next six months is only about 15 percent. Thus, among women who are working during pregnancy, the career interruption associated with childbirth is either relatively short (less than six months) or rather extended.

Factors other than the wage that a woman is offered could also influence the length of a career interruption following childbirth. For example, the effect of a career interruption on future earnings may differ across jobs. When a woman drops out of the labor market, her skills may depreciate, thus driving up the cost of her career interruption and reducing her reservation wage. Mincer and Polachek (1974) argue that women who plan frequent or lengthy withdrawals from the labor market will choose occupations that accommodate such withdrawals best, and that such considerations are largely responsible for the "occupational segregation" of the sexes. Women who expect more intermittent careers will choose occupations with skills that are not specific to a particular employer, and skills that do not rapidly depreciate during periods of nonemployment. Desai and Waite (1991) report that women in jobs with more flexibility (such as part-time work) and social support (such as other women with young children) return to work more quickly after childbirth.

Since World War II, the percentage of women employed has increased every decade. The evolution of this increase in the labor force participation rate is described by Cherlin (1990). During the 1950s, the increase was primarily among women with children already in school. In the 1960s and 1970s, the increase was largest among women with preschool-aged children. In the 1980s, the increase has been largest among women with infants. According to U.S. Bureau of the Census data (1991), in 1970 only 30 percent of married women with children under age six participated in the labor force; by 1988 the figure had almost doubled to 57 percent. Moreover, the increase in employment has been especially pronounced among women with infants. In 1971, only 23 percent of women were working (either part or full time) within twelve months of delivery; by 1987 this figure had increased to 42 percent.

Not only has employment of women with infants increased in recent decades, but many more women are maintaining ties to their original employer by using maternity or vacation leaves. Klerman and Leibowitz (1994) show that the percentage of women on vacation or maternity leave following childbirth rose dramatically during the 1980s. Although the United States is the only major industrialized country without a national maternity-leave policy, many firms are providing maternity leaves without the mandate (Kammerman et al. 1983). However, coverage is not uniform across employees. Even (1992) shows that women with greater amounts of employer-provided training who are employed by large or unionized firms are most likely to be covered by a maternity-leave policy.

The trend toward increased employment following childbirth has important implications for the future of women in the labor force. Shapiro and Mott (1994) provide evidence that the employment behavior of women surrounding their first childbirth is a very strong indicator of whether they will be employed as much as fifteen years later. For example, of women who had their first child between 1968 and 1973, those who were employed in the six months before and after childbirth had accumulated 4.5 more years of labor market experience by 1987 than those who were not employed in this time surrounding childbirth. This effect persists even after controlling for differences in years of schooling. Given this result, the increased employment of women with young children in the 1980s should signal greater labor-market attachment of women in the 1990s and beyond. Moreover, O'Neill and Polachek (1993) show that the greater attachment of women to the labor force in the past two decades has assisted in reducing wage differences between men and women.

*William E. Even*

## Bibliography

Cherlin, Andrew. 1990. "Recent Changes in American Fertility, Marriage, and Divorce." *The Annals of the American Academy of Political and Social Science* 510:145–54.

Desai, Sonalde, and Linda Waite. 1991. "Women's Labor Force Participation before and after Their First Birth: The Effect of Occupational Characteristics and Work Commitment." *American Sociological Review* 56:551–66.

Even, William E. 1987. "Career Interruptions following Childbirth." *Journal of Labor Economics* 5: 255–77.

———. 1992. "Determinants of Parental Leave Policies." *Applied Economics* 24:35–43.

Gronau, Reuben. 1973. "The Effect of Children on the Housewife's Value of Time." *Journal of Political Economy* 81:168–201.

Heckman, James. 1974. "Effects of Child-Care Programs on Women's Work Effort." *Journal of Political Economy* 82:136–63.

Kammerman, Sheila B., Alfred J. Kahn, and Paul Kingston. 1983. *Maternity Policies and Working Women.* New York: Columbia University Press.

Klerman, Jacob A., and Arleen Leibowitz. 1994. "The Work-Employment Distinction among New Mothers." *Journal of Human Resources* 29:277–303.

Leibowitz, Arleen, Jacob A. Klerman, and Linda Waite. 1991. "Time Trends in Recent Mothers' Labor Supply." Mimeographed.

Mincer, Jacob, and Solomon Polachek. 1974. "Family Investments in Human Capital: Earnings of Women." *Journal of Political Economy* 82:76–108.

O'Neill, June, and Solomon Polachek. 1993. "Why the Gender Gap in Wages Narrowed in the 1980s." *Journal of Labor Economics* 11:205–28.

Shapiro, David, and Frank Mott. 1994. "Long-Term Employment and Earnings of Women in Relation to Employment Behavior Surrounding the First Birth." *Journal of Human Resources* 29:248–75.

U.S. Bureau of the Census. 1991. *Statistical Abstracts of the U.S.: 1991.* 111th Ed. Washington, D.C.: Government Printing Office.

## The "Mommy Track": Impact of Family Life on Women in the Professoriate

A recent article (Schwartz 1989) examines the issue of professional women and men and their differences regarding commitment, turnover, promotability, and career interruptions. The conclusion is that because many of the gender differences relate to maternity rather than socialization issues, two separate (and unequal) tracks should be created within organizations. These tracks, labeled "career-primary" and "career-and-family," are designed to give women with families the opportunity to maintain their career positions but on a less-than-equal footing with positions of men. The career-and-family track, labeled the "mommy track," is suggested to be part time, possibly job-shared, and with fewer benefits and financial and promotional opportunities. Schwartz maintains that these two tracks are essential because the "career-primary" woman needs opportunities to perform like men without the stigma attached of being associated with other, potentially mothering, women who cast negative aspersions on all women within the corporate environment. The "career-and-family" women need to acknowledge the strength of the family commitment and this can best be accomplished with organizational accommodations made for her. The organization will ultimately benefit by keeping the "mommy track" woman who otherwise may have opted out of the workforce for a period of years to devote herself full-time to parenting.

This issue of the roles of women with and without family is important to examine within the context of the professoriate. Women have become increasingly represented in higher education. Women have increased in the professoriate from 1 percent in 1950 to an estimated 40 percent in 1990 (National Center for Education Statistics 1988). In addition, fully 64 percent of the women in the labor force in 1987 had children under age eighteen and 54 percent had children under age three (Datatrack 1987). Of those women who work, two in three have full-time jobs.

The increasing representation of women in the professoriate, coupled with women in the workforce in general also being parents of young children, means that this issue of a dual-track path for women may be salient in academe as well. There may be a difference in commitment, ability, and motivation for childless women compared with their counterparts with families. Previous research has suggested the presence of children for women disadvantaged their career, although the issue has been dealt with largely through the comparisons of males and females in various professions.

Graddick's and Farr's study (1983) of male and female scientists, for example, found that men were more committed to the organizations than women. Men had lower levels of work-family conflicts than women, and women saw themselves as being treated worse than the men. The greater the number of children women had living at home, the lower was the women's level of job involvement, a relationship less true for men. This study illustrated both gender differences at work, and within those gender differences further differences based on family status.

Chusmir (1982) reports that gender differences such as those cited above are perhaps due to a function of occupational level or other situational characteristics and not gender. In general, women hold more lower-level positions than do men, and turnover and absenteeism rates are higher for these lower-level jobs than for jobs with high pay and high status.

The family sociology model presents another view. Fogarty et al. (1971) show differences between women with children and those without, but in the opposite direction. Working women without children are less committed to work than are those with children, because of weaker networks of support.

Notably, Bruning and Snyder (1983) found only slight differences by sex. They conclude that although certain differences are present, "such differences may not be as pervasive as the organizational literature suggests" (p. 489), and other factors such as organizational position or proportionality of representation in the workforce may be as important as sex in determining differences ordinarily attributed to sex alone.

The authors undertook a study to examine issues surrounding dual tracks in the professoriate by surveying women marketing educators. Previous research had suggested these women with children will fare worse than women without children. Also, marketing as a discipline has been dominated by men and only recently experienced an increasing representation of women. In 1980 women constituted only 16 percent of the doctorate recipients; by 1990, the percent was estimated to be 40 percent (National Center for Education Statistics). For this reason, then, the issues facing the marketing professoriate are similar to those facing the corporate community regarding increasing representation of women.

Women marketing educators were surveyed with regard to their status, commitment, and job satisfaction. Of those surveyed, 93 percent were full-time faculty members and were concentrated at the assistant- and associate-professor levels; one-third had achieved tenure. More than half were between thirty-four and forty-three years old and approximately half of the women had children; of those, 75 percent had children of either preschool or elementary-school age.

Women with and without children were compared with regards to status, professional activity, type of institutional affiliation, and levels of satisfaction. We found that those with children were more likely to be associate or full professor than those without children and were more likely to have tenure. Family status, then, did not appear to influence professional achieved status. Also, family status did not appear to make a difference in their levels of professional activity, such as presentation of papers at national or regional conferences and publication of a book or journal articles or job satisfaction. Finally, we considered whether institutional size represented a proxy for a dual track. That is, larger institutions with more advanced degree programs typically require faculty members to produce more research. One possibility was that women with children are found less frequently at those institutions. Yet women with and without children were equally likely to be found at all types of institutions.

In essence, research by the authors showed that among female faculty, there was no career disadvantage created by the presence of children. A possible explanation for the lack of difference may lie in the issue of job entry. As Clark and Corcoran (1986, p. 20) note, women who have persevered in sustaining successful academic careers are "survivors who have gone against the grain of occupational stereotyping to enter a primarily male profession." Overcoming the barriers to occupational entry, these women are likely to give their occupational position primary importance in their lives. The strength of occupational socialization may supersede the issue of role stereotyping. In addition, the family may actually act as support for one's career, and may become a stabilizing base from which other life issues are explored. A final explanation may lie with the nature of the academic profession itself. The professoriate allows women to have far more autonomy concerning the structure of their worklife than does corporate America. Professors can often work at home, for example, or utilize campus-based day care, and so on.

The results of the authors' research in conjunction with previous research prompt questions about the need for dual career tracks implied by Schwartz (1989). Further, empirical work in this area would lead to a better assessment of the need for dual tracks in the corporate environment as well.

*Ellen J. Kennedy*

*Mary Carsky*

*Mary Ellen Waller Zuckerman*

## Bibliography

Bruning, Nealia S., and Roberta A. Snyder. 1983. "Sex and Position as Predictors of Organizational Commitment." *Academy of Management Journal* 26(3):485–91.

Chusmir, Leonard H. 1982. "Job Commitment and the Organizational Woman." *Academy of Management Review* 7(4):595–602.

Clark, Shirley M., and Mary Corcoran. 1986. "Perspectives on the Professional Socialization of Women Faculty: A Case of Accumulative Disadvantage?" *Journal of Higher Education* 57(1):20–43.

Cohen, Aaron G., and Barbara Gutek. 1988. "The Division 35 Survey: Early Career Experiences." Paper presented at the American Psychological Associate convention, Atlanta, Georgia.

*Datatrack.* December 1987. No. 17, 33.

Fogarty, M.P., R. Rapaport, and R.N. Rapaport. 1971. *Career, Sex and Family.* London: Allen and Unwin.

Graddick, Miriam Massengerg, and James L. Farr. 1983. "Professionals in Scientific Disciplines: Sex-Related Differences in Working Life Commitments." *Journal of Applied Psychology* 68 (4):641–45.

National Center for Education Statistics. September 1988. 181–212.

Schwartz, Felice N. 1989. "Management Women and the New Facts of Life." *Harvard Business Review* 67(1):65–76.

# VIII

# Cross-Cultural Issues
and International Studies

# Cross-National Comparisons

## Women's Labor-Force Participation in Advanced Industrial Countries

The past few decades have witnessed a dramatic change in the G-7 countries: The pronounced increase in women's economic activity rates and the simultaneous decline in men's activity rates has meant that the "average" worker is as likely to be female as male. Recent studies, however, point to the contradictory results of women's entry into wage labor. Increasingly, many sectors and industries are experiencing a feminization of their labor force, yet women's employment still remains less secure than men's. This fact is reflected in their concentration in atypical or nonstandard forms of employment, such as part-time work.

Some authors have suggested that casualization and other structural adjustments in labor markets may be leveling down the work conditions of many men to women's levels (Standing 1989). The earlier trend of a narrowing of the earning gap between women and men has also slowed down or, in some cases, been reversed. Two trends in particular can be said to characterize women's economic security over the 1980s and into the 1990s: one of uniformization and convergence, the other of segmentation and differentiation. On the one hand, the narrowing of the formal activity gap between women and men and women's continuity of working career signal a convergence; on the other hand, uniformization has not necessarily led to greater equality, since structural change and economic crisis have reinforced inequalities between women and men concerning pay, unemployment and precariousness, and widened differences within the female labor force.

Women's and men's employment patterns reflect both changes in the economic structure and factors on the labor-supply side. The latter includes levels of education, demographic changes including declining fertility and the increase in female-headed households, inflationary pressures, and institutional interventions in the labor market such as equal pay and comparable worth policies (equal pay for work of equal value). Participation rates are a helpful first indicator of women's economic activities. Over the last two decades, female participation rates rose steadily, experiencing a leveling off by the late 1980s to early 1990s. Female participation rates in 1973 ranged from a low of 34 percent in Italy to a high of 54 percent in Japan; by 1992, Italy's female labor-force participation rates were at 46 percent (still the G-7 low) and at 69 percent in the United States (Baden 1993). The highest participation rates were found in the Scandinavian nations, with Sweden leading the way at 79 percent.

The greatest increase in women's activity rates occurred for women between the ages of twenty and fifty-nine (the core labor supply). The "core" female labor supply increased in all European Community (EC) countries, with the larger activity rate increases taking place in the United Kingdom (9 percent) and Germany (8.2 percent) (Commission of the European Communities 1992). We can add to this the case of Canada, which experienced an increase in core female labor activity rates of 10.4 percentage points (from 65.1 percent in 1983 to 75.6 percent in 1990); the United States (an increase of 6.9 percentage points from 67 percent to 73.9 percent); and, Japan (an increase of 4.7 percentage points from 59.5 percent to 64.2 percent). Activity rates for the core group of women aged twenty to fifty-nine with children indicate that while family responsibilities still influence women's participation, the patterns of activity across countries are so variable they suggest that differences in women's participation from men's cannot be reduced to their role as mothers. Other factors such as the nature of women's employment (for example, temporary work), the level and form of welfare support for families with children, and the social organization of child care may be explanatory factors for breaks in women's working career. In terms of increased demand for women's employment, most industrialized economies have seen a rapid growth in services and a relative decline in industrial production over the last two decades. Recession in the early 1990s has, as in previous recessions, been reflected in concentrated job losses in manufacturing and construction (Baden 1993). Approximately 15 to 20 percent of women workers in the industrialized economies are concentrated in "women's industries" such as clothing, footwear, leather, and food processing, and around 5 percent in agriculture. The majority of women in the G-7 countries are concentrated in the service sector, with about 60 to 75 percent of their share of total employment concentrated in this sector. While most continue to work in clerical, service, sales, and middle-level professional occupations, there has been a perceived upward trend in the last decade or so in the representation of women in managerial and administrative categories and in the professional and technical categories, relative to their share in total employment.

A factor closely associated with the expansion of female employment in services is the growth of part-time work. Women are disproportionately found among the part-time ranks, with the proportion varying from about 65 to 90 percent of the total. In general, so-called "atypical" forms of employment (part-time, self-employment, subcontracting, fixed contracts, homework) continue to correlate with feminization of the labor market, being twice as common among women as men (OECD 1993). Increasingly, men are entering part-time employment as manufacturing jobs disappear and recession results in a decline in overall employment. As such, part-time employment has emerged as an important employer and state-driven instrument of economic and labor-market adjustment.

How part-time work is organized does vary a great deal across countries and sectors. In some countries (Middle Europe and the United States), the majority of part-time work is unregulated, marginal, often involuntary, and not covered by social insurance. In others (Nordic) this form of employment is fully regulated, optional for older workers and working parents, and concentrated between twenty and thirty-four hours per week (OECD 1993). Whether part-time employment is marginal or fully integrated into the forms of regulation and the policy initiatives of governments and collective-bargaining processes (for example, white-collar workers) is a crucial factor determining the structure and development of part-time work.

Part-time workers generally earn lower hourly rates than full-time workers and receive fewer fringe benefits and employment protection. Baden's ILO report (1993) notes that an increasing amount of part-time and temporary work is involuntary and that there is a growing incidence of underemployment and less job security and earning capacity for women workers. Analysts have suggested that this raises concerns about labor-market restructuring and flexibility in employment. So long as flexible employment is associated with marginalization of the workforce, then there is a higher probability that workers in these positions (mostly women and ethnic minorities) are bearing an unequal burden of the costs of structural change. For example, involuntary, part-time employment for women is primarily due to their inability to secure a full-time job; for their male counterparts, working part time involuntarily is mainly for economic reasons (Baden 1993). Relatedly, so long as social investment in the caring for children and other dependents is not recognized or granted sufficient priority, women will likely continue to bear a disproportionate share of these tasks, as is partly reflected in their overrepresentation in involuntary part-time work and as discouraged workers. In this sense, women may be providing the flexibility that allows men's working patterns to remain less flexible. Women's lack of bargaining power within and outside of the household limits their labor-market power and tends to bias their participation toward low-skill, part-time work.

A reflection of women's limited bargaining power is the persistence of gender pay differentials. In recent years, rising wage inequality has characterized most industrialized countries, with explanations varying from general factors to the unique features within each country such as the nature of the labor force. For example, in some countries the decline in women's average earnings relative to men's over the last decade and a half was seen to be an effect of the government's wage policies: wage hike ceilings, ending indexing of wages to inflation, decentralization of wage determination, privatization of state-owned companies. The European Community links the economic and social policies related to the employment crisis in the 1980s to changes in compensation for low-wage workers. Consequently, the wages of women and gender-based pay differentials (Commission of the European Communities 1992). On average, women's earnings are at 50 to 90 percent of those of men, depending on the country in question (Baden 1993).

Persistent vertical and occupational segregation continues to lie at the source of pay differences. Skill valuation and the influence of bonus systems also play a significant role in certain aspects of pay differentials (Commission of the European Communities 1992). According to the Organization for Economic Co-operation and Development (OECD 1993), rising wage inequality in the public sector also contributes to the overall trend of steady or rising inequality in women's earnings. Explanations vary from continuing occupational segregation to the contracting out of consulting and support services. Some authors have argued that shifts in employment away from manufacturing toward services are contributing to income polarization. As a result, wages and earnings are no longer clustered around the middle of the wage distribution but are moving toward an hourglass configuration, where wages tend to be clustered at the top or the bottom. Emerging jobs are polarized according to earnings and skills, which favors the feminization of employment (Standing 1989). This may be a gain for women in terms of overall economic participation but results in the incidence of more precarious and low-income forms of economic activity.

Another implication of earning, skill, and job polarization is that, as women continue to be drawn to either pole of employment, the disparity among them will increase. This has economic as well as political implications. Pay equity (equal pay for work of equal value) and equal-employment-opportunity legislation, for example, assume a commonality of interests among women, but economic restructuring appears to be creating both material differences and skill divisions within female ranks. The increasing polarization or segmentation among women signals, for some authors, a class-based divergence of interests among women in the labor force (Bakker 1990).

What all of these trends suggest are both new opportunities for women to be economically active and new structures of inequality exacerbated by the process of restructuring. The policy implications of this are far-reaching and will require a rethinking of standard employment-equality legislation to address not only differences between women and men but also to target women who are at the lower end of the workforce in terms of job stability and remuneration. For example, if polarization leads to more men in "bad" jobs, or overall employment conditions are lowered, then parity of male and female wages (pay equity) could be realized. However, such equality could be taking place at lower average wage levels. Given women's concentration in the service sector and the continued importance of this area of economic activity in the future, the public sector can play an important role in shaping the mix of services and the structure of employment. Analysts of women's employment patterns are increasingly expanding their focus to encompass broader economic policies. For example, macroeconomic strategies that target deficit reduction via public expenditure cuts should also incorporate a gender-based analysis of costs and benefits. Shifting caring activity from the paid to the unpaid economy may result in increased pressures on women's "choices" in the labor market, influencing their participation in more precarious forms of employment (Elson 1994).

*Isabella Bakker*

## Bibliography

Baden, Sally. 1993. *The Impact of Recession and Structural Adjustment on Women's Work in Developing and Developed Countries.* Geneva: ILO Working Paper, Equality for Women in Employment, December.

Bakker, Isabella. 1990. "Pay Equity and Economic Restructuring: The Polarization of Policy?" In *Just Wages: A Feminist Assessment of Pay Equity,* edited by Judy Fudge and Patricia McDermott. Toronto: University of Toronto Press.

Commission of the European Communities. 1992. *The Position of Women on the Labour Market.* Brussels: Women of Europe Supplements, No. 36.

Elson, Diane. 1994. "Micro, Meso, Macro: Gender and Economic Analysis in the Context of Policy Reform." In *The Strategic Silence: Gender and Economic Policy,* edited by Isabella Bakker. London: Zed.

Jenson, Jane, Elizabeth Hagen, and Ceallaigh Reddy, eds. 1988. *Feminization of the Labour Force: Paradoxes and Promises*. Cambridge, Mass.: Polity.

McDowell, Linda, and Rosemary Pringle, eds. 1992. *Defining Women: Social Institutions and Gender Divisions*. Cambridge: Polity/Open University.

Organization for Economic Cooperation and Development. 1993. *Women and Structural Change in the 1990s*. Report by Gunther Schmid. Paris: OECD.

Standing, Guy. 1989. "Global Feminization through Flexible Labour." *World Development* 17(7): 1077–95.

## Women and Agriculture in the Developing World

The United Nations has estimated that women grow half of the food of the world but own less than one-hundredth of its land. In Africa, women perform almost 80 percent of agricultural work, and in both Asia and Africa almost all employed women work in agriculture. In the poorest countries, where they grow, harvest, process, and prepare virtually all the food consumed by their families, their work is seen largely in terms of subsistence and is essentially unpaid. Although a surplus may produce items for exchange or some cash, subsistence agricultural labor is not considered income-generating in the same sense as when women are employed for wages. More important, women in subsistence agriculture are unlikely to be counted as members of the labor force, which not only undervalues their vital role in family and community survival but also distorts the economic reality of the country as a whole.

As the pace of development accelerates there is a movement away from subsistence to cash crops for those who remain on farms as well as the out-migration of males seeking paid, often seasonal, employment elsewhere. Although subsistence farming is less valued in most of the world when compared with any other activity allowing for cash income, it has provided women with a measure of respect and control over an essential productive process, especially if women become even temporary heads of households while their husbands are employed elsewhere. Many farms are female-managed even if they are not female-owned. This is not to underestimate the exhausting demands faced by women who are responsible for both farming and household tasks, but to emphasize their critical productive roles.

Yet the traditional economic definition of labor is consistent with the view that only those functions that create a surplus for profit in the marketplace are considered aspects of productive work. Thus as Waring (1988, p.30) suggests, the international economic system imposes a reality that excludes the majority of the work women perform, such as raising children and domestic labor, as well as subsistence farming.

Since the subsistence farming roles of women have been deemphasized if not ignored in evaluating labor-force activities in the Third World, development policies have also largely ignored their contributions as well. Such policies are designed to upgrade the economic standards of families by concentrating on the male head of household, who is seen as the breadwinner, with his dependent wife in the homemaker role. It is reasoned that by improving the employment situation of the husband, the position of the entire family would also be upgraded. By failing to even acknowledge the varied productive roles of rural women, many development programs have not only fallen short of goals but have actually undermined the already fragile nature of the subsistence activities of these women. A simple example of this is the introduction of mechanization to oxen and plow or hoe farming. Such technology may decrease the workload of men, who either now produce cash crops or who seek employment on other farms away from home, but it increases the burden on women, who not only lose male help in their remaining subsistence farming but who also lose control over their own farming activities in the conversion to cash crops. Cash cropping competes with subsistence agriculture for land, labor, and resources.

The economic options of rural women relative to men vary widely according to culture and stage of economic development. When development opportunities are extended to women, compared with men they not only face more intractable barriers for accessing them but find that this assistance is primarily directed to their status as mothers (maternal and child-health programs) and preparing for motherhood (family planning). This emphasis on reproduction again discounts their roles in agricultural production. The assumption that women and children will be cared for by male heads of households has continued to bolster the view that the economic activities of women are marginal. Although women would benefit immensely from agricultural extension programs, these are typically directed to men. Again, the process of development often downgrades the position of women in the subsistence sector, increases their total work burden, and lessens their control over resources relative to that of men.

There is growing recognition among policy planners that development projects must take serious notice of all the productive roles of rural women if they are to be successful. The focus here is on the agricultural role, but all the daily childcare and household production activities should also be included. It is also clear that the definitions of labor and production need to be revised to become more inclusive of women's work activities. Agriculture, women as a productive workforce, food security, and family maintenance are inseparable components of development. Since subsistence farming is the primary means of livelihood for women in the developing world, it must be protected, extended, or realistically evaluated and modified. At a minimum it must be acknowledged. To eliminate it without considering alternative sources of income can have disastrous consequences for the family, especially if these women are now household heads because of desertion, divorce, or widowhood.

Finally, development assistance programs need to be evaluated according to their degree of success in empowering women. Rural women who are provided with welfare or access to educational programs are unlikely to upgrade their position unless such assistance also allows for increased control over their productive and reproductive lives. While the gender-based division of agricultural tasks may continue, women can more actively participate in and influence the economic life of their families and communities.

*Linda L. Lindsey*

## Bibliography

Abraham, M. Francis, and P. Subhadra Abraham, eds. 1988. *Women, Development and Change*. Bristol, Ind.: Wyndham Hall.

Brydon, Lynn, and Sylvia Chant. 1989. *Women in the Third World: Gender Issues in Rural and Urban Areas*. Hants, England: Edward Elgar.

Dixon-Mueller, Ruth. 1985. *Women's Work in Third World Agriculture*. Geneva: International Labour Organization.

Kandiyoti, Deniz. 1985. *Women in Rural Production Systems: Problems and Policies*. Paris: United Nations Educational, Scientific and Cultural Organization.

Kardam, Nuket. 1991. *Bringing Women In: Women's Issues in International Development Programs*. Boulder, Colo.: Lynne Rienner.

Tinker, Irene, ed. 1990. *Persistent Inequalities: Women and World Development*. New York: Oxford University.

United Nations. 1985. *The State of the World's Women, 1985*. World Conference to Review and Appraise the Achievements of the United Nations Decade for Women: Equality, Development and Peace. Nairobi, Kenya (July 15–26). Oxford, England: New Internationalist Publications.

Waring, Marilyn. 1988. *If Women Counted: A New Feminist Economics*. San Francisco: Harper.

## Gender Inequality in Labor-Force Participation across Nations (circa 1980)

Inequality in the rate of women's and men's labor-force participation exists across nations. Ratio measures of economic activity (the number of women per one hundred men in the formal labor force) indicate that higher levels of national income do not reduce gender inequality in the labor force. The difference between women's and men's representation in the industrial sector remains relatively constant regardless of level of national income; at best, women's rate of industrial employment is only two-thirds that of men's. Women's relative participation in agriculture drops with higher national income; only in low-income countries do more women than men work in agriculture. In all but the poorest nations, women dominate the services; their representation in this sector is $1^1/2$ times that of men.

Women's empowerment requires access to and control over material resources (Blumberg 1988). In particular, female labor-force participation rates have been used widely in cross-national research as measures of women's status (Clark et al. 1991; Johnston 1985; Ward 1984). However, scholars have begun to replace the notion of "women's status" with the concept of "gender inequality" because it offers a fuller depiction of gender relations in society (Momsen and Townsend 1987).

Gender inequality can be defined as the departure from parity in the representation of women and men in valued aspects of social life—such as economic activity. This requires the use of ratio measures that clearly focus on the situation of women relative to men. For example, in Table 1, the average ratio of women to men in the labor force in low-income countries is sixty-six. This means that in the labor force there are sixty-six women for every one hundred men; in addition, this number takes into account the number of women and men in the population. For more discussion of the concept of gender inequality and the measurement strategy as well as a list of countries in various income categories see Young et al. (1994).

The analysis in Table 1 assesses the distribution of economic resources to women and men in societies at varying levels of per capita income and thereby offers a different, gendered, perspective on the connection between economic growth and the situation of women. The table presents two indicators of gender inequality in labor-force participation (for people aged fifteen to fifty-nine, and for the fifteen to twenty-four age group) and three indicators of gender inequality in the main economic sectors (agriculture, industry, and services) by level of national income. The statistics used in calculating the ratio measures come from the United Nations's Women's Indicators and Statistics (WISTAT), which contains employment data for 103 countries for the 1980 census round (United Nations Statistical Office 1988, 1991). The income level classification comes from the World Bank's *World Development Report 1982;* it excludes high-income oil-exporting nations and the nonmarket industrial nations of Eastern Europe and the former Soviet Union.

TABLE 1. Averages for Economic Activity Indicators for 103 Countries by Level of National Income, 1980

| | Low N=28 | Low-Mid N=39 | Up-Mid N=17 | High N=19 |
|---|---|---|---|---|
| *Labor-Force Participation Ratios* | | | | |
| All workers, age 15–59 | 66 | 47 | 45 | 62 |
| Young workers, age 15–24 | 71 | 52 | 57 | 83 |
| *Sector of Economic Activity Ratios, All Ages* | | | | |
| Agriculture | 115 | 95 | 63 | 70 |
| Industry | 45 | 60 | 69 | 50 |
| Services | 64 | 131 | 150 | 153 |

Examination of Table 1 reveals how gender inequality in the labor force varies by level of national income. The labor-force participation ratios indicate curvilinear relationships between national income and gender inequality. For all workers in the formal (counted) labor force, the highest ratio of women to men workers (sixty-six) is found in the poorest countries. The ratios drop at middle-income levels, reaching their lowest point in the upper-middle-income countries. Then, in the high-income countries the ratio of women to men in the labor force increases, although it is still less than in the low-income countries.

The pattern differs somewhat for women and men in the fifteen to twenty-four age group, a life stage that offers women important alternatives in terms of education, work, marriage, and parenting. Labor-force participation ratios are highest for young women in the high-income countries (rather than the low-income countries) but are still lowest in the middle-income nations.

Material and cultural forces operate to reduce women's labor-force participation. Processes of urbanization and industrialization expand opportunities and modify expectations for young women. Cultural preferences are most markedly revealed in comparisons of young workers to all workers. The difference in the gender ratios for younger workers and for all workers appears in the upper-middle income countries, with a difference of twelve points. The preference for younger women in the labor force widens in the high-income countries to twenty-one points, four times that in lower-income countries.

Turning, then, to gender ratios in sectors of economic activity, women's representation in industry is highest in the upper-middle-income countries, but drops considerably in high-income nations. However, there is less variation in the ratios in industry by income level than exists in the sectors of agriculture and services. In fact, the industry ratio is the only indicator where the difference across income levels is not statistically significant.

A ceiling appears to exist on the ratio of women to men in the industrial sector regardless of national income level. This is unfortunate, as industrial work presents the greatest potential to empower women because it is the sector most likely to be organized and to offer better terms of employment. Moreover, national resources have been deployed away from agriculture to industry, and the gender-based division of labor operates less forcefully in industry than in services (Joekes 1987).

In agriculture, the apparent pattern of decline in the gender ratios with higher national income is best understood in the context of the transformation of farming. With economic growth, the proportion of the population engaged in farming generally decreases, as does the rural population. As mechanization and commercialization of agriculture become more intense, they exclude women because they replace the system of household-based food production in which women dominate. It is important to note that the higher than expected ratio of women in agriculture in high-income countries (given the pattern of general decline) results from the persistence of small-scale family farming in Germany, Austria, Italy, and Japan. Excluding these countries from the calculation results in a mean ratio of fifty-one, which follows the general pattern of decline in women's representation across levels of national income.

An opposing pattern of women's overrepresentation appears in services. Women dominate service employment, except in the poorest countries, and their dominance is greater in higher-income countries. The process of urbanization in concert with national income growth results in expansion of work opportunities in the service sector, in particular personal and social services. Service employment for women generally constitutes an extension of their domestic activities even when tied to the growth of the state and public employment. Aside from a small number of professional women, mainly in high-income countries, women's service work is overwhelmingly poorly paid and of low status. Thus, women's overrepresentation in this sector signifies no advantage.

The empirical analysis leads to some broader conclusions. The general lack of parity in participation in formal economic activity, the apparent preference for women prior to marriage and motherhood, their displacement from modern agriculture, the ceiling they experience in industrial employment, even their overrepresentation in services, all indicate the strength of the gender-based division of labor. The complexity of the relationship between economic growth and women's employment contradicts the assumption that higher levels of national income automatically translate into better relative positions for women. Only relative measures—that is, measures of gender inequality—can reveal disparities due to unequal distribution of resources between women and men.

> Gay Young
>
> Lucía Fort
>
> Mona Danner

## Bibliography

Blumberg, Rae. 1988. "Income under Female versus Male Control." *Journal of Family Issues* 9:51–84.

Clark, Roger, Thomas Ramsbey, and Emily S. Adler. 1991. "Culture, Gender and Labor Force Participation." *Gender & Society* 5:47–66.

Joekes, Susan. 1987. *Women in the World Economy.* New York: Oxford University Press.

Johnston, Denis. 1985. "The Development of Social Statistics and Indicators on the Status of Women." *Social Indicators Research* 16:233–61.

Momsen, Janet H., and Janet G. Townsend. 1987. *The Geography of Gender in the Third World.* Albany, N.Y.: SUNY Press.

United Nations Statistical Office. 1988. *Women's Indicators and Statistics Microcomputer Data Base (WISTAT), Version 1*. New York: U.N. Statistical Office.

——. 1991. *The World's Women 1970–1990*. New York: United Nations.

Ward, Kathryn. 1984. *Women in the World System: Its Impact on Status and Fertility*. New York: Praeger.

World Bank. 1982. *World Development Report 1982*. New York: Oxford University Press.

Young, Gay, Lucía Fort, and Mona Danner. 1994. "Moving from 'The Status of Women' to 'Gender Inequality': Conceptualization, Social Indicators, and an Empirical Application." *International Sociology* 9:55–85.

## The Division of Household Labor in Cross-Cultural Perspective

The concepts of "housework" and "household labor" create an image of boring, repetitive, and distasteful chores that need to be attended to on a daily basis. Numerous studies have sought to explain the division of household in terms of its correlates, history, and future. However, one common trait among these studies is that wives, or women in general, typically do much more work within the home than do husbands (Blair and Lichter 1991).

One additional trait shared by most research into the division of household labor is that it has focused primarily on the United States. Household labor most certainly exists outside the boundaries of the United States, yet there is a paucity of research that addresses the allocation of housework in other countries and cultures. Does the allocation of household chores differ across cultures? In order to more fully comprehend the nature of the division of work within the home, it is necessary to consider the variations that may exist in other, particularly non-Western, cultures. By this means, a more complete understanding of the division of household labor, as well as its accompanying ideologies, will be achieved.

### Understanding Household Labor

Many studies have used "household labor" as a broad descriptive of virtually any activity within the home environment. One obvious, yet seemingly unanswered question, is, What constitutes household labor? Although there is relative consensus among researchers as to where the labor takes place, there is some diversity among the categories or types of labor that are considered "housework." Blair and Lichter (1991) included the following categories in their assessment of household labor: meal preparation, washing dishes, cleaning house, outdoor tasks, shopping, washing and ironing, paying bills, and auto maintenance. Other researchers have added such tasks as taking care of children, punishing children, taking care of pets, garden care, making arrangements for doctor and dentist visits, and clothing construction.

Studies of the division of household labor in non-Western cultures appear to be both similar to the definition of household labor in the United States yet also to bear their own culture-specific dimensions of housework. For example, in Northern Ireland (Curry and McEwen 1989), household labor also includes bringing in fuel for the stove or furnace. In Ghana, household labor is perhaps more true to the terminology, as housework also includes the actual building of houses (Tripp 1982). South African families appear to utilize servants in the performance of the less desirable chores (such as cleaning floors and washing [Smedley 1978]). Hence, what is actually considered housework seems to vary somewhat from one culture to the next.

Meissner (1977) offers a more qualitative assessment of household labor by noting the different traits of typically "masculine" and "feminine" tasks in the home. Male tasks tend to have the following qualities: (1) a well-defined beginning and end; (2) personal discretion as to when the task should be performed (lack of a solid time frame); and (3) a leisure component. Females, however, spend the majority of their household labor time in tasks that contain the opposite qualities. Washing dishes, cooking, and child-care are tasks that must be performed daily, at specific times, and do not allow much discretion as to when the tasks should be done. Hence, the qualities of female chores are in sharp contrast to those chores commonly performed by males. Female chores tend to be routinized, repetitive, boring, and dirty.

### Cross-Cultural Comparisons of Household Labor

To what extent, then, do differences exist in the division of household labor across countries and cultures worldwide? In keeping with results shown in previous studies in the United States, Blair and Lichter (1991) find that American women average about thirty-three hours per week in household labor, while men contribute approximately fourteen hours per week. In general, the allocation of household chores among American couples is highly segregated by sex, and its division is largely associated with women's employment (that is, employed and better-educated women appear more able to control the allocation of labor within the home). Using the United States as a basis for comparison, variations and similarities in the division of household labor can be easily noted.

In Australia, men and women seem to follow a pattern of family labor allocation that is quite similar to that of American couples. Australian women contribute about twenty-eight hours to housework weekly, while men perform about seven hours per week (Presland and Antill 1987). Employment is again cited as a central factor in the division of labor, such that husbands contribute more time to household chores when wives are actively employed outside the home. Interestingly, the majority of wives state that they are satisfied with the allocation of work in the family.

Indeed, it would appear that the trends evident in the United States and Australia seem to typify Westernized cultures. For example, in the United Kingdom, Canada, Sweden, and Israel, women clearly seem to bear a disproportionate share of housework. Women in these countries perform between two to five times as much housework as do men. Yet what can account for these differences? The answer again appears to be associated with Western cultures. Gershuny and Robinson (1988) posit that the changes in the division of household labor in the United Kingdom are largely due to increases in the availability of labor-saving appliances (such as microwave ovens and automatic dishwashers). Some studies find that wives' contributions to household labor are strongly associated with their employment status (Blair and Lichter 1991; Presland and Antill 1987), while others conclude that the employment of women decreases their time in household labor, yet does not actually increase men's time in housework (Douthitt 1989; Shamir 1986).

Whether the allocation of housework is associated with the employment status of women, their earnings, or with the availability of labor-saving appliances, the constant among all of the research studies conducted among Westernized cultures again demonstrates the intransigent nature of the division of household labor. But what of non-Western cultures?

In Japan, wives are again overly burdened in the distribution of domestic chores. Women have almost exclusive responsibility for cooking, mending clothes, dish-washing, and other tasks that clearly are among the most repetitive and unsought chores in the home. Interestingly, Morinaga et al. (1992) conclude that Japanese society still maintains traditional domestic role expectations for women, such that it is generally assumed that females bear the larger burden of family labor. Morinaga et al. further posit that there is very little association between the division of household labor and marital satisfaction, suggesting that women in Japanese society are socialized into the acceptance of an inequitable set of domestic responsibilities.

Women in Ghana share a similar set of responsibilities as men in labor outside the home (that is, farming), yet these women also perform a considerably larger share of household labor than men. Ghana women spend about four hours per day in domestic labor, yet they also spend approximately two-thirds as much time, on average, as men do working in the fields (Tripp 1982). This again seems to suggest that there is a sex-based set of role expectations that is common to all cultures (or at least those whose distribution of labor has been examined).

Russian women, as compared to American women, also appear to bear the responsibility for a disproportionate share of household labor. Russian husbands spend an average of fifteen hours per week in household chores, while wives average about thirty-three hours weekly (Patrushev 1982). As with the allocation of household chores in the United States, there appears to be little improvement in the distribution of household tasks as a result of advances of Russian women into the paid labor force. Patrushev (1982) suggests that although Russian workers, both male and female, have experienced an overall decrease in their time spent in paid labor, men's contributions to household labor have remained relatively constant. Women's share of household labor is expected to decrease toward the end of this century, yet this seeming improvement will likely result from a reduction in women's overall time spent in household labor, and not from an actual increase in men's participation in housework.

The decrease between men's and women's level of household labor is also illustrated by the allocation of household chores in Norway. Gronmo and Lingsom (1983) conclude that the difference between men's and women's daily participation in household labor decreased significantly between 1971 and 1981, yet this change in the difference between men's and women's housework is primarily due to a decrease in women's household labor.

## Conclusion and Discussion

The division of household labor, as compared across cultures, appears to share several qualities with studies of the allocation of housework in the United States. First, it would appear that the entire division of household labor is largely sex-based. Specifically, numerous cultures seem to maintain a division of labor that is quite inequitable in that women perform a significantly larger share of housework than do men.

Second, it would appear that the division of household labor is not only sex-based, but it is also maintained within cultures via ideological constraints. In many of the studies cited here, the division of labor in the home was primarily based upon adherence to traditional domestic roles. Men were expected to be "providers," while women were expected to bear responsibility for housework. Although the participation of women in paid employment affected the distribution of housework in several cultures, the resultant changes typically include a reduction in women's time spent in housework, and not an increase in men's participation in housework.

These findings have profound implications for the status of women. As women achieve statuses equivalent to those of men in their respective societies, it would seem necessary that they also secure equal status within the home. Although women have made significant advances into the paid labor force in numerous societies, advances toward equality in the home and family environments must be made in order to ensure a change in domestic roles and societal expectations for men and women in future generations.

*Sampson Lee Blair*

## Bibliography

Blair, Sampson Lee, and Daniel T. Lichter. 1991. "Measuring the Division of Household Labor: Gender Segregation of Housework among American Couples." *Journal of Family Issues* 12(1):91–113.

Curry, C.A., and A. McEwen. 1989. "The 'Wendy House' Syndrome: A Teenage Version." *Research in Education* 41:53–60.

Darque, Martine Berlan. 1988. " The Division of Labour and Decision-Making in Farming Couples: Power and Negotiation." *Sociologia Ruralis* 28(4):271–92.

Douthitt, Robin A. 1989. "The Division of Labor within the Home: Have Gender Roles Changed?" *Sex Roles* 20(11/12):693–704.

Gershuny, Jonathan, and John P. Robinson. 1988. "Historical Changes in the Household Division of Labor." *Demography* 25(4):537–52.

Gronmo, Sigmund, and Susan Lingsom. 1983. "Household Work and Sexual Equality: Changing Time Use Patterns in the 1970s." *Tidsskrift for samfunnsforskning* 24(5):415–39.

Meissner, Martin. 1977. "Sexual Division of Labor and Inequality: Labor and Leisure." In *Women in Canada*, edited by M. Stephenseon, pp. 160–80. Toronto: Women's Education.

Morinaga, Yasuko, Kiriko Sakata, and Ryoko Koshi. 1992. "Marital Satisfaction and Division of Family-Related Tasks among Japanese Married Couples." *Psychological Reports* 70:163–68.

Patrushev, Vasilii. 1982. "Possible Changes in the Utilization of Time Budgets." *Sotsiologicheskie Issledovaniya* 9(1):28–35.

Presland, Pauline, and John K. Antill. 1987. "Household Division of Labour: The Impact of Hours Worked in Paid Employment." *Australian Journal of Psychology* 39(3):273–91.

Shamir, Boas. 1986. "Unemployment and Household Division of Labor." *Journal of Marriage and the Family* 48:195–206.

Smedley, Linda N. 1978. "White Housewives: An Introductory Study." *South African Journal of Sociology* 17:61–72.

Tripp, Robert B. 1982. "Time Allocation in Northern Ghana: An Example of the Random Visit Method." *Journal of Developing Areas* 16:391–400.

# Women in Advanced Industrial Societies

## Australian Women in Paid Employment

In May of 1989, Australia had an estimated work force of 7.7 million employed persons, of whom 3.1 million were women (41 percent of the overall total and 78 percent of the part-time total). The unemployment rate was 7 percent for women and 6 percent for men. The labor-force participation of all women has increased steadily over the past forty years, from 30 percent in 1947 to 52 percent in 1991. For married women the increase over the same period was sevenfold from 6.5 percent to 49.5 percent. In the 1980s there was a great increase in the proportion of part-time jobs in Australia. By 1989, 40 percent of women in the workforce were employed part time. Many of them cared for young children and worked in jobs that often do not provide opportunities for training or promotion and are poorly paid (ABS 1990; Bittman 1991; Smyth 1991, 1991a).

In 1990, the average earnings of women employed full time were 83 percent that of men. When part-time workers are included, women earned around 65 percent of men's earnings. Only 38.5 percent of women had superannuation (retirement plan) at the end of the 1980s, compared with 65.3 percent of men (DEET 1990; NWCC 1990).

Australian women are clustered in relatively low-paying industries and occupations with flat career paths. Australia has one of the most sex-segregated workforces of all OECD countries. In 1989, about 85 percent of women workers were employed in five of twelve industrial divisions (community services, recreation, sales, finance, and manufacturing), in contrast with men who were spread more evenly. Women constitute 65 percent of the community services sector (health, education, welfare) and 56 percent of the recreation, personal, and other services sector (hospitality, hairdressing, and so forth), which together accounted for nearly 40 percent of the female workforce but only 25 percent of the total workforce (ABS 1990; DEET 1990).

A high degree of occupational segmentation is also evident. Over 50 percent of women in the workforce find employment in clerical or sales jobs. Women are 89 percent of receptionists and telephonists, 63 percent of sales and personal service workers, and 77 percent of clerical workers. Excluding hairdressing, only 3 percent of apprentices in the skilled trades are women. The proportion of women managers has doubled since the 1960s, but women still occupy only 25 percent of managerial jobs, mostly at the lower levels. Women are 94 percent of nurses, 40 percent of paraprofessionals, 10 percent of parliamentarians. Only 9 percent of women lawyers are partners in law firms, compared with 41 percent of men. However the proportion of women engineers increased from 3 percent to 9 percent over the course of the 1980s (ABS 1990; DEET 1990; Smyth 1991).

Most legislative and administrative obstacles to employment in what were traditionally men's jobs have been removed and antidiscrimination laws and affirmative-action policies introduced. Women are now represented in most occupations, but a high degree of segmentation remains, partly due to differentiation in the educational system based on gender. The high school completion rate increased for women from 49.5 percent in 1985 to 62.5 percent in 1989. Many women now go on to higher education but most go into traditionally female areas such as the humanities, nursing, and education (Smyth 1991).

Australia has an active trade-union movement that enjoys a high participation rate and has a complex bureaucratic and legal system that manages industrial relations and sets minimum wages and work conditions (or awards) for different types of work. In recent years, negotiators for traditional women's occupations such as nursing, child-care, education, and secretarial work have argued that the skills involved in these jobs have not been properly recognized or appropriately remunerated.

Accordingly, union representatives have argued before the Industrial Relations Commission that award restructuring should involve developing career paths, recognition and encouragement of multiskilling (Field 1990), the provision of child-care facilities and flexibility in hours of employment and career structures to account for family obligations, and the removal of discrimination. This process, known as the movement for "pay equity," has some similarities with a form of the "comparable worth" process pursued in the United States in the 1980s. This strategy is meeting with some success. Recently a new award for secretarial workers was announced that included pay raises and a six-tier career structure (Smyth 1991, 1991a; Windsor 1991).

In recent years, more women than men have begun their own businesses. Currently 262,000 women own small businesses, which is 32 percent of the total. While these are usually smaller and less likely to expand into large businesses than men's, they are less likely to fail. Women are far less likely to borrow capital from a financial institution to set up a small business. Instead they use their savings, sell assets, or borrow from family and friends (Hely 1990; Smyth 1991a).

Women are more likely than men to be involved in home-based or outwork. While this provides flexible hours in which to care for children and run a household, the disadvantages are isolation and lack of job security and benefits (Smyth 1991a).

Although 44 percent of women with a child under five years of age engage in some paid employment, only 1 percent of companies have child-care facilities. The federal government gives some tax concessions to employers who provide child-care and provided funds for the establishment of community-based child-care services. There is no tax deduction for families for money spent on child care, but fee relief is available on a means-tested basis. It is a common pattern for women, after the birth of their first child, to reenter the workforce as part-time employees so that they can raise their children, contribute economically to the household, and retain employment skills.

As their children become more independent, many women return to the labor force. A recent survey by the Australian Institute of Family Studies found that the percentage of mothers working in paid employment for thirty or more hours weekly increased from 19 percent for those with preschool-age children to 54 percent for women whose youngest child was thirteen or older. A further 21 percent of these women worked part time. In recent years, the number of job-share and permanent part-time positions has increased considerably (Glezer 1991).

In 1990 Australia ratified International Labour Organization Convention 156, which recognizes that male workers also have family responsibilities. Later that year, the Industrial Relations Commission granted paternity leave to fathers, who now have the right to take up to one year of unpaid leave on the birth or adoption of a child (Glezer 1991).

Women are still in a very disadvantaged position in the Australian labor force, but slowly women's work conditions are improving. Generous family-leave provisions have also been negotiated with some public sector employers that allow mothers or fathers up to seven years' unpaid leave to care for children. Less progress has been made in altering gender relations at home, which is essential if women are to gain equality in the workplace (Bittman 1991; Smyth 1991a).

*Gerard Sullivan and Karen Herne*

### Bibliography

Australian Bureau of Statistics. 1990. *The Labour Force Catalogue* No. 6203.0. Canberra: Commonwealth Government Printer.

Bittman, Michael. 1991. *Juggling Time: How Australian Families Use Time*. Canberra: Australian Government Publishing Office for Office of the Status of Women, Department of Prime Minister and Cabinet.

Burton, Clare. 1991. *The Promise and the Price: The Struggle for Equal Opportunity in Women's Employment*. Sydney: Allen and Unwin.

Department of Employment, Education and Training (DEET). 1990. *Occupational Segregation, Women's Work, Women's Pay*. Canberra: Australian Government Publishing Service.

Field, Laurie. 1990. *Skilling Australia: A Handbook for Trainers and TAFE Teachers*. Melbourne: Longman-Cheshire.

Glezer, Helen. 1991. "Juggling Work and Family Commitments." *Family Matters* 28(April):6–10.

Hely, Susan. 1990. "Working Women." *Charter* 61(8):20–21, September.

Lever-Tracy, Constance, and Noel Tracy. 1988. "Gender Differences in Participation Rates and Hours of Work in the Paid Work Force." *Australian and New Zealand Journal of Sociology* 24(1):124ff.

National Women's Consultative Council (NWCC). 1990. *Pay Equity for Women in Australia*. Canberra: Australian Government Publishing Service for the Labour Research Centre.

Smyth, Maggie. 1991. *Women and Work: An Overview*. Sydney: New South Wales Women's Advisory Council.

———. 1991a. *An Uphill Battle: Women and Paid Work*. Sydney: New South Wales Women's Advisory Council.

Windsor, Kim. 1991. *A Fair Deal for Women: A Practical Guide to Women's Priorities in Award Restructuring*. Canberra: Australian Government Publishing Service for the Department of Industrial Relations.

## Australian Men and Women Managers

Women are underrepresented in managerial ranks in Australia, although they have increased in managerial, professional, and administrative occupations from 11.23

percent in 1975 to 17.67 percent in 1985 and 25.09 percent by 1991 (*Australian Bureau of Statistics* 1986, 1991). International evidence on men and women managers (for example, Davidson and Cooper 1987) has found that men and women differ on factors thought important to hierarchical advancement in organizations. Differences have been found in work and home environments, work-relevant experiences, early backgrounds, and personal dispositions. Identification of such differences between men and women managers assists in understanding why women are underrepresented in management and, hence, in the formulation of strategies to redress their underrepresentation.

Researchers have argued against the emphasis of the 1960s and 1970s that women's lack of career advancement is caused by their "deficient" personal qualities in comparison to men's, or that women's advancement is caused by the special personal qualities, early experiences, and backgrounds of "exceptional" women. More recently (for example, Crawford and Marecek 1989), researchers have argued that women's lack of career advancement can be explained by the structure of social systems, rather than by personalistic explanations. Building on Kanter's earlier identification (1977) of women's career barriers as less opportunity, power, and numerical representation, gender is thought to be a principle of social organization influencing the structure of relations and the distribution of resources. If this is so, then the salient differences between women and men managers should be work and home factors and work experiences, rather than early backgrounds and personal dispositions. The authors surveyed 654 women and 616 men Australian managers of six managerial levels from supervisor to chief executive to provide information on such gender differences. The results showed a very strong similarity with international evidence comparing British men and women managers (Davidson and Cooper 1987) and, except for the findings for age and education, with those for U.S. managers (Harlan and Weiss 1982).

**Work Environment**

Australian women managers' work environments show that gender is a principle of social organization, resulting in more obstacles and different relationships than for men. In comparison to the men, the women have been to fewer formal training courses, report more obstacles preventing their course attendance, and have received fewer development opportunities (Table 1). The latter include representing their organizations at outside meetings and conferences and temporarily acting in positions at higher levels when incumbents are unavailable. Their work is, however, as challenging as men's. Women managers are also likely to be in more female managerial hierarchies than the men, with more women bosses and colleagues. Women report receiving more encouragement for their career development from within the organization from bosses and colleagues, but this is more likely to be from other women. Hence, they are more marginalized than men. Work structures are also less favorable. Women have fewer positions available to them for promotion, and thus shorter career ladders within their organizations.

**Hierarchical Advancement**

Similar to international evidence, Australian women managers have had both favorable and unfavorable hierarchical advancement. They have been promoted less,

TABLE 1. Summary of Gender Differences

| Category | Summary of Differences on Items* |
|---|---|
| *Advancement* | |
| Promoted | More women than men not received promotion (35–44), taken fewer years in organization to current position (35–44, 45–54), with similar numbers of each having applied. |
| Managerial Level | More women than men middle level (35–44) and fewer senior (45–54) managers and executives (45–54), women earned less than men (35–44, 45–54, >54), with fewer subordinates (35–44, 45–54). |
| Magnitude of Advancement | Trend for women to have less difference in managerial level from first to current job. |
| Chance of Promotion | More women than men reported very good chance (25–34), fewer years since promotion (35–44, >54), with similar expected position at career's end. |
| *Experience* | |
| Work Experience | Women had fewer years than men as full time employees in lifetime (25–34, 35–44, 45–54, >54), organization (25–34, 35–44, 45–54) and occupation (35–44, 45–54). |
| Work Continuity | Fewer women than men worked full time continuously (25–34, 35–44, 45–54, >54), and work full time as opposed to part time now (35–44, 45–54). |
| Moved | Fewer women than men relocated for promotion (25–34, 35–44, 45–54, >54) and similar numbers of men and women moved organizations for promotion. |
| Age | Women younger than men, with more 25–34 (14.4%, 7.5%) and fewer 45–54 (8.3%, 16.0%). |
| Education | Fewer women than men with technical college qualifications (2.4%, 6.5%) and more with undergraduate degrees (19.8%, 15.9%) and postgraduate diplomas (9.7%, 5.0%) (35–44, 45–54). |
| *Early Socialization* | |
| Parents' Education | Women's mothers (35–44) and fathers (25–34, 35–44, 45–54) more educated than men's. |
| Educational Encouragement | More women than men reported more encouragement from father for tertiary education (35–44) and from mother for tertiary education (25–34, 35–44, 45–54, >54) and year 12 (35–44), with similar from father for year 12 (<25, 35–44). |

*(continued on next page)*

TABLE 1   (continued)

| Category | Summary of Differences on Items |
|---|---|
| Education on Entry to Work | Fewer women completed grade 10 (6.0%, 12.3%) or 12 (7.8%, 17.3%) and more completed undergraduate degrees (21.9%, 12.2%) and postgraduate diplomas (4.9%, 1.4%) than men (35–44, 45–54). |
| Relationships with Parents | More women than men had closer relationships with both father (35–44) and mother (45–54). |
| First Born | Nonsignificant difference for first-born status for men and women. |
| Maternal Employment | Nonsignificant difference for maternal employment for men and women. |
| Secondary School | Nonsignificant difference in public and private school attendance. |

*Home Environment*

| Category | Summary of Differences on Items |
|---|---|
| Role Conflict | Women reported more times than men of family roles incompatible with work roles (35–44), with similar interference of home responsibilities with work (35–44). |
| Spouse Support | Women reported more times than men for spouse support for work as career path (25–34, 35–44), similar levels for work as income (35–44), and less domestic assistance by spouse (25–34, 35–44, 45–54, >54). |
| Spouse/Children | More women (19.2%) than men (5.8%) without spouses (35–44, 45–54, >54), and women with fewer children (25–34, 35–44, 45–54). |
| Child-Care | Fewer women than men reported convenient child-care (35–44), and regular unpaid dependent help (25–34, 35–44, 45–54). |
| Financial Responsibility | More men than women had all financial responsibility for dependents and more women share (25–34, 35–44, 45–54). |
| Spouse Salary | Women's spouses earn more than men's (25–34, 35–44, 45–54). |

*Work Environment*

| Category | Summary of Differences on Items |
|---|---|
| Training and Development | Women had fewer times than men on internal committees (35–44, 45–54), selection/promotion panels (<25, 45–54, >54), external (35–44, >54) and internal (35–44, 45–54) training courses, acting in a higher position for 3 or > months (35–44, 45–54), with similar times as representative at outside meetings (<25, 35–44, >54). |

TABLE 1 *(continued)*

| Category | Summary of Differences on Items |
|---|---|
| Challenging Work | Women and men had similar times on challenging assignments in first 3 months of present job, and since then (45–54). |
| Prevention of Training | More women's than men's participation in training courses prevented (35–44, 45–54, >54), with similar refusal of paid study leave (25–34, 35–44). |
| Organizational Encouragement | Women encouraged more times than men for career development by more senior person (35–44) and organizational colleagues (35–44, 45–44) and for promotion by others in organization (>54). |
| Network Encouragement | Women reported more times of external peer network assistance (35–44, 45–54) and of encouragement from external senior for career development (25–34, 35–44, 45–54). |
| Career Ladder | More women than men had no positions available for promotion in the same (<25, 25–34, 35–44, >54) and in a different (35–44, 45–54, >54) organizational category. |
| Gender in Hierarchy | More women than men in all women hierarchies (35–44, 45–54, >54), with all women colleagues and both sexes (35–44, 45–54, >54), and work closely with a woman manager (35–44). |
| Employer Category | Women and men similarly represented in public and private sectors. |

*Cognitions*

| | |
|---|---|
| Prepared to Move | Fewer women than men prepared to relocate for promotion (25–34, 35–44, 45–54), and similar number prepared to change organizations for promotion. |
| Self-Confidence | Similar self-confidence levels for performance of their job for men and women. |
| Internal Attributions | More women than men attributed job success to effort and ambition, but similarly for ability, experience, and qualifications. |
| External Attributions | More women than men attributed success to luck, but similar numbers to ease of task. |

*Note: Gender differences were tested by chi-squares, except for magnitude of advancement and self-confidence, which were t-tests. Differences between women and men were tested for the total sample and for the sample split into five age groups (<25, 25–34, 35–44, 45–54, >54). Where a significant difference for the total sample also occurred for an age group, that age group is given in brackets after the item. Where age groups are given in brackets after a nonsignificant gender difference, there was a significant gender difference for that age group.

but have taken fewer years to reach their current level. They are more likely to be middle than senior managers or senior executives, and are more likely to earn less and have fewer subordinates.

The hierarchical advancement of women managers is noteworthy when the obstacles these women face are considered. For women managers, especially those in the thirty-five to forty-four and forty-five to fifty-four age groups, in comparison to men more disadvantageous circumstances occur at home and at work. These include receiving less training and development, having more obstacles to training attendance, having shorter career ladders, having less work experience and continuity, more incompatible work-family roles, less domestic assistance, and less convenient child-care and dependent help.

Similar to findings in other countries, Australian women managers have had much less work experience and less work continuity but are more educated at the tertiary level than male managers. Women have relocated less for promotion than men, but have changed organizations for promotion as much as men. In keeping with British studies (Davidson and Cooper 1987), women are younger and more educated than the men. U.S. studies (Harlan and Weiss 1982) have indicated that women managers may be older and less educated than men managers.

**Home Environment**

Consistent with international evidence (Davidson and Cooper 1987; Gutek 1988), women managers are more likely than men to be of single status and childless. If not, they have more home responsibilities and work conflict through family roles, but they do share financial responsibilities. Surprisingly, they perceive their spouses to be more supportive than do men. Gender has structured social relations at home. Specifically, women with children report less child-care and dependent help. Although women report more spouse career support, they receive less domestic assistance and report more incompatibility of family roles with work. Those with spouses do report higher spouse salaries and more sharing of financial responsibilities than do men.

At the same time, Australian women managers do not appear to be deficient in the attitudes thought necessary for progression, in comparison to men. Thus women's underrepresentation in management does not appear to be determined by personal dispositions. Although they attribute their job success more to luck than do men, they also attribute it more to effort and ambition.

In all, the authors found that Australian men and women managers have very similar gender differences in work and home environments, work-relevant experiences, and attitudes to their British and U.S. counterparts. This pattern suggests that very similar factors are operating to result in women's underrepresentation in management within English-speaking, Western cultures. The findings do support the view that gender is a principle of social organization influencing resources and relations in disadvantageous ways for women, with situational factors of much greater influence on women's hierarchical advancement than individual factors, especially attitudes.

*Phyllis Tharenou*
*Denise K. Conroy*

## Bibliography

Alban Metcalfe, B. 1985. "The Effects of Socialization on Women's Management Careers." *Management Bibliographies and Reviews* 11:1–50.

Australian Bureau of Statistics. January 1991. *The Labour Force,* Catalogue No. 6203.0. Canberra: Commonwealth Government Printer.

————. 1986. *The Labour Force, Australia* ABS Catalogue No. 6204.0. Canberra: Canberra Publishing and Printing.

Betz, N.E., and L. Fitzgerald. 1987. *The Career Psychology of Women.* New York: Academic.

Cockburn, C. 1985. *In the Way of Women.* London: Pluto.

Crawford, M., and J. Marecek. 1989. "Psychology Reconstructs the Female." *Psychology of Women Quarterly* 13:147–65.

Davidson, M., and C. Cooper. 1987. "Female Managers in Britain." *Human Resource Management,* 26:217–42.

Gutek, B.A. 1988. "Sex Segregation and Women at Work: A Selective Review." *Applied Psychology: An International Review* 37:10–27.

Harlan, A., and C.L. Weiss. 1982. "Sex Differences in Factors Affecting Managerial Career Advancement." In *Women in the Workplace,* edited by P.A. Wallace, pp. 59–100. Boston: Auburn House.

Kanter, R.M. 1977. *Men and Women of the Corporation.* New York: Basic Books.

Lemkau, J.P. 1979. "Personality and Background Characteristics of Women in Male-Dominated Occupations: A Review." *Psychology of Women Quarterly* 4:221–40.

Riger, S., and P. Galligan. 1980. "Women in Management: An Exploration of Competing Paradigms." *American Psychologist* 35:902–10.

Tharenou, P., and D.K. Conroy. 1988. "Opportunities for and Barriers to Managerial Role Attainment." In *Readings in Australian Personnel Management,* edited by G. Palmer, pp. 179–221. Sydney: Macmillan.

## Australia: Immigrant Women and Work

In 1986 the Australian population reached sixteen million; it had more than doubled since World War II. Almost 40 percent of this growth was due to migration. The major source of immigrants to Australia is the United Kingdom and Ireland, but after 1945 large numbers of immigrants arrived from most European countries. In the 1970s nondiscriminatory immigration policies were introduced and by the mid 1980s 43 percent of Australia's immigrants came from Asia, 43 percent from Europe, and 13 percent from Oceania, mostly New Zealand. Presently the Australian population contains ethnic groups representing over 130 cultures and nations, and over 20 percent of the population was born overseas. One-eighth of the overseas-born arrived as refugees.

Immigrants are more often men than women. Women, however, are more likely to migrate as part of the family reunification program or as dependents rather than as independent migrants or principal applicants. (Independent migrants apply on the basis of occupational skills, while "principal applicants" apply to migrate either on the basis of family reunification or in other immigration programs.) The male to female ratio for overseas-born Australians has altered from 133:100 in 1954 to 105:100 in 1986 as family migration has become more frequent. Immigrant women are more likely to have children than Australian-born women but family sizes tend to be smaller.

It is common for a distinction to be made between immigrants from English-speaking countries and those of non-English-speaking countries. The socioeconomic status of immigrants from English-speaking countries is comparable to that of the Australian-born population. However, patterns of disadvantage, difference, and discrimination have been documented for those from non-English-speaking countries, who constitute 56 percent of the overseas-born population (Inglis et al. 1992; Jupp 1988).

Immigrants from non-English-speaking countries (NESC) are often at a disadvantage in the Australian labor market because of discrimination, language difficulties, and the nonrecognition of educational qualifications obtained overseas. These factors, and because many immigrants from NESC are unskilled workers, results in their concentration in blue-collar jobs that have higher occupational health hazards. Workers from NESC are therefore more likely to sustain work-related injuries and consequently retire earlier. Women from non-English-speaking countries are often doubly disadvantaged and face additional problems because of poorer access to education and a greater burden of unpaid work (Alcorso 1991).

In 1987, immigrants made up 25 percent of the 7.1 million people employed. In 1992, the overall labor-force participation rate for those born in Australia was 55 percent for women and 76 percent for men. The corresponding figures for immigrants were 48 percent and 73 percent. While the rate for women from English-speaking countries was the same as for Australian-born women, the labor-force participation rate for women from non-English-speaking countries was 44 percent. Unemployment rates follow a similar pattern: 9.4 percent for Australian-born women, 9.6 percent for women from English-speaking countries, and 14.0 percent for women from non-English-speaking countries. Unemployment rates were particularly high for those from Southeast Asia (20.7 percent) and the Middle East and North Africa (30.6 percent). In general, the labor force participation rate increased and unemployment rate declined as length of residence increased (ABS 1989, 1991).

Participation rates also varied by educational attainment: While 63 percent of women from English-speaking countries with postschool qualifications were employed, only 48 percent of those without were employed. The figures for women from non-English-speaking countries were 55 percent and 37 percent, respectively. Among these four groups, the unemployment rate was highest for women from non-English-speaking countries with postschool qualifications (9.3 percent). This reflects the difficulty of gaining recognition of these credentials.

Of those employed, a higher proportion of people from non-English-speaking countries work full time than their English-speaking-country or Australian-born counterparts. While over 90 percent of men in all categories are employed full time, only 60 percent of Australian-born women and those from English speaking countries (but 67 percent of women from non-English-speaking countries) are full-time employees. Only half (51 percent) of Australian-born women who were employed and married worked full-time in 1987, but 63 percent of women from non-English-speaking countries did so. These rates were especially high for women from Asia and 92 percent for married women born in Vietnam (ABS 1989; Pittaway 1991).

Immigrants from non-English-speaking countries were more likely to be employers or self-employed than Australian-born or those from English-speaking countries. Nine percent of employed women from non-English-speaking countries were self-employed and 4.6 percent were employers. In general, the employment pattern of women from non-English-speaking countries and English-speaking countries was consistent with those of Australian-born women. A notable exception is the concentration of women from non-English-speaking countries in the manufacturing sector (23 percent, compared with 10 percent of women from English-speaking countries and 9 percent of Australian-born women). To a lesser degree, women from non-English-speaking countries are also overrepresented in the transport and communication industry (ABS 1989).

Occupational stratification figures show an underrepresentation of women, and especially those from non-English-speaking countries, in the professions, management, and trades in Australia, and overrepresentation in clerical work, sales, and personal service. Immigrants from non-English-speaking countries, and particularly the women, are concentrated in lower-skilled, "dirty, dangerous, or degrading" occupations such as janitorial or production work: 12 percent of women from non-English-speaking countries work as plant and machine operators and 22 percent as laborers or in related occupations, compared with 2 percent and 12 percent respectively of employed, Australian-born women (Wood 1990).

In all industries, 75 percent of the workforce is Australian-born. However, in manufacturing industry, Australian-born make up only 58 percent of the employed women and 63 percent of employed men. Within this sector, women from non-English-speaking countries are concentrated in the clothing, textile, and footwear industries. These industries in particular have been seriously hurt by the downturn in Australian manufacturing, which has disproportionately affected the employment prospects of women from non-English-speaking countries and forced many into outwork, or piece-rate work according to market demand, conducted in the worker's home (Fincher et al. 1991).

When it comes to wages and salaries, gender appears to put workers at a greater disadvantage than ethnicity (defined here in terms of language spoken at home), at least in aggregate terms. For full-time workers in 1986, men from non-English-speaking countries could expect to earn 91 percent of the wages paid to Australian-born men. Australian-born women and those from non-English-speaking countries earned 79 percent of Australian-born men's earnings. Though proportionally there are far fewer of them, women from non-English-speaking countries in full-time, professional, para-professional, or white-collar jobs actually earned more than Australian-born women in similar jobs. Overall there were no appreciable wage differentials for immigrant and nonimmigrant women working full time in a trade or blue-collar job. In large part this is due to the strong union movement and centralized wage-fixing system. Comparable data regarding earnings for part-time work have not been published.

In general, immigrants' income is clustered in the middle of that earned by Australian-born workers. While 32 percent of Australian-born employees earned more than AUD$400 per week in 1986, only 29 percent of those from non-English-speaking countries did so. However, while 16 percent of Australian-born employees earned less than AUD$160 per week, only 9 percent of those from non-English-speaking countries did so (ABS 1989). Comparable data broken down by gender have not been published. Another indicator of standard of living does not show great disadvantage to immigrants: The rate of home ownership or purchase is almost the same for immigrants from non-English-speaking countries (72 percent) as for the Australian-born population (73 percent). However, Asian home ownership or purchasing rates are low (58.5 percent), especially for Vietnamese (38.7 percent), most of whom came to Australia as refugees and have very high un- and underemployment rates. While wages for individuals in similar jobs are comparable, because women from non-English-speaking countries are more likely to be employed in jobs at lower skill, and therefore pay levels, as a group their income is likely to be less.

Government policy has been influenced by findings that the major factors influencing labor-market status by immigrants from non-English-speaking countries are English-language competency, education level, length of residence, and lack of familiarity with the Australian labor market, discrimination, recognition of overseas qualifications, and, especially for women, access to suitable child-care facilities. In recent years much greater efforts have been made to set up mechanisms to properly assess overseas trade and professional qualifications. The Adult Migrant English Service provides a variety of English-language classes. Funding has also been provided to ethnic community organizations to establish child-care services. Antidiscrimination legislation has been passed in most states, and multicultural policies have been implemented in an attempt to ensure equality of access to public services. In addition, some workers' unions and the Industrial Relations Commission have taken an interest in outworkers and attempted to have standard industry conditions and pay rates extended to include them, but the deregulation of industry makes this difficult (Wooden 1990).

The pattern of interaction between workforce participation and family life is often different for immigrants and the Australian-born population. Communities from many non-English-speaking countries display a relatively strong traditional division of labor on the basis of gender, with husbands in employment and wives as homemakers. Women from non-English-speaking countries have been found to spend the least amount of time in leisure and most time doing unpaid work compared with Australian-born women, men, and other immigrants. They spend 40 percent more time on child care than Australian-born women, which includes substantially more time caring for others' children. Men from non-English-speaking countries also spend more time in caring for children than Australian-born men. Both women and men from non-English-speaking countries spend slightly less time than average in the care of sick and disabled relatives. These patterns are explained to a considerable degree by structural conditions of high unemployment rates for women from non-English-speaking countries, the fact that many immigrants do not have extended family they can rely on to assist in unpaid work, and immigration policies that recruit physically healthy families (Bittman 1991; Eliadis et al. 1990).

Migrants from non-English-speaking countries have a low utilization rate of formal child-care services, relying more on alternating shifts with spouses to allow child care. Day-care centers often do not meet the needs of this group in the community because of language, diet or religious differences, and the lack of care at the times that shift workers are employed (Yeatman 1988).

While the Australian government has taken steps to integrate immigrants into the mainstream of society and in particular in the workforce, more efforts need to be made to ensure equal participation, particularly for those who are especially disadvantaged. Women from non-English-speaking countries are in this category, and those from refugee backgrounds especially so.

*Gerard Sullivan*
*Joanne Travaglia*

## Bibliography

Alcorso, Caroline. 1991. *Non-English Speaking Background Immigrant Women in the Work Force: Working Papers in Multiculturalism No. 4*. Canberra: Office of Multicultural Affairs, Department of Prime Minister and Cabinet and Centre for Multicultural Studies, University of Wollongong.

Australian Bureau of Statistics. 1991. *Labour Force Status and Other Characteristics of Migrants. Australia, September 1990*. Catalogue No. 6250.0.

————. 1989. *Overseas Born Australians, 1988: A Statistical Profile*. Catalogue No. 4112.0

Bittman, Michael. 1991. *Juggling Time: How Australian Families Use Time*. Canberra: Australian Government Publishing Service for the Office of the Status of Women, Department of Prime Minister and Cabinet.

Eliadis, Maria, Rosetta Colanero, and Patricia Roussos. 1990. *Issues for Non-English-Speaking Background Women in Multicultural Australia*. Canberra: Office of Multicultural Affairs, Department of Prime Minister and Cabinet.

Fincher, Ruth, Michael Webber, and Iain Campbell. 1991. *Immigrant Women and Manufacturing Work*. Occasional Paper No. 25. Centre for Multicultural Studies, University of Wollongong.

Inglis, Christine, S. Gunasekaran, Gerard Sullivan, Chung-Tong Wu, eds. 1992. *Asians in Australia: The Dynamics of Migration and Settlement*. Sydney: Allen and Unwin.

Jones, Frank L. 1992. *Sex and Ethnicity in the Australian Labour Market: The Immigrant Experience*. Canberra: Australian Bureau of Statistics, Catalogue No. 6252.0.

Jupp, James, ed. 1988. *The Australian People: An Encyclopedia of the Nation, Its People and Their Origins*. Sydney: Angus and Robertson.

Pittaway, E. 1991. *Refugee Women: Still at Risk in Australia*. Canberra: Australian Government Publishing Service for Bureau of Immigration Research.

Wood, Gavin A. 1990. *Occupational Segregation by Migrant Status in Australia*. Murdoch University.

Wooden, Mark. 1990. *Migrant Labour Market Status*. Canberra: Australian Government Publishing Service for Bureau of Immigration Research.

Yeatman, Anna. 1988. *A Review of Multicultural Policies and Programs in Children's Services, with Particular Emphasis on Child Care Services*. Canberra: Office of Multicultural Affairs, Department of Prime Minister and Cabinet.

————. 1990. *Immigrants and the Australian Labour Market: An Annotated Bibliography*. Canberra: Australian Government Publishing Service for the Bureau of Immigration Research.

## French Women's Educational Opportunities

The education of female children in nineteenth-century France was shaped by a social prejudice toward women. Even though the program of education administered by the state differed in many respects from the earlier one established by the church (for example, the curriculum was less traditional and more intellectual or liberal-arts oriented), there were still enormous differences between the instruction given to girls and the one given to boys. In both the church and state educational systems, young ladies did not receive a comprehensive education nor were they prepared to attend college. This restriction of women's studies helped preserve the traditionally low-status position of women (Mayeur 1981). However, this situation did change. Thanks to innovators such as Mathilde Salomon, young women were provided the opportunity to participate in educational programs reserved for boys. Because of these important developments, they were able to attend college and eventually acquire a wider range of occupations and a more dominant role within French society.

Napoleon's comment about the "weakness of women's brains" was a belief shared by many in early modern French society. In this period, the primary role of a woman was to be a good wife and child-rearer. Such an ideology was rigidly adhered to and shaped young women's education.

During most of the nineteenth century young ladies received a religious education. In fact, the church almost exclusively controlled the education of the young female population until the Camille Sée law of 1880. Its program was based on very narrow views concerning women's place in society. The "arts of agreement" (music, dance, sewing, and so forth) heightened the attractiveness of the young lady to her husband or his family. A basic knowledge of arithmetic, writing, and reading enhanced her ability to be a competent housewife. The young girl was also taught how to become a good hostess and how to speak eloquently. Moreover, since a pious Catholic woman was expected to exhibit highly moral behavior, biblical and theological knowledge was considered indispensable (Mayeur 1981).

It should be noted that while girls born in privileged families were raised in convents, the rest of the population attended public schools, where most teachers were nuns as well. In both public and private schools, however, the education received was at an elementary-school level. Although the instruction provided in public schools was actually superior to and more practical than the one given in bourgeois institutions, it was still quite limited. Attendance was also poor, as the young girl would often return home in order to take care of a sibling or to help in the fields at harvest time. Furthermore, education was not considered essential, because even in the larger and less privileged classes the girl was destined to assume primarily a domestic role. Besides, if the young woman had to work outside the home, such as in a factory or a workshop, she would learn her trade in that setting. Toward the end of the century, with the advent of the New Republic, the church's monopoly of girls' education was strongly shaken. The state attempted to weaken the influence of the church politically and transform the entire educational system. In order to remove nuns from public schools, the state created a series of new laws. For example, in 1883 children were to be taught only by accredited teachers. Until then, nuns had not needed teaching credentials, as a letter of recommendation written by the Mother Superior was sufficient for instructing children (*lettre d'obédience*). A year later a law banned church persons from public schools by requiring the personnel of public schools to be nondenominational. Finally, the state prohibited all instruction by members of religious congregations in 1904.

With the rise of modern industrial society, the perceived need for a more advanced, secondary education for women began to emerge, one that would continue to be free from the clergy's control. Thanks to Camille Sée and Jules Ferry, the structure of female education took a more modern turn; in 1880, girls' *lycées* and *collèges*—that is, high-schools—were created, offering to girls for the first time a more substantive education (Crubellier 1979). The task was not accomplished without controversy. Because women had never received a secondary education and were not granted diplomas to teach at that level, the instruction had to be provided by men. The closeness of the sexes in the classroom concerned many families. The members of the bourgeois class also resented seeing their daughters sharing the same classroom bench with girls from the lower classes. Moreover, many did not believe that women should receive further education. Although the beginnings were difficult, these schools grew every year. Paralleling their growth was the creation in 1881 of the *Ecole Normale Supérieure* of Sèvres, which trained future female high-school teachers (Margadant 1990).

If girls were better educated, they still did not receive an education similar to the one boys received in *lycées* and *collèges*. In order to graduate at the completion of their schooling, young men had to pass an examination, the *baccalauréat*, which was the only diploma that guaranteed entrance into the university. In contrast, there was no preparation for such an examination in the girls' *lycées* and *collèges*. Upon graduating, young women received a type of high-school diploma certifying that they did graduate but which was otherwise useless. Women could not attend universities, nor could they pursue careers. For the state, as for the church, the woman's first mission was still that of marriage and motherhood (Ozouf 1963).

Certain women played the major role in changing this situation. It was essentially due to the initiatives taken by a bold innovator, Mathilde Salomon, director of the Collège Sévigné, a private institution for girls, that profound changes occurred. As director of this school from 1883 to her death, twenty-six years later, Salomon accomplished more for women than might have seemed possible. She surrounded herself with excellent teachers who provided her students with a superior education. Being adept at foreign languages she added both German and English to the curriculum. These were not, however, her only innovations. In 1885 she created evening classes, *cours du soir,* for young women who wanted to become teachers and had not been able to register at Sèvres. Furthermore, she created in her school in 1904 the first kindergarten in France (Salomon 1907).

Among Salomon's many initiatives one surpasses all the others. While other high schools limited girls' studies by not preparing them for the entrance exam to universities, the Collège Sévigné allowed young ladies to study for the *baccalauréat*. Thus, in 1894 two of the school's students took the *baccalauréat* exam and passed it. This first success inspired the director to prepare all her students for the *baccalauréat*. Taking advantage of the exam's new format, which offered a section in Latin and languages, she instituted an accelerated study of Latin that gave her pupils the same chance as male students to obtain the diploma. Beginning in 1905, all Collège Sévigné students prepared to take the *baccalauréat* exam (Collège Sévigné 1980).

It is important to recognize that, although the state did not prevent women from taking the *baccalauréat* (fifteen young ladies had been authorized to take the exam between 1861 and 1873), it never prepared them for it (Mayeur 1979). Thus, Salomon pursued a program of feminine emancipation by providing her students with a much more comprehensive education that enabled them to take the university entrance examination. A few years later, other private schools for girls followed the example created by Salomon and began preparing their students for the *baccalauréat*. For instance, Madame Daniélou, a former student and teacher at the Collège Sévigné, created her own Catholic school using Sévigné as a model. The Institut Adeline Désir, where Simone de Beauvoir studied, was also part of this trend.

Thanks to the influence of these private schools, a growing number of young women tried to attain the *baccalauréat*. Confronted with the success of these new schools, the state was forced to modify its own curriculum so that by 1924, in public girls' *lycées* and *collèges,* the number of students who obtained the *baccalauréat* was twice the number of those who received the simple high-school diploma. From that time on, universities were opened to both sexes. While other changes in the educational system, such as the sexual desegregation of primary and secondary schools, would not occur until later in the twentieth century, these earlier transformations were crucial in altering the stereotyped role of women, their work opportunities, and their overall life chances in modern French society.

*Frédérique Van de Poel-Knottnerus*

### Bibliography

Collège Sévigné. 1980. *Le livre du centenaire, 1880–1980*. Paris: Fernand Nathan.

Compayré, Gabriel. 1907. *L'enseignement secondaire des jeunes filles: Législation et organisation*. Paris: P. Dupont.

Crubellier, Maurice. 1979. *L'enfance et la jeunesse dans la société française, 1800–1950*. Paris: Librairie Armand Colin.

Margadant, Jo Burr. 1990. *Madame le professeur: Women Educators in the Third Republic*. Princeton: Princeton University Press.

Mayeur, Françoise. 1981. *De la révolution à l'école républicaine*. Vol. 3 of *Histoire générale de l'enseignement et de l'éducation en France*. 4 vols. Paris: Nouvelle librairie de France.

———. 1979. *L'éducation des jeunes filles en France au XIX siècle*. Paris: Hachette.

———. 1977. *L'enseignement secondaire des jeunes filles sous la Troisième République*. Paris: Presses de la fondation nationale des sciences politiques.

Ozouf, Mona. 1963. *L'école, l'église et la république, 1871–1914*. Paris: Librairie Armand Colin.

Prost, Antoine. 1968. *Histoire de l'enseignement en France, 1800–1962*. Paris: Librairie Armand Colin.

Salomon, Mathilde. 1893. *A nos jeunes filles: lectures et leçons familières de morale, d'après le programme des écoles primaires supérieures de jeunes filles*. Paris: L. Cerf.

———. 1907. *L'enseignement secondaire des jeunes filles en France, 1880–1907*. Paris: Administration et rédaction de la revue de l'enfant.

### Women in East Germany

At the end of World War II, Germany was divided into four occupied zones: The western zones, occupied by the United States, France, and England, became the Federal Republic of Germany (FRG); the eastern zone, occupied by the Soviet Union, became the German Democratic Republic (GDR). During its forty years of existence (1949–1989), the communist regime of the GDR brought nearly all women into the workforce. Despite remaining gender inequalities at work and in the division of labor at home (Gysi and Speigner 1983), women experienced extraordinary changes in their social position and in their self-understanding. These gains were real, though compromised by other features of the regime. They are now threatened by the unification of the two Germanies. Women have been especially affected by unemployment; by 1993, they constituted 64 percent of the unemployed. Subsidies for childcare centers as well as other supports for dual-career families and families headed by women have also been reduced (Rueschemeyer 1994).

The need for women to participate in the reconstruction of the German economy and society after World War II was intensified by the shortage of male labor; there were three million more women than men in the area of the GDR (Rueschemeyer and Schissler 1990). The Soviet military administration established equal pay for equal work, and in 1949 the new constitution established gender equality in all spheres of social life. Though women entered the labor force in large numbers in the 1950s, there were neither nurseries nor kindergartens to care for the children; at first, these were often improvised by women's committees in the factories. The system of Krippen (for children under three) and kindergartens (for children three to six) became fully developed only in the 1960s.

By 1971, the time of the Eighth Party Congress, it was clear that more supports were needed if women were going to have more than one child and remain active in the workforce. Women's labor continued to be important because massive emigration led to a decline of the GDR's population from over eighteen million in 1950 to under seventeen million and to an unfavorable age structure. (The Wall, erected in 1961, was designed to prevent further emigration.)

During the 1970s, a number of important supports for working parents were initiated, and housing and other necessary services expanded. The supports included a year's leave with pay at the birth of the first child and a guarantee of returning to the same job (later an option for men as well, though rarely used) with increased time for each additional child, a work week of forty hours (rather than $42^3/4$) with children under sixteen, one household day a month, paid days if a child was ill, and increased vacations for shift-workers. Single parents were given priority in the allocation of nursery places and apartments.

By the early 1980s, over three-quarters of the children under three were in Krippen and over 90 percent of the children between three and six were in kindergartens. At the same time, nearly 70 percent of all women had completed an apprenticeship or more advanced vocational training. Half of the students in the university were women; women of forty years or younger had achieved the same educational level as men. Over 90 percent of women eligible to work were either studying or in the workforce, a third part time (typically working six rather than eight hours a day).

However, even with the entry of women into a number of traditionally "male" occupations such as medicine and law (they constituted approximately half of the doctors and judges and a third of the lawyers) and despite their participation in engineering, metallurgy, and other technical fields, they remained segregated to a considerable degree in traditionally female occupations. And within their professions they were rarely found in the highest leadership positions. Although they represented a third of the managerial personnel, the higher the position, the lower the percentage of women. This was true at the workplace and in the union as well as in the party and in government (Meyer 1986).

Both women and men were strained by the demands of work and the difficulties of taking care of household chores after the end of the workday. Although younger and more educated men shared much of the work, women had by far the larger share of the burden. Divorce rates were high; approximately one in three marriages ended in divorce. A large number of women had children outside of marriage: A third of the children born had single parents. The supports that these women—and dual-career families—had have been severely reduced. The closing of enterprises and cultural institutions in which women were highly represented, combined with greater discrimination in the workplace, have severely affected women. Women are also affected by more restrictive abortion regulations. In East Germany, abortion was legal during the first three months of pregnancy. The arguments about a unified code for both Germanies were severe and the compromise proposed by parliament was rejected by the Constitutional Court and returned with further stipulations. Because approximately 20 percent of deputies in the German parliament are women, some of these issues continue to be addressed. As of now, however, the laws against gender discrimination in hiring are relatively weak, and the state funding for day care is inadequate without federal aid (Rueschemeyer 1994).

*Marilyn Rueschemeyer*

**Bibliography**

Gysi, Jutta, and Wulfram Speigner. 1983. "Changes in the Life Patterns of Families in the German Democratic Republic." Paper of the Academy of Sciences of the GDR, Institute of Sociology and Social Policy, Berlin.

Meyer, Gerd. 1986. "Frauen in den Machthierarchien in der DDR." In *Deutschlandarchiv* 293–311.

Rueschemeyer, Marilyn. 1994. "Women in the Politics of Eastern Germany: The Dilemmas of Unification." In *Women in the Politics of Post-Communist Eastern Europe*, edited by Marilyn Rueschemeyer, pp. 87–116. New York: M.E. Sharpe.

Rueschemeyer, Marilyn, and Hanna Schissler. 1990. "Women in the Two Germanys." In *German Studies Review*, DAAD Special Issue 1990, 71–85.

## Japanese Women: A Historical Overview

Women in Japan have, over the past two thousand years, occupied a wide range of symbolic, occupational, and familial statuses. In the earliest recorded history, Japanese women appear to have had political, social, and religious influences in society. Even in peasant communities, until relatively recently, women have been powerful, expressive, and even publicly recognized as decision-makers. Internal and external sources of change have over time affected women's influence and status, sometimes enhancing and valuing their roles, and sometimes reducing their visibility and access to status and power.

Anthropologists and scholars of folklore note that Japanese creation myths and early cultural practices gave women high status and power. Early family structure was matricentric and matrilocal, and women inherited property and status from their women families. In the sixth to eighth centuries, empresses ruled Japan, although some appear to have been "regional" rather than national rulers (Pharr 1977). Women were also shamans, mediating between humans and the gods, and women's importance in the native Shinto religion remains today in various rites and in the presence at shrines of the *miko*, or shrine-maidens. In the Heian Period (793–1185), women of the court were noted writers and poets, the most famous of these, Lady Murasaki Shikibu, the writer of the first vernacular novel, *The Tale of Genji* (Brazell 1973). However, there were countervailing forces in the borrowed cultural and religious models from China. Confucian and Buddhist values, imported from the Asian mainland, place women low on the social and moral hierarchy of status and virtue, and Confucian social ethics influenced legal codes.

Gradually, Confucian patriarchal social codes and hierarchical models began to characterize Japanese aristocratic and *samurai* families, and over time these practices spread to lower classes through the process called "samuraization," or the emulation of upper-class values by merchant and rich peasant families. In such families, women were seen as possessions of the male lineage, and the phrase "borrowed womb" (*hara no karimono*) referred to the fact that the bride's chief duty in service to the family into which she married was to bear sons to carry on the line. Women lost property rights as well and became socially and financially dependent on their husbands' families.

These tendencies were exaggerated among samurai families during the period of internal warfare, from the twelfth through the sixteenth centuries, for men were valued for their ability to fight and women became pawns in strategic marriage alliances. The sequestering of women in such families was a response to the problem of security in warfare: A woman marrying into a warrior household was seen as a potential traitor and her access to her own family was limited to control the spread of strategic secrets.

During the Tokugawa Period (1603–1868), a period of relative peace and political and social consolidation, women's roles were to some degree morally and culturally constrained further by Confucian norms. An eighteenth century treatise, the *Onna Daigaku* by Kaibara Ekken, emphasized that women must obey fathers when young, husbands in their marriage, and sons in their old age, though the formula stresses "family" loyalty rather than specific duties to men. In the countryside and in lower-class families, women had more freedom and, working alongside men in the fields, often experienced greater equality in decision-making and status as well (Smith and Wiswell 1982). This period of peace also saw the growth of the entertainment industries, the *mizu shobai,* in which women were notable as performers, dancers, singers, and as *geisha,* polished artistes and courtesans. Prostitution and entertainment service jobs occupied women at the lower rungs of the "entertainment" ladder.

The Meiji Period (1868–1912) introduced many aspects of Western work to Japan, affecting women economically, culturally, and legally. In response to the opening to the West, Japanese leaders further sought to consolidate and strengthen Japanese society and culture, and the creation of the Meiji Civil Code (1898) institutionalized the Confucian family structure of the upper classes as a legal standard for the family (Bernstein 1991). While education for women lagged behind that of men, at all levels women participated in learning. The earliest industries employed women in great numbers, and up to 80 percent of the textile industry workforce was female. Participation in the workforce, however, did not mean independence and professional development for these women: Most worked only for a few years before marriage, and most sent most of their earnings home to their families, or set them aside for their wedding costs.

During the Taisho Period (1912–1926), urban, educated women were often influenced by Western trends in fashion and literature, and the *moga,* or "modern girl," was the Japanese "flapper." Women also joined political and social reform movements, and the feminist movement was led by the Bluestocking Society (Seitosha), a group of activist poets and writers, followed by other groups of women involved in labor, birth control, suffrage, and other reforms (Ishimoto 1984). The women's movements of the 1920s, however, like other movements for social and political reform, were suppressed in the 1930s as dangerous and potentially treacherous. In the war years, Japanese women's groups were mobilized to provide support for the troops and government campaigns. A pronatalist government policy attempted to increase the birth rate and to discourage the use of birth control.

Postwar reforms, established by the Allied Occupation and by the Japanese after the Occupation (1945–1952), gave women the vote, legal equality with men, full coeducational opportunities in the schools, and more access to a range of employment. Family law allowed women equal access to divorce, property, and inheritance rights. In fact, in some areas, the American constitution enacted in Japan exceeded legal codes in the United States in their wide-ranging guarantees of equality to women.

*Merry White*

## Bibliography

Bernstein, Gail. 1991. *Recreating Japanese Women, 1600–1945*. Berkeley: University of California Press.

Brazell, Karen. 1973. *The Confessions of Lady Nijo*. Stanford: Stanford University Press.

Ishimoto, Shiduzue. 1984. *Facing Two Ways*. Stanford: Stanford University Press.

Lebra, Joyce, et al. 1976. *Women in Changing Japan*. Stanford: Stanford University Press.

Pharr, Susan. 1977. "Japan: Historical and Contemporary Perspectives." In *Women: Roles and Status in Eight Countries*, edited by Janet Z. Giele and Audrey C. Smock, pp. 219–55. New York: Wiley.

Smith, Robert J., and Ella Wiswell. 1982. *The Women of Suye Mura*. Berkeley: University of California Press.

## Contemporary Japanese Women: Family, Education, and Workplace

Women in postwar Japan have seen far-reaching changes in their lives. Legally and institutionally, women have been granted full access to educational, social, and occupational equality with men. However, mobility through educational credentials, the postwar meritocratic basis for career success, has been notably lacking for women, as has any significant change in attitudinal and domestic patterns that might free women for wider participation in society. In spite of this apparent lag, women have created pervasive changes in their work and family lives. These efforts, it is said, are stimulating reconsideration of workforce and family practices for both men and women (Iwao 1992).

Under the constitution instituted by the Allied Occupation of Japan in 1947, gender biases in family and education laws were removed. Women no longer were seen as possessions of their families, to be given to the families of their spouses on marriage, and women could inherit and divorce on equal terms with men. Other constitutional provisions for the equality of the sexes make Japanese law fundamentally more progressive than that of most modern nations.

Seen from other perspectives, however, one aspect of the 1947 laws appeared to reinforce separate standards for women rather than full equality. The Labor Standards Law overall created better working conditions for women but in its emphasis on protection now is seen as placing restrictions on women. The idea of "protection" (including such stipulations as "no late-night overtime work," "no physically demanding work," "no work demanding overnight travel," and the guarantee of menstrual leave) reinforced the gender-role typing that strikingly characterizes most institutional considerations of women and divides especially middle-class families by sphere of authority and activity.

While the Labor Protection Laws of 1947 were finally repealed in the Equal Employment Opportunity Act of April 1986, the underlying notion of "man's work, women's place" still characterizes women's occupational lives and their domestic arrangements. For example, although overtime work, one of the requisites for promotion on a management track, is now theoretically available to women, few can make it onto the track, in the first place and, once on, few are actually encouraged to join the after-hours cohesion-promoting sessions known as *nomunikeshon*, or "communication through drinking," seen as necessary for a man's advancement. And those women who in theory might join in often in practice must rush home to fulfill their role as homemaker to husband and children. Most working women are "pink-collar" employees, known as "O.L.," or office ladies, who perform clerical and service tasks and who work fixed hours.

With the "separation of spheres" of middle-class, white-collar lives and perpetuated, divided role assignments within the home, men are unlikely to share domestic responsibilities even with a full-time working wife. Family life is influenced by a conservative cultural lag, and few women are not fully responsible for their households (Imamura 1987). In spite of the double life many women must lead, the workplace rarely provides resources such as child care, and most government-authorized day care centers require parents to pick up children no later than six P.M. Moreover, men may receive salary increases when their wives give birth, but working women receive only (in most cases) a very short maternity leave. Where child-care leave is mandated (since 1992 for full-time workers in larger firms only), only half the women eligible actually take long-term leave, because of the pressure of the work or because they do not want to burden their work-mates. One alternative, practiced by most women over the past thirty years, is to leave work altogether when they become pregnant (or visibly pregnant) and to reenter the workforce when the youngest child is in school. The second entry is almost invariably at a lower-status job, for less money, than was the first, but this "M-Curve" pattern has been common for women not on a professional career track. For those who have higher aspirations, there is a trend to take only the briefest leave time and to create elaborate, stressful, child-care arrangements, often a patchwork of day care, family aid, and neighbor support.

Women often resort to part-time work or piece work done at home. Employers in many cases prefer a large part-time force because these workers are paid low wages, are not union members, receive no benefits, and can be laid off in slack periods. Other women create their own jobs as freelancers, or their own companies. In 1992 there were forty-four thousand companies headed by women, a fourfold increase over a decade ago.

The gender-defined dual-track workplace has not eroded significantly since the passage of the Equal Employment Opportunity Act in 1986, for the law incorporates little enforcement power. Passed after a year of negotiation, the compromise achieved represents symbolic more than actual advances in work conditions. While some say that more leverage for women might emerge from a labor shortage, these predictions are not yet clear, and shortages in unskilled and semi-skilled work may actually be met by hiring retirees and foreign laborers rather than by acceding to demands for structural change from the female labor force.

The work of the home is culturally defined as women's work, and, although household technology has reduced the time needed to complete tasks, women still have the responsibility for conforming their housework to very high cultural standards. With most husbands working very late hours, women do almost four hours per day of housework, compared with an average of eight minutes of tasks performed by their husband. Domestic work also means child-rearing tasks demanded by the competitive educational system. Beginning at least by junior high school, most middle-class children prepare for entrance examinations to high school and college, and the role of the mother is viewed as significant. As "homework coach," as supervisor of professional tutoring and cram school participation, and as provider of general support and solace, the mother is actively involved (Vogel 1978). The success or failure of the child is seen as her responsibility, and many women who had worked outside the home now quit at this point in their children's lives to devote themselves to this activity. A popular home-study desk epitomizes their role: Equipped with a full assortment of pencil sharpeners, lights, and calculators, it also has a button to be pushed ringing a bell in the kitchen to summon mother for help or a snack.

The division of labor often leaves the husband and father outside many aspects of home life, leading to discussions of the "absent father syndrome" among psychologists. Among some women, however, especially those whose children have grown and left home, there is a saying that "the good husband is healthy and absent." Similar attitudes have led to an increase in divorces initiated by middle-aged wives, often just at the moment of their husband's retirement. To these women, a husband's retirement brings not a second honeymoon but a return to the caretaking role, this time tied to the needs of a dependent, helpless man (White 1992).

Demographic change and cultural norms may now be diverging for women. The traditional work for wife, *okusan*, or "woman in the interior," is scarcely now applicable to most women of any age. There is a range of opportunities and experiences open to and sought by Japanese women. The social forces and value given to women in their role as mothers continues to determine their lives during their child-rearing years. The financial independence of full-time, working women has contributed to their choice to delay marriage, and the practice of splitting a man's lump-sum pension at divorce similarly liberates the older women. Life expectancies for women and men have risen greatly, and a woman can expect to live into her eighties, while the birth rate now has dropped to about 1.5 births per family. The low birth rate, a concern for government officials, is said to be related to the high costs of education and land, and the availability and safety of birth control and abortion technology. However, with fewer children and a longer life span, women now have a greater period of relative freedom: From the time of their last child's entry into full-time schooling to their own deaths, there are typically more than forty years. With good health care and continuing relative affluence, Japanese women find themselves, at least in terms of legal and demographic realities, better positioned than ever to create fulfilling lives.

*Merry White*

### Bibliography

Imamura, Anne E. 1987. *Urban Japanese Housewives*. Honolulu: University of Hawaii Press.
Iwao, Sumiko. 1992. *The Japanese Woman*. New York: Free Press.
Lebra, Takie. 1984. *Japanese Women: Constraint and Fulfillment*, Honolulu: University of Hawaii Press.
Pharr, Susan. 1981. *Political Women in Japan*. Berkeley: University of California Press.
Saso, Mary. 1990. *Women in the Japanese Workplace*. London: Hilary Shipmen.
Vogel, Suzanne. 1978. "Professional Housewife: The Career of Urban Middle Class Japanese Women." *Japan Interpreter* 12(1):16–43.
White, Merry. 1991. *Challenging Tradition: Women in Japan*. New York: Japan Society of New York.
———. 1992. "Home Truths: Women and Social Change in Japan." *Daedalus* 121(4)61–82.

## Occupational Sex Segregation in New Zealand, 1971, 1976, 1981

Occupational sex segregation is a significant feature of employment that has been shown to have negative consequences for the position of women in many countries. Lower earnings (both for men and for women) and unequal access to authority, on-the-job training, promotions, and lateral transfers within firms, as well as physical and social distance in the workplace, are all associated with employment in female-typed occupations (Reskin 1984; Roos 1981; Taylor et al. 1986). Explanations of the origins and persistence of occupational sex segregation include discrimination and women's own choices (see England 1992 for a detailed review). Explanations of change in occupational sex segregation include changing structural features of the social organization of work (Oppenheimer 1970; Reskin and Roos 1990; Williams 1979) and changing demographic characteristics of the labor force (Beller 1984; Lewis 1985). The findings reported below follow the latter tradition (Gwartney-Gibbs 1988).

New Zealand presents an interesting test case for studying change in occupational sex segregation. It is unique among advanced industrial economies because, despite its strong market and cultural ties to North America and Europe, it maintains a relatively large production-agricultural sector and has a relatively small, but growing, service sector. Moreover, female labor-force participation in New Zealand remains substantially lower than in North America and most of Western Europe. Thus, despite New Zealand's shared cultural heritage with Australia, North America, and Western Europe, and associated similar patterns of economic and social organization, it maintains distinct features that may influence levels and patterns of change in occupational sex segregation. These features make New Zealand an interesting test case for cross-national comparison.

New Zealand census data from 1971, 1976, and 1981 reveals, first, that levels of occupational sex segregation in New Zealand were higher than those of several other industrialized nations, but comparable to the degree and the decline of occupational segregation found in Australia and the United States (Blau and Hendricks 1979; Jacobs 1989; Lewis 1985). The index of segregation in eighty occupations showed that in 1971, 62.5 percent of employed women would have to change occupations in order to have the same occupational distribution as men. As female labor-force participation increased from 34 percent to 39 percent in the decade (an increase of 120,000 female workers), the share of women in sixty-seven out of eighty occupations also increased. By 1981, the index of segregation declined slightly to 57.6 percent.

Second, there were marked increases in the proportion of the female labor force in highly sex-segregated occupations. In 1981, the majority (51.6 percent) of women workers were employed in occupations two-thirds or more female, and this was almost twice the proportion of the female labor force in highly sex-segregated jobs in 1971 (26.5 percent). The growth of highly female-concentrated occupations in the decade was so great as potentially to absorb all new female labor-force entrants in the period. The largest and most highly sex-segregated occupations were stenographer and typist, tailor, medical and dental assistant, cook and waitress, general clerical, bookkeeper and cashier, and retail salesperson.

Third, very high—and increasing—proportions of young women moved into sex-typical occupations. About two-thirds of the women in the labor force less than twenty-four years old worked in occupations two-thirds or more female in 1981, compared with roughly 42.9 percent in 1971. As female cohorts age, they move increasingly into sex-typical occupations. In 1981, all age cohorts were in more sex-typical occupations than when their cohort entered the labor market. These results suggest that observed declines in the index of segregation are associated more with men entering female-typed and mixed-sex occupations than with women moving into men's more advantageous occupations. Such a pattern parallels changes in U.S. occupational structure (England and Farkas 1986).

Many of these patterns parallel patterns found in prior research on other countries, particularly Australia. This suggests, first, that similar patterns underlie the sex structure of occupations in industrialized nations, despite considerable latitude in economic and social organization, and second, that the forces that govern change in those patterns also may be similar. Unfortunately, there exists no systematic cross-national examination of the antecedents, correlates, and consequences of change in patterns of occupational segregation (see, however, Roos 1985).

*Patricia A. Gwartney-Gibbs*

## Bibliography

Beller, Andrea H. 1984. "Trends in Occupational Segregation by Race and Sex, 1960–1981." In *Sex Segregation in the Workplace: Trends, Explanations, Remedies*, edited by Barbara F. Reskin. Washington, D.C.: National Academy.

Blau, Francine D., and W.E. Hendricks. 1979. "Occupational Segregation by Sex: Trends and Prospects." *Journal of Human Resources* 14:43–55.

England, Paula. 1992. *Comparable Worth: Theories and Evidence*. New York: Aldine de Gruyter.

England, Paula, and G. Farkas. 1986. *Households, Employment, and Gender: A Social, Economic, and Demographic View*. New York: Aldine.

Gwartney-Gibbs, Patricia A. 1988. "Sex Segregation in the Paid Workforce: The New Zealand Case." *Australia and New Zealand Journal of Sociology* 24:263–78.

Jacobs, Jerry A. 1989. "Long-Term Trends in Occupational Segregation by Sex." *American Journal of Sociology* 95:160–73.

Lewis, D.E. 1985. "The Source of Changes in the Occupational Segregation of Australian Women." *Economic Record* 61:719–36.

Oppenheimer, Valerie K. 1970. "The Female Labor Force in the United States." Population Monograph Series No. 5. Berkeley: University of California, Institute of International Studies.

Reskin, Barbara F., ed. 1984. *Sex Segregation in the Workplace: Trends, Explanations, Remedies*. Washington, D.C.: National Academy.

Reskin, Barbara F., and Patricia A. Roos. 1990. *Job Queues, Gender Queues: Explaining Women's Inroads into Male Occupations*. Philadelphia: Temple University Press.

Roos, Patricia A. 1985. *Gender and Work: A Comparative Analysis of Industrial Societies*. Albany, N.Y.: SUNY Press.

———. 1981. "Sex Stratification in the Workplace: Male-Female Differences in Economic Returns to Occupation." *Social Science Research* 10:195–224.

Taylor, Patricia A., Patricia A. Gwartney-Gibbs, and R. Farley. 1986. "Changes in the Structure of Earnings Inequality by Race, Sex and Industrial Sector, 1960–1980." *Research in Social Stratification and Mobility* 5:105–38.

Williams, G. 1979. "The Changing U.S. Labor Force and Occupational Differentiation by Sex." *Demography* 16:73–87.

## Efforts toward Gender Equity in Sweden

Sweden is known for its many efforts at promoting gender equality in education, in the family, and in employment. Through legislation and social programs, the Swedish government has been the primary force behind these efforts. While these state actions have yet to bring full equality for Swedish men and women, the policies have shown success in certain areas, such as in increasing the involvement of women in paid work. As such, Sweden provides a unique example of government attempts to achieve gender equity.

Since World War II, the Swedish government has established a variety of public programs to allow men and women the means easily to combine both family and paid work roles (Moen and Forest 1990; Widerberg 1991). Many of the policies have been aimed at easing the traditional burden on women in fulfilling family roles at the cost of employment activity. For example, the Swedish government provides some economic support to families with children, as well as an extensive system of child care.

Important within these policy efforts is the parental-leave program, which allows parents a period of paid leave from their work so they can spend time with their children (Widerberg 1991). Begun in 1955, this state-sponsored program was initially for mothers only. In 1974, Sweden became the first country to introduce a parental leave program for both mothers and fathers. By 1990, employed parents were together eligible for up to fifteen months' leave, during which time they would receive roughly 90 percent of their gross earnings.

Family and paid work roles also are more easily combined in Sweden through the extensive supports for part-time workers (Sundstrom 1991). Among women workers, there is a high percentage who work part-time (43 percent in 1986) and still retain job security, receive full social benefits, and are highly unionized. In addition, during the 1970s, the Swedish government initiated tax reforms so as to encourage wives and husbands both to be employed (Carlson 1990).

Some social scientists suggest that these various social policies have led to increases in the number of children born, as well as the greater involvement of women in paid work (Hoem 1990). Sweden currently has one of the highest total fertility rates (2.13 in 1990) and one of the highest female labor-force participation rates (86 percent in 1990) in Western Europe. Certainly, in the past twenty-five years since the major government reforms were instituted, there has been a steady increase in the proportion of Swedish women in paid work (Gustafsson and Jacobsson 1985). In 1970, 59 percent of adult women were employed. This had risen to 84 percent by 1990. At the same time, the level of unemployment among Swedish women remained at around 1 to 2 percent. These statistics indicate a dramatic increase in women's labor-market activity in Sweden. While some predict that gender differences in labor-market activity will disappear by the end of this century, Swedish men and women continue to differ in the type of jobs they perform and the level of income they earn (Rosenfeld and Kalleberg 1990). Part of this may be due to the government focus on full employment of women, rather than specifically promoting the advancement of women in all areas of paid work.

One effort to encourage men's and women's entry into nontraditional occupations has been a series of reforms aimed at removing gender bias from the entire educational system, including adult vocational training and universities (Boucher 1982; Thelin 1990). Starting in 1956, Swedish policy-makers began re-designing school programs so as to remove the effects of gender, as well as economic or class background, on educational achievements. For example, boys and girls are no longer taught separately, nor are they taught separate curricula. In the short term, these educational reforms have not led to substantial change in the segregation of men and women into different occupations. Still, combined with other social reforms, schooling based on gender equality may still contribute to gender equality in the labor market over the long term.

So even with substantial government efforts to achieve gender equality, important differences persist in Swedish men's and women's lives. For example, in Sweden wives (even employed wives) do more household work than their husbands (Haas 1981), and women are less likely to be employed in higher-status occupations than are men (Rosenfeld and Kalleberg 1990). The Swedish experience, thus, provides a useful measure of the potential, as well as limits, of state action in producing gender equality.

*Lisa A. Cubbins*

## Bibliography

Boucher, Leon. 1982. *Tradition and Change in Swedish Education.* Oxford: Pergamon.

Carlson, Allan. 1990. *The Swedish Experiment in Family Politics: The Myrdals and the Interwar Population Crisis.* New Brunswick, N.J.: Transaction.

Gustafsson, Siv, and Roger Jacobsson. 1985. "Trends in Female Labor Force Participation in Sweden." *Journal of Labor Economics* 3:S256–74.

Haas, Linda. 1981. "Domestic Role Sharing in Sweden." *Journal of Marriage and the Family* 43:957–67.

Hoem, Jan M. 1990. "Social Policy and Recent Fertility Change in Sweden." *Population and Development Review* 16:735–48.

Moen, Phyllis, and Kay B. Forest. 1990. "Working Parents, Workplace Supports, and Well-Being: The Swedish Experience." *Social Psychological Quarterly* 52:117–31.

Rosenfeld, Rachel A., and Arne L. Kalleberg. 1990. "A Cross-National Comparison of the Gender Gap in Income." *American Sociological Review* 96:69–106.

Ruggie, Mary. 1984. *The State and Working Women: A Comparative Study of Britain and Sweden.* Princeton: Princeton University Press.

Sundstrom, Marianne. 1993. "The Growth in Full-Time Work among Swedish Women in the 1980s." *Acta Sociologica* 36:139–50.

———. 1991. "Part-Time Work in Sweden: Trends and Equality Effects." *Journal of Economic Issues* 25:167–78.

Thelin, Annika Andrae. 1990. "Working towards Equal Opportunities: The Swedish Context." In *The Primary School and Equal Opportunities: International Perspectives on Gender Issues*, edited by Gaby Ueiner, pp. 9–34. London: Cassell Educational.

Widerberg, Karin. 1991. "Reforms for Women—On Male Terms—The Example of the Swedish Legislation on Parental Leave." *International Journal of the Sociology of Law* 19:27–44.

# Women in Newly Industrialized Societies

## Women, Work, Patriarchy, and Development in India

The majority of Indian women are involved in regular economic activity or productive work. This is in addition to their domestic work, which patriarchal ideology defines as women's responsibility, in India as elsewhere. Cross-culturally, the sexual division of labor is taken as natural and allocates to women those jobs that are poorly rewarded, onerous, and labor-intensive. Yet, without the work of women, family survival would be in jeopardy. Their contribution to the national and world economy is crucial.

There is tremendous diversity in the work of Indian women, and in the incidence of the double burden of work (Anant et al. 1986; Lebra et al. 1984). "Modernization" strategies sponsored by the postcolonial state in India and supported by the international political economy have changed but not improved women's roles, rights, or status. The condition of the majority of working women in India is characterized by poverty, lack of education and training, lack of access to technology and credit, uncertain employment (caused by agricultural seasonality, for example) or lack of it, excessive work burdens, and appalling working conditions. There is, however, some hope in the efforts of women's movements and organizations in India to improve women's daily lives and challenge the structures of patriarchy (Everett 1986; SEWA 1988; Sen 1990).

Patriarchy is a powerful system in India. It is constantly reinforced through religious and cultural practices and educational systems. At the base of the patriarchal system is denial of women's access to and control over productive resources, such as land and labor. The operation of patriarchy in structuring the form and extent of women's work participation varies with class, caste, residence, and region. For upper-class, upper-caste, rural, North Indian women, for example, it takes the form of restrictions on physical mobility and sexuality (through *purdah*, or veiling, and not allowing women to be seen in public spaces like the market). At the bottom of the socioeconomic grid, in contrast, it may take the form of longer and harder work; for example, poor, low-caste, rural, South Indian women form the bulk of casual laborers in agriculture. The double burden of work is lessened for upper-class women because they employ lower-class women as domestic help; for the women in lower classes the double burden is experienced acutely, because even tasks such as fetching water or fuel-wood can take many hours (Agarwal 1988).

Despite the overwhelming evidence that Indian women are actively involved in economic activity, their work is often rendered invisible and unrecognized in official statistics (Agarwal 1989). There was little recognition by male development planners that the problems of poverty are gender-specific until the U.N. Decade for the Advancement of Women (1975–1985). This conceptual bias can be traced to mainstream social theory adopted by development agencies that assume that "modernization" through economic development will lead to the production of greater output and wider participation in economic activity, and that these processes will automatically include women and improve their status, rights, and roles. This assumption was also made by the British colonial government, which ruled India for nearly two hundred years, until independence was won in 1947. Boserup (1970) first questioned this assumption. She showed that female poverty increased during the colonial era because colonial rulers disfavored women in access to land, credit, technology, and employment. But the patriarchal ideology of colonists was only part of the problem. The other legacy of colonization is that through private-property creation, commercialization, and export-oriented production it created and enhanced inequalities among nations (like India and Britain) and impoverished large numbers of men and women within nations. Within nations, women suffered more because of patriarchy (Sen and Grown 1987).

While the biases of male development planners in India are reflective of their position as privileged men, the interests of powerful nations—the former colonizers from the First World—are also enmeshed in development strategies and inequitable structures (Mies et al. 1988). Three "crises" in the world political economy that have real and detrimental consequences for poor women in India and elsewhere in the developing world are: (1) the excessive emphasis on global trade and national food production, leading to the neglect of local food, fuel, and water availability; (2) the balance of payments and debt crisis, leading to adoption of "structural adjustment" policies imposed by agencies such as the International Monetary Fund, leading to cuts in social-service expenditures and other domestic austerity measures; and (3) growing militarization, fundamentalism, and violence, all of which divert scarce resources away from the fulfillment of basic needs and subjugate women to new forms of patriarchy (Sen and Grown 1987, pp.50–74).

State-sponsored, internationally aided development in India has proceeded at differing rates and has affected different sectors and men and women differently (Government of India 1975). About 80 percent of the female labor force is employed in agriculture (Government of India 1984). Most of these women are employed as casual, daily laborers, or work as unpaid helpers on family farms. In all regions, the jobs defined as female are the most laborious and the least remunerative; for example, paddy transplanting, which involves standing ankle deep in water and bending down to plant each seedling, is exclusively women's work in South India. Agriculture has been transformed through the adoption of the Green Revolution, a strategy to transform "traditional" farming through a package of high-yielding varieties of seeds (mainly wheat and rice), irrigation, chemical fertilizers, and pesticides. The Green Revolution has increased the amount of foodgrains produced in India: In the year 1966, India imported 15 percent of its foodgrains, but by 1984–1985 it was able to send food to famine victims in Ethiopia. In addition, the Green Revolution has led to greater employment in a few well-endowed areas (such as the northern state of Punjab, equipped with irrigation and infrastructure). In areas such as the southern states of Andhra Pradesh, Karnataka, Tamil Nadu, and Kerala, women's employment has increased through the increase in the number of crops planted, the number of operations on each crop (such as weeding and fertilizing), and harvesting and processing activities. However, the Green Revolution has had many adverse effects (Farmer 1986; Shiva 1988). Because it requires a heavy investment of funds and labor, poorer, smaller cultivators have often sold their land and become landless, agricultural laborers. More women now work on the lands of others, earning a wage to feed their families. Further, the Green Revolution has often displaced women's labor through mechanization; for example, where twenty women may have been employed for hand-milling rice, one skilled man may be employed to run the electric mill. Last, although the availability of food has increased, the disposable income of the poorest rural families has not, so they have not increased their levels of consumption (Lipton and Toye 1990).

About 8 percent of working women in India are employed in the industrial sector; this percentage has increased dramatically in the last few decades. Yet, whether in industries where the employment of women has been customary for some time (like the textile industry in Bombay) or newer, export-oriented industries like electronics and garments, women are employed because they are cheap and manipulable (Banerjee 1991). Again, the sexual division of labor discriminates against women, resulting in their placement in dead-end, poorly paid, low-skilled jobs, with long hours of repetitive work and abysmal working conditions. Industrial work is being increasingly decentralized: Women are subcontracted to work at home and are paid by the piece. They are even more vulnerable to exploitation because they work in isolation. Because their work is vital for family survival, women in these jobs too have no option but to continue. The record of trade unions is dismal. These trends are likely to intensify as the Indian economy, which was more inward oriented than those of most other developing countries and had strict restrictions on foreign capital, has recently jumped on the liberalization bandwagon.

About 12 percent of the female labor force is employed in the service sector (Census of India 1981). In this sector, a few women are highly educated professionals and work as lawyers, doctors, managers, politicians, and so forth; they also form the bulk of teachers and nurses. The majority of women (94 percent of the workforce), however, are self-employed or work in the "informal" realm of the service sector (SEWA 1988). The self-employed include women who are small-scale vendors, traders, and hawkers of goods such as food, vegetables, and fish, women who are home-based producers such as potters, milk producers, garment stitchers, and processors of agricultural produce, and women who sell their labor such as construction workers, agricultural laborers, head loaders, cooks, sweepers, and washers of clothes. The self-employed are among the poorest of workers; often they cannot meet even basic needs: food, housing, water, health, and education. A majority of these women contribute as much as 50 percent of total family income; in female-headed households, 100 percent. Low income, uncertain or no work, exploitation by middlemen, lack of credit, and poor working conditions were some of the difficulties reported by the women themselves (SEWA 1988).

In conclusion, patriarchal ideology, the sexual division of labor, the world political economy, and development strategies aimed at "modernization" all contribute to the exploitation and undervaluation of women and their work in India. However, past and recent experiences with women's movements and organizations in India offer some hope; they reveal women as actors who can recognize, defend, and advance their own interests. These organizations occupy a wide range of political and social spaces. Thus, agricultural peasant-worker organizations have fought for higher agricultural wages, but in addition link matters of family survival to issues of women's self-respect (Everett 1986; Sen 1990). Other organizations, such as the Self Employed Women's Association, have developed innovative ways to organize self-employed women to improve their daily lives: by stopping harassment by the police for street-vending, setting up a bank to provide cheap credit, upgrading women's skills, and improving women's access to health care (SEWA 1988). Still other movements, such as Chipko-to, which stops the contract felling of trees by literally hugging them, are linking issues of gender to the fight for environmental conservation and human rights (Shiva 1988). These organizations, and many more, not only offer hope, they also provide directions for changing the unequal division of labor between the sexes, providing basic subsistence needs, achieving a more equitable distribution of resources, and ensuring a better quality of life not just for working women in India but for underprivileged men and women the world over.

*Priti Ramamurthy*

## Bibliography

Agarwal, Bina. 1988. "Neither Sustenance nor Sustainability: Agricultural Strategies, Ecological Degradation and Indian Women in Poverty" In *Structures of Patriarchy*, edited by Bina Agarwal. New Delhi: Kali for Women.

———. 1989. "Work Participation of Rural Women in the Third World: Some Data and Conceptual Biases." In *Serving Two Masters: Third World Women in Development*, edited by Kate Young. Ahmedabad: Allied.

Anant, Suchitra, S.V. Ramani Rao, and Kabita Kapoor. 1986. *Women at Work in India: A Bibliography.* New Delhi: Sage.

Banerjee, Nirmala, ed. 1991. *Indian Women in a Changing Industrial Scenario.* New Delhi: Sage.

Boserup, Esther. 1970. *Women's Role in Economic Development.* London: George, Allen and Unwin.

Everett, Jana. 1986. "We Were in the Forefront of the Fight: Feminist Theory and Practice in Indian Grass-Roots Movements." *South Asia Bulletin* 6(1):17–23.

Farmer, B.H. 1986. *Understanding Green Revolutions: Agrarian Change and Development Planning in South Asia.* Cambridge: Cambridge University Press.

Government of India. 1975. *Towards Equality: Status of Women in India—A Synopsis of the Report of the National Committee on the Status of Women (1971-74).* New Delhi: Indian Council of Social Science Research.

———. 1984, *Census of India, 1981.* New Delhi: Registrar General of India.

Lipton, Michael, and John Toye. 1990. *Does Aid Work in India? A Country Study of the Impact of Official Development Assistance,* London: Routledge.

Lebra, Joyce, Joy Paulson, and Jana Everett, eds. 1984. *Women and Work in India: Continuity and Change.* New Delhi: Promilla.

Mies, Maria, et al. 1988. *Women: The Last Colony.* London: Zed.

Self Employed Women's Association (SEWA). 1988, *Annual Report.* Ahmedabad: SEWA.

Sen, Ilina. 1990. *A Space within the Struggle: Women's Participation in People's Movements.* New Delhi: Kali.

Sen, Gita, and Caren Grown. 1987. *Development, Crises, and Alternative Visions: Third World Women's Perspectives.* New York: Monthly Review.

Shiva, Vandana. 1988. *Staying Alive: Women, Ecology and Survival in India,* London: Zed.

### Women's Earnings in Israel

Approximately 42 percent of women aged fifteen and over participate in the Israeli labor force (compared with 57 percent of women aged sixteen and over in the United States). On average, in 1987 Israeli women earned a wage rate of $3.90 per hour and worked approximately thirty-five hours per week (Israeli Central Bureau of Statistics 1990).

One would not expect much gender-based earnings discrimination to be present in Israel, in view of the formal egalitarian ideology claimed to be the cornerstone of the Israeli society. Furthermore, legislative action prohibiting discrimination has been taken lately. The Equal Opportunity in Employment Law, the most recent and comprehensive legislation in this area, was passed in 1988. Moreover, the Israeli public sector and a substantial portion of the private sector are covered by labor agreements in which wages and conditions of employment are collectively determined. Empirical results, however, do not live up to such egalitarian expectations.

Women's hourly wage rate in Israel approaches only about 75 percent of the wage rate of their male counterparts. This wage gap, which has remained stable over the years, cannot be explained by differences in education, labor-market experience, and other human-capital variables, or by differences in occupational distributions between male and female workers. For example, men's median years of schooling is lower than that of their female counterparts (11.9 years of schooling versus 12.6, respectively). Neither does the advantage of men in terms of labor-market experience explain the 25 percent "premium" added to their wage rate. In fact, the entire 25 percent wage gap between Israeli men and women remains "unexplained" after accounting for gender-based differences in productivity-related variables (Semyonov and Kraus 1983). Moreover, some of the studies conducted in Israel have indicated that if women were compensated for their human capital level similarly to men, they should have earned slightly more than men. This indicates a higher average level of human capital accumulated by women.

Most working women in Israel are segregated into a small number of "female-type" jobs, mainly secretarial, teaching, and nursing. Their share in the high-paying "male-type" jobs is small (Izraeli and Gaier 1979). For example, women constitute only 15 to 20 percent of the population of Israeli managers, and approximately 20 percent of Israeli scientists employed in academia (as compared with 40 and 30 percent respectively in the United States). Not only are the average wages in the "female-type" jobs lower than those paid in the "male-type" jobs, but also women earn less than men who work in similar jobs.

This phenomenon of an "unexplained" earning gap, which is found in both the private and public sectors in Israel, is usually attributed to market discrimination (Cain 1986). It should be noted, however, that researchers have been more successful in explaining portions of the wage gap between men and women through analyses of data collected at a single firm rather than data gathered from national samples, probably because such firm-level data provide better and more detailed information about jobs and organizational positions, and because a one-firm analysis controls for variability in organizational policies and environments. In several cases, Israeli researchers have been able to explain between one-half and two-thirds of the 25 percent wage gap between males and females working in the same firm (Haberfeld and Shenhav 1987).

Two differences emerge from a comparison of the gender-based earnings gaps in Israel and in the United States and should be clearly stated. The 25 percent gap between the average hourly wage rates of men and women in Israel is smaller than the gap in the United States, where it reaches approximately 30 to 35 percent (Marini 1989).

However, the entire earnings gap in Israel remains "unexplained" after controlling for gender-based differences in human capital and job characteristics, thus resulting in an estimated 25 percent wage discrimination against women. Studies in the United States, on the other hand, have explained approximately half of the 30 to 35 percent gap by differences between working men and women in human capital and job characteristics. As a result, the estimated discrimination against women in the American labor market is lower than in Israel and stands at a level of 15 to 20 percent.

*Yitchak Haberfeld*

**Bibliography**

Ben-Porath, Yoram, and Reuben Gronau. 1985. "Jewish Mother Goes to Work—Trends in the Labor Force Participation of Women in Israel, 1955–1980." *Journal of Labor Economics* 3:S310–27.

Cain, Glen G. 1986. "The Economic Analysis of Labor Market Discrimination: A Survey." In *Handbook of Labor Economics*, edited by Orley Ashenfelter and Richard Layard, pp. 693–785. New York: Elsevier.

Haberfeld, Yitchak, and Yehouda Shenhav. 1987. "Gender-Based Wage Discrimination or Level of Analysis? Aggregated vs. Organizational Data." In *Academy of Management Best Papers Proceedings*, edited by Frank Hoy, pp. 364–68. Columbia, S.C.: The Academy of Management.

Israeli Central Bureau of Statistics. 1990. *Statistical Abstracts of Israel*. Vol. 41. Jerusalem: Government Press.

Izraeli, Dafna, and Kalman Gaier. 1979. "Sex and Interoccupational Wage Differences in Israel." *Industrial Relations* 18:227–32.

Marini, Margaret Mooney. 1989. "Sex Differences in Earnings in the United States." *Annual Review of Sociology* 15:343–80.

Semyonov, Moshe, and Vered Kraus. 1983. "Gender, Ethnicity and Income Inequality: The Israeli Experience." *International Journal of Comparative Sociology* 24:258–72.

## Women and Work in Mexico

An understanding of women's work roles in Mexico must be viewed in the context of Latin America's rigid typing of gender, as defined by the machismo cult. Although women have made slight advances in their status in the late twentieth century, they are subordinate to the male both in the home and in industry, in which they find marginal positions despite a higher literacy rate than men. They are relegated predominantly to service roles and to the assembly line, often in factories belonging to multinational corporations.

The history of Latin America offers a classic example of gender discrimination. This tradition is rooted in Western culture but also represents much of the Third World today. Because of the slower rate of social change and its adherence to male dominance on the Iberian peninsula for most of its history, Latin America has only recently become sensitized to the concepts of egalitarian gender relationships. This development is related to the peculiar development of a feudalism based on quasimedieval institutions that were removed from the rationalistic innovations from which Latin America was even more isolated than were Spain and Portugal. These vestiges of patriarchalism have lingered on into the twentieth century. However, any generalization has to be tempered by considerable adjustment to the subcultures fashioned by nation, region (urban-rural), social class, education, and generation. Of course, the individual family regime and personality differences must also be considered.

### Marriage, Family Socialization, and Identity

Through much of Latin America, marriage has varied between the formal system (with the choice of either a civil or a civil-religious ceremony) and the consensual union or union libre. The choice is dictated by a number of factors—social class, urban or rural residence, and local traditions. Although not as popular in Mexico as in several other countries, the consensual union permits the woman more freedom to dissolve an oppressive relationship in a male-dominated society. In reality, especially in rural areas, the union tends to be fairly permanent.

The family structure is basically nuclear but notably in the middle and upper class has extended overtones. The *compadrazgo* system means considerable stress on ceremonial kinship and in certain areas the godmother may receive as much attention as does the natural mother. In any event, the mother plays the central role in the family, both instrumentally and expressively.

Obviously the family structure cannot be understood without an explanation of the formidable differentiation in sex roles as compared with the larger sweep of Western cultures. Both genders are socialized into certain models that begin with the early years. The distinction represents a curious balance between the aggressiveness and dominance of the male and the fragile subordination and fragility of the female. After all, in her ideal form the woman personifies the Virgin Mary and hence the magic meaning of the madre. In keeping with the Judeo-Christian tradition the male is central and is to embody machismo. This concept includes several traits: (1) preeminence of the male; (2) his stronger sex interest and the freedom to develop this capacity; and (3) the need to demonstrate his power and masculinity. This includes the privilege of maintaining the casa chica or the periodic visit to the bordello. Again, the difference varies enormously among the countries. Chile shows a minimum and Mexico a relative maximum, but even here many men do not adhere to the cultural norm.

Inevitably women are caught in a dilemma. They fall into three variants: (1) chastity and purity; (2) the mother, inspired by the Virgin Mary, who remains chaste but is technically no longer virginal; and (3) the fallen. In urban areas this typology is gradually adjusting to the norms of Western society. But the literature, both research and fictional, documents the degree to which women are made to feel different from men. Even in infancy and the preschool years, the boy may appear in the street only partially clad, but his sister must be fully clothed even in the tropics. From infancy to marriage the female is to be protected from the potential ravages of the male (Franco 1989). Indeed, for both genders a confusion of models becomes a problem: The family is considered sacred, assuming that it is intact. If the father is present, the son follows the lordly and remote pose of his father. If the father is absent, the boy overcompensates in order to protect his masculinity, and indeed by his mid teens may become the ruling male figure of the household. In any instance, the mother is forced into an acutely insecure role of being the chief socializing agent of the family, but with her powerlessness and dubious status provides an ambivalent model for the daughter.

In Mexico the female role is further complicated by the conquistador heritage and in part by the warrior cult of the Aztec and other indigenous sources, not to mention the aftermath of the Moorish occupation of Spain. The model contains the ideals of violence and boisterousness. The Mexican male must inflict "actions by chingar (doing violence to others), or else he suffers them himself at the hands of others" (Paz 1961, p.78). As the male is the active, dynamic agent, the female is confined to a passive and masochistic role. Moreover, intellectuals have been responsible for the perpetuation of a number of stereotypes as well as protests and guilt about these misrepresentations. Especially since 1968—a somewhat revolutionary year in which Mexicans began to rethink their social norms and ideals—a revision of the woman image has been a high priority (Franco 1989, p.175f).

Studies of immigrants to the United States underline the identity problems they face. Male dominance, the twilight of the extended family, lack of network of friends, and barriers to their entry into meaningful employment prevent them from forming a secure self-image. Even so, they apparently have greater freedom than do the women who remain in Mexico. For instance, in a study of decision-making among a national sample of married couples, in ten of the eleven areas men made the final decision. As one example, the wife's working outside the home, 74 percent of the husbands said they made the decision, and 57 percent of the wives agreed with that assessment (Elu de Lenero 1969).

**Women in the World of Work**

The late twentieth century has seen a marginal advance in women's rights. For example, the vote did not come to women in Mexico until 1953. Despite a major role women played in the Mexican Revolution and in social and political reform in much of Latin America, their status has been seldom enhanced (Hahner 1980). Moreover, despite the image of the political conservatism of women, they are found to be more liberal than men and increasingly aware of their inferior position in the political and economic world. As one symbol of this submerged position, women are seldom sought out by census-takers (most of whom are male), even though in many barrios the majority of homes are headed by women (Butler Flora and Santos, 1986). The limited access women have to a career and to power in general is reflected in the educational attainment they are allowed. Males are somehow permitted lengthier schooling. As result, of Mexico's recorded illiterates in 1980, 2.5 percent were male, 3.9 percent were females (Tunon 1987).

Three different viewpoints surround the status of women in Latin America (Tiano 1986): (1) the integration thesis holds that industrialization precedes emancipation and achievement of equality as women assume their place in the economic world; (2) marginalization presumes that women can at best enter a subordinate role in industry; (3) the exploitation thesis claims that women are inevitably confined to a proletarian role in the capitalist search for profits. It is possible to rephrase the debate as the articulation versus exclusion arguments (Phillips 1990).

The research findings in the field have not resulted in any final answer to the dilemma. What does seem clear is that industry has increasingly taken women from the home. In Mexico they moved from being less than 4.6 percent of the workforce in 1930 to over 24 percent in 1980, but research reveals that they have not been elevated from a subservient role (Tunon 1987). The three dominant areas of their employment are service, 46 percent (especially domestic, yet they are also 57 percent of the nation's teachers); commerce and sales, 22 percent; and industry, 21 percent. Interestingly, the most active employment period is between ages fifteen and twenty-four. At the same time, official unemployment records point to nearly twice the unemployment rate for women than for men.

Several studies have focused on the maquiladora industries that constitute the "export processing zone" (a "global assembly line" attached to multinational organizations), as found in border towns such as Ciudad Juarez as well as in the major industrial centers of central Mexico (Fernandez-Kelly 1983). Redkau (1984) points to the segregated role of women in industry, yet they provided more than half the income in over a third of the families studied.

Several lines of inquiry have been directed to the status of women in a changing social order, not least the relative position of women in the urban versus the rural milieu. On this question Chaney and Schmink (1976) point out that in much of the hemisphere women have more equality in the indigenous cultures, notably hunting and gathering societies (where they have access to the technology) than they do in the Westernized ones. Women obviously have more entrée to employment in the city, as reflected in their rate of cityward migration, which is higher than men's. A number of experiments have emerged in order to resolve the problem of women's limited horizons in rural areas, particularly in land-reform programs (Butler Flora and Santos 1986).

Another dimension in the status and employment of women has centered on the relevance of the economic system. Even though capitalist regimes have hardly favored the role of women, neither are Marxist regimes very inviting, as they only add to the burdens of the woman as she is expected to follow her traditional roles of homemaking and child-rearing in addition to economic ones, for which she is as underpaid as she is under capitalism (Chant and Brydon 1989).

The question remains as to why women's labor, particularly in areas of low pay, is highly desired, and yet in other areas few career opportunities are available (Tiano 1986). In the rural area, progress may be more visible than in the urban, but it has the longest way to go (Phillips 1990).

*Robert C. Williamson*

## Bibliography

Butler Flora, Cornelia, and Blas Santos. 1986. "Women and Farming Systems in Latin America." In *Women and Change in Latin America: New Directions in Sex and Class,* edited by June Nash and Helen Safa, pp. 208–28. South Hadley, Mass.: Bergin and Garvey.

Chaney, Elas M., and Marianne Schmink. 1976. "Women and Modernization: Access to Tools." In *Sex and Class in Latin America,* edited by June Nash and Helen Safa, pp. 160–82. New York: Praeger.

Chant, Sylvia, and Lynne Brydon. 1989. "Introduction: Women in the Third World: An Overview." In *Women in the Third World: Gender Issues in Rural and Urban Areas,* edited by Lynne Brydon and Sylvia Chant, pp. 1–46. New Brunswick, N.J.: Rutgers University Press.

Elu de Lenero, Maria del Carmen. 1969. *Hacia Donde va la Mujer Mexicana?* Mexico, D.F.: Instituto Mexicano de Estudios Sociales.

Fernandez-Kelly, Maria P. 1983. *For We Are Sold, I and My People: Women and Industry in Mexico's Frontier*. Albany: State University of New York Press.

Franco, Jean. 1989. *Plotting Women: Gender and Representation in Mexico*. New York: Columbia University Press.

Hahner, June E. 1980. *Women in Latin American History*. Rev. ed. Los Angeles: Latin American Center Publications, University of California.

Nash, June. 1986. "A Decade of Research on Women in Latin America." In *Women and Change in Latin America: New Directions in Sex and Class*, edited by June Nash and Helen Safa. pp. 3–21. South Hadley, Mass.: Bergon and Garvey.

Paz, Octavio. 1961. *The Labyrinth of Solitude*. New York: Grove.

Phillips, Lynne. 1990. "Rural Women in Latin America: Directions for Future Research." *Latin American Research Review* 25:89–107.

Redkau, Verena. 1984. *"La Fama: y la Vida: Una Fabrica y sus Obreras*. Tlapan, Mexico, D.F.: Centrol de Investigaciones y Estudios Superiores en Antropologia Social.

Tiano, Susan. 1986. "Women and Industrial Development in Latin America." *Latin American Research Review* 21:151–70.

Tunon, Julia. 1987. *Mujeres en Mexico: Una Histora Olvidada*. Mexico, D.F.: Planeta.

## Filipino Women's Educational and Occupational Opportunities

In recent years, women in the Philippines have had increasing access to educational and occupational opportunities. Education enrollment rates for females at all levels shows moderate increases, and women continue to gain advantage in college and graduate school enrollments (Smock 1981). Female employment also has been increasing. Between 1978 and 1983, female employment registered a 30 percent growth. There are now two female workers for every male worker in the Philippines (*Women's Decade in the Philippines* 1985).

Cultural tradition and the family structure serve as catalysts in promoting women's access to opportunities outside the home. Filipinos observe a cultural tradition that extends deference, equality, and respect for women. The evidence derived from popular folk beliefs and fragments of recorded history suggests that the prehistoric people who inhabited the group of islands now known as the Philippines accorded respect and equality to women. One folk belief relates the story of creation showing the first man, *Malakas,* and the first woman, *Maganda,* emerging simultaneously from a bamboo trunk split in the middle. Historical narratives, from the Chinese chronicler Chao-Ju-Kua to the handful of Spanish historians such as Morga, Loarca, and Padre Chirino, recorded the role of Filipina women as heiress to the sultanate, as property owners, and as priestesses and healers. According to Agoncillo and Alfonso (1967), customary law gave women the right to assume leadership of the *barangay,* the right to own and inherit property, the right to engage in trade and industry, and the right to give names to their children.

Colonial rule under Spain lasted three hundred years (through the 1890s) and introduced a legal system that classified women together with infants and idiots. If unmarried, a woman could not leave home without the consent of her parents. If married, she needed the consent of her husband to enter into contracts. Blair and Robertson (1903) noted that colonial education instructed girls in the work of their sex, namely sewing, embroidery, cleaning, cooking, washing clothes, and so forth. But more important, girls were also subjected to religious and moral indoctrination. Colonial education run by religious orders defined the choices of roles for Filipino women: motherhood or service to God.

Nakpil (1963), however, disputes the image of Filipinas during the Spanish regime as submissive and dependent. She argues that women of that period were hard working and industrious. Middle-class women were engaged in trading and lower-class women were farm workers, weavers, hat makers, potters, cigar-makers, and wooden-shoe handcrafters. Nakpil also argued that the oppressive colonial rule taught women to become more self-sufficient and independent, because the male provider in the family often was forcibly taken by Spanish authorities to render *polos y servicios* obligation.

Unlike the oppressive Spanish colonial rule, the American rule (1898–1946) proclaimed "benevolent assimilation" as the cornerstone of its colonial authority. The policies were aimed at preparing the Filipinos to embrace a democratic form of government. There was no conscious effort to exclude women's participation in nation building. Hence, the ideals of freedom and equality benefited both men and women, but particularly women's opportunities in education and in employment. Castillo (1942) reports increases in enrollments at all levels of education during the American rule. While there are no available statistics classifying male and female enrollments to show equal opportunity in education, there are indications that the female population had considerable representation in the school system. Nakpil (1963) noted that in less than twenty-seven years of American indoctrination, thousands of Filipinas became physicians, dentists, pharmacists, optometrists, nurses, and school teachers.

The introduction of freedom and equality as ideals in a democratic country contributed to women's active political participation. In 1933, the Suffrage Law was passed by the national legislature. Women obtained the right to have a voice in selecting individuals passing laws affecting their lives. Yet three years later, however, the United States–sponsored Commonwealth Constitution of 1936 excluded women's right to vote. Organized women's groups such as the Asossacion de Damas Filipinas, Catholic League, YWCA, and the Women's Club engaged in an aggressive political campaign against the exclusion and were successful in restoring women's suffrage.

While the colonial regime passed laws and adopted policies denigrating the status of women and limiting their opportunities, the family preserved the remnants of a cultural tradition that accepted and approved women's seeking opportunities outside the home. Generally, a family's meager resources allow any able family member to pursue educational and occupational goals to improve the family's economic security. Female members almost always are the beneficiaries. Thus, the increasing visibility of women in educational institutions and in the workplace is primarily due to the family.

The goal of every family, and particularly lower-class families, is to attain financial security and material comfort. The family as a unit strives to reach that goal. Thus, any family member can expect cooperation and mutual aid benefit from other family members in the nuclear family and the extended family—including both maternal and paternal relatives. The family places a high value on education to improve their social and financial standing. Education is regarded as a means for avoiding distasteful manual labor and gaining prestige (Lawless 1967) or the path to a prestigious white-collar or professional future (Holnsteiner 1970).

By pulling together its available resources, a lower-class family can send a son or daughter to college. The family looks up to the individual household member who has the potential for success and achievement regardless of gender, age, or chronological position in the family. Pido (1986) states that support and preferential treatment are invested in a family member identified as the "brightest."

Very often girls are the beneficiaries of such preferential treatment. Young girls undergo discipline and responsibility training. Girls benefit from helping at home, cooking meals, cleaning the house, and baby-sitting younger siblings, while the boys venture outside the home and engage in rough games (Fox 1963). Because girls are more disciplined, they earn better grades than boys (*Filipino Women in Education* 1985). Parents feel confident that daughters will finish their college degrees and then get jobs to help finance the educational expenses of younger siblings (Jacobson 1974) or provide financial support to aging parents as well (Holnsteiner 1970).

With regard to employment there is a wide range of occupations open to Filipino women. They are highly visible in the government and the private sector. But the majority of working women are found in the rural areas of the country. Indeed, the typical working woman is a paid or unpaid family farm worker. Finally, a large number of Filipino women work overseas. Overseas women workers have taken advantage of manpower markets for medical personnel in North America, and since the 1970s as service workers bound for the Middle East and other Asian countries (*Women's Decade in the Philippines* 1985).

The educational and occupational opportunities open to and sought by Filipino women are insufficient for them to attain full equality with men. Working outside the home means balancing of dual roles for women but not for men. Working women receive lower wages than men, are seldom promoted, and suffer poor working conditions.

There are an abundance of laws and public policies that directly address the unique position of women as workers. For instance, the Labor Code of the Philippines requires that married women are entitled to 120 days maternity leave with pay and without loss of job or seniority. The Family Code of 1987 grants the right of women to make decisions regarding property, children, and choice of occupation and residence. Republic Act 6725 provides that women should have equal access to promotion and advanced training or study grants, and it eliminates low wages for women.

While the existence of these and other laws beneficial to women is important, an adequate implementation and enforcement of the laws is badly needed. Besides the rampant graft and corruption of government officials charged with the implementation of these laws, there is also the persistent view that the husband is still the main provider of the family and the wife's income is supplementary. As such, the economic status of women in the Philippines is more vulnerable than might be expected, given the legal statutes that have been enacted.

*Sonia D. Carreon*

## Bibliography

Agoncillo, T., and O. Alfonso. 1967. *History of the Filipino People*. Quezon City: Malaya Books.
Blair, E., and J. Robertson. 1903. *The Philippine Islands 1493–1898*. Cleveland, Ohio: Clark.
Castillo, G., and S. Guerrero. 1969. "The Filipino Woman: A Study in Multiple Roles." *Journal of Asian and African Studies* 4:18–29.
Castillo, T. 1942. *The Changing Status of the Filipino Women during the American Administration*. Ph.D. dissertation. University of Southern California.
*Filipino Women in Education*. 1985. Manila: National Commission on the Role of Filipino Women.

Fox, R. 1963. "Men and Women in the Philippines." In *Women in the New Asia: The Changing Social Roles of Men and Women in South and Southeast Asia*, edited by B. Ward. Paris: UNESCO.

Holnsteiner, M. 1970. "The Filipino Family Confronts the Modern World." In *Responsible Parenthood in the Philippines*, edited by V. Gorospe. Manila: Ateneo de Manila University.

Jacobson, H. 1974. "Women in Philippine Society: More Equal than Many." In *Many Sisters: Women in Cross-Cultural Perspective*, edited by C. Matthiason. New York: Free Press.

Lawless, R. 1967. "The Foundation for Culture and Personality Research in the Philippines." *Asian Studies* 5:101–36.

Nakpil, C. 1963. *Woman Enough and Other Essays*. Manila: Vibal.

Pido, A. 1986. *The Pilipinos in America*. New York: Center for Migration Studies.

Smock, A. 1981. *Women's Education in the Developing Countries*. New York: Praeger.

*Women's Decade in the Philippines*. 1985. Manila: National Commission on the Role of Filipino Women.

## Women and Work in Singapore

According to the Singapore Yearbook of Labour Statistics (1992), in 1991 there were 2.4 million people living in Singapore aged fifteen years and over, of whom 51.1 percent were women. The labor-force participation rate was 79.8 percent for men and 50.5 percent for women. By international standards the unemployment rate was very low, at 1.8 percent for women and 2.0 percent for men.

Between ages twenty and twenty-four the labor-force participation rate was 82.6 percent for women and 83.1 percent for men. The participation rate for women was lower in all other age groups and decreased as the age increased. Part-time workers constituted only 3 percent of the employed workforce in 1991, but of these 65 percent were women and 76 percent were married, widowed, or divorced. This suggests that many women do not return to paid employment once their children reach school age. However, the labor-force participation of women aged thirty-five and over has been increasing in recent years.

In contrast, in 1991 men's labor-force participation rate was well over 90 percent for ages twenty-five to fifty-four. Age fifty-five is still the official retirement age in many organizations, but 19.8 percent of men continue to participate in the labor force beyond age sixty-five, compared with 4.1 percent of women. The retirement age is a residue of days when life expectancy was considerably lower than it is at present, and the high labor-force participation rate of older men is partly due to limited public-welfare programs. Older, never-married men without family support are particularly likely to continue in employment beyond the usual retirement age.

Almost one-third of women (31.2 percent) in paid employment worked in manufacturing. One-quarter (25.4 percent) worked in the community, social, and personal services sector, and 22.7 percent in commerce. Industrial segmentation for women is not very different from that for men. The same proportion of women and men in the labor force (22.7 percent) were employed in the commercial sector. Over one-quarter of men (26.2 percent) worked in the manufacturing sector and 18.3 percent in the community, social, and personal sector.

On the other hand, there are some substantial differences between women and men in occupational segmentation. In 1991 only 3.6 percent of women were administrative, managerial, or executive workers, compared with 12.6 percent of men. Over one-quarter (27.7 percent) of women in paid employment were clerical or related workers, compared with only 6.3 percent of men. Large proportions of women and men worked as production and related workers, and transport equipment operators and laborers (36.6 percent and 43.0 percent, respectively). Similar proportions of women and men were professional, technical, or related workers (17.5 percent and 17.1 percent, respectively), and sales and service workers (14.5 percent of women in paid employment and 13.9 percent of men).

There were considerable differences in the earnings of female and male workers in Singapore in 1991. While 11.0 percent of men earned S$3,000 or more per month, only 4.1 percent of women in paid employment did so. (In 1991 US$1 = S$1.7 approximately.) Women were overrepresented in the lower income brackets: While 34.0 percent of women earned less than S$600 per month, only 17.4 percent of men in the workforce were paid so little. Women's earnings were less than men's in all occupational categories. The average gross wage of women managers was S$3,937 per month, or 75.4 percent of what male managers earned. Women professionals earned 79.5 percent of what their male counterparts earned. Income inequality was slightly less for women clerical workers, service and sales workers, and cleaners, laborers and related workers, who earned 86.7 percent, 85.9 percent, and 83.9 percent respectively of what men in similar occupations earned. However, income disparity for production workers, machine operators, and assembly-line workers was high: In 1991 women in these occupations were paid only 61 percent of what men in these occupations were paid.

The number of women enrolled in institutions of higher education in 1991 increased by a factor of 2.8 to over twenty-five thousand compared with a decade earlier. (Male enrollments were up by 2.3 times to almost thirty-five thousand.) The proportion of women among all students in higher education increased from 37.3 percent to 42.2 percent during this period. Inequities in this area continue to exist. In 1991, only 47.7 percent of students enrolled at the two universities were women, and women accounted for only 37.3 percent of students in polytechnics. Examination of higher education fields of study shows that occupational segmentation is likely to continue: 29.6 percent of the women who graduated in 1991 were in the fields of business and accounting compared with 8.6 percent of men. Similarly, 16.5 percent of the women graduates majored in arts (humanities) and social sciences compared with only 4.7 percent of men, and 11.6 percent of women majored in education compared with only 3.3 percent of men. Fields in which men predominated included engineering, which accounted for 65.8 percent of male graduates but only 20.4 percent of female graduates, and medicine. In 1991, 114 (1.4 percent) men graduated in medicine compared with only 53 (0.8 percent) of women. Men constitute the great majority of those trained in trades as well: In 1991 only 12.4 percent (2,967) of those who graduated with trade certificates were women.

In the field of law, 830 women have graduated over the past decade but only 783 men. Women lawyers have formed an association that functions as an education and advocacy group to improve women's working conditions. There is plenty for them to do. Currently there is no legislation in Singapore protecting women from discrimination in employment. Singapore is not a signatory to the United Nations conventions concerning equal opportunities and equal treatment for men and women workers, concerning equal remuneration for men and women workers for work of equal value, or on the elimination of all forms of discrimination against women. No legislation has been enacted regarding leave to care for children, paternity leave, child-care facilities, flexi-time, part-time work, or job sharing. To some degree the lack of legislation in this area is a product of the policy to make Singapore an attractive place for foreign investment and manufacturing, much of which in the past has been labor intensive.

The Association of Women Lawyers is particularly concerned about retrenchment practices, which it argues hurt women more than men. Women are more likely to be employed in industries most affected by downturns in demand, but some employers "retrench their women production operators, [and] simultaneously or shortly thereafter, recruit new women workers at lower starting salaries" (SAWL 1986, p.35). Unions do not have the right to question the basis or necessity of retrenchment. Employers are not required to give reasons for retrenchment and there is no minimum period of notice. Retrenchment benefits need only be paid to employees who have been in continuous service with the same employer for three years or more.

Women (and men) with family responsibilities sometimes find that their terms of employment make it difficult for them to care adequately for their dependents. However, in recent years the Civil Service has instituted new policies designed to make it easier for mothers to be employed. Mothers of children under six years of age who are employed by the Civil Service are now entitled to five days leave per year per child to care for sick children (up to a maximum of fifteen days per year). They are also entitled to one year of unpaid leave to care for each child (up to a maximum of four years), and up to three years part-time work.

Women are entitled to eight weeks' paid maternity leave for each of their first two children if they have worked for the same employer for six months prior to delivery. Women cannot be dismissed during maternity leave or in the preceding three months without a good reason. However, while employers are required to provide a safe working environment, a mother does not have the right to sue an employer even if her child is born with a deformity that can be traced to the workplace.

Singapore does not have a well-developed social-welfare system. The government promotes reliance on self and family, and administers mandatory savings schemes that people draw on in times of ill health and old age. Women bear much of the responsibility of running households and caring for children and elderly relatives. In 1991, the great majority (72.9 percent) of those over fifteen years of age who were not in paid employment or looking for it were homemakers. Only 2.2 percent were retired and 15.9 percent were full-time students. (The corresponding figures for men were 0.1 percent, 37.9 percent, and 44.0 percent respectively.)

Due to the rapid aging of the population and labor shortage, women are being encouraged to marry and have children and mothers to continue in paid employment. Relatively long working hours and limited child care and services for the elderly and disabled make this difficult. Many families have solved the dilemma by hiring foreign maids, who take over many domestic duties. Maids are exclusively women and come from neighboring countries that have excess and inexpensive labor, particularly the Philippines, Indonesia, Thailand, and Sri Lanka. There are strict immigration and labor laws governing the hiring and tenure of foreign maids but relatively few regulations concerning conditions of employment such as wages, duties, and work hours. At present there are approximately sixty-five thousand foreign maids employed in Singapore.

*Gerard Sullivan*

*Mui Teng Yap*

## Bibliography

Chinen, Joyce N., and Uhn Cho. 1982. "Female Wage Workers in the Export-Oriented Manufacturing Sector: The Situation in Singapore and Korea in the 1970s." Mimeograph. Department of Sociology, University of Hawaii.

Lau, Cynthia. 1991. *Women and Housework in a HDB Estate*. Academic exercise. Department of Sociology, Faculty of Arts and Social Sciences, National University of Singapore.

Quah, Stella. 1988. *Between Two Worlds: Modern Wives in a Traditional Setting*. Field Report Series No. 19. Singapore: Institute of South East Asian Studies.

Quah, Tiong Ewe Euston. 1987. *Household Production and Social Accounting: A Study of the Household Economy of Singapore*. Ph.D. thesis. Department of Economics and Statistics, Faculty of Arts and Social Sciences, National University of Singapore.

Singapore Association of Women Lawyers. 1986. *Legal Status of Women*. Singapore: Asia Pacific Books and Legal Aids.

Toh, Mung Heng. 1988. "The Interaction between Fertility and Female Labour Force Participation Rates in Singapore." Paper presented at the Symposium on Population Issues in Singapore, Faculty of Arts and Sciences, National University of Singapore.

Wong, Aline K. 1981. "Planned Development, Social Stratification and the Sexual Division of Labor in Singapore." *Signs: Journal of Women and Culture in Society* 7(2):434–52.

———. 1992. *1991 Singapore Yearbook of Labour Statistics*. Singapore: Research and Evaluation Department, Ministry of Labour, 1992.

———. *Yearbook of Statistics, Singapore 1991*. Singapore: Department of Statistics.

# Women in Developing Societies

## African Women in Economic Development

Most West African writers have focused on the culture and its implied limitations on the economic roles of women (Akubue 1993; Mufuyai 1991). Some North African authors decry the inevitable veils, servitude, and domesticity of the Moslem women, while southern activists speak about economic repression and racism for all blacks (Bruner 1984).

The problems that women face the world over are not as distinct as might be concluded from the above paragraph. However, the issues that are emphasized differ by the level of development in the country or continent. In general, women receive less formal education and are regarded as the minority (despite their larger population) in all societies.

The roles of women in Africa have changed over the period. Several factors such as inadequate educational programs, cultural norms, stereotyping, and so forth have been cited as variables that influenced the various roles of women over time (Finney and Parpart 1989). For example, precolonial and colonial periods saw women in different roles.

### Precolonial Period (Before 1800s)

Most sub-Saharan cultures in the precolonial era regarded women as chattels, especially ones that are old enough to be contracted into marriage (marriage through various forms of dowry). Nonetheless, women were instrumental to both social and economic development. Women were the mainstay of family life, child-rearing, discipline, and so forth, and also major contributors to economic survival and development. Women were responsible for feeding the family, a responsibility they accomplished through farming, preservation of seasonal crops, and exchange (barter).

Women's contribution to economic development was even more outstanding in some matriarchal societies such as Ghana (some tribes), Sierra Leone, Cameroon, and Kenya. These societies recognize and respect women's participation and leadership in policy-making and implementation. Societal norms and violations were set and settled by councils led by older women members. Unlike patriarchal societies (Nigeria, Côte d'Ivoire, Niger, and so forth) women inherit and own land and other tangible properties, which they often apply for economic development.

### Colonial Period (1800–1950s)

Sub-Saharan women in this period had less formal education than the men. Only one out of eight women received formal education, compared with two men. Women were expected to get married early, raise a family, and help on the farm. Most families were more willing to offer a male child an opportunity for a formal education, as education was the main channel to paid work. The society expected the man to take care of the family and, therefore, women did not need a high level of formal education for work within the family. However, for the few women who worked (mostly women in the cities) outside the home, they received the same pay as their male counterparts.

By the 1950s, statistics show that the number of urban, middle-class women with a high-school education and in civil service had risen from 5 percent in the 1920s to over 25 percent (Omoleye 1989). Religious beliefs (in Moslem societies) and other norms did not favor women working outside the home.

Women were not always inactive nor dominated by men. This view is exemplified in the "famous" women's riot of 1929. This organized protest initiated and carried out by West sub-Saharan women in protest of the colonial government's legislation requiring women to pay a flat tax on cash crops. The government expected trouble from men and not women. There were other incidents of women's demonstration against authority, mostly in relation to their business activities, such as income from cash crops, dress-making, farm labor, and others (Anyansi-Archibong 1985).

### Postcolonial Period (Independent States, 1940s–the present)

By the postcolonial period (after the 1940s), with the growth of formal education and declining parental pressure for early marriage, women began to choose their future more carefully. By the end of 1983, statistics show that for every ten students in a university there were four females (Anyansi-Archibong 1985). This increased enrollment in formal education has also led to increased numbers of women in the labor force. Furthermore, the increasing cost of living has also forced more women to work outside the home, including individuals with minimal or no formal education. This change in traditional roles of women did not occur among the Moslem societies.

The most dramatic change in the economic role of women is occurring in the management and ownership of private family enterprise. However, the evolution has expanded beyond family firms. Approximately fifteen of every one thousand private firms are owned and controlled by women (Anyansi-Archibong 1985).

This entrepreneurial status of women in most sub-Saharan African countries became noticeable in the early 1970s when women became active as major construction contractors. After civil unrest in the West African countries, reconstruction projects were predominant and women, especially those who had husbands in the army or were widowed, began to organize small business operations. These women later diversified into other growing industries, such as import/export activities following the ECOWAS trade agreement in 1976.

In addition, a recent study, "Women Managers and Their Managerial Role Profile" (Parikh 1985), indicates that there are growing numbers of women who have seized existing educational opportunities and the changing societal and cultural expectations to gain authority positions in the labor market.

The sub-Saharan African woman is constantly contributing to national economic development, directly, through her involvement in the economic system (farming, business activities, and so forth) and indirectly by nurturing of children. These efforts often go unrecognized or sometimes criticized by patriarchal societies as irrelevant.

However, African women's most difficult challenge seems to be their conscience. Intrapersonal conflict resulting from the internalized traditional roles has continued to plague the group. Several women who have succeeded in making significant economic contributions in any of the various ways have had hard times dealing with their maternal instincts. They see their desire to make direct contributions to the economic growth as an abandonment of their traditional roles. Furthermore, most of the formally educated women work in the government, which is the largest employer. Few are affiliated with private organizations, and fewer still have become established entrepreneurs and small business owners.

To whatever category the women belong, most urban dwellers are aware of the implicit and explicit (education for all, property ownership, divorce) role modifications in the societies.

A major concern for women currently is the issue of whether to accept or reject this new set of roles, especially when the package arrived with such problems as stress and unequal division of household chores.

*Chi Anyansi-Archibong*

## Bibliography

Akubue, A.I. 1993. "Technology, Women and Development." In *16th National Third World Studies Conference Proceedings*. Neb.

Anyansi-Archibong, C. 1985. "Evolution of Firms: Strategy and Structure of Enterprise in a Third World Country." Dissertation. School of Business, University of Kansas, Lawrence.

Bruner, C. 1984. *Unwinding Threads: Stories by Women in Africa*. Exeter, N.H.: Heinemann.

Bullwinkle, D. 1989. *African Women, A General Bibliography*. New York: Greenwood.

Finney, G., and J. Parpart. 1989. *Women and Development in Africa: Comparative Perspective*. Lanham, Md.: University Press of America.

Mufuyai, M. 1991. *Social Economic Analysis of Culture and Women in Agriculture*. Unpublished master's thesis. Greensboro, N.C.: North Carolina Agricultural and Technical State University.

Omoleye, A. 1989. *But for the Grace of Women*. Chicago: C and D.

Parikh, I. 1985. "Women Managers and Their Managerial Role Profile." Paper prepared for the Women and Development Programme, Commonwealth Secretariat, London.

Strobel, M., and S. Mirza. 1989. *Three Swahili Women*. Bloomington: Indiana University Press.

Waciuma, C. 1969. *Daughter of Mumki*. Nairobi: East African Publishing House.

## Changing Roles of Chinese Women: 2000 B.C. to 1949

Although the history of China extends back well into the Neolithic era, the first written records began during the Shang Dynasty (c. 1766 B.C.). From these early times women have occupied a low social position with respect to men. Women were traditionally viewed as possessions and were often bought and sold to benefit and reinforce the patriarchal system. Women worked only to increase the status of the husband and family. The primary mission of women was to produce a son for the husband, to raise children, and to keep an orderly house. As China's dynastic era drew to a close, women began to protest their low social position and discriminatory treatment. Although still badly treated during the time of the Republic of China (1912–1949), they continued to make modest progress in education and occupational goals, and to increase awareness of their needs.

## Cultural Factors Shaping Women's Roles

The second-class status of women was reflected in many Chinese social institutions, including language, religion, and education (Peterson 1991). Chinese language retains many remnants of symbolic patriarchy (as do English and other Western languages). In Chinese, these remnants are particularly noticeable because of the symbolic form of writing. For example, the character *hao*, meaning "good," is a combination of the characters *nu* (meaning woman) and *zi* (son). The implication is that a woman who has produced a son is "good." Similarly, the character *an* (peace) is created by placing *nu* (woman) under the symbol for roof, an ancient suggestion of "women's place." Other examples are abundant.

China's three major religions reflect the inferior status of women. Confucianism (c. 470 B.C.–present) is a major Chinese religion that stresses the importance of family loyalty and gender roles. Confucian philosophy promotes male superiority and the place of the woman as a support for the aspirations of her husband or son. From Confucianism comes the idea of the "three obediences" of women. She must first be obedient to her father. When she marries, she must be obedient to her husband. After the death of her husband, she must be obedient to her son, who is obligated to care for her (Creel 1937; Wei 1989).

Buddhism spread to China from India during the Western Han Dynasty (c. 139 B.C.). The religion, although not specifically antifemale, excluded women from participation. The Chinese philosophical tradition upon which Chinese Buddhism was based was completely male. Mainstream Buddhism itself excludes women from becoming priests or monks and concentrates on the resolution of ethical dilemmas of men (Wei 1989).

The third major religion of China is Taoism. Taoism took its place with Confucianism and Buddhism during the Wei Kingdom (220–265) and the Jin Dynasty (265–420). Taoists believe in two modalities of the universe, the *yin* and *yang*, meaning literally "dark side" and "sunny side." Women are the *yin* of the universe; illuminated by the *yang* of men. While necessary as a universal, balance, taoism sees women as passive, devious, and created primarily to serve and nurture men (Creel 1937; Wei 1989).

Another major institution that repressed women was education. Traditionally, Chinese women were not thought worthy to receive an education. School was generally preparation for China's competitive examinations. Those scoring highest on the examinations would be rewarded with public office. Since women were not allowed to hold public office, there was little need to train them in the arts, sciences, or humanities. Consequently, during China's long dynastic history (until 1912), it was rare for women to attend school.

## Women's Status during the Late Dynastic Era (1890–1912)

By the end of China's dynastic era, women had become victims of traditions that promoted men and repressed women. Although unhappy with their lot, they were powerless to change their condition. A woman's status was at all times linked with her husband's. Husbands could legally beat their wives to death. Wives became the passive receiver of the husband's wrath, cruelty, or arbitrary whims. Wives became members of the husband's family forever; they could not divorce, and widows could not remarry.

The result of the low status of women was "son preference." Women learned from an early age that they were "worthless" in comparison to men. Many committed suicide to escape cruel and unreasonable husbands or in-laws. Since men were a valued commodity, able to work, produce an income, and increase the family size (since married wives would leave their family to live with the husband's family), sons were vastly preferred to daughters. Families with limited food and resources often committed female infanticide. Chinese folklore is filled with cases of wives being beaten to death because they could not produce a son. The son preference persists even today. In spite of governmental attempts to control female infanticide, rural census reports indicate a much higher number of male births than female. If the daughter survives infancy, selling is not uncommon (Parsons 1906).

One visible manifestation of the low position of women was "foot-binding." Toward the end of the dynastic period, Chinese men became enamored of dainty women's feet. In attempts to reduce the size of women's feet artificially, parents bent the toes of their young daughters back under their feet and tied them. The goal was to produce the ideal "golden lotus" of approximately three to five inches. The process was painful and made it impossible for women to walk unaided. Originally a status symbol for rich men, the custom filtered into the peasant class. This had the function of keeping women at home where they could work, and presumably kept them from running away. Unfortunately, they could no longer work in the fields or do the simplest chores for themselves. Footbinding was outlawed around 1900 but continued well into the 1930s, due to the strong influence of tradition (Levy 1966).

## Women's Liberation Efforts

By the nineteenth century, women began developing an awareness of their low status and worked to change it. China's earliest "women's liberation" movement was during the Taiping (Heavenly Kingdom) Rebellion (around 1850). The leader of the movement, Hong Xiuquan taught equality and fought against sexual discrimination. Among other things, the movement demanded economic equality between men and women, the assembly of a female army, women's education, and an end to mercenary marriages, rape, and prostitution. Although the movement was repressed, it sparked an awareness of women as human beings and suggested a place in the workforce.

Footbinding was the symbolic "last straw" for many Chinese women in the late nineteenth century. In 1898, a second "women's liberation movement" attempted to abolish footbinding and establish equality for women. Although it failed to achieve all of its goals, the Reform Movement of 1898 was successful in establishing the first female school in Shanghai. Shortly thereafter, Shanghai established a women's association and a women's newspaper.

Partially because of demand from Chinese women and partially from pressure from the Western countries, in 1902 the Empress Dowager Tz'u-hsi passed the Anti-footbinding Edict. The edict was partially successful in abolishing footbinding in the cities, although it continued for several decades in the countryside.

In 1912, the army of Dr. Sun Yat-sen successfully conquered the crumbling Qing Dynasty. Sun was a believer in democracy and equality, and he worked quietly for women's equality.

Under the early "Republic of China," women felt more freedom to express their unhappiness. In 1912, eighteen provincial women's groups established the Women Suffrage Alliance and petitioned the government for social equality, family reform, education for women, monogamy, free-choice marriage, and the end of selling females, but they were largely unsuccessful in establishing favorable legislation (for a discussion of the history of women's progress in China, see Chipp and Green 1980; Watson and Ebrey 1991).

On May 4, 1919, major demonstrations were held in Peking denouncing "feudalistic thinking," which still pervaded the republic. The demonstrations were largely anti-Confucian in nature and symbolized a breaking away from the harsh constraints of Chinese religious tradition, which had oppressed women.

As Sun Yat-sen slowly lost control of the Koumintang Party, and lost power in China, women's equality suffered. "Natural Footed Societies" arose to take up women's causes. Many women cropped their hair short as a symbol of their equality and emancipation. Unfortunately, the ruling Koumintang under Chiang Kai Shek saw these progressive women as dangerous, and imprisoned or executed them.

During the years of the Republic of China, steps toward complete women's equality were very small and uncertain. The country was in political turmoil made worse by a corrupt government and a war with Japan. Women's status evolved slowly. In spite of the problems and uncertainty, there could be no doubt that enlightened Chinese women would never return to the oppressive status experienced under feudalism.

*Michael R. Ball*

**Bibliography**

Arnold, Fred. 1989. "Sex Preference, Fertility and Family Planning in China." *Population and Development Review* 12(2):221–46.

Chipp, Sylvia A., and Justin J. Green, eds. 1980. *Asian Women in Transition*. University Park: Pennsylvania State University Press.

Creel, Herrlee Glessner. 1937. *The Birth of China*. New York: Frederick Ungar.

Gasster, Michael. 1973. *China's Struggle to Modernize*. New York: Alfred A. Knopf.

Hsu, Francis L.K. 1955. *Americans and Chinese*. London: Cresset.

Levy, Howard S. 1966. *Chinese Footbinding: The History of a Curious Erotic Custom*. New York: Rawls.

Parsons, Elsie Clews. 1906. *The Family: An Ethnographical and Historical Outline*. New York: G.P. Putnam's Sons.

Peterson, Elizabeth A. 1991. *The Status of Women in Modern China*. Unpublished master's thesis. Lincoln: University of Nebraska.

Watson, Rubie S., and Patricia Buckley Ebrey, eds. 1991. *Marriage and Inequality in Chinese Society*. Berkeley: University of California Press.

Wei, Zhangling. 1989. *Status of Women in China*. Bangkok: UNESCO Principal Regional Office for Asia and the Pacific.

## Women in the People's Republic of China (1949–the Present)

The long and colorful history of China has seen women as the servants of often unreasonable and brutal husbands and fathers. Slight progress was made after the Revolution of 1912, but a corrupt government and political turmoil prevented any real progress for women. The 1949 Liberation of China by Mao Tse Tung and the Communist Party in 1949 promised women full equality with men. Mao instituted educational, occupational, and family reforms to strike at the heart of gender discrimination and accorded women unprecedented human rights. Although great strides have been made in women's rights, the recent introduction of capitalism into China has created a formidable obstacle to women's progress.

### The Promise of the 1949 Revolution

The collected theories of Karl Marx and Frederick Engels were the inspiration for the Chinese Revolution of 1949. Engels believed that the family was organized for little more than the "concealed domestic slavery of women." He adamantly supported women's equality as necessary to give women an economic base for freedom from domestic slavery. In short, women were viewed as a repressed class, and communism's promise to women was similar to its promise for the proletariat: full equality and participation in society (Engels 1978).

As a firm advocate of Marxism and Leninism, Mao believed that the absolute equality of women was not only economically desirable but necessary for the reduction of misery and abuse brought about by capitalism and the earlier rule of the Koumintang (1911–1948). Mao observed that "women hold up half the sky" and should therefore share equally in all social rewards.

Mao welcomed women to participate in the new government, taking as a first step the drafting of Article 48 of the Constitution of the People's Republic of China. Article 48 guaranteed women "equal rights with men in all spheres of life, in political, economic, cultural, social, and family life." It further promised to protect the rights and interests of women, to guarantee equal pay for equal work, and to select women for positions as "cadres" (middle-level governmental officials) (*Constitution of the People's Republic of China* 1982).

In order to mobilize these high ideals, Mao established the All China Women's Federation to advise the party of the needs and problems of women and to make recommendations to correct inequalities. In the early days of the People's Republic, the All China Women's Federation adopted the phrase "anything a man can do, a woman can do." Women began working as miners and heavy laborers.

Another radical step Mao made toward women's equality was the institution of the Marriage Law of 1950. It demanded an end to arranged marriages, child betrothals, concubinage, the selling of women, and female infanticide. This law helped change the idea that women were property to be sold or disposed of as a father or husband saw fit, and reflected a more humanized image of women. For the first time women could divorce their husbands. The law provided for complete social equality between the sexes in marriage and affirmed the right of women to divorce and to remarry and allowed women to own property (Wei 1989).

In the 1950s, China adopted a system of farm collectivization that helped women establish economic independence. Under this system, the farms were owned by the state rather than the family. Women and men who worked in the fields both received work points that could be traded for goods. Since the women were no longer under the direct supervision of their husbands, and were able to earn their own money. It gave them a certain amount of economic freedom and helped to destroy the feudalistic patriarchal tradition in the countryside. Still, pay systems reflected a great deal of inequality. Women consistently received less pay than men, as it was reasoned that they were weaker and could do less work (Yang 1959).

Shortly after Chinese Liberation (1949), Mao advocated increasing China's population. He believed that more workers were necessary to build China. Child-raising responsibilities effectively kept many women out of the workforce, defeating Mao's equality goal. By the mid 1950s, Mao realized the disastrous problems created by unchecked population growth and instituted a two-child-per-family policy (Sidel 1972). After Mao's death, Deng Xiaoping instituted a one-child-per-family policy in an attempt to reduce China's population by the end of the century. The reduction in family size linked with better child care facilities allowed Chinese women to rejoin the workforce and contribute to the increased Chinese standard of living (Watson and Ebrey 1973).

**Current Status of Chinese Women**
The status of women in China has skyrocketed since 1949. Women have progressed from near slavery with the family system to a position of near equality with men. Still, many problems remain.

China's educational system improved dramatically after 1949, and with this improvement came unprecedented opportunities for women to attend school on an equal footing with men. However, many obstacles stand in the way of equal educational opportunity. Census figures and other investigations report that in the countryside women illiterates outnumber male illiterates two to one. The reason is that only about one-third of eligible girls aged seven to eleven attend elementary school; the rest are discouraged from doing so by their families. On the other hand, nearly 100 percent of eligible boys attend schools (Shell 1977).

In higher education the figures are similarly discouraging. While 36 percent more males have a primary education, 60 to 70 percent more males have a secondary education and three times as many males attend college as females. Much of the problem stems from the fact that colleges require higher scores on entrance examinations or higher high-school GPAs for women. Although the Ministry of Education has created strict sanctions against schools that discriminate, it cannot change the strongly entrenched cultural traditions favoring males.

After graduation, women's struggle continues. Many work units have refused to accept women college graduates even though they may be much more highly qualified than their male counterparts. Employers believe that women will miss more work because of childbirth and child-rearing responsibilities, and they want to avoid the cost of child-care facilities in their workplace. To counteract this problem, the Chinese Communist Party has focused a propaganda campaign on equality in hiring and has issued minimum quotas for women in work units. The All China Women's Federation no longer advocates that women and men do equal work but has come to accept the popular position that women can be "hurt" by heavy labor. It now focuses on encouraging better working conditions for women and seeking strong legal sanctions against offending work units. It has also been instrumental in sponsoring night schools and vocational training programs for women in the workplace (Peterson 1991).

Since liberation women have made great strides in employment. Currently almost 44 percent of the workforce consists of women. In addition, the party promotes equal pay for equal work within the state bureaucracy and in state-run enterprises and organizations. At the same time, women's employment conditions are not as rosy as they might first appear. While more women than ever before are employed, they are overrepresented in service work and in clerical-sales jobs. They are also highly underrepresented in leadership positions. In spite of party rhetoric, only about 10 percent of leading cadres of state-run organizations and enterprises are female, and virtually none of the national leaders are women (Peterson 1991).

China's new-found capitalism has created discrimination problems beyond the easy control of authorities. Individual and joint-venture enterprises fall outside the control of antidiscrimination legislation, and authorities are hesitant to pressure such enterprises for fear of losing precious investment money or upsetting the fragile balance of China's neocapitalism. Since the 1980s, China has been slowly decollectivizing the countryside and returning to a system of partial family capitalism. This places women once more directly under the supervision of their husbands and reestablishes the patriarchal system.

In addition to the above problems, household chores and child care continue to fall almost exclusively upon the women of China. They carry the "double burden" of employment outside the home and maintenance work within the home (Chance 1984; Sidel 1973).

China has long been characterized as a land of contrasts, and nowhere is it clearer than in women's progress. On the one hand, women occupy low positions at work, suffer discrimination in education and occupation, and retain the nurturing stereotype that bars them from admission to leadership positions. They are daily victimized by China's long-standing patriarchal traditions. On the other hand, in less than a century they have progressed from footbound possessions of husbands and fathers to be bought, traded, or killed at whim to a legal status of near equality.

*Michael R. Ball*

### Bibliography
Chance, Norman A. 1984. *China's Urban Villagers: Life in a Beijing Commune.* New York: Holt, Rinehart, and Winston.
*Constitution of the People's Republic of China.* 1982. Beijing: Foreign Languages Press.
Engels, Frederick. 1978. *The Origin of the Family, Private Property and the State.* Peking: Foreign Languages Press.
Peterson, Elizabeth A. 1991. *The Status of Women in Modern China.* Unpublished master's thesis. Lincoln: University of Nebraska.
Rau, Margaret. 1989. *Young Women in China.* Hillside, N.J.: Enslow.
Shell, Orville. 1977. *In the People's Republic.* New York: Random House.
Sidel, Ruth. 1973. *Women and Child Care in China: A Firsthand Report.* New York: Hill and Wang.
Watson, Rubie S., and Patricia Buckley Ebrey. 1973. *Marriage and Inequality in Chinese Society.* Berkeley: University of California Press.
Wei, Zhangling. 1989. *Status of Women in China.* Bangkok: UNESCO.
Women of China. 1987. *New Trends in Chinese Marriage and the Family.* Beijing: China International Book Trading.
Yang, C.K. 1959. *Chinese Communist Society: The Family and the Village.* Cambridge: M.I.T. Press.

### Nicaraguan Women in the Formal and Informal Economy
Traditional perspectives on the "informal" sector in developing countries have downplayed its significance for the larger economy, choosing to focus more intensely upon the "formal" sector of wage laborers. Such views are influential on Third World policy-makers, who have tended to favor formal-sector employees,

often at the neglect of informal-sector workers. In many cases, women constitute the majority of workers in the informal sector of developing economies. As can be seen in Nicaragua, government policies during the 1970s through the 1990s had a dramatic impact on informally employed women and the economic viability of their households. The resulting political tensions eventually helped undermine popular support for the revolutionary Sandinista government (1979–1990), this despite its commitment to radical reforms designed to improve the social conditions of women. The case of Nicaragua underlines the need for further research on the informal sector so as to provide correctives to traditional approaches while contributing to more informed policy-making.

## Perspectives on "Informal" Work in Development

The notion of the "informal sector" refers to the sum total of occupations in a given society involving work carried out on a self-employed basis conducted largely outside of legal regulation. Broadly defined as such, the informal sector includes the production and distribution of a wide range of goods and services where work is not remunerated by wages but rather by the direct receipt of wealth generated by workers' economic activities vis-à-vis their self-regulated connection to the enterprise formed by their work. This can, therefore, refer to street vendors, home-based manufacturing, prostitution, domestic work, and many other enterprising activities that provide goods and services of both legal and illegal status to an economic chain that ultimately connects up with consumers. Understanding the nature of informal work has proved elusive to development theory, which only recently has begun to appreciate the productive potential of such activities.

Development studies were largely dominated by the modernization paradigm from the early post–World War II period up until the 1960s. Theorists such as W.W. Rostow, Bert F. Hoselitz, and numerous other intellectuals residing in the industrialized West argued that a capitalist industrialization strategy was the only rational strategy of economic development. This implied that a modernizing economy would increasingly draw "marginalized," traditional sectors of the population into the wage-earning, "formal" sector as modern, capitalist social relations became institutionalized. Work in the informal sector was, therefore, seen as largely "backwards" and "irrational" vestiges of traditional, precapitalist society.

During the 1960s, an alternative paradigm arose among Third World intellectuals in opposition to modernization perspectives. Eventually becoming known as "dependency" theories, this view emerged from a comprehensive critique of modernization strategies where they had been actually employed. Dependency theorists argued that "underdevelopment" rather than development was the deformed product of modernization strategies, a social formation that was profoundly exploited by foreign capital and characterized by a "dependent capitalism" that generates extreme social inequalities. This critical approach to modernization policies stressed the need to comprehend the economic and political implications of foreign capitalist investment, unequal trade relations, and development "assistance" programs being offered to developing countries on a highly conditional basis.

Despite its many attractive qualities, the dependency perspective remained too simplistic in its view of the informal sector. Although a provocative approach to exploitative relations in development was advanced, dependency theory tended to overgeneralize about the nature of informal work, seeing it as either a subordinate, superexploited appendage to the wage-earning sector (which it helps subsidize) or as a parasitic sector, siphoning off wealth from the wages of the working class. In either scenario, the informal sector was viewed negatively by dependency theorists, thereby denigrating the importance of a sector that in many cases is predominantly female. This bears an unlikely resemblance to modernizationists such as Boserup (1970), who argued, albeit for different reasons, that women would only advance through their systematic integration into the formal sector. In short, both modernization and dependency theorists failed to conceptualize the possibility that informal-sector work could compose a productive and viable part of an economic strategy of development.

### Informally Employed Women in Rural and Urban Settings

A growing number of empirical studies conclusively point to the need to differentiate between rural and urban varieties of informal-sector work and its significance for women. Analysts such as Carmen Diana Deere (1990) have convincingly shown that rural women who become landless and eventually forced into the formal, wage-earning sector most frequently encounter a more tenuous level of subsistence. In contrast, formal-sector employment in some urban settings can offer higher standards of living and a series of benefits such as social security, minimum wage levels, and so forth that can prove both attractive and elusive for women seeking work.

Yet, Helen I. Safa (1987) and others have shown that the incorporation of women into the formal sector often occurs as a means of heightening the exploitation of labor, resulting in inferior pay and highly discriminatory work conditions. In some cases, younger women become employed in high-paced work settings that are simply unsustainable for prolonged periods, producing a high rate of turnover and employment instability. Perhaps the greatest similarity between rural and urban settings is the consistency with which women employed in both the formal and informal sectors remain disproportionately tied to household work responsibilities.

Understanding the overall significance of formal versus informal work for women ultimately requires analysis of the larger political economy that characterizes any particular developing area. The progressive incorporation of rural women into formal agricultural work may signify greater exploitation and impoverishment, particularly when implemented by transnational corporations in a militarized, dependent capitalist setting such as the Philippines, El Salvador, and Guatemala. However, it may also mean higher social status, increased access to social services, and better working conditions when carried out in a society developing in a revolutionary, mixed-economy such as Grenada (1979–1983) or with a socialist development strategy such as Cuba, Mozambique, or Vietnam. As can be seen in the Nicaraguan Revolution of 1979, even the best intentions of a domestic state committed to the advancement of women can become thwarted once caught up in the contradictions of social development.

### Women and Work in Nicaragua

The case of Nicaragua provides an excellent means to illustrate the social complexity and significance for women of state policies aimed toward the informal sector in the context of development. During the 1950s through the 1970s, the informal sector became pronounced in the urban areas of Nicaragua as the result of a dramatic trend of urbanization. By 1980, Nicaragua was the most urbanized nation in Central America, with around one-third of the total population living in the capital city of Managua. The migration to the city essentially reflected socioeconomic changes in the countryside, where landlessness grew as a result of the "modernization" of rural agriculture and its creation of an agro-export, capitalist sector far less labor intensive than the traditional farming that had preceded it.

The majority of those arriving in the cities became dependent upon informal-sector work for their livelihood, making up half of the economically active urban population, with a majority of this sector being female and engaged in such diverse informal occupations as domestic work, home production of confectioneries for street vendors, and prostitution. In 1972, a major earthquake devastated the city of Managua and contributed still further to the growing informal sector, this precisely due to the fact that informal economic activities proved far more capable of self-reactivation amidst the destruction of the city's former infrastructure. In the later 1970s, the growth of a guerrilla insurgency and ensuing waves of state repression further fueled internal migration to Managua as civilians fled hostilities throughout the countryside.

With the Sandinista Revolution of mid 1979, dramatic changes took place in Nicaragua's development strategy. The new Sandinista administration created a revolutionary mixed-economy that conformed to its prosocialist platform, propelling it to consolidate the unionized, wage-earning working class and devote resources toward elevating the status of formal-sector workers. Women were widely encouraged to join and did in fact enter the formal sector of employment in large numbers, increasing their representation from slightly less than a third to almost half of the total wage force, resulting in their enjoyment of many new benefits including free health care, education, and the improved social security being offered to all wage workers.

In the early years of the revolution, the Sandinista government attempted to regulate and "formalize" informal-sector employment, illegalizing those activities such as prostitution, black marketing, and so forth, that were deemed antisocial, while seeking to rationalize other sectors by organizing them into legally recognized cooperatives. Social services such as day-care centers, expanded access to public schools, and active programs sponsored by youth-based, mass organizations offered simultaneous relief from heavy household workloads as the benefits for formal-sector workers sharply improved.

As the U.S.-financed contra war against Nicaragua intensified during the mid 1980s, migration to the city from the countryside accelerated still further, flooding the urban labor market and overwhelming the fragile social infrastructure created by the revolution. With the agricultural, export-oriented base of the country being undermined by the war at the same time that the national defense budget drained an increasing portion of Nicaragua's resources, the economy progressively deteriorated and eventually went into a tailspin, with hyperinflation soon rendering formal-sector work valuable only in terms of the access it offered to state-rationed goods. At one point, government workers were paid directly in rice and beans, providing dramatic evidence of the essential worthlessness of wages being offered many formal-sector employees.

During the mid to later 1980s, many wage-earning households became increasingly involved in informal-sector occupations as an economic "survival strategy." Before long, this informal sector became a major provider of goods and services to urban, formal-sector employees, including homemade-food vendors, artisan-produced consumer goods and crafts, money changing, and many others.

Under tremendous economic pressures, the Sandinista government sought to improve the conditions for its historically reliable political base in the urban working class by a series of abortive moves toward heavy regulation designed to curtail "parasitic" practices in the informal sector. At different points in time, for example, the government sought to strictly control the skyrocketing prices charged by street vendors, prohibit unlicensed domestic workers from selling their services, and levy various forms of taxes on informal-sector producers of goods and services. Although well intentioned so as to protect the "working-class," the strong regulatory policies were inadvertently coming down squarely upon the Sandinistas' main political base among the working urban majority.

A published study by sociologists at the Central American University in Managua (Escuela de Sociologia 1988) showed that a large portion of the economically active population of Managua had become regularly involved in informal-sector employment. Informal work had become a "survival strategy" for many families, particularly those headed by women, thus providing a means either to supplement their declining real income earned through formal-sector employment or to replace income lost through growing unemployment. The revolutionary state, squeezed by the contradictions of a transitional development strategy under constant external attack, was unwittingly taking aim at a sector that both guaranteed the means of subsistence for increasing numbers of the poorest workers and indeed produced a growing portion of the goods and services available to the working majority. Given that informal-sector workers in urban Nicaragua were predominantly female, such policies disproportionately affected women, helping to further undermine the organized women's movement in Nicaragua, which for years had provided a solid base of support for the Sandinista revolution.

In summary, the case of Nicaragua shows that even the most well-intentioned state that seeks to improve the relative position of women cannot guarantee a consistent policy toward all women workers once caught up in the contradictions of development. The fact that informal-sector activities massively involve the work of women throughout the developing world signifies its importance for future research. Understanding the dynamics of women and work in development requires an adequate conceptualization of informal and formal work—that is, one that examines the larger political-economic context in which the role of the state and the overall logic of development being pursued is taken into account.

*Richard A. Dello Buono*

## Bibliography

Angel, Adriana, and Fiona Macintosh. 1987. *The Tiger's Milk: Women of Nicaragua.* New York: Henry Holt.

Boserup, E. 1970. *Women's Role in Economic Development.* New York: St. Martin's.

Chamorro Zamora, Amalia. 1989. "La Mujer: Logros y Limites en 10 Anos de Revolucion." *Cuadernos de Sociologia* 9/10.

Chamorro Zamora, Amalia, and Richard Dello Buono. 1990. "The Political Economy of the Sandinista Electoral Defeat." *Critical Sociology* 17:93–101.

Deere, Carmen Diana, et al. 1990. *In the Shadows of the Sun*. Boulder, Colo.: Westview.

Escuela de Sociologia. 1988. "Survival Strategies in the Popular Sectors of Managua." *Critical Sociology* 15:5–32.

Etienne, Mona, and Eleanor Leacock. 1980. *Women and Colonization: Anthropological Perspectives*. New York: Praegar.

Hoselitz, Bert F. 1960. *Sociological Factors in Economic Development*. New York: Free Press.

Leacock, Eleanor, Helen Safa, et al. 1986. *Women's Work: Development and the Division of Labor by Gender*. Westport, Conn.: Bergin and Garvey.

Rostow, W.W. 1960. *Stages of Economic Growth: A Non-Communist Manifesto*. New York: Cambridge University Press.

Safa, Helen I. 1987. "Urbanization, the Informal Economy and State Policy in Latin America." In *The Capitalist City*, edited by Michael P. Smith and Joseph Feagin. New York: Basil Blackwell.

United Nations. 1991. *The World's Women 1970–1990: Trends and Statistics*. New York: United Nations Publications.

## Nigerian Women

Successful entrepreneurship depends on several environmental factors. The formal and informal economic factors play major roles among women entrepreneurs. The terms entrepreneurship and small business are used in this report to reflect both formal (registered) and informal (nonregistered) business activities started, owned, controlled, and operated by a woman in the Nigerian society (INCH Handbook 1983).

### Informal Entrepreneurship Activities

Nigerian women are generally enterprising. They are responsible, through the traditional bazaar markets, for bringing the much-needed products (crops) to consumers. Traditionally, Nigerian women have less formal education than men; in the late 1930s only one out of eight women received formal schooling.

Males were encouraged and supported for formal education, as this offered them opportunity to get employment with the colonial government. Males were heads of families and ensured continuity of family names, contrary to females who changed their names upon marriage.

While the males were supported with capital for trade or assigned large portions of farmland, women often turned to the marketplace as major small retail business owners. These activities by women were so profitable that the colonial government elected to tax the profit (flat tax). (The Women's Revolt of 1929 across the country was in protest of this flat tax.) In 1984 there was another demonstration, against the Nigerian military government for imposing a flat tax on every female independently pursuing a business venture. Women-owned and -controlled businesses between the 1930s and 1970s were mostly unstructured and nonregistered enterprises. Most consisted of retail (sales of crops), dressmaking shops, hair salons, and so forth.

### Formal Entrepreneurship Activities

Nigerian women entrepreneurs of the 1980s engage in interstate enterprises, registered (or incorporated) business, and they are managers of large businesses and they own businesses. In one survey of women entrepreneurs, the results indicate that out of one thousand incorporated businesses in Nigeria, six (0.6 percent) were owned and directed by women (Anyansi-Archibong 1987). Fifty-nine (5.9 percent), mostly family-owned or controlled, had wives of the founders listed as members of the board of directors. There were no data to indicate whether these women were in any way involved with the management of the business. However, thirty-eight (3.8 percent) of the businesses had women listed as major shareholders, again without any involvement in the management. Furthermore, forty-one businesses (4.1 percent) listed women as professional members of the board of directors.

With regard to industry, building construction, insurance, and consultancy services had more women directors than other service areas. There are two management consulting firms owned and controlled by women out of a total of six. Average share capital in the six businesses owned and controlled by women was $24,000.

It is difficult to determine the performance of these businesses without data on the volume of sales over a period of at least five to ten years. Also, lack of information on other factors such as profits, total assets, liabilities, and other financial data makes it difficult to determine the strengths and weaknesses of these women entrepreneurs and, therefore, types of assistance needed.

## Success Factors

So far, women entrepreneurs claim that the Economic Organization of West African States (ECOWAS) treaty, with its free-trade provisions, has made a major difference to their success as formal entrepreneurs. Free and improved education for all came second, while business training and financing programs came a distant third (Ahmed 1988).

Women entrepreneurs in Nigeria have benefited immensely from government regulations that allow them to compete vigorously with men (Anyansi-Archibong 1985). In addition, Western education, currently available to both men and women, has made it possible for women to improve their formal business skills. (Only 11 percent of the women surveyed had a high-school diploma.) Marketing issues were blamed on their inability to organize adequate market surveys.

Nigerian women entrepreneurs are challenged by the government to contribute to effective economic development through DFRRI. The government has developed programs to help support women entrepreneurs in the 1990s financially through investment banks and technically through Ministry of Small and Medium Enterprise training.

*Chi Anyansi-Archibong*

## Bibliography

Ahmed, A.A. 1988. "Issues and Problems of Small Scale Industries Financing." *Nigeria Trade Journal* 31:3.

Alahaji, Amed. 1987. "The Role of Central Bank in Small Scale Enterprise Financing." *Nigeria Trade Journal* 31:3.

Anka, A.I.M. 1987. "Outlets for Marketing of Excess Grains from the Peasant Farmers." *Nigeria Trade Journal* 31(December):3.

Anyansi-Archibong, Chi. 1985. "Evolution of Firms: Strategy and Structure of Enterprise in a Third-World Country." Dissertation study. School of Business, University of Kansas.

———. 1985. "The Changing Role of Women in Africa." Paper presented at the Women Researcher Conference, Kalamazoo, Michigan.

———. 1987. "The Role of Entrepreneurs in Economic Development: An Analysis of Remote and Operating Environment in Africa." In *The Spirit of Entrepreneurship*, edited by Robert G. Wyckham, Lindsay No. Meridith and Gervase R. Bushe. Vancouver: Simon Fraser University.

Bascom, W. *The Yoruba of Southwestern Nigeria.* 1969. New York: Holt, Rinehart and Winston.

"Better Life Fair for Rural Dwellers." 1988. Address by Gen. I.B. Babangida, president and com-
mander-in-chief of the armed forces. *Nigeria Trade Journal* 32(September).

*Economic Prospects: SAP*. EPD Series. Lagos: Federal Ministry of Information and Culture.

*Guidelines of the Fourth National Development Plan*. 1981–1985. Lagos: Federal Ministry of National
Planning.

INCH Handbook. 1983. *Jikonzult Management Services Limited*.

"West Africa's Franc Zone." *Economist*. 1990. June 2:48.

## Palestinian Women in the Israeli-Occupied West Bank and Gaza Strip

Israel's 1967 occupation of the West Bank and Gaza Strip, held respectively by
Jordan and Egypt since 1948, had a profound impact in transforming the role of
Palestinian women. Proletarianization became one of the main features of this
occupation, as both men and women were forced in large numbers into the paid
labor force (Samed 1976). Wages earned by Palestinian women would often be
used to supplement the income of male family members. In cases where their
menfolk were imprisoned, killed, or deported, women became the sole providers for the subsistence needs of their families. By the mid 1980s, women constituted close to 18 percent of the labor force in the West Bank and some 6 percent of that in the Gaza Strip. In the decade before the *intifada* (1987), some 4.5
percent of these women worked in Israel (Fishman 1989). This figure declined
by more than half in the years after the uprising. These developments had a variety of consequences, on women and on Palestinian society generally. The effects on refugee and lower-class women and their families were particularly acute,
due in part to Israeli restrictions on work in Israel in the aftermath of the Gulf
War (1990–1991) and to the cutoff of remittances from family members in the
Gulf during the same period.

In addition to their regular household duties in the West Bank prior to
1967, women's work was generally confined to unpaid agricultural labor on family plots of land. The situation in the Gaza Strip differed, in that its socioeconomic
infrastructure had been largely destroyed as a result of the huge influx of refugees that followed the establishment of the State of Israel in 1948. In the Gaza Strip,
close to 70 percent of the total population are refugees, a fact that indicates the
extent of their pauperization and adds to the significance of the work of women.
Israel's policies of land expropriation and settlement, coupled with restrictions to
indigenous economic ventures in both industry and agriculture, led to a situation
where Palestinians were increasingly dispossessed of their traditional means of livelihood and forced into a position of dependence on Israel (Siniora 1990). In the
resulting economic and social dislocation, Palestinian women began joining the paid
labor force in larger numbers as unskilled seasonal workers in Israeli agriculture
and as low-paid workers in Israeli garment and food-processing industries (Rockwell 1985; Siniora 1990; Young 1992). Such Israeli industries were typically subcontracted in the West Bank and Gaza Strip. In the West Bank, about half of the
female labor force is employed in such ventures. Women are overrepresented in
the service sector (65 percent in the Gaza Strip and 35 percent in the West Bank)
and agricultural work (about 13 percent in the Gaza Strip and 50 percent in the
West Bank) (Fishman 1989). Statistics on women's participation are not always
reliable, as often they do not include seasonal laborers, women under fourteen
years of age, and women who do not secure work through the official Israeli labor exchanges (Siniora 1990).

Because of the forced abandonment of their traditional roles, Palestinian women were increasingly exposed to exploitation on the basis of nationality and class as well as gender. Women formed a reserve pool of cheap labor that could be tapped by Israeli entrepreneurs (Rockwell 1985). Generally, women earned less than men and were expected to perform their traditional household duties in addition to their paid work. As they increased their visibility in the public sphere, women also began to transform their roles in other areas of society. Their enrollment in education, including higher education, increased as Palestinian women sought to improve their chances of securing well-paid jobs. Based on their membership in professional unions, Palestinian working women constitute about 13 percent of dentists, 30 percent of pharmacists, 7 percent of journalists, 8 percent of physicians, 6 percent of lawyers, 8 percent of agronomists, and 4 percent of engineers (Young 1992).

Women assumed active political and social roles. Between 1978 and the early 1980s, four grassroots women's committees were established, each affiliated to a major faction within the Palestine Liberation Organization (PLO): the Union of Palestinian Women's Work Committees (affiliated to the Democratic Front for the Liberation of Palestine [DFLP] and known also as the Palestinian Federation of Women's Action Committees); the General Union of Palestinian Working Women's Committees (affiliated to the Communist Party); the General Union of Palestinian Women's Committees for Social Work (affiliated to *Fatah*); and the Union of Palestinian Women's Committees (affiliated to the Popular Front for the Liberation of Palestine). These committees were formed to address women's daily concerns and enhance their political awareness, with a view toward creating a mass women's movement in the Occupied Territories (Kuttab 1993). By the early 1990s there were five broad women's committees in the Occupied Territories, reflecting the split of the DFLP into two factions. There are a combined total of fifty-eight branches of these committees (thirty-five in the West Bank and twenty-three in the Gaza Strip)(Directory of Palestinian Women's Organizations 1993). Unlike established voluntary and charitable societies that tend to be urban-based and dominated by middle- and upper-class women, these committees invited the direct involvement and participation of dispossessed and lower-class women in designing activities and setting priorities.

The rights of working women were taken up by several of these committees, notably the Union of Working Women's Committees (established in 1980), which addressed women's rights in the workplace for better pay, equality, benefits, and membership in trade unions. Grassroots committees also concentrated on providing training for women in vocational skills in order to enhance their self-sufficiency, both as individuals and as members of their communities. These programs include, for example, sewing, weaving, ceramics, hairdressing, and others. Together there are 193 such projects in the West Bank and 49 in the Gaza Strip (Directory of Palestinian Women's Organizations 1993). These include programs offered by the eighty-two voluntary societies in the West Bank and Gaza Strip.

In the years since the *intifada*, women have been active in establishing economic ventures administered and run exclusively by local women. By 1992 there were eleven women's projects in the West Bank, including the undergarment factory in the Balata refugee camp near Nablus, the baby food and health project in Beit Hanina near Jerusalem, the copper and embroidery project in Beit Hanina, and the vegetable-drying project in Arrabeh village near Jenin. These were set up to serve and benefit local women, especially refugees and villagers. There were also twelve women's cooperatives in the West Bank and one in the Gaza Strip, such as Production is Our Pride, the Beitello food-production cooperative in the Ramallah area. This was established in 1986 to develop alternatives to Israeli products and to provide job opportunities to local village women (*Directory of Palestinian Women's Organizations* 1993; Strum 1992). Reliable statistics are difficult to obtain, as membership fluctuated over the years. Other women's cooperatives are organized around handicrafts (for example, in the Gaza Strip) and other ventures.

By the early 1990s, three women's studies and research centers were operating in the Occupied West Bank, one of which has a branch in the Gaza Strip. These centers have undertaken a series of studies designed to investigate the conditions of Palestinian women in the occupied areas. One area of investigation is how to address the growing influence of radical Islamic religious groups such as *Hamas* (the Islamic Resistance Movement) (Holt 1992). In the Gaza Strip in particular, this group exerted pressure on women to abandon public roles and resume their traditional duties as wives and mothers. In response, Palestinian women activists began articulating a women's agenda that can be carried out alongside the struggle for national liberation (Kuttab 1993; Strum 1992).

In the two years between the opening of the Madrid Conference (October 1991) between Israel and the Arab states (including the Palestinians) and the signing of the Declaration of Principles between Israel and the PLO (September 1993), Palestinian women actively pursued their goal of advancing the social, political, and economic rights of women. A technical team on women's issues was created to provide the Palestinian negotiators at the peace talks with accurate information concerning women.

Meantime, the activities of women's committees turned increasingly to issues of everyday life, such as early age of marriage, wife abuse, women peddlers, and rights of women at the workplace. Separate centers were established to address these issues, such as the Women's Center for Legal Aid and Counseling in Jerusalem. Many Palestinian women openly began to describe themselves as feminists and struggled to ensure that democratic principles will be safeguarded during the interim autonomy phase and that they will enjoy social equality in a future Palestinian state.

*Souad Dajani*

## Bibliography

Bauman, P., and R. Hammami. 1989. *Annotated Bibliography on Palestinian Women*. Jerusalem: Arab Thought Forum.

*Directory of Palestinian Women's Organizations*. 1993. Ramallah, West Bank: Women's Studies Committee, Bisan Center for Research and Development.

Fishman, Alex. 1989. "The Palestinian Woman and the Intifada." *New Outlook*. 22(June/July):9–12.

Hammam, M. 1981. "Labor Migration and the Sexual Division of Labor." *MERIP Reports* 96:3–12.

Holt, Maria. 1992. *Half the People: Women, History and the Palestinian Intifada*. Jerusalem: Palestinian Academic Society for the Study of International Affairs.

Kuttab, Eileen S. 1993. "Palestinian Women in the Intifada: Fighting on Two Fronts." *Arab Studies Quarterly* 15:69–87.

Rockwell, S. 1985. "Palestinian Women Workers in the Israeli Occupied Territories." *Journal of Palestine Studies* 14:114–37.

Sabbagh, S., and G. Talhami, eds. 1990. *Images and Reality: Palestinian Women under Occupation and in the Diaspora*. Washington, D.C.: Institute of Arab Women's Studies.

Samed, A. 1976. "The Proletarianization of Palestinian Women in Israel." *MERIP Reports* 50:10–16.

Siniora, R. 1990. *"Palestinian Labor in a Dependent Economy: Women Workers in the West Bank Clothing Industry."* *Cairo Papers in the Social Sciences* 12, Monograph 3. Cairo: American University.

Strum, P. 1992. *The Women are Marching: The Second Sex and the Palestinian Revolution*. New York: Lawrence Hill.

Young, Elise. 1992. *Keepers of the History: Women and the Israeli-Palestinian Conflict*. New York: Teachers College Press, Columbia University.

## Birth Control and Development in Three Latin American Countries

Social policies concerning birth control share in all societies an inextricable linkage with the larger political economy. This is particularly true in Third World countries, where birth-control policies are often used in various ways by the state and development agencies to promote a particular strategy of development. A massive birth-control campaign carried out in Puerto Rico during the 1970s used surgical methods of sterilization in attempt to control population growth, ostensibly as a means of reducing poverty and "modernizing" the island economy. Socialist Cuba, by way of contrast, pursued a policy of radically liberalized birth control methods beginning in the 1960s, in order for women to optimize their participation in the labor force. In Nicaragua, birth-control policies have become a contested terrain in the shifting national politics that began with the 1979 overthrow of the Somoza dictatorship. In all three Latin American cases, it becomes clear upon investigation that the social content as well as the relative success in implementing birth-control policies display a clear linkage to the larger political economy that surrounds national development.

### Birth Control in Latin America

The starting point for analysis of Latin American societies is to be found in their common experience with colonialism. Military conquests by the Spanish in the sixteenth century, similar to those of the other great European colonizers, established colonies throughout the Americas and created tightly controlled regimes designed to enrich the "mother country." As part of its conquest over new sources of raw materials, colonialism imposed a social structure designed to tightly control the labor supply. This in turn meant a strongly pronatalist ideology, which, consistent with Euro-Christian ideology, provided the social basis for a legal order hostile to birth control. Antiabortion legislation was nearly universal in the colonies, just as traditional women's organizations, the former catalyst for traditional birth-control methods and child-spacing, were forcibly disbanded by the colonizers (Etienne and Leacock 1980).

Despite the departure of Spanish colonialism from the Americas, its patriarchal legacy has persisted into the modern era and continues to pose obstacles for women's equality in development throughout Latin America. It is important to realize that either the absence or extremely poor accessibility to safe birth-control methods for the majority of the world's women is their single greatest health risk, leading to approximately one-fourth to one-third of all deaths of females of child-bearing age (United Nations 1991). These fatalities are typically caused by complications arising from pregnancy, difficulties in childbirth itself, problems induced by unsafe contraceptive methods, and, most notoriously, by the need to rely upon improper, usually illegal abortion methods (Bell and Reich 1988).

While much discussion in the developed world has centered upon the health hazards of modern contraceptives, such risks are actually quite marginal in Third World settings when compared with the magnitude of suffering and maternal mortality caused by the generalized inaccessibility to adequate means of contraception. It is precisely this lack of accessibility to contraceptive methods in the modern era that points us back toward the political economy of Latin America.

The national governments of developing nations frequently formulate repressive birth-control policies as a mechanism for shaping the rate of population growth. Yet comprehensive attempts at raising the status of women and their full reincorporation into all societal spheres is ultimately the only just and truly effective means of regulating fertility rates. This essentially involves restoring to all women their complete control over fertility in the context of universal access to the technological means of contraception available to a given society. It is the wide array of political economic constraints on developing societies that makes progress in the struggle for women's equality in the Third World so difficult. As can be seen in the following Latin American cases, birth-control policies pursued by the state in developing countries invariably reflect the larger logic of social control that corresponds to their particular strategy of development.

## Puerto Rico

In the case of Puerto Rico, colonialism continues to impose its imprint upon birth control on this Caribbean island. Since 1898, when the Spanish were driven out following the Spanish-American War, the United States has retained its own colonial hold over Puerto Rico. Despite the imposition of U.S. citizenship in 1917, Puerto Ricans have retained their Latino culture and strong sense of nationality in the face of legal domination by U.S. federal authorities. For most of the twentieth century, Puerto Rican politics have revolved around the tensions associated with Washington's rule over Puerto Rican affairs, and this eventually came to include the issue of birth control.

During the early 1970s, an undersecretary for family planning was established in Puerto Rico who presided over a massive campaign to encourage "voluntary" sterilization. The goal of the aggressive campaign was to achieve zero population growth on the island. Surgical sterilization as a birth-control strategy first began in Puerto Rico during the 1930s with the construction of sixty-seven clinics located in all areas of the island. By 1947, 7 percent of Puerto Rican women had been sterilized, and by 1949, 18 percent of hospital births were followed by sterilization. In 1954, the percentage of sterilized women reached 17.5 percent (Presser 1973).

Seeking to build upon the "successes" of the past, the 1970s campaign involved a massive propaganda effort that included door-to-door canvassing, advocating surgical sterilization as a means to promote the "modernization" of families and the "eradication of poverty" on the island. Funded with $1.3 million from the U.S. Department of Health, Education and Welfare, this neo-Malthusian approach to Puerto Rico's development problems soon resulted in the sterilization of roughly one-third of the island's women of child-bearing age (Mass 1977). Almost from the outset, however, many Puerto Ricans opposed the program and before long it was sharply cut back in response to intense national and international criticism, including charges of genocide made by Puerto Ricans invited to speak at the United Nations. "Informed consent," the key to voluntary decision-making regarding surgical sterilization, was reportedly absent in an alarming number of cases. A substantial number of women later reported that they believed the procedure, which had become known throughout the island as "la operación," to be reversible. By 1981, 39 percent of Puerto Rican women had nonetheless been sterilized, the highest rate in the world with the lowest average age of sterilization (at twenty-five years) (Mass 1977).

### Cuba

Sharing a similar colonial history with Puerto Rico, Cuba radically broke away from U.S. hegemony in 1959 when it overthrew the U.S.-supported Batista dictatorship and consolidated a popular revolution that declared itself socialist by 1961. Prior to Cuba's revolution, abortion was illegal, the infant mortality rate was very high, and contraception was inaccessible to most women, as it was stigmatized in a staunchly macho Cuban society. During the 1960s, the Cuban revolution made radical changes in this situation, creating guarantees for employment of all citizens and giving a high priority to incorporation of women into the labor force.

Along with these economic changes, Cuba fully legalized abortion and guaranteed its availability on demand at no cost to all Cuban women alongside of making a variety of forms of free contraceptive devices available throughout the island. These policies, in conjunction with remarkable improvements in health care and education, had dramatic results in the standards of living for all Cubans and among women of child-bearing age in particular. The maternal mortality rate fell from 125.3 (per thousand pregnancies) in 1958 to 26.1 in 1988 (United Nations 1991). By the period 1975–1980, Cuba experienced a natural rate of population growth that was among the lowest in Latin America (13.2 per thousand population), with a birth rate of 19.5 (per thousand population), as opposed to Puerto Rico's, which was still above 24. The figure settled in to be consistently below 17 in the 1980s (Murray 1978; United Nations Population Division 1991).

### Nicaragua

In Nicaragua, like most of Central America, the standard of living has always been considerably lower than in the Spanish-speaking Caribbean. The 1979 Sandinista Revolution brought the issues of women's equality directly on the government's agenda for the first time in the region's history. Once in power, the Sandinista Front (FSLN) committed itself to the liberation of women and a national women's organization was formed to advocate on behalf of women's issues (Randall 1981).

In practice, however, the FSLN ran into serious obstacles in implementing its political programs. Met with unprecedented hostility from the United States under the successive Reagan administrations, the initial successes of the revolution were reversed by a devastating war fought by U.S.-funded "contras."

It should be noted that with a relatively sparse population density, Nicaragua never felt the kinds of overpopulation pressures encountered in many other developing areas.

Despite this lack of a population imperative, the Sandinista government throughout its decade in power (1979–90) pursued the strategy of education concerning family planning, so as to promote a fuller incorporation of women's participation in Nicaraguan society. Contraceptives circulated widely in Nicaragua, and the number of abortions increased because of the government policy of refusing to prosecute physicians who practiced abortions, its illegality notwithstanding. Many observers pointed to the steadfast opposition of the Catholic Church in preventing the full legalization of abortion. Moreover, the huge loss of life that occurred just prior to the revolution and then again as a result of the contra war led some Sandinista leaders to emphasize the need for maintaining high fertility rates, something that Nicaragua has indeed maintained (Chamorro Zamora 1989).

Following the political defeat of the FSLN in the 1990 elections, the conservative government that succeeded it restored emphasis upon traditional values and has attempted to reverse the progress made during the revolutionary period. Consistent with the new government's close relationship with the traditional Catholic sectors, one of the first policies of 1991 included a standardized new textbook for the public-education system that refers to abortion as "murder" and criticizes the use of contraceptives as "unnatural." Despite these shifts in official ideology, considerable social struggle continues in Nicaragua over women's issues, including the issue of abortion. As of the early 1990s, Nicaragua remained a desperately poor nation with one of the highest birth rates in Latin America (United Nations Population Division 1991).

The experience of each of the three Latin American cases discussed above shows that fertility and family planning are inextricably linked to traditional cultural values, employment practices, educational attainment, women's legal rights, and their political participation in social development. It has been established that the cultivation of women's political power, the equalization of women's access to birth control, and the fuller development of women's social potential that results constitute the critical variables necessary to lower the birth rate while elevating the status of women in developing countries. It is precisely this fundamental kind of change in social relations that can promote the optimal deployment of the available technologies of birth control in conjunction with state policies dedicated to guaranteeing their access to all sectors of the population.

*Kathryn Stout*
*Richard A. Dello Buono*

## Bibliography

Bell, David E., and Michael R. Reich, eds. 1988. *Health, Nutrition, and Economic Crisis: Approaches to Policy in the Third World*. Dover, Mass.: Auburn.

Chamorro Zamora, Amalia. 1989. "La Mujer: Logros y Limites en 10 Anos de Revolucion" ("Women: Achievements and Limits after 10 Years of Revolution"). *Cuadernos de Sociologia* 9/10.

Etienne, Mona, and Eleanor Leacock, eds. 1980. *Women and Colonization: Anthropological Perspectives*. New York: Praegar.

Leacock, Eleanor, Helen Safa, et al. 1986. *Women's Work: Development and the Division of Labor by Gender*. Westport, Conn.: Bergin and Garvey.

Mass, Bonnnie. 1977. "Puerto Rico: A Case Study of Population Control." *Latin American Pespectives* 14(Winter):66–81.

Murray, Nicola. 1978. "Changes in the Position of Women in Cuban Society." Thesis. Cambridge University.

Presser, Harriet B. 1973. *Sterilization and Fertility Decline in Puerto Rico*. Berkeley: Institute of International Studies.

Randall, Margaret. 1981. *Women in Cuba: Twenty Years Later*. New York: Smyrna.

Ross, John A., Marjorie Rich, Janet P. Molzan, and Michael Pensak. 1988. *Family Planning and Child Survival: 100 Developing Countries*. New York: Center for Population and Family Health, Columbia University.

Stone, Elizabeth, ed. 1981. *Women and the Cuban Revolution*. New York: Pathfinder.

United Nations. 1991. *The World's Women 1970–1990: Trends and Statistics*. New York: United Nations Publications.

United Nations Population Division. 1991. *Measuring the Dynamics of Contraceptive Use*. New York: United Nations Publications.

# Contributors

Rodolfo Alvarez is professor of sociology at the University of California, Los Angeles. His research includes the empirical measurement of institutional discrimination. His research in the present volume was funded in part by a grant from the Academic Senate of UCLA.

Chi Anyansi-Archibong is associate professor of strategic management at North Carolina A&T State University. She has published extensively in the area of international management development, with special emphasis on women entrepreneurs and women in economic development.

Douglas D. Baker is professor of management and systems at Washington State University. His research interests include organizational strategy and structural change; cycles of cognition, goal setting, and affect; and sexual harassment.

Isabella Bakker is a political economist at York University, Toronto, Canada. She is the author of *The Strategic Silence: Gender and Economic Policy* (Zed Press, 1994) and a contributor to Jenson, Hagen, and Reddy, *The Paradox of Women's Employment* (Polity Press, 1988).

Michael R. Ball is associate professor of sociology at the University of Wisconsin, Superior. He has published articles on popular culture, women's issues, the history of sociology, and teaching methodology.

Melissa A. Barker is assistant professor at the State University of New York at Potsdam, where she teaches in the Industrial Labor Relations Program. She also has served as the technical consultant for the State of Michigan's Equitable Classification Plan.

Colleen S. Bell is associate professor and Gordon B. Sanders Chair in education at Hamline University. Her research interests focus on gender and educational leadership, and since 1986 she has been collaborating with Susan

E. Chase on a nationwide study of women's experience in the K–12 superintendency.

Cynthia Berryman-Fink is professor of communication at the University of Cincinnati. She has published two books and over fifteen articles on gender and communication and has served as consultant to numerous corporations and government agencies.

Michael Betz is professor of sociology at the University of Tennessee. His primary research interests are in work and occupations and health care, including herbal medicine and its revival in Thailand.

Denise D. Bielby is professor of sociology at the University of California, Santa Barbara. Her research interests include the dynamics of the workplace and gender and issues in popular culture. She is co-author of *1989 Hollywood Writers' Report: Unequal Access, Unequal Pay* with William T. Bielby.

Sampson Lee Blair is assistant professor of sociology at the University of Oklahoma. He has published numerous papers on the division of household labor performed by both adults and children.

Margaret Anne Bly, Ph.D., is professor of psychology and human services, Edison Community College, Ft. Myers, Florida.

Rosemary Booth is assistant professor of management at the University of North Carolina at Charlotte. She has her Ph.D. in organizational communications from the University of Kentucky.

Sandra Boyd-Davis received her Ph.D. in sociology from the University of Southern California. She currently works as a research analyst for the Kaiser Permanente Health Plan in Pasadena, California.

Kathleen C. Brannen is associate professor of management at Creighton University. She wrote her doctoral dissertation on "Women in Management" and served for two terms on the editorial review board of the *Journal of Small Business Management*.

Barbara G. Brents is associate professor of sociology at the University of Nevada, Las Vegas. Her current research is on prostitution.

Christina Christenson Brush is associate professor of management at Kennesaw State College. She conducts research in the areas of career-family conflict, the impact of unemployment on professionals, and college faculty roles/performance.

David F. Bush is professor of psychology and human resource development at Villanova University, where he teaches courses in organizational psychology and organizational change. His research interests include the relationships among gender, organizational influence, and organizational reward systems.

Silvia Cancio received a master of arts degree in religious studies from the Atheneaum of Ohio and is presently obtaining her doctorate in sociology at the University of Cincinnati.

Sonia D. Carreon holds a Ph.D. from the University of Cincinnati. Her research interest focuses on immigrant women and work. She is editorial assistant of this encyclopedia.

Mary Carsky is professor of marketing at the University of Hartford. She has published several articles examining the roles of women in the professoriate.

Susan E. Chase teaches sociology and women's studies at the University of Tulsa. She researches professional women's stories about accomplishment and discrimination at work. Her book, *Stories of Power and Subjection: The Work Narratives of Women Educational Leaders* (University of Massachusetts Press), examines how women narrate these contradictory experiences.

David Cheal is professor of sociology at the University of Winnipeg, Canada. His publications include *The Gift Economy* (Routledge) and *Family and the State of Theory* (University of Toronto Press).

Joyce N. Chinen is assistant professor of sociology at the University of Hawaii, West O'ahu, and a research associate in the Social Science Research Institute at the University of Hawaii, Manoa. Her research interests are in the sociology of work, especially women and work, and race and ethnic relations.

Jeanette N. Cleveland is associate professor of psychology at Colorado State University. She has published several research articles on age and gender bias in personnel decisions and co-edited two books on performance appraisal in organizations, including *Performance Measurement and Theory* (with F. Landy and S. Zedeck) (Erlbaum).

Rosalie A. Cohen obtained her Ph.D. in sociology from the University of Pittsburgh. She has published a number of books, monographs, and papers on women's issues.

Samuel Cohn is associate professor of sociology at Texas A&M University. His research has been in the areas of gender and human capital theory, and theories on the labor process.

Denise K. Conroy is senior lecturer at the School of Economics and Public Policy, Queensland University of Technology, Australia.

Daniel B. Cornfield is professor of sociology at Vanderbilt University. His research has addressed several issues in labor sociology, including the development and resolution of gender and ethnic-racial conflict in the labor movement. Among his publications are "The U.S. Labor Movement: Its Development and Impact on Social Inequality and Politics" *Annual Review of Sociology* (1991).

Constance Counts holds a Doctorate in human development from the Harvard Graduate School of Education. She is an associate professor at Lesley College in Cambridge, Massachusetts, where she teaches courses in human development, education, management, and cultural diversity.

Teresa Joyce Covin is associate professor and chair of the Department of Management and Entrepreneurship at Kennesaw State College. Her teaching and research interests are in the areas of human-resource management and organizational change.

LouEllen Crawford is professor in the Arts and Management Department at Colorado Technical College, Colorado Springs, Colorado, teaching in both the graduate and undergraduate programs. Her teaching includes business ethnics, sociology of work, and women in society.

Lisa A. Cubbins is currently assistant professor of sociology and a research associate in the Institute for Policy Research at the University of Cincinnati. Her current research focuses on gender differences in education and work in Sweden, and the links between employment and health.

Susan M. Cunningham is a visiting assistant professor of sociology at Wheaton College in Norton, Massachusetts, and has held a post-doctoral position at the Center for Alcohol and Addiction Studies at Brown University. Her research interests include the structural determinants of drinking-related problems for men and women and the drinking-family violence connection.

Souad Dajani is assistant professor of sociology at Allegheny College. Her areas of interest include the Intifada, women and family in the Occupied Territories, and other issues pertaining to the situation in the West Bank and Gaza Strip under occupation.

Mona Danner is assistant professor in the Department of Sociology and Criminal Justice at Old Dominion University. Most recently, she has carried out a cross-national investigation of the relationship between gender inequality and criminalization mechanisms in the social control of women.

Richard A. Dello Buono is associate professor of sociology and Latin American studies at Rosary College in Chicago. He has done field research in Cuba, Nicaragua, and Puerto Rico over a period of ten years.

Vasilikie Demos is associate professor of sociology at the University of Minnesota, Morris. Her research areas are gender and aging as well as race and ethnic studies. Her articles have appeared in the *Journal of Marriage and the Family* and the *Gerontologist*. With Marcia Texler Segal, she coedited *Ethnic Women: A Multiple Status Reality* (General Hall).

Gregory H. Dobbins is associate professor of management at the University of Tennessee. His research interests are in the areas of performance appraisal, leadership, and women in management. He has published over forty articles in his field.

Dana Dunn is assistant professor of sociology at the University of Texas at Arlington. Her major research interests are women and work, women and politics, gender stratification, and women and development.

Margaret A. Eisenhart is professor of educational anthropology and research methodology in the School of Education, University of Colorado, Boulder. Her areas of research include the study of gender, ethnic, and academic identities in schools and peer groups. She is co-author of *Educated in Romance: Women, Achievement and College Culture* (with D. Holland, 1990).

Paula England is professor of sociology at the University of Arizona. She has published numerous articles on gender and labor markets and with George Farkas is the author of *Households, Employment, and Gender* (Aldine, 1986). *Comparable Worth: Theories and Evidence* (Aldine, 1992). From 1994-96 she is serving as the editor of the *American Sociological Review*.

Melissa Evans-Andris is assistant professor of sociology at the University of Louisville, Kentucky. She is currently working on a longitudinal study of the process of innovation with computer technology in elementary schools.

William E. Even is associate professor of economics at Miami (Ohio) University. His past research has been devoted primarily to gender differences in the labor market and the role of pensions in employment contracts.

Jeffrey D. Facteau is a doctoral candidate in industrial and organizational psychology at the University of Tennessee in Knoxville. He is working on his dissertation, which examines motivational processes underlying the performance-appraisal process. His work has been published in the *Journal of Research in Personality*, the *Journal of Management*, and *Human Resource Management Review*.

Catherine A. Faver is professor of social work at the University of Tennessee, Knoxville. Her interests include social welfare history, women's spirituality, and the social consequences of religious worldviews. She currently is studying factors that account for women's social activism in the early twentieth century.

Anne E. Figert is assistant professor of sociology at Loyola University, Chicago. Her teaching and research interests focus on the linkage between science, medicine, and gender, including the recent definition of PMS as a psychiatric disorder and the gender politics of AIDS research and treatment.

Juanita M. Firestone is assistant professor of social and policy sciences at the University of Texas, San Antonio. Her teaching and research interests include formal organizations, military sociology, family, gender roles, and women in management.

Lucía Fort is a Peruvian citizen who did her undergraduate studies at the Pontificia Universidad Catolica in Lima, Peru, and currently is a graduate student in the Department of Sociology at the American University. She was conference coordinator at the Institute for Women's Policy Research (Washington, D.C.) for the Fourth Women's Policy Research Conference (1994).

Sandra French is associate professor of sociology at Indiana University Southeast. She has published in *Sociological Focus*, *Journal of Drug Issues*, and *Sociological Inquiry*.

Allie Funk is professor of sociology at Appalachian State University, where her research and teaching have been in the areas of gender studies, family, social deviance, and theory. Her Ph.D. is from Emory University.

Joan V. Gallos is associate professor of urban leadership and policy studies at the School of Education, University of Missouri, Kansas City. She is the editor of the *Journal of Management Education* and recipient of the 1993 Radcliffe College Award for Teaching Excellence and the 1990 Fritz Roethlisberger Memorial Award for the best published paper on management education.

Aleta Esther Geib is a Ph.D. candidate in the department of sociology at the University of Akron. Her research interests include feminist theory, social psychology, and work and occupations. Her dissertation is entitled *The Amazon Complex: News Media Representations of Women Warriors*.

Rosalie G. Genovese, Ph.D., is the editor of *Families and Change: Social Needs and Public Policies* and has published articles on planning, self-help networks, advocacy in professions, and dual-career couples. Her research interests include the impact of public policies on families and the assessment of policies and programs to improve the economic status of women.

Annette M. Girondi graduated with a master's degree in general/experimental psychology from Villanova University. She currently is completing her doctorate in industrial/organizational psychology at the University of Akron.

Roberta Goldberg is assistant professor of sociology at Trinity College in Washington, D.C. She has written about labor organizing among clerical workers and the relationship of work and family in her book *Organizing Women Office Workers: Dissatisfaction, Consciousness and Action.*

Heidi Gottfried is associate professor of sociology and women's studies at Purdue University. Her most recent publications include "The Impact of Skill on Union Membership: Rethinkng Gender Differences." Her book entitled *Feminism and Social Change: Bridging Theory and Practice* is forthcoming from the University of Illinois Press.

Cherlyn Skromme Granrose is associate professor of human resource administration at Temple University. Her research has focused on the interaction between the goals and plans of individuals and the organizations employing them. She is co-author of *Science, Sex and Society,* and *Job Saving Strategies: Worker Buyouts and QWL.*

Linda Grant is associate professor of sociology and faculty associate of the Institute of Behavioral Research at the University of Georgia. Her current research focuses on careers of women and men physicians and scientists, and her recent articles have appeared in *American Sociological Review, Sociological Quarterly,* and *Social Problems.*

Patricia A. Gwartney-Gibbs is associate professor of sociology and director of the Oregon Survey Research Laboratory at the University of Oregon. She and Denise Lach have published extensively in the area of gender and workplace dispute resolution, with articles in *Law and Society Review, Negotiation Journal, Human Relations,* and *American Sociological Review.*

Yitchak Haberfeld holds a Ph.D. from the University of Wisconsin, Madison, and is now a senior lecturer in the Department of Labor Studies at Tel Aviv University. He has published extensively in the area of wage discrimination in the labor market both in Israel and the U.S.

Cynthia Riffe Hancock is adjunct professor of sociology at Methodist College in Fayetteville, North Carolina. Her current research interests include the role of women in traditionally male occupations—specifically, women in the military and in religious settings.

Susan Hanson is professor of geography and director of the School of Geography at Clark University. She has been grappling with the geography of home and work firsthand since the birth of her first child in 1966, when she was a Peace Corps volunteer in Kenya.

Karen Herne is a graduate student in education at the University of Sydney and works as a research assistant in the Multicultural Centre at the Univer-

sity of Sydney. She is currently investigating industrial relations management in a multicultural workforce.

Joni Hersch is associate professor of economics at the University of Wyoming. Her
research interest focuses on wage differential, job promotion, and job
benefits for women.

Randy Hodson is professor of sociology at Indiana University. His research interests are in the sociology of work and social stratification, and he is currently studying the maintenance of dignity in the workplace and the
changing patterns of social organization in the former Yugoslavia. His
recent publications are in *Work and Occupations* and the *American Sociological Review*.

David G. Hogan received his doctorate in American history from Carnegie Mellon
University and is currently assistant professor of history and American
studies at Heidelberg College. He writes in areas of social and cultural
history.

Pierrette Hondagneu-Sotelo is assistant professor of sociology at the University of
Southern California. Her research focuses on the intersection of gender
and migration among Mexican undocumented immigrants. She currently
is involved in research on employers of domestic workers, and she is the
author of articles that have appeared or will appear in *Gender & Society*
and *Social Problems*.

Margaret McLean Hughes is presently working on her Ph.D. at Georgia State University. Her primary research interest is in the effect of mother's work
on child development.

Jerry A. Jacobs is associate professor and chair of the graduate program in sociology at the University of Pennsylvania. His book *Revolving Doors: Sex Segregation and Women's Careers* was published in 1989 by Stanford University Press, and an edited collection, *Sex Segregation at Work*, was published
by Sage Press in 1994.

Ellen J. Kennedy is professor of marketing at St. Thomas University. She has published several articles examining the roles of women in the professoriate. She has also done extensive work in the field of business ethics.

Barbara Stanek Kilbourne is assistant professor of sociology at Vanderbilt University. Her research interests are race and gender stratification in the labor
market. She has a 1995 article in *American Journal of Sociology* and has
recently published an article in *Social Forces*.

Denise H. Lach, Ph.D., is a research sociologist at Battelle Seattle Research Center.
She is currently involved in research on environmental dispute resolu-

tion and has published articles on gender and workplace dispute resolution in *Law and Society Review, Negotiation Journal,* and *Mediation Quarterly.*

Sue A. Lafky received her Ph.D. in mass communication from Indiana University and currently is an assistant professor in the School of Journalism and Mass Communication at the University of Iowa. Her research areas include gender and the media work force, gender and cultural studies, and feminist pedagogy. She is one of the founding members of the Feminist Teacher Editorial Collective.

Phylis Lan Lin is professor of sociology and director of Asian programs at the University of Indianapolis. She is the author or co-author of a number of articles and books focusing on the family; most recently, she co-edited two books, *Families East and West* and *Selected Readings in Marriage and the Family: A Global Perspective.*

Ann Leffler is professor of sociology at Utah State University, where she also directs her university's general education reform. Once active in the U.S. women's liberation movement, she now teaches the sociology of gender. With colleagues, she is writing a book, *Passionate Avocations,* about stratification in leisure life.

Kevin T. Leicht is assistant professor of sociology at Pennsylvania State University. His research interests include organizational stratification and the political economy of deindustrialization. His current research explores the organizational context surrounding gender stratification and career mobility in corporate law (with Mary L. Fennell).

Lisa Licausi is a recent women's studies graduate of UNLV. She has been involved in research on prostitution with Barbara Brents.

Linda L. Lindsey is professor of sociology at Maryville University, St. Louis. Her research has included gender in the developing world, the leadership qualities of women, and mate selection among college students. She is the author of *Gender-Roles: A Sociological Perspective* now in its second edition.

Lloyd B. Lueptow is professor emeritus in the Department of Sociology, University of Akron. He has specialized in the study of sex roles since the early 1970s and is the author of *Adolescent Sex Roles and Social Change* and numerous articles on gender patterns.

David A. Macpherson is currently an associate professor of economics and a research affiliate of the Pepper Institute on Aging and Public Policy at Florida State University. His major research interests include the labor market effects of unionism and pensions and the causes of gender differences in the labor market.

Dayle A. Mandelson is associate professor of economics at the University of Wisconsin, Stout. She previously served as assistant to the chancellor for affirmative action (1984–1988).

Elizabeth Maret is associate professor of sociology at Texas A&M University, where she has taught and done research in the area of women and work for eighteen years. Her publications include two research monographs, *Women's Career Patterns* (1983) and *Women of the Texas Range* (1993), and more than thirty research articles.

Richard F. Martell is assistant professor in the Department of Social and Organizational Psychology at Teachers College, Columbia University. His research on occupational sex discrimination is directed toward better understanding the organizational factors responsible for biased personnel assessments and the social-cognitive processes that mediate discrimination.

Susan R. Martin Macke is associate professor in education and community, Indiana State University. She received her Ed.D. in educational foundations at the University of Cincinnati in 1992.

Jonathan Marx is assistant professor of sociology at Winthrop University, Rock Hill, South Carolina. His research interests include organizational recruitment strategies and minority job acquisition, and his publications have appeared in *Work and Occupations, Sociological Focus,* and *Sociology and Social Research.*

H. Virginia McCoy is associate professor of public health at Florida International University. She has published numerous journal articles and serves as consultant to FIU Center on Aging. Her research focus includes HIV and drug abuse.

Elizabeth G. Menaghan is professor of sociology and director of graduate studies in sociology at Ohio State University. Her early research focused on social stressors and adults' emotional well-being, while her recent research more directly examines the intergenerational consequences of adult occupational and family experiences in shaping children's development.

Vicki Meredith is currently associate professor of accounting at Indiana University Southeast. Her primary research area is on gender research as it applies to accounting, and she is the author of "Women in Public Accounting: Growth and Advancement" in *Critical Perspectives in Accounting* (1993).

Albert J. Mills is associate professor of management at Saint Mary's University, Halifax, Nova Scotia. His research focuses upon the impact of organizational culture on discriminatory practices, and he is the co-author/editor of four books including *Gendering Organization Theory* (with P. Tancred) (Sage, 1992).

William A. Mirola is assistant professor of sociology at Marian College. His works in progress include "A Refuge for Some: Gender Differences in the Relationship between Religious Involvement and Depression."

Lynda L. Moore is associate professor of management at Simmons College. She has published and consulted in the field of women in management and is active in many professional organizations.

Mary C. Moore is currently dean of the College of Arts and Sciences, University of Indianapolis. She received her Ph.D. in sociology from York University. Her research interests are in ethnic studies, focusing primarily on Hispanic women and issues of identity.

Susan E. Moreno is a Ph.D. student in sociology at the University of Texas at Austin. Her research interests include Mexican Americans, race and ethnic relations, education, and quantitative methods.

Gayle Morris is currently completing degrees in women's studies and psychology at the University of Nevada, Las Vegas. She is also involved in research on prostitution.

Chandra Muller is a lecturer in sociology at the University of Texas at Austin. Her current research interests are in parent involvement and the interface of families, peers, and schools in the lives of adolescents.

Stephanie D. Myers is a Ph.D. student in industrial/organizational psychology at the University of Tennessee. Her research interests are in the areas of performance appraisal, women in management, and leadership.

Paula D. Nesbitt is assistant professor of sociology of religion at Iliff School of Theology, Denver, Colorado, and a member of the core faculty for the joint Ph.D. program between Iliff and the University of Denver. She earned her Ph.D. in 1990 from Harvard University (Department of Sociology), following ten years' experience in organizational communications and public relations.

Lenahan O'Connell is assistant professor of sociology at Transylvania University. In addition to his interest in gender and work, he is conducting research on discrimination in law enforcement and income differences between the races.

Marie Withers Osmond is associate professor of sociology at Florida State University. Her recent publications include articles in *Gender & Society, Journal of Marriage and the Family,* and *Journal of Family Issues.*

Angela M. O'Rand is associate professor of sociology at Duke University. She has published several articles over the past fifteen years on women's pension opportunities and retirement patterns. Her current projects include cross-national comparisons of pension systems and their implications for older women's economic well-being.

Laura L. O'Toole is assistant professor of sociology and anthropology at Guilford College in Greensboro, North Carolina. Her current research focuses on corporate women's networks in two multinational organizations.

Irene Padavic is associate professor of sociology at Florida State University. Her research has been in the areas of gender and work, economic restructuring, and the labor process. She recently completed a book with Barbara Reskin called *Women and Men at Work*.

Nanette Page is completing her Ph.D. in sociology at the University of Connecticut at Storrs. Her area of interest centers on work and the family, as well as on issues surrounding the working poor.

Toby L. Parcel is a professor of sociology and associate dean of the College of Social and Behavioral Sciences at the Ohio State University. She is co-author (with Elizabeth Menaghan) of *Parents' Jobs and Children's Lives*, published in 1994 by Walter de Gruyter.

Carolyn C. Perrucci is professor of sociology and associate dean of the graduate school at Purdue University. Her current research focuses on race and gender differences in retirement income, and factors in retention of U.S. minorities in graduate education.

Daniel Poor received his Ph.D. in sociology from the Graduate Center of City University of New York. He has researched the work lives of solo, small firm, and large corporate law firm lawyers in the New York area, and his present work examines alternative legal work group models and their effects on the career paths of large law firm professionals.

Geraldine Pratt is associate professor of Geography at the University of British Columbia and editor of *Environment and Planning D: Society and Space*.

Priti Ramamurthy is an adjunct faculty member in the Departments of Anthropology, Social Science and Women's Studies at Syracuse University. Her publications include *Managing Irrigation* (with Norman Uphoff and Roy Steiner) and articles on women and agricultural intensification in India.

Barbara F. Reskin is professor of sociology at the Ohio State University. She has published a score of chapters and articles and three books on gender and work, including *Women's Work, Men's Work: Sex Segregation on the Job* (with Heidi Hartmann) and *Job Queues, Gender Queues* (with Patricia Roos).

Sabine Rieble is a Ph.D. student at Indiana University. She is currently working on her dissertation about the role of unions in vocational education, comparing Germany and the U.S.

Leah Robin is a Ph.D. candidate at the University of California, Los Angeles. Her research interests are gender and the sociology of medicine and mental health.

Stacy J. Rogers is assistant professor of sociology at the University of Nebraska, Lincoln. In addition to her research on the impact of maternal working conditions on children's well-being, she has done research examining the effects of gender-disproportionate representation on women's persistence in undergraduate fields of study.

Mary Ann Rossi, Ph.D., was appointed to the Wisconsin Governor's Commission on the Status of Women and was elected to serve as legislative chairperson of that commission (1976–1980). As a teacher/scholar, she works for equality of rights for women under the law and is an honorary research fellow of the Women's Studies Research Center, University of Wisconsin, Madison.

Marilyn Rueschemeyer is professor of sociology at the Rhode Island School of Design, an adjunct professor at Brown University, and a fellow at the Russian Research Center, Harvard University. Her books on Eastern Europe include the edited books *Quality of Life in the German Democratic Republic* (with C. Lemke, 1989), and *Women in the Politics of Post-Communist Eastern Europe* (1993).

Beth Rushing is chair of sociology and anthropology at the University of Tennessee, Martin. Her research focuses on gender and race differences in health, and includes work on social roles and health, health care, and reproduction.

Terri A. Scandura is associate professor of management at the University of Miami. She obtained her Ph.D. in organizational behavior from the University of Cincinnati.

Jennifer A. Schmidt is a graduate student, Department of Psychology: Human Development, University of Chicago. She is conducting research on adolescents' conceptions of work with an emphasis on what activities are defined as "like work," how much time is invested in such activities, and the quality of the work experience as perceived by the individual.

Barbara Schneider, Ph.D., is senior social scientist, Ogburn Stouffer Center for the Study of Social Organizations, University of Chicago. Her main fields of interest are the social organization of schools and school-to-work transitions. She is now studying adolescents' conceptions of work and how they are influenced by opportunity structures in schools and in local labor markets.

Beth Anne Shelton is associate professor of sociology at the University of Texas, Arlington. Her research interests are in the area of gender, primarily work and family. Recent publications include "Measuring Household Work: Recent Experience in the United States" (with Margaret Marini) in *Social Science Research*.

Yehouda Shenhav holds a Ph.D. degree from Stanford University and is now senior lecturer in the Department of sociology and Anthropology at Tel Aviv University. He has published in the area of organizations and labor-market inequality.

Martha L. Shockey is a Ph.D. candidate in sociology at the University of Iowa in Iowa City. Her research interests include the intersection of labor markets and social control and its effect on women; she is currently investigating the link between changing labor market factors and female criminality.

Amily Shui-I Huang is an undergraduate at the University of California, Berkeley. She is pursuing a dual major in sociology and architecture.

Layne A. Simpson is a doctoral candidate in sociology at the University of Georgia where she is completing a dissertation on effects of affirmative-action policies on municipal employment practices. Her published works have appeared in *Journal of Marriage and the Family* and the *Journal of Behavioral Medicine*.

Patricia Sotirin teaches organizational communication at Michigan Technological University. Her current research reconceptualizes organizational and labor resistance from a feminist perspective, showing how women in secretarial and clerical positions have been written out of conventional histories about labor resistance.

Judith Stepan-Norris is assistant professor of sociology at the University of California, Irvine. Her recent research analyzes political relations within Congress of Industrial Organizations (CIO) unions, and she is working on a book on United Auto Workers Local 600.

David L. Sterling is associate professor of history at the University of Cincinnati and holds both a Ph.D. degree and J.D. degree. He has written several articles on legal topics and most recently has edited, along with professor Herbert Shapire, an autobiography of Rose Paster Stokes (University of Georgia Press).

Kathryn Stout is assistant professor of criminal justice at Northeastern Illinois University in Chicago. Her work includes research on social movements and a field study in the border region of the southwest United States as part of an investigation of the Sanctuary Movement.

Dana L. Stover is assistant professor of management at the University of Idaho. Her research interests include intraoccupational gender segregation, sexual harassment, and team work.

Robin Stryker is associate professor of sociology at the University of Iowa. Her research focuses on the politics of policy-making. She currently is examining the politics of science in equal-employment opportunity and environmental law.

Lori K. Sudderth is a visiting assistant professor of sociology at Albion College. Her primary interests include the sociology of gender, criminology, sexuality, and emotions, with a special focus on surviving and coping with sexual violence.

Gerard Sullivan is currently senior lecturer in health sociology at the University of Sydney in Australia. Previously he was a postdoctoral fellow at the Institute of South East Asian Studies in Singapore and held a research position in Multicultural Centre at the University of Sydney.

Russel J. Summers is assistant professor and chairperson of the Department of Management at Saint Mary's University, Halifax, Nova Scotia, Canada. His two primary research areas concern judgment and perceptual processes as they relate to dealing with complaints of sexual harassment and decisions associated with affirmative action.

Dena B. Targ is associate professor and extension specialist, Department of Child Development and Family Studies, Purdue University. Her research concerns the intersection of social problems and family problems, including the impact of plant closings on displaced workers and their families.

Phyllis Tharenou is senior lecturer in psychology, University of Queensland. Her previous positions include the director of human resource management, Public Sector management Commission, in Brisbane. Her consulting, course responsibilities, and academic research have been in the areas of organizational behavior and human-resource management.

Joanne Travaglia is lecturer in the Multicultural Centre at the University of Sydney. Her research interests include differential utilization of education, health-care facilities, and social services by ethnic minorities, and cross-cultural communication.

Diana Gullett Trevino, M.A., is currently teaching for the Cincinnati Public School System. She recently published in *From Mountain to Metropolis*, edited by Kathryn Borman and Phil Obermiller, and is a member of the Appalachian Studies Conference.

Mia Tuan is a doctoral student at the University of California, Los Angeles. Her research interests include ethnic/racial relations in school settings and the persistence of ethnic identity among second-generation populations in the United States.

Frédérique Van de Poel-Knottnerus is assistant professor of French, Department of Foreign Languages and Literatures, Oklahoma State University. She has published in the *Humboldt Journal of Social Relations* and *Sociological Inquiry*, and her current research focuses on the role of children, education, and women in nineteenth- and twentieth-century French literature and history.

Chris Von Der Haar is a visiting assistant professor of sociology at Indiana University. From 1989 to 1991 she worked on the CBS/*New York Times* polls as the manager of surveys for CBS News.

Kathryn B. Ward is professor of sociology and former coordinator of the Women's Studies Program at Southern Illinois University at Carbondale. She is the author of *Women Workers and the World System* and editor of Women Workers and Global Restructuring.

Sandy Welsh is assistant professor of sociology at the University of Toronto. Her main research interests are in the sociology of work and gender, and she currently is studying the organizational context of sexual harassment. Her recent publications include a collaborative piece, "Is Workplace Solidarity Undermined by Autonomy and Participation?" *(American Sociological Review)*.

Regina E. Werum is a Ph.D. candidate in sociology and American studies at Indiana University, Bloomington. Her research areas include gender, race/ethnicity, educational stratification, social movements, and historical sociology.

Merry White is professor of sociology at Boston University, and associate in research, Reischauer Institute of Japanese Studies at Harvard University. She has written several books on Japan, including *The Japanese Educational Challenge* (Free Press, 1986) and *The Material Child: Coming of Age in Japan and America* (Free Press, 1993).

Diane E. Wille is associate professor of psychology at Indiana University Southeast. Her research focus is on factors that impact infant social-emotional development, including maternal employment, child care, and prematurity.

Robert C. Williamson is adjunct professor of sociology, Lehigh University, and the author or co-author of a number of books, including *Marriage and Family Relations, Sex Roles in Changing Society,* and *Early Retirement: Promises and Pitfalls*.

Alice C. Wilson received her B.G.S. from Indiana University Southeast in 1991. She is currently a graduate student at Indiana University-Purdue University at Indianapolis.

David Wright is assistant professor of sociology, Wichita State University. His current research focuses on the changing industrial and occupational structures involved in the transition from Fordist to post-Fordist production systems.

Wu Xu's first lesson on gender was discovering that having an uninspired name ("Number 5"), instead of meaningful ones typically given by Chinese, was because of her being an "unwanted girl." Her perspective on the gender/ethnicity intersection developed as a graduate student at Utah State University, where she is completing her dissertation.

Mui Teng Yap is currently senior fellow at the Institute for Policy Studies in Singapore. She has conducted research at the East West Center Population Institute and for the Population Planning Unit in Singapore.

Young-Hee Yoon is a senior research associate at the Institute for Women's Policy Research. She currently studies unemployment insurance benefit recipiency rates, with special attention to the barriers faced by women, part-time workers, and the self-employed.

Gay Young is assistant professor of sociology at the American University in Washington, D.C. She is co-editor (with Bette J. Dickerson) of *Color, Class, and Country: Experiences of Gender*. She is preparing a book-length manuscript on social responses to Mexico's economic crisis based on field work in Ciudad Juarez funded by the National Science Foundation (with Beatriz E. Vera).

Mary Ellen Waller Zuckerman is professor of marketing at SUNY, Genesee. She has published several articles examining the roles of women in the professoriate. She has also done extensive work in the history of women as consumers.

# Subject Index

Gays, organizational intolerance for, 324
Gender roles: dispute resolution and, 342; in
     Mexico, 477–78; socialization into
     (*see* Socialization)
Gender-role stereotypes. *See* Sex stereotypes
Gender-socialization perspective, on work
     interests, 284–85
Generalization perspective, on drinking prob-
     lems, 298–99
Geographic factors, 105–7
Ghana, division of household labor in, 442
Glass ceiling, 121, 139–40, 338–40, 357–58
Greek ethnic women, 51–54; immigrants, 51–
     53; native-born, 53–54

Health-care professionals, 162–63. *See also*
     specific disciplines
Higher education. *See* Academia; Academic
     mentors; Education
Hispanics. *See* Latinas
Homemaking responsibilities. *See* Childrearing
     responsibilities; Domestic responsi-
     bilities; Work-family interface
Housecleaning cooperatives, 46–47
Human capital: earnings gap related to, 61–62,
     107; occupational segregation re-
     lated to, 107, 319. *See also* Educa-
     tion; Training
Human capital perspective, on women's ad-
     vance to academic administration
     positions, 355–56
Human resource professionals, work-family
     interface and, 314–15

Identity approach, to work commitment, 288
Immigrant women: in Australia, 453–55; in
     garment industry, 219–20; Greek,
     51–54; illegal immigrants, 42, 219–
     20; labor-force participation of, 41–
     44; Latinas' labor-force participa-
     tion and immigrant status and, 40–
     41; from Mexico, 478
Income: possession of, in couples, 81–82. *See
     also* Earnings; Earnings gap
India, women's employment in, 471–74
Industrial countries: women's labor-force par-
     ticipation in, 431–34. *See also* spe-
     cific countries
Industrial sector: gender inequality in labor-
     force participation across nations
     and, 438–39; immigrant women in
     Australia in, 455; in India, 473;
     Palestinian women in, 502. *See also*
     Factory workers; specific industries
Industrial Workers of the World (IWW), 30,
     44, 219
Industrialization, work-family interface and,
     385–91
Institutional changes, labor-force participation
     of women and, 6
Integrated women, 128–30
International Committee for Prostitutes Rights,
     223

International comparisons, 431–508; agricul-
     tural labor in developing countries
     and, 435–36; of division of house-
     hold labor, 440–43; of gender in-
     equality in labor-force participa-
     tion, 437–39; of labor-force partici-
     pation in advanced industrial
     countries, 431–34. *See also* specific
     countries
International Labour Organization Convention
     156, 447
International Ladies Garment Workers Union
     (ILGWU), 31–32, 219
Interpersonal support, women's advancement
     into management positions and,
     351
Interrupted careers. *See* Career interruptions
Israel: Palestinian women in areas occupied by,
     502–4; women's earnings in, 475–76

Japanese women, 462–66; contemporary, 464–
     66; division of household labor
     and, 442; historical background of,
     462–63
Job analysis, comparable worth and, 375–76
Job characteristics, job satisfaction and, 292
Job classification, comparable worth and, 377–
     78
Job concept, comparable worth and, 375
Job descriptions, comparable worth and, 376–
     77
Job evaluation, comparable worth and, 76,
     378–81
Job placement bias, 339–40
Job satisfaction, 245, 292–94; family character-
     istics and, 293; job characteristics
     and, 292; personal expectations
     and, 293–94
Job searches, networks and, 312–14
Journalism, 189–92
Judeo-Christian ideologies, women's roles and,
     238–41

Knowledge, professional, 119

Labor-force attachment (LFA), 103–4
Labor-force participation: of adolescents, 17–
     20; of African-American women,
     35–36; of Appalachian women, 49;
     of Chinese women, 494; demand
     for domestic workers related to, 46;
     gender inequality in, across na-
     tions, 437–39; growth of, 395–96;
     household labor time and, 111–12;
     of immigrant women in Australia,
     454; of immigrant women in the
     United States, 41–44; of Latinas,
     38–41; part-time work and, 7–10;
     religion and, 240–41; self-employ-
     ment and, 10–12; in Singapore,
     483; in Sweden, 469; of teenagers,
     17–20; in the United States, 3–6,
     41–44; of women in industrial

countries, 431–34; of working-class women, 13–16. *See also* Unemployment; Unions

Labor movement: women's status in, 30–33. *See also* Unions

Lack of fit model, of sex bias in performance evaluations, 336–37

Language: Chinese women's roles and, 490; computer, effects on educational and career choices of women, 235–37; male-female communication and, 310–12

Latin America. *See* specific countries

Latinas: birth control and, 505–8; as domestic workers, 47; labor-force participation of, 38–41; in Mexico, 476–79

Lawyers. *See* Legal profession

Leadership Conference of Women Religious (LCWR), 187

Leadership styles: gender comparison of, 358–60; sex stereotypes and, 125; of women school superintendents, 178

Leaves: for childbirth, 423–24, 485; under Family and Medical Leave Act, 274–77; parental, in Sweden, 469; in Singapore, 485

Legal profession, 195–98; increase in women in, 120, 195; in Singapore, 484–85; women's practice patterns in, 196–97

Legislation: Family Support Act (*see* Family Support Act [FSA] of 1988); governing comparable worth, 75; governing discrimination, 203–4; governing sexual harassment, 264; governing women in the military, 210; governing women's rights, 255–56. *See also* Protective legislation

Lesbians: discrimination against, 183–84; organizational intolerance for, 324

Management positions, 357–64; in Australia, 447–52; determinants of women's advancement to, 351–54; gender bias in personnel decisions and, 338–40; in journalism, 191–92; leadership styles of men versus women and, 358–60; research directions for study of women's advancement into, 361–64; sex stereotypes as barriers to women's advancement into, 357–58

*Maquiladora*, 219, 479

Marine Corps, 209

Marital status: African-American women's labor-force participation and, 36; of Appalachian women, 48–49; discrimination against married women and, 332–34; integrated women and, 129–30; labor-force participation of married women and, 4; in Mexico, 477; money-

management style of couples and, 81–82; teaching profession and, 174–75

Market structure, demand for part-time workers related to, 8

Marriage bars, 332–33

Mathematics, reasons women choose not to pursue careers in, 234

Maximum-hour laws, 252

Medical leave, under Family and Medical Leave Act, 274–77

Medical profession, 153–55; discrimination in, 154; personal-life values in, 155; practice structures and work patterns in, 153–54; professional orientations and values in, 154–55; women's distribution in, 153

Mental health: of children, maternal working conditions and, 419–21; maternal role conflict and, 408–9; unemployment and, 22–23

Mentors: women's advancement into management positions and, 363. *See also* Academic mentors

Mexican women, 476–79. *See also* Latinas

Midwives, 159–62; contemporary, 161–62; before 1930, 160–61

Military occupations, 209–11; in combat, 211

Minimum-wage legislation, 252–53

Minority women: in academia, 165–66, 168–72; resistance by, 368. *See also* Race; Racial discrimination; specific minority groups

Modernization perspectives, on Third World economic development, 496

Money-management style, of couples, 81–82

National Association of Religious Women (NARW), 187

National Conference of American Nuns (NCAN), 187

National Task Force on Prostitution, 223

National Training School for Girls, 231

Navy Nurse Corps (NNC), 209

Networks, 187, 256–57; communication styles and, 310–11; job searches and, 312–14

New Zealand, occupational segregation in, 466–68

Newly industrializing countries (NICs), 471–86; garment industry in, 219. *See also* specific countries

Nicaraguan women: birth control and, 507–8; in formal and informal economy, 495–99

Nigerian women, entrepreneurship of, 500–1

Nine to Five, 256–57

Nontraditional occupations: blue-collar, 147–50; gender stereotypes and, 244; problems faced by women in, 139–41; role models as factors in choosing, 242–43; sexual harassment as means of keeping women

Racial discrimination: against African-American women in professional fields, 37–38; sex discrimination compared with, 300–302; in the South, 55; against women clergy, 183

Rape, 325–26

Recruitment bias, 339–40

Religious ideologies: Chinese women's roles and, 490; women's roles and, 238–41

Religious professions, 181–88; American Catholic sisters, 185–88; clergy, 181–84, 239

Research: women's productivity in, 166–67. *See also* Scientists

Reservation wage, return to work following childbirth and, 422–23

Reserve Officer's Training Corps (ROTC), 210

Resistance: feminist perspective on, 367–70; of working-class women, 16

Resource hypothesis, of domestic responsibilities, 98

Retirement, 25–27; pensions and, 26–27, 77–80

Role models, occupational choice and, 242–43

Roles. *See* Gender roles; Social roles

Roman Catholic Church, on ordination of women, 182

Russia, division of household labor in, 442

Satisfaction, with job. *See* Job satisfaction

School principals, women as, 295–96

School superintendents, 176–78, 295–96; career paths leading to positions as, 177; leadership strategies used by women and, 178

Scientists, 141–43, 156–57; reasons women choose not to pursue careers as, 234

Second Vatican Council, 186–87

Segregation. *See* Racial discrimination; Sex discrimination

Self-employment, 10–12

Self-perceptions, effects of sex-based selection on, 258–59

Service sector, 143–47; gender inequality in labor-force participation across nations and, 439; in India, 473–74; Palestinian women in, 502; women's economic importance in, 134; working-class women in, 13–14

Sex discrimination, 329–44; against African-American women, in professional fields, 37–38; in China, 495; college women's career plans and, 234; in dispute resolution, 341–44; earnings gap related to, 62; factors promoting, 329–31; in Latin America, 476–77; legislation governing, 203–4; against married women, 332–34; against older women, 334; organizational culture and, 321–22; in

performance evaluations, 330, 334–37; in personnel decisions, 338–40; pregnancy as basis of, 256, 301; protective legislation as, 252; racial discrimination compared with, 300–302; against women clergy, 182–84; against women doctors, 154; against women scientists, 157; work orientations and, 286–87

Sex-role spillover, 324; sexual harassment and, 261

Sex segregation, 116–17; in blue-collar jobs, 148–50; intergroup contact and, 117; occupational (*see* Occupational segregation); in organizational communications and public relations, 200–1; in scientific disciplines, 156

Sex stereotypes, 123–26; as basis of discrimination, 329–31; communication patterns and, 311; job satisfaction and, 245; nontraditional occupations and, 244; occupational segregation based on, 320; personnel decisions and, 340

Sexual harassment, 260–66, 303–6; coercion based on, 325–27; corporate programs for preventing, 371–74; as discrimination, 301; effects on women's careers, 304–6; filing complaints of, 265–66; judging complaints of, 262; legal and policy issues regarding, 256, 264–66; models of, 260–62; power and, 323; reactions to, 262–63, 303–6

Sexual orientation: discrimination on basis of, 183–84; organizational intolerance for preferences other than heterosexuality and, 324

Sexuality, organizational manipulation of, 323–24

Sharecropping, 54–56

Shift work, child care and, 406–7

Singapore, women's employment in, 483–86

Sister Formation Conference (SFC), 186–87

Skills: demand for, earnings gap and, 68–70; firm-specific, exclusion of women from positions requiring, 108

Social changes, labor-force participation of women and, 6

Social class: work-family interface and, 388–89. *See also* Working-class women

Social cognition theory, of determinants of women's advancement into management positions, 351

Social/nurturant skills, demand for, earnings gap and, 68–70

Social roles, work-family interface and, 396

Social Security Act of 1935, 267

Social Security System, retirement and, 26

Social stigmatization, of sexual harassment victims, 305

Work-family interface, 314–16, 385–427; in
academia, 424–27; in China, 495;
early industrialization and, 385–
91; in East Germany, 461;
eldercare and, 397–400; gender
segregation of housework and,
391–95; of immigrant women in
Australia, 456; in India, 471; interdependence of family responsibilities and paid work and, 110–13;
in Japan, 465–66; life course
patterns and, 395–97; in
Singapore, 485. *See also*
Childrearing responsibilities;
Domestic responsibilities
Work-force participation. *See* Labor-force
participation
Working conditions, children's behavior problems related to, 419–21
Working-class women, 13–16; work-family
interface and, 387–88. *See also*
Blue-collar jobs

# Author Index